Using AutoCAD®

2nd Edition

Robert L. Knight
and William Valaski

with Brenda L. Fouch
Craig W. Sharp
Brent Ring

CORPORATION
LEADING COMPUTER KNOWLEDGE

Using AutoCAD®
2nd Edition

Copyright © 1989 by Que® Corporation

Library of Congress Catalog Number: 89-61810

ISBN 0-88022-469-X

93 92 91 90 89   8 7 6 5 4 3 2 1

Interpretation of the printing code: the rightmost double-digit number is the year of the book's printing; the rightmost single-digit number, the number of the book's printing. For example, a printing code of 89-4 shows that the fourth printing of the book occurred in 1989.

Using AutoCAD, 2nd Edition, is based on Release 10 of AutoCAD.

ABOUT THE AUTHORS

Robert **L. Knight** graduated from the University of Cincinnati with a degree in Architectural Engineering. For the past three years, Bob has worked at LOM Corporation, Indianapolis, where he is the CAD Operations Manager. He is involved with the CAD Users' Group in Indianapolis.

William **Valaski** graduated from the University of Cincinnati with a degree in Architectural Engineering. Bill is CAD Operations Manager for CDS Associates in Cincinnati, Ohio, where he has worked for three years. A computer applications programmer, Bill programs in several languages and is active in the Cincinnati CAD Users' Group.

Brenda **L. Fouch** is a Purdue University graduate in Industrial Illustration Technology. Author of the first edition of *Using Auto-CAD*, Brenda has taught AutoCAD for several years and has been an independent AutoCAD consultant. She is also an AutoLISP programmer.

Craig **W. Sharp**, a registered architect in Florida and Indiana, earned a Bachelor of Architecture degree from Ball State University. Craig, the author of *AutoCAD Advanced Techniques*, has used AutoCAD since Release 2.1. As a CAD consultant, Craig has provided such services as AutoLISP programming, custom menu design, and instruction in the use of AutoCAD and AutoCAD AEC.

Brent **Ring** has used AutoCAD for more than three years. He is a Systems Engineer for CAD/CAM Engineering, Inc., a CAD consulting firm in Indianapolis.

Publishing Manager

Allen L. Wyatt, Sr.

Product Development

Linda W. Sanning

Editors

Gail S. Burlakoff
Gregory Croy
Tim Huddleston
MS Editorial Service
Elizabeth M. Rehfus
Rebecca Whitney

Editorial Assistant

Ann K. Taylor

Technical Editors

Michael W. Ellis
Alan Hooper

Index

Brown Editorial Service

Book Design and Production

Dan Armstrong
Brad Chinn
Corinne Harmon
Dave Kline
Lori A. Lyons
Jennifer Matthews
Jon Ogle
Jenny Renbarger
Patricia Maupin Riggs
Dennis Sheehan
Mary Beth Wakefield

Composed in Garamond and OCRB
by Que Corporation and Precision Printing

CONTENT OVERVIEW

TABLE OF CONTENTS ▼

I   The Ground Floor

II   Making AutoCAD Work for You

IV   Working in the Third Dimension

V   Branching Out

18   Using AutoShade and AutoFlix.................... 437

ACKNOWLEDGMENTS

Books about difficult or complex software programs are often the collaborative effort of many people. It should come as no surprise, then, that a comprehensive book about AutoCAD is the result of hours of work by many people. Que Corporation thanks the following people for their outstanding efforts in relation to *Using AutoCAD*, 2nd Edition:

Gail Burlakoff, for managing the editorial development of *Using AutoCAD*, 2nd Edition. Gail has been associated with both editions of this book; she has contributed excellence and a sense of bringing order out of chaos. How she has done so with grace and finesse remains a mystery.

Gregory Croy, for editorial versatility and responsiveness. Greg stepped in many times when the going got tough. His sense of loyalty, professionalism, and team spirit is a worthy example to all of us.

Allen Wyatt, for his developmental efforts. In addition to being publishing manager and product line director for the book (like being chief cook and bottle washer), Allen researched, wrote, and expanded many portions of the Command Reference section. Most of the error messages there are an outgrowth of his childlike desire to play with something until it breaks.

Linda Sanning, for jumping into the deep end of the development pool to help with the Command Reference section, and for her work with the many AutoCAD users' groups across the country. Most of the plotted drawings in the book are a result of Linda's telephone calls.

Patricia Peper, for her excellent support. To many publishers, Patricia (who works in corporate communications at Autodesk) is the personification of corporate communications and, by extension, of Autodesk. Thanks for taking the time to talk.

This list is far from comprehensive; the acknowledgment section would be longer than prudence dictates if we named every person who contributed materially to this book. Those individuals know who they are; Que Corporation hopes that they will accept our sincere and heartfelt thanks for contributing to a work of which we are proud. You all make being associated with this business exciting.

*T*RADEMARK
*A*CKNOWLEDGMENTS

Que Corporation has made every attempt to supply trademark information about company names, products, and services mentioned in this book. Trademarks indicated below were derived from various sources. Que Corporation cannot attest to the accuracy of this information.

386-to-the-Max is a trademark of Qualitas, Inc.

Apple, Mac, and Macintosh are registered trademarks of Apple Computer, Inc.

AutoCAD, AutoCAD AEC, Autodesk, AutoLISP, and AutoSketch are registered trademarks of Autodesk, Inc. AUI, AutoFlix, AutoShade, and AutoSolid are trademarks of Autodesk, Inc.

COMPAQ Deskpro 386 is a registered trademark of COMPAQ Computer Corporation.

CompuServe Information Service is a registered trademark of CompuServe Incorporated and H&R Block, Inc.

dBASE III Plus is a trademark of Ashton-Tate Corporation.

Epson FX-286 is a trademark of Epson America, Inc.

Hercules is a registered trademark of Hercules Computer Technology.

IBM, PS/2 Model 70, and PS/2 Model 80 are registered trademarks of International Business Machines Corporation.

LETTEREASE is a trademark of CAD Lettering Systems, Inc.

Lotus and 1-2-3 are registered trademarks of Lotus Development Corporation.

Microsoft, MS-DOS, and XENIX are registered trademarks of Microsoft Corporation.

NEC Multisync is a registered trademark of NEC Home Electronics (USA) Inc.

Norton Editor is a trademark of Norton Computing.

PostScript is a registered trademark of Adobe Systems Incorporated.

Quarterdeck QEMM is a trademark of Quarterdeck Office Systems.

UNIX is a trademark of AT&T.

VAX/VMS is a trademark of Digital Equipment Corporation.

WordStar is a registered trademark of MicroPro International Corporation.

Xerox is a registered trademark of Xerox Corporation.

Introduction

Today's CAD (Computer-Aided Design) has made a quantum leap beyond the T-squares and drafting tables of 20 years ago. From its beginnings as a simple tool used exclusively on mainframe computer systems, CAD has evolved into a powerful design and engineering tool and is still evolving today. As hardware technology improved, CAD moved into the PC market, bringing its design and drafting capabilities to smaller businesses.

AutoCAD is the leading software package in the personal computer CAD field. With Release 10, AutoCAD has true 3-D capabilities and becomes a powerful tool for designers and engineers. Some reasons for AutoCAD's popularity are the following:

❑ With AutoCAD's 3-D capabilities, design and engineering specs can be checked easily on the computer. You do not have to build models or prototypes.

❑ Architectural projects can be checked for aesthetics as well as for function and presented to clients while still in the preliminary design stage.

❑ Projects can be dealt with on any level. With AutoCAD, you can examine specific construction points or simply ''walk through'' a project.

An important enhancement to Release 10 is the *flexible construction plane*, in which a drawing has normal X and Y axes, with a Z axis perpendicular to the X-Y plane. AutoCAD's capability to move the construction plane to different orientations adds an additional dimension of understanding and gives you a drawing freedom that far exceeds anything offered by other CAD software.

1

Using AutoCAD, 2nd Edition, is written and designed to help both experienced and first-time CAD users become more proficient with the AutoCAD program. First-time users will quickly learn to use AutoCAD and to feel more comfortable with the CAD equipment. Experienced users will learn to use the more advanced features of AutoCAD and to exploit the capabilities of Release 10. Users at all levels will realize the benefits of the comprehensive reference sections of this book.

Why Use AutoCAD?

AutoCAD is an impressive drafting package. Those who see AutoCAD in action are amazed at the ease with which an object—a gear, for example—can be drawn. Before the advent of AutoCAD and other CAD programs, many "war stories" circulated about people who spent tedious hours painstakingly drawing the same projects over and over by hand. Such stories are a thing of the past.

Why use AutoCAD rather than another computer-assisted design package? Basically, for the following reasons:

- ❏ Cost savings
- ❏ Compatibility
- ❏ Flexibility
- ❏ An industry standard

Let's look briefly at each of these factors.

Cost Savings

Economy is the main reason for buying a CAD system. You want to be more competitive, save time, use your time more efficiently, and reduce drafting costs. When approached correctly, a CAD system can help you do all of these.

For approximately what you would spend to hire a new draftsman for one year, you can have a CAD system set up and running for many years. The system is an efficient tool that—for an investment equivalent to one year's wages (minus insurance and taxes)—will allow you to do two or three times the work of the operator you could have paid with those wages! Essentially, you are substituting long-term capital for short-term cost.

AutoCAD by itself is quite affordable. Priced in the middle range of CAD packages, it gives you programmability combined with ease of use and the capability of working on a PC. This is an impressive combination.

Compatibility

The term *compatibility* is used here to refer to how easily something you develop can be picked up and worked on by another person on another system. When selecting a CAD drafting package, it is imperative that you consider compatibility with anyone who may need to access your work. Compatibility can range from the computer you use to the language you speak. We are most interested in system compatibility and drawing compatibility.

System compatibility with your clients is extremely important. System compatibility is the ease with which you can move information from computer to computer or system to system. Because AutoCAD runs on a variety of hardware and software platforms, AutoCAD drawing files can be transferred between computers regardless of their operating systems. This is not always true of other CAD software packages.

If you are looking for drawing compatibility, AutoCAD is an excellent selection. Generally, you can transfer an AutoCAD drawing to most other packages. Be aware, however, that the process of transferring drawings from one CAD program to another is not foolproof. You may lose part of the drawing during translation. To solve the problem of incompatibility, you must either use the same CAD package as your clients or draw your entire drawing with simple entities. The former is usually the better solution.

Flexibility

AutoCAD is a powerful tool for both drafting and design. Part of AutoCAD's power comes from the program's flexibility. It is quite impractical for any software developer to write a CAD package that will perfectly fit the needs of every user "out of the box." Autodesk has written a program that by itself is quite powerful, but the program's real strength lies in its adaptability; AutoCAD is easily customized to fit a user's specific needs.

Other aspects of AutoCAD's flexibility include the following:

- ❏ Its wide range of commands
- ❏ Its support of many types of hardware
- ❏ The availability of third-party tie-ins
- ❏ The AutoLISP programming language

The program is easy to learn and use for standard drafting. AutoCAD prompts are easy to understand and use, and as you will see, editing is not difficult. To aid drawing, you can create temporary construction lines, which won't show in your final output. With AutoCAD's menu systems, you can access the commands quickly and efficiently.

Whether you use the standard AutoCAD program by itself or with the aid of AutoLISP routines, AutoCAD has the potential to be used as an exceptional design tool. From a mechanical drafting standpoint, you can check clearances on parts that move together, or you can design parts as complex as modified sine cams. From an architectural point of view, you can evaluate structures in perspective or isometric from any location, inside the building or out. AutoCAD handles all of these functions quickly and cleanly. Combined with your ingenuity and creativity, AutoCAD's power is virtually unlimited.

An Industry Standard

Currently the industry standard for PC-based CAD systems, AutoCAD is an excellent tool for drafting, a good tool for design, and is fairly easy to learn and use. Some reasons AutoCAD has become such a strong standard are the following:

❑ A strong network of user groups
❑ Journals devoted specifically to its use and promotion
❑ An extensive array of dealers across the country
❑ A direct line to users, dealers, and Autodesk itself for questions and support

If you would like to have personal interaction with people who use AutoCAD, users' groups specifically created to share experiences with the program are located throughout the country. Such groups exemplify AutoCAD's strong following.

Should you prefer a broader, more detailed analysis of the latest tips and tricks on AutoCAD, both *CADalyst* and *CADENCE*, two excellent journals devoted to AutoCAD, are useful for both the novice and the advanced user. These magazines provide information for various disciplines that use the software.

Your AutoCAD dealer is also a good source of support. Autodesk has worked to make their dealers the best and most informed in the industry. If you are experiencing difficulties, your dealer has probably already seen the problem, or at least knows where to get the answer, and will be happy to help you out.

In addition to the users' groups, printed material, and your dealer, an AutoCAD forum is available on CompuServe. This is your "direct line" to people who are exposed to AutoCAD everyday. Here you will find the people who are striving to keep AutoCAD the industry standard. They will respond to your questions with a quicker and potentially more accurate answer than any other source.

Part VI, this book's Reference section, includes a complete listing of how you can find and take advantage of groups and other means of support for AutoCAD, the industry-standard CAD package.

Assumptions about the Reader

Certain assumptions have been made about you—the reader. It is assumed that you have AutoCAD Release 9 or 10 installed and running, that you have the equipment necessary to run CAD, and that you know certain basic computer-related information.

What You Should Have

In order to run AutoCAD, you must have the following basic hardware:

❏ 286 or 386 IBM-compatible computer with at least 640K of RAM; a Macintosh; or 32-bit workstation platforms

❏ Math coprocessor

❏ Hard disk (at least 40M)

❏ Monitor (at least EGA)

❏ Digitizing pad or mouse

❏ Plotter or printer plotter

What You Should Know

You must be familiar with computers and have a basic working knowledge of DOS, directories, and files. You should know how to reference different disk drives. Chapter 4, "Dabble in DOS," will discuss DOS commands, especially those that apply to the typical workstation. For more information about DOS, consult *Using PC DOS*, 2nd Edition, or *MS-DOS User's Guide*, Special Edition, both published by Que Corporation.

You should know something about menu-driven software. You do not need to know a great deal about menus, but you should be familiar with them because AutoCAD uses many types of menus.

Important software concepts in Chapters 1, 2, and 3 of *Using AutoCAD*, 2nd Edition, are not described elsewhere in the book. You should familiarize yourself with these concepts so that when the terms defined in these chapters are used in later chapters, you will know what they mean.

About This Book

As you look through this book, you will notice certain conventions. AutoCAD commands are in uppercase: the LINE command, for example. AutoCAD prompts and messages are in a `monospace type`, and information that you type at the AutoCAD prompt line is in **boldface**; you can see at a glance what actions to take as you use the program. Numerous examples supplement and clarify the text, which is written so that any architect, designer, draftsman, or engineer can use AutoCAD correctly and efficiently.

To help you learn the commands, you are introduced to the entire prompt sequence. Each command, listed as though you had typed it from the keyboard, is shown with all pertinent prompts. For example:

Prompt:	Response:	Explanation:
`Command:`	**CIRCLE**	Starts CIRCLE command
`3P/2P/TTR/<Center point>:`	Move crosshairs to circle's center point; pick it.	
`Diameter/<Radius>:`	**.25**	Indicates a radius of .25 inch

Explanations of the selections you can make at each prompt are also provided.

Examples follow the explanations of most commands. Projects for most of the commands follow the examples. Each set of projects builds on your knowledge of the commands covered earlier in the book.

What Is in This Book

Using AutoCAD, 2nd Edition, describes all drawing, editing, and specialty commands. After reading this book, you should be able to create, edit, and plot a drawing to your specifications. You will be able to set up and use a symbol library and create basic drawings on which to pattern other drawings. You will know how to develop and edit simple and complex three-dimensional models. You will be able to customize AutoCAD to your specific working environment, and you will have information on using two add-on packages (AutoShade and AutoFlix) as well as AutoCAD's programming language, AutoLISP.

Because *Using AutoCAD*, 2nd Edition, has been written for both the novice and the experienced AutoCAD user, your level of proficiency with AutoCAD should determine where you begin reading the book. If you are a novice, you should begin with Chapter 1 and continue through each chapter. This will help you establish a firm command of the concepts on which AutoCAD is based. If you are familiar with the equipment, DOS, and the computer environment, and if AutoCAD is already installed on your system, you may want to skip Part I, "The Ground Floor," and go from Chapter 1, "A Quick Start in AutoCAD," to Chapter 6, "The Basics of Drawing in AutoCAD."

If you have more experience as a CAD user, you will see that this text is arranged in a series of progressions. The book begins by demonstrating the concepts and commands necessary to draw in two dimensions, then expands those same principles into three-dimensional work. There are also chapters on customizing AutoCAD and using add-on packages to enhance your drawings.

Finally, a complete reference section provides invaluable information for users of all levels. The following synopsis should help you decide where to begin reading and where to find specific information.

❏ **Chapter 1: A Quick Start in AutoCAD**

This chapter provides step-by-step instructions to get into AutoCAD, do some minor drawing, and get out. Designed for the novice, this get-your-feet-wet chapter is a painless and quick introduction to AutoCAD.

❏ **Part I: The Ground Floor**

This Part covers basic information that you need to know before you begin to work with AutoCAD. There is a discussion of the benefits of Computer-Aided Design/Drafting over the "old-fashioned," manual method. Instructions on installation are provided as well as an overview of the CAD equipment. There is an explanation of how to best use DOS to your advantage.

❏ **Chapter 2: Manual versus Computer Drafting**

This chapter discusses the benefits of Computer-Aided Design/Drafting over manual drafting. It also covers some of the preparations that must be considered in order to transfer manually created drawings into AutoCAD drawings.

❏ **Chapter 3: Know Your CAD Equipment**

In this age of great technological leaps, the more you know about the hardware components in your system, the more productive you can be. This knowledge also enables you to take better advantage of future products because you will see how they could affect you. This chapter is devoted to increasing your awareness of the equipment that is designed to make your job easier and more productive.

❏ **Chapter 4: Dabble in DOS**

The operating system you use controls the programs you run as well as how those programs are able to access files, control the screen, and get information from the keyboard. Some hardware knowledge, a little insight into how your disk is set up, and knowing how to ensure the safety of your drawings can make your life much easier.

❏ **Chapter 5: Installing AutoCAD and AutoShade**

Complete instructions on the installation of AutoCAD and AutoShade are provided in this chapter. Also included are detailed directions on how to configure AutoCAD to fit your specific requirements.

❏ **Part II: Making AutoCAD Work for You**

This Part shows you how to use AutoCAD. Instructions and the accompanying examples teach you how to make drawings, edit drawings, view your drawings from different perspectives, and plot your drawings. Explanations are provided for all the AutoCAD commands used to perform the different tasks.

❏ **Chapter 6: The Basics of Drawing in AutoCAD**

The use of AutoCAD as a drawing tool begins in this chapter. The commands used to perform CAD drafting are shown. This chapter also discusses AutoCAD's screen, pull-down, and tablet menus.

❏ **Chapter 7: Editing Your Drawing**

In CAD, unlike manual drafting, it is often quicker and easier to revise and modify than to draft from scratch, because of the flexibility the editing commands offer. This chapter shows you how to edit the work you have on-screen.

❏ **Chapter 8: Advanced Editing Commands**

AutoCAD has other editing commands that permit sophisticated modification of your drawings. The PEDIT, CHANGE, and LAYER commands are covered in this chapter. The commands are demonstrated by building on an example developed in the previous chapter.

❏ **Chapter 9: Ways To View Your Drawing**

This chapter presents the options available for viewing your drawing. These options range from seeing your drawing on-screen through enlargements to hard-copy output such as prints and plots.

❏ **Chapter 10: Plotting Your Drawing**

Plotted drawings from AutoCAD are impressive. This chapter covers the commands and procedures for producing hard-copy output.

❑ **Part III: Mastering Your AutoCAD Environment**

The information in this Part is designed to make your work with AutoCAD more efficient and quick. The Part covers the commands you can use to customize your drawing environment and build a symbol library. Working with text and controlling dimensions with system variables are also covered.

❑ **Chapter 11: Customizing Your Drawing Environment**

AutoCAD has a broad variety of additional commands that allow for easier data manipulation and expand your control over your CAD environment. In this chapter, you learn to take advantage of those commands and customize your drawing environment.

❑ **Chapter 12: Expanding Your Horizons**

Some of the more involved drawing commands are discussed in this chapter. These commands demonstrate how to work with text and emphasize techniques such as dimensioning, hatching, and sketching.

❑ **Chapter 13: Creating a Symbol Library**

In this chapter, you learn more about how to use the basic drawing commands to build a library of parts and to use the parts in a drawing. You also learn how to break library parts into their original entities.

❑ **Part IV: Working in the Third Dimension**

With Release 10, AutoCAD has true three-dimensional capabilities. This part discusses all the commands and functions that support 3-D. Examples show how to use the 3-D commands and how three-dimensional entities affect commands that were previously used in two-dimensional drawings.

❑ **Chapter 14: Entering the Third Dimension**

This chapter explains the methods of taking the data you've created in two dimensions and transforming it into a three-dimensional image. You also learn the steps needed for drawing in three dimensions, as well as the basic three-dimensional entities.

❑ **Chapter 15: More 3-D Drawing Tools**

More 3-D drawing commands are presented in this chapter. Useful tips on how to model in three dimensions for presentation or design studies are explained.

❑ **Chapter 16: Editing Your Three-dimensional Drawing**

You should consider different approaches when working in the third dimension. This chapter explains the different approaches as well as the special precautions you must take when editing a three-dimensional model.

❏ **Chapter 17: Ways To View Your Three-dimensional Drawing**

This chapter expands on the methods for viewing conventional two-dimensional drawings, with examples of how to generate the picture with the view point and perspective you want. This chapter shows how to get the most out of some of the older commands and explains the newer options available with Release 10.

❏ **Part V: Branching Out**

There are numerous programs that supplement AutoCAD. This Part discusses two Autodesk add-ons, AutoShade and AutoFlix. You are also introduced to AutoCAD's programming language, AutoLISP.

❏ **Chapter 18: Using AutoShade and AutoFlix**

AutoShade is an add-on package with the capability to make full-color renditions of your AutoCAD drawings. AutoShade includes AutoFlix, an animation program. This chapter explains how to install and use these programs to enhance your AutoCAD work.

❏ **Chapter 19: An AutoLISP Primer**

AutoCAD is completely programmable through the AutoLISP language. This chapter introduces you to this full-fledged programming language.

❏ **Part VI: Reference**

This Part is a complete reference to AutoCAD commands, system variables, and pull-down menus. It includes a troubleshooting guide and a section on where to find help. There are appendixes on AutoCAD menus and useful add-on programs; one appendix presents a portfolio of plotted AutoCAD drawings.

❏ **AutoCAD Troubleshooting Guide**

This section identifies many problems that you may encounter when using AutoCAD and offers solutions. Using this section when you are in trouble can result in significant time savings.

❏ **Where To Get Help**

This section provides you with information on where to turn for help with AutoCAD. Here you will find ways to get answers if you run into trouble as you begin to work with AutoCAD.

❏ **Quick Reference to AutoCAD's System Variables**

This section is a convenient reference to the variables that give you complete control over the AutoCAD drawing environment.

❏ **AutoCAD Command Reference**

This section is an alphabetical listing and explanation of the entire set of AutoCAD commands.

❏ **Appendix A: AutoCAD's Menus**

This appendix touches on the main programs found in AutoCAD's screen and pull-down menus.

❏ **Appendix B: Useful Additional Programs**

This lists a collection of supplemental programs that greatly enhance the power and flexibility AutoCAD offers.

❏ **Appendix C: A Portfolio of Plotted Drawings**

In this appendix, you can examine completed drawings produced by AutoCAD users around the country. This portfolio shows you just some of the drawing and design possibilities that can be achieved with AutoCAD.

Also provided are a glossary and an extensive index, to help you find information quickly.

Summary

Using AutoCAD, 2nd Edition, is designed to make you more productive in your use of AutoCAD. This book will help you become familiar with the equipment used for your CAD station and AutoCAD's 2-D commands. In addition, you will learn 3-D drafting, undoubtedly the most exciting aspect of Release 10.

A Quick Start in AutoCAD

This chapter shows you how easy it is to get into and out of AutoCAD; it also gives you a chance to become comfortable with the AutoCAD environment. If you are just beginning and have never been exposed to CAD, this quick demonstration of how easy it can be to draw with a computer may be invaluable. The capabilities and complexities of this environment can be overwhelming, but as you work with AutoCAD you will be amazed at how quickly you learn what you need to know and grow comfortable with the program.

The following subjects are discussed in this chapter:

❏ The Main Menu
❏ The AutoCAD Coordinate System
❏ The Drawing Editor

The following AutoCAD commands also are briefly described:

❏ CIRCLE   ❏ LINE
❏ END   ❏ OOPS
❏ ERASE   ❏ QUIT
❏ HELP   ❏ U

Once you finish reading this chapter and complete the example presented, you should feel comfortable with starting a new AutoCAD drawing. You should also understand the AutoCAD coordinate system and the different methods of giving point information to AutoCAD commands. This information will prove valuable as you move on to the more complex example that begins in Chapter 6, "The Basics of Drawing in AutoCAD."

Starting AutoCAD

There are many ways to set up your computer so that you can access different programs. Batch files may be used alone or with elaborate menus. Because the standards of your business determine how your system is set up, you need to find out how to set up and access AutoCAD. If you do not have a batch file or menu set up on your computer, you can use the following basic method to work in AutoCAD.

To start the AutoCAD program, first go to the subdirectory where AutoCAD is stored (on most IBM-compatible computer systems, this is set up as C:\ACAD). At the DOS prompt type **ACAD**, then press Enter. This starts the program.

On some computer systems, a menu system may already be set up. A menu system allows you to start different programs without knowing the specifics of the program's name or location. Typically, a menu system is set up so that when your computer is not running a program, a screen is displayed showing the programs you can run. If AutoCAD is available to you from a menu system installed on your computer, an option labeled AutoCAD should be visible. Pick that option to start AutoCAD.

Once AutoCAD has been started (regardless of the method), one or two preliminary screens are displayed, followed by the AutoCAD Main Menu.

The AutoCAD Main Menu

From AutoCAD's Main Menu you can access each of AutoCAD's main commands. These commands, among other options, allow you to start a new drawing, continue with a previous drawing, plot your drawing, set up AutoCAD and its different devices, or leave AutoCAD entirely. The menu displayed on your screen should be similar to that shown in figure 1.1, although they may not match exactly.

REAR (SOUTH) ELEVATION

Drawing courtesy of Peterson + Habib consultants, inc.
engineer and architect
Thunder Bay, Ontario, Canada

Fig. 1.1. *The Main Menu.*

```
Main Menu
     0.   Exit AutoCAD
     1.   Begin a NEW drawing
     2.   Edit an EXISTING drawing
     3.   Plot a drawing
     4.   Printer Plot a drawing

     5.   Configure AutoCAD
     6.   File Utilities
     7.   Compile shape/font description file
     8.   Convert old drawing file

Enter selection:
```

At the top of the screen you will notice some important information: the AutoCAD release number (if this is not Release 9 or 10, parts of this book may not apply to you), copyright and ADE (Advanced Drafting Extension) information, and the program's serial number. If you need to contact Autodesk for technical assistance, you will be asked to provide this information.

Several AutoCAD commands are run from the Main Menu; these commands allow you to edit existing drawings, plot drawings, and execute such DOS commands as COPY and DELETE. If you enter an invalid response to one of the command prompts, AutoCAD tells you of your error and lets you try again.

Most of the Main Menu options will be covered later in this chapter. The first two Main Menu options allow you to exit AutoCAD or begin a new drawing.

Option 0 — Exiting AutoCAD

Be sure to use Main Menu Option 0 to exit AutoCAD *before* you turn off your computer. AutoCAD keeps several files open. If you turn off your computer before you exit AutoCAD, those files will not be closed properly and the information in them can be lost or corrupted (mixed up or partially erased).

> **Sharing Drawings between Different Versions of AutoCAD**
>
> The Main Menu information is important if you are sharing drawings with other people who are using AutoCAD. As AutoCAD has grown, changes have been made to the way graphical information is stored in drawing files. As a result of these changes, you cannot use AutoCAD Release 10 to work on a drawing created with Version 2.62. To avoid this, make sure that everyone is using the same version of AutoCAD or that you can locate a drawing translator to convert new format drawings to an older format. (Drawing translators usually are available on most AutoCAD bulletin board systems, which are accessible by modem.) Fortunately, this problem occurs only when you change from a newer version of AutoCAD to an older one. Drawing files are *upwardly compatible*, which means that files created by an older version of AutoCAD can be read by newer releases of the program. For more information on translator programs, see Appendix B, "Useful Additional Programs."

If a file is corrupted, AutoCAD may no longer be able to use it, and your entire drawing may be lost. Remember to select Option 0, `Exit AutoCAD`, when you finish an AutoCAD session.

Option 1 — Beginning a New Drawing

When you are ready to start a new drawing, use Main Menu Option 1. An on-screen message then prompts you for the name of the drawing. This name, which is the name of the file in which information about the drawing is stored, must correspond to the requirements for DOS, UNIX, or whatever operating system you are using with AutoCAD. The DOS specifications follow:

❏ Drawing names can be up to eight characters long. You do not need to add an extension because AutoCAD automatically provides the extension *.DWG* for drawing files.

❏ Drawing names can contain numbers, letters (both upper- and lowercase), and the dollar sign ($), hyphen (-), or underscore (__) characters.

No spaces are allowed in a file name. To simulate a space, use a hyphen or an underscore character. AutoCAD treats the space bar the same as another Enter key; if you try to insert a space by pressing the space bar, AutoCAD assumes that you have finished entering the name and calls up the Drawing Editor.

If you want your drawings to reside in an existing directory (other than the current one), or on another drive, you must indicate the appropriate path, as you would at the DOS level. When AutoCAD prompts you for the name of the drawing, be sure to put the path in front of the name. For example, if your drawing (ELEV01) were stored in the JONES subdirectory of the ACAD directory, you could respond to the prompt as follows:

Enter NAME of drawing:**\ACAD\JONES\ELEV01**

If the drawing name you enter already exists, AutoCAD will let you know. Then you can either choose a new name, rename the existing file, or copy over (delete) the existing file, effectively replacing the existing drawing with the new one you are about to create. For information on subdirectories and how your hard disk might be set up, be sure to read Chapter 4, "Dabble in DOS."

With your drawing's name successfully entered, you will see AutoCad's Drawing Editor (see fig. 1.2). This is the area in AutoCAD where all drawing occurs.

Fig. 1.2. The AutoCAD Drawing Editor screen.

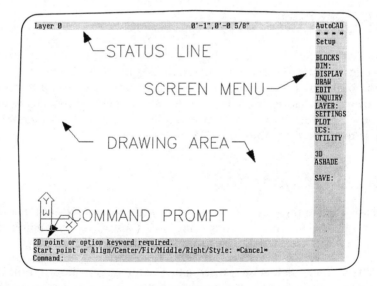

The Drawing Editor screen consists of these parts:

Drawing Area: The area in which AutoCAD places the entities you draw. To show the location of your input device within this area, AutoCAD will display crosshairs. As you move your input device, the crosshairs follow on-screen.

Command Prompt: Located at the bottom of the screen, this area displays everything you type when you use an AutoCAD command. AutoCAD also uses this area when it requests information from you, information which may relate to a specific command.

Screen Menu: The screen menu serves as another way to enter AutoCAD commands. (You can also press the Insert [Ins] key to use these commands from the keyboard if you don't have a mouse or a digitizer.) By moving the crosshairs into the screen menu area, you can pick the commands you want to use instead of entering them from the keyboard.

Status Line: This line, located at the top of your screen, displays important information about the status of your drawing. Information displayed on this line may include the layer you currently are on, the coordinate position of the crosshairs, and which of AutoCAD's modes are active.

A Short Drawing Exercise

Now that you have been introduced to the Drawing Editor, your next step is to see just how easy drawing with AutoCAD really is. At this point, you'll learn the basics of a few commands; in later chapters, you will find detailed explanations of what these commands do. By following this drawing exercise (from now on referred to as *the example*), you will begin to understand how easy it is to work with AutoCAD's Drawing Editor.

The LINE Command

Perhaps the simplest command to start with is the LINE command. This command does just what it sounds like (most AutoCAD commands are like that)—it draws a line from point to point until you tell it to stop.

After you enter this command sequence, your screen should look like the screen shown in figure 1.3. The coordinate locations are shown so that you can understand where the numbers you typed place the LINE endpoints.

Prompt:	Response:	Explanation:
Command:	**LINE**	Starts LINE command
From point:	**1,1**	Absolute starting point for the line
To point:	**5,7**	Next point. This draws first line.
To point:	**9,3**	Last point. This draws second line.
To point:	Press Enter.	This ends the LINE command.

Fig. 1.3. *The Drawing Editor after the previous example.*

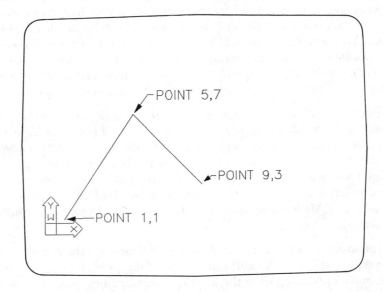

AutoCAD's Coordinate Systems

AutoCAD normally uses a fixed Cartesian coordinate system, referred to as the *World Coordinate System* (WCS). This system uses three axes (x,y,z) to locate any point in three dimensions. The origin of this coordinate system is 0,0,0

(X=0, Y=0, and Z=0). Three-dimensional drawing and the X,Y,Z coordinate system will be covered in greater depth in Chapter 14, "Entering the Third Dimension." Because you will want to work first in two dimensions, the following descriptions are restricted to the X,Y coordinate system.

In two-dimensional drawing, you usually draw as if you were looking straight down on your project from above (this is called *plan view*). Every object that you choose to draw in AutoCAD has some sort of X,Y coordinates associated with it. Those coordinates can be the X,Y locations of a line endpoint (as shown previously), or they can be the location for the center of a circle (as will be demonstrated later in the example). The origin of this coordinate system is located at 0,0 (which should correspond to the lower left corner of the Drawing Window).

Entering Points in AutoCAD

You can enter points in several ways, the easiest of which is called *picking*. By picking, you randomly but accurately indicate points in a drawing. In this method, you use a pointing device (a puck, mouse, or stylus) to pick the location of points. Typically, points entered by picking are two-dimensional. Points may also be located in three-dimensional space. Chapter 11, "Customizing Your Drawing Environment," explains how to set certain AutoCAD variables so that the points you pick are not restricted to the X,Y coordinate system.

On pucks and mice, you locate a point by pressing the pick button; styluses are either spring-loaded (you press down to indicate a point) or have a single button that you press. Pucks and styluses generally are used with a *digitizing tablet*. Mechanical mice are moved across a smooth, hard surface; optical mice are moved across a reflective pad. For more information about using mice and styluses as input devices, see the appropriate sections in Chapters 3 and 6 ("Know Your CAD Equipment" and "The Basics of Drawing in AutoCAD," respectively).

As you move the device, the crosshairs that appear on the AutoCAD screen correspond to the position and movement of the pointing device. To locate points, move the crosshairs to the location you want and then pick the points by pressing the pick button on your puck or mouse, or by pressing down on your stylus.

Another way to enter points is to use the keyboard. You can enter points from the keyboard in two ways: by using the arrow keys to control the cursor on-screen or by typing the point's X,Y coordinates, as in the previous example of the LINE command.

Point information can be Cartesian or polar. In the Cartesian system, you identify the X,Y coordinates. Type the X value, followed by a comma, then type the Y value. When you press Enter, AutoCAD accepts the point.

To indicate a *polar* coordinate, enter a distance and an angle (using the format @*d*<*A*, in which *d* = distance and *A* = angle). For polar coordinates, the angle is measured around the most recently picked point (whether by pick with a mouse or tablet, or by entry from the keyboard). Angles are calculated counter-clockwise from three o'clock (unless AutoCAD's default settings have been changed through the use of the UNITS command, explained in Chapter 6, "The Basics of Drawing in AutoCAD").

If you use relative coordinates, you can draw entities by referencing points instead of calculating all the absolute coordinate points. In the previous example of the LINE command, absolute coordinates were used to locate the endpoints of the line. Relative coordinates also can be used to locate these endpoints. In figure 1.4, the lines drawn are the same as those in figure 1.3, except that relative coordinates, rather than absolute coordinates, have been used to find the endpoints.

Fig. 1.4. *Lines drawn using relative coordinates.*

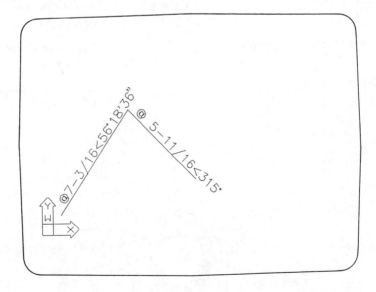

The difference between absolute and relative coordinate entry will become clearer as you work through the example beginning in Chapter 6, "The Basics of Drawing in AutoCAD." Cartesian coordinates *may* be used for relative input, but polar coordinates are *always* entered in relative input form. You should remember, though, that either of these different types of point input can be used whenever you are prompted for location information.

The CIRCLE Command

As mentioned previously, most of AutoCAD's command names are indicative of the function they perform; the LINE command draws lines, the CIRCLE command draws circles, and so on. AutoCAD has been designed to be easy to use, as the command names indicate.

Unlike the LINE command, which is extremely simple to use, the CIRCLE command has several variations. These variations are explained in more detail in Chapter 6, "The Basics of Drawing in AutoCAD." For now, the following command sequence shows only the default option of the CIRCLE command: to pick the circle's center and then give a radius.

Prompt:	Response:	Explanation:
Command:	**CIRCLE**	Starts CIRCLE command
3P/2P/TTR/<Center point>:	**6,3**	Center of circle at point 6,3
Diameter/<Radius>:	**2**	Indicates a radius of 2 inches

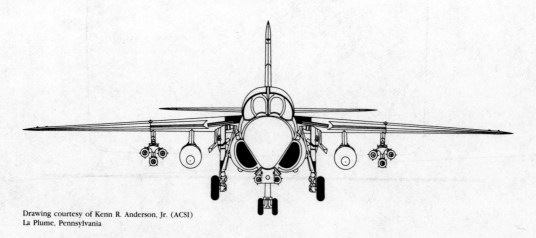

Drawing courtesy of Kenn R. Anderson, Jr. (ACSI)
La Plume, Pennsylvania

Now your screen should look like the one shown in figure 1.5.

Fig. 1.5. Your first drawing—lines and a circle.

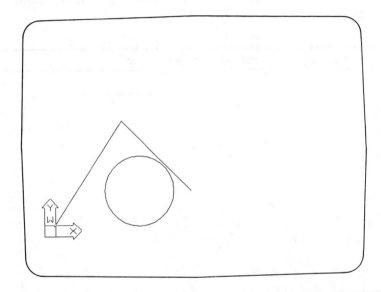

The ERASE Command

AutoCAD not only allows you to draw entities easily, but also allows easy editing of the objects you have drawn. Of the many editing commands available, the ERASE command probably will be the one you use most often. Everyone makes mistakes, but in AutoCAD it is easier to "erase" them!

Prompt:	Response:	Explanation:
Command:	**ERASE**	Starts ERASE command
Select Objects:	**Last**	Chooses the last entity drawn (the circle)
Select Objects:	Press Enter.	Erases the entities selected (the circle)

When AutoCAD picks an object during an edit command, it creates what is known as a *selection set*. The selection set contains all the entities chosen for an edit command. The entities in the selection set are highlighted, which has the effect of turning the entities from their typical solid lines and circles into a dotted outline (see figure 1.6). This "ghosting" is done simply to show which entities you have chosen to edit.

Fig. 1.6. A highlighted entity in a selection set.

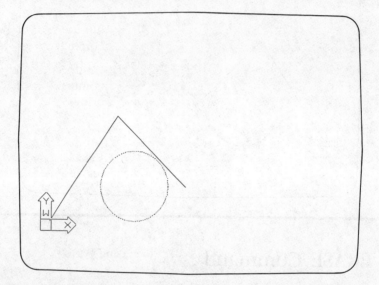

Correcting Your Mistakes (OOPS and U)

It may sound odd, but sometimes you can make mistakes by erasing your mistakes. If you erase too many entities, for example, you can lose information that you need in your drawing. To correct this, AutoCAD provides two commands to help you retrieve information you may have erased accidentally. These commands, OOPS and U (for *UNDO*), allow you to "step back" one or more commands and recover entities that you may have altered inadvertently.

The difference between the OOPS and U commands may not be apparent at first. OOPS brings back the last group of entities erased, whereas U causes the last step you took to be undone. The following example should help clarify the differences between these commands:

Prompt:	Response:	Explanation:
Command:	**OOPS**	Puts the circle back on the screen

The U command allows you to step backwards through all the commands you have entered, even if you want to go all the way back to the point at which you entered the Drawing Editor. The following example shows how it works:

Prompt:	Response:	Explanation:
Command:	U	Re-erases the circle that we un-erased (un-does the OOPS command)
Command:	U	Un-does the ERASE command and brings back the circle
Command:	U	Un-does the CIRCLE command, leaving only the lines
Command:	U	Un-does the LINE command

If you have followed this example, you can see that using U to step back through the drawing commands leaves you with the blank screen you saw when you entered the Drawing Editor.

Finding Help (HELP)

If you are in the Drawing Editor and are not sure about the command you need to use, AutoCAD provides a simple help facility to explain the available commands and what they do. The HELP command provides a limited amount of on-line assistance within AutoCAD. You use it to get general information about AutoCAD or specific information about a command. To get general help for all AutoCAD commands, press Enter at the Command: prompt. This action will initiate AutoCAD's HELP facility.

To enter the HELP system, enter **HELP** at the Command: prompt. AutoCAD will respond with the following prompt:

Command name (RETURN for list):

You have two choices. If you enter a command, you will receive help for that specific command. If you press Enter, you will see a series of screens similar to the one shown in figure 1.7. These screens contain information for which AutoCAD command help is available, as well as help on point entry and the coordinate system. To advance through the screens, you must press Enter when prompted.

Fig. 1.7. *An AutoCAD help screen.*

```
     AutoCAD Command List  (' = transparent command)

  APERTURE    CHANGE      DIVIDE      EXPLODE     IGESOUT
  ARC         CHPROP      DONUT       EXTEND      INSERT
  AREA        CIRCLE      DOUGHNUT    FILES       ISOPLANE
  ARRAY       COLOR       DRAGMODE    FILL        LAYER
  ATTDEF      COPY        DTEXT       FILLET      LIMITS
  ATTDISP     DBLIST      DVIEW       FILMROLL    LINE
  ATTEDIT     DDATTE      DXBIN       'GRAPHSCR   LINETYPE
  ATTEXT      'DDEMODES   DXFIN       GRID        LIST
  AXIS        'DDLMODES   DXFOUT      HANDLES     LOAD
  BASE        'DDRMODES   EDGESURF    HATCH       LTSCALE
  BLIPMODE    DDUCS       ELEV        'HELP / '?  MEASURE
  BLOCK       DELAY       ELLIPSE     HIDE        MENU
  BREAK       DIM/DIM1    END         ID          MINSERT
  CHAMFER     DIST        ERASE       IGESIN      MIRROR

  Press RETURN for further help.
```

If you want help with a command, enter the name of that command at the HELP prompt; AutoCAD will display a help screen for the command (see fig. 1.8). Remember that you can advance through the help screens by pressing Enter.

To use HELP inside other commands, type **'HELP** (notice the apostrophe), or enter a question mark (**?**) at the prompt for which you need help. In AutoCAD, the apostrophe has special meaning. It is used to perform one command *transparently* while you are in the middle of another command (to get help, for instance).

After you finish viewing a help screen, you are left in AutoCAD's text mode. To view your drawing again, press the F1 function key. This key "flips" you between *graphics mode* (which shows the drawing screen) and *text mode* (a full screen that shows your latest responses to the Command: prompt). Many CAD

Fig. 1.8. A help screen for the INSERT command.

```
The INSERT command inserts one occurrence of a defined Block into the
current drawing at a designated point, applying scale factors and
rotation.  If the named Block is not defined in the current drawing, but
another drawing exists with that name, a Block Definition is first
created from the other drawing.

Format:     INSERT Block name (or ?) <default>:
            Insertion point:
            X scale factor <1> / Corner / XYZ:
            Y scale factor (default = X):
            Rotation angle <0>:

The X/Y scales may be specified simultaneously by using the insertion point
as the lower left corner of a box, and a new point as the upper right corner;
just enter the new point in response to the "X scale factor" prompt.

You can enter "DRAG" to dynamically specify the insertion point, X/Y scales,
and rotation angle.  You can preset the scale and rotation for the dragged
image by using the "Scale" or "Rotate" option at the "Insertion point:"
prompt.

Press RETURN for further help.
```

systems use what is called *dual-screen mode* with AutoCAD; all of your graphic information can be placed on one screen and all your responses to the Command: prompt can be placed on another. For more information on dual-screen configurations and other hardware, see Chapter 3, "Know Your CAD Equipment."

Exiting the AutoCAD Drawing Editor (END/QUIT)

Getting out of the AutoCAD Drawing Editor is as easy as getting into it. To get back to AutoCAD's Main Menu, you can type either **END** or **QUIT**.

The END command saves your drawing and returns you to the Main Menu. This is the command you will use 95 percent of the time to get out of the AutoCAD Drawing Editor.

The QUIT command does not save your work; it simply exits directly from the Drawing Editor back to the Main Menu. AutoCAD asks whether you are sure you want to exit without saving your changes. If you are sure, type **Y** (for Yes) and press Enter. Be careful with this command—once you say "yes," the work you have done will be lost forever.

Whether you realize it or not, you have just finished your first drawing in AutoCAD. Even though what you have done is fairly simple, you are now on a path that will show you how to use the AutoCAD drawing commands to create complex drawings.

The Other Main Menu Options

AutoCAD has a total of nine Main Menu options (numbered 0 through 8). Option 0, Exit AutoCAD, and Option 1, Start a New Drawing, were covered earlier in this chapter (before the drawing exercise). The remaining Main Menu options are discussed briefly in the following sections.

Option 2 — Editing an Existing Drawing

Select Main Menu Option 2 if you want to work with a drawing that already exists. If AutoCAD cannot find the drawing, you will see the following message:

```
**Drawing (name) is not on file.
Press RETURN to continue.
```

Press Enter to go back to the Main Menu, and try again. You may have to access the File Utility Menu (Main Menu Option 6) to see which drawing files are available.

If the drawing you want to edit is in another directory or another drive, you must indicate the path and the drawing's name (see the explanation of Main Menu Option 1, earlier in this chapter, for a description and example of this process).

When you choose to edit a drawing that already exists, all the settings are retained and the drawing appears on-screen as it did when you ended your last editing session. All settings retain their values and all toggles retain their settings. This part of AutoCAD is convenient: you can end a drawing and then, without having to reset values, resume working from the exact stage at which you stopped.

Option 3 — Plotting a Drawing

One way to produce hard copy of your drawing is to select **3** from the Main Menu; doing so is effectively the same as entering the PLOT command from within the Drawing Editor (as described in Chapter 10, ''Plotting Your Drawing''). The only difference is that when you choose to plot from the Main Menu, you do not have a chance to see the drawing before you plot it. If you consider this a drawback, enter the Drawing Editor and use the PLOT command.

Because plotting from the Main Menu is the same as from the Drawing Editor, you can produce uniform plots with either method. For an in-depth discussion of plotting, see Chapter 10.

Option 4 — Printer Plotting a Drawing

To create a hard copy of your drawing on a printer that allows graphics, select 4 from the Main Menu. This option is effectively the same as issuing the PRPLOT command from within the Drawing Editor; both correspond closely to Main Menu Option 3 and the PLOT command. For more information, see the preceding section and Chapter 10.

Option 5 — Configuring AutoCAD: A Brief Look

Before you can use AutoCAD, you must let the program know what hardware you want to run. Presumably, you have the software designed for your computer (an IBM-compatible machine or a Macintosh). Choose Option 5, Configure AutoCAD, and set up your monitor, graphics card, digitizing device, printer, plotter, and any other peripherals you will use. After you set up your equipment, you can return to the Main Menu.

If you change your monitor, printer, or any other peripheral, you must reconfigure AutoCAD. The software needs accurate information about each peripheral. Otherwise, the hardware may not work.

AutoCAD configuration is explained more fully in Chapter 5, "Installing AutoCAD and AutoShade," and in the *Installation and Performance Guide* that comes with AutoCAD. If you follow all the instructions in these references, you should have no problem. If a problem should occur, you can check to see whether the peripheral is hooked up. If you are familiar with your computer, look behind it and make sure that the cable from the device is connected to the correct port. Check to see whether the device is turned on and whether the correct cable connects the device to the computer. If you are not comfortable with these steps, or if they do not work, call your service representative. If your system was configured by an authorized AutoCAD dealer, it should work properly. Your dealer should be able to correct any problems.

Option 6 — File Utilities

Use Main Menu Option 6 to access the File Utility Menu (see fig. 1.9). From this menu you can exit to the Main Menu, list the drawing files, list any files, or delete, rename, and copy files. Most of these functions are duplicates of the operating system's functions. For more information on these commands and their effects on your computer and its hard disk, see Chapter 4, "Dabble in DOS."

Fig. 1.9. *The File Utility Menu.*

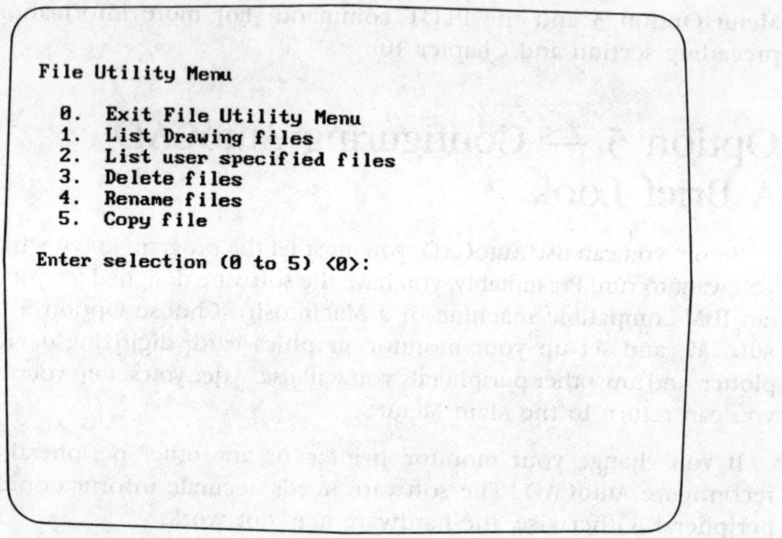

```
File Utility Menu

   0.  Exit File Utility Menu
   1.  List Drawing files
   2.  List user specified files
   3.  Delete files
   4.  Rename files
   5.  Copy file

Enter selection (0 to 5) <0>:
```

Use Option 0 when you want to exit the File Utility Menu and return to the Main Menu. Option 1 lists the drawing files in any directory you specify. If you want to know which drawing files are in the current directory, simply press Enter at the Enter drive or directory: prompt.

You also can list the drawing files on another drive. To list files from drive A:, for example, type **A:** at the Enter drive or directory: prompt and then press Enter.

Option 2 on the File Utility Menu lets you list any type of file. Before you select **2**, however, you should be aware of certain conventions. First, DOS file names can have two parts: a file name and an extension that indicates what type of file it is. The file name can be up to eight characters long; the file extension can have up to three characters. The file name and extension are separated by a period. The following are examples of common AutoCAD file names:

File name	Type of file
ACAD.DWG	An AutoCAD prototype drawing
ACAD.EXE	An AutoCAD executable file
ACAD.MNX	An AutoCAD menu file (compiled)
ACAD.MNU	An AutoCAD menu file (not compiled)

AutoCAD and other programs use many other files. If you want to list a group of related files, you can substitute *wild-card* characters for the letters in the file names and extensions. The computer reads a question mark (?) as "any character in this position"; an asterisk (*) is read as "any characters from here until the end of the name or extension." If you want to list a series of five drawings (DRAW1.DWG-DRAW5.DWG), enter the following information:

```
Enter selection (0 to 5): 2
Enter file search specifications: DRAW?.DWG
```

You are telling AutoCAD to list all the files with names that start with *DRAW*, followed by any other single character, and end with the *.DWG* extension.

To list *all* the files that start with DRAW, you would type **DRAW*.*** at the `Enter file search specifications:` prompt. *DRAW*.** tells AutoCAD to list all files that begin with DRAW, followed by any characters before and after the period. By using wild-card characters, you can list groups of files whose names or extensions have common parts.

You must use both the file name and its extension when you work in the File Utility Menu. During other AutoCAD activities, you do not have to specify the file extension because AutoCAD looks for a certain type of file and provides the extension for you.

Choose File Utility Menu option **3** to delete files from any drive or directory. Again, you can use wild-card characters to help with the file names, but if you do, be very careful: when you use wild-card characters with the `Delete files` selection, you can accidentally delete files you did not intend to delete.

The prompts for this selection are

```
Enter file deletion specification:
Delete (filename.ext)? <N>:
Delete (filename.ext)? <N>:
```

Type the file name at the first prompt and then respond to the other prompts. As you may have guessed, `filename.ext` represents the name of the file you have specified for deletion. If you specified a wild card (the * or ? character) and AutoCAD found more than one file to delete, you will be asked to individually confirm the deletion of each file. The default is N; if you press Enter to accept the default, the file remains intact. You must type **Y** to delete the file.

Option 4 lets you rename a file. This step is important if you have not yet established a naming convention. If you misname a drawing, simply rename the file by entering appropriate names at the following prompts:

```
Enter current filename: filename.ext
Enter new filename: newname.ext
```

You can also rename files in other directories or in other drives.

Choose Option 5 when you want to duplicate a file. This is handy for copying files from your hard drive to a floppy disk. You must provide the file name and the destination, as indicated by the following prompts:

```
Enter name of source file: filename.ext

Enter name of destination file: A:filename.ext
```

This example copies *filename.ext* to the floppy disk in the A: drive. Remember that you must include both the file name and the extension.

After you have worked with the File Utility options, return to the Main Menu to continue learning about that menu's options.

Option 7 — Compiling Shape/Font Description Files

Main Menu Option 7 compiles programmed shape and font files created in separate DOS files outside AutoCAD. These programmed files must be compiled before you use them. Because shapes and font descriptions are advanced AutoCAD techniques and part of AutoCAD programming, they are not covered in this book. If you are interested in these aspects of AutoCAD, we recommend *AutoCAD Advanced Techniques*, published by Que Corporation.

Option 8 — Converting Old Drawing Files

Main Menu Option 8 updates old file formats to the current release of AutoCAD. The drawing file format was changed dramatically after AutoCAD Release 2.0. Some types of entities were removed and new ones were added.

(The change from Release 9 to Release 10 is not as dramatic—it involves some major additions, but no major subtractions).

As stated earlier in this chapter, you usually need to use a translation program to convert drawings from a newer version of AutoCAD to an older version. Option 8 does just the opposite: it takes an older version of a drawing and updates it. Because AutoCAD contains all the necessary routines to perform this conversion, there is no need for a translation program to perform this step.

If you plot or printer plot from the Main Menu, the file is updated automatically. If you try to edit an old file in a new release of AutoCAD, and the file is rejected because it is old, simply use Option 8 to convert the file; then edit it.

Summary

This chapter has introduced you to AutoCAD. You have learned about the Main Menu and its options. You have also learned the basics of entering and exiting the AutoCAD Drawing Editor and working in the AutoCAD coordinate system. We have also covered the following commands:

- ❏ CIRCLE
- ❏ END
- ❏ ERASE
- ❏ LINE
- ❏ HELP
- ❏ OOPS
- ❏ QUIT
- ❏ U

Although AutoCAD is an extremely powerful and versatile drafting tool, it is not so complex that a casual user cannot use it to create simple drawings. This chapter has demonstrated the basis for creating all drawings. The upcoming chapters will further explain the equipment you will use and demonstrate how you can put AutoCAD's commands to work for you.

Part I

EAST ELEVATION
SCALE 1/4"=1'-0"

235 ASPHALT SHINGLES

FACE BRICK

Drawing courtesy of R.L. Tomlinson Drafting & Blueprinting, Inc.
Thunder Bay, Ontario, Canada

The Ground Floor

2

AutoCAD—Manual versus Computer Drafting

Many firms are switching from existing manual drafting techniques to computer-aided drafting and design. Although computers offer many advantages over typical manual drafting methods, only by becoming aware of the differences between manual and computer drafting techniques can you make CAD productive for you and your company.

The purpose of this chapter is to illustrate the differences between manual and computer drafting and to highlight the advantages CAD offers. To this end, the following CAD concepts are discussed:

❑ Precision drawing
❑ Working with scale
❑ The relativity of CAD
❑ Templates and symbols
❑ Reusability of previous work
❑ Quick changes
❑ Diversity and the multidiscipline drawing
❑ Final output
❑ Training

When you have finished reading this chapter you should be familiar with the similarities and differences between CAD and manual drafting, and the advantages of each method.

Precision Drawing

Clearly, there is a large conceptual difference between drawing manually and drawing in AutoCAD. This difference begins with the concept of *drawing precision*. Unless you take time to think through the concept, it can cause several problems when you first convert your manual system to AutoCAD.

When drawing manually, most people start with a rough sketch and then fill in the details. Saying that a widget will be about one inch long or that a wall will be about 16 feet long is acceptable because you know you will go back and finish the drawing with accurate dimensions. This method substantially speeds up the process of the first draft, but forces the user to come back later to dimension his or her work. This takes time and can be costly if a mistake slips through.

Even with a powerful tool like AutoCAD, you will need to do thumbnail sketches or at least have an idea of what you are drawing before you start. But as with any new tool, after you learn the basics of AutoCAD you will think of many new areas in which it can make you more productive.

Drawing in AutoCAD is much easier if you draw precisely from the day you start using the program. AutoCAD is an extremely exact tool. When you draw a one-inch square in CAD, it is *exactly* 1.00000000 inch square. AutoCAD works at a precision of 16 decimal places. Some of the advantages of such precision follow:

❑ Conflicting elements are easier to notice.

❑ AutoCAD can automatically manage your drawing's dimensioning.

❑ Specific information (such as room volumes, linear feet of steel, etc.) is easier to extract from the drawing later.

❑ Others can more easily work with your drawings.

❑ Sharing your drawings with other people off-site is easier.

If you take these points into account, you can understand how the precision of a drawing can affect your work.

A brief explanation of how AutoCAD "sees" entities may help you understand the importance of drawing precisely within AutoCAD. Each AutoCAD entity is stored in a database as individual pieces of information. The information stored depends on the type of entity. When a line is stored, for example, AutoCAD keeps track of the line's endpoints, length, and direction. Information stored for a circle includes its center point and a radius from which the circumference is derived. These elements are stored as numbers to a precision of 16 decimal places, even though AutoCAD may not display all 16 decimal places. (The number of displayed decimal places is controlled through the UNITS command, which is discussed in Chapter 6, "The Basics of Drawing in AutoCAD.")

Because these numbers are stored so precisely within the database, AutoCAD can reflect *very* accurately any imperfections in your work (such as one edge of a wall being 0.00000001 inch shorter than the other edge of the same wall). Suppose that you need to do clearance-checking later (something AutoCAD is well suited for). By using precision from the beginning of your drawing session, you will make the task much easier.

This precision shouldn't keep you from using AutoCAD as a sketch pad for your ideas. Because AutoCAD is an exact tool, you may want to use pencil and paper for the creative process and then put your roughed-out ideas into AutoCAD, using precise dimensions. The more experienced you are as a designer and engineer, the easier you will find this method.

Working with Scale

When you begin an AutoCAD drawing, one of the things you need to consider is how you will scale your drawing. Scale is used all the time in manual drafting: a gear may be drawn at a 5:1 scale; a floor plan, at 1/8″=1′-0″. In AutoCAD, you can work with scale in two ways.

In the first method, you draw everything full-scale and then, when you are ready to plot your drawing, you tell the computer the scale at which you want to plot the drawing. If you choose this method, you can work full-scale in your drawing without having to worry about calculating the scaled measurements of every entity as you enter that entity.

The second method of scaling involves drawing to a scale other than full-scale and then plotting exactly what you have drawn. This method is good for users who have title blocks in their drawings and who continually work with paper of one size. People who need to know the boundaries of their drawings benefit from drawing with a title block because doing so most resembles their work before they used a CAD system. As you become more familiar with AutoCAD, you will find that this scaling method does not take advantage of some of the features CAD offers.

There are three primary advantages to working at full-scale. The first is that maintaining an accurate drawing is easier. Assume, for example, that you are creating a site plan for a house. The drawing scale that you want to use is 1″=20′-0″. If you are drawing in full-scale, when you tell AutoCAD to draw a 24′-4″ wall for your garage, the wall line is exactly 24′-4″. On the other hand, if you are using a scaling method, you must first find out how many inches 24'-4" will be at 20 scale (1.21666667 inches), and then have AutoCAD draw the line that length. Such calculations, repeated over the course of an entire project, can become tiresome.

The second advantage to working at full-scale relates directly to AutoCAD Release 10. Working in true 3-D is easier if you draw in full-scale and plot at a reduced scale. The three-dimensional aspects of AutoCAD Release 10 are covered later in this book, starting with Chapter 14, "Entering the Third Dimension." New 3-D commands, such as VPORT, allow you to draw an object in its entirety and then pull different views from the object. This capability to fully use the drawing after it is in the database is one of the marks of a good CAD system.

The third benefit of working at full-scale has to do with what everyone else is doing. Most AutoCAD users have adopted the standard of working at full-scale for all drawings because, by doing so, they can take advantage of symbol libraries created by other companies or third-party manufacturers. Thus, working in something other than full-scale isolates you from the vast majority of the AutoCAD community.

The Relativity of CAD

Although the expression "Everything is relative" may not always hold true, it certainly applies to CAD, and especially to AutoCAD. Remember—one of the most important concepts of CAD is that *nothing is set in concrete!* AutoCAD is an extremely dynamic environment, designed to be tailored to your specific needs. If a hatch pattern (what draftsmen refer to as *poché*) is not right, modify it. If a particular linetype is incorrect, change it. If you need drawings that are two different scales on the same sheet, it's a piece of cake.

As you can see, this flexibility places computer-aided drafting significantly ahead of manual drafting in this area. All you need is an understanding of the resources AutoCAD draws from to create your drawings.

Templates and Symbols

Any good draftsperson knows that hundreds of drawing templates are available to help him or her produce an accurate drawing quickly. Circle and ellipse templates, bathroom, kitchen, steel shapes, and shrubbery have all been immortalized in plastic cut-outs available from your local drafting supply. Typically, every discipline has its own set of symbols that graphically represent items of importance. Center lines of circles, slots to be cut out of a steel plate, the pattern of a wooden parquet floor, or a symbol that represents a water valve or a fire hydrant on a utility map are other examples of items that may be important to your clients.

As you will see in Chapter 13, "Creating a Symbol Library," AutoCAD provides an easy way to insert graphic symbols within your drawings—even easier than using the old-fashioned drafting templates. And AutoCAD gives you the flexibility to create your own frequently used symbols. For instance, you can define a center line that exactly matches the one you have been using in your office. A symbol that you recognize as a fire hydrant can be created and then "rubber stamped" throughout your drawing. You can also design your own poché to give your drawing a little extra flair.

Should you not have the time or the desire to create your own symbol sets, hundreds of designers are working to create symbols to suit a variety of needs. As an AutoCAD user, you just need to be aware of the products you need—the vendors will seek you out!

Reusability of Previous Work

When you use computer-aided drafting, one of the biggest boosts to productivity is the ability to reuse previous work in a new drawing. You will find that, with CAD, modifying an existing drawing is often quicker than starting a new one. This simple feature can save hours of time, compared to typical manual methods of recreating previously drafted information.

AutoCAD stores drawings electronically. Until your drawing is plotted on paper, all the drawing information is simply an electronic collection of bits and bytes, held together under a common file name (which may be as simple as CHAIR-1.DWG). You can reuse this electronic information in a fraction of the time needed to redraw it from scratch.

Let's look at a simple example of how reusing your AutoCAD-generated work can save time. If you use a drawing of an auditorium chair often, possibly to show all the seats in a movie theater, you can create it once and then reuse it as a standard part of the rest of your drawings. By doing so, you could save hours of drafting—you don't have to draft each of the 150 chairs. Many such examples will become apparent as you work within the electronic drawing environment.

Quick Changes

The second greatest boost to productivity that you get from using AutoCAD instead of a traditional drafting method is that drawings can be changed easily.

Most manual draftsmen use layout sheets in order to "lay out" the different elements of their drawings. Doing so allows them to organize the information as best they can when they start drafting onto the mylar. But as we all know, things are never as smooth as we'd like them to be. A drawing changes, notes are added, details change or are removed. After many of these revisions are incorporated into a drawing, you have spent a great deal of time on a single sheet of Mylar and the quality of the final product is often compromised.

In contrast, AutoCAD drawings can be changed quickly. Details can be updated or erased almost instantly; entities can be moved so that the drawing is not cluttered. Even the text size of all your notes can be altered with minor disruption to the rest of your drawing. The ease with which you can modify your work and still produce a clean, easily-read product cannot be duplicated in manual drafting.

Diversity and the Multidiscipline Drawing

A good draftsperson uses different line weights, unique text, and artistic license to give his or her work "readability." Computer-aided drafting can usually be tailored to do the same. Undoubtedly, CAD excels in this area of drawing. One of its most important tools is *diversity*.

CAD's diversity means that a drawing can contain any number of elements that emphasize best the ideas that you, the creator, are trying to convey. The text you use for titles can be different from that which you use for notes. You can use a hatch pattern that shows exactly how you want a custom brick walkway to look. In fact, AutoCAD offers so much in the way of diversity that distinguishing CAD work from hand-drafted projects is becoming increasingly difficult.

As more firms that collaborate on projects begin to use AutoCAD, they will want to share files in much the same way that they currently share drawings. By using AutoCAD to establish the base sheets used by each firm, everyone involved in a project builds from the same basic information. Although this can also be said for manual drawings, the advantage of CAD in this situation is that if the base sheets change, all that has to be done is to distribute new base sheets and copy them over the earlier versions of the same base sheet. None of the information that the firms have since drawn is lost (as it would be if the drawings had been created manually). Only minor modifications are needed to match any design changes in the new base sheets.

Final Output Considerations

Whether you are using AutoCAD or drafting manually, no drawing is complete until you hand it to the client. But as an AutoCAD user, you have to be more sensitive to the timing—*when* to plot is important.

One of the most difficult decisions a project manager makes is when to plot his or her work. Most people think that only one plot, at the end of the project, will do. Sometimes this may be correct, but more often than not your work needs to be reviewed during different stages of development. Therefore, because people usually are more comfortable looking at paper than at a video screen, you may have to produce a progress plot. You need to learn how to decide when to make that progress plot. The decision will be easier with proper management and if everyone involved has adequate experience. You must find the proper balance between making a plot whenever you make a change and making a plot only when your drawing is complete.

Training Considerations

An additional consideration in the planning process is the cost of training. A company should plan on a substantial initial investment in training employees to use AutoCAD. There is a never-ending need to update this training as new features are added. Anyone who thinks ''I know AutoCAD. I don't need to be taught,'' is limiting his or her potential.

Telling people that using a computer for their specific application can make them 300 to 400 percent more productive is easy. But few people can tell you with any degree of accuracy *how long* you have to work with CAD to reach this level of productivity. Some users should realize that, in many of their initial applications, they probably will be *faster on a drawing board* for quite a while (depending on how customized the system is).

As a rule however, training time can be reduced if you follow two basic concepts. First, concentrate on the basics. If you are comfortable with the commands you use frequently, you will be able to use AutoCAD effectively.

The second (and most important) way to reduce training time is consistency. If you can work on your AutoCAD system at least one hour a day, five days a week, you are making headway. Crash courses (an eight-hour day, once a week) typically overload you with information. This crash method seldom gives you time to feel comfortable with one topic before you have to move on to the next. Again, the secret here is to learn the basics. As you will see, learning to draw with a computer is more complex than learning to draw with a parallel bar and a triangle.

Summary

Almost anything you draw on a piece of paper can be drawn with a computer. As you have seen, computer-aided drafting can provide advantages that are not possible with a manual drawing system.

Many of AutoCAD's greatest advantages come from its ability to expedite frequently used symbols and to make quick changes to a drawing. With CAD, work that might take days of manual drafting may easily be done in hours.

Nevertheless, don't let the outstanding advantages of AutoCAD blur your vision or objectivity. Clearly, you must weigh high-technology drafting methods against the cost of the system, plot time, and training considerations.

In Chapter 3, "Know Your CAD Equipment," we will look more closely at the computer equipment used with AutoCAD.

3

Know Your CAD Equipment

E very CAD system is only as good as the equipment on which it is run. This chapter explains the different hardware options available for any computer, as well as the hardware you most likely will see on CAD systems.

After you finish reading this chapter you should be able to recognize the major components of your computer; you will have a basic understanding of the work these components perform and their usefulness to your CAD system.

The Computer Hardware

All computer systems have one main box which houses the components that do the "thinking" and run the software. With IBM PC-compatible computers, that box typically measures approximately 24 inches wide by 8 inches high by 18 inches deep. The box houses the central processing unit (CPU), an Intel 80286, 80386 or 80486 chip; probably a numeric coprocessor; one or two floppy disk drives; a hard disk; the Random Access Memory (RAM); and one or two additional cards that allow you to connect your computer to a printer, plotter, and a video screen.

Figure 3.1 shows a typical computer system and a few of the components mentioned in the preceding paragraph. Let's take a brief look at each of these parts so that you can better understand the function of each component.

Fig. 3.1. *A typical CAD station.*

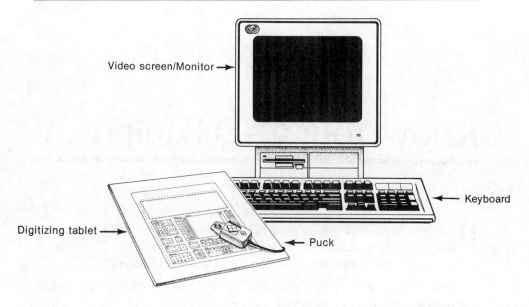

Video screen/Monitor →

← Keyboard

Digitizing tablet →

← Puck

The Microprocessor (CPU)

The main processor of your computer, commonly called the CPU, is located on the computer's *motherboard*. The motherboard has all the connections from your peripheral device slots, power supply, and speaker to the main processor.

The *main processor* is the chip that does almost all the work in your computer. It translates requests from your programs (requests for file access, screen writing, keyboard buffering, and memory management) into the hardware instructions needed to get the job done. As a program user, you do not need to understand exactly what those instructions are—just that they work. If the software is properly written, your program should run smoothly.

The Numeric Coprocessor

In order to run AutoCAD Release 10, your computer needs one additional chip—a *numeric coprocessor*. This chip, which is usually an option when you buy your system, helps with the mathematical calculations AutoCAD performs. Because AutoCAD uses mathematical functions to locate intersections of lines, draw arcs, and calculate planes in three-dimensional space, drafting is faster if your system includes a coprocessor. In fact, without this chip, AutoCAD would be too slow to serve as an adequate computer drafting tool.

Many programs—especially spreadsheets and mathematical analysis programs—are being written to take advantage of the coprocessor's capabilities. You probably will see this chip in many computers due to its capability of speeding up most programs' throughput.

Machines that use the Intel 80486 as the main processor are an exception to the coprocessor rule. The 80486 chip is designed to incorporate the coprocessor and the main processor into a single chip, thus eliminating the need for additional chips that take up precious space on the motherboard.

The Hard Disk and Disk Drives

Files typically are stored on floppy disks or on the computer's hard disk. Information (your drawings, for example) can be placed on either medium, each of which has advantages and disadvantages.

The floppy disk, sometimes called a *diskette*, is a portable plastic disk. Any information on a permanent storage device, such as a hard disk, can be copied to a floppy disk. The only limitation is the amount of information the floppy disk can hold.

The storage capacity of floppy disks varies, as does the disk size. Currently, 5 1/4-inch floppy disks (the most common format for PCs) can hold 360K (approximately 360,000) or 1.2M (1.2 million) bytes of information; the newer 3 1/2-inch disks can hold either 720K or 1.44M (see fig. 3.2). Although these capacities may seem substantial (and there was a day when they *were*!) in modern personal computer CAD work, a large drawing can easily exceed storage space on the lower capacity disks. For example, the two lines and the circle drawn in Chapter 1 were 1,731 bytes. You can see that storage will quickly be exceeded as drawings get complex.

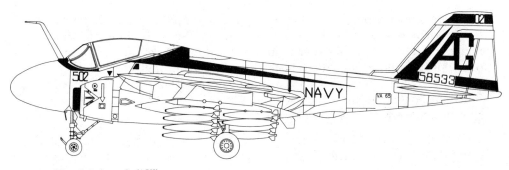

Drawing courtesy of Kenn R. Anderson, Jr. (ACSI)
La Plume, Pennsylvania

Fig. 3.2. 5 1/4-inch and 3 1/2-inch disks.

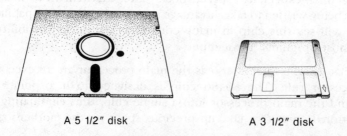

A 5 1/2″ disk   A 3 1/2″ disk

Distinguishing between a 3 1/2-inch disk and a 5 1/4-inch disk is easy, but how do you tell whether a disk is double density or high density? One way is that high density floppies can be formatted to hold either 360K or 1.2M (as in the case of a 5 1/4-inch disk) whereas a double density (low density) disk can only be formatted accurately for 360K. The difference is also shown as *DD* or *HD* on the disk label, and is *always* reflected in the price.

> **Compatibility with Floppy Disks**
>
> You may think that having an IBM computer, running DOS V3.3, and using AutoCAD Release 10 makes your disks compatible with *everyone* else's. Not so! Even though 360K disks (and 720K as well) may be a dying breed, there are still four standard disk formats (360K, 720K, 1.2M, and 1.44M, as mentioned previously). These formats could pose a problem with data circulation. It is commonplace for most serious CAD offices to be able to store and retrieve every disk format, especially if they receive or send information to other firms.

Storage is not the only limitation of floppy disks; speed is a major drawback to any extensive use of floppy disks. The floppy disk is the slowest form of storage and retrieval on your system. As a result, floppy disks are used primarily for archival purposes and for transferring information between computers. Therefore, while floppy disks are a limited form of storage, they do offer something for the modern CAD station. What floppy disks lack, *hard disks* (sometimes referred to as *fixed disks*) provide.

Hard disks usually have storage capacities ranging from 20M to 320M. A *megabyte* is equivalent to 1,048,576 bytes of information, or almost three low-density (360K) floppy disks. The hard disk usually cannot be removed from your computer, as floppy disks can, but offers a substantial advantage in speed. The typical hard disk can store or retrieve information 10 to 20 times faster than a floppy disk drive. What this means to you is faster loading of drawing and data files, as well as faster overall execution of programs such as AutoCAD that frequently access the disk.

With the advantage of speed comes the disadvantage of cost. Although the hard disk might seem expensive if you were to itemize the cost of each of your system's components, its importance must be emphasized. Choosing the right hard disk for reliability, speed, and storage capacity can make all the difference in the life of your CAD station. The right hard disk can affect whether a station is used for CAD *at all*. CAD is disk-intensive. The difference between trying to work with an 18ms (*ms* stands for *millisecond*) hard drive and an 80ms hard drive is incredible.

Although a hard drive has a major impact in the operation of your system, other factors, such as the microprocessor and the numeric coprocessor, influence speed and overall performance. An additional factor that can boost speed is the amount of random access memory (RAM) available on your system.

Random Access Memory (RAM)

RAM is the area from which your program is executed. Many people tend to confuse RAM memory with the storage capacity of a hard disk. If you have 30M of storage and only 256K of RAM, you may not be able to run AutoCAD (or many other programs).

Maybe the best way to explain it is that a hard disk is used to hold your programs when they are *not* running. When you want to run your program, it must be loaded from the hard disk into RAM and then executed. This transfer of the program from storage into RAM occurs whenever you run a program, but is transparent to you, the user.

Many IBM-compatible computer systems come with 640K of RAM, which is usually enough to run almost any program. The 640K standard has come about due to the limitations of the disk operating system (DOS), which typically is unable to use memory above the 640K barrier for the execution of programs.

Programmers, who are more intelligent than the software they write, have found ways to get around this limit imposed by DOS. In AutoCAD, any memory located above the 640K limit is used by AutoCAD for *page space*, a temporary storage area for drawing information. Page space helps reduce the amount of disk access AutoCAD must make when it is working on a drawing.

The Video Screen, or Monitor

The video screen is an integral part of AutoCAD. The proper video screen can make a significant difference in your productivity as a CAD draftsperson. Video screens range in size from 13 to 36 inches; the typical CAD screen measures 14 inches diagonally.

Video cards and screens also have different resolutions that affect their "look." *Monochrome screens* (generally black-and-white) offer good resolution but poor contrast with a program such as AutoCAD in which different information can be assigned colors. Color cards and screens offer a variety of resolutions and colors that are limited only by your budget. Those colors and resolutions boil down to the following basic categories:

❑ CGA 640 x 200 resolution with 2 colors
❑ EGA 640 x 350 resolution with 16 colors
❑ VGA 640 x 480 resolution with 256 colors

Color Graphics Adapter (CGA)

The *color graphics adapter*, or *CGA*, is the oldest form of graphics device for CAD work. It was was one of the original screen displays introduced by IBM when their line of personal computers was first released. As mentioned previously, the lack of color support at an acceptable resolution for CAD work tends to limit the ability to discern different types of entities in a drawing.

Enhanced Graphics Adapter (EGA)

The *enhanced graphics adapter*, or *EGA*, has become the standard color video card in use today. It offers a higher resolution with more colors than the CGA, which makes it the choice of users who need their programs displayed in full color. In AutoCAD, entities can be displayed in different colors, thus allowing you to differentiate between entities.

Video Graphics Array (VGA)

The *video graphics array*, or *VGA*, is slowly becoming the standard for users who need both high resolution and multiple colors for optimum display of their programs. Many of today's programs are designed to take advantage of the higher resolution of these screens in order to display information with greater clarity.

Resolution and Colors: the Dilemma

The type of resolution you need depends on how you want to spend most of your time. If you are using a low-resolution monitor and card, you will have to zoom in quite often in order to discern details of the objects you are drawing. If you spend more time zooming and than drawing, your productivity plummets.

If you can't discern certain details that are too close together, you can magnify a portion of the overall drawing by *zooming in*, a technique that allows you to view a portion of the overall drawing on the entire screen. While zoomed in, you can do anything you might have done from the original view, move from one portion of the drawing to another (called *panning*), or *zoom out* to the original view of the entire drawing.

The number of colors you need depends on the type of drawings you will create. If you plan to use a rendering package to make a three-dimensional drawing of your house look sharp, you will probably want 256 colors in order to get good definition from your drawing. If, on the other hand, you simply use colors to discern different layers in your drawing, 16 colors should be plenty.

As with anything in computer hardware, the bottom line is the cost. Clearly, high resolution with 256 colors costs much more than medium resolution and 16 colors. You need to know how you plan to use your CAD station. Buying an EGA card, with its support of only 16 colors at an acceptable resolution for CAD work, will not help you when you have to produce a rendering of your newest office layout.

Input Devices

AutoCAD currently supports more than 50 different input devices; new ones are added whenever AutoCAD releases a new version. Although there are many different input devices, they all fall into one or more common categories. Those categories include:

- Keyboards
- Mice
- Joysticks
- Track balls
- Digitizing tablets
- Touch screens and light pens

Each of these devices has good and bad points; all have features that make them acceptable as AutoCAD input devices. For information on how to use these devices for input into AutoCAD, see Chapter 6, "The Basics of Drawing in AutoCAD."

Keyboards

Keyboards, the most overlooked input devices available today, typically are not thought of as input devices. Although using a keyboard is not as elegant as picking points on the screen with a mouse or a digitizer, any command you can execute from a mouse can also be executed from the keyboard. The keyboard's advantage over any other input device is that every computer has one—it is not an additional piece of equipment that must be bought with your CAD package. Figure 3.3 shows a typical computer keyboard.

Fig. 3.3. *The keyboard.*

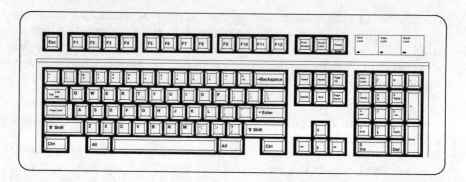

Keyboards are being designed for greater flexibility. Many computer systems now have special keyboards that are part "normal" keyboard and part track ball or joystick. In CAD and computer paint programs, these new keyboards combine normal keyboard input with the ease of graphic drawing associated with track balls or joysticks.

Mice

Mice could easily become the second "keyboard" of the nineties. They are being picked up as an alternative method of input for many programs, not just CAD. Many programmers are beginning to incorporate support for mice in the software they write, thanks in part to the incredible range of usefulness mice have on the Macintosh.

The mouse was originally designed by Xerox at the Palo Alto Research Center in the early seventies. Since that time, the mouse has slowly crept into almost every aspect of computer use. Many computers (most notably the Macintosh) have been designed to work their fastest if a mouse, rather than the keyboard, is used for input.

The look of a mouse is pretty much standard across the industry. Basically, a mouse looks like a bar of soap with a cord connecting it to your computer, and with one to three buttons for command input (see fig. 3.4). Most mice are *mechanical mice*; they have small wheels on their underside that allow the computer and its software to track the mouse's movements. A new breed of mice, called *optical mice*, is slowly emerging. The movement of an optical mouse is tracked by light, reflected from a special pad to the mouse's sensors.

Fig. 3.4. *A mouse.*

Several factors determine whether you should buy a mouse or a different type of input device. You need to consider the following:

- ❏ The cost of the mouse
- ❏ How much room you have for the mouse
- ❏ Whether the software is designed for mouse input
- ❏ Whether you will be using other software that takes advantage of a mouse

Joysticks

The computer joystick is just like its arcade counterpart—a thin stick topped by a firing button (see fig. 3.5). Basically, a joystick is the poor man's input device. Most people buy them in order to play computer games. If you have a joystick, using it for CAD is convenient. To use a joystick with your computer, all you need is a *game port* to plug in the joystick. Game ports are not standard on most computers, but can easily be ordered and installed.

Fig. 3.5. *A joystick.*

Track Balls

The *track ball* can be used in much the same fashion as a mouse. A track ball, which looks like a large billiard ball set into a square base, is like a mouse that has been flipped onto its back. As you rotate the ball with the palm of your hand, sensors in the track ball's base track the cursor's movement across the screen.

Digitizing Tablets

Of all input devices, the digitizer is the one used most for entering commands and picking points in AutoCAD. A *digitizer* is a square pad that is used to emulate the screen. With this pad, you use a *puck* (which looks like a mouse). As you move the puck across the surface of the digitizer, crosshairs on the screen track the cursor's movements within AutoCAD.

Digitizers vary in size from the typical 12-inch by 12-inch tablet (see fig. 3.6) to tablet surfaces that measure 48 inches by 60 inches. Usually the larger digitizers are used for tracing existing plans into the computer. If a small digitizer is used to do this, you will need to break up your original drawing into many smaller pieces and match them together later. Small tablets are convenient because they don't take much room. A small tablet can be place on any table surface and used without hindering the surrounding work surfaces.

Fig. 3.6. A 12-inch by 12-inch tablet with a four-button puck.

Touch Screens and Light Pens

Touch screens and light pens are probably the least used of all CAD input devices because they are not comfortable to use. *Light pens* require you to place a pen-like device in contact with the video screen. As the electron beam that creates the picture on your video screen travels down the screen, it allows a lens within the pen to locate the x,y coordinates of the pen and then transmit that information to your program.

Touch screens use infrared light beams or the electrically conductive surface of the video screen to determine where your finger has touched the screen. Neither type of input was designed with physical comfort in mind. Most video screens are set at eye level, which means that when you point at something with your finger or a light pen, your arm will always point at the screen. When a program like AutoCAD requires you to have your arm at screen level most of the time, you will tire quickly.

Output Devices

Once all the information is *in* your program, you need to plot it *out* onto some form of hardcopy. Clients request copies of drawings, you need something to check against, etc. Many types of output device can be used with your computer and with AutoCAD. This book describes the following output devices:

❑ Dot-matrix printers
❑ Laser printers
❑ Pen plotters
❑ Laser plotters
❑ Electrostatic plotters

Dot-matrix Printers

These low-cost printers have many uses in general computer applications as well as AutoCAD. *Dot-matrix* printers print characters and graphics as a series of dots—hence the name. The more dots a printer can print, the finer your characters and pictures will be.

The two basic types of dot-matrix printers are 9- or 24-pin printers (see fig. 3.7). The number of pins in the print head determines how well circles and arcs will be printed. Circles and arcs printed with a 9-pin printer tend to look jagged; circles and arcs printed with a 24-pin printer will look smoother, because a 24-pin printer can print more dots.

Fig. 3.7. *A dot-matrix printer.*

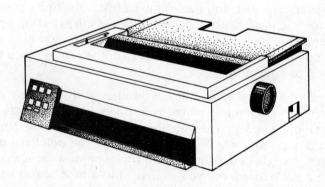

Dot-matrix printers are not limited to CAD. They can be used also to print information typed in response to a command, and to print letters from a word processing program, and results created from an analysis program.

Laser Printers

Laser printers are much like dot-matrix printers. Both laser printers and dot-matrix printers use a series of dots to make up characters and pictures being printed. However, laser printers offer resolution that cannot be matched by any conventional dot-matrix printer. Dot-matrix printers usually maintain a resolution of only 200 dot-per-inch (DPI). Laser printers typically print with 300 DPI resolution, thus allowing for professional graphics with little loss in quality. Laser printers tend to be used more for desktop publishing, where high-quality output is necessary, than for CAD. Although CAD can take advantage of the high resolution offered by laser printers, most laser printers only use 8 1/2 inch by 11 inch paper, which tends to be much too small for most drawings. The typical laser printer looks like the one shown in figure 3.8.

Fig. 3.8. *A laser printer.*

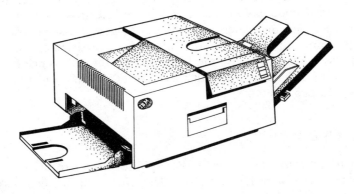

Pen Plotters

Pen plotters offer the best plotted output. As the name implies, the plotter uses an ink pen to draw the information on your screen. Pen plotters typically offer resolutions of more than 1,500 steps per inch, thus making all circles and arcs as smooth as possible—even to the most discriminating eye.

Pen plotters typically allow several types and sizes of pens during a plot. AutoCAD can map its colors to different pens when performing a plot. This gives you the flexibility to make specific colors map to thinner or bolder pens as you need them, instead of having one line weight for the whole plot.

Pen plotters also give you the flexibility of plotting onto different media of different sizes. Most typical drafting media available today (bond, vellum, and Mylar) are available for most plotters, but in a special format. Plotter ink differs from normal drafting ink; the plotter media also tend to be slightly different. On most pen plotters, you can plot sheet sizes up to 24 inches by 36 inches; on a few, you can plot up to 36 inches by 48 inches (even longer, if you buy a roll-feed type plotter).

Laser Plotters

Laser plotters are much like their siblings (laser printers), only bigger. Laser plotters typically offer 300 DPI resolution; they also allow you to plot at much the same sizes as pen plotters. The laser plotter's one big advantage over the pen plotter is speed.

Pen plotters are sometimes referred to as vector plotters because the information they plot out is in vector form: a line is plotted as one entity with a beginning and an ending point. Laser plotters and electrostatic plotters, on the other hand, are sometimes referred to as *raster plotters*. A raster plotter converts the vector information, such as a line, into a picture made up of dots, and then prints the dot picture. Because the laser plotter only has to print a series of dots, instead of each individual entity, it can print a picture 5 to 10 times faster than a typical pen plotter.

Electrostatic Plotters

Electrostatic plotters are much like laser plotters. Both are raster devices that are incredibly fast at producing plots. The greatest difference between an electrostatic plotter and a laser plotter is ink. An electrostatic plotter uses ink to create the raster image of a plot, whereas a laser plotter uses a toner (similar to that used in copiers) that adheres to the plot.

Output Device Image Quality

Each output device creates plots with a different resolution and therefore a different quality. The quality you need depends mostly on who will see your drawings. A printer or laser plot may be good enough for in-house review. If you want to send drawings to a client, we recommend using a pen plotter to achieve the finest quality drawings (see fig. 3.9).

Fig. 3.9. *The sample drawing, plotted with a pen plotter.*

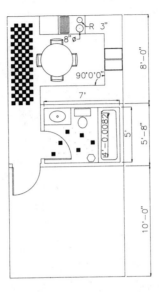

Summary

This chapter explained each piece of hardware in your CAD system and its function. Armed with this knowledge, you can start taking advantage of these devices to speed up your work and produce output that for your firm and your clients.

Chapter 4, ''Dabble in DOS,'' explains how your computer's operating system allows you to do the work you want to do. By itself, hardware is useless. But under the control of a fairly intelligent operating system, the hardware does the work that makes you more productive.

CHAPTER 4

Dabble in DOS

This chapter covers the *disk operating system* (called *MS-DOS* or *PC DOS*) of IBM-compatible computers. If your CAD station is based on any other operating system (such as UNIX, VAX/VMS, XENIX, Mac/OS, or AEGIS), the information in this chapter is not applicable.

Whether you want to admit it or not, your computer's operating system (DOS) has to be dealt with. For those of you who are not familiar with DOS (rhymes with "sauce"), this chapter emphasizes the importance of good DOS practices and some of the more commonly used DOS commands. Those of you who are already comfortable with DOS can go on to the next chapter.

This chapter covers aspects of DOS that are important to today's CAD stations—specific commands you could easily use every day. The full capabilities of DOS are beyond the scope of this text. For complete coverage of MS- and PC DOS, we recommend *MS-DOS User's Guide*, 3rd Edition, and *Using PC DOS*, 3rd Edition, both published by Que Corporation.

This chapter assumes that you are using DOS V2.0 or later; versions now go as high as 4.0. Basically, PC DOS (written by IBM for their "true-blue" computers) and MS-DOS (written by Microsoft for "compatibles") are the same.

After finishing this chapter, you will be able to do the following:

❏ Back up your drawings for safety

❏ Circulate drawings "out of house"

❏ Provide an organized storage system for your drawings

❏ Pick up almost any DOS guide and easily build on this foundation

Before You Begin

Although you've probably heard horrifying stories about getting hopelessly lost in DOS, it is important to realize that DOS will not bite you. Repeat after me: *"DOS is good, DOS is my friend."* DOS does, however, show little patience or mercy if you type the wrong thing. For example, there is a substantial difference between the following lines:

DIR C:*.DWG
DEL C:*.DWG

The former will list all your drawings and the latter will destroy them.

About DOS

Computers would be expensive paperweights if there were no software to tell them what to do. Chapter 3, "Know Your CAD Equipment," discussed hardware ranging from monitors to computers to mice. Most people consider a floppy disk to be hardware, because it stores information the same way a hard drive does. But software is quite different. *Software* is the program (or group of programs) which is *on* the disk and interacts with the hardware to accomplish your task. The AutoCAD program is software.

Just as AutoCAD bridges the gap between you (the draftsman) and your computer, DOS acts as a moderator between programs and your system's storage devices or disks. If you didn't run DOS when you turn on your system, you would not be able to access any data or programs stored on your disks. Among other things, DOS allows you to do the following:

❏ "Talk" directly to your computer's equipment (printers, modems, monitor, disk drives, etc.)

❏ Transfer data or programs from one device to another

❏ Provide an environment in which you can store and organize information

❏ Run programs, such as AutoCAD

DOS itself will not do certain things for you—it won't draw, do mathematical calculations, or compose music. DOS simply provides the foundation for your interaction with the computer.

The DOS Commands

The way you interact with almost any program, including AutoCAD, is to give it a command. DOS is no exception to this rule. This chapter explains *some* of the commands DOS recognizes, and what these commands do. Not all DOS commands are covered here—just those you should be aware of as a CAD operator. The commands are separated into the following areas of usage:

- ❏ The DOS prompt
- ❏ Commands that influence disks
- ❏ Commands that influence files
- ❏ Commands that affect the directory structure
- ❏ Commands that allow you to "talk" with your hardware

Upper- or Lowercase Letters Make No Difference in DOS

It is important to realize that when you are working with DOS and DOS file names, you can use any series of upper- and lowercase letters. DOS will always interpret your characters as uppercase and execute your command or access your files accordingly.

AutoCAD works in a similar fashion. If you want to work on a drawing called FLOORPL.DWG, you can type **floorpl**, **FLOORPL**, or **FloorPL** at the AutoCAD Main Menu.

The DOS Prompt

Just as most applications will ask you for a command, DOS will *prompt* you for input. The prompt is where you give DOS a function to do. In AutoCAD, the prompt is Command:. With DOS, however, you can change the prompt message to whatever you want, by using the PROMPT command.

Setting the DOS Prompt (PROMPT)

The default setting for the DOS prompt displays a C> to indicate that drive C: is the current disk drive. The standard prompt seen on most computers is C:*[path]*>. C: is the current drive, *[path]* is the active path, if any, and > is the end of the prompt.

You can make your computer's prompt look like the standard by using the following command:

PROMPT pg

If you want a custom prompt for your operating system, it is easily accomplished. The options available are listed in table 4.1. Any combination of these can be used (as in the preceding example) by preceding the letter with a *$* symbol.

Table 4.1. *Special characters for the PROMPT command.*

Character	Returns
d	The date
n	The default drive letter
p	The current directory of the default drive
t	The time
v	The DOS version number
b	The | character
e	The Escape character (sends an ASCII 27 character used for interaction with a device driver such as ANSI.SYS)
g	The > character
l	The < character
q	The = character
$	The $ character
h	A backspace (erases the character to the left of the cursor)
_	A carriage return and a line feed (goes to the beginning of the next line on the screen)

Any character other than those listed in table 4.1 will not be recognized by DOS. There will be a *null prompt*, which means that no DOS prompt will appear on the screen; you will just see a blinking cursor.

Text (such as This is the DOS Prompt>) can easily be reflected in the prompt. You simply do *not* precede the text with a $. For example:

If you enter:	*The prompt will be*
PROMPT This is the DOS Prompt$g	This is the DOS Prompt>
PROMPT CAD Station #1$_$p$g	CAD Station #1 C:\>
PROMPT $a	*(nothing at all)*

The prompt is "home base" for DOS. You (and everyone using your system) should recognize the DOS prompt, especially if it has been customized.

Another standard command that you will use quite often is the CLS command.

Clearing the Screen (CLS)

Often, after running a program or executing commands, you want to clear the screen of information. You can do this by typing **CLS** at the DOS prompt. This command clears the display and shows the DOS prompt at the top of the screen.

PROMPT and CLS are simple commands you might execute to control what you see of DOS. Other DOS commands are more commonly used for interaction with disks, files, and the directory structure, and for communicating with hardware.

Commands that Influence Disks

When you work with disk storage, it is important to have as much control over the medium as possible. DOS offers features with which you can prepare a disk for storage and verify the reliability of the disk. These commands work with either floppy or hard disks.

Preparing the Disk for Data (FORMAT)

In order for a new disk to hold data, it must first be *formatted*. When formatting a disk, the computer writes on the entire area of the disk and verifies that it is able to hold information. This procedure organizes the disk and creates a structure that permits the disk to hold data.

Important things to remember about the FORMAT command include the following:

❑ A disk must be formatted before it can hold information.

❑ Formatting a disk that already has data on it WILL DESTROY ALL THE INFORMATION on that disk.

❑ If a disk is having read or write errors, and you don't need the information on the disk, a FORMAT may allow you to fix the disk for future use.

❑ DO NOT format your hard disk. (Hard-disk formatting should be done ONLY if you are proficient in the use and applications of your system.)

To format a new disk in drive A:, type:

FORMAT A:

at the C:\> prompt. The following information will be displayed on-screen:

```
Insert new diskette for drive A:
and strike any key when ready

Formatting...

Formatting...Format complete
xxxxxx bytes total disk space
xxxxxx bytes available on disk

Format another (Y/N)?
```

If you don't want to format additional disks, just type **n** and then press Enter.

Some of the additional FORMAT command parameters (not covered here) allow you to transfer DOS to the floppy disk after formatting or to attach a description (called a label) to the disk. For further information on these functions, consult your DOS manual.

After formatting a disk, DOS displays the integrity and storage capacity of the disk. You can check a formatted disk (whether or not it it contains information) by using the CHKDSK command.

Checking Your Disks (CHKDSK)

With this command, you can verify the data on a disk, determine the disk's free space, or find out how many files are on the disk. To start the command, type **CHKDSK** at the C:\> prompt.

A sample of the CHKDSK command's output follows:

```
730112 bytes total disk space
 54272 bytes in 2 hidden files
513024 bytes in 10 user files
162816 bytes available on disk

655360 bytes total memory
528496 bytes free
```

Now you know how to prepare and check a disk. While we all can appreciate the importance of having control over your disks, some of the more frequently used DOS commands are those which affect the files on those disks.

Commands that Influence Files

The term *files* can apply to any file on a disk, from an AutoCAD program file to one of your drawings. Therefore, you can interpret the following explanations of how to manipulate files as explanations of how to manipulate your drawings.

Some of the following commands can be accessed from within AutoCAD. From AutoCAD's Main Menu, press **6** for File Utilities: you will see a selection of DOS choices. The DOS commands AutoCAD allows you to execute from inside the AutoCAD program include COPY, DIR, DELETE, and RENAME. All of these options are discussed in this chapter, but for the time being, let's concentrate on the commands that influence files.

Changing File Names (RENAME)

You use the RENAME command (REN, for short) to modify the name you have given a specific file or drawing. As you learned from Chapter 1, "A Quick Start in AutoCAD," all file names in DOS are restricted to eight characters. DOS helps computer users by either providing or allowing you to provide a three-character *extension* to the file name; DOS uses a period to separate the file name from the extension. The benefit of file-name extensions is that they let you know what a specific file should be used for.

As an example, all AutoCAD drawing files are given the extension *DWG* to signify that they are drawings. When you create a file in Lotus 1-2-3, on the other hand, the file name is given an extension of either *WKS* or *WK1*, depending on which version of 1-2-3 you have.

Suppose that you have a drawing file called FLOORPL.DWG and that you want to change the name to indicate that it is the plan of the first, not the second, floor. With the eight-character limit (with no spaces) for file names, you could choose a new name, such as 1ST_FLPL.DWG. To change the original file name (*FLOORPL.DWG*) to *1ST_FLPL.DWG*, type:

RENAME FLOORPL.DWG 1ST_FLPL.DWG

at the `C:\>` prompt.

Although you can use the RENAME command to change the name of a specific file, you cannot change the file's location. Nor can you create multiple copies of a file. The COPY command enables you to perform these (and other) functions.

Duplicating Files (COPY)

You need to be able to move a file from one location to another. The COPY command lets you copy a file to another disk, to another name on the same disk, or (as you will see in the next section) to a different directory on the same disk. To copy a file from your hard disk to a floppy disk, type:

COPY C:*filename.ext* A:

at the `C:\>` prompt. The message:

`1 File(s) copied`

will be displayed on-screen.

Use this command when you want to copy your drawing to a floppy disk. If someone else needs to work with one or more of your drawings, for example, COPY is the easiest command to use.

There are many options to this command. In fact, this seemingly simple DOS command is so flexible that to cover it in full detail could fill this chapter. For more detailed information, refer to a DOS manual or reference book.

Removing Files (DEL and ERASE)

So far, this chapter has covered how to place drawings on another disk and how to erase everything on a disk with the FORMAT command. It has not, however, explained how to delete a specific file from your disk.

Erasing a file from your disk is easy. Just type

DEL *filename.ext*

at the `C:\>` prompt.

In the preceding example, using ERASE causes the same results.

You need to be able to delete unneeded files so that you have room for active drawings. While a 60M hard disk may seem large, there definitely will be a day when you need to erase older, unneeded files to free up space. But *be careful*. Deleting files throws them into the electronic "bit bucket"—never to be seen again.

Deleting Backup Files

Many software products, including AutoCAD, will duplicate your original file for backup purposes. This feature is helpful if you want to see the previous edition of the current drawing.

If you work on your FLOORPL.DWG file, for instance, AutoCAD will copy the original file to a new file called *FLOORPL.BAK*. The backup file is there in case you need to "go back" to that version of your drawing. AutoCAD does this automatically for every drawing you work on, whenever that drawing file is saved. These .BAK files will accumulate, and you will want to delete the outdated version so that your hard disk has more room. This backing up of your file should not be confused with the DOS BACKUP command, discussed later.

If you want to remove a file from your hard disk, but would like to keep a copy of it for future use, you have several options. One option is to COPY the file to a floppy disk. But if you have a large group of files that will not fit on a single disk, you may want to consider using the BACKUP and RESTORE commands.

Insurance for Your Files (BACKUP)

The BACKUP command lets you place a group of files on a set of disks. Let's say that you have 10 drawings whose combined size is 2M. Copying the files individually would not be practical, as they would not fit on one disk. The BACKUP command could save you much more time in this situation, especially if you will be doing this often for archival purposes.

BACKUP is different from COPY in several ways. First, unlike the COPY command, the information placed on the floppy disks is unusable in the new (backup) form. In order to work on any of these drawings, you must first restore the files to the hard disk. (RESTORE is discussed later in this chapter.)

The BACKUP routine is best understood if you imagine DOS temporarily grouping all your files into one big file. After this, the BACKUP command begins copying this big file to the floppy drive. When the first floppy disk gets full,

DOS will ask you to insert the next disk in the drive and press a key. DOS is copying the files to what it *thinks* is one large floppy disk, made up of many little ones. Depending on how many files you want to back up, and what type of disks you use, the stack could have a many as ninety disks! For this reason, it is important to label the disks sequentially, in the order in which they were inserted.

Cashing Your Insurance (RESTORE)

The BACKUP and RESTORE commands work together. You use DOS's BACKUP to copy files to floppy disks and you need the RESTORE command to copy the files back to the hard disk so that they can be used.

The main advantage to the BACKUP and RESTORE commands is the ability to group all the drawings from one project on one set of disks. The speed and ease offered by BACKUP and RESTORE make this a powerful set of commands for retaining archival sets of inactive projects.

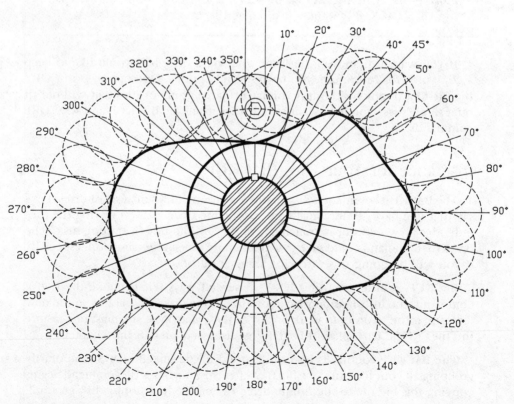

Drawing courtesy of Greg Kidder
Kennebunk, Maine

File Names and Wild-card Characters

DOS allows you to reduce the amount of typing needed when you enter file names. You can use *wild-card* characters (the ? and * symbols) which represent (for DOS) one or more undefined characters in the file name. The *?* represents a single character, whereas the * reflects a group of characters. To better understand their uses, let's look at the following example.

Suppose that you have 10 files on a disk, with the names:

DRAWING1.DWG   SPELL.DOC
DETAIL-1.DWG   TEST-2.DWG
DRAWING2.DWG   TEST-2.BAK
DETAIL-1.BAK   TESTING.DWG
QUARTER.WKS   DRAW.DWG

Entering **DIR DRAWING?.DWG** will display:

```
DRAWING1.DWG
DRAWING2.DWG
```

Entering **DIR *.DWG** will display:

```
DRAWING1.DWG
DETAIL-1.DWG
DRAWING2.DWG
TEST-2.DWG
TESTING.DWG
DRAW.DWG
```

Entering **DIR *.d??**, which is the same as entering **DIR *.d***, will display:

```
DRAWING1.DWG
DETAIL-1.DWG
DRAWING2.DWG
SPELL.DOC
TEST-2.DWG
TESTING.DWG
DRAW.DWG
```

With wild cards, you can delete all backup files with:

DEL *.BAK

You may want to consider the power of wild cards as you select your file names. By choosing an organized system of file names, you can more easily copy, delete, or find the appropriate files.

Commands that Affect the Directory Structure

One DOS feature that enables you to be better organized is the *directory structure*. The directory structure is basically a series of specific areas on your disk to which you can copy files and from which you can move files; each of these areas is called a *subdirectory*. After the files are placed in a subdirectory, you can access them as you have before. Subdirectories allow you to create a unique area for related files from the same project.

If there were no allowance for a directory structure, *all* of your files would be placed in one location. Finding a specific drawing would be difficult, and selecting a file name would be challenging (given the eight-character limitation).

Figure 4.1 shows a graphical representation of a disk's directory structure. Notice that some directories are *parents* to others. This term refers to the fact that the subdirectories are related to one another in location. In order to get to the NORTON directory, for example, you would have to go first to the UTILITY directory.

Fig. 4.1. *A disk's directory structure in graphic form.*

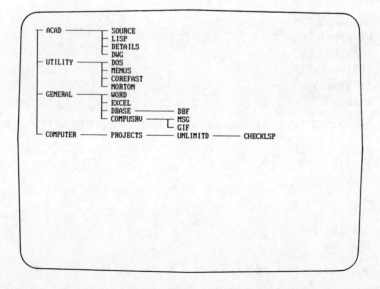

The layout of the directory structure has led to the terms *directory tree* and *tree structure*. If you can visualize the directory structure in this manner, you will have an easier time getting around in your disk's directory structure.

DOS gives you a series of commands with which you can:

❏ Make a subdirectory.
❏ Change the current subdirectory.
❏ Find out what is in a subdirectory.
❏ Remove an unneeded subdirectory.

Creating a Subdirectory (MKDIR or MD)

In order to create a subdirectory, you would go to the directory you want to be the parent (using the CHDIR command, discussed in the next section of this chapter), and type **MKDIR** *filename* (*filename* must conform to the DOS file-name requirements mentioned in Chapter 1, ''A Quick Start in AutoCAD'').

Let's assume that you are at the *root* directory. (This term emphasizes the *tree structure* concept by giving the base directory the name *root* and by showing it on your computer as a \.) To create a new directory (called *PRACTICE*) off the root, you would type **MKDIR PRACTICE** or **MD PRACTICE** at the DOS prompt.

Setting the Current Subdirectory (CHDIR or CD)

Once you have created a new directory, you will want to go into that area and do your work. To do so, you change the current directory by using the CHDIR command. Continuing the preceding example, after you create the PRACTICE directory you can change the current directory to PRACTICE by typing **CHDIR PRACTICE** or **CD PRACTICE**.

Seeing What Is in a Subdirectory (DIR)

At any time, and from any directory, you can look at a listing of the files in that directory. You can also find out what is in any other directory.

You can get a list of all the files in the current directory by typing **DIR**. Should you want a listing of all your *drawings* in the current directory, type **DIR *.DWG**.

You can find the files of another directory by entering **DIR** *[path]*. The *[path]* is made up of the names of the directories, usually starting at the *root*, each separated from the next by a backslash (\). If you wanted to know what is in the PAINT directory, for example, you could find out with the following command:

DIR DRIVERS\MOUSE\PAINT

Removing a Subdirectory (RMDIR or RD)

You've seen how to create a directory, change directories, and find out what is in an existing directory, but what about removing an unwanted directory? Well, it is just as easy as the other options.

To remove a directory, you must first DELETE *all* the files in that specific directory. Then you must be in the parent directory of the one you want to remove. If you wanted to remove the PRACTICE directory you created earlier, for instance, you would have to be in the root directory. Finally, you would enter the following command: **RMDIR PRACTICE** or **RD PRACTICE**.

Tips for Using Subdirectories

To optimize the performance of your CAD station and create an efficient and organized workplace, you need a strong directory structure. By using well-named directories, you will be able to locate, store, and retrieve drawings related to one project easily. You can BACKUP and RESTORE entire projects with little trouble. As an added bonus, if you make good choices with the eight characters DOS allows, you will have a well-organized structure that anyone can use to find a drawing easily.

For an example of a directory structure for drawings, see figure 4.2. In this example, the hard drive is divided into many different projects. The directory names leave little doubt as to where you might find the drawings for the tenants of Building 79 in Park 100.

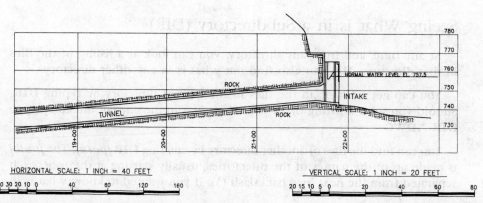

HORIZONTAL SCALE: 1 INCH = 40 FEET

VERTICAL SCALE: 1 INCH = 20 FEET

Drawing courtesy of R.L. Tomlinson Drafting & Blueprinting, Inc.
Thunder Bay, Ontario, Canada

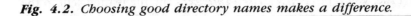

Fig. 4.2. Choosing good directory names makes a difference.

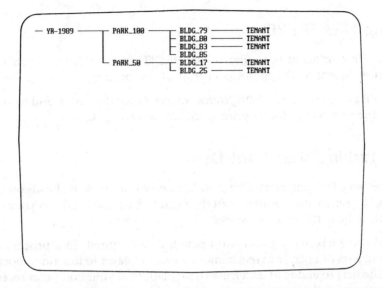

Commands that Let You "Talk" with Your Hardware

So far, this chapter has explained some of the basic DOS commands that allow you to organize your disks and files, and shown you how to work with directories. DOS also lets you communicate with your computer equipment. In this section, you will learn how to "talk" to your printer, monitor, and hard disk.

Printing Files (PRINT)

You can print a file with your printer by using the PRINT command, provided that the file is in readable format. *Readable* format means that a file can be viewed with the PRINT or TYPE command (TYPE is discussed next) and understood by a person. A computer program is not readable after it has been compiled, or reduced to a language only a computer can understand. The AutoCAD program and the drawing files are in this format. If you were to PRINT a compiled file, you literally would get garbage.

To print a file, you type: **PRINT** *filename.ext*. The file is then sent to the printer and printed on paper.

Viewing Files (TYPE)

The TYPE command is similar to the PRINT command, except that the information is sent to the monitor instead of the printer.

To TYPE a file, you type **TYPE** *filename.ext*. Once this command has been entered, the text in the file is printed on the screen.

Safely Parking Your Hard Drive

Another way DOS interacts with your hardware is to *park* the heads on your hard disk. If you are not familiar with the need to park the heads on your hard drive, this is how the process works.

A hard drive has many *platters* on which data is stored. In a process that is similar to a record player in mechanics and a tape player in function, movable heads write data to and read data from these platters. If your computer receives a strong bump while it is on or off and if the heads touch the platters, you could easily damage data. This shock to the hard disk could permanently destroy part or all of your hard disk.

While the computer is on, it is more susceptible to shock. But when you are finished for the day, you can park the heads by moving them to a "safe" area on the platters. If the computer receives a bump while the heads are parked, your hard disk and its data will be safe. By all means, when you want to move your computer, whether down the hall or across the street, park the heads.

Most of the newer computers automatically park the heads when you turn off your computer. Unfortunately, some brands still do not. In order to park your hard disk, you can run a program at the DOS prompt. The computer store from which you bought your system probably will be able to provide you with this type of utility.

If you are not sure whether you have the utility, which is specific to your particular hardware, call your dealer. You will also be able to locate this type of program from some of the sources discussed in the "Where To Get Help" section of Part VI, this book's reference section.

Checking Your DOS Version (VER)

You can use the VER command to ask the computer what version of DOS you are running. If you type **VER** at the DOS prompt, you should see a response similar to the following:

```
MS-DOS Version 3.30
```

This can be helpful if you try to run a DOS command and receive an error message because you are using a later version of DOS. The message displayed would be

```
Incorrect DOS Version
```

Summary

The information in this chapter pertains strictly to PC DOS and MS-DOS. If your CAD station is based on another operating system, you should research the ways that operating system emulates the commands in this chapter. Furthermore, the information in this chapter is intended to introduce you to some of DOS's functions; it is in no way a complete list of the operating system's capabilities.

You have learned how to you can back up your drawings, copy a drawing to a disk, and use directories to create an organized storage system for your drawings. Hopefully, you have found that DOS did not bite you. With a little more practice and patience, perhaps you soon *will* be saying "DOS is good. DOS is my friend."

5

Installing AutoCAD and AutoShade

The last few chapters have given you basic information that will help you capitalize more fully on your experiences with AutoCAD.

Chapter 2, "AutoCAD—Manual versus Computer Drafting," focused on *why* you should use AutoCAD. Chapter 3, "Know Your CAD Equipment," described the equipment you might use, and Chapter 4, "Dabble in DOS," took you through some simple DOS commands. Now it is time to apply this information and to learn how to install AutoCAD (and AutoShade) on your computer system. If your system has been set up already, and the software has been installed by someone else, this chapter probably will be of little interest to you. If this is the case, you can skip ahead to Chapter 6, "The Basics of Drawing in AutoCAD." If you want to learn the AutoCAD installation process, however, you should continue with this chapter.

In addition to explaining *installation*, the process of transferring the software to your computer system, this chapter also explains the steps involved in configuring the software. *Configuration* simply means telling AutoCAD which peripheral equipment or hardware extras you are using. Many of these hardware devices were described in Chapter 3, "Know Your CAD Equipment." Your collection of peripherals may include a graphics adapter, mouse, digitizer, plotter, or printer plotter. The "Configuring AutoCAD for Your Hardware" section of this chapter addresses memory (RAM) usage and ADI (Autodesk Device Interface) considerations for your peripherals.

Before Installation

Chapter 3, "Know Your CAD Equipment," focused on the various types of computer hardware and peripherals you *could* have attached to your system. What follows is a list of the minimum basic hardware components you *must* have in order to run your CAD system. (Refer to Chapter 3 if you need more information on a specific piece of equipment.)

❑ IBM PC, XT, AT, or PS/2, or 100 percent IBM-compatible computer with the following:

   ❑ 512K (*K* stands for *kilobyte*) of memory (640K to use AutoLISP)

   ❑ A disk drive and a hard disk drive

   ❑ An Intel 8087, 80287, or 80387 math coprocessor

   ❑ A video display adapter (such as a CGA, EGA, or VGA card)

   ❑ A video monitor

   ❑ DOS (Disk Operating System) V2.0 or later (V3.3 or later for the PS/2). DOS is covered in Chapter 4, "Dabble in DOS."

   ❑ An asynchronous communications adapter, or COM port. This usually is an add-in card, which is placed inside your computer, and is used to connect peripherals like a digitizer or mouse, plotters, and a hardware lock. Normally, you will need two adapters if you want to use more than one of the peripherals listed below. The adapters usually come standard with one LPT (line printer) port, to which a printer plotter can be attached. A dealer can help you make the best selection.

   ❑ A digitizer or mouse. These are optional; it's difficult to imagine using AutoCAD effectively without one of them. That is why they are listed here as a minimum requirement.

   ❑ A hardware lock, if you are using the international version of AutoCAD. This is a small box with an electrical connection at each end. It is shipped with AutoCAD, along with your program manuals and disks. The international version will not work unless the lock has been installed. This device comes with instructions for installing it on your computer.

Remember, this is simply a list of the minimum equipment requirements for running AutoCAD. Further system enhancements will make AutoCAD an even more productive and beneficial tool. You might consider adding the following replacement components as components of your system:

❏ IBM PS/2, IBM 386 or 486 or 100 percent IBM-compatible computer. (As of this writing, 486-based machines are not available. This should be remedied soon, perhaps by the time you read this.)

❏ 2M to 4M (*M* stands for *megabytes*) of extra memory, in addition to the 1M of memory that is standard for most 286- and 386-based computers.

❏ A 40M or larger hard disk with a maximum access time of 30 milliseconds. If possible, this should be ESDI controlled. (*ESDI* stands for *Enhanced Small Device Interface.*)

❏ A video graphics adapter with display-list processing capability. This capability allows your drawing to be stored in memory as a vector list that can be manipulated very, very quickly by a special graphics coprocessor on the video adapter. The result is a faster, higher-resolution display than is possible with either an EGA or VGA card.

❏ A video display to match display adapter's capabilities

❏ A plotter or printer plotter

❏ A memory-manager program to provide expanded memory for display-list processing. Programs like QEMM, from Quarterdeck, or 386 to the Max, from Qualitas, are good examples. Most of the recommended computers come with some type of program to provide these capabilities.

Your AutoCAD program's productivity will vary in proportion to the type of hardware you use. Do not skimp on any part of your system. In time you will learn that the benefits of increased productivity outweigh the dollars you might have saved by buying slower or inferior equipment. An authorized AutoCAD dealer can be helpful in this area.

Regardless of the type of hardware you choose, you should read the instructions that came with your computer hardware (not just the computer itself, but the peripherals as well) before installing your software. Most contain clear-cut directions for using the item with AutoCAD and are helpful when configuring the AutoCAD program to your system.

Beginning the Installation Process

This chapter deals with the installation of AutoCAD in general, and the installation of AutoCAD on the IBM PC and compatibles in particular. The text cannot attempt, however, to cover all the hardware platforms for which AutoCAD is currently available, like the Sun Microsystems products, Digital

Equipment's offerings, or the Macintosh. For detailed information on these platforms, refer to the software's installation guide or talk to your authorized AutoCAD dealer.

Remove the shrink wrap from your program master disks, or take them out of the plastic storage box that Autodesk provides. Somewhere on the AutoCAD disks you will see an indication (*360Kb* or *1.2Mb*) of the disks' capacity.

The format of your AutoCAD disks determines the number and type of disks that come with your AutoCAD system. The common AutoCAD formats are packaged as follows:

Format	Size	Disks
360K	5 1/4"	11
720K	3 1/2"	6
1.2M	5 1/4"	4

One K (kilobyte) is approximately 1,000 bytes; a 360K disk can store about 360,000 bytes. One M (megabyte) is approximately one million bytes; a 1.2M disk will hold approximately 1,200,000 bytes of information.

As you begin the installation process, be sure you have an equal number of blank disks of the same format, and some disk labels. You will need these to make backup copies of your AutoCAD disks.

Next, you should view (or print out) a copy of the file README.DOC. This file is important. It may contain notes and installation and configuration instructions that are not included in the AutoCAD manuals.

The README.DOC file's location depends on the disks' format, as follows:

Format	Disk Number	Disk Name
360K	10	Driver Disk 1
720K	6	Driver Disk
1.2M	2	Executable/Drivers

Place the appropriate disk in drive A:. If you just want to view the file on your video monitor, type the following command:

C:\>TYPE A:README.DOC |MORE

If you have a printer, and want a printed copy of the file, type either of the following lines (both do the same thing):

C:\>TYPE A:README.DOC >LPT1

or

C:\>TYPE A:README.DOC >PRN

After you read the file, you should begin making backup copies of your AutoCAD disks.

Making Backup Copies of Your AutoCAD Disks

When making backup copies of your AutoCAD disks, you will follow the same steps for each disk in the original set. Remember—it takes time to make the copies, but your time will have been well spent if the original disks are ever lost or damaged.

To make a copy of a disk, follow these steps:

1. Type the following command:

   C:\>DISKCOPY A: A:

   This should look familiar from the discussion of the DISKCOPY command in Chapter 4, "Dabble in DOS." After entering the command, you will see this response:

   ```
   Insert SOURCE diskette in drive A:
   Press any key when ready . . .
   ```

2. Place your first AutoCAD disk (labeled "1 of x", where x is the total number of disks in the set, based on the format) in drive A:.

3. Press any key to start the copying process.

   A message will appear, giving some technical information about the copying being done. This is purely for your information. Information is now being read from the AutoCAD disk to the computer's memory.

   After a few moments you will see a message similar to the following:

   ```
   Insert TARGET diskette in drive A:
   Press any key when ready . . .
   ```

4. Remove the AutoCAD disk from drive A: and replace it with a blank disk.

5. Press any key to continue the copying process.

   Now the new disk is receiving the information that was read into the computer's memory during Step 3. Another message may appear on the screen:

   ```
   Formatting while copying . . .
   ```

Again, this is just for your information. It indicates that your computer is formatting the new disk while the copying process takes place.

In a few moments you may see another message, similar to the following:

```
Insert SOURCE diskette in drive A:
Press any key when ready . . .
```

6. Remove the disk from drive A: and replace it with the same AutoCAD disk you removed in Step 4.

7. Press any key to continue the copying process.

From this point, you will repeat Steps 3 through 6, until you see a message similar to the following:

```
Copy another diskette (Y/N)?
```

This means that all the information on the source disk (the original AutoCAD disk) has been copied onto the target disk (the previously blank disk).

8. Remove the newly copied backup disk from the disk drive. Copy the information from the label of the original AutoCAD disk onto one of your blank labels, and place the label on the backup disk.

9. If you have more disks to copy, press **Y** (for *yes*). Again you will see this familiar message:

```
Insert SOURCE diskette in drive A:
Press any key when ready . . .
```

Repeat Steps 2 through 8 for each remaining disk in your AutoCAD set.

When you are finished, you will have a complete backup set of your AutoCAD disks. The reason for making backups is simple. If the data on the masters (the original disks) is ever corrupted, you can use the backups. If the hard disk's copy of the program becomes corrupted, or if your hard disk crashes, you have your backups.

When you have made your backups, store your master disks in a safe, static-free, antimagnetic environment. A disk holder is ideal. Take care not to place disks on your digitizing tablet; the digitizer has a magnetic field that can quickly destroy a disk's stored data. Be careful where you place your disks.

Transferring AutoCAD to Your Hard Disk

With the backup disks made and the program masters safely stored away, it is time to create a storage location on your hard disk for the AutoCAD program.

This is the copy you will use daily. The procedure for making the storage location is simple. At the prompt, type the following:

MKDIR \ACAD
CHDIR \ACAD

The first command tells DOS to create a directory named ACAD on the hard disk; the second command sets the current directory to ACAD. For a refresher course on directories, refer to Chapter 4, "Dabble in DOS."

Next you must copy the information from each of your AutoCAD program disks into this new hard disk directory. One by one, place each of your backup AutoCAD disks in drive A: and type the following command:

`C:\ACAD\>COPY A:*.* /V`

You will see a list of the files as they are copied.

When you have done this for each of the AutoCAD disks, installation of AutoCAD on your computer is complete. All that remains is to configure the program—then you will be up and running.

Configuring AutoCAD for Your Hardware

This probably is the most imposing task in the AutoCAD installation process. Besides the fact that there are literally hundreds (maybe thousands) of different AutoCAD-compatible hardware devices, there are nearly as many variations that can be made in the configuration. For the purposes of instruction, however, we will keep it simple. This sample configuration assumes that you have the following equipment:

- ❏ A computer from the recommended list
- ❏ A Video Graphics Array Adapter (VGA)
- ❏ An NEC Multisync 2A Video DIsplay
- ❏ A Kurta IS/ONE digitizer
- ❏ A Hewlett-Packard E-sized plotter
- ❏ An EPSON FX-286 printer plotter

This is not to be interpreted as a shopping list. Rather, the list represents an easily set-up configuration and is intended to familiarize you with the configuration process. *If your hardware is different from that in the sample configuration, refer to the owner's manuals and installation documentation for specific instructions. Substitute those instructions for the ones given here.*

Some short notes before moving on. Autodesk provides *driver files* (a program for interfacing AutoCAD with a particular piece of hardware) for many standard pieces of equipment. Autodesk also provides a standard driver file around which other hardware manufacturers can write or program their own driver files for certain pieces of equipment. This standard driver file is called the ADI (Autodesk Device Interface). Most display-list graphics adapter manufacturers and some plotter and printer plotter manufacturers take advantage of this feature to provide additional enhancements. This book cannot attempt to address every kind of ADI interface. Refer to your equipment manuals for specific instructions concerning your hardware.

Memory usage also is important. This book covers the basic setup recommended for use with AutoCAD. Remember, however, that AutoCAD has the capability to use extended or expanded memory. Examples are a virtual disk (or RAM drive) and/or expanded memory for a display-list graphics adapter. This chapter does not attempt to explain all the different options for memory usage; refer to Chapter 4 of the *Installation and Performance Guide*, which came with your copy of AutoCAD. The guide provides a complete, detailed explanation of options available and a couple of sample configurations, based on memory amounts.

The AUTOEXEC.BAT File

All computers should have a file called AUTOEXEC.BAT. Each time you turn on or reboot your computer, this file gives the computer a sequence of instructions to complete before turning control over to you. AUTOEXEC.BAT is a simple ASCII (American Standard Code for Information Interchange) file, and can be edited with any text editor, such as Norton Editor, EDLIN, or WordStar. We will use EDLIN because it usually comes with DOS-based computers.

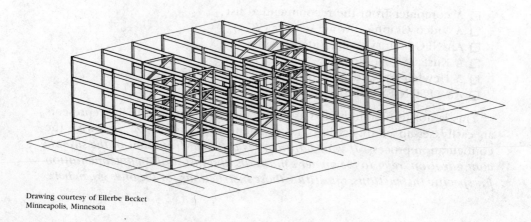

Drawing courtesy of Ellerbe Becket
Minneapolis, Minnesota

AutoCAD's environment variables must be set if the program is to function efficiently. These variables are

ACADFREERAM
LISPHEAP
LISPSTACK

To set these environment variables, enter the following command sequence:

Prompt:	Response:	Explanation:
C:\>	**EDLIN C:\AUTOEXEC.BAT**	Starts EDLIN using the AUTOEXEC.BAT file
*	**L**	Tells EDLIN you want a list of the lines in the file. A numbered list of the lines in the file will be displayed on-screen.
*	*xx*i	Replace *xx* with a number that is 1 greater than the number of lines listed in the preceding step. For instance, if 10 lines are listed, replace *xx* with *11*.
*11:	**SET ACADFREERAM=28**	
*12:	**SET LISPHEAP=40000**	
*13:	**SET LISPSTACK=5000**	
*14:	Press F6.	Tells EDLIN that you have finished adding lines to the file
*	e	Tells EDLIN that you have finished working with the file

Your AUTOEXEC.BAT file is now modified. The changes simply provide memory-paging space for AutoCAD and AutoLISP to function effectively. To initialize the changes you have just made, you need to *cold boot* the computer (turn it off and then turn it back on) in order to effectively clear memory and initialize the new settings. (A *warm boot*, in which you simply press the Ctrl-

Alt-Del keys simultaneously, does not always flush memory banks and reset the computer.)

Now you can continue with the configuration process.

Starting AutoCAD for the First Time

When you configure AutoCAD for the first time, you should execute or start AutoCAD normally. The following is the step-by-step process for executing AutoCAD:

1. Type:

   C:\>chdir acad

   The prompt will change to:

   `C:\ACAD\>`

2. Type the following:

   C:\ACAD\>acad

   You should see a screen of information concerning AutoCAD and first-time users (see fig. 5.1). This ACAD.MSG file, which will display whenever you execute AutoCAD, should be read and heeded, and then deleted.

3. After reading the ACAD.MSG file, press Enter twice.

   You will see the AutoCAD header at the top of the screen, along with the following message:

   ```
   AutoCAD is not yet configured.
   You must specify the devices to which AutoCAD will interface.
   Press RETURN to continue:
   ```

You will then be prompted for a display adapter.

Configuring AutoCAD for Your Display Adapter

Next you should see a list of display adapters. This list will fill more than one screen; you must press Enter to see the entire list. After the list has been displayed, you will be prompted to enter the number corresponding to your video display adapter:

```
Select device number or ? to repeat list <1>:
```

Fig. 5.1. *The ACAD.MSG file.*

```
A U T O C A D
Copyright (C) 1982,83,84,85,86,87,88 Autodesk, Inc.
Release 10 c2 (10/26/88) IBM PC
Advanced Drafting Extensions 3
Serial Number: 79-224868
NOT FOR RESALE

Thank you for purchasing AutoCAD.

If you are a new AutoCAD user, you may want to begin with the
two-dimensional drawing exercise in the "AutoCAD Tutorial."
Veteran users are encouraged to try the 3D exercises, which
highlight Release 10's new features.

For compatibility with applications developed prior to Release
10, you may need to set the FLATLAND system variable to 1. See
README.DOC for details.

In addition to the regular version of AutoLISP, a new Extended
AutoLISP is now supplied. For details, see the "AutoCAD
Installation and Performance Guide" and Chapter 2 of the "AutoLISP
Programmer's Reference."

- Press RETURN for more -
PLEASE SEE README.DOC FOR DETAILS ON THESE AND OTHER SIGNIFICANT
CHANGES.

Be sure to return the installation certificate and registration
card if you haven't already done so. Registered users receive
notices of updates.

This message is in the file ACADMSG. You can delete it or replace
it with a customized version, if you like.

Press RETURN to continue:
```

For this example, we will use number 19, a Video Graphics Array Adapter (VGA). Type:

19

AutoCAD gives you the opportunity to adjust a square on your graphics screen:

```
If you have previously measured the height and width of
a "square" on your graphics screen, you may use these
measurements to correct the aspect ratio.

Would you like to do so? <N>
```

Since (in this example) you have not yet even seen a square on-screen, type **N**. If, when you get to the Drawing Editor, you notice that objects are skewed in one direction or another, you can come back and adjust the aspect ratio, after measuring a square on-screen. This adjustment normally is not necessary; it does not affect plotted output.

Continue the configuration by answering **Y** to the following prompts:

```
Do you want a status line? <Y>
Do you want a command prompt area? <Y>
Do you want a screen menu area? <Y>
```

Your answers to these three questions define the normal AutoCAD drawing screen. Normally, you would want all these things to provide all the options of command entry. Moving right along, type **N** at the next prompt:

```
You may select either a dark (black) or a light graphics area
background. If you select a light graphics area background, then
lines drawn in color 7 will be drawn in black instead. This choice
most closely resembles a black ink drawing on paper.

Do you want dark vectors on a light background field? <Y>
```

This question is self-explanatory; your response is a matter of personal preference. If you find that you do not like your selection here, you can later change the configuration to use the other type of display.

The next prompt:

```
Do you want to supply individual colors for parts of the graphics
screen? <N>:
```

allows you to color-customize your screen's appearance. Again, it is not necessary for normal operation and is a matter of user preference. Type **N**.

The next screen shows the different colors available and the number that corresponds to each. If you specified a monochrome monitor earlier, you will be prompted for color assignments using shades of gray.

Now the video display portion of the configuration process is complete. You will be prompted to press Enter to continue.

Configuring AutoCAD for Your Pointing Device

Next, you should see a list of pointing devices. Because this list fills more than one screen, press Enter to see the entire list. After the list has been displayed, you will be prompted to enter the number corresponding to your pointing device. Most of these devices fall into two categories: digitizers and mice.

There are important usage differences between a digitizer and a mouse. A mouse provides pointing capabilities for on-screen use only. You can point to and select on-screen menu functions and work in the graphics screen. You also can use the AUI (Advanced User Interface), which provides pull-down menus at the top of the screen in the Drawing Editor.

A digitizer has all the capabilities of a mouse and also lets you use tablet menus. After you send in your registration card, Autodesk provides a plastic digitizer tablet overlay that will allow you to select most commands by simply securing the overlay on the digitizer and configuring the menu areas. (This configuration is covered near the end of this chapter.)

Once you are familiar with AutoCAD and the menu structure, you can even program spaces on the tablet to perform functions or macros of your own design. Some digitizers also offer ADI options that are not available with mice; these options allow additional user functions. Some even provide mouse emulation, causing the digitizing puck or pen to perform like a mouse! While this is not intended to be a sales pitch for digitizers, their features far outweigh their additional cost.

At the prompt:

```
Select device number or ? to repeat list <1>:
```

enter the number that corresponds to your pointing device. For this sample configuration, type **22** (a Kurta IS/ONE digitizer).

Depending on the type of pointing device you select, you may see the following display on your screen:

```
Connects to Asynchronous Communications Adapter port.

Standard ports are:

   COM1
   COM2

Enter port name, or address in hexadecimal <COM1>:
```

If the question is displayed, type the name of the communications port used by your digitizer tablet. (This should have been determined by whoever connected your digitizer to the computer.) For the example, we will assume that the default, COM1, is acceptable. You can select the default by pressing Enter.

Next you will see a prompt similar to the following:

```
You may configure one of two different digitizers

   0 - 8.5 x 11
   1 - 12 x 12

Select your digitizer size, 0 or 1 <0>:
```

Again, this may be different, or even optional, depending on the pointing device you selected. For this example, type **1** to specify the 12 × 12 tablet. (If you see a similar prompt for your pointing device, your response should be consistent with the equipment you actually have.)

At this point AutoCAD may display additional prompts for information about your pointing device. If so, answer each question as it appears. When the pointing-device portion of the configuration process is complete, you will be prompted to press Enter to continue.

Configuring AutoCAD for Your Plotter

Next you see a list of plotters. If this list fills more than one screen, you must press Enter to see the entire list.

After the list has been displayed, you will be prompted to enter the number that corresponds to your plotter:

```
Select device number or ? to repeat list <1>:
```

For the example, select **8**, which corresponds to a Hewlett-Packard E-sized plotter.

A Word about ADI Plotter Interfaces

Many plotters (the JDL 850+ and some of the CALCOMP line of plotters, for example) provide an ADI driver to speed up the vectorization process AutoCAD uses to provide hard-copy output. The JDL driver allows all data to be processed in its native vector format, thus reducing processing time by as much as 70 percent! The CALCOMP driver improves the data-transmission rate from computer to plotter by a factor of 2 over normal data transmission rates. These are just two plotting improvements provided by ADI drivers. An authorized dealer can provide information and good advice concerning these drivers.

An additional thought about plotters: They are delicate devices, and preparing a plotter for use can be confusing. You should contact your dealer or the manufacturer if you have questions.

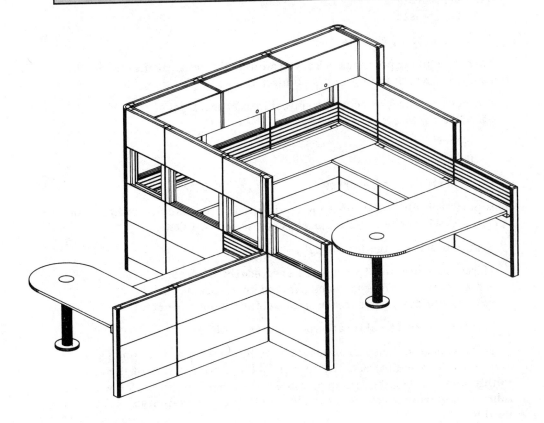

Drawing courtesy of Lillian Ey & McQuiddy Office Designers
Nashville, Tennessee

If AutoCAD needs more information about your particular plotter, a list of available models appears:

```
Supported models:
 1. 7220
 2. 7470
 3. 7475
 4. 7550
 5. 7580
 6. 7585
 7. 7586
 8. 7600 240D
 9. 7600 240E
10. Colorpro
11. Draftpro
12. Draftpro DXL
13. Draftpro EXL
14. Draftmaster

Enter selection, 1 to 14 <1>: 6
```

Then, as with the pointing device, you are asked to designate the communications port to which the plotter is connected:

```
Connects to Asynchronous Communications Adapter port.
Standard ports are:

  COM1
  COM2

Enter port name, or address in hexadecimal <COM1>:
```

This port typically is the next port available. For the sample configuration, specify **COM2**, because the digitizer is connected to COM1.

Next you will see the following:

```
If you have previously measured the lengths of a horizontal
and a vertical line that were plotted to a specific scale,
you may use these measurements to calibrate your plotter.

Would you like to calibrate your plotter? <N> N
```

This is similar to the square measurements message on your graphics screen. You probably have not used your plotter yet and are not sure of the answer to this question. For the example, type **N**, the default response. As with the other configuration items, you can always change your responses later if you need to.

The next series of questions deals with defaults AutoCAD will use when doing a plot. You will be able to change them when you plot, but AutoCAD has to have values to use as defaults.

```
Write the plot to a file? <N>
```

Your answer here determines whether AutoCAD will direct plotter output to the plotter or to a disk file. If you decide to have the output go to a file, AutoCAD automatically assigns to plot files the extension *.PLT*. Some plot spoolers (or plot queuing devices) require the use of a plot file. You can accept the default response by pressing Enter.

```
Size units (Inches or Millimeters) <I>:
```

Here your answer indicates whether you want to use metric or English units of measure. The selection, which is based on user preference, will affect the remaining plotting prompts. To choose the default response, press Enter.

```
Plot origin in Inches <0.00,0.00>:
```

Plot origin indicates the position on the drawing where AutoCAD should begin plotting. Changing this option typically requires substantial experimentation. Normally, no change is required. You can accept the default response by pressing Enter.

```
Standard values for plotting size

Size    Width    Height
A       10.50     8.50
B       16.00    10.00
C       21.00    16.00
D       33.00    21.00
E       43.00    33.00
MAX     44.72    35.31

Enter the Size or Width,Height (in Inches) <MAX>:
```

Here you specify what size paper you want. If you want to take full advantage of your plotter's size, select **MAX**.

```
Rotate 2D plots 90 degrees clockwise? <N>
```

This prompt is fairly self-explanatory. There may be times when you want some two-dimensional plots rotated. You can change this setting for individual plots.

```
Pen Width <0.010>:
```

Your response here depends on the type of pens you are using with your plotter. Check with your pen manufacturer to determine the correct response.

```
Adjust area fill boundaries for pen width? <N>
```

When you are filling plotted entities, your plotter can spend a great deal of time moving the pen back and forth. Your answer here will affect the quality of your plot's filled areas.

```
Remove hidden lines? <N>
```

Hidden lines typically are removed for three-dimensional plots. If you specify that hidden lines should be removed, AutoCAD will calculate and remove lines (from the plot only) that normally would not be seen because of obstructing objects.

```
Specify scale by entering:
Plotted Inches=Drawing Units or Fit or ? <F>:
```

At this point, you should select the default response. Chapter 9, ''Ways To View Your Drawing,'' discusses plotting in detail. Since this response can be changed at that point, your answer here is not critical.

Now the plotter portion of the configuration process is complete. You will be prompted to press Enter to continue.

Configuring AutoCAD for Your Printer Plotter

You should now see a list of printer plotters. This list may fill more than one screen; if it does, press Enter to see the entire list. After the list has been displayed, you will be prompted to enter the number that corresponds to your printer plotter.

A *printer plotter* is simply a normal printer that can print graphics. Many printer plotters can plot graphics but are limited as to the paper size they can accept. In most cases, the printer plotter is limited to the resolution at which drawings can be plotted. ADI software packages (such as FAST PLOT, from Code Lab, or ADIPRINT) provide an ADI driver to improve the speed and resolution of printer-plotter drivers used with AutoCAD. An authorized dealer can advise you about this kind of software. Also, contact your printer plotter's manufacturer to see if you can use this software with your equipment.

At the prompt:

```
Select device number or ? to repeat list <1>:
```

enter the number that corresponds to your printer plotter. For the sample configuration, select **5** (EPSON).

The following printer models are supported:

1. Epson FX-80
2. Epson FX-100 or 286

Select desired model <1>: 2

As with other choices when you configure AutoCAD, this prompt may or may not appear, depending on the printer plotter you specify. Your response should be consistent with your hardware.

Next, you will be asked the same series of questions that you answered to configure AutoCAD for your plotter. Answer them using the same general guidelines provided in the preceding section, ''Configuring AutoCAD for Your Plotter.''

The Main Configuration Menu

After you finish configuring AutoCAD for your printer plotter, you will be returned to the Configuration Menu. Most of the configuration work is complete.

As you can see from figure 5.2, the main Configuration Menu includes nine options (counting Option 0), each of which is covered individually in the following sections.

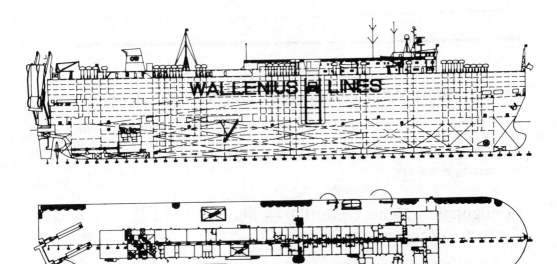

Drawing courtesy of The ACADemy
Sausalito, California

Fig. 5.2. The Configuration Menu.

```
Copyright (C) 1982,83,84,85,86,87,88 Autodesk, Inc.
Release 10 c2 (10/26/88) IBM PC
Advanced Drafting Extensions 3
Serial Number: 79-224868
NOT FOR RESALE

Configuration menu

  0. Exit to Main Menu
  1. Show current configuration
  2. Allow detailed configuration

  3. Configure video display
  4. Configure digitizer
  5. Configure plotter
  6. Configure printer plotter
  7. Configure system console
  8. Configure operating parameters

Enter selection <0>:
```

Configuration Menu Option 0 — Exit to Main Menu

This option does two things. It lets you save the changes you have made during your configuration session, and it also is the only way to return to AutoCAD's Main Menu. You should choose this option when you have finished configuring AutoCAD.

Configuration Menu Option 1 — Show Current Configuration

This option simply displays on-screen the current configuration settings used by AutoCAD (see fig. 5.3). It displays the current video display adapter, the current digitizer, and the current plotter, and then prompts you to press Enter to return to the Configuration Menu.

Fig. 5.3. Show current display screen.

```
Copyright (C) 1982,83,84,85,86,87,88 Autodesk, Inc.
Release 10 c2 (10/26/88) IBM PC
Advanced Drafting Extensions 3
Serial Number: 79-224868
NOT FOR RESALE

Current AutoCAD configuration


  Video display: IBM Video Graphics Array

  Digitizer: Kurta Series I
             12 X 12

Port: Asynchronous Communications Adapter COM1 at address 3F8 (hex)

  Plotter: Hewlett-Packard Rev.3 7585
  Port: Asynchronous Communications Adapter COM2 at address 2F8 (hex)

  Printer plotter: Epson FX-100 or 286


Press RETURN to continue:
```

Configuration Menu Option 2 — Allow Detailed Configuration

Options 3 through 7 let you adjust many device parameters and typical operation modes. Some devices have fine-tuning parameter prompts that are suppressed during normal configuration. An example is pen motion optimization for multipen plotters. By selecting Option 2, you can perform fine adjustments beyond the normal requirements.

Configuration Menu Option 3 — Configure Video Display

This option's name is misleading. It refers to your computer's video display adapter card, not to the video display (monitor) attached to the adapter. Select this option if you decide later to change adapters. The procedure is the same as described earlier in this chapter.

Configuration Menu Option 4 — Configure Digitizer

Use this option to configure a different digitizer, if you decide to change some time in the future. The procedure is the same as that described earlier in this chapter.

Configuration Menu Option 5 — Configure Plotter

Use this option to select a different plotter. The prompts generally are the same as those mentioned previously, depending on which plotter you choose. The procedure is the same as that described earlier in this chapter.

Configuration Menu Option 6 — Configure Printer Plotter

This option lets you select a different printer plotter. The prompts will be the same as those indicated previously, depending on which printer plotter you choose. The procedure is essentially the same as the one for setting up a plotter, described earlier in this chapter.

Configuration Menu Option 7 — Configure System Console

Because the IBM PC has no configurable system console options, this option does not apply. Some of the other hardware platforms, such as the Sun 386, have configurable system console parameters. But with the IBM PC, if you choose Option 7 you will see an error message and will be returned to the Main Configuration Menu.

Configuration Menu Option 8 — Configure Operating Parameters

This option takes you to a secondary configuration menu (see fig. 5.4). These options are covered separately.

Fig. 5.4. *The Operating Parameter Menu.*

```
Copyright (C) 1982,83,84,85,86,87,88 Autodesk, Inc.
Release 10 c2 (10/26/88) IBM PC
Advanced Drafting Extensions 3
Serial Number: 79-224868
NOT FOR RESALE

Operating parameter menu

  0. Exit to configuration menu
  1. Alarm on error
  2. Initial drawing setup
  3. Default plot file name
  4. Plot spooler directory
  5. Placement of temporary files
  6. Network node name
  7. AutoLISP feature

Enter selection <0>:
```

Option 0 — Exit to Configuration Menu

This option takes you back to the Main Configuration Menu.

Option 1 — Alarm on Error

If you select this option you will see the following display:

```
Do you want the console alarm to sound when you make an
    input error? <N>
```

Unless you are a sadist and like noise, or want to frustrate your coworkers, simply press Enter to accept the default. This will spare everyone (including you) a headache.

Option 2 — Initial Drawing Setup

If you choose this option you will see the following:

```
Enter name of default prototype file for new drawings
    or . for none <acad>:
```

If you have a drawing that you use as a prototype for all your drawing work, it may behoove you to use this feature so that you don't have to do a lot of repetitive work (such as standardized layers, grid aspect, snap ratio, and other functions) to set up the drawing environment. If you do not specify a drawing along with the correct path, ACAD.DWG will be used as the default prototype drawing.

You do not have to change this the first time you use AutoCAD. You can change it at any time.

Option 3 — Default Plot File Name

If you choose Option 3, you will see the following:

```
Enter default plot file name (for plot to file)
    or . for none <.>:
```

If you want to specify a standard plot output file name for all the files you generate using the plotting menu's plot-to-file feature, you can enter that name here. Otherwise, before beginning the vectorization process (basically the last step before the plotter does its job), AutoCAD will prompt you for a name.

Option 4 — Plot Spooler Directory

Choosing this menu option causes the following message and prompts to be displayed:

```
When plotting to a file, AutoCAD writes the output to the plot
spooler directory if the special name AUTOSPOOL is
given as the plot file name. The plot spooler directory
is ignored for normal plotting.

Enter plot spooler directory name
<\spfiles\>:
```

This feature will come in handy if you are using a plot spooler. Otherwise, ignore this option.

Option 5 — Placement of Temporary Files

Changing this option will prompt you as follows:

```
Enter directory name for temporary files, or DRAWING to
place them in the same directory as the drawing being edited.
<DRAWING>:
```

When you work on a drawing in AutoCAD, the program keeps constant tabs on the memory available both for the program itself and for the drawing being edited. In almost all cases, the computer's memory is not large enough to hold both AutoCAD and the drawing. AutoCAD creates a backup copy of the drawing and creates temporary files on disk. These files are storage locations to and from which AutoCAD can page pieces of drawing information. This allows the program to function effectively and efficiently without damaging the integrity of the original drawing file. When you save or end an editing session, these temporary files are deleted automatically.

Obviously, paging to and from a temporary file takes time. This is one area in which extra memory configured as a *Virtual Disk* or *Vdisk* (synonymous with *RAM drive*) can help increase productivity. A Vdisk is a "pseudo disk drive" by which a chunk of system memory is set aside to hold data, just like a disk drive. With these files placed on a Vdisk, paging occurs much faster than with ordinary disk-to-memory and memory-to-disk paging.

This option allows you to specify the drive and path of that Vdisk or a faster hard disk if your computer has two hard drives.

Option 6 — Network Node Name

Selecting Option 6 prompts you:

```
On network and multiuser systems, a unique "network node
name" should be specified for each user. This name is added
to certain temporary files and to plot spooler output files
to ensure uniqueness.
```

```
Enter network node name (1 to 3 characters) <AC$>:
```

For instructional purposes, ignore this option. Much of today's CAD environment is networked, but networking is beyond the scope of this book.

Option 7 — AutoLISP Feature

If you select Option 7, you are asked:

```
Do you want AutoLISP enabled? <Y>

Do you want to use Extended AutoLISP? <N>
```

This is an important option because many of AutoCAD's main drawing menus use a substantial amount of the LISP programming language, which is integral to AutoCAD. For those who have extra memory, Extended AutoLISP improves performance of the LISP functions already defined. It also provides extra stack space for users of third-party software packages derived from AutoLISP.

Saving Your Configuration Changes

As was stressed earlier in this chapter, it is important that you save your AutoCAD configuration changes properly. To save changes made during this initial configuration, be sure that the Configuration Menu is displayed on-screen. If it is not displayed, return to this menu. Then choose Option 0, Exit to Main Menu. You will see the following prompts:

```
If you answer N to the following question, all configuration
changes you have just made will be discarded.
```

```
Keep configuration changes? <Y>
```

If you want to save your changes (AutoCAD assumes that you do), simply press Enter. This completes the configuration of AutoCAD on your computer.

If you have just completed the entire process of installing and configuring AutoCAD, it is a good idea to do the following:

1. Exit AutoCAD (select 0 from the Main Menu).

2. Turn your computer off.

3. Turn your computer on again.

4. Restart AutoCAD (as described earlier in this chapter and in Chapter 1, "A Quick Start in AutoCAD").

These steps make absolutely sure that any changes (particularly changes to memory use) are fully initialized.

One more thing needs to be done before you install and configure AutoShade on your system. You need to set up your digitizer overlay.

Setting Up Your Digitizer Overlay

If you do not have an overlay for your digitizer tablet, this section will be of little use. If you plan to get an overlay in the future, you can refer to this section then.

If you have a tablet overlay, follow these steps to set it up:

1. Place the digitizer overlay on your tablet.

2. Fasten the overlay to the tablet so that it will not move. If you are using the tablet overlay shipped with your AutoCAD Bonus Pack (shipped after you return your AutoCAD registration card), you can use the fasteners provided.

3. Start AutoCAD normally. If you need help, refer to the beginning of this chapter or to Chapter 1, ''A Quick Start in AutoCAD.''

4. Choose to edit an existing drawing by selecting Option 2 from the Main Menu. Specify the drawing name as **acad**.

5. Once you are in the Drawing Editor, move your puck or pen around a bit. You should see the crosshairs move on the screen. If you do not, something probably is wrong with your configuration of AutoCAD. Proceeding from this point will be useless; you should not go any further until you can find and correct the problem.

6. The screen menu is at the screen's right side. Highlight the SETTINGS option and press Enter.

7. A new set of screen menu options will appear. Pick the NEXT option.

8. Another set of screen menu options will appear. Pick the TABLET option.

9. Again, the screen menu options will change. This time, pick the CONFIG option.

10. Following the diagram shown in figure 5.5, configure your tablet by answering the questions presented on the screen.

11. When you have finished answering the questions, type **SAVE** at the Command: prompt to save your changes to disk.

12. Use the END command to leave the Drawing Editor.

Now you are all set. If you ever change your template, or if you move the template on your digitizer, you must repeat these steps to configure the tablet again. The process may seem long (it really isn't), but the results are well worth the trouble.

Fig. 5.5. Configuring the tablet menu areas.

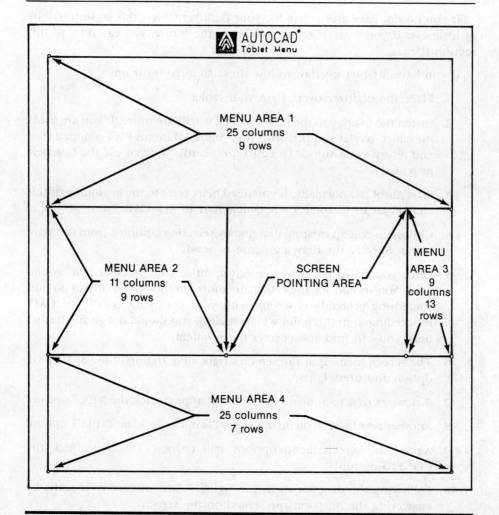

Installing AutoShade on Your Computer

AutoShade lets your drawings shine. It lets you change perspectives, explore different angles, and take advantage of all the options you might have with a camera and film (but with greater accuracy).

AutoShade is a post-processor to AutoCAD. It operates outside the AutoCAD drawing environment, providing features that can be added to previously developed AutoCAD drawings. Similarly, there are post-processors to AutoShade that provide photo-realistic renderings. Autodesk recently acquired PIXAR Corporation, which received an Academy Award in 1989 for best computer-generated movie, *Tin Toy*. Some of the software used to create *Tin Toy* will be used in conjunction with AutoShade to provide photo-realistic imaging.

This section shows you how to install and configure AutoShade on your computer. Chapter 18, ''AutoShade and AutoFlix,'' focuses on using AutoShade with your AutoCAD drawings.

The installation instructions given here are applicable to the two currently available versions of AutoShade (AutoShade and AutoShade 386). The installation procedures are essentially the same for both versions, but their configurations are different. This section covers the configuration of standard AutoShade.

Because the AutoShade 386 memory management schemes are so complex, you should refer to the AutoShade *Installation and Performance Guide* for AutoShade 386 configuration instructions and ask an authorized dealer to help you with the AutoShade 386 configuration process.

AutoShade's hardware requirements are basically the same as those listed earlier in this chapter for AutoCAD. The hardware requirements for AutoShade 386 are a bit more restrictive:

❏ COMPAQ Deskpro 386, PS/2 models 70, 80, or a true 386-compatible computer. (Note: Your 80386 computer CPU must be step B0 or higher. Your dealer can help you determine whether your machine meets this requirement.)

❏ An Intel 80287 or 80387 math coprocessor

❏ 2M of RAM, 1M of which is set up as extended memory

❏ A hard disk with a capacity of at least 20M

The math coprocessor, video display, pointing device, and output device requirements for AutoShade 386 are the same as those for AutoShade and AutoCAD.

Remember: Autodesk supports only the COMPAQ Deskpro 386 and the two IBM PS/2 models (70 and 80), but other 80386 computers can run AutoShade 386. If your hardware is different from that listed here, refer to Appendix A of the AutoShade *Installation and Performance Guide* for specific configuration instructions for AutoShade 386.

Beginning the Installation Process

AutoShade installation is similar to AutoCAD installation, described earlier in this chapter. You should begin by removing your program master disks from their shrink wrap or plastic storage box. The disks' capacity (360K or 1.2M) should be indicated on the disk labels.

The number and size of your AutoShade disks depends on their format. The common AutoShade formats require the following sizes and numbers of disks:

Format	Size	Disks
360K	5 1/4"	7
720K	3 1/2"	4

Before you begin the installation process, be sure you have an equal number of the same size disks, and a few disk labels. You will need these to make backup copies of your program disks.

Like AutoCAD, your AutoShade disks may contain a README.DOC file, which you should read on-screen or print out. This file may contain additional installation and configuration instructions that may not be in the AutoShade manuals.

The README.DOC file's location depends on the disks' format, as follows:

Format	Disk Number	Disk Name
360K	3	Support Disk
720K	2	Support/Filmroll Disk

Place the appropriate disk in drive A:. If you just want to view this file on your video monitor, type the following command:

C:\>TYPE A:README.DOC |MORE

If you have a printer and want a printed copy of this file, type either of the following commands (both do the same thing):

C:\>TYPE A:README.DOC >LPT1

or

C:\>TYPE A:README.DOC >PRN

If you receive a File Not Found error message, Autodesk did not consider README.DOC to be necessary and did not include it on your disk. If you find the file, read it carefully. Now you can make backup copies of your AutoShade disks.

Making Backup Copies of Your AutoShade Disks

To make backup copies of your AutoShade disks, follow the same steps you took when copying your AutoCAD disks (refer to the "Making Backup Copies of Your AutoCAD Disks" section of this chapter). Simply substitute your AutoShade disks for the AutoCAD disks called for in the instructions.

After you have made your backup copies, store the program master disks with the AutoCAD masters in a dry, static-free, antimagnetic environment.

Transferring AutoShade to Your Hard Disk

AutoShade is easy to install on your hard disk. The AutoShade Install disk has a simple installation program. To execute the program, place your backup copy of the Install disk in drive A: and then type the following command at the prompt:

C:\>a:install

Because this chapter covers only the installation of standard AutoShade, type **N** at the next prompt:

`Do you want to install AutoShade 386 <N>`

If you wanted to install AutoShade 386, you would enter **Y**.

The next prompt:

`Enter AutoShade source diskette drive letter <A>`

asks for the disk drive from which you intend to copy AutoShade. For this sample installation, type **A**.

Also for the sample installation, AutoShade will be installed in the same subdirectory as AutoCAD. At the prompt:

`Enter path in which AutoShade will be installed <c:\SHADE>`

type **C:\acad**. With both programs installed in the same directory, they can interface more easily. Furthermore, AutoShade's support files must reside in the AutoCAD subdirectory.

The next installation step simply purges old AutoShade software (from an earlier version, for example) from the AutoCAD subdirectory. Before responding to this prompt:

```
Any existing AutoShade program and utility files in the
target directory "c:\acad" will be overwritten.
Do you want to continue? <Y>
```

think for a moment: Do you have in your ACAD subdirectory any AutoShade rendering files that you want to keep? If so, you should choose not to continue. Copy the "keeper" files to another disk so that they will not be lost. Once those files are safe, you can restart the installation program, answering the prompts until you get to this point again.

When you answer **Y** to this prompt, the installation program starts copying the AutoShade disks to the hard drive. You are prompted to change disks as required. The procedure is relatively easy to follow. When you are finished with the installation, you can start the AutoShade configuration process.

Configuring AutoShade for Your Hardware

Like the sample AutoCAD configuration earlier in this chapter, the following sample AutoShade configuration has been devised under certain assumptions that affect the answer to each configuration prompt. These hardware assumptions were detailed earlier. If you have different hardware (and you probably do), answer each AutoShade configuration prompt with the appropriate response for your hardware.

If your hardware uses any ADI drivers or mouse drivers, they must be loaded into memory before you execute AutoShade; otherwise, the program will not function. Follow the instructions specific to your hardware.

To configure AutoShade for the first time, type **SHADE** at the DOS prompt. Later, if you want to change your AutoShade configuration, you will type the command **SHADE -r**.

Configuring AutoShade for Your Display Device

You are asked first to configure a pointing device. The screen will look like this:

```
Select pointing device:

    1.   Autodesk Device Interface Pointer
    2.   Microsoft Mouse
    3.   Joystick / Koala pad
    4.   Keyboard cursor keys
```

Pointer Selection: **2**

For the sample configuration, select **2**. The Kurta IS/ONE digitizer (remember our hardware assumptions) has the capability to emulate a Microsoft mouse. When you actually configure AutoShade for your pointing device, your answer should be appropriate to your hardware.

Next, you are prompted to specify your display device:

```
Select display device:

    1.   Autodesk Device Interface display driver
    2.   Hercules graphics card
    3.   IBM Color Graphics Adapter (CGA - Monochrome mode)
    4.   IBM Enhanced Graphics Adapter (EGA)
    5.   IBM Video Graphics Array (VGA)
    6.   IBM Alphanumeric Display
    7.   None
```

Display Selection:

This is the display used by AutoShade for menus, dialogue boxes, and plan view or wireframe images. Select **5**.

Now you need to specify another display device. AutoShade uses this one to display renderings, or the shaded images. Select **5**.

```
Select rendering display device:

    1.   Autodesk Device Interface display driver
    2.   Hercules graphics card
    3.   IBM Color Graphics Adapter (CGA)
    4.   IBM Enhanced Graphics Adapter (EGA)
    5.   IBM Video Graphics Array (VGA)
    6.   IBM Professional Graphics Controller (PGC)
    7.   Orchid TurboPGA
    8.   None
```

Rendering Selection:

Notice that the last option is None. AutoShade can run in *batch mode*, which is used for making slides or renderings without displaying them on-screen. Batch mode cannot be used with the IBM CGA, EGA, or VGA adapters. Thus, if you plan to automate your renderings in batch mode, you should inform AutoShade that no display device will be used. Chapter 18, "AutoShade and AutoFlix," covers batch processing in more detail.

The installation procedure continues with the following prompt:

```
Do the display and rendering display devices share a single
screen (default = no)
```

For some hardware configurations, the display device and the rendering device can be the same adapter, or can be interchanged. For a list of possible combinations, see Chapter 2 of the AutoShade *Installation and Performance Guide*. For the sample configuration, type **Y** to select the single screen option.

The last display prompt is

```
Does FLIPSCREEN require a redraw (default = no):
```

Some adapters have enough memory on the card to store both the display screen and the rendering screen. Because the displays selected for this sample configuration do not have sufficient memory to store both screens, a redraw will occur when you switch between renderings and the interactive screen. Answer **Y** to this question.

You have finished configuring AutoShade for your display device. Next, you will be asked about hard-copy output.

Configuring AutoShade for Your Hard-Copy Device

The final configuration step for AutoShade is to specify a hard-copy device for renderings.

```
Select rendering hard copy device:
```

```
1.  Autodesk Device Interface rendering driver
2.  Postscript Device
3.  Rendering file (256 color map)
4.  Rendering file (continuous map)
5.  None
```

```
Rendering hard copy Selection:
```

For the sample configuration, type **5**; we plan to view our renderings on-screen only. If you are actually configuring AutoShade, you should respond according to your hardware configuration. Select the output device or file format you will use with AutoShade.

Your configuration of AutoShade is complete. The interactive AutoShade screen should appear. Try moving the pointing device. If the small on-screen arrow moves, AutoShade is ready for use. If you want to learn more about how AutoShade works, see Chapter 19, ''An AutoLISP Primer.''

A final reminder about AutoShade 386: Many memory variables come into play when you configure AutoShade 386. This information, which is quite technical, is beyond the scope of this book. For more information, consult an authorized dealer and refer to Appendix A of the AutoShade *Installation and Performance Guide*.

Summary

The AutoCAD and AutoShade installation and configuration is over. This chapter has covered a lot of ground. It may have been redundant or unnecessary for some readers. That's OK; the information is optional, because your dealer may have installed and configured AutoCAD (and AutoShade). The information has been covered here for two reasons: First, many readers will install AutoCAD and AutoShade by themselves. Second, every AutoCAD user should have a firm grasp of AutoCAD's use, from start to finish.

To recap a few important points about installing AutoCAD and AutoShade:

❏ Make sure that you have the proper equipment for using AutoCAD and AutoShade.

❏ Be sure to read the instructions for your peripheral equipment *before* you install AutoCAD and AutoShade.

❏ Read the README.DOC files that may be on your AutoCAD and AutoShade disks. These files are very important; they contain additional installation information.

❏ Make backup copies of the program master disks.

❏ Configure the software for your hardware, based on the instructions for the hardware.

❏ Most of all, enjoy your equipment and software and have fun.

Installation and configuration can be confusing. If you get in a hurry or let it get the best of you, you will feel frustrated. Take your time. Enjoy learning about your equipment and software; they will reward you with years of production.

Now you're ready for Part II, ''Making AutoCAD Work for You.'' In Chapter 6, ''The Basics of Drawing in AutoCAD,'' you will begin learning the powerful drawing commands available in AutoCAD's Drawing Editor.

Part II

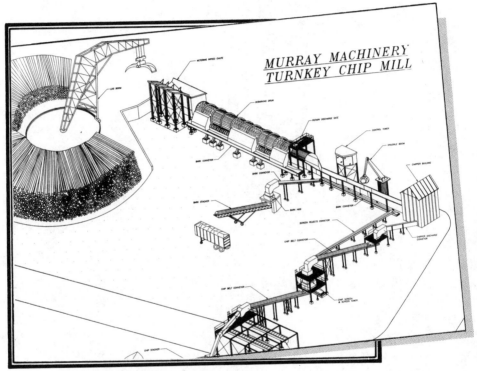

MURRAY MACHINERY
TURNKEY CHIP MILL

Drawing courtesy of Bobby Benson, FMP/RAUMA Company

Making AutoCAD Work for You

6

The Basics of Drawing in AutoCAD

This chapter is designed to give you a thorough understanding of how to use the AutoCAD drawing commands and work with the different methods of command input available. The following methods of command input are covered:

- ❏ Keyboard
- ❏ Programmed buttons
- ❏ Screen menus
- ❏ Tablet menus
- ❏ Pull-down menus
- ❏ Repeating commands

Some of these methods are used to demonstrate the following drawing commands:

- ❏ UNITS
- ❏ LINE
- ❏ PLINE
- ❏ ARC
- ❏ OSNAP
- ❏ ELLIPSE
- ❏ CIRCLE
- ❏ POLYGON
- ❏ DONUT
- ❏ SOLID
- ❏ POINT

After you have finished reading this chapter and have worked through the example, you should have a good understanding of how to use AutoCAD's drawing commands. Try using a few of the different methods for entering your commands in AutoCAD. When you are familiar with AutoCAD's different input methods, you can choose the easiest one for you.

Entering Commands in AutoCAD

AutoCAD supports many devices for entering commands and displaying information. Therefore, a variety of methods are available for entering AutoCAD's commands. Although no one particular method is always best, you should be familiar with each form of command input so that you can determine which method is the most productive for you.

Many of these methods are tied to specific hardware devices such as digitizers, mice, and pucks. These devices are covered in greater depth in Chapter 3, "Know Your CAD Equipment." If you are uncertain about the hardware options on your system, you should read Chapter 3, which gives complete coverage of any CAD system equipment.

From the Keyboard

The keyboard is an integral part of every computer; it is one of the pieces of hardware provided when you buy your computer. Whether you are using AutoCAD or not, the keyboard is the usual manner by which you communicate with the programs you will be running. As such, it is the most often used of all input devices that AutoCAD uses for entering commands.

When using the keyboard, you type each AutoCAD command and then press the Enter key or the space bar (both keys do the same thing in AutoCAD) to tell AutoCAD to execute the command.

The keyboard can be used also to access the screen menus (described later in this chapter). When you press the Insert (Ins) key, one of the screen menu bars is highlighted. You can then use the arrow keys to move the highlighted bar up or down to the command you want to execute. When the command you want to use is highlighted, simply press the Enter key to start execution.

The Poor Man's Mouse

Even though they are not as versatile as using a mouse or tablet, the arrow keys found on all keyboards can be used to move the crosshairs around the screen. Simply press the appropriate arrow key to move the crosshairs in one direction or another. When you press the PgUp or PgDn keys, you increase or decrease the space the crosshairs will move when you press one of the arrow keys.

From the Digitizing Tablet

You use a *stylus* or a *puck* (sometimes mistakenly referred to as a mouse because their shapes are similar) to enter commands from the digitizing tablet. (If you are not sure what these devices look like, please refer to Chapter 3, "Know Your CAD Equipment.") At the top of the puck is an extension, made of coiled wire, with crosshairs through the center. AutoCAD uses this crosshair to track exactly where you are pointing on the digitizing tablet. When the crosshairs are placed over the box on the tablet that corresponds to the command you want to execute, you press the puck's pick button to start the command.

The stylus looks like a fancy pen with a spring-loaded or electronic tip and a button on its side. To select a command with the stylus, move the tip so that it is inside the menu square you want to select and then either press down on the pen or push in the button on the side of the pen.

The tablet menu contains only the most commonly used AutoCAD commands. Figure 6.1 shows a drawing (supplied by Autodesk) of the tablet menu with the different menu areas indicated.

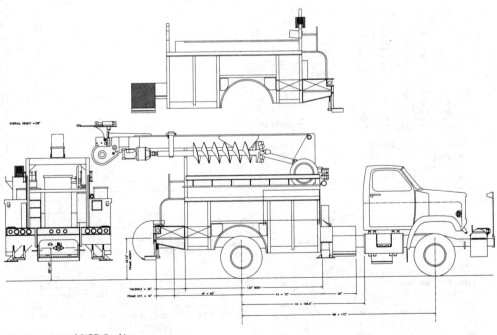

Drawing courtesy of CADD Graphics
Raleigh, North Carolina

Fig. 6.1. *Autodesk's tablet overlay for the digitizer.*

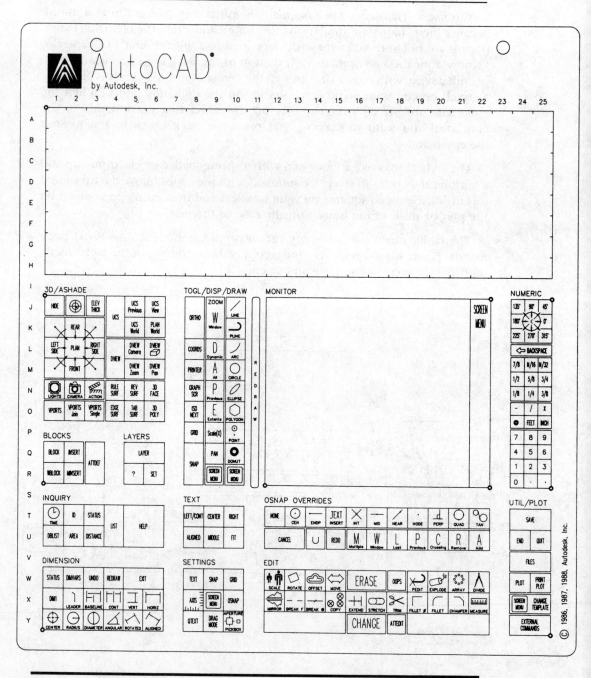

With Programmed Buttons

The programmed buttons on pucks and mice are easy to use. The *pick* button is used for selecting commands from the tablet or menu screen and for choosing entities or locations on the drawing screen. This button is different, depending on whether you are using a mouse or a puck. If you are using a mouse, the pick button is usually the one on the left. If you are using a puck, the pick button typically is found near the top of the puck. Common settings for the other buttons are Enter, Cancel, and Snap On/Off. Mice are limited to three buttons: one is used exclusively for picking; the other two can be programmed to do almost anything.

Some pucks have as many as 16 buttons. Because all menus are programmable, these descriptions may not correspond to the buttons on your puck. You should experiment with your puck or mouse to determine the command for each button. To check the buttons, simply press each button and watch for an on-screen effect. If you don't see one, try again. Make sure that the puck is on the digitizing tablet when you press the button. (If you are using an optical mouse, make sure that it rests on its reflective pad.)

The Screen Menu

In Chapter 1, you saw a picture of the AutoCAD Drawing Editor screen (refer to fig. 1.2). The menu on the side of the screen interacts with the digitizing tablet as well as the other input devices. When you execute a command from the digitizing tablet, for example, the screen menu conveniently shows that command and lists all appropriate menu options.

The screen menu hierarchy shown in figure 6.2 is taken from Autodesk's MENUTREE sample drawing.

When you enter the Drawing Editor, the screen menu that appears is called the *Root Menu*. From this menu you can access many others, including the menus of editing commands, drawing commands, and display commands. If you want to draw a line, for example, you select DRAW. The Root Menu is then replaced by the Draw Menu and you can select a drawing command such as LINE.

To make a selection from a screen menu, move the crosshairs into the menu area. The menu options are highlighted as the crosshairs pass over them. To select an item, use the pick button on your input device.

Fig. 6.2. *The screen menu hierarchy.*

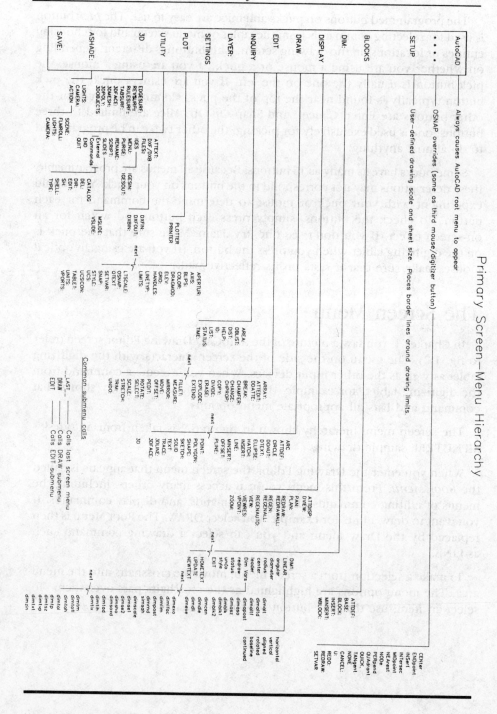

Primary Screen–Menu Hierarchy

Most screen menus offer the following special options:

❏ NEXT
❏ PREVIOUS
❏ LAST
❏ ACAD
❏ ****

If there is more than one screen of commands, an item labeled NEXT will appear at the bottom of the screen menu. The NEXT option takes you to the next page of menu commands. PREVIOUS returns you to the previous menu page. LAST lets you backtrack through the menus, whereas the ACAD option always returns you to the Root Menu. To access special frequently used commands, such as REDRAW and the Object Snap Overrides, you select the menu entry denoted by four asterisks (****).

Pull-Down Menus

If your monitor and video card use the Autodesk Device Interface (ADI) driver, you will be able to use AutoCAD's pull-down menus. When you move the crosshairs to the top of the screen, the pull-down menu headings appear. To select a particular menu, highlight and "pick" its heading. The menu will appear below the heading.

To make a selection from the pull-down menu, move the cursor vertically through the menu, highlight the command you want, and then "pick" that command. To remove the pull-down menu from your screen without entering a command, you can do one of the following:

❏ Use Ctrl-C from the keyboard.
❏ Use the Cancel button on your puck.
❏ Pick in a blank slot in the menu.
❏ Pick in an area of the screen not covered by the pull-down menu.

Some commands on the pull-down menus are programmed to repeat themselves. This built-in capability is convenient if you want to execute a command several times in succession. When you are finished, press Ctrl-C to return to normal AutoCAD operations.

Other commands executed from the pull-down menus provide a dialogue box that appears as an overlay of your drawing (see fig. 6.3). Within this box you can respond to the command in several ways: you can enter values or settings, you can answer yes or no questions, or you can easily modify areas of your drawing.

Fig. 6.3. *An example of a dialogue box.*

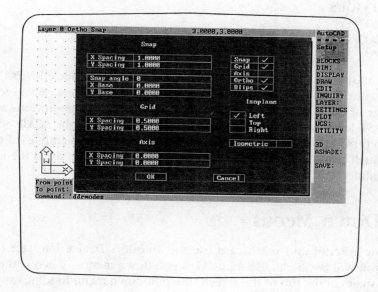

Even if you do not understand all of the AutoCAD commands, familiarize yourself with how to use the pull-down menus and where the commands in the menus are located. The advantages to using the pull-down menus are that they allow for "heads up" choosing of commands (your eyes never have to leave the screen) and you can use dialogue boxes to enter and manipulate drawing information. The diagram of pull-down menus shown in figure 6.4 is taken from the MENUTREE drawing supplied by Autodesk.

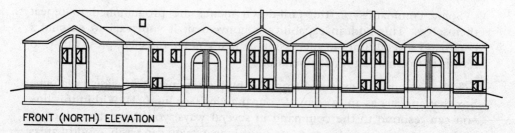

FRONT (NORTH) ELEVATION

Drawing courtesy of Peterson + Habib consultants, inc.
engineer and architect
Thunder Bay, Ontario, Canada

Fig. 6.4. Autodesk's diagram of pull-down menus.

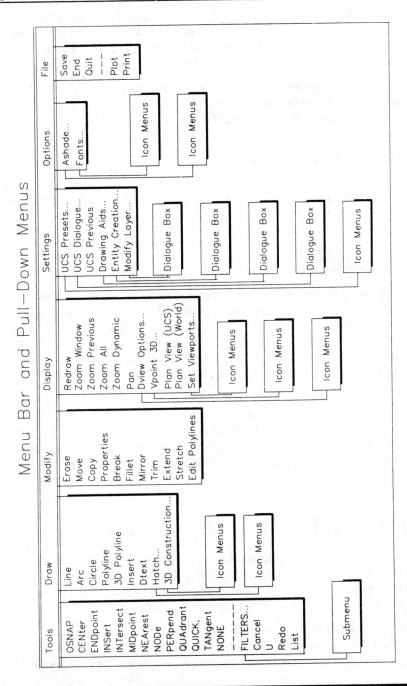

Repeating Commands

AutoCAD's built-in command-repeat feature is helpful when you want to repeat a command two or three times. AutoCAD will repeat the last-executed command if you press the Enter key or space bar on the keyboard (or the pick button on the mouse or puck) at the Command: prompt.

If you want a command to be repeated many times, use the MULTIPLE command prior to the command to be repeated. For example, you can repeat the CIRCLE command (described later in this chapter) as many times as necessary by typing the following response to the command prompt:

Command: **MULTIPLE CIRCLE**

You will then be prompted in the normal manner for drawing a circle, but the command will automatically repeat after each circle is finished. To cancel the repetition, press Ctrl-C.

The Example

You will create a drawing by using various AutoCAD drawing and editing commands. This sample drawing will demonstrate all of the commonly used AutoCAD commands. As with any drawing, you will work with simple elements, building on them to create a complex drawing. You will start by creating a bathroom, using only the AutoCAD drawing commands. In Chapter 7, "Editing Your Drawing," you will use the editing commands to create the full floor plan with a minimum of work.

To prepare for drawing the example, you must create a new drawing with Option 1 in the AutoCAD Main Menu. As demonstrated in Chapter 1, "A Quick Start in AutoCAD," this will start you with a clean drawing. Call the drawing *EXAMPLE*, so that you will be able to differentiate it from other drawings on your computer.

The AutoCAD Drawing Commands

The AutoCAD drawing commands form the basis for almost anything you create. They are the blocks from which you can build complex drawings. Most AutoCAD commands are named to indicate the function they perform. The LINE command draws lines and the CIRCLE command draws circles, for example.

AutoCAD commands have what is known as a *default response*. All of the commands expect you to input point information or select pieces of your drawing that they may manipulate. After any command, AutoCAD supplies a default response that is displayed enclosed in arrow brackets (<>). If the default is the correct response, you choose it by pressing the Enter key on your input device. Default responses help speed up your work because they decrease the amount of typing required.

Setting Display Format and Precision (UNITS)

The UNITS command is used to set the display format and precision of your drawing units. You can set up your own standards, work with them, and change them while you are drawing or editing. The UNITS command allows you to change any of the following:

❏ Unit display format
❏ Unit display precision
❏ Angle display format
❏ Angle display precision
❏ Angle direction

You probably will want to set at least one of these items whenever you start a new drawing. Since you have just begun a new drawing, enter **UNITS** at the Command: prompt and press Enter. AutoCAD displays the following menu of available formats, with examples of how each is displayed:

```
Systems of units:      (Examples)

   1. Scientific        1.55E+01
   2. Decimal           15.50
   3. Engineering       1'-3.50"
   4. Architectural     1'-3 1/2"
   5. Fractional        15 1/2

Enter choice, 1 to 5 <2>:
```

With the exception of the Engineering and Architectural formats, these formats can be used with any basic unit of measurement. For example, Decimal (the default) is perfect for metric units as well as decimal English units. If you are accustomed to using units with a specific format, the UNITS command tells AutoCAD to use that format. Press Enter if you want to use the default format. To choose one of the other formats, enter the appropriate number.

For the floor plan example, select 4 to set the units to Architectural (because entering 4'6" as a distance or a coordinate value is easier than entering 54"). Both the engineering and architectural formats show feet and inches. If you select 5 (Fractional), the displayed units and fractions may represent either inches or millimeters.

The next prompt depends on which system of units you select. When you select 1, 2, or 3, the following prompt appears:

```
Number of digits to right of decimal point (0 to 8)<current>:
```

If you select 4 or 5, the following prompt is displayed:

```
Denominator of smallest fraction to display
   (1, 2, 4, 8, 16, 32, or 64) <current>:
```

After you have selected the system and precision, AutoCAD prompts you for an angle format:

```
Systems of units:          (Examples)

  1. Decimal degrees        45.0000
  2. Degrees/minutes/seconds 45d0'0"
  3. Grads                  50.0000g
  4. Radians                0.7854r
  5. Surveyor's units       N 45d0'0" E

Enter choice, 1 to 5 <1>:
```

The example to the right of each selection shows the syntax to use when you enter an angle within AutoCAD. Choose a system of angle measurement and press Enter.

Next, AutoCAD will prompt you for the following:

```
Number of fractional places for display of angles (0 to 8)<current>:
```

You can specify a precision of up to eight places. If you are working with degrees/minutes/seconds, the number you enter determines the accuracy of the minutes and seconds. If you type **0**, for example, only degrees are displayed; if you specify **1** or **2**, minutes also are displayed; type **3** or **4** to get degrees, minutes, and seconds (5 to 8 cause display of additional fractional seconds).

Next, AutoCAD prompts you for the direction for angle 0. The default is for angle 0 to be at 3 o'clock, with other angles calculated counterclockwise. You can change both angle 0 and the direction in which other angles will be calculated.

Indicate the direction for angle 0 at the following prompt:

```
Direction for angle 0.0000:
   East   3 o'clock  =   0
   North 12 o'clock  =  90
   West   9 o'clock  = 180
   South  6 o'clock  = 270
Enter direction for angle 0.0000 <current>:
```

Note that the display will vary depending on the angle format you previously specified. You should indicate a direction for angle 0 which is consistent with the angle format you have specified.

If you want to specify an angle that is not listed in the preceding prompt, press the F1 function key to flip to the graphics screen; then indicate the angle with two points. A word of caution: if you indicate an angle in this way, remember what you have done. Using a nonstandard angle as your 0 angle can lead to major confusion.

The final prompt controls how the other angles are measured (clockwise or counterclockwise). The prompt follows:

```
Do you want angles measured clockwise? <N>:
```

Press **Y** if you want the angles to be measured clockwise.

The UNITS command allows you to specify what format is used to enter and view distances and angles. This can help eliminate confusion if you are used to working with units in a particular fashion. UNITS lets you customize AutoCAD for your specific needs.

Drawing Lines (LINE)

As demonstrated in Chapter 1, "A Quick Start in AutoCAD," AutoCAD provides an easy way to create lines—the LINE command. To draw a line, you provide AutoCAD with a beginning and ending point. The LINE command also has an option called *Close*; this option will close a polygon by drawing a line from the last point specified to the starting point of your first line.

You will use the LINE command to create the walls of the bathroom (see fig. 6.5). Enter the following responses to AutoCAD's prompts. (Be sure to press Enter after each response.)

Prompt:	*Response:*	*Explanation:*
Command:	**LINE**	Starts LINE command
From Point:	**0,0**	Starting at point 0,0
To Point:	**@7'0"<0**	First wall line
To Point:	**@7'0"<90**	Second wall line
To Point:	**@7'0"<180**	Third wall line
To Point:	**C**	Draws last line back to starting point

If the wall lines in the preceding example extend beyond the edge of the screen, type **ZOOM E**. This command (which is discussed in Chapter 9, "Ways To View Your Drawing") will bring all of the elements in your drawing into view.

Fig. 6.5. Bathroom walls created using the LINE command.

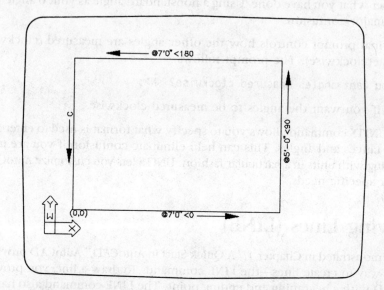

The concept of absolute and relative point entry was discussed in Chapter 1, "A Quick Start in AutoCAD." In the series of keystrokes you just entered, you applied what you learned about this concept. In this series of keystrokes, you entered both absolute and relative coordinates (the relative coordinates begin with the @ symbol; the absolute coordinates are the X,Y pairs).

While you're at it, go ahead and draw the tub. The tub is simple to create. At this stage all the corners are still sharp and all the inner lines are parallel to the outer lines, which normally doesn't happen with tub design. The editing commands in Chapter 7, "Editing Your Drawing," will make the tub look "real." For now, remembering to press Enter after each response, follow along with the example:

Prompt:	Response:	Explanation:
Command:	**LINE**	Starts LINE command
From Point:	**5′0″,0**	Starts tub edge line
To Point:	**@5′0″<90**	Draws it up to other wall
To Point:	Press Enter.	
Command:	**LINE**	Starts LINE command
From Point:	**6′9″,3″**	Draws inner tub line (3″ inside wall and tub lines)
To Point:	**@1′6″<180**	Draws first of four sides
To Point:	**@4′6″<90**	Second side
To Point:	**@1′6″<0**	Third side
To Point:	**C**	Finishes with last side

Your drawing should now contain the elements shown in figure 6.6.

Fig. 6.6. The bathroom with tub.

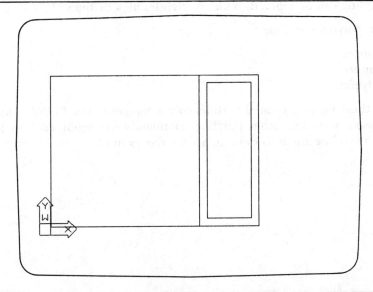

The final use of the LINE command will be to draw the edges of the sink. You will start drawing the sink here; later, you will use the ELLIPSE command to draw the sink's basin. The following command sequence walks you through the process of drawing the sink edges:

Prompt:	Response:	Explanation:
Command:	**LINE**	Starts LINE command
From Point:	**0,5'0"**	Starts lines showing sink edges
To Point:	**@1'6"<270**	Continue drawing sink lines
To Point:	**@2'6"<0**	
To Point:	**@1'6"<90**	
To Point:	**C**	

Figure 6.7 shows the partially created bathroom with its wall lines, lines for the tub, and lines showing the edge of the sink. The upcoming commands will continue to "flesh out" the drawing.

For the next element of the bathroom, you will use a variation of the LINE command, called PLINE (for polyline). *Polylines* are special entities in AutoCAD—they are lines and arcs (segments) which are connected end-to-end to form one entity. Polylines are extremely versatile: the individual segments of a polyline can be tapered, wide, or slender arcs or lines.

Other polylines include:

❑ Ellipses
❑ Donuts
❑ Polygons

Each of these items is created with its own command. The PLINE command is discussed next. The other polyline commands are examined later in the chapter as we use them to draw items for our example.

Fig. 6.7. The newly created sink and tub.

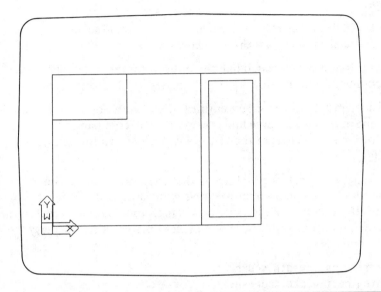

The Basic Polyline Command (PLINE)

PLINE (pronounced *P line*) is the basic command for creating polylines. Polylines have many advantages. One of them is that a polyline creates a single object or entity. When you use the PLINE command to draw the door in the bathroom, you will be creating that door from four lines. Since the PLINE command creates only one entity, editing the door will be easier. When you edit the door (moving or rotating it to fit the opening), you can pick any piece of the door—AutoCAD will select the entire door.

The initial prompt for the PLINE command is similar to the prompt for the LINE command. When you enter **PLINE**, AutoCAD prompts you (From point:) for the starting point of the polyline. When you have entered that point, the following prompts appear on-screen:

```
Current line width is ___
Arc/Close/Halfwidth/Length/Undo/Width/<Endpoint of line>:
```

The PLINE command's default drawing segment is a line. You can either indicate the line's endpoint or choose one of the other options, which are explained in the following paragraphs.

If you want to draw arc segments, select Arc by picking it from the drawing menu or by typing **A** and pressing Enter. AutoCAD displays the following prompt:

```
Angle/CEnter/CLose/Direction/Halfwidth/Line/Radius
   /Second pt/Undo/Width/ <endpoint of arc>:
```

These options are very much like the options for creating a standard arc. (The ARC command and its options are discussed in the next section.)

Because polylines are single entities, they can be open or closed. Closing a polyline performs the same function as the LINE command's C option; it draws a line or arc segment from the last point you entered to the beginning of the polyline.

A special property of polylines is that they can have thickness, or width. The width can be specified in two ways: you can specify either the total width or a specific width on either side of a center line. The Halfwidth option uses a specified width on either side of a center line. AutoCAD displays the following prompts:

```
Starting half-width <current>:
Ending half-width <current>:
```

If you want the segment to be a uniform width, enter the same starting and ending halfwidth. Halfwidth is one way to specify the width of a polyline. Width, discussed later in this section, is the other way.

Select Length if you want to enter the length of the next segment. This segment will be drawn with the same angle as the last segment, and with the length you entered.

Select Undo when you want to undo the last segment you drew. The effects of Undo are the same in PLINE as they are in the LINE command.

You can assign widths to polyline segments—differing widths, if you want. When you select Width, AutoCAD prompts you for both the beginning and the ending width. By entering different beginning and ending widths, you can create tapered segments.

With the default, Endpoint, AutoCAD is looking for the end of the line segment. As in the LINE command, endpoints can be entered as either absolute or relative coordinates.

Now it's time to use the PLINE command to create the door (see fig. 6.8):

Prompt:	Response:	Explanation:
Command:	**PLINE**	Starts PLINE command
From Point:	**0,4**	Starting point of the door
/<Endpoint of line>:	**@2′6″<0**	Length of door is 2′6″
/<Endpoint of line>:	**@1<90**	Width of door is 1″
/<Endpoint of line>:	**@2′6″<180**	Draws third and final sides
/<Endpoint of line>:	**C**	Closes polyline back to beginning

Fig. 6.8. The bathroom door.

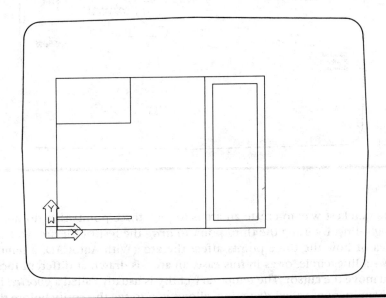

In the next section, you will use the ARC command to show the door's path when it opens.

Drawing Arcs (ARC)

The ARC command is one of the most complex AutoCAD drawing commands, second only to PLINE. ARC has eight different options for creating the Arc entity type. In the next example, you will use the `Start/Center/Included Angle` option to create an arc. The other arc-creating options are shown in figure 6.9.

Fig. 6.9. *Examples of the different types of arcs.*

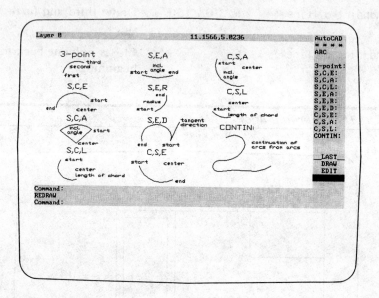

The quickest way to create an arc is to pick three points that do not lie on a straight line. By using the third point to *drag* the rest of the arc, you can get an idea of how the three points affect the arc. (With AutoCAD, a temporary entity—a line, circle, or as in this case, an arc—is drawn at different locations as you move the cursor. The temporary entity is usually called a *ghosted* image; the phenomenon, called *dragging*, allows you to see the entity before the last point is indicated.)

Now, using the ARC command, draw the door's path of travel (see fig. 6.10).

Prompt:	Response:	Explanation:
Command:	**ARC**	Starts ARC command
Center/<Start point>:	**Int**	Starts arc at inter-section point of door lines
Center/End/<Second point>:	**C**	We want to specify the center point of the arc
Center:	**Int**	Specifies that center point will be located where door and wall meet
Angle/Length of chord /<End point>:	**A**	Specifies that you want to enter the arc angle
Included angle:	**90**	Shows arc for fully opening door

Fig. 6.10. An arc used to show the door's path of travel.

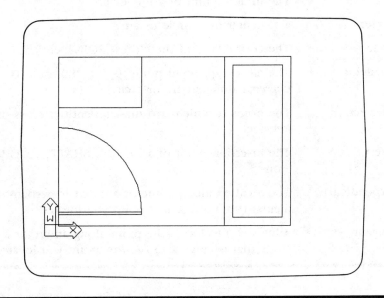

Choosing What You Want: The Object Snap Overrides

AutoCAD provides a capability that let's you choose exact locations of drawing entities and then use those points as input into a command. This capability was demonstrated in the preceding example: when you typed *Int* in response to prompts for certain points, AutoCAD located the intersection point of two lines in the door and used that point as input for the ARC command. This capability, called *Object Snap Override*, gives you great flexibility. You can draw entities without having to be intimately familiar with every X,Y coordinate around which the entities are drawn.

The Object Snap Override capability is not limited to locating intersections of drawing entities. AutoCAD has 10 Object SNAP modes, some of which you may never use, but *all* of which can be helpful. These Object Snap modes and the points they locate are listed in table 6.1.

Table 6.1. *AutoCAD's Object Snap Modes*

Mode	*Points located*
Nearest	A point on the closest line, arc, or circle entity
Endpoint	The nearest end of a line or arc
Midpoint	The middle point of a line or arc
Center	The center of a circle or arc
Node	The coordinates of the closest POINT entity
Quadrant	The closest quadrant point (0, 90, 180, or 270 degrees) along an arc or a circle
Intersection	The point at which two drawing entities cross or intersect
Insert	The insertion point of a BLOCK, SHAPE, or TEXT entity
Perpendicular	The location along a line or arc that is perpendicular (90°) to the *last* point you located
Tangent	Allows you to locate the point along an arc or a circle that is tangent to the *last* point you located

The Object Snap modes give you great flexibility. The ability to locate points without knowing their coordinates can come in handy. You should be familiar with and understand what all the modes do, even if you don't use some of them. You will continue to use Object Snap modes as you develop the sample drawing.

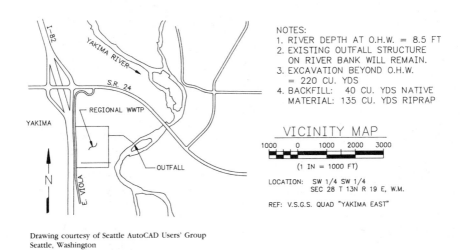

NOTES:
1. RIVER DEPTH AT O.H.W. = 8.5 FT
2. EXISTING OUTFALL STRUCTURE
   ON RIVER BANK WILL REMAIN.
3. EXCAVATION BEYOND O.H.W.
   = 220 CU. YDS
4. BACKFILL: 40 CU. YDS NATIVE
   MATERIAL: 135 CU. YDS RIPRAP

VICINITY MAP

1000   0   1000   2000   3000

(1 IN = 1000 FT)

LOCATION: SW 1/4 SW 1/4
            SEC 28 T 13N R 19 E, W.M.

REF: V.S.G.S. QUAD "YAKIMA EAST"

Drawing courtesy of Seattle AutoCAD Users' Group
Seattle, Washington

The ELLIPSE Command

Now it's time to add to the outline of the bathroom sink. You will use AutoCAD's ELLIPSE command to draw an elliptical shape for the basin.

Prompt:	Response:	Explanation:
Command:	**ELLIPSE**	Starts the command
<Axis endpoint 1>/Center:	**6",4'3"**	Locates starting point of first axis
Axis endpoint 2:	**@1'6"<0**	Length and direction of first axis
<Other axis distance> /Rotation:	**@6"<90**	Length and direction of second axis

Now use the ELLIPSE and LINE commands to draw the toilet:

Prompt:	Response:	Explanation:
Command:	**LINE**	Starts LINE command
From Point:	**2'10",4'11"**	Starts drawing toilet tank
To Point:	**@1'6"<0**	Next line
To Point:	**@8"<270**	Next line
To Point:	**@1'6"<180**	Next line
To Point:	**C**	Draws final line back to beginning
Command:	**ELLIPSE**	Starts the command
<Axis endpoint 1>/ Center:	**3'9",4'2"**	Starts drawing toilet bowl
Axis endpoint 2:	**@12"<270** or **@1'<270**	Second endpoint
<Other axis distance>/ Rotation:	**@5"<90**	Minor axis length

Figure 6.11 shows the bathroom with all the objects you have drawn, including the basin and the toilet.

To create an ellipse, you first specify the length of its major axis; then you specify a distance for the minor axis. The length of the major axis will be the length, tip-to-tip, of the longest section of the ellipse. Using two unequal axes creates the egg shape of an ellipse.

A second way to create an ellipse in AutoCAD is to specify the location of the center of the ellipse by choosing the Center option, and then visually choosing the locations for the major and minor axis endpoints. Use the first method if your ellipse must be accurate.

Fig. 6.11. The bathroom with all its fixtures.

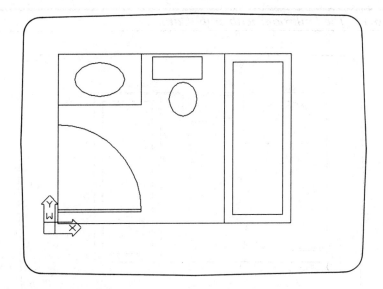

Drawing Circles (CIRCLE)

You will use the CIRCLE command to create one of the drains for the bathroom. Later in this chapter, you will use the DONUT command for the other drain.

Circles can be drawn in several ways; you can specify a center point and radius, center point and diameter, or two- and three-point circles created by choosing points on the edge of the circle. At this point, you will draw the circles by using the command's default options: picking a center point for the circle and then specifying a radius.

Prompt:	Response:	Explanation:
Command:	**CIRCLE**	Starts CIRCLE command
3P/2P/TTR/ <Center point>:	**1'3",4'3"**	Locates center of sink drain
Diameter/<Radius>:	**1"**	Drain has a radius of 1"

Your bathroom should now look like the drawing in figure 6.12.

Fig. 6.12. The bathroom with sink drain.

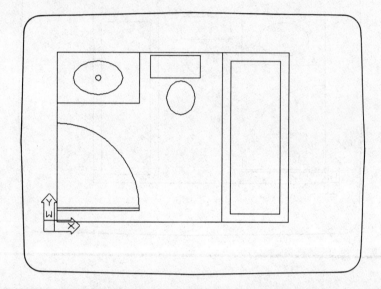

Regular Polygons (POLYGON)

A *polygon* is a special polyline entity. The POLYGON command creates a figure with up to 1,024 sides of the same length. The typical polygon is created by first specifying the number of sides to draw and then telling AutoCAD whether the entity is to be drawn inside or outside a circle with a certain radius.

The command is most useful when you need to draw an entity with sides that are all equal in length. In the example, you will use the POLYGON command to create a unique decorator wastebasket with six sides (see fig. 6.13).

The command format is

Prompt:	Response:	Explanation:
Command:	**POLYGON**	Activates command
Number of sides:	**6**	Indicates the number of sides

Prompt:	Response:	Explanation:
Edge/<Center of polygon>:	Pick a point.	Center of polygon
Inscribed in circle/ Circumscribed about circle I/C:	C	Draws polygon outside circle
Radius of circle:	4	Radius of circle is 4″

Inscribed means that the lines making up the polygon are contained entirely within the circle upon which that polygon is based; *circumscribed* means that the lines are outside the circle. You enter either **I** or **C**, depending on which type of polygon you want to create. AutoCAD then displays a *ghosted* polygon (an image of what the polygon might look like) and prompts for Radius of circle:. Enter the radius in whatever way you prefer.

Fig. 6.13. *A unique decorator wastebasket created by using POLYGON.*

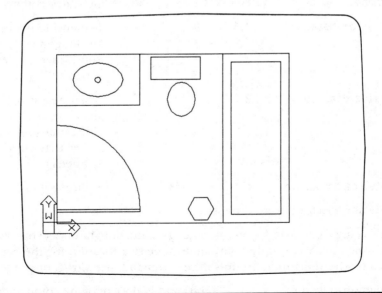

If you want to create a polygon by first specifying the length of its sides, select Edge. This causes AutoCAD to ask you for the two endpoints of the polygon side. Respond to the following prompts:

```
First endpoint of edge:
Second endpoint of edge:
```

As you can see, a ghosted polygon appears after you specify the first endpoint. It can help you to select the second endpoint by showing you what the polygon will look like when you choose the second endpoint.

Rings and Solid Filled Circles (DONUT)

Rings and solid filled circles (doughnuts) are another adaptation of the polyline. To draw them, use the DONUT command. AutoCAD also recognizes the alternate command spelling: DOUGHNUT. Both spellings result in the same prompts and exactly the same entities are created. By using DONUT, instead of DOUGHNUT, you can cut down on the amount of typing required to specify the command.

Now you will now use DONUT to draw the drain for the tub. The command sequence for DONUT is

Prompt:	Response:	Explanation:
Command:	**DONUT**	Activates command
Inside diameter:	**1.5**	Sets inside diameter of doughnut. For solid filled circles, set to "0".
Outside diameter:	**2**	Sets outside diameter of doughnut (must be larger than inside diameter)
Center of doughnut:	**6'0", 1'3"4'3"**	Indicates point
Center of doughnut:	Press Enter.	

With a single command, you can enter as many doughnuts as you want, all of the same size. You simply continue to specify a location for the center of each successive doughnut. To finish the command, use Ctrl-C or press Enter.

To demonstrate the uses of the SOLID and POINT drawing commands, you will use them to create patterns of 4-by-4 inch tiles on the floor.

Solid Areas (SOLID)

To draw large solid rectilinear and triangular areas filled with color, use the SOLID command.

When you draw solids, you indicate three or four corners of the area to be filled. Indicating these corners in a specific order is important if you are to achieve the shape you want. To draw a rectilinear solid, the first and third points must lie on the same edge; if you indicate the points in a clockwise or counterclockwise direction, you will get a bow tie (see fig. 6.14). Look carefully at the figure, focusing on the order in which corners were indicated.

Fig. 6.14. *An incorrectly drawn solid.*

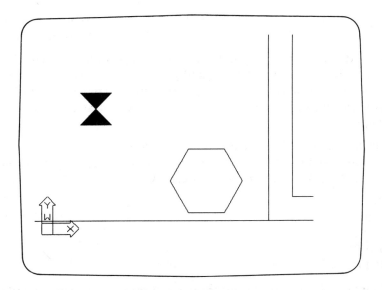

The following example demonstrates the proper method of entering information for the SOLID command:

Prompt:	Response:	Explanation:
Command:	**SOLID**	Activates command
First point:	2'0",2'8"	Corner point of first tile
Second point:	2'0",3'0"	Second point is 4' up
Third point:	2'4",2'8"	Third point is 4" to the right and 4" down
Fourth point:	2'4",3'0"	Last point is 4" to the right and 4" up. This draws the SOLID.
Third point:	Press Enter.	Completes command sequence

Notice this last prompt. AutoCAD continues to cycle through the Third point: and Fourth point: prompts until you complete the command. For each additional third or fourth point you specify, AutoCAD will draw another solid, using the previous third and fourth points as the first and second points for this shape.

By using the SOLID command, you have laid the first tile in the bathroom. Use the same command sequence to lay five other tiles, with their lower left corners at the following coordinate locations:

8",8"
16",20"
3'4",2'4"
3'0",1'0"
4'4",1'8"

You figure out the X,Y locations for the other three corners of each tile. Once these tiles are laid, your drawing should look like figure 6.15.

Perhaps the best advice for using the SOLID command is to experiment. As you work with the command you will start to understand how AutoCAD implements it. Remember that the first point is always connected to the third; if there is a fourth point, the second is connected to it.

Fig. 6.15. Bathroom's tile floor, drawn using solids.

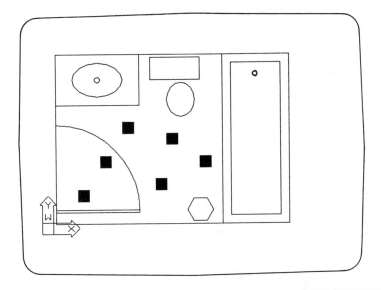

Indicating Locations (POINT)

Points can be used for many different purposes. They can be used, for example, to represent the following:

- ❏ The centerlines of structural beams
- ❏ Intersections of entities
- ❏ Problem areas with parts that fit together
- ❏ Crucial points within blocks
- ❏ Points of contact and centers of rotation for mechanical parts

Whenever you need a special entity to indicate something, use a point.

Typically, the point entity is used for temporary purposes until another entity can be laid in over it. Many programs that send information to AutoCAD use the point to show the location of information, such as the corners of a surveyed lot. Once an entity is placed over that point, the point is erased or removed from the drawing screen.

To insert point entities in a drawing, you simply enter **POINT** at the Command: prompt, press Enter, and then, at the Point: prompt, indicate the point's location. That's all there is to it—the point is inserted. Point locations may be indicated in either absolute or relative coordinates. They may also be indicated using the Object Snap modes discussed at the beginning of this chapter.

Now try using the POINT command to lay a random pattern on the tile floor (see fig. 6.16).

Fig. 6.16. *Placing points at random to enhance the floor's appearance.*

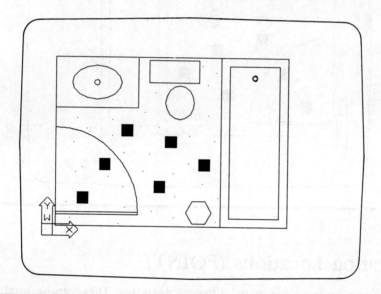

Prompt:	Response:	Explanation:
Command:	**POINT**	Starts the POINT command
Point:	Pick a location for your point	

A system variable (PDMODE) controls what a point looks like. Setting PDMODE makes all points in a drawing identical. If you change the setting, all point entities change to the new variable setting. To change this variable, you use the SETVAR command as follows:

Prompt:	Response:	Explanation:
Command:	**SETVAR**	Starts SETVAR command to change system variable
Variable name or ?:	**PDMODE**	Specifies that you want to change PDMODE
New value for PDMODE<0>:	Enter the number that corresponds to display mode selected from figure 6.17.	

Fig. 6.17. *Settings for the system variable PDMODE.*

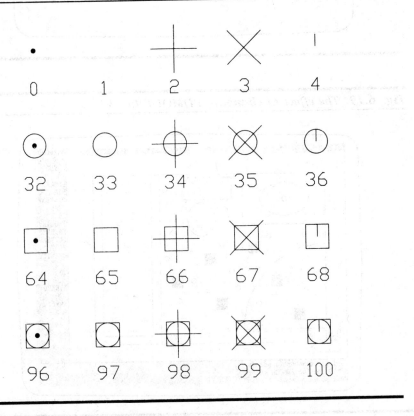

The effects of different settings for PDMODE are shown in figures 6.18 and 6.19.

Fig. 6.18. *The effect of changing PDMODE to 35.*

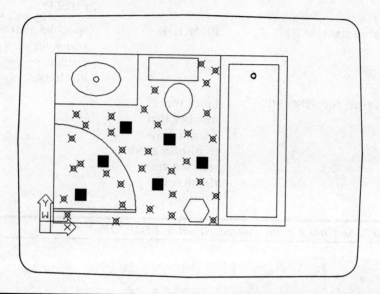

Fig. 6.19. *The effect of changing PDMODE to 53.*

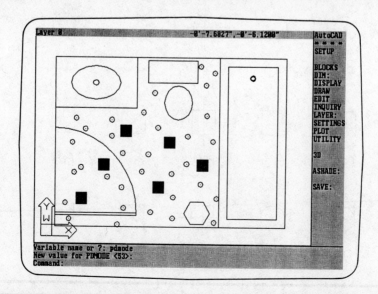

Figure 6.18 shows what happens when you change the PDMODE variable to 35; figure 6.19 shows what will happen when you change the PDMODE variable to 53.

Ending Your Example

You have now finished the drawing example for this chapter. At this point you have two options: you can use the END command to save your drawing and exit the Drawing Editor, or you can go on to Chapter 7, "Editing Your Drawing," and continue building the example. By choosing the END command, you can take a break and then come back to your drawing at a later time.

Summary

This chapter has shown you how the fairly simple drawing entities can be combined to create a complex drawing. At this point, you have used only drawing commands to create a sample drawing. These commands include the following:

- ❑ UNITS
- ❑ LINE
- ❑ PLINE
- ❑ ARC
- ❑ OSNAP
- ❑ ELLIPSE
- ❑ CIRCLE
- ❑ POLYGON
- ❑ DONUT
- ❑ SOLID
- ❑ POINT

You have learned about the different ways to enter commands and how to locate *specific* points on a drawing entity by using the Object Snap Overrides. And you have learned how to set AutoCAD's UNITS command so that you can enter points in the most convenient way for your profession.

The work you have completed sets the stage for Chapters 7 and 8 ("Editing Your Drawing" and "Advanced Editing Commands," respectively). With the information in these chapters, you will be able to complete the floor plan.

7

Editing Your Drawing

In Chapter 6, "The Basics of Drawing in AutoCAD," you learned how to use AutoCAD to create drawings. As you know, every drawing is made up of a series of objects—lines, arcs, circles, and polylines. In the AutoCAD environment, these objects are known as *entities*. In addition to AutoCAD's many commands for creating entities, the program provides a series of powerful editing commands with which you can *change* entities. In some cases these editing commands will allow you to create new entities from previously created entities.

The majority of AutoCAD's editing commands are discussed in this chapter. Two editing commands that are not presented here (CHANGE and PEDIT) are discussed in depth in Chapter 8, "Advanced Editing Commands." By reading and working through the examples in this chapter, you will not only add many commands to your collection of AutoCAD tools but also gain a firmer grasp of the way AutoCAD views and manipulates objects in a drawing.

The commands discussed in this chapter are

❏ COPY   ❏ MOVE   ❏ SCALE
❏ OFFSET   ❏ TRIM   ❏ MEASURE
❏ ZOOM   ❏ STRETCH   ❏ DIVIDE
❏ FILLET   ❏ BREAK   ❏ CHAMFER
❏ EXTEND   ❏ MIRROR   ❏ ARRAY
❏ ROTATE   ❏ ERASE

Your Sample Drawing

In Chapter 6, "The Basics of Drawing in AutoCAD," the sample drawing demonstrating the AutoCAD drawing commands consisted of a small part of a floor plan. You started by using the drawing commands to lay out the first room, the bathroom. In this chapter, you will add a bedroom and kitchen to the example. This will allow you to "flex your muscles" a little and show you how easy it is to expand a drawing with AutoCAD's editing commands.

If, as suggested, you ended your drawing so that you could take a small break, you can get the drawing back on-screen by choosing Option 2, Edit an Existing Drawing, from AutoCAD's Main Menu. When it asks you for your drawing file name, type **EXAMPLE** and then press the Enter key. This will take you into the AutoCAD Drawing Editor and display the bathroom floor plan.

Selecting AutoCAD Entities

Each of AutoCAD's editing commands performs a different type of editing function on the entities that make up your drawing. A group of entities on which AutoCAD is to perform a function is known as a *selection set*. As you issue an editing command, AutoCAD typically responds by allowing you to specify the entities on which the command will have an effect. AutoCAD will proceed only when you indicate that you have finished specifying the selection set.

When you execute an editing command, the AutoCAD crosshairs change to a small box, called a *pickbox*. You use this box to choose entities to be added to the selection set. Whenever AutoCAD asks you to choose entities, which occurs in all of the edit commands, you can either use the pickbox to select each entity individually or you can use additional options to modify the way you build your selection. These options (see table 7.1) allow for a variety of ways in which entities may be added to or deleted from a selection set.

Table 7.1. Options used in building selection sets.

Option	Function
A point	Allows you to pick a single entity and add it to the current selection set.
Multiple	Causes AutoCAD to scan the drawing database only once when choosing a set of entities to edit. AutoCAD ordinarily scans the database whenever you pick an entity. If you have a complex drawing, this can slow you down.

Option	Function
Window	When you use this option, AutoCAD asks you to pick two corners of a rectangle that surrounds the entities you want to edit. Once you have entered the second corner point, AutoCAD chooses all entities that were *completely* within the area of your defined window.
Crossing	Almost exactly like the Window option, except that any entity that *touches* the window border is chosen, as well as those within the window border.
Last	Tells AutoCAD to choose the last entity drawn.
Previous	Uses the last group of entities (the last selection set) you chose to form the current selected set.
Undo	Allows you to step back through the entity selection process and remove entity groups in the reverse order of that in which you chose them. For example, if you were to add a set of entities by using the Window option, and then decided you didn't want to edit them, the Undo option will remove those entities from the selection set.
Remove	If you have selected a few entities that you really don't want to edit, you can use this option to remove those entities from the selection set. When you enter **Remove**, AutoCAD asks you to Remove objects:. To do so, you may use the options listed here to remove entities from the selected set.
Add	If you are in Remove mode, this option returns you to the Select objects: prompt; you can resume adding entities to the selection set.
Return	Pressing Enter causes AutoCAD to stop picking entities to be edited and begin to perform the edit.
Ctrl-C	This is a quick way to cancel an AutoCAD command, as well as the process of selecting entities or picking endpoints for the LINE command. Press Ctrl-C to return immediately to the Command: prompt.

Any of these options may be used in any sequence at any time. For example, you may build a selection set by picking some entities individually and using the Window option to add others. Now that you know how to build a selection set, let's look at several of the basic editing commands.

The Editing Commands

AutoCAD's editing commands are the most powerful commands available within the Drawing Editor. They not only allow you to make changes to your drawing but also, when used in conjunction with the drawing commands discussed in Chapter 6, "The Basics of Drawing in AutoCAD," let you quickly create and enhance your drawing. These commands give you much greater speed than using only the drawing commands to create your drawing.

Before you begin the practice session for the editing commands, take a moment to ensure that you have loaded the sample drawing (EXAMPLE) and that you are within the Drawing Editor.

Copying Entities (COPY)

The COPY command is used for making copies of entities that already exist within a drawing. You will use the COPY command to give a width (4″) to the bathroom walls. Like other editing commands, the COPY command allows you to create a *selection set* that contains the entities you will copy. The selection set can be made up of one entity or 1,200. In this case, you will copy only one wall section at a time.

To begin using the COPY command, enter the following command sequence. As you enter these commands, notice how the crosshairs change to a pickbox.

Prompt:	Response:	Explanation:
Command:	**COPY**	Starts COPY command
Select objects:	Pick wall.	Select the wall you want to copy.
<Base point or displacement> /Multiple:	Pick a point near wall.	The point from which you will be copying
Second point of displacement:	@4″<90	The point to which you are copying

As you can see, this operation copied the wall line 4 inches up (90 degrees). Now use the COPY command to copy each of the other walls out 4 inches from the bathroom. The three other directions you will specify—**180, 270,** and **0** degrees (remember, you just completed the 90-degree copy)—represent *left*, *down*, and *right*, respectively. When you are done, your screen should look like the one in figure 7.1.

Fig. 7.1. *The bathroom walls after COPY has been used.*

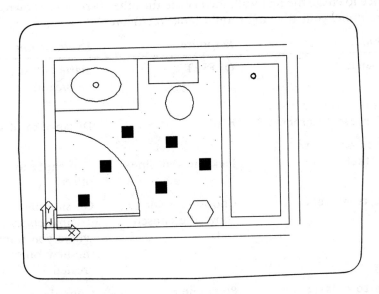

This exercise showed you that after you finished the selection set you had to pick the base point to copy *from* and the point to copy *to*. Many of the editing commands work this way (selecting a base point and a second point). Although it may feel a little odd, after you practice this method a few times it works easily.

The COPY command has another option (Multiple) that allows you to make several copies of the entities in your selection set. After your Base point: has been chosen, you can give several Second point: locations to which the entities are to be copied.

Offsetting Entities (OFFSET)

The OFFSET command is similar to COPY except that the new entities created are always parallel to the original entity. The new entity is either placed a specified distance from the original or drawn through a point you choose.

You will use OFFSET to create more rooms and a hallway for your sample floor plan. The wall located at the top of the screen needs to be offset up 8′0″ to form part of the kitchen. The wall near the bottom of the screen needs to be offset 10′0″ to create the second wall for the bedroom. The outer bathroom wall (where the door is currently located) needs to be offset 3′0″ outward (to the left) to form a hallway to connect all these pieces. Follow the command sequence to create the first wall; then create the other two on your own. When you are done, your drawing should look like figure 7.2.

Prompt:	Response:	Explanation:
Command:	**OFFSET**	Starts OFFSET command
Offset distance or Through <current>:	**8′0″**	Distance to offset
Select object to offset:	Pick the wall line.	The entity to offset
Side to offset:	Choose a point above the chosen wall.	On side of original entity where you want the new one created
Side to offset:	Press Enter.	Quits the command

REAR (EAST) ELEVATION

Fig. 7.2. Creating the rest of the walls, using OFFSET.

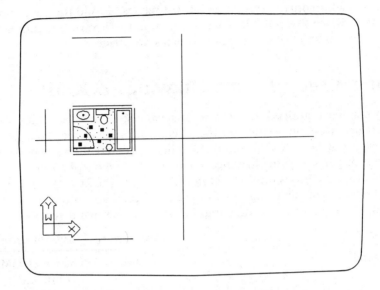

You can enter a distance to offset by typing in an exact number (as previously illustrated), picking two points, or typing **T** (for Through). The Through option allows you to specify an offset distance *after* you have chosen an entity to offset. The offset entity will then pass *through* the point you chose.

When AutoCAD prompts you to:

`Select object to offset:`

use your pointing device to select the entity you want to offset. Although AutoCAD will not let you choose more than one entity at a time, after this first offset you can perform additional offsets on other entities in your drawing. AutoCAD will repeat this prompt until you cancel the command or press Enter.

After you select the entity you want to offset and specify an offset distance, you are asked for the `Side to offset:`. The side you choose determines where the new, offset entity will be placed. For instance, if you are offsetting a circle, you should select a point either inside or outside the circle. The offset copy of the circle will be concentric to the original.

A problem occurs when you try to offset complex curves such as ellipses and other complex polylines and arcs: if you offset to the interior of the curve, AutoCAD will eventually reach a point that passes beyond the centerpoints of these arcs. When this point is reached (the point will vary, depending on the entity being offset), AutoCAD approximates an offset.

Seeing More of Your Drawing (ZOOM)

You may have noticed that as you offset the specified wall lines, the new lines created were not visible on the screen. In order to see those lines, you must use AutoCAD's ZOOM command. This command allows you to "zoom" in or out of parts of your drawing, much as you'd take a photograph through a telephoto lens. This is only a brief introduction to the ZOOM command. For more information on using ZOOM, read Chapter 9, "Ways To View Your Drawing." To see your full drawing, follow this command sequence:

Prompt:	Response:	Explanation:
Command:	**ZOOM**	Starts ZOOM command
All/Center/Dynamic/Extents/Left /Previous/Window/<Scale>:	**.02**	Enter scale factor to zoom by

In this example, you use the Scale option to zoom out of the drawing area a little. When you provide a scale value, remember that a number greater than one will zoom in on the drawing and a number less than one will zoom out. The two other ZOOM commands you will need are ZOOM WINDOW and ZOOM PREVIOUS.

With the ZOOM WINDOW command, you can pick the two corners of a rectangle encompassing the area you want to examine. Use the ZOOM PREVIOUS command to back out of zoomed windows to the previous viewing area.

Experiment with these commands and become familiar with the way they work. The ZOOM command does not change your drawing in any way; it simply allows you to examine your drawing at various distances. Its purpose is to help you to get a better view of the areas in which you will be drawing. As you continue through the example, you will want to use ZOOM to make your screen match the figures in this chapter.

Filleting Entities (FILLET)

FILLET trims or extends two lines until they are tangent to an arc of a specified radius. The two lines must intersect at some location within the drawing, because AutoCAD cannot fillet parallel lines. You can fillet lines, arcs, circles, and polylines You are not limited to filleting only two similar entities; you can fillet a line and a circle, for example. FILLET trims or extends the two entities until the fillet fits. The FILLET command sequence goes like this:

Prompt:	Response:	Explanation:
Command:	**FILLET**	Starts the FILLET command
Polyline/Radius/ 　<Select two 　objects>:	Select the two wall lines shown in figure 7.3.	Select object to fillet

---

Fig. 7.3. *Two lines to be filleted.*

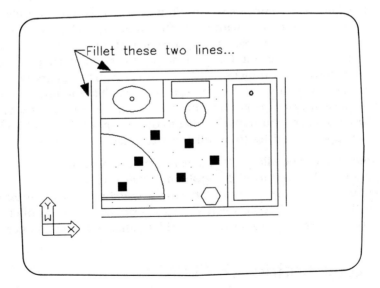

To specify a radius to fillet, select Radius. The default fillet radius is normally set to 0. If you fillet two lines with a 0 radius, AutoCAD produces a sharp corner. As you can see, this routine is nifty for cleaning up wall intersections on floor plans (or for anything that requires sharp corners). The radius value, which is set with this command, is stored in an AutoCAD system variable called FILLETRAD. For an explanation of system variables and the values they hold, see the ''Quick Reference to AutoCAD's System Variables'' section of Part VI.

Select two objects is the default selection. When you entered the FILLET command, you may have noticed that AutoCAD changed the on-screen crosshairs to a pickbox. This pickbox is used to select the two entities to fillet. The points you pick when you select these entities determine where the fillet will be placed. This is especially noticeable when you fillet arcs and circles. The point with which you indicate the entity is the area in which AutoCAD will try to place the fillet.

Because you will use the FILLET command to produce sharp corners for the wall lines, you should set the fillet radius to 0 (as indicated above). Then execute the FILLET command again and select the two objects (entities) you want to fillet. In this example, these are the intersecting wall lines. Don't forget—if you make a mistake, you can always use **U** to undo your error and try the command again.

An interesting occurrence may crop up more often when you fillet circles or arcs than when you work with lines. Depending on where you select the two entities, it may be possible (and equally correct) to produce either of two fillets. In such an instance, AutoCAD will place a fillet on the first entity, closest to the point at which you picked the second entity. The results may not be what you want. To get the results you want, you may have to undo a fillet and try again. In such cases, make sure that you select the entities at a different point, closer to where you want the fillet to occur. Figures 7.4a and 7.4b show what can happen if entities to be filleted are picked at different locations.

Polylines also can be filleted. If you want to fillet a polyline, select Polyline. When AutoCAD is asked to fillet a polyline, each vertex (the point at which two sections of a polyline meet) is filleted to the specified radius. One exception to this is that the distance between vertexes is smaller than the fillet radius. In this instance vertices shorter than the fillet radius will remain unchanged.

Extending Entities (EXTEND)

The EXTEND command changes the length of entities to a boundary defined by another existing entity. The entities used as boundaries must be visible on-screen. When you enter **EXTEND**, you will see the following prompts:

```
Select boundary edge(s)...
Select objects:
```

Fig. 7.4a. *Picking an entity at one location.*

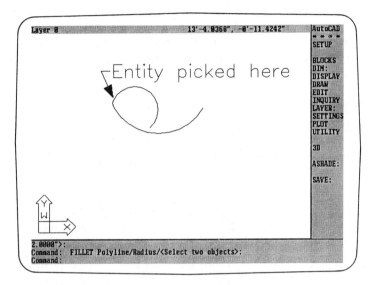

Fig. 7.4b. *Picking the same entity at a different location.*

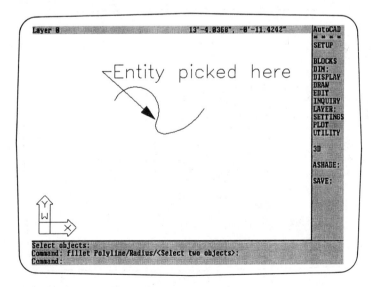

AutoCAD is asking you to create a selection set that will be used as the boundaries to which other items (that you specify) are to be extended. Figure 7.5 shows the wall lines you need to extend to. AutoCAD will highlight the entities you have chosen as boundaries. When you select the entity you want to extend, AutoCAD immediately extends it to the closest boundary. In this case, you will extend the two walls that make up the bathroom wall (see fig. 7.6). You extend these walls so that you can later create an opening for a door.

Follow this command sequence:

Prompt:	Response:	Explanation:
Command:	**EXTEND**	Starts the EXTEND command
Select boundary edge(s)..	Choose the left and right wall lines.	Selects the entities to which you will extend
Select objects:	Choose the lines to extend.	Selects the entities to extend

Fig. 7.5. The lines to extend.

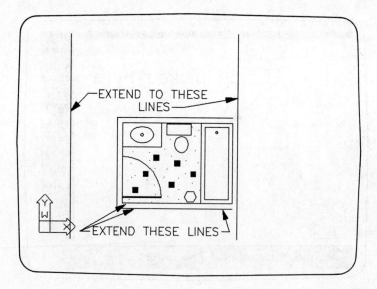

***Fig. 7.6.** The lines extended.*

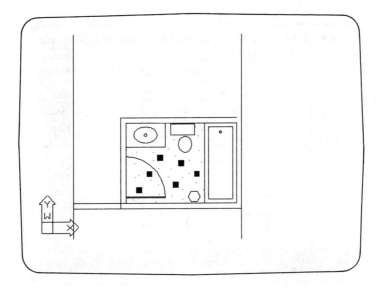

Before you begin using the next command, you need to prepare your sample drawing by making a copy of the door and the arc that represents its path of travel. Use the COPY command to pick those two elements (the door, which was created as a polyline, is a single item) and copy them from their current location in the bathroom to the bedroom (see fig. 7.7). Once in the bedroom, these two elements can be used to demonstrate the ROTATE command.

Rotating Entities (ROTATE)

You can use the ROTATE command to rotate lines, arcs, circles, polylines, and any other entity drawn on the screen. All that you need, after the selection set is chosen, is to provide AutoCAD with a base point and an angle through which to rotate the entities. The following command sequence illustrates how the ROTATE command works.

Fig. 7.7. *Copy the door from the bathroom into the bedroom.*

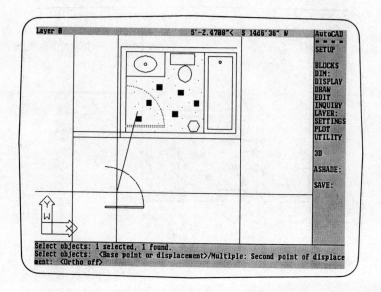

Prompt:	Response:	Explanation:
Command:	**ROTATE**	Starts the ROTATE command
Select objects:	Pick the door and arc.	Choose the objects to rotate.
Base point:	Pick near corner of door.	Choose point around which you will rotate objects.
<Rotation angle> /Reference:	**−90**	Give rotation angle.

As with most other editing commands, after you enter **ROTATE** at the Command: prompt AutoCAD displays the pickbox and asks you to create a selection set of the entities you want to rotate. Pick the two entities you just copied into the bedroom (the door and the arc). When you have finished creating the selection set, press Enter at the Select objects: prompt.

Next, AutoCAD asks you for the Base point:. This is the point around which the entities will be rotated. It works in much the same way as the COPY command's Base point/Second point prompts (discussed earlier in this chapter). In this case, however, a ghosted image is displayed on-screen (after the base point is chosen) to give you an idea of what the rotated entities will look like. Figure 7.8 shows the original entities and the ghosted image as you prepare to perform the rotation.

Fig. 7.8. Rotating the door.

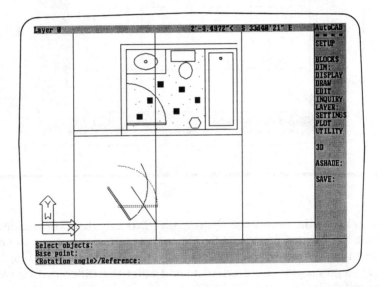

You can enter a rotation angle or work with referencing. Usually you will want to enter a rotation angle, either by entering a value from the keyboard or by using your pointing device to accept the ghosted image. Don't forget, when you provide an angle to AutoCAD, you typically will use the format *DDdMM'SS"*, where *d* stands for degrees.

You need to rotate the door and the arc 90 degrees clockwise so that you can place it in the wall opening. If you enter a positive value for the angle, AutoCAD rotates the image counterclockwise; if you enter a negative value, rotation is clockwise. Therefore, you need to rotate the door −90 degrees. After you respond to the prompt, your drawing should look like figure 7.9.

Fig. 7.9. The new door after it has been rotated.

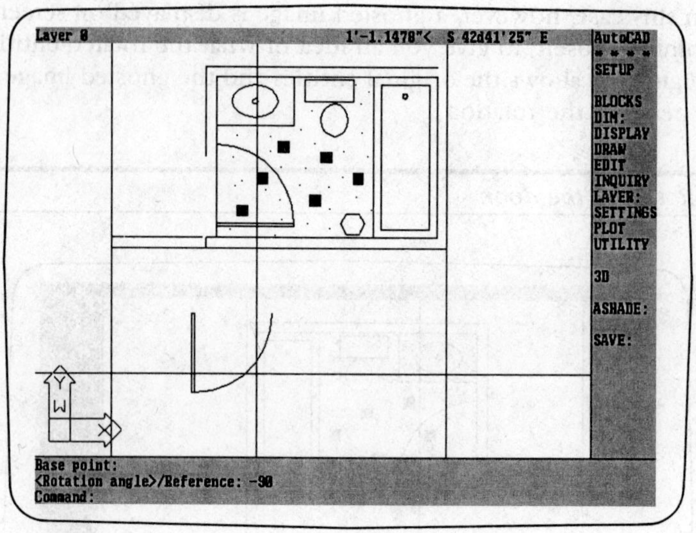

If you choose the Reference option, AutoCAD calculates the rotation angle based on a reference you provide. For instance, if you wanted to continue rotating an image from its current rotation value of 45 degrees to a new values of 27.25 degrees, you could calculate and enter the difference between the current and desired angles (−17.75 degrees), or you could let AutoCAD perform the calculation for you. You simply choose the Reference option and, at the prompt:

    Reference angle <current>:

enter 45 (the current angle of the image). When AutoCAD asks for a New angle:, enter the angle you want (27.25 degrees). When you use this option, you just tell AutoCAD what you want and the program does all the work.

If you do not know the angle of the entity, you can specify a reference angle by using your pointing device to select the endpoints of a line on-screen. Use OSNAP mode (as you did in the examples in Chapter 6) to lock onto the ends of the reference entity. After you indicate the reference, type the angle you want the entity to be.

Moving Entities (MOVE)

The MOVE command is similar to the COPY command, except that instead of making a copy of the selection set at the point specified by the `Second Point:` prompt, MOVE moves the original entities to the point you have chosen.

Now that you have correctly rotated the door, you will use the MOVE command to position the door along the wall. The first time you move the door, you will grab one of its corner intersections and move it to the intersection of two walls. The second move will shift the door four inches to the right so that it is placed correctly. The following command sequence, as well as figures 7.10 and 7.11, illustrate the actions needed to complete this part of the example.

Prompt:	Response:	Explanation:
Command:	**MOVE**	
Select objects:	**P**	Uses the door and arc selected in the previous command (ROTATE)
Base point or displacement:	**Int**	Choose INTersection of door.
Second point of displacement:	**Int**	Choose INTersection of wall.

EAST ELEVATION
SCALE 1/4"=1'-0"

Drawing courtesy of R.L. Tomlinson Drafting & Blueprinting, Inc.
Thunder Bay, Ontario, Canada

Fig. 7.10. *The door being moved into position.*

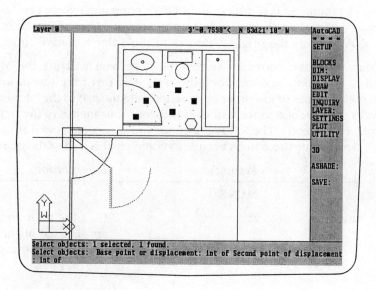

Fig. 7.11. *The door in its final position.*

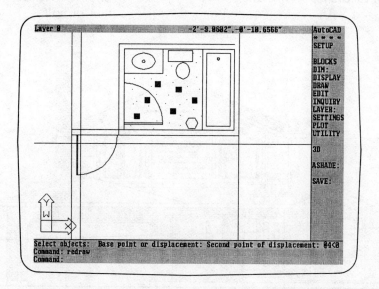

After correctly positioning the door, you need to show an opening that people can walk through. Use the LINE command to draw two lines from the points on the door (see fig. 7.12).

Fig. 7.12. *Lines illustrating the door frame.*

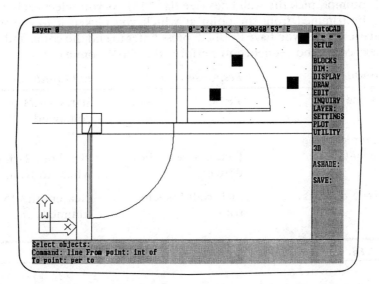

When you draw these lines to the opposite wall, use the Object Snap PER function (discussed in Chapter 6, ''The Basics of Drawing in AutoCAD'') to draw the lines exactly perpendicular to the opposite wall. Once this is finished, you will be ready to learn the next command, TRIM.

Trimming Entities (TRIM)

If you want to trim entities so that they do not extend beyond a specified boundary, use the TRIM command. (TRIM is the opposite of EXTEND.) As with the EXTEND command, the entities you select as boundaries must be visible on-screen.

The prompts for TRIM are similar to those for EXTEND. When you enter **TRIM** at the Command: prompt, AutoCAD responds with

```
Select cutting edge(s)...
Select objects:
```

You are asked to create a selection set composed of the entities you want to use as cutting edges. The selection set will consist of the two lines you drew at the end of the last example. After you have selected the lines, press Enter. The boundaries will remain highlighted and you will see the following prompt:

    Select object to trim:

At this prompt, pick the wall lines (see fig. 7.13). As you select each wall line, it will be trimmed from the point at which you picked it to the specified boundaries. When you have finished, press Enter to end the command. Follow the next command sequence to perform the TRIM command.

Prompt:	Response:	Explanation:
Command:	**TRIM**	Starts TRIM command
Select cutting edge(s)...	Pick last two lines drawn.	Pick boundaries to which to trim.
Select objects:	Pick wall lines to trim.	Pick entities to be trimmed.

Fig. 7.13. *Creating the door frame.*

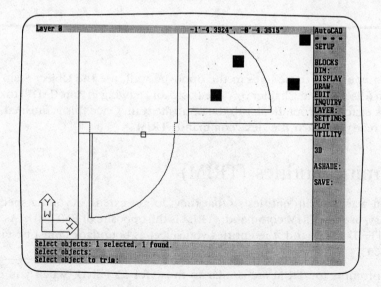

Stretching Parts of Your Drawing (STRETCH)

The STRETCH command moves portions of your drawing without disturbing connections between entities. Entities can be stretched to elongate or shorten their lengths, or their alignment can be changed.

You may recall that when you created the tub in your drawing (in Chapter 6, "The Basics of Drawing in AutoCAD,") you were told to wait until this chapter to make the tub look real. Well, the time has come. You will use the STRETCH command to alter the angle of the tub's inner lines; then you will use FILLET to remove the sharp corners that would have made bathing in this tub a rotten experience!

Prompt:	Response:	Explanation:
Command:	**STRETCH**	Starts STRETCH command
Select objects to stretch by window...	**C**	Choose crossing window to select entities.
Select objects:	Select lines in upper right corner of tub.	
Base point or displacement:	Pick point near corner.	
Second point of displacement:	**@1<180**	Stretch lines 1″ to the left.

This command sequence outlines AutoCAD's prompts when you use the STRETCH command. When you enter **STRETCH** at the Command: prompt, the following prompt appears:

```
Select objects to stretch by window...
Select objects:
```

In the STRETCH command, you may specify two different sets of entities: those that are moved, but remain intact, and those that are stretched. The way you select an entity determines which group that entity belongs in. If you use a window to select a group of entities, those entities are moved (similarly to the MOVE command) but not stretched. Entities chosen by the Crossing option will be stretched.

You can stretch only one selection set at a time. If you choose a second window or crossing, AutoCAD will ignore the first selection set. In other words, only the most recent selection set will be used by the STRETCH command.

Using the Crossing option, *grab* the corner of the tub as shown in figure 7.14. After you have selected the objects that make up the tub corner, press Enter. Then, when AutoCAD asks you for a Base point:, specify a point to be used as a reference point for the stretch. If you pick a point fairly close to your original entities, you will not be limited to stretching in any direction as you stretch those entities around the screen. When you do this, AutoCAD will show your entities "ghosted in," so that you can see the way they will look when you finally specify a New point:. For this example, the new point will be 1″ to the left (the 180-degree direction).

Fig. 7.14. *Using STRETCH on the tub corner.*

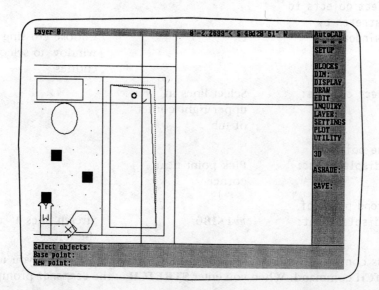

Figures 7.14, which shows the corner of the bathtub being stretched around the screen, and 7.15, which shows the tub with one of its corners stretched inward by an inch, are examples of how you should be using the STRETCH command. Now use the STRETCH command to make the other tub corners correspond to the first.

Fig. 7.15. *The tub after stretching.*

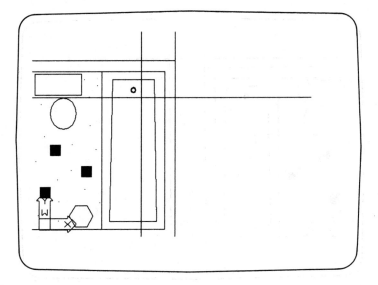

Now the lines look a little more like a bathtub, but you still have the problem of those sharp corners. Here is an instance where the FILLET command really pays off. Set the fillet radius to 3″ and try filleting two of the lines. Suddenly the sharp corners are smoothed out! You can use the FILLET command to take the sharpness out of the other corners, or you can try playing with the FILLET command by specifying radii of different sizes and really smoothing out the bathtub! Whatever you do, the drawing in figure 7.16 shows what the tub looks like with all its corners filleted with 3″ radii.

Up to this point, you have had fairly detailed, step-by-step guidance in the use of AutoCAD's editing commands. Now you can strike out on your own, putting your new knowledge to work. The next step is to add countertops in the kitchen. The countertops are located 20″ from the wall lines. To complete this exercise, you may want to refresh your memory of the OFFSET and EXTEND commands.

Fig. 7.16. *The tub after using FILLET to smooth the corners.*

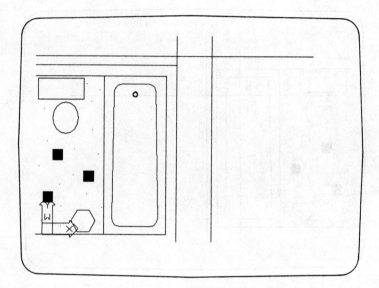

Erasing Parts of Entities (BREAK)

The BREAK command lets you remove sections of an entity or break an entity into two pieces without removing either of the resulting parts. You can use BREAK on lines, arcs, circles, and polylines. If you work with an Autodesk tablet menu, two BREAK command selections are available on the menu:

❏ BREAK, which removes pieces of entities
❏ BREAK @, which divides an entity into two pieces

You will use the BREAK command to finish the basics of the kitchen counters you created earlier. Entering **BREAK** at the Command: prompt will produce the following prompts:

Prompt:	Response:	Explanation:
Command:	**BREAK**	Starts BREAK command
Select object:	Select line.	Select counter line you want broken.

Prompt:	Response:	Explanation:
Enter second point (or F for First):	**F**	You are going to pick two break points.
First point:	Choose INT of first indicated point.	
Second point:	Choose INT of second indicated point.	

AutoCAD begins by asking you to select the entity you want to break, which in this case will be the counter line shown in figure 7.17. After you select that line, AutoCAD asks you to:

Enter second point (or F for First):

Here you have two options. First, you can specify a second point. If you enter this second point, the BREAK command is completed and AutoCAD returns to the Command: prompt. In other words, AutoCAD accepts the first point (the one used to indicate the entity) and the second point as the two points that define which part of the entity should be broken out.

Fig. 7.17. Location for breaking the counter line.

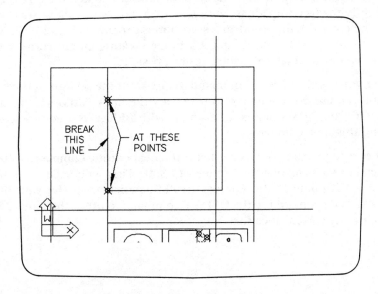

Your other option is to enter **F**, signifying that you want to explicitly define the first point at which the break should be made. This is the option you will use to create the kitchen counters. Use the points shown in figure 7.17 to indicate the first and second points you will use to make the break.

The tablet menu's BREAK @ selection is useful for creating hatching boundaries. When you use this menu selection, you are prompted for only one point, the point at which the entity will be divided.

To use BREAK @ from the keyboard, indicate a first point and type @ for the second point. As explained in Chapter 1, "A Quick Start in AutoCAD," the @ symbol is used for relative input. By using @, you are telling AutoCAD that you want to do something *in relation to the last point chosen*. Here, the last point chosen is the point at which you want to break the entity. The **BREAK F** selection on the screen menu is the standard BREAK command.

If you are breaking a line, arc, or polyline, the portion of the entity between the two specified break points is removed. If one point is past the end of the entity, the entity is deleted from the first break point to the endpoint nearest the second break point.

When you break a circle, remember two things:

1. AutoCAD calculates breaks on a circle as it calculates many other circular operations: counterclockwise. The portion removed from the circle will extend counterclockwise from the first break point to the second break point.

2. BREAK @ cannot be used on circle entities. When a circle is broken, it is changed into an arc entity. AutoCAD does not allow arc entities to be created with 360 degrees or more of rotation. Using BREAK @ on a circle would cause AutoCAD to try creating an arc entity with 360 degrees of rotation, which is not possible.

After you use the BREAK command to break out the section of the countertop, you can use this command to trim back the lines. Although this is easier to do with the TRIM command, doing it with BREAK is a good exercise for learning this new command.

In order to prepare your example for the next editing command (MIRROR), you need to start creating the outline of a sink. First, you need to draw a line from the MIDpoint of the counter to PERpendicular to the wall line (see fig. 7.18). Then you can use the OFFSET command to offset that line 12″ above and below its current location.

***Fig. 7.18.** The sink area.*

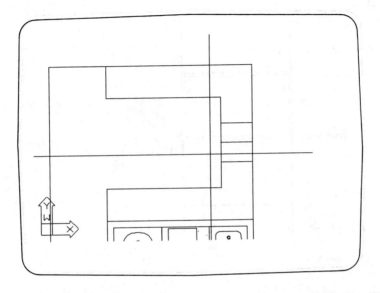

In the upper rectangle of the sink you just created, you will place the sink basin lines. These lines are offset 1/2″ from the four surrounding sides. After these lines have been offset, you will need to trim back the left and right inner-sink lines to the upper and lower inner-sink lines. Then use **FILLET** with a radius of 0 to square off all the inner-sink lines. Your drawing should now look like figure 7.19.

Creating Mirror Images (MIRROR)

AutoCAD's powerful MIRROR command produces a mirror image of your entities along what is called a *mirror line*. A mirror line is just what it sounds like—a line that shows where the "mirror" is held in order to project the reflection that will become a new image. AutoCAD does not restrict you to a specific mirror line. You can specify this line at any angle, not simply horizontal or vertical to the entity being mirrored.

While you are drawing, you frequently will become aware of interrelationships between entities—the way many things you draw are simply mirror images of each other. If you need to create symmetrical entities, MIRROR is the best command to use.

Fig. 7.19. *Using OFFSET to create sink lines.*

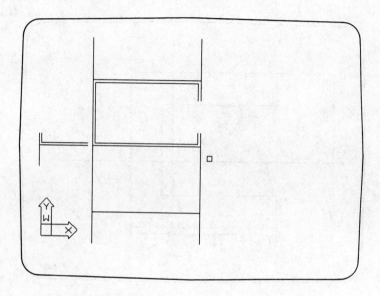

When you enter **MIRROR**, you are prompted for a selection set of the entities you want to mirror. You will be mirroring the lines and arcs that make up the sink you just created. After you have specified these entities and pressed Enter at the Select objects: prompt, you will see this prompt:

    First point of mirror line:

Now you begin to specify the mirror line. The mirror line, a line of symmetry, is not restricted in either location or angle. You can have a mirror line at any position you want. Figure 7.20 shows the locations for the start and end of the mirror line used in the next example.

Fig. 7.20. Setting up to mirror the sink.

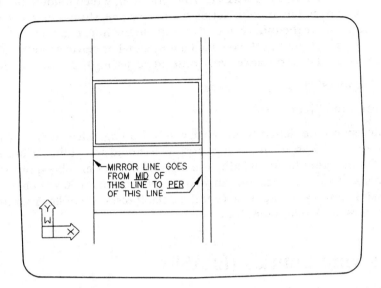

To mirror the sink's lines and arcs, use the following command sequence:

Prompt:	Response:	Explanation:
Command:	**MIRROR**	Starts MIRROR command
Select objects:	**W**	Use a window box so that only the entities *inside* the boundaries are chosen.
First point of mirror line:	(See fig. 7.20)	
Second point:	(See fig. 7.20)	
Delete old objects?<N>	Press Enter.	Do not delete the original entities.

After you enter the first endpoint for the mirror line, you will notice a ghosted reflection of the entities you selected. This reflection, which follows the changes in the rubber-band line used to define the mirror line, should help you set the other endpoint for the mirror line. To complete the line, enter an endpoint at the Second point: prompt. If you want a horizontal or vertical mirror line, you can specify a relative distance with your angle set to 0, 90, or 180 degrees.

Finally, AutoCAD asks:

Delete old objects? <N>:

Your decision here depends on what you are doing. Clearly, if you want a symmetrical duplicate of an existing entity, you should accept the default answer of No. On the other hand, deleting the original entities may be appropriate in certain instances or applications. In your sample drawing, you want both copies of the sink; just press Enter to accept the default response of No. Your drawing should now look like figure 7.21.

Removing Entities (ERASE)

As you learned in Chapter 1, "A Quick Start in AutoCAD," ERASE is an editing command that eliminates unwanted entities. All AutoCAD needs to know is which objects you want to erase.

To initiate the ERASE command, enter **ERASE**. The prompt Select objects: will appear. Notice that the crosshairs turn into a pickbox. As mentioned earlier in this chapter, AutoCAD is waiting for you to create a selection set. This set becomes the object of the ERASE command—each entity in the selection set will be removed from the drawing. By following the next command sequence, you will erase the first line you drew when you began creating the sink (the line between the two basins).

Fig. 7.21. The sink, completely drawn.

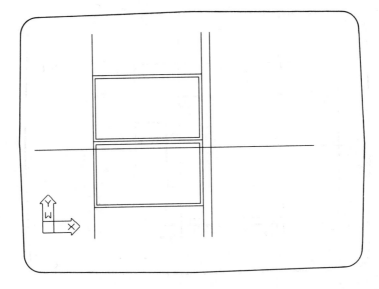

Prompt:	Response:	Explanation:
Command:	**ERASE**	Starts the ERASE command
Select objects:	Select first-drawn sink line.	Select the entities to be erased.
Select objects:	Press Enter.	Erases selected entities

In order to use the next editing command, SCALE, you need to do a little preparation. The next object you create for the kitchen will be a range top with a couple of burners. To draw in the range top, you first need to draw a line from the MIDpoint of the upper counter line to PERpendicular to the upper wall line. This step is similar to that used for the sink. Then offset that line 15″ left and right to create the extents of the cooking area. Finally, erase the middle line. Your drawing should be similar to that shown in figure 7.22.

Fig. 7.22. *Drawing in the range top.*

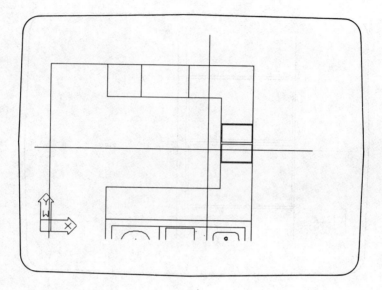

Next, you will place the two burners (each with a 4″ radius) with their centers located at 3′5″,12′2″ and 3′5″,12′11″. Your drawing should now look like figure 7.23. Now you are ready for the next editing command.

Scaling Parts of a Drawing (SCALE)

To adjust the size of entities proportionally, you use the SCALE command. The command prompts for SCALE are similar to those for ROTATE. In order to scale an object, you need a *base point*, which is used as the reference for creating the new entity's location. After that base point is positioned you can either reference part of the object or indicate the scale factor.

When you enter **SCALE** at the Command: prompt, AutoCAD asks you to create a selection set of entities to be scaled. The command sequence for SCALE is similar to the following example:

Fig. 7.23. *A range top with burners.*

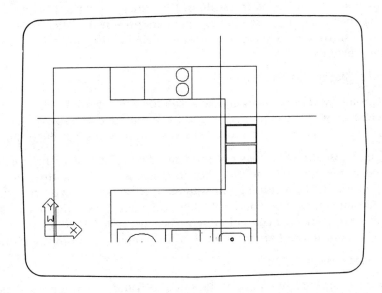

Prompt:	Response:	Explanation:
Command:	**SCALE**	Executes SCALE command
Select objects:	Choose upper burner and press Enter.	
Base point:	**CEN**	Base point is center of burner.
<Scale factor>/ Reference:	**R**	By using Reference, you let AutoCAD compute the scale factor.
Reference length <current>:	**8**	Current diameter
New length:	**6**	New diameter

Next, AutoCAD asks you for the `Base point:`, the reference point by which the entity is scaled. A base point somewhere on or within the entity is held static (it does not move) as the scale of the entity is changed. After the base point has been set, a ghosted image appears on-screen. This image can be dragged to show approximate sizes for the scaled entity. You will also see the following prompt:

`<Scale factor>/Reference:`

At this prompt you can either enter an absolute scaling factor or choose to work with referencing. If you enter a scaling factor, it multiplies the size of the original entity: 1 represents the original size, whereas .5 represents half the original size.

If you choose the `Reference` option, AutoCAD will calculate the scale factor, based on a reference you provide. For instance, if you knew that the side of a polygon was 1.37 units long, but wanted to scale the entity so that the side was 3.785 units long, you could calculate and enter the scaling factor (2.763). Scale-factor referencing makes more sense because AutoCAD does all the work. When you choose the `Reference` option, the following prompt is displayed:

`Reference length <1>:`

Simply enter the current length of the side (1.37) and, when AutoCAD asks for a `New length:`, enter the final length (3.785). You do not have to do any calculating.

If you do not know the current length, you can reference the length of the entity by using an OSNAP mode to indicate the endpoints and then, at the next prompt, entering the new length.

Partitioning Entities

When you need to divide an entity into several sections of equal length, AutoCAD provides two commands (DIVIDE and MEASURE) that make the job both quick and easy. The DIVIDE and MEASURE commands both work on any basic drawing entity, including lines, arcs, circles, and polylines.

To see the effects of these commands, it will be helpful if you change the way AutoCAD displays points. As you may recall from the discussion of points in Chapter 6, "The Basics of Drawing in AutoCAD," AutoCAD has several ways to display points. We suggest that you change the point display in the following manner:

Prompt:	*Response:*	*Explanation:*
Command:	**SETVAR**	Initiates the command to set a variable
Variable name or ? <current>:	**PDMODE**	Specifies that you want to change the point display-mode variable (PDMODE)
New value for PDMODE <current>:	35	Sets a new value of 35

If you follow this sequence of commands, each point will be displayed as a circle with a "plus sign" through it. Setting the PDMODE in this manner will help you visualize and understand how the MEASURE and DIVIDE commands work.

Measuring Distances along Entities (MEASURE)

The MEASURE command is used to place objects (either points or entities known as *blocks*) at a certain measured distance along a selected entity. You must define the interval length that AutoCAD uses to measure the entity.

Before you use the MEASURE command, you need prepare for creating the grill in the next example. Draw a line from 1'7",13'3" to 2'5",13"3" and then offset this line 18" down (see fig. 7.24).

When you enter **MEASURE** at the Command: prompt, AutoCAD asks you to Select object to measure:. You can select only one entity, but that entity can be of any type. After you select the entity you want to measure, follow the rest of this command sequence:

Prompt:	*Response:*	*Explanation:*
Command:	**MEASURE**	Starts the MEASURE command
Select object to measure:	Choose top line of grill.	
<Segment length>/Block:	1	This is the distance between measured points.

Fig. 7.24. Laying in lines for the range-top grill.

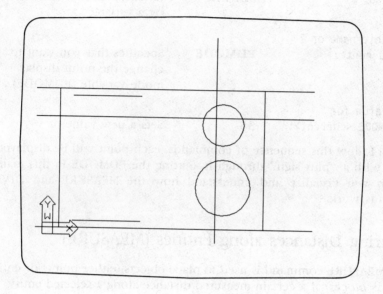

After you select the entity you want to measure, you have two choices. You can specify a distance to use as the segment length, or you can choose the Block option, which means that you will indicate the measured distances with a block entity instead of a point entity. Blocks are discussed in detail in Chapter 13, "Creating a Symbol Library."

You can enter a segment length either by typing a value or by using your pointing device to select two points on-screen. The distance between the two points is the segment length. Figure 7.25 shows what happens when you measure the top line of the burner with one-inch segments.

You should use the UNDO command to reverse what you have just done. Then you will use DIVIDE to perform a similar function.

Dividing Entities into Equal Parts (DIVIDE)

The DIVIDE command, which divides an entity into equal parts, is similar to the MEASURE command, which places them at specified lengths. You can use either points or blocks to indicate the parts. Instead of prompting you for a length, AutoCAD asks how many parts you want.

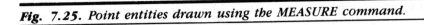

***Fig. 7.25.** Point entities drawn using the MEASURE command.*

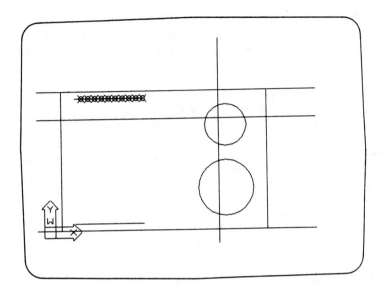

At the Command: prompt, enter **DIVIDE**. When AutoCAD asks you to Select object to divide:, you can select only one entity but it can be any type of entity. After you select the entity, follow the rest of the prompts:

Prompt:	Response:	Explanation:
Command:	**DIVIDE**	Starts DIVIDE command
Select object to divide:	Choose top line of grill.	
\<Number of segments\> /Block:	**8**	This is the number of pieces into which you are dividing the entity.

You have two options: you can specify the number of segments or choose Block, notifying AutoCAD that you want to use blocks to divide the entity.

If you choose the Block option, AutoCAD prompts you for the name of the block to use. (Blocks are discussed in Chapter 13, "Creating a Symbol Library.") When you enter the block name, AutoCAD will display the following prompt:

Number of segments:

As mentioned earlier, you should enter the number of segments into which you want to divide the entity. Figure 7.26 shows how the DIVIDE command is used in this example.

Fig. 7.26. Point entities drawn using the DIVIDE command.

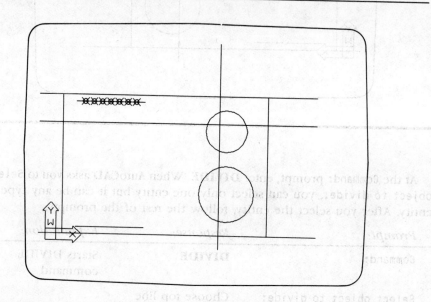

Use the LINE command to draw the grill lines (see fig. 7.27). The lines extend from the NODe of the point created in the MEASURE command to PERpendicular to the lower grill line. After drawing these lines, you can use the ERASE W command to remove the points created by the DIVIDE command. Erasing these points will help clean up the drawing.

Fig. *7.27. The range-top grill.*

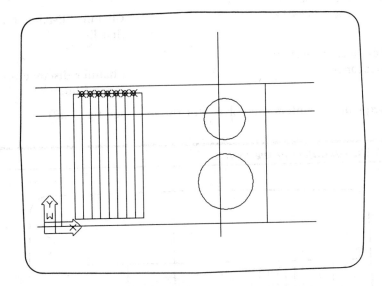

Chamfering Lines (CHAMFER)

AutoCAD's CHAMFER command trims or extends two lines a specified distance from the point at which they would intersect, and then connects the lines with a line segment. Because the two lines must at some time intersect, AutoCAD cannot chamfer parallel lines. The CHAMFER command works with distances from an intersection, rather than with angles. Because of the way the CHAMFER command works, only lines and polylines may be chamfered.

The following command sequence is an example of how to set the distances from the intersection for the new line:

Prompt:	Response:	Explanation:
Command:	**CHAMFER**	Starts the CHAMFER command
Polyline/Distance/ <Select first line>:	**D**	Set chamfer distances first.

Prompt:	Response:	Explanation:
Enter first chamfer distance <5E-01>:	.5	Chamfer distance for first line
Enter second chamfer distance	.5	Chamfer distance for second line

This sequence chamfers the corners of the grill (see fig. 7.28).

Fig. 7.28. *Chamfering the grill.*

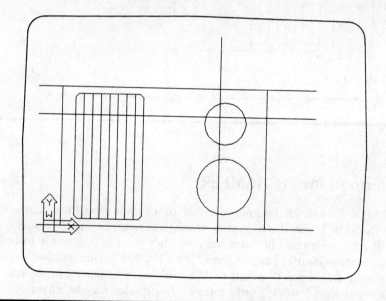

When you enter **CHAMFER** at the Command: prompt, AutoCAD displays the following prompt:

Polyline/Distance/<Select first line>:

Select Polyline if you want to chamfer an entire polyline. With CHAMFER, as with the FILLET command, a vertex that is not large enough to be chamfered remains unchanged.

To set the distances for the chamfer, select `Distance`. AutoCAD then prompts you for two chamfer distances. The first distance you enter is applied to the first entity you indicate for the chamfer operation. The distance you enter is stored in the CHAMFERA system variable. The second distance is applied to the second entity selected for chamfering and is stored in the CHAMFERB system variable. When you chamfer a polyline, the first distance is applied to the first segment of the vertex.

The default for both distances is 0; if you use this value, chamfering two lines will result in a sharp corner. This is the same as setting the FILLET command's radius to 0.

`Select first line` is the default option. If you want to chamfer two lines, use your pointing device to select one and then, when AutoCAD prompts you for a second line, select it. The chamfer is completed when you choose the second line—you do not need to press Enter.

Arrays of Entities (ARRAY)

Unlike most of the previously discussed editing commands (which modify an existing entity), the ARRAY command allows you to make multiple, uniformly placed copies. Using an *array* is definitely the easiest way to produce multiple copies of entities. You can create circular arrays, called *polar arrays*, or the more-often used rectangular arrays.

Arrays are used for any repetition of entities in a circular or rectangular pattern. The repetition must be at a consistent distance (otherwise, the ARRAY command won't produce the results you need). The prompts displayed by the ARRAY command depend on whether you are working with rectangular or polar arrays.

Rectangular Arrays

Rectangular arrays are based on columns and rows: *columns* are the vertical series of entities in an array; *rows*, the horizontal series. This is similar to the way a spreadsheet is described—by columns and rows. Also similar to a spreadsheet is the concept of a *cell*. In an array, the distance between rows is referred to as the *row distance*; that between columns, as the *column distance*. These two distances, together with the entity used in the array, make up a *unit cell*.

You will use the ARRAY command to create a floor pattern in the kitchen. This pattern is similar to the pattern used in the bathroom, except that the tile layout in the kitchen will be uniform rather than random.

To create the entities to be arrayed, use the SOLID command to create two
4×4 tiles as you did in Chapter 6, "The Basics of Drawing in AutoCAD." The
lower left corners of these tiles will be at the points $3'0'',5'4''$ and $2'8'',5'8''$.
Figure 7.29 shows the tiles placed properly.

Fig. 7.29. *The starting tiles for the kitchen floor.*

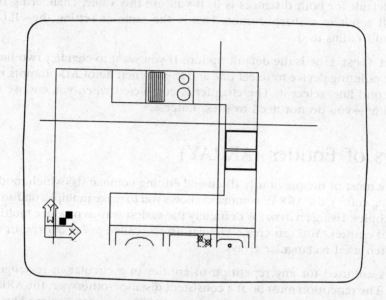

To create your pattern, you want to make a rectangular array of the two tiles.
The following command sequence shows the procedure for creating a rectangular array.

Prompt:	Response:	Explanation:
Command:	**ARRAY**	Starts the ARRAY command
Select objects:	Choose the two tiles you created.	Choose the entities to be arrayed.
Rectangular/Polar array (R/P):	**R**	Create a rectangular array.

Prompt:	Response:	Explanation:
Number of rows (---) <1>:	**11**	Indicate number of rows.
Number of columns (|||) <1>:	**3**	Indicate number of columns.
Unit cell or distance between rows (---):	**8″**	Specify distance between rows.
Distance between columns (|||):	**8″**	Specify distance between columns.

As you can see, you specify a rectangular array by typing **R**. AutoCAD will ask you first for the Number of rows (---): and then for the Number of columns (\|\|\|):. (The graphics represent lines in either the horizontal [---] or vertical [\|\|\|] direction.) Enter the appropriate number at each prompt, pressing Enter after each entry. AutoCAD then asks for the distance between rows and columns in the array and promptly begins creating the array. If you enter a positive number, AutoCAD will calculate the rows and columns upwards and to the right from the entities being arrayed. If you enter a negative number, row and column calculation will proceed down and to the left from the selected entities. Your kitchen floor should now look like figure 7.30.

Polar Arrays

Polar arrays are multiple copies (arranged in a circular pattern) of a group of entities. In order to satisfactorily create a polar array, you need to know any two of the following three pieces of information: how many items you want to create, the center point and angle specifying the arc along which the entities should be replicated, or the angle between individual items.

You will use AutoCAD's polar array feature to copy chairs around a circular table. But first you need to create the table and one chair. The table is simply a circle with an 18″ radius; its center point is located at 1′3,9′4. Create the chair by using lines and an ellipse (see fig. 7.31).

Fig. 7.30. The finished floor pattern.

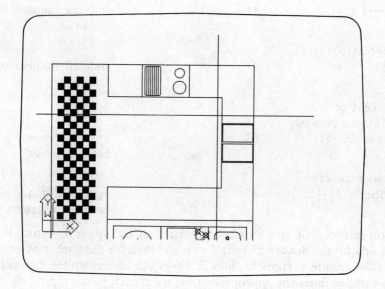

Fig. 7.31. A kitchen table and chair.

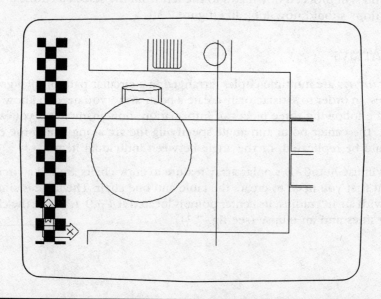

After you have added the table and chair to your drawing, follow this procedure for the polar array:

Prompt:	Response:	Explanation:
Command:	**ARRAY**	
Select objects:	**W**	A window makes selecting entities easier.
Rectangular/Polar array (R/P):	**P**	Polar array
Center point of array:	**CEN**	Center of array is at center of table.
Number of items:	4	Make 4 copies of chair.
Angle to fill (+=CCW, -=CW) <360>:	Press Enter.	All copies will be spaced equally within 360 degrees.
Rotate objects as they are copied?<Y>:	**Y**	All entities will be rotated as they are copied.

You start out just as you do with a rectangular array. Enter **ARRAY** at the Command: prompt, create a selection set of the entities to be used within the array and, when you have finished selecting the entities, press Enter at the Select objects: prompt. When AutoCAD asks whether you want to create a rectangular or polar array, type **P**. AutoCAD then prompts you for the Center

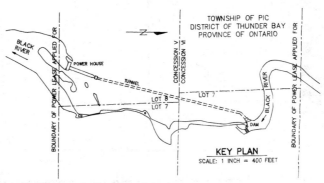

Drawing courtesy of R.L. Tomlinson Drafting & Blueprinting, Inc.
Thunder Bay, Ontario, Canada

point of array:. Remember that the specified entities will be replicated along an arc that uses this center point. AutoCAD will ask you to supply the number of items you want to create. You must provide a whole number that represents the number of repetitions you want created. Then you will be asked either for the Angle to fill or for the Angle between items.

The Angle to fill (+=CCW, -=CW) <360>: prompt asks for the angle defining the length of the arc created around the specified center point. A negative number causes a clockwise rotation, whereas a positive number causes counterclockwise rotation. The Angle between items: prompt asks for the displacement angle between items in the array.

After you have entered this array-definition information, AutoCAD asks one final question:

Rotate objects as they are copied? <Y>:

If you answer **Y**, the replicated entities will be rotated individually as they are placed around the arc of the array.

The chairs in figure 7.32 were rotated as they were copied; those in figure 7.33 were not.

Fig. 7.32. *The chairs, properly rotated as they were arrayed.*

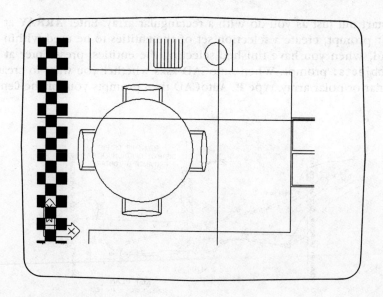

Fig. *7.33. The effects of not rotating entities as they are arrayed.*

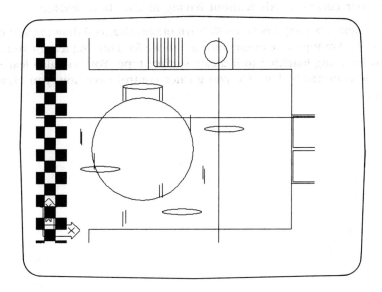

Summary

This chapter has shown you most of AutoCAD's editing commands. (Three editing commands not covered in this chapter—CHANGE, PEDIT, and LAYER—are discussed in Chapter 8, "Advanced Editing Commands.") The commands covered in this chapter include:

❏ COPY	❏ MOVE	❏ SCALE
❏ OFFSET	❏ TRIM	❏ DIVIDE
❏ ZOOM	❏ STRETCH	❏ MEASURE
❏ FILLET	❏ BREAK	❏ CHAMFER
❏ EXTEND	❏ MIRROR	❏ ARRAY
❏ ROTATE	❏ ERASE	

You have used these commands to enhance your basic floor plan.

As you work with the editing commands, you will discover that AutoCAD is truly versatile. Unlike manual drawing systems, in which you must "begin anew" whenever you have to make changes to a basic drawing, AutoCAD allows you to modify previously created entities. You can create a basic set of drawings and, with the capabilities of the editing commands, modify the entities to suit your current needs without having to start from scratch.

In the next few chapters you will learn other advanced drawing and editing commands. Among these commands are those for entering text in your drawing and for using hatching to indicate surface type. You will also learn more about the commands that give you greater control over how you view your drawing.

8

Advanced
Editing Commands

Chapter 7, "Editing Your Drawing," discussed AutoCAD's editing commands. You used the commands to manipulate existing entities and to make entirely new entities without having to draw them. The editing commands expand your ability to work within AutoCAD's Drawing Editor.

Chapter 7 described all but two of the editing commands. Those two editing commands (CHANGE and PEDIT) are fully discussed in this chapter. Both commands have so many options that a chapter of explanations and examples is needed to cover them completely.

This chapter also covers AutoCAD's most important *control* command—the LAYER command. The LAYER command is an important addition to your AutoCAD toolkit. With it you can begin to control the way your drawing is displayed.

When you finish this chapter you will have a working knowledge of the following commands:

❏ PEDIT   ❏ CHANGE   ❏ LAYER

Your Sample Drawing

By the end of Chapter 7, you had modified the sample floor plan considerably. (You probably were ready to start cooking breakfast in your new kitchen!) In this chapter, you continue to build the sample drawing as the concepts of the PEDIT, CHANGE, and LAYER commands are illustrated.

Editing Polylines (PEDIT)

Because of the special nature of polylines, AutoCAD provides a command (PEDIT) designed specifically for editing them. You can use PEDIT to do the following:

❑ Create a new polyline from a line or arc entity
❑ Open or close polylines
❑ Join entities to form a polyline
❑ Add new segments to an existing polyline
❑ Select a uniform width
❑ Separate a polyline into segments
❑ Insert new vertices
❑ Move and eliminate vertices
❑ Fit a curve or a spline
❑ Take the curves out of a polyline
❑ Change the width of segments

PEDIT is a versatile command that makes editing polylines easy. To begin learning this command, you will change one of the wall lines into a polyline. Figure 8.1 shows which wall line to change; the following command sequence shows the steps you need to take:

Prompt:	Response:	Explanation:
Command:	**PEDIT**	Starts the PEDIT command
Select polyline	Choose a bedroom wall line.	

At the final prompt:

Entity selected is not a polyline.
Do you want to turn it into one? <Y>:

press Enter to turn the line into a polyline.

If the entity you choose is not a polyline, AutoCAD will proceed as though you want to change it into one. If you type **Y** or press Enter (to tell AutoCAD that you accept the default), the entity is changed into a polyline and the PEDIT command continues. This is a handy way to change entities into polylines.

In some cases, polylines have certain advantages over normal line and arc entities. One of these advantages is the ability to string together several different arc and line entities to form one polyline entity. Copying, offsetting, and moving one entity (created from several entities) is easier than having to choose and manipulate 57!

Fig. 8.1. *The line you want to turn into a polyline.*

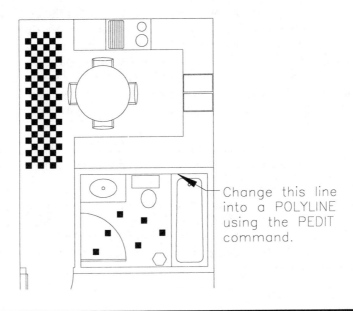

Change this line
into a POLYLINE
using the PEDIT
command.

Another area in which polylines have an advantage is that of showing entity widths. No width information is associated with entities that are not polylines. A polyline, on the other hand, can have a uniform width over its entire length or differing widths in different segments. The next section deals with these advantages and how you can put them to good use.

The PEDIT Subcommands

When you select the polyline you want to edit, AutoCAD displays the following prompt:

```
Close/Join/Width/Edit vertex/Fit curve/Spline/Decurve/Undo/eXit<X>:
```

Each of these options is an editing command, but these commands work only with polylines. The following descriptions and examples illustrate what these commands do.

Close and *Open*

If you select a polyline and the word `Close` appears in the command line, the polyline is *open*. An open polyline is one in which the ends do not touch—there is a visible beginning and end to the polyline. Conversely, a *closed* polyline is one in which there are no easily identifiable endpoints—the ends touch. An example of a closed polyline is the POLYGON entity you used to create the waste basket (refer to Chapter 6, ''The Basics of Drawing in AutoCAD''). To create a closed polyline, use the `Close` option when you are drawing and using the PLINE command.

If you pick a polyline that is already closed, the word `Open` will appear in the PEDIT prompt. Use `Open` to remove the last polyline segment created (the one that closed the polyline).

In many cases, the closing segment of a polyline is a temporary entity that may disappear if the polyline is edited using the `Edit vertex` command (explained later in the chapter). When a section of the polyline is removed, or simply broken, the link connecting the endpoint and beginning point of the polyline disappears.

Join

The `Join` option allows you to extend a polyline by stringing together polylines, lines, and arc segments. The entities you want to connect to the polyline must touch end-to-end, otherwise the polyline will not extend through the new entities.

When you select `Join`, if the polyline is not closed AutoCAD will prompt you to `Select objects:` that you want to join to the polyline. As they are added to the polyline, the entities will take on different attributes of the original polyline such as its current layer (discussed later in this chapter), color, and thickness. The resulting polyline is the same as any polyline created with the PLINE command. Figure 8.2 shows the lines you should join with the polyline.

Width

The `Width` option allows you to set a uniform width for all segments of the polyline. The width can be specified in either of two ways: by giving AutoCAD a numeric value (such as 3'-6") for the width or by specifying a point near the polyline through which you want the thickness to pass.

When you want to change the width, AutoCAD will prompt you to `Enter new width for all segments:`. Figure 8.3 shows the effect of giving your polyline a 4" width.

Fig. 8.2. Using Join *to add entities to a polyline.*

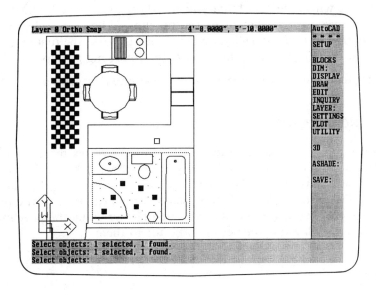

Fig. 8.3. The polyline with a 4" width.

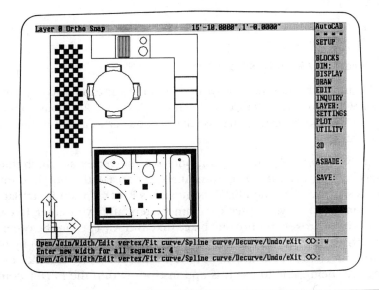

Editing Polyline Vertices

No matter what type of polyline you are editing, you can edit the individual vertices between each segment of the polyline. When you select the Edit vertex option from the PEDIT prompt, AutoCAD marks the first vertex of the polyline with a graphical X and displays the following prompt:

Next/Previous/Break/Insert/Move/Regen/Straighten/Tangent/Width/eXit<N>:

Next and *Previous*

You can move the vertex indicator (the *X*) from vertex to vertex by using the Next or Previous commands. As you use these commands, the vertex indicator will travel forwards or backwards one vertex at a time along the polyline. The vertex indicator always starts at the beginning of the polyline. If the segments you need to edit are located farther along the polyline, Next and Previous will move the vertex indicator to them.

Break

The Break command is very much like the "normal" BREAK command that you use from the Command: prompt. With Break, you can either break the polyline into two pieces (which is like the BREAK @ command), or you can break out a section of the polyline between two vertices of your choice (similar to BREAK F).

When you choose the Break option, you will see a new prompt that lists several suboptions:

Next/Previous/Go/eXit <N>:

The beginning break point always occurs at the vertex marked by the vertex indicator when you type **Break**. You can use Next and Previous to move the *X* indicator to another vertex; then use that second vertex as the ending location of your break.

When the vertex indicator is positioned on the vertex at which you want the break to end, use the Go option. AutoCAD breaks the polyline into two pieces. As stated earlier, the PEDIT command's Break option is similar to the BREAK command. If you enter **Go** immediately after you enter **Break**, the polyline will be broken in only one place (like BREAK @). On the other hand, you can break out a section of the polyline (much like BREAK F) by moving the vertex indicator backward or forward after you enter **Break**, and then entering **Go**. Being able to use this option from within the PEDIT command gives you flexibility. You can edit a polyline with one command rather than with several different commands.

Insert

The `Insert` option creates a new vertex between the current vertex (where the vertex indicator is located) and the next vertex in the polyline. The `Insert` option places two new polyline line segments to connect the new point to the current and the next vertex. At the `Enter location of new vertex:` prompt, pick the new point. Figure 8.4 shows the result of using the `Insert` option.

Fig. 8.4. Inserting a new vertex into the polyline.

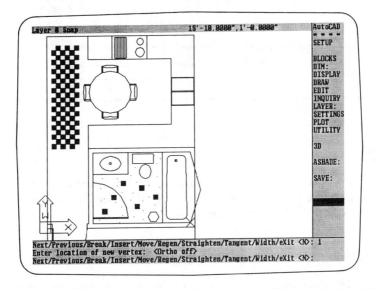

Move

To move the current vertex to a new location, type **M** (for *Move*). AutoCAD will prompt you to `Enter new location:`. After you pick the point where you want the current vertex to be located, the vertex will be moved to that location and the polyline adjusted accordingly. Figure 8.5 shows what will happen if you move the vertex you just created.

Fig. 8.5. *Using the* Move *option to move the new vertex.*

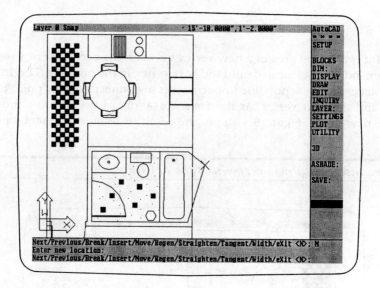

Regen

The Regen option will redraw the entire polyline. This command is useful when the polyline has not been redrawn entirely after an edit operation such as Spline, Width, Fit curve, or Decurve.

Straighten

Straighten allows you to remove all of the vertices between two points and replace them with a single polyline segment. This is handy when you need to remove extraneous vertices. After you have chosen Straighten, the following prompt appears:

Next/Previous/Go/eXit <N>:

As with the Break command, you can use Next and Previous to move through the vertices. When you have positioned the vertex marker on the last vertex for the Straighten option, select Go. AutoCAD will remove the vertices between the two you have indicated and replace them with a straight polyline segment. Figure 8.6 shows how Straighten is used to remove the previously entered vertex.

Fig. 8.6. Straightening the segment where you inserted the vertex.

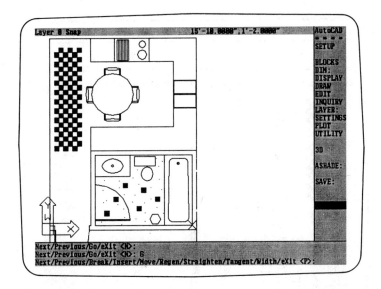

Tangent

Tangent gives the polyline tangent information used by the Fit curve command. Fit curve (discussed later in this chapter) inserts two arcs to define a curve from one vertex to the next. With the Tangent option, you are overriding the original polyline and defining the tangent direction for the curve. You can define the angle to which the curves are tangent, thereby influencing the way Fit Curve affects the original polyline. The Tangent option will not affect the generation of a spline curve. An example of how Tangent works is provided in the discussion of the Fit curve option, later in this chapter.

Width

The Width option lets you change the width of individual segments of the polyline. When you use this option, AutoCAD will prompt you to Enter starting width: and Enter ending width:. Figure 8.7 shows how a starting width of 6″ and an ending width of 2″ can be used to modify the segment width. You must use the Regen option to see the changes in the width of the polyline.

The Width command is useful for modifying or creating tapered entities (those that have different beginning and ending widths).

Fig. 8.7. *Using the* Width *option to modify a single segment.*

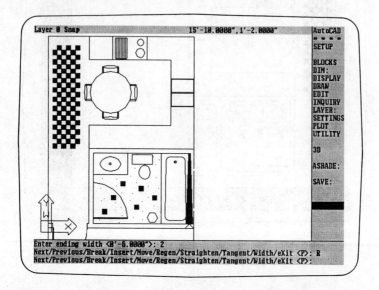

eXit

The eXit option returns you from the Edit vertex option to the main PEDIT prompt. As with the main PEDIT eXit command (discussed later), all changes you have made to the polyline during the editing session are permanent, whether you exit or cancel PEDIT. If you want to reverse the effects of your individual edits, use the PEDIT Undo option. You can also use AutoCAD's UNDO command to reverse the effect of all of the PEDIT editing you just performed.

Fit Curve

Fit curve computes a smooth curve that will fit each vertex of the polyline. This curve is made up of a series of arcs that pass through all the vertices of the original polyline. Two curves are used to connect one vertex to the next; one of these curves is tangent to the first vertex; the second curve is tangent to both the first curve and the second vertex, and down the polyline it goes. Figure 8.8a shows the effects of Fit curve on the polyline. The look of the curve can be altered by editing the individual vertices of the polyline first, using the Edit vertex option discussed earlier, and then using Fit curve. You can also change the look of the curve by using the Tangent suboption located under Edit vertex. Figures 8.8b and 8.8c show the effects of altering the tangent direction of the polyline vertex.

Fig. 8.8a. Using Fit curve *on a polyline.*

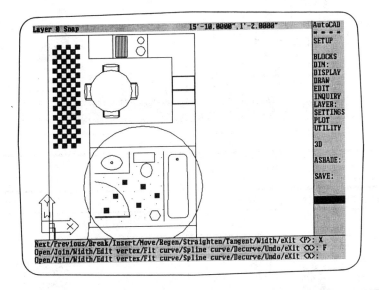

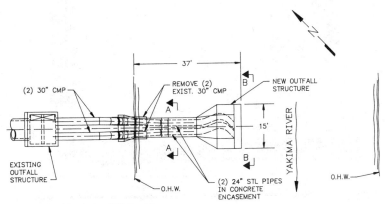

Drawing courtesy of Seattle AutoCAD Users' Group
Seattle, Washington

Fig. 8.8b. *Altering the tangent direction.*

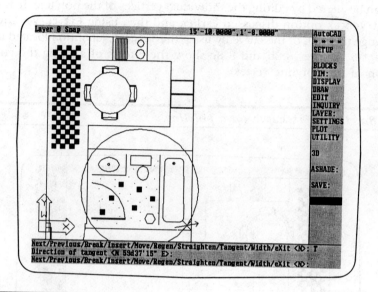

Fig. 8.8c. *The resultant fit curve.*

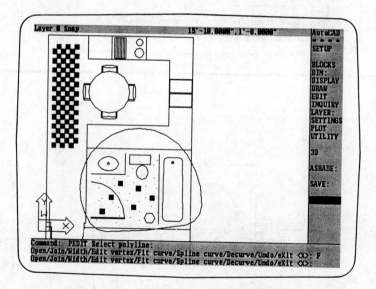

Spline Curve

Splines are curve-fit polylines that are mathematically smoothed and follow (more faithfully than a normal Fit-curve polyline) the underlying frame on which they are based.

The frame is made up of all the original vertices connected by line segments. Because splines pass through the first and last vertices and are "pulled" toward the remaining vertices as the curve passes near them, the spline of a polyline with many segments will be smoother than that of a polyline with only a few segments. The frame is the definition of the spline and is modified as the spline is modified.

Figure 8.9a shows the sample polyline after it has been "splined."

Fig. 8.9a. *Using the* spline *option on your polyline.*

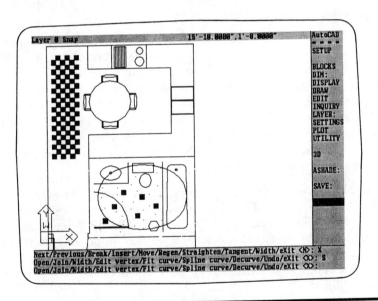

Spline Curve Variables

Two of AutoCAD's system variables, SPLINETYPE and SPLINESEGS, control the way a spline curve is generated. (For more information about system variables, see the "Quick Reference to System Variables" in Part VI of this book.) To change these variables, you type **SETVAR** at the Command: prompt, press Enter, and then type the variable name. SPLINETYPE controls whether the spline created (technically called a *B-spline*) is cubic or quadratic. SPLINESEGS controls the resolution (fine or coarse) of generating the spline. An additional variable, SPLFRAME, is used to show the frame on which the spline is created.

The difference between the two types of splines is one of mathematics and smoothness—a *cubic* B-spline, because it is generated differently mathematically, will be smoother than a *quadratic* B-spline. The value of the SPLINETYPE variable controls which type of B-spline is generated. If SPLINETYPE is set to 6, the spline will be cubic; if the value is set to 5, the spline will be quadratic.

AutoCAD uses the SPLINSEGS system variable to determine how many line or arc segments to use in constructing a spline curve. The default setting (8) draws eight line segments from one vertex to the next. If you change SPLINSEGS to a larger or smaller value (by using the SETVAR command), the number of segments increases or decreases accordingly. With a larger number of segments, an increased amount of time (and file space) is needed to generate the spline. If the value is set to a negative number, two arcs define where one of the default line segments would be creating the same effect as fit curve.

The SPLFRAME system variable controls the display of the spline frame (the original polyline). SPLFRAME is used to show a spline-creating frame as well as invisible edges of 3DFACEs. If SPLFRAME is set to zero, only the spline is displayed; if nonzero, both the spline and its frame are displayed. Figure 8.9b shows the effect of setting SPLFRAME to 1 so that the spline frame is shown. (This is covered in Chapter 15, "More 3-D Drawing Tools.")

Editing a Spline

Generally, splines can be edited like other entities. Both the spline and its frame (the original polyline) can be moved, erased, copied, mirrored, rotated, and scaled. You can make a slpine permanent by using BREAK, TRIM, or EXPLODE to remove the frame. OFFSET generates a new polyline from the

Fig. 8.9b. The spline and its frame.

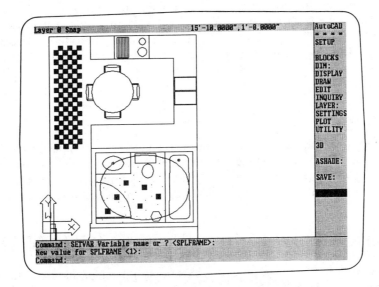

original spline. With STRETCH, the frame is stretched and the spline refitted when the operation is complete. The spline (not the frame) is used when you DIVIDE, MEASURE, use the AREA command, select entities, HATCH, FILLET, and CHAMFER.

Splines are used to define irregular curves. You may need to use trial and error in order to find the correct curve. Use the Decurve option if you want to return to the original polyline so that you can make changes.

Decurve

Decurve does the opposite of Fit curve and Spline curve; it takes the polyline that has been curve fit, removes the arcs, and replaces them with the original straight polyline segments. If you have used the BREAK, TRIM, or EXPLODE commands on either a fit curve or spline polyline, the original frame is gone; Decurve can no longer be used.

Undo

Undo undoes the most recent PEDIT operation; using it is similar to using UNDO from the Command: prompt. With this option, you can step back to the beginning of the PEDIT editing session. Undo allows you to test a modification and then, if it doesn't work as you want it to, restore the original state of the polyline.

eXit

The eXit option returns you to AutoCAD's Command: prompt. Choosing eXit takes you back to the Command: prompt and locks in (saves) all changes you have made to the polylines. Changes made at any time from within the PEDIT command, even if the command is canceled, are permanently saved.

Changing Drawing Entities (CHANGE)

Although the PEDIT command is extremely powerful, its use is limited to modifying polylines. To change some of the aspects of an entity (whether a polyline or not), you should use the CHANGE command. CHANGE, one of the most used editing commands, modifies the *properties* of entities.

CHANGE is commonly used for the following:

❏ Changing an entity's properties
❏ Using change points
❏ Changing an entity

In each of these categories, a different type of *change* is made to the entities selected. Each type of change is discussed in the next few sections.

Changing an Entity's Properties

When you enter the **CHANGE** command at the AutoCAD prompt, AutoCAD will first ask you to select the entities you want to edit. Once you have created your selection set, AutoCAD will then ask you:

    Properties/<Change point>:

If you select Properties, the following prompt appears:

    Change what property (Color/Elev/LAyer/LType/Thickness) ?

Color, layer, linetype, elevation, and thickness are properties of almost every entity in an AutoCAD drawing. As this prompt indicates, each of these individual properties may be altered for the entities you have selected. The next few sections cover the effects of changing these properties.

Changing an Entity's Color

If you select Color, AutoCAD will change the color of the entities you have chosen. Typically, the color you have assigned to the layer on which the entity resides (discussed in the next section), governs the color of the entity. With this option, however, you can mix entities of different colors on the same layer. When you choose Color, AutoCAD will ask you to indicate a new color. You can respond with either a color name (red, yellow, green, cyan, blue, magenta, or white) or number corresponding to a color (1–255). If you want to change colors to the default layer's color, enter **BYLAYER**. This tells AutoCAD to use the color of the layer on which the entity resides.

Blocks (discussed in Chapter 13, ''Creating a Symbol Library'') may have colors specific to their individual entities, which may differ from the layer colors. You can specify a color of BYBLOCK, which causes the entities within the block to assume the color of the block in which they reside. You can use the setting BYBLOCK also to override the layer color.

Changing an Entity's Elevation or Thickness

Elev (which stands for *elevation*) allows you to give a two-dimensional drawing entity a location within three-dimensional space. This elevation is always parallel to the current Z axis. The use of the Elev option will become more apparent as you learn about three-dimensional drawing and editing, beginning in Chapter 14, ''Entering the Third Dimension.''

Thickness is another property of the third dimension. Essentially, it is the *extrusion*, or stretching, of an entity from flat two-dimensional space into three-dimensional space, where the entity takes on a thickness. A positive thickness extends *up*; a negative thickness extends *down*. Because elevation and thickness are related to each other and to three-dimensional drawing, they are discussed together in more detail in Chapter 16, ''Editing Your Three-dimensional Drawing.''

Changing an Entity's Assigned Layer

The ability to place entities from one layer onto another layer is provided through the LAyer option. When an entity is moved from one layer to another, it takes on the default properties of the new layer, such as color, linetype, and state. This is true unless these individual properties have been overridden with the CHANGE command. Each of these properties is discussed later in this chapter in the section that deals with the LAYER command.

Changing an Entity's Linetype

The LType option allows you to change the a line's appearance. As with Color, LType can be established by using the LAYER command and later overridden with the CHANGE command. The linetype of an entity can be changed back to that of its native layer by using the BYLAYER linetype.

BYBLOCK is necessary only when an entity is used within a block; then it will take on properties specific to the block as it is inserted. BYBLOCK is discussed further in Chapter 13, ''Creating a Symbol Library.''

Using Change Points

A *change point* is a point that defines a new location for any of the following:

❏ The endpoint of a line
❏ The endpoint of a polyline
❏ The circumference of a circle
❏ The endpoint of an arc
❏ The insertion point of a block
❏ The insertion point of text

You can use a change point to modify an entity's size or physical position within a drawing. When you enter **CHANGE** at the Command: prompt, AutoCAD prompts you to create a selection set. After you have done so, the following prompt is displayed:

Properties/<Change point>:

By picking a location within the drawing, you are specifying a change point. AutoCAD uses this point as the new endpoint of the entities in your selection set. The endpoint changed is the one closest to the change point. Note that this will not work on splines.

If your selection set contains a circle, the radius of the circle is changed so that the change point lies on the circumference of the circle.

If your selection set contains entities that have an insertion point (such as blocks or text), the insertion point is moved so that it coincides with the change point. Blocks are beyond the scope of this chapter but are discussed further in Chapter 13, "Creating a Symbol Library." Information about text is covered in Chapter 12, "Expanding Your Horizons."

Changing an Entity

Finally, you can change an entity (Change Entity, for lack of a better description) by changing individual pieces of information that are a part of the entity. Due to the simplistic nature of many of the entities within the Drawing Editor, this command works only on circle, text, block, and attribute entities.

When you enter **CHANGE** at the `Command:` prompt, AutoCAD prompts you to create a selection set. After you have done so, the following prompt is displayed:

`Properties/<Change point>:`

If you press Enter at this prompt, AutoCAD allows you to modify some of the underlying values of the entities mentioned in the preceding paragraph. These values, which are different for each of the entities, are explained further in the following sections.

Change entity will allow you to change the tag, prompt string, and value of an attribute definition before it is combined with other entities to form a block. Attribute definitions may also be moved so that their insertion point passes through the change point. Attribute definitions are discussed in Chapter 13, "Creating a Symbol Library."

Changing Circles

Only one property of a circle, its radius, may be changed by pressing Enter at the `Properties/<Change point>:` prompt. If you have done this, AutoCAD will ask you to specify the new value to use for the circle's radius.

The results of changing a circle in this way are the same as those produced by using a change point with a circle in your selection set. The only difference is that this method allows you to use the keyboard to provide an exact radius for the circle. You should use whichever method best fits your needs.

Changing Text

You can change almost all aspects of a text entity. If you press Enter at the `Properties/<Change point>:` prompt, AutoCAD prompts you, in turn, for each of the following:

❏ A new text style (or font)
❏ A new text height
❏ A new rotation angle
❏ A new text string

Note that if the text style has been defined with a fixed height (as explained in Chapter 12, "Expanding Your Horizons"), you will not be allowed to change the height of that particular font. Also, if you are changing the text to a different style, the new style must already have been defined.

You should be aware also that using the CHANGE command on a text string could result in a fair amount of typing. Even if you need to change only one character in a text string, you must enter the entire text string again.

Chapter 12, "Expanding Your Horizons," covers text in greater detail.

Changing Blocks and Attributes

If your selection set contains either a block or a block that contains library attributes, only two items can be changed. Blocks have only one property that may be changed in this way: their rotation angle. If your selection set contains a block, AutoCAD simply asks you to specify a new rotation angle.

If a block is combined with attribute definitions, change entity allows you to change the current value of an attribute. Attributes are discussed further in Chapter 13, "Creating a Symbol Library."

Working With Layers (LAYER)

Layers within AutoCAD are similar to the sheets of mylar used in overlay drafting. In overlay drafting, common elements are placed on the same sheet of mylar; different sheets may contain anything from furniture layouts to structural grids. AutoCAD is no different in its use of layers. Each layer in an AutoCAD drawing can be used to hold different entities. The advantages to using layers within AutoCAD are that the LAYER command allows you to show different layers *only* as you need to see them, and the properties of the entities residing on those layers may all be changed at once to meet your needs.

In AutoCAD, you can modify and create layers from the Command: prompt or through dialogue boxes. As you know from Chapters 2, "AutoCAD — Manual Versus Computer Drafting," and 6, "The Basics of Drawing in AutoCAD", in order to use dialogue boxes, your video device must be able to use the Advanced User Interface (AUI). For information about using dialogue boxes, specifically the layer dialogue boxes, see Chapter 9, "Ways To View Your Drawing."

When you enter **LAYER** at the Command: prompt, AutoCAD displays the following prompt line:

    ?/Make/Set/New/ON/OFF/Color/LType/Freeze/Thaw:

Each option controls a different aspect of how you work with layers; each is described fully in the following sections.

This section shows you how to manipulate layers and change the properties of entities on those layers. The following LAYER commands are covered:

❏ COLOR
❏ LINETYPE

As you may have noticed, both COLOR and LINETYPE deal with properties that affect entities. While the LAYER command is used to globally alter entity properties, there are also commands in LAYER that affect what is called the "state" of the layer, as well as commands that create new layers and place you on those layers. These commands are

❏ ON   ❏ NEW
❏ OFF   ❏ SET
❏ FREEZE   ❏ MAKE
❏ THAW

The "state," entity-property, and layer-creation commands all affect how layers work. In the next few pages, you will learn how to make the LAYER command work for you. The basics of using layers will be covered first. Next, the "state" of a layer and its effects will be discussed. Finally, you will see how to change the properties of all the entities on a given layer.

Layer Basics

AutoCAD is designed to work with many layers. No matter what you are drawing, or when you are drawing, you are always drawing your entities on a certain layer.

Every drawing has at least one layer. This layer, called 0, is the AutoCAD default layer whenever a new drawing is created. It is not the *only* layer you can work with, but is ordinarily the *first* layer you work with. As a default, layer 0 has the following properties:

❑ The color is white.
❑ The linetype is continuous.
❑ The layer is turned on.

You can draw on only one layer at a time. The layer on which you are working is considered the *current* layer. If you look at the upper left corner of the Drawing Editor, you will notice the name of the current layer displayed in the status line. Although layer names can be up to 31 characters long, only the first 8 of those characters are shown on the status line (see fig. 8.10).

Fig. 8.10 *The layer name displayed on the status line.*

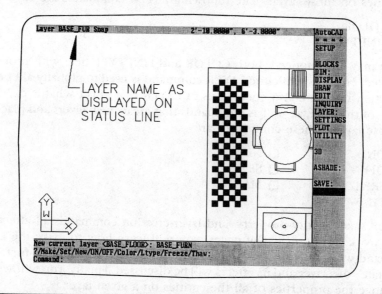

As you begin to work with layers, you will find that developing a layer scheme that is repeated throughout all your drawings is an excellent idea. This scheme should include the layers most common to your field of work. (You do not have to include all layers that might ever be needed.) For example, the scheme for an architectural project might include layers for the structure, the electrical layout, plumbing, and HVAC. Other kinds of projects will have other layers in common.

Not only is a standard layer scheme across drawings a good idea, but you should also get in the habit of giving common layers the same first characters. This will simplify your ability to manipulate these common layers simultaneously. Such a naming scheme is consistent with the draft guidelines for CAD layering, as prepared by the Task Force on CAD Layer Guidelines. This task force is sponsored by the following organizations:

- ❑ The American Institute of Architects
- ❑ The American Consulting Engineers Council
- ❑ The American Society of Civil Engineers
- ❑ The International Facility Management Association

A copy of the draft guidelines is available from the American Institute of Architects.

The following section shows you how to create new layers and change the current layer.

Creating, Changing, and Listing Layers

The LAYER command has many different options. When you enter **LAYER** at the `Command:` prompt, AutoCAD displays the following prompt line:

`?/Make/Set/New/ON/OFF/Color/LType/Freeze/Thaw:`

Right now, the first four layering options (`?`, `Make`, `Set`, and `New`) are of concern to us. Let's look at each one, but in an order that approximates the order in which they ordinarily are used.

The `New` option allows you to create new layers. When AutoCAD prompts you for a layer name, you can enter more than one name at a time by separating the names with a comma. If you need to simulate a space, use the underscore (_) character instead of pressing the space bar (remember—pressing the space bar is like pressing Enter).

Every new layer you create will always begin with the layer properties set to the following:

- ❑ The color is white.
- ❑ The linetype is continuous.
- ❑ The layer is turned on.

These properties may look familiar; they are the default values used for layer 0 when you begin a drawing. It is up to you to use the LAYER options to customize the layers to suit your needs.

The `Set` option tells AutoCAD which layer you want to draw on. When this option is invoked, AutoCAD prompts you for the name of the layer. Enter the layer's name (it must be an existing layer) and press Enter. This layer becomes the current layer. Its name is placed on the status line in the upper left corner.

The Make option effectively combines both the Set and New options. When this option is invoked, AutoCAD prompts you for a layer name. Once you enter a name, Make does the following:

1. Searches for the layer to determine whether it exists
2. If the layer does not exist, creates it and gives it the default attributes
3. Makes the requested layer the current layer

Be careful when you use the Make option. If you mistype the name of the layer you want (assuming that you want an existing layer), you could end up inadvertently with a brand new layer.

Regardless of how you set the current layer (using either the Set or Make commands), all subsequent drawing activity will occur on the current layer. In order to place entities on other layers, you must either change the current layer or use the CHANGE command to move an entity to another layer.

Once you have created a number of layers, remembering their names can be confusing. The ? option allows you to get a list of all layers within a drawing. AutoCAD first asks:

```
Layer name(s) for listing <*>:
```

The default (*) lists all the layers within the drawing. As with the DOS commands (explained in Chapter 4, "Dabble in DOS"), the * character is used as a wild-card character. If the names of several layers in your drawing began with *BASE-*, for example, you could list the layers in which the first five characters of the layer name were *BASE-* by entering **BASE-***.

Layer States

As was mentioned earlier, the "state" of a layer can affect the way it is viewed within a drawing. This section discusses how to manipulate the state of a layer and make this concept of layer states work for you.

When you enter **LAYER** at the Command: prompt, AutoCAD displays the following prompt line:

```
?/Make/Set/New/ON/OFF/Color/LType/Freeze/Thaw:
```

Several of these options control the state of the current layer. These options are ON, OFF, Freeze, and Thaw.

The entities in a layer that is turned ON are visible on-screen. You can use Set to change the current layer to one that is turned on. If you draw entities on a layer that has been turned on, those entities are visible as you draw them.

A layer that is turned OFF is not visible on-screen. AutoCAD will recognize that the entities are "there," it will just not show them. You can use Set to change the current layer to one that is turned OFF, but any entities you draw there cannot be seen until you turn the layer back ON.

The Freeze option goes a step beyond OFF. It does *not* display the layer's entities, and AutoCAD will *not* recognize the existence of those entities when performing edits and displaying the drawing. The original state of the layer may be ON or OFF, but a layer that is frozen is no longer displayed on the screen.

You may wonder what advantages a FROZEN layer has. The principal advantage is that the entities on a frozen layer are not recalculated during edits, ZOOMs, or PANs (ZOOMs and PANs are discussed in the next chapter). This can greatly speed up the way AutoCAD shows information in the drawing after an edit, ZOOM, or PAN. If you work frequently with a couple of layers, you probably will want to just turn them ON and OFF. But if you will be using certain layers infrequently, your best bet is to FREEZE them and thus speed up AutoCAD for your other operations.

The Thaw option simply reverses the effects of freezing a layer. The layer goes back to its original state of ON or OFF.

The following chart summarizes the effects of the various layer states within AutoCAD:

	ON	OFF	Freeze
Set layer as current	Yes	Yes	No
Draw entities on layer	Yes	Yes	No
Entities visible	Yes	No	No
Edit entities on layer	Yes	No	No
CHANGE entities to layer	Yes	Yes	No
Entities calculated	Yes	Yes	No

The Properties of Layers

Let's take a detailed look at two important properties (color and linetype) that affect all the entities on a layer. One of several ways to change the properties of entities is to use the CHANGE command to override the properties assigned by the LAYER command. Two other methods, the COLOR and LINETYPE commands, are discussed in Chapter 11, "Customizing Your Drawing Environment."

Understanding Layer Color

When a color is assigned to a layer, all entities on that layer will be that color. As you may recall, this color originally defaults to white. But you may find it easier to keep track of what is displayed on-screen if each layer is set to a different color. If you are using a monochrome monitor, AutoCAD cannot display in color. Instead, these colors will be different shades of the same color.

To set the color of a layer, first enter **LAYER** at the Command: prompt. AutoCAD then displays the following prompt line:

?/Make/Set/New/ON/OFF/Color/LType/Freeze/Thaw:

Select the Color option. When you are prompted for a color, you may enter either the name of one of seven colors or a number that represents the color you want.

AutoCAD is capable of creating and using 256 colors. Your display will be slightly limited only if your graphics card and monitor are not capable of handling the full range of 256 colors. Typically, 256 colors are useful only for presentation rendering. AutoCAD can use only colors 1 through 15 when it produces plots. The following standard colors are available for all color monitors:

Number	Color
1	Red
2	Yellow
3	Green
4	Cyan
5	Blue
6	Magenta
7	White

On monitors that can handle 256 colors, the hue is determined by the first two digits of the color number; the intensity (saturation) is determined by the third digit. The basic colors are

Color #	Color
010	Red
050	Yellow
090	Green
130	Cyan
170	Blue
210	Magenta

If you want orange, use 030 (020 is a reddish orange; 040 is a yellowish orange).

The last digit gives the color its intensity, or brightness. This digit can be 0 (the brightest), 2, 4, 6, or 8 (the dimmest). The remaining color numbers (250–255) are the levels of gray, with 250 the weakest and 255 the brightest.

When AutoCAD prompts you for a new color, enter either the number or the color name. You are then prompted for the names of the layers this change should affect. You can enter multiple layer names by separating the layer names with commas (not spaces). When you press Enter, the color of the entities on the specified layers is changed (if not explicitly overridden).

Understanding Layer Linetypes

Each layer has an assigned linetype which is used to draw all of the entities that use lines (lines, circles, and arcs) on the layer. You can specify the linetype to be used from the following list of standard linetypes:

- Border
- Center
- Continuous
- Dashdot
- Dashed
- Divide
- Dot
- Hidden
- Phantom

All but Continuous (the default linetype) are in the ACAD.LIN library file. Figure 8.11 shows examples of each of these linetypes.

When you enter **LAYER** at the `Command:` prompt, AutoCAD displays the following prompt line:

`?/Make/Set/New/ON/OFF/Color/LType/Freeze/Thaw:`

Select `LType` to set the linetype for a layer. At the prompt:

`Linetype (or ?) <CONTINUOUS>:`

enter the name of the linetype you want to use. The REGEN command (explained fully in Chapter 9, ''Ways To View Your Drawing'') may be needed in order to display the entities with the linetype properly changed. To get a list of all the linetypes loaded in the drawing, type **?** and press Enter. The list produced will be similar to that shown in figure 8.11.

Fig. 8.11. *The different AutoCAD linetypes.*

```
File to list <acad>:

Linetypes defined in file C:\ACAD\ACAD.lin:

      Name            Description
   -----------     --------------------
DASHED          _ _ _ _ _ _ _ _ _ _ _ _ _
HIDDEN          - - - - - - - - - - - - - - - - - -
CENTER          ___ _ ___ _ ___ _ ___ _ ___ _
PHANTOM         ___ _ _ ___ _ _ ___ _ _ ___
DOT             ....................................................

DASHDOT         _ . _ . _ . _ . _ . _ . _ . _ .
BORDER          _ _ . _ _ . _ _ . _ _ . _ _ .
DIVIDE          _ . . _ . . _ . . _ . . _ . .
1DASH           ___ ___ ___ ___ ___
2DASHES         ___ _ _ ___ _ _ ___

3DASHES         ___ _ _ _ ___ _ _ _ ___
1DOT            ___ . ___ . ___ . ___
2DOTS           ___ . . ___ . . ___ . . ___
3DOTS           ___ . . . ___ . . . ___ . . .

?/Create/Load/Set:
```

LAYER, CHANGE, and
the Sample Drawing

Up to this point, only the CHANGE and LAYER commands have been explained. Now it's time for you to put what you've learned to work. First, use the LAYER command to set up layers with the following names, states, and properties:

Name	State	Color	Linetype
PLAN-WALLS	ON	CYAN	CONTINUOUS
PLAN-FURN	ON	WHITE	CONTINUOUS
PLAN-FLOOR	ON	GREEN	CONTINUOUS
PLAN-FIXTURE	ON	MAGENTA	CONTINUOUS

After setting up these layers, you use the CHANGE command to change the following entities to the specified layers:

Entities to change	Layer to use
All wall lines	PLAN-WALLS
Floor tiles and ''dots''	PLAN-FLOOR
Bathroom fixtures, sink, and range	PLAN-FIXTURE
Countertops, table, and chairs	PLAN-FURN

Summary

This chapter finished the discussion of the editing commands by explaining how to work with CHANGE and PEDIT. These commands have many options that can make a big difference in the editing and display of entities in your drawing. The numerous options available make these two commands extremely powerful, but they frequently are misunderstood.

This chapter also covered the LAYER command's features and benefits. The ability to layer entities in your drawing gives you better control over the way certain information is presented. Also, if your layer usage is well-planned, some of AutoCAD's functions are accelerated.

Chapter 9, ''Ways To View Your Drawing,'' shows you techniques for accessing different views and areas of your drawing. The three commands presented in that chapter (ZOOM, PAN, and VIEW) will give you the flexibility to change displays rapidly and make the most of your AutoCAD time.

Ways To View Your Drawing

In this part of the book, you have learned that CAD work basically consists of creating entities and then modifying them to suit your needs. Just as important, however, is the ease with which you can see your computerized drawing. This chapter will discuss the options you have for *viewing* your drawing. Here you will learn how to get out the information you put in.

As you can imagine, there are many ways to view a CAD drawing. These viewing options vary from on-screen viewing to hard copy plots (draftsmen who don't know CAD usually are more comfortable with the latter). The hard copy options are discussed in Chapter 10, "Plotting Your Drawing." After reading this chapter and the next, you will be able to select the output method that best suits your needs.

This chapter will show you how to look at your drawing on-screen. By letting you see your drawing in different ways, AutoCAD gives you the means to draft faster, more easily, and more accurately. AutoCAD also allows separate image presentation on-screen through the use of slides, which also are covered in this chapter.

After describing the different screen-control commands, the chapter progresses through the Display Dialogue boxes to AutoCAD's presentation capability. (Commands covering the display of three-dimensional entities are discussed in Chapter 17, "Ways To View Your Three-dimensional Drawing.") This chapter covers the following commands:

- ❏ DDEMODES
- ❏ DDLMODES
- ❏ REGEN
- ❏ Transparent commands

- ❏ DDRMODES
- ❏ MSLIDE
- ❏ PAN
- ❏ REDRAW

- ❏ VIEW
- ❏ VSLIDE
- ❏ ZOOM
- ❏ SLIDELIB

Screen-Control Commands

An important aspect of CAD drafting is the ability to see what you are working on. Although this almost goes without saying, it should not be taken lightly. The following exercise will demonstrate the importance of being able to see your drawing as you work on it.

Call up the sample drawing you put together as you studied the previous chapters. (You can call up any drawing, for that matter.) At the Command: prompt enter **ZOOM .0001**.

Where did it go? You drawing should have almost disappeared. It is still there; you just told AutoCAD to look at your work from much farther away. You probably see a tiny speck near the center of the screen. This small dot is your drawing! The drawing has not changed; rather, you have changed the way you are looking at it.

If you were drawing a picture this small, it would be difficult to tell what you were doing, or whether you were doing it correctly. The following sections will discuss the commands you can use to get views that will help you draft accurately and easily. These commands are

- ❏ PAN
- ❏ REDRAW
- ❏ REGEN
- ❏ VIEW
- ❏ ZOOM

Magnifying Parts of the Drawing (ZOOM)

Like the zoom lens on a camera, AutoCAD's ZOOM command magnifies your drawing so that you can perform detailed work. With the aid of ZOOM, you can enlarge any area of your drawing (making it as big as you need) and then ZOOM back to view the entire working area. This capability provides the means for accuracy and detail, no matter how minute.

In Chapter 7, "Editing Your Drawing," you had a brief introduction to AutoCAD's zooming features which taught you how to use the ZOOM command to draft more quickly and easily. You probably have guessed, however, that this command has more power and flexibility than have been demonstrated so far in this text.

Let's look at the command, its options, and its use. When you enter **ZOOM** at the Command: prompt, the following line is displayed:

```
All/Center/Dynamic/Extents/Left/Previous/Window/<Scale(X)>:
```

Choose ZOOM All to return to your drawing's limits or the extents, whichever is larger. You can think of a drawing's *limits* as the edges of the drawing paper; the area in which you have drawn (enclosed in a box) is the *extents*. (The X and Y values make up the extents of your drawing.) For this exercise, a ZOOM All will display your drawing as shown in figure 9.1.

Fig. 9.1. *The sample drawing after a* ZOOM All.

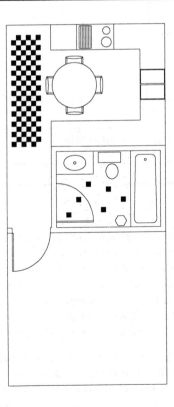

If you select ZOOM Center, you will be prompted for a new center point of the screen. In other words, AutoCAD asks what should be located at the screen's center. Then you are prompted for the height, which determines the zoom scale.

ZOOM Dynamic can be harder to understand. When you select Dynamic, a new screen appears on the monitor (see fig. 9.2). You will work on this new screen. For AutoCAD to be able to do the dynamic zoom, you must work within the part of the drawing displayed on-screen.

Fig. 9.2. *The* ZOOM Dynamic *screen.*

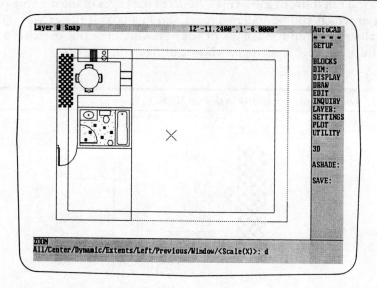

The ZOOM Dynamic command makes use of what is known as a virtual screen. This type of screen allows you to see the extents of your drawing (indicated by a large white box), the current screen location (a dotted green box), the area you may zoom into without causing a regeneration (signified by four red corner marks), and a box (with an *X* in its center) which represents the area that will be drawn next on the screen. Even if you do not have a color monitor, these areas are distinct enough to be easily recognizable.

The advantage to using a virtual screen is speed. AutoCAD can quickly show you the important zooming information (drawing extents and regeneration limits) and let you choose the location for your next screen, all before it has to start drawing any entities. If you know where you need to go in the drawing, in relation to where the screen is currently looking, using ZOOM Dynamic is much faster than performing a ZOOM Previous and then a ZOOM Window.

To choose your new screen location, move the pointing device to the area you want to draw on the screen. The box with the *X* in its center (called the *view box*) will follow your movement. If necessary, you may adjust the size of the box by pressing the pick button. When you do this, the *X* in the center of the box will change to an arrow, and any movement to the left or right will increase or decrease the size of the box. When the box is the size you need, press the pick button again. The *X* will reappear.

ZOOM Dynamic can also be helpful by showing you which drawing area you must stay within in order to avoid a regeneration (a *regen*). Regens (discussed later in this chapter) force AutoCAD to re-create the drawing entities from the .DWG file, which tends to be very slow. By displaying an hourglass in the screen's lower left corner (see fig. 9.3), ZOOM Dynamic will warn you when the view box is placed in an area that will cause a regen. Whenever the hourglass is not displayed, your ZOOM will happen as quickly as possible because the drawing information is re-created from entity data kept in memory.

Fig. 9.3. *The* ZOOM Dynamic *window: a regeneration is about to occur.*

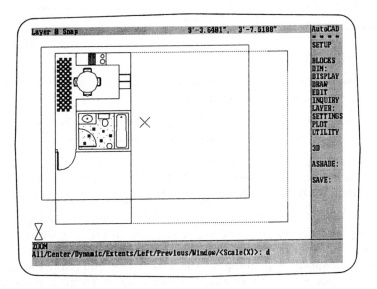

ZOOM Extents lets you see your entire drawing on-screen. The extents of the drawing are the precise area that you have drawn (see fig. 9.4).

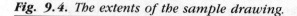

Fig. 9.4. *The extents of the sample drawing.*

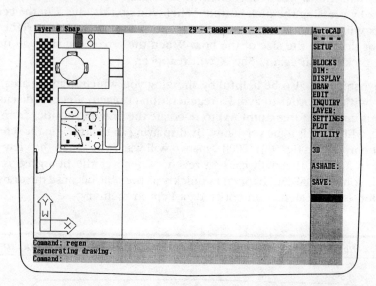

If you choose ZOOM Left, AutoCAD will ask what you want to see in the lower left corner and then prompt you for a height.

Select ZOOM Previous to return to the preceding screen. This can be repeated up to 10 times so that you see a series of the last views.

ZOOM Window lets you put a window around your work area. This window is similar to the one used to gather information for the selection set when you edit your drawing (refer to Chapter 6, ''The Basics of Drawing in AutoCAD'').

Another ZOOM command selection, Scale, allows you to zoom in or out while keeping the same view of the screen. When you use this option, the objects in the center of the screen remain there; their apparent size is either enlarged or reduced, depending on the scale factor entered. As a result, the smaller the scale factor, the smaller your drawing will appear on-screen.

A scale can be entered in either of two ways. The first method acts on the zoom scale of the whole drawing. For example, if you enter **2** at the prompt, the on-screen picture is enlarged to twice its size; if you enter a scale factor of .5, the image is reduced to half the original size.

In the second method, you enter a positive number followed by an X. This method will calculate the new zoomed view based on the current display.

Your familiarity with the ZOOM options will grow as you experiment and practice. For now, practice applying some of the commands to the exercise. The following ZOOM commands are the ones you most likely will use in your everyday drafting.

Indicating a Specific Area (ZOOM Window)

As mentioned before, when you want to work on one part of a drawing, you can single out that area by enclosing it in a *window*. To issue a ZOOM Window, follow these steps:

Prompt:	Response:	Explanation:
Command:	**ZOOM**	Starts ZOOM command
All/Center/Dynamic /Extents/Left /Previous/Window /<Scale (X)>:	**W**	Indicates that ZOOM Window has been selected
First corner:	Move crosshairs to an area that represents a corner, such as the bottom left corner of the bathroom sink.	
Other corner:	Move crosshairs to opposite corner of sink.	

This exercise should result in a picture similar to that shown in figure 9.5. From this view, you can add a significant amount of detail to the drawing.

Fig. 9.5. *Using* ZOOM Window *to enlarge an area of the drawing.*

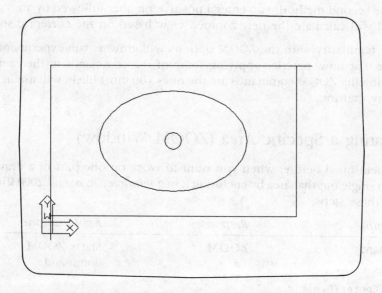

Seeing the Entire Drawing (ZOOM All)

After zooming in on different areas of the drawing, you probably will want to see the whole drawing again. To do this, use the ZOOM All command sequence. To execute the ZOOM All command from the keyboard, type **A** at the ZOOM prompt and press Enter. The magnification level should return to normal, and your complete drawing should appear on-screen.

Backing Up through Screens (ZOOM Previous)

Sometimes, after you ZOOM in to magnify your drawing, you need to return to the view you had before. Use the ZOOM Previous command sequence to move back to the previously displayed screen. AutoCAD allows you to issue up to 10 ZOOM Previous commands in a row. Each time, AutoCAD takes you back to the preceding view. These views can be different ZOOMed areas, or views created with the PAN command, which is discussed next.

Moving Around in the Drawing (PAN)

PAN often works in conjunction with the ZOOM command. Suppose, for example, that you want to see the view just to the right of the one currently on the screen. This can be done with the ZOOM command by ZOOMing out and then selecting a new window to ZOOM in on. The PAN command is much better for this application, however, because PAN allows you to move around in the drawing without ZOOMing in and out. If you are working in one part of the drawing and need to work in an adjacent part, you can PAN from one area to the other.

When you enter **PAN** at the `Command:` prompt, AutoCAD prompts you for `Displacement` and for a `Second point`. At the first prompt, you enter a point of reference. After choosing the first point you indicate a second point. When you indicate a point, this will tell AutoCAD the direction and displacement to PAN.

If you decide to pick two points for reference, the points indicate the direction and distance you want to move the drawing. Think of it this way: the first point represents placing your hand on the drawing sheet; the second represents dragging the sheet in the desired direction. When finished, the on-screen image will reflect the sheet as it was moved. The PAN command moves the screen in relation to the drawing.

Using VIEW

Zooming and panning do not take much time if your drawing is small, but they can slow you down if you are working with many entities. To speed up your work, you can use the VIEW command to create specific views of your enlarged work areas. Then you can quickly flip between these views.

When you enter **VIEW** at the `Command:` prompt, the following line is displayed:

`?/Delete/Restore/Save/Window:`

Select `?` to list all views currently defined in the drawing.

If, after you finish working with a view, you want to remove its reference from the list, select `Delete`. Only the view's name and reference are removed; the drawing remains intact.

Select `Restore` when you want to call up another view. This selection will restore a defined view to the screen.

To save the current on-screen image as a view, choose Save. AutoCAD will prompt for a view name. You use this name—which can be 31 characters long and contain letters, numbers, and the dollar sign ($), hyphen (-), and underscore (_) symbols—to reference the view. For example, you might create and name views such as "bathroom" or "kitchen."

The VIEW Window command gives you greater flexibility than VIEW Save by allowing you to create a view from the two corners of a window box. This method is much easier, and faster, than having to first zoom to the area you want to save, then using VIEW Save, and then zooming to the area for your next view. As you can see, if you have several views to save, VIEW Save will waste much of your time. If, on the other hand, you can perform a ZOOM Extents and then window each area you want to save as a view, you can dramatically reduce the time spent performing this process.

Using ZOOM, PAN, and VIEW Transparently

ZOOM, PAN, and VIEW can be used *transparently* as you work with other commands. For example, if you are drawing a line that must be extended beyond the area encompassed by the current screen, you can pan over (without stopping the LINE command) and continue drawing the line.

To do this, execute the LINE command as usual. When you need to use the PAN command, type 'PAN at any prompt and press Enter. The leading apostrophe alerts AutoCAD that you are executing one command inside another; AutoCAD temporarily suspends the first command and prompts you with the normal PAN command prompts. When you finish using the transparent command (in this case, PAN), the original command (LINE) resumes from the point at which it was interrupted.

To use commands transparently at any point in the current command, type an apostrophe (') and the name of the command you want to execute. The PAN, VIEW, and ZOOM commands cannot be used transparently, however, while the following commands are in use:

❑ DVIEW
❑ VPOINT
❑ another PAN, VIEW, or ZOOM

(DVIEW and VPOINT are discussed in Chapter 16, "Editing Your Three-dimensional Drawing.")

You must be careful when using a command transparently, because it could force a regeneration. The regeneration will cancel the transparent command. (Because ZOOM All and ZOOM Extents always force a regeneration, they are not included in the transparent ZOOM prompt.)

The transparency of these commands gives you greater flexibility with the screen image. There may be times, though, when the on-screen image needs to be refreshed. For those situations, use the REDRAW command.

REDRAW

The REDRAW command tells the computer to redraw the on-screen image. You should use this command if, for some reason, the image on the screen has partial data, or if the drawing seems to contain garbage that was not there before.

The computer can redraw the screen image in just a moment or two, and sometimes this is helpful. When, for example, you turn off a layer, or a group of layers (as discussed in Chapter 8, "Advanced Editing Commands"), the computer automatically redraws the screen image. If the computer did not do this, you would not see the drawing correctly.

You can issue a REDRAW at any time, even transparently. This gives the REDRAW command great flexibility because you can use it to clean up the screen (even during commands that dirty the screen). For example, you can use 'REDRAW to clear the screen of blip marks created while you are creating a complex polyline.

If the image still is not displayed correctly (for example, with entities of the wrong color), a complete regeneration of the drawing might be in order. Because REDRAW is significantly faster than the REGEN command, a REDRAW should be issued first.

REGEN

The REGEN command (for REGENeration) is used to regenerate the drawing's data on the screen. An automatic REGEN is issued when you FREEZE or THAW layers, or when you initially call up an existing drawing. A regeneration also occurs automatically if you use any ZOOM command that causes a significant change to the drawing's on-screen view (such as ZOOM All or ZOOM Extents).

As a general rule, you should use the REGEN command manually if the image presented by REDRAW does not correctly reflect your drawing.

Because REGEN goes through the drawing's *entire* database and projects the information on the screen, this command will give you the most accurate image possible. The image is presented, however, at the cost of speed. Because of the manner in which it functions, a REGEN takes significantly longer than a REDRAW.

Automatic Screen Regeneration

If your computer does not automatically regenerate the screen image after a LAYER THAW, you may need to tell AutoCAD to do so. To do so, type **REGENAUTO** at the `Command:` prompt. The message displayed will be similar to:

`On/Off <Off>:`

At this prompt, type **ON**. This causes AutoCAD to regenerate the screen automatically whenever it determines that a regeneration is necessary. With REGENAUTO set to OFF, AutoCAD still determines when a regeneration is needed, but asks your permission before doing it.

Dynamic Dialogue Boxes

If the Advanced User Interface (AUI) is installed with your version of AutoCAD, you can take advantage of pop-up dialogue boxes. There are five such boxes, but this chapter covers only those that interact with the commands discussed so far in this text. AutoCAD's five dialogue-box control commands are

❏ DDATTE
❏ DDEMODES
❏ DDLMODES
❏ DDRMODES
❏ DDUCS

The "DD" in each command name stands for *D*ynamic *D*ialogue. Only DDEMODES, DDLMODES, and DDRMODES are discussed here. (For a discussion of DDATTE, see Chapter 13, "Creating a Symbol Library." DDUCS is covered in Chapter 14, "Entering the Third Dimension.")

You can use any of these commands by typing the command name at the `Command:` prompt. You may need to respond to further prompts to complete the command. Finally, you will see a box with which you can interact to change AutoCAD settings. This box contains the drawing's current settings. By moving your pointing device and picking a specific area in the box, you can *graphically* select any setting you want to modify.

Near the bottom of each box is an area labeled `OK`, and another labeled `Cancel`. After making modifications to the information in the dialogue box, you can make the changes permanent (OK), or tell AutoCAD not to make any changes and stop the command (Cancel).

Dialogue boxes make it easier, and often faster, to alter your AutoCAD drawing's settings. If your system does not have the Advanced User Interface (AUI), do not fret. All of the Display Dialogue boxes' functions are provided within AutoCAD through other commands, and are covered elsewhere in this text.

Let's take a look at the three commands that invoke the dialogue boxes.

Modifying Entities with DDEMODES

With the DDEMODES command you can see and modify several attributes of an entity. DDEMODES lets you change the following properties:

- ❏ Color
- ❏ Elevation
- ❏ Layer
- ❏ Linetype
- ❏ Thickness

Obviously, these properties also can be changed with individual AutoCAD commands. The effect of using the DDEMODES command is the same as that of using the following commands:

- ❏ COLOR
- ❏ ELEVation
- ❏ LAYER Set
- ❏ LINETYPE Set

When you type **DDEMODES** at the Command: prompt, your screen should look like the one shown in figure 9.6.

If you select Color, Layer, or Linetype, a *subdialogue* box is displayed to allow for easier input. If Elevation or Thickness is selected, AutoCAD expects you to type the information.

The DDEMODES command may be used transparently, by typing **'DDEMODES** at the Command: prompt. The modified information does not take effect, however, *until the next command is given*.

Modifying Drawing Settings with DDRMODES

The DDRMODES command lets you view and modify the current drawing settings. When you type **DDRMODES** at the Command: prompt, your screen should be similar to the one shown in figure 9.7.

Fig. 9.6. The DDEMODES dialogue box.

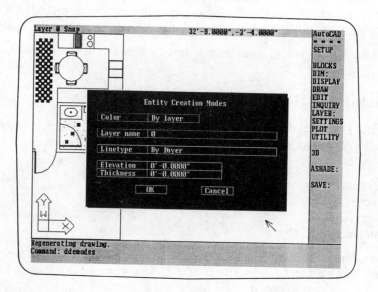

Fig. 9.7. The DDRMODES dialogue box.

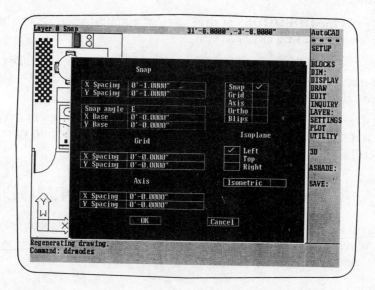

As you probably can tell from figure 9.7, DDRMODES affects several settings, including the following:

- ❏ Axis settings
- ❏ Grid spacings
- ❏ Isoplane settings
- ❏ Snap angle
- ❏ Snap spacing

The DDRMODES command does all the functions of the following commands:

- ❏ AXIS
- ❏ BLIPMODE
- ❏ GRID
- ❏ ISOPLANE
- ❏ ORTHO
- ❏ SNAP

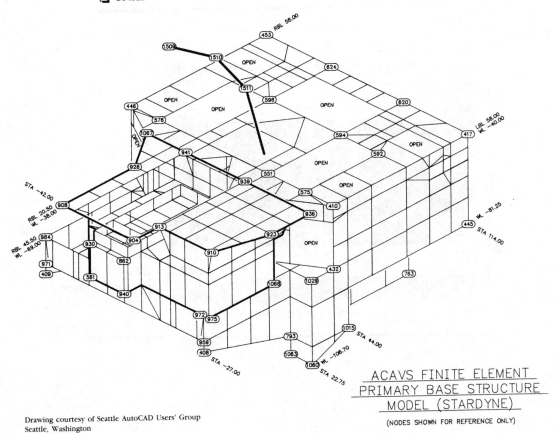

ACAVS FINITE ELEMENT
PRIMARY BASE STRUCTURE
MODEL (STARDYNE)

(NODES SHOWN FOR REFERENCE ONLY)

Drawing courtesy of Seattle AutoCAD Users' Group
Seattle, Washington

Modifying Layer Settings with DDLMODES

The DDLMODES command gives you all the power of the LAYER command (and more) in an easy-to-use form. With this dialogue box you can do the following:

❏ Alter a layer's linetype
❏ Change a layer's color
❏ Change the current layer
❏ Freeze or thaw a layer
❏ Rename a layer
❏ Turn layers on or off
❏ Add new layers

Figure 9.8 shows the dialogue box presented when you enter the DDLMODES command.

Fig. 9.8. *The DDLMODES dialogue box.*

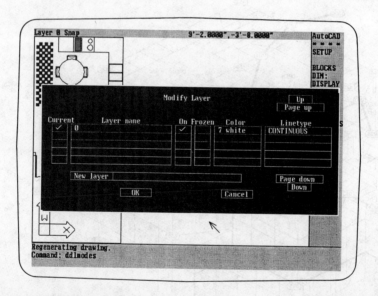

LAYER versus DDLMODES: Should You Use Only One?

Even though the DDLMODES command is powerful, it should not replace the LAYER command. This is especially true if your drawing uses many layers, such as those used by Autodesk's AEC-A or AEC-M templates (see Appendix B, "Useful Additional Programs," for more information).

The decision of when to use DDLMODES and LAYER is based strictly on speed. Suppose, for example, that you are working on a drawing with more than 50 layers (typical for many disciplines), and you want to set the current layer to ARWALL. Using the LAYER command, you can do this with just 16 keystrokes. Even a CAD operator with 10 thumbs would be surprised at how fast this can be done. If you were to do the same thing using the DDLMODES dialogue box, you could find yourself scrolling through a series of screens until the correct layer is found. This is much slower than simply using the LAYER command directly.

You can use the DDLMODES command transparently, by typing **'DDLMODES** at the Command: prompt. Changed information does not take effect, however, until the next command is issued.

When you work with transparency, one command is suspended temporarily while you execute another (the transparent DDLMODES command). Once the transparent command is completed, the original command is resumed until it also is completed. The next command entered then will be affected by any modifications made during the 'DDLMODES.

Creating Slide Shows

AutoCAD gives you the views you need to construct your drawing, as well as several features for modifying its settings. It also lets you create presentation images, called *slides*, on-screen. AutoCAD slides are snapshots of drawings; in many ways, they are similar to the VIEW command discussed earlier.

These snapshots are separate files that you create and save. A slide is the exact image you see on-screen when you create the snapshot. The advantage of slides is that you can look at a slide or series of slides whenever you are in the Drawing Editor. The disadvantage is that you cannot edit slides; they are just pictures, not drawings.

Another important advantage of slides is that they are quickly projected on-screen. Further, you can automate the slide display through script files. These features let you animate, or present different options for evaluation.

Beginning with Release 9 (and continuing with Release 10), slides can be combined into slide libraries. A *slide library* is a collection of similar slides in one big file. You can retrieve a specific slide from this library. The advantage to this approach is that you can group an entire project of similar slides into one file, thus reducing the risk of losing or misplacing an individual slide.

The command that creates the libraries is executed from the DOS prompt. After creating the slides, as described later, you can combine them to form a library. You also can build a library from slides created in previous releases of AutoCAD.

Making Slides (MSLIDE)

To make a slide of any drawing (or any part of a drawing), call up the drawing in the Drawing Editor and zoom in on the area that you want for the slide. Once you have the view you want to capture, you use the MSLIDE command.

At the `Command:` prompt, type **MSLIDE**. AutoCAD responds by asking the following:

`Slide file:`

AutoCAD wants to know the slide file's name (a DOS file name up to eight characters, with the standard DOS limitations). When you enter a valid file name, AutoCAD will create the slide from the image currently displayed on-screen. This slide is saved on disk as an individual slide file (using the file name you supplied). You can combine the slide with others to form a library, or you can view it separately by using the VSLIDE command.

Viewing Your Slides (VSLIDE)

After you have created a slide, you can use the VSLIDE command to display it on your monitor. When you enter **VSLIDE** at the `Command:` prompt, AutoCAD prompts you for the name of the slide you want to view:

`Slide file:`

If the slide is part of a library, enter the name of the library and, in parentheses, the name of the slide (without spaces). For example, if you want to view a slide called 5 in a slide library called *HOUSE_1*, enter **HOUSE_1(5)** as the slide file's name.

Remember that slides are simply snapshots of drawings. You can view them at any time while you are working on any drawing. Your current drawing is not changed, nor is it removed from the Drawing Editor. To remove a slide's image from the screen and bring back the image you had before, use the REDRAW or REGEN commands.

Creating Slide Libraries (SLIDELIB)

As you may recall, AutoCAD can group a series of slides into *slide libraries*. These libraries are simply collections of .SLD files placed together in a large file with a .SLB extension.

Slide libraries have the advantage of grouping many slide files under one file, thus allowing you to reduce file clutter on your hard disk. Unfortunately, putting your slide files into a library does not reduce disk space significantly. Also, the SLIDELIB program allows very little interaction with the slides placed within the library.

SLIDELIB is a program called from the DOS prompt; its command line looks like this:

SLIDELIB *Slidelibname Slidefiles*

Slidelibname is the name you want to give to the slide library. *Slidefiles* is the name of the slide you want added to the slide library. If you want to incorporate more than a few slide files into the library, you can create an ASCII file and use the DOS redirection facilities (<) to have SLIDELIB take the slide names from the ASCII file rather than the command line. The following example would create a slide library called EXAMPLE, made from slides called BATH and KITCHEN:

SLIDELIB EXAMPLE BATH KITCHEN

Once you have created the slide library file, you can view the slides that were placed in it. Just type the name of the library and then (in parentheses) type the original slide name. To call up the BATH slide from the library you created, for example, you would follow this command sequence:

Command:	*Response:*	*Explanation:*
VSLIDE	**EXAMPLE(BATH)**	Calls up BATH slide from library

While the SLIDELIB program is a good start for organizing the many slide file you may have in your computer, it does very little for efficient slide-library management. Once slides are in the library, SLIDELIB offers no method for finding out their names. Slides within the library cannot be removed, even if they are unnecessary. To accomplish efficient slide-library management, you may want to get a copy of John Intorcio's SlideManager program, available from bulletin boards and CompuServe. For more information about SlideManager, see Appendix B, ''Additional Useful Programs.''

Summary

This chapter discussed many of the ways to view drawings within AutoCAD. These options range from the ways you can look at your drawing on-screen, to the different screen-control commands, to information on capturing screen images in slide files. As you can see, being able to control both the visual aspects of CAD and the drafting environment is important.

The following commands were discussed in this chapter:

❏ DDEMODES   ❏ REGEN
❏ DDLMODES   ❏ Transparent commands
❏ DDRMODES   ❏ VIEW
❏ MSLIDE   ❏ VSLIDE
❏ PAN   ❏ ZOOM
❏ REDRAW   ❏ SLIDELIB

Chapter 10, ''Plotting Your Drawing,'' discusses how to get the picture you want, covering the procedures needed to place your image on hard copy.

Plotting Your Drawing

When you work on a CAD drawing, there will come a time when you need to see the image on paper. Your boss may want to see how your work is progressing, you may want to check that each of the drawing elements is in proper scale or location, or you may be ready to produce final drawings for a client. Whatever the reason, you will learn in this chapter how to get this output.

As was mentioned in Chapter 9, "Ways To View Your Drawing," there are many reasons for wanting to reproduce your CAD image on hard copy as opposed to on-screen. The term *hard copy* describes a tangible reproduction of a screen image. This could apply to many things including pictures, videotape, prints, or plots; this chapter discusses the most commonly used form—the plotted image.

The commands introduced in this chapter are

❏ PLOT   ❏ PRPLOT

After completing this chapter, you will be able to place any screen image on a tangible medium by using the PLOT or PRPLOT command. You also will be familiar with the many considerations specific to producing a proper plotted image. These considerations, which range from selecting media, pens, and colors to obtaining the proper combination of plotted linetype widths, are examined in the following sections.

The Reason for Plots

Someone once said: "You will never get rid of paper." In this age of computers and electronically stored information, you might expect that saying to be less valid. But the need for a paper copy seems to be greater than ever. As you will see, there are a number of reasons for this.

The most obvious thing about computers is that electronic information storage provides us with a compact source of information that is easy to access. A single floppy disk, which weighs less than eight ounces and can fit in the pocket of your jacket, can hold all the files that went into creating this book. The final product is a bit bulkier. As with many things, CAD has disadvantages. Some of the main disadvantages to CAD drawing are

❏ Unless a drawing is on-screen at a given time, there is a delay between loading the drawing and viewing it.

❏ You may lose track of scales and relationships among drawing elements. Text may be too large, an object's detail might be overdone, or the pieces of the drawing may be arranged incorrectly.

❏ A drawing may pick up unnecessary information (such as lines or text that you thought had been erased). These may not be noticed until a plot is run.

For these and other reasons, *progress prints* (also known as *check plots*) of CAD work are needed. In many offices, a project leader delegates drafting work (CAD or not) to many draftsmen. As the project continues, progress prints document the current status of the project. The project leader reviews these prints and adds information for the draftsmen to add to the master drawing. This process continues until the project is complete.

As this "draft, mark-up, draft" procedure continues toward the finished drawing, many prints accumulate. To reduce the number of check plots and thus save time and expense, the draftsman should complete as much of the drawing as possible before running a plot. This is probably the most important of all good plotting practices. More of these habits and considerations are discussed in the next section.

Good Plotting Practices

Completing as much of a drawing as possible before plotting is a concept that cannot be overemphasized. Plot times for drawings can range from two minutes to over an hour. Therefore, you must learn to do as much of the drafting as you can before you produce a plot. If you do not follow this guideline, you may waste time by plotting unnecessarily.

A new AutoCAD user needs to become familiar with how the drawing looks after it goes from *screen* to *paper*. AutoCAD's scales and the relationships among drawing elements take time to grasp completely. This knowledge comes only from frequent use of AutoCAD and timely creation of plots of your work.

If you are new to CAD drafting, you may suddenly become aware of the need to have a tangible copy of your current work. We have all felt this way. As you become more familiar with CAD, you should find less of a need to plot your drawing. In fact, many people will not plot a drawing until it is either substantially completed or someone else wants to see it.

Another good practice is to set up a regular plotter-maintenance schedule. Maintenance does not mean cleaning the circuit boards or checking the chip relays. The type of maintenance you should be doing includes removing the pens after you finish plotting, using the proper plotter media, replacing worn ribbons or used toner, and periodic cleaning of moving parts. These common-sense types of maintenance will all help you avoid potential problems.

Good plotter management is another consideration that must be emphasized. Knowing *when* to plot can often save tremendous amounts of time, energy, and money. Scheduling the needed plots around lunch time, for example, turns otherwise idle time to more productive use.

The key to good plotter management is knowing your plotter's limitations. The most important limitation probably is *time*. You frequently may need to run a progress set of a 10-sheet project. With plot times that can run from two minutes to an hour, depending on the complexity of your drawing, you may have to set aside five to six hours just to make the *originals*. This is, without question, one of the major drawbacks to plotting your drawings in house. Careful management of the plotter and the use of plotting service bureaus, when necessary, can be key to making tight deadlines instead of missing them.

Hard-copy Output

To produce a hard copy of your CAD work, you need AutoCAD's plot commands, a printer, or a plotter. As you may recall, the different types of hardware that you can use to produce printer or plotter hard copy are discussed in Chapter 3, ''Know Your CAD Equipment.'' Plot devices produce hard copy from either vector or raster information. *Vector* information deals with actual coordinates of entity data, whereas *raster* information is generated by transforming the entity into a series of dots.

Electrostatic plotters and laser plotters both create plots from raster data but are too costly for most firms. This discussion will focus on using the basic eight-pen plotter (and AutoCAD's PLOT command) and the wide-carriage dot-matrix graphics printer, with the PRPLOT command.

Although the procedure is similar for obtaining output from either the printer or the plotter, certain differences must be considered. For example, although a *printer plot* will lose line quality, line weight, color, and reproducibility, its speed and convenience make it fit certain needs. Typically, printer plots are used for quick checks of your work. A *pen plotter*, on the other hand, offers superior line quality, color plotting, excellent reproduction, and uses a variety of media. These benefits must be balanced against the drawbacks of higher equipment cost and longer processing time.

The main reason plotting takes so long is that the plotting device cannot process the information from the computer as fast as the computer can send it. There are ways to speed up this process, of course, but even the fastest method will take some computer time.

Most CAD systems can calculate the entity vector information and send it to the plotter faster than the plotter uses it. To help the plotter take in the information more rapidly, people are now beginning to use hardware buffers. A *hardware buffer* is a device that stores the information coming from a computer and going to a printer or plotter. Because the buffer has a larger storage capacity than the output device, it is able to free up the computer faster so that you can continue working while plotting progresses. The buffer then sends the stored information to the printer or plotter.

Note that hardware buffers are not the same as spoolers. (A *spooler* basically sets aside RAM to emulate a hardware buffer.) Because spoolers rob AutoCAD of the memory it needs to run fast, hardware buffers often are preferred in CAD applications.

One last note before you plot: because many things can happen during a long plot, it is a good idea to save your drawing before you use the plot commands. Make sure that the information you want to plot is displayed on the monitor and that your plotter is ready. The plotter should be turned on, hooked up to your computer, and equipped with paper and pen.

Producing Your Drawing on a Plotter (PLOT)

To use the PLOT command, your CAD station should be connected with a pen plotter. If your station is *directly* connected to a plotter, you are ready to start using the PLOT command. If you are plotting through a hardware buffer or a Local Area Network (LAN), consult the appropriate documentation so that you can begin plotting.

This section discusses the PLOT command and how you use it to get a tangible, hard-copy reproduction of your CAD drawing. Begin by calling up the drawing, and then enter **PLOT** at the Command: prompt. You will then be prompted with:

What to plot? Display, Extents, Limits, View, or Window <D>:

The Display option allows you to plot the image displayed on-screen. Should you select either the Extents or Limits of your drawing, the plotted image would be similar to the image seen on-screen after a ZOOM Extents, or a ZOOM Limits. (If you need to refresh your memory of how to use ZOOM, refer to Chapter 9, "Ways To View Your Drawing.")

By choosing to plot a previously created View, you would get an image similar to the screen image after a VIEW Restore. Or you can plot only a specified Window of the current screen's area. The effects of this option would be similar to those of ZOOM Window.

Because you want to plot the information displayed on-screen, enter **D**. AutoCAD then displays information similar to the following:

```
Plot will NOT be written to a selected file
Sizes are in Inches
Plot origin is at (0.00,0.00)
Plotting area is 43.00 wide by 33.00 high (E size)
Plot is NOT rotated 90 degrees
Pen width is 0.010
Area fill will NOT be adjusted for pen width
Hidden lines will NOT be removed
Plot will be scaled to fit available area

Do you want to change anything? <N>
```

The information on your screen probably will be different from that shown here, depending on the way your plotter has been configured. This information shows the data AutoCAD will use to project the image to the plotter. Because you need to modify any discrepancies between your information and that in the book, press **Y** at the Do you want to change anything? <N> prompt.

The following segment represents the information you will be prompted for and the data you will need to enter. After you have worked through the following command sequence, each of these prompts will be discussed.

This section also shows AutoCAD's responses when configured for the Calcomp 104x series of plotters. This configuration is used because the Calcomp 104x series is by far the most popular pen-plotting device in the CAD industry. The responses shown here may not reflect those you see if your AutoCAD package is configured for a different plotter. (For more information about configuring AutoCAD, refer to Chapter 5, "Installing AutoCAD and AutoShade.")

```
Entity        Pen   Line      Entity       Pen   Line
Color         No.   Type      Color        No.   Type
1 (red)       1     0         9            1     0
2 (yellow)    2     0         10           2     0
3 (green)     3     0         11           3     0
4 (cyan)      4     0         12           4     0
5 (blue)      5     0         13           5     0
6 (magenta)   6     0         14           6     0
7 (white)     7     0         15           7     0
8             8     0

Line types    0 = continuous line

Do you want to change any of the above parameters? <N> n
Write the plot to a file? <Y> n
Size units (Inches or Millimeters) <I>: i
Plot origin in Inches <0.00,0.00>: 0,0

Standard values for plotting size

Size    Width    Height

A       10.50    8.00
B       16.00    10.00
C       21.00    16.00
D       33.00    21.00
E       43.00    33.00
MAX     64.50    36.00

Enter the Size or Width,Height (in Inches) <E>: e
Rotate 2D plots 90 degrees clockwise? <N> n
Pen width <0.010>: .01
Adjust area fill boundaries for pen width? <N> n
Remove hidden lines? <N> n

Specify scale by entering:
Plotted Inches=Drawing Units or Fit or ? <F>:  1/4"=1'
Effective plotting area:  8.74 wide by 7.07 high
Position paper in plotter.
Press RETURN to continue or S to Stop for hardware setup
```

To start the plot, press Enter. The following line (and eventually the last two lines) will be displayed:

```
Processing vector: xxx
Plot finished.
Press RETURN to continue
```

What you now have is a 1/4″ = 1′-0″ scale hard-copy image of your computer drawing.

Plotting From AutoCAD's Main Menu

By plotting your drawings from AutoCAD's Main Menu, you circumvent having to enter the Drawing Editor. In certain situations, this can save time. Simply choose Option 3, Plot a drawing, at the Main Menu. The procedure is similar to that discussed in the preceding section.

The PRPLOT command is explained later in this chapter. If you want to produce a printer plot from the Main Menu, choose Option 4, Printer Plot a drawing. Again, the procedure is similar to that described for PLOT.

The PLOT Command Prompts

In the preceding section you produced a plot of the sample drawing you have been creating. You used the PLOT command, told AutoCAD what you wanted to plot, and then had to answer a few questions regarding specifics about producing the plot. In this section, you will learn what each of those questions means and how they can affect plotted output.

After telling AutoCAD what you want to plot, you are presented with the following table:

Entity Color	Pen No.	Line Type	Entity Color	Pen No.	Line Type
1 (red)	1	0	9	1	0
2 (yellow)	2	0	10	2	0
3 (green)	3	0	11	3	0
4 (cyan)	4	0	12	4	0
5 (blue)	5	0	13	5	0
6 (magenta)	6	0	14	6	0
7 (white)	7	0	15	7	0
8	8	0			

and then asked:

Do you want to change any of the above parameters? <N>

AutoCAD allows you to assign an entity color to a certain pen number within your plotter. If you respond with a **Y**, AutoCAD asks you to correlate an entity color with a pen positioned in your plotter. Suppose, for example. that you have a wide pen in position 4 of your plotter. You would type **4** at the `Color 1 <1>:` prompt. Now AutoCAD will use this pen whenever it plots a red entity.

You have the option of either plotting to an external device (typically your plotter) or plotting to a disk file. When you are asked:

`Write the plot to a file? <Y>`

AutoCAD wants to know where to send the plot information. Plot files are convenient if you are sending a plot to a service bureau. The bureau can send a plot file directly to the plotter without needing the original drawing file.

To specify the size of your plots in metric units, you would answer **M** to the question:

`Size units (Inches or Millimeters) <I>:`

The default unit is inches.

To specify the location of the lower left corner from which the plotter should begin plotting, enter an X,Y coordinate at the prompt:

`Plot origin in Inches <0.00,0.00>:`

As the plotter loads the media, it scans for the edges of the sheet. It then will know the location of the lower left corner from which all plotting starts. This prompt is handy if you are placing several small plots on one sheet of paper and you want each plot to start at a different place.

AutoCAD then shows you a chart of standard AutoCAD sheet sizes and asks you to specify the size of the sheet on which you are plotting:

`Enter the Size or Width,Height (in Inches) <E>:`

This helps AutoCAD establish the largest area within which a plot may be created. Later, when you are asked for a plot scale, if AutoCAD calculates that the drawing will exceed the plot boundaries, the size of the plot will match the dimensions of the sheet you chose.

The next two prompts:

`Pen width <0.010>:`

and

`Adjust area fill boundaries for pen width? <N>`

are related to the way filled areas are generated on the plot. This is what happens: from the pen width you enter, AutoCAD calculates how many pen strokes will fill a solid area. If you are using very wide pens, you should adjust this value so that fewer strokes are used. The `Adjust area fill` prompt tells AutoCAD whether to pull in a half-pen width so that the boundaries of filled areas are as accurate as possible.

The `Remove hidden lines? <N>` prompt is necessary when you are producing a readable three-dimensional drawing. By entering **Y**, you ensure that lines which should be hidden by other objects are not shown on the final output.

Respond to the final plot prompt:

`Specify scale by entering: Plotted Inches=Drawing Units or Fit or ? <F>:`

by entering the scale at which you want the drawing plotted. AutoCAD will display the area within which the drawing will be plotted, wait for you to press Enter, and then start the plotting process.

Plotting Your Drawing on a Printer (PRPLOT)

If you have a printer for your CAD station, you can get a *printer plot* of your drawing. The advantage of a printer plot is that the time required to get a tangible image is greatly reduced. The disadvantage of a printer plot is the line quality. Although the quality of a printer plot is increasing with improved technology, few people will use a printer plot as their final output.

To get a printer plot of the drawing, use the PRPLOT command. The PRPLOT and PLOT commands have almost identical prompts. If you want a printer plot, enter **PRPLOT** and then proceed in exactly the way shown for the PLOT command.

Once again, to produce a hard-copy image of your drawing, use the PLOT command if you have a plotter; if you have a printer plotter, substitute the PRPLOT command for PLOT. The prompts for both commands are the same.

Summary

This chapter has explained how to obtain a hard copy of your drawing. You have learned the two fundamental commands used to obtain plots and printed plots. These commands are

❑ PLOT ❑ PRPLOT

Chapter 11, "Customizing Your Drawing Environment," will expand your knowledge of drawing, editing, and viewing. You will learn ways to make CAD drafting easier, faster, and more accurate. AutoCAD has become one of the most popular CAD packages because it allows modification of the CAD setup. This easy customization can improve your efficiency and personalize the final product.

Part III

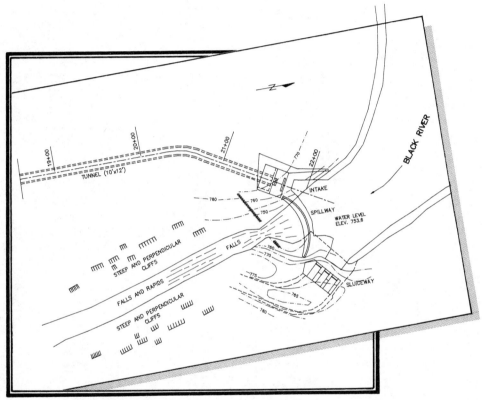

Drawing courtesy of R.L. Tomlinson Drafting & Blueprinting, Inc.
Thunder Bay, Ontario, Canada

Mastering Your AutoCAD Environment

CHAPTER 11

Customizing Your Drawing Environment

In Part II, you read about AutoCAD's drawing, editing, and view commands. These commands are important parts of your foundation for working in AutoCAD's Drawing Editor.

In this chapter, you will learn about some of the available shortcuts that you can use when working on a drawing. These shortcuts include handy commands that let you pick certain points on entities, keyboard toggles that change coordinate display or invoke printer output, and commands that can be used transparently from within other commands.

This chapter introduces several commands that will help you speed up your work within the AutoCAD environment. These drawing enhancement commands are

- ❏ GRID
- ❏ ORTHO
- ❏ ISOPLANE
- ❏ COLOR

- ❏ SNAP
- ❏ OSNAP
- ❏ AXIS
- ❏ LINETYPE

You will learn also about commands that retrieve information from the drawing database, and commands that can be used from within AutoCAD to manipulate or run files in the operating system. These commands include:

- ❏ LIMITS
- ❏ LIST
- ❏ DIST
- ❏ STATS
- ❏ RENAME

- ❏ ID
- ❏ DBLIST
- ❏ AREA
- ❏ TIME
- ❏ PURGE

❏ FILES   ❏ SHELL
❏ SH   ❏ CATALOG
❏ DIR   ❏ DEL
❏ TYPE

First we will look at the commands that speed up the drawing and editing process within AutoCAD. These commands, called *mode commands*, are AutoCAD drawing aids, just as T-squares and graph paper are aids to manual drafting; they relieve you of the drudgery of basic drafting techniques.

AutoCAD's Mode Commands

You already have used several AutoCAD mode commands while working on the sample drawing you have developed in the past few chapters. Whenever you used the INT function (to grab the intersection of two entities), or the PER function (to locate a point perpendicular to the point you are drawing), you used a subset of AutoCAD's Object Snap Mode, called Object Snap Override. AutoCAD supplies these functions as mode commands to simplify your work within the Drawing Editor.

This section discusses several AutoCAD mode commands: GRID, SNAP, ORTHO, OSNAP, ISOPLANE, and AXIS. You also will learn how to toggle these commands from the keyboard.

Setting a Grid (GRID)

When you invoke the GRID command, AutoCAD creates a grid that is similar to a sheet of graph paper. But AutoCAD's grid has no lines; it has points to indicate where its invisible lines would intersect. Further, AutoCAD's grid can be set to a different size at any time, or its points can be spaced unevenly. Try that with a piece of graph paper!

The grid has several uses within the Drawing Editor. First, it gives you an idea of your drawing's size. If your drawing if more than 200 dots long, for example, and you know that the grid dots are 12 inches apart, you have a better sense of the drawing's size than if it were on a blank background.

Second, using the grid with the SNAP command (discussed in the next section) is helpful when you create modular designs. If the sample drawing (the floor plan) had been designed on a 4-inch module, you could have set the grid points and the Snap increment to 4 inches and continued designing the rooms. Snap mode would make sure that all the points occurred at 4-inch intervals.

If you were at all unsure that what you were drawing was centered on your 4-inch grid, you could check your drawing visually by comparing the locations of the grid dots and the crosshairs.

When you type **GRID** at the `Command:` prompt and press Enter, you see the following option line:

`Grid spacing(X) or ON/OFF/Snap/Aspect <current>:`

The default selection, which is the current grid spacing shown within elbow brackets, lets you set the grid's X and Y values. If you enter a value representing a new `Grid spacing` and press Enter, the default is overridden and the grid spacing is set to the unit value you enter. The grid is turned on automatically when you either accept the default grid spacing or enter a new grid-spacing value. Figure 11.1 shows a drawing with a grid spacing of 12 inches.

Fig. 11.1. *The sample drawing with a 12" grid spacing.*

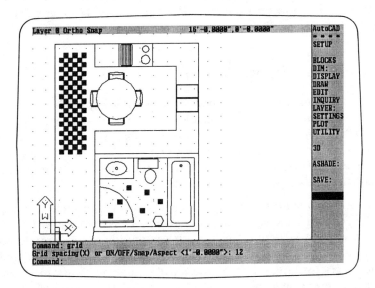

The `ON` option has the same effect as accepting the default grid-spacing value—it turns on the grid with the current grid spacing. `OFF` turns off the grid. You can turn the grid on or off from the command line, or by using one of two keyboard toggle switches: either the F7 function key or the Ctrl-G key combination. As the grid is switched on or off, the words <GRID ON> or <GRID OFF> are displayed on the Command: prompt line.

The grid spacing can be set to the same value as the Snap spacing. As mentioned earlier, the GRID and SNAP commands can complement each other to help you draw. If you want your grid to default to the Snap setting, type an uppercase **S** (for *Snap*) and press Enter.

Use the Aspect option if you want to set different X and Y values for the grid. AutoCAD prompts you first for the X value and then for the Y value. Remember to respond to both prompts. This is handy if you are dealing with modules of unequal dimensions, such as a 2-by-4-foot module that might be used in a drawing with a ceiling grid.

When you work with a large drawing area, you probably will need to set the grid spacing to a larger value. In an architectural application, for example, you may need to set your grid to 1, 2, or 4 feet, whereas in a mechanical application you might set the grid to 0.0125 inch. If your grid value is too small, based on your current view, AutoCAD may tell you Grid too dense to display. If this happens, use a larger value for your grid spacing. If the grid is no longer too dense, AutoCAD will redisplay it.

Using Snap Mode (SNAP)

The SNAP command provides an invisible reference grid. Because the SNAP and GRID commands are set separately, their values may differ. You can set your grid (the dots) for one value that remains visible on-screen, setting a smaller value for SNAP. The main difference between the SNAP and GRID commands is that the grid display is only for reference, whereas SNAP physically places the crosshairs at the specified increments.

The SNAP command's value is that it lets you easily lock onto a precise spacing interval for drawing commands. Snap mode is used also when you need to draw in a rigidly structured area. With Snap mode set on, you do not have to worry about the accuracy of your point placement because you are locked onto the precise spacing set up by the SNAP command. You can override the Snap spacing by entering absolute or relative points from the keyboard, or you can simply toggle off Snap mode by pressing F9 or Ctrl-S.

When you enter **SNAP** at the Command: prompt and press Enter, you see the following prompt:

Snap spacing or ON/OFF/Aspect/Rotate/Style <current>:

As in the prompt for the GRID command, the default Snap spacing is shown within elbow brackets. This command lets you set the snap spacing X and Y values. If you enter a value representing a new Snap spacing and press Enter, the default is overridden and the Snap spacing is set to the unit value you enter. The grid is turned on automatically when you either accept the default spacing or enter a new Snap-spacing value.

The ON option has the same effect as accepting the default Snap-spacing value; it turns on the Snap grid with the current Snap spacing. Likewise, OFF turns off Snap mode.

Snap mode, like Grid, can be turned on and off as you need it. You can toggle the Snap grid by typing **ON** or **OFF** at the Snap prompt, or by pressing F9 or Ctrl-B. When you activate Snap mode, the word SNAP appears on the status line; if you use the keyboard toggles, the words <SNAP ON> and <SNAP OFF> are displayed as Snap mode is turned on or off.

With SNAP, as with GRID, Aspect sets the X and Y spacings to different values. You are prompted first for the X value and then for the Y value.

You can rotate the grid and snap if you need to draw at an angle other than horizontal. By selecting Rotate, you affect both the visible grid and the invisible Snap mode. AutoCAD prompts you for a base point (the point around which the grid will be rotated). If you want to align the point with an entity, indicate the entity. Otherwise, leave the base point at 0,0. The Snap grid can be rotated at any angle from – 90 degrees to 90 degrees. When you finish drawing, always remember to rotate the grid back to 0 degrees.

The Style option lets you choose between standard drawing mode (the default) or isometric. (The isometric Snap mode is covered later in the chapter, in the discussion of ISOPLANE.)

Using Ortho Mode (ORTHO)

AutoCAD's Ortho mode lets you draw lines that are exactly perpendicular to each other within the drawing. This command is helpful when you need to draw lines that are strictly horizontal or vertical.

The ORTHO command is a toggle (ON or OFF); it has no other features. The status of Ortho mode, like that of AutoCAD's other modes, can be changed by toggle keys. Ortho mode can be turned on or off with either the F8 function key or the Ctrl-O key combination.

If you type **ORTHO** at the Command: prompt, the defaults are displayed:

ON/OFF <current>:

When Ortho mode is turned on, the word ORTHO appears in the status line at the top of your screen. If Ortho is toggled from the keyboard, the words <ORTHO ON> and <ORTHO OFF> are displayed on the Command: prompt line.

You can draw only horizontally or vertically when Ortho mode is active, regardless of the cursor's on-screen position. (Notice that the rubber-band line, which usually travels from the first point you picked to the crosshairs, will be drawn as a straight horizontal or vertical line only—not a diagonal line.) The direction in which you draw is determined by the change in the X value of the cursor movement compared to the change in the cursor's Y value. If you are drawing horizontally, the change in X is greater than the change in Y; conversely, the change in Y is greater than in X if you are drawing vertically.

If the Snap grid is on while you work with ORTHO, the crosshairs will be locked onto the grid and limited to horizontal or vertical lines. This can speed up your drawing. Using Ortho mode can save you a great deal of time when you need to draw perpendicular lines.

Locking onto Objects (OSNAP)

One form of the OSNAP command was discussed in Chapter 6, "The Basics of Drawing in AutoCAD." That form of OSNAP, called Object Snap Override, lets you pick certain points on an entity in response to a command prompt. With the OSNAP command, you permanently set the type of entity selection you want to perform. The OSNAP command works like this:

Prompt:	Response:	Explanation:
Command:	**OSNAP**	Starts OSNAP
Object snap modes:	Pick an OSNAP mode.	

You may recall (from Chapter 6) that the OSNAP modes include NEArest, ENDpoint, MIDpoint, CENter, NODe, QUAdrant, INTersection, INSert, PERpendicular, and TANgent. These modes give you the flexibility of being able to choose a specific point on an entity when AutoCAD prompts you to choose a point. Two other modes, QUIck and NONe, are applicable only when used with OSNAP. QUick mode forces AutoCAD to choose the first entity that matches the OSNAP request. NONe mode turns off OSNAP if it is using one of the other OSNAP modes to pick entities.

To use OSNAP, you type the name of one (or more) of the modes at the Object snap modes: prompt. When this happens, the on-screen crosshairs change to include a box centered on the crosshairs' intersection. This box, called an *aperture*, is used for targeting entities you want OSNAP to lock on to. When you pick an entity that is within the aperture box, AutoCAD will try to lock on to a point on that specific entity that matches the OSNAP mode you specified.

Creating Isometric Drawings (ISOPLANE)

Although AutoCAD has many advanced three-dimensional commands that let you build models of your plans, many disciplines still use isometric drawing as a method of showing an object in three dimensions. Isometric drawings are not "true" three-dimensional drawings because the lines in these drawings remain parallel to each other as they go back to the horizon. In a true three-dimensional drawing, usually called a *perspective* drawing, the lines converge at a point called the *vanishing point*.

In AutoCAD, isometric drawing is aided by the ISOPLANE command. This command sets the current isometric plane on which you are drawing. The command line for ISOPLANE looks like this:

Prompt:	Response:	Explanation:
Command:	**ISOPLANE**	Starts ISOPLANE
Left/Top/Right/(Toggle):	Specify which isometric plane.	

The Left isometric plane is defined by the 90- and 150-degree axis pair. The Top isometric plane is defined by the 30- and 150-degree axis pair, and the Right plane uses the 90- and 30-degree axis pair. The (Toggle) option lets you use the Enter key to move from one isoplane to the next. To toggle isoplane from the keyboard, use the Ctrl-E key combination.

The SNAP command can help you draw isometric entities. As mentioned earlier, the SNAP command has an option called Style. This option determines whether you use a normal Snap grid, arranged horizontally and vertically, or an isometric Snap grid whose points are rotated to help with your isometric drawing.

Temporary Ruler Lines (AXIS)

To place a temporary ruler line along the right side and the bottom of the drawing area, use the AXIS command. This command sets up ruler lines with tick marks at any increment you specify. The AXIS command prompts look like this:

Prompt:	Response:	Explanation:
Command:	**AXIS**	Starts AXIS
Tick spacing (X) or ON/OFF/Snap/ Aspect <current>:	Specify axis spacing.	

The options allow you to turn the AXIS line on and off, set the tick marks to the same spacing as the SNAP command, and set different X and Y tick spacings.

Overriding Layer Color (COLOR)

The LAYER command lets you set the color for a specific layer. The color's value determines the color of the entities residing on that layer. The specified layer color will apply also to any entities changed to that layer or drawn on that layer.

AutoCAD's COLOR command lets you override the default layer color for an entity. You can use this command to give a specified color to any entity you draw.

When you enter **COLOR** at the Command: prompt you will see the following prompt:

```
New entity color <current>:
```

You have several options at this prompt. If you press Enter, the current default color setting is accepted. If you want to change the color, enter the name or number of the color you want. Your two remaining options are BYLAYER and BYBLOCK, neither of which is case sensitive (you can enter them in any combination of upper- and lowercase letters).

If you type **BYLAYER**, any new entities drawn will default to the layer's color setting. Typing **BYBLOCK** causes the color of the entities to default to the color set for the block definition. (The color of a block is determined when you create the block, as you will learn in Chapter 12, "Expanding Your Horizons.")

Remember that after you override the color for a layer, the entities you draw with the new color will be set to override the current layer's color setting. If you change the color of the layer, the entities will not change color. If you want the entities to be the same color as the layer, use the CHANGE command to switch the color setting of the entity to BYLAYER. (CHANGE is discussed in Chapter 8, "Advanced Editing Commands.")

Overriding Layer Linetype (LINETYPE)

The linetype for entities can be overridden in the same way colors are overridden. By using the LINETYPE command, you can override the default layer linetype and create your own linetypes while working in AutoCAD. The creation of customized linetypes is beyond this book's scope. For more information, see Appendix B in the *AutoCAD Reference Manual*.

When you type **LINETYPE** at the `Command:` prompt, AutoCAD displays this prompt:

`?/Create/Load/Set:`

For a list of the linetypes available in a linetype file, select `?`. Then, at the `File to list <current>:` prompt, type the file's name. AutoCAD displays the list of linetypes and then returns you to the LINETYPE prompt.

Select `Create` if you want to create a linetype while working within a drawing. Once you create the linetype, you can use it within your drawing.

If the linetype you want to use is located in a file other than ACAD.LIN, you must load it before you can use it. To load a linetype, select `Load`; then tell AutoCAD the name of the linetype you want loaded. Linetypes are stored in files on disk. AutoCAD prompts you for the `File to search <current>:`. The default file will be either ACAD or a file you specify. You do not have to specify a file extension because AutoCAD assumes the .LIN extension. If the linetype is in the ACAD.LIN file, AutoCAD will load it automatically.

Use the `Set` option to set the linetype with which you will work. This option lets you override the default layer linetype. The specified linetype will then apply to all the entities you draw. *A word of caution:* If you draw a block in which some entities are set to layer default linetypes, others are set with linetype overrides, and still others are set to linetype BYBLOCK, inserting that block will result in a confusing mess. Some entities will retain the linetype you want but others will change to the layer default. To set the linetype, type its name at this prompt:

`New entity linetype (or ?) <current>:`

You have several options at this prompt. If you press Enter, the default (the current linetype setting) is accepted. If you want to change the linetype, type the name of the linetype you want. The two remaining options are BYLAYER and BYBLOCK, neither of which is case sensitive (you can enter them in any combination of upper- and lowercase letters).

As with all overrides, be careful about changing your drawing's entities. When you are first learning AutoCAD, overriding layer settings can cause confusion. You can expect a dashed linetype on the DASHED layer, for example, but if you use the LINETYPE command to set dashdot as the current linetype, you will be drawing with a dashdot linetype. If you are not sure whether the linetypes are overridden or defaulting to the layer linetype, use the CHANGE command to change every entity's linetype to BYLAYER. Then use CHANGE again to alter only specific entities to the linetype you need.

Consistent Linetypes at Any Scale (LTSCALE)

You can create a linetype by specifying a pattern definition in the file ACAD.LIN. This pattern tells AutoCAD the dash length, space length, and dot placement that make up a specific linetype. When you use different linetypes in large drawings, you may not see the linetype because the system variable that AutoCAD uses when scaling the linetypes for larger size drawings is set too small. This variable, called *LTSCALE*, controls the spacing of dashes and spaces in the linetype, in relation to the drawing's scale.

The LTSCALE variable's value should be set properly whenever you start a new drawing. Unfortunately, the AutoCAD SETUP routine, called from the screen menu, does not change this variable from its starting value of 1. To change the scale, enter **LTSCALE** at the Command: prompt. AutoCAD responds with the following prompt:

```
New scale factor <current>:
```

The new scale factor must be a value greater than *0*. LTSCALE typically is calculated by 12 × drawing scale. Thus, if your scale is 1″ = 20′-0″, your value for LTSCALE should be 240 (12 × 20). After you set the LTSCALE, be sure to execute a REGEN so that the linetypes are redisplayed with the new spacing. To do so, type **REGEN** at the Command: prompt, and press Enter.

Other Toggles

As you have seen, many mode commands can be toggled from the keyboard. Two other features (printer echo and coordinate display) can be toggled also.

The *printer echo* toggle, which is activated by the key combination Ctrl-Q, sends all AutoCAD prompts and responses to the printer as well as to the screen. This function is useful if on-screen information (such as a list of layers) is too complex simply to be written down. By typing Ctrl-Q and then using the usual AutoCAD commands, everything you type (and that AutoCAD answers) will go to the printer.

Coordinate display, which you can toggle by typing Ctrl-D, changes the coordinate readout in the upper right corner of the status line from static display to dynamic display. Static display shows only the crosshairs' coordinates when you use the pick button to respond to an AutoCAD command. Dynamic display, on the other hand, constantly tracks the crosshairs' position as they move around the screen. A ''distance < angle'' format also is displayed when the rubber-band cursor is on-screen (possibly when going from endpoint to endpoint of a line).

The F6 key, or Ctrl-D, will toggle through a three-step ''ring'' of possibilities: First is static, of course. Second is dynamic, tracking the cursor in relative Cartesian coordinates (or X,Y). Third is tracking in relative polar coordinates, or ''@dist <angle'' format. This is always the case.

Using Commands Transparently

Typically, AutoCAD allows only one command to be run at a time. But certain commands, called *transparent* commands, can be used within another command that is already running. Transparent commands can be used simply by typing an apostrophe (') at the beginning of the command's name.

The most frequently used transparent commands probably are the ZOOM, PAN and VIEW commands. These commands can be called from within drawing and editing commands; they expand AutoCAD's usefulness by not forcing you to have your full drawing shown in order to draw or edit entities.

To understand how a transparent command works, suppose that you are drawing a polyline, but the next point is off the screen. What do you do? Do you end the polyline, then use PAN to shift the screen over and start PLINE again? No way! You use 'PAN or 'ZOOM from *within* the PLINE command to move your view over to the new drawing area. It's that easy.

The following are some of the commands that can be used transparently:

- ❏ ZOOM
- ❏ PAN
- ❏ VIEW
- ❏ SETVAR
- ❏ HELP
- ❏ REDRAW

Commands that use pull-down menus and flip between the graphics and text screens also can be used transparently. The only restriction to using transparent commands is that they *cannot* force AutoCAD to perform a regeneration of the screen (like zooming outside the current drawing extents). AutoCAD will let you know if this occurs and cancel the transparent command.

Determining the Size of Your Drawing (LIMITS)

The *limits* of a drawing are the boundaries that define the drawing area. A drawing's limits are used by commands to make you aware of the area you have specified that you wish to draw within. These commands include GRID, ZOOM ALL, ZOOM DYNAMIC, and the commands used for drawing and editing entities.

To set these limits, use the LIMITS command. When you type **LIMITS** at the Command: prompt, AutoCAD displays the following prompt:

```
ON/OFF/<Lower left corner> <current>:
```

The LIMITS command lets you set a *limits check*—a beeping alarm that alerts you if you draw outside the limits. You use the first two options to turn this alarm on and off. As mentioned in Chapter 9, "Ways To View Your Drawing," two ZOOM command options (ALL and Dynamic) use limits to show viewing areas restricted by the imposed boundaries. The GRID command also uses LIMITS to determine the area within which to draw the grid.

The LIMITS command's default response is a coordinate specifying the lower left corner of your drawing area. The standard lower left corner for LIMITS is (0,0); it can actually be anywhere to the lower left of your drawing. If you want to accept 0,0 as the lower left corner, press Enter. If you want to indicate a different lower left corner, either digitize a point or type the point's X and Y values in X,Y fashion.

After you indicate the lower left corner, AutoCAD prompts you for the drawing's upper right corner:

```
Upper right corner <current>:
```

Remember to enter the X value first, followed by the Y value. If you want to set the limits so that your drawings fit an 8 1/2-inch-by-11-inch sheet of paper, with the long side horizontal, type **11,8.5** at this prompt. For larger sizes, simply type the horizontal length, a comma, and the vertical length; then press Enter. You can indicate this corner also by picking a point in the drawing's upper right corner. To see the new drawing size, do a ZOOM ALL. You can practice using the LIMITS command by setting the limits in your sample drawing.

The LIMITS command is useful because it tells you when you are drawing outside your drawing's designated boundaries. If you know that you can draw in a limited area only, and that you must stay within certain boundaries, turning the limit checking to ON will alert you if you exceed those boundaries. Remember, you do not *need* to have limit checking enabled. It is there for your convenience.

Getting Information from AutoCAD

You probably have noticed that AutoCAD keeps a great deal of information about each entity in a drawing. For AutoCAD to function as expected, several other pieces of information (system variables, for example) also must be maintained.

AutoCAD keeps all this information in a *database*. This database, which is maintained within the drawing file, is simply an organized structure designed to store the information generated by AutoCAD. You can use a variety of informational commands to extract and view this information.

Identifying Points (ID)

The ID command can be used to return positional information about a specified point in your drawing. When you type **ID** at the Command: prompt, AutoCAD responds with the following prompt:

Point:

If you use your pointing device to select a point in your drawing, the X,Y,Z coordinates for the point are returned. Typically, the Z coordinate will be equal to the current elevation for the plane on which the point is located (usually the current UCS). However, if you use an OSNAP mode to snap to a point of a three-dimensional object, the Z coordinate will be the true elevation for the selected point.

If, instead of selecting a point, you enter the point's X,Y,Z coordinates, AutoCAD places a blip on-screen to indicate the point's position. Note that this is different from points created with the POINT command. ID does not insert a point. It simply indicates the location of the coordinates you entered.

Retrieving Entity Information (LIST and DBLIST)

When you need information about entities within your drawing, use the LIST and DBLIST (DataBase LIST) commands. The needed information appears on-screen after the Command: prompt. (The information will NOT appear on the graphics screen after the Command: prompt. The screen will flip to text, clear itself, and then display the requested information.)

Use the LIST command to get information about specific entities within the drawing on which you are working. When you type **LIST** at the Command:

prompt, AutoCAD asks you to choose the entities you want to list. If you were to ask LIST for information about one of the lines in the tub in the sample drawing, for example, the following information might be returned:

```
      LINE
from point,   X= 6'-8 1/16"  Y=4'-6 1/16"
  to point,   X=6'-8 15/16"  Y=0'-6 1/16"
    length   =       4'-0", angle = S 1d3'39" E
   delta X   = 0'-0 7/8", delta Y=      -4'-0"
```

The information returned by LIST will contain any specific details regarding the entity you select. (*Specific*, in this instance, means information about line endpoints, current layer, color or linetype overrides, and the exact type of entity.)

Using DBLIST is similar to using LIST, but DBLIST selects and reports on every entity in your drawing. The information returned is the same for each entity as it is in LIST, as is the formatting. Although DBLIST may list a whole drawing (a process that can take anywhere from 10 minutes to 2 hours), it usually is too cumbersome to be used effectively.

The Ctrl-Q toggle would be handy in this instance. You just toggle on the printer and type in **DBLIST**. In a few minutes, your entire database will be printed. This can be handy for finding things like nested blocks whose names you have forgotten, comparing the structure of one block with the printout of another, and so forth.

If you want to stop the listing, press Ctrl-S. Then press any key to resume listing. Or you can press the Pause key to stop and then press Enter to resume. To cancel the listing, press Ctrl-C.

Getting Distances (DIST)

The DIST command gives you the distance between any two points that you pick within a drawing. This function is handy for checking clearances between different objects.

When **DIST** is entered at the Command: prompt, AutoCAD asks for a first and second point; then it provides you with information similar to the following:

```
Distance = 4'-6 1/2", Angle = S 1d3'39" E
delta X  =  0'-0 7/8", delta Y=      -4'-0"
```

Calculating Area (AREA)

The AREA command is used for calculating the area of any object. AutoCAD maintains a running total of the area at all times. Any "holes" in objects like circles or polylines can be subtracted from this running total so that only the area you need is calculated.

When you type **AREA** at the `Command:` prompt, AutoCAD displays the following prompt:

`<First point>/Entity/Add/Subtract:`

The `First point` option is the default. You can enter points clockwise or counterclockwise. You do not have to indicate the first point again because AutoCAD retains it as the original starting point. AutoCAD automatically closes the area back to your starting point.

The `Entity` option calculates the area of a specific circle or polyline. If you choose this option, AutoCAD prompts you to

`Select circle or polyline:`

If you choose a circle, its circumference and area are displayed; if you choose a polyline, AutoCAD displays its perimeter length and area.

Using the `Add` and `Subtract` options, you can add or subtract, respectively, the results derived from the current area calculations to or from the results of earlier calculations. AutoCAD keeps a running total of the area, based on the entities you select.

You can use the AREA command to find out the square footage of the bathroom in the sample drawing. To do so, follow this command sequence:

Prompt:	Response:	Explanation:
`Command:`	**AREA**	Starts AREA
`<First point>/Entity/Add/` `   Subtract:`	**INT**	First corner of bathroom walls
`Next point:`	**INT**	Second corner
`Next point:`	**INT**	Third corner
`Next point:`	**INT**	Fourth corner
`Next point:`	Press Enter.	Back to start point

`AREA = 5040.00 square in. (35.0000 square ft.) perimeter = 24'-0''`

Getting the Status of Your Drawings (STATUS)

The STATUS command is important because of the information it provides about your drawing. STATUS generates the following information:

❑ Toggle settings
❑ Drawing extents
❑ Drawing limits
❑ Disk space available
❑ I/O page space available
❑ Layer settings

To use the command, type **STATUS** at the Command: prompt and press Enter. The following example is the report AutoCAD generated based on our sample drawing. Yours may be slightly different, but this gives you an idea of the output provided:

```
 321 entities in EXAMPLE
Limits are         X:    -3'-8"        7'-9"   (Off)
                   Y:   -10'-9"       13'-10"
Drawing uses       X:    -3'-4"        9'-4 7/8" **Over
                   Y:    13'-4"       30'-0 1/16"
Display shows      X:    -4'-11 3/16" 30'-0 1/16"
                   Y:   -11'-3 1/2"   16'-3 1/2"
Insertion base is  X:     0'-0"    Y:   0'-0"        Z:    0'-0"
Snap resolution is X:     0'-1"    Y:   0'-0"
Grid spacing is    X:     0'-0     Y:   0'-0"

Current layer:     0
Current color:     BYLAYER -- 7 (white)
Current linetype: BYLAYER -- CONTINUOUS
Current elevation:    0'-0"  thickness:     0'-0"
Axis off  Fill on  Grid off  Ortho off  Qtext off  Snap off
Tablet off
Object snap modes: None
Free RAM: 8672 bytes      Free disk: 19361792 bytes
I/O page space:  81K bytes  Extended I/O page space: 256K bytes

Command:
```

Working with Time (TIME)

AutoCAD's internal clock keeps track of the current time and date and uses this for maintaining key information about your drawing. The information displayed by the TIME command contains:

- ❏ Date and time the drawing was created
- ❏ Date and time the drawing was last updated
- ❏ Date and time used on an elapsed timer

AutoCAD's clock is based on the DOS clock. If you rely on this AutoCAD feature, be sure your DOS clock is set correctly.

When you type **TIME** at the Command: prompt, AutoCAD returns several pieces of information. The display on your screen will be similar to the following:

```
Command: time

Current time:            12 Oct 1988 at 16:25:03.180
Drawing created:         03 Oct 1988 at 13:59:51.000
Drawing last updated:    12 Oct 1988 at 12:38:20.770
Time in drawing editor:  0 days 02:46:46.990
Elapsed timer:           0 days 02:46:46.990
Timer on.
Display/ON/OFF/Reset:
```

Notice the prompt that appears right after the display:

```
Display/ON/OFF/Reset:
```

If you want to see the display again (updated for the elapsed time, of course), choose the Display option. ON turns on the elapsed timer if it has been turned off. OFF turns off the elapsed timer. Select Reset to reset the elapsed timer to 0 and turn it on.

The TIME display itself contains the following information:

Drawing created is the date and time the current drawing was created. This prompt is set when you execute Main Menu Option 1 (Begin NEW Drawing) or use the WBLOCK command (discussed in Chapter 13).

Drawing last updated is the last time you updated the current file. This prompt, which is set initially when you create the drawing, is updated whenever you use the SAVE or END commands.

Time in drawing editor is the total amount of time spent in the Drawing Editor with this drawing. This includes all times that the drawing was started and ended. (If the QUIT command was used at any point, however, the time in the Drawing Editor is unaccounted for.)

Elapsed timer is the amount of time you have spent in the Drawing Editor this session (provided that you have not reset the timer). Whenever you reset the timer, it starts from 0. This also is a nice timer if you keep track of your time within the drawing. If you need to step away from the drawing (to go to lunch, for example) but do not want to END it, use Reset and then issue the Display command when you get back. The elapsed time will show you how long you have been away from the drawing.

Changing Names (RENAME)

As you know, you can name several AutoCAD components: library blocks, views, layers, text styles, etc. But what happens if you want to change the name you have been using for one of these objects? You use the RENAME command!

You can use the RENAME command to change the name of any of the following objects:

- ❏ Layers
- ❏ Library blocks
- ❏ Linetypes
- ❏ Text styles
- ❏ User Coordinate Systems (UCS)
- ❏ Views
- ❏ Viewport configurations

This supposes, of course, that you already have named the object you want to rename. For example, you can create a UCS, but you do not necessarily have to give it a name. The RENAME command works only on objects you have named. Note also that RENAME cannot be used to change the name of layer 0 (it must remain layer 0) or the CONTINUOUS linetype.

When you enter **RENAME** at the Command: prompt, AutoCAD responds with the following prompt:

Block/LAyer/LType/Style/Ucs/VIew/VPort:

This lets you specify the type of object you want to rename. For instance, if you want to rename a layer, you enter **layer** (or simply type **LA**).

After you select the type of object you want to rename, AutoCAD asks for the object's old name. The exact prompt will vary according to the type of object you are renaming. If you enter a name that refers to a nonexistent object, AutoCAD generates an error message and ends the RENAME command.

After you enter the object's old name, AutoCAD asks for the new name. Enter a valid AutoCAD object name. That's all there is to it. If the name you enter is currently being used for another object, AutoCAD will tell you so and will not make the change.

Removing Unwanted Baggage (PURGE)

After you have worked with a drawing for some time, you no longer need certain objects that you have named. For instance, that library block of a widget (which took you ages to create) has been been rendered unnecessary by a recent change in specifications. The problem is that the block is still in the drawing database, taking up space and slowing down AutoCAD's operation.

The PURGE command allows you to remove groups of named objects from a drawing. This command can be used to remove the following types of *unused* objects:

- ❑ Layers
- ❑ Library blocks
- ❑ Linetypes
- ❑ Shapes
- ❑ Text styles

Notice that fewer types of named objects can be deleted than can be renamed with the RENAME command. (The commands for certain named objects [such as viewports, views, and UCSs] have their own built-in deletion capabilities.)

PURGE removes only objects that are *not* being used in a drawing. Thus, if you want to remove 15 defined library blocks, PURGE will delete only those that are not inserted in your drawing.

When you type **PURGE** at the Command: prompt, AutoCAD responds in the following manner:

Blocks/LAyers/LTypes/SHapes/STyles/All:

Again, specify the type of objects you want to delete. For instance, if you want to delete all unreferenced library blocks, type **blocks** (or simply **B**).

After you select the type of objects you want to delete, AutoCAD goes into action. It checks the AutoCAD database to see whether any named objects of the specified type are not referenced within the drawing and, if one is found, deletes it.

PURGE checks through the database just once (whenever the command is invoked). Thus, if you choose the All option to delete all unreferenced objects, and a text style is used only within a library block that is to be deleted, AutoCAD does not recognize that the text style is no longer needed. To be sure that all extraneous objects actually are deleted, you need to do several purges, saving your drawing and exiting/restarting AutoCAD between the purges.

AutoCAD File Operations (FILES)

Frequently, you may need to get a list of files, delete a file, or rename a file while you are working in the Drawing Editor. You can do any of these functions (and others) by using the FILES command.

When you type **FILES** at the Command: prompt, you are taken immediately to AutoCAD's File Utility menu (the one described in detail in Chapter 1). From this menu you can do the following tasks:

❑ List drawing files
❑ List other files
❑ Delete files
❑ Rename files
❑ Copy files

If you need help using the File Utility menu, refer to Chapter 1, ''A Quick Start in AutoCAD.''

Accessing DOS (SHELL, SH)

If you want to access DOS while you are working in AutoCAD, you can do so with AutoCAD's SHELL or SH command. Both commands let you exit the Drawing Editor temporarily so that you can execute DOS commands.

SHELL, the more fully functional of the two commands, allows you to execute virtually any DOS command. SHELL allocates more memory than does SH— memory in which the DOS commands can function.

When you type either **SHELL** or **SH** at the Command: prompt, AutoCAD displays this prompt:

DOS command:

Here you have two choices. If you enter a DOS command, it will be executed and you will be returned to the Command: prompt. (You can use spaces and commas in your response to the DOS command: prompt.)

If, instead of typing a DOS command, you simply press Enter, you are allowed repeated DOS commands. A portion of your computer's memory is set aside for a new copy of DOS. This copy of DOS is loaded and executed and a regular DOS prompt is displayed. At this point, you can enter virtually any DOS command you want. You will be returned to the `Command:` prompt only when you type **EXIT** at the DOS prompt.

If, when you try to execute a DOS command by using SH, you receive an error message indicating that there is not enough memory available, try the same command with SHELL. If you receive the message again, you are trying to execute a command or program that takes too much memory to function. You must exit AutoCAD to run the other program or command.

Because the SH command allocates less memory for execution of a command than does SHELL, you need to understand that SH works only for DOS commands that require very little memory. Examples of such commands are COPY, DEL, DIR, and TYPE. These commands, which DOS manuals call *internal DOS commands*, are an integral part of DOS. You may want to refer to a good DOS book for more information on this topic.

Other DOS Operations

A few miscellaneous external commands come with AutoCAD. They closely parallel DOS commands.

CATALOG and DIR both allow you to view a file directory. When you type **CATALOG**, you will see the following prompt:

`Files:`

When you type **DIR**, this prompt appears:

`File specification:`

In both instances, you should give a file specification for the files you want to view. (You can use the wild-card characters * and ?.)

The difference between CATALOG and DIR is that DIR (which corresponds to the DOS command of the same name) gives you a normal DOS directory, whereas CATALOG (which corresponds to the DOS command DIR /W) simply gives you a list of files, arranged in columns.

DEL deletes files for you. When you type **DEL** at the `Command:` prompt, AutoCAD responds:

`File to delete:`

Specify the name of the file you want to delete. As with the directory commands, you can use wild-card characters in the file specification. This command corresponds directly to the DOS DEL command.

Beware: If you type **DEL *.***, you are telling DOS to delete *all* files. Be sure that you really want to do this. To clear a floppy disk, insert the disk in the drive and type **DEL a:*.*** or **DEL b:*.*** to indicate the floppy disk drive rather than the hard drive. A prompt asks whether you are sure. Answer **Y** or **N** and press Enter.

The EDIT command causes execution of EDLIN, the DOS line editor. EDLIN (a capable editor, but extremely limited in what it will do) should be used only for *very* short files. When you type **EDIT** at the Command: prompt, AutoCAD will ask:

File to edit:

You should specify a full file name. Do not use wild-card characters. The use of EDLIN is beyond the scope of this book but is covered in many DOS books.

You use the TYPE command when you want to view the contents of a normal ASCII file. When you enter **TYPE** at the DOS prompt, AutoCAD responds:

File to list:

Here, as with the EDIT command, you should enter the full name of the file. No wild cards are allowed. This command corresponds directly to the DOS TYPE command.

Summary

This chapter has shown you a few AutoCAD commands that will speed up your work by providing many of the tools used in manual drafting. To make these tools easier for you to use, AutoCAD provides keyboard toggles that give you the flexibility of turning on and off the tools you need without having to issue a new command.

You also have learned many AutoCAD commands that give you specific information about entities, drawing boundaries, and drawing status. Used properly, these commands will help you make more efficient use of the time you spend working in AutoCAD. They relieve you of the guesswork associated with keeping track of time, calculating areas of odd-sided figures, and monitoring your drawing's status.

Chapter 12, "Expanding Your Horizons," will discuss many other ways to enhance your drawing. These methods include using AutoCAD to figure all the dimensioning of a floor plan, as well as labeling key parts of the floor plan.

Expanding Your Horizons

So far, working on the sample drawing has shown you how to use AutoCAD to turn basic lines, arcs, and circles into entities with meaning. You have seen how to use AutoCAD's editing commands to reproduce and enhance these objects, and how to use some of AutoCAD's more helpful drafting aids. And you have learned ways to view different parts of your drawing.

Essentially, however, all you have is a pretty picture. It still lacks *body*. This chapter will show you ways to give your drawing some depth and meaning through the use of text, hatch patterns, and dimensions. All of these will work toward making your drawing a more complete document.

This chapter introduces you to the following commands:

❏ TEXT   ❏ HATCH
❏ DTEXT   ❏ SKETCH
❏ QTEXT   ❏ DIM
❏ STYLE   ❏ DIM1

By using these commands, you can draw your audience's attention to specific elements of your drawings and make your design's purpose clear. These commands will also help you give your drawings a finished look.

Working with Text

No drawing is complete until important information has been labeled. On a floor plan, for example, rooms need to be given names. Machine shop drawings require notes about assembly procedures, and computer chip blueprints must give detailed information about transistor materials or electrical capacities. This section will show you how to add such text to your drawings.

285

AutoCAD's text facilities are powerful. They give you the ability to assign different font styles to your text, enter notes in any fashion, and even to alter the property of text in order to speed up drawing regeneration.

The following pages will show you how to enhance your sample drawing by adding text labels. As with the previous chapters, your sample drawing should be on-screen and you should be ready to go to work. If not, load the sample drawing and start learning the intricacies of working with text in AutoCAD.

Inserting Text into A Drawing (TEXT)

Currently, there are only two AutoCAD commands for entering notes and labels into your drawing: TEXT and DTEXT. DTEXT is discussed in the next section. The TEXT command is the basic method of adding text entities to your drawing.

The TEXT command offers several options for fitting text within the drawing. These options are displayed on the command line after you enter **TEXT** at the `Command:` prompt. The TEXT option line looks like this:

`Start point or Align/Center/Fit/Middle/Right/Style:`

The first six options—`Start point`, `Align`, `Center`, `Fit`, `Middle`, and `Right`—deal with the method by which text strings are formatted. These options, which give you tremendous flexibility in creating your text's "look," will be discussed shortly.

The `Style` option lets you change the style, or font, of the text AutoCAD inserts into your drawing. The AutoCAD program includes more than 15 font styles, ranging from single-stroke Roman to multistroke Gothic lettering. A little preparation is required before you can use many of these styles; this will be covered in the section on the STYLE command.

`Start point` is AutoCAD's default method for inserting text strings in a drawing. To use this option, you simply choose a starting point (either by picking a point or giving an X,Y coordinate) for your text. Any text that you enter will start at this point and continue to the right. The start point is, in effect, the text's extreme left position. Once you have chosen the start point, AutoCAD will ask for the following:

`Height<default>:`
`Rotation angle<0>:`
`Text:`

`Height` refers to the height of the text you want to place in the drawing. This value, which can range from 1/32 inch to two miles (and more!), depends mainly on the size of the plot you plan to create. The text height's <default> value is simply the same as the size of the last text entity entered.

The Rotation angle prompt allows you to rotate your text to any angle. This can be especially helpful for entering text along sloped lines. To have your text rotated 90 degrees, for example, you would enter **90** at this prompt.

The final prompt, Text:, asks for the text to be entered into the drawing. A variation on these three prompts (rotation, height, and text) is used by AutoCAD regardless of the TEXT option you choose for entering text.

Justifying Text (TEXT *Align* and TEXT *Fit*)

The TEXT prompt's Align option will place text between two specified points while adjusting the text's height so that it looks natural. This keeps the text string from appearing oddly stretched as it is made to fit between the two points.

AutoCAD asks first for a start and finish point, and then for the text string itself. Although you can specify a rotation when you enter the two points, AutoCAD will not ask for the Rotation angle<0>:. Further, because AutoCAD adjusts the height to make the text appear natural, you will not be asked to specify a text height.

The Fit option is similar to Align. AutoCAD prompts you for beginning and ending points, but then allows you to specify a text height. As with Align, AutoCAD adjusts the text's width so that the text string is stretched or compressed to fit between the two points. The only difference is that Fit does not alter the text's height (as Align does). It remains at the height you specify.

Figure 12.1 shows text that has been placed in a drawing by the Align and Fit options. Both have the same width, but the Fit option distorts the text font, based on the specified height.

Centering Text (TEXT *Center* and TEXT *Middle*)

To center the text, select Center: and enter a center point. The text is placed in your drawing with the center point of the text's baseline at the point you specify. Once a center point is chosen, AutoCAD will ask the three questions described in the section on the Start point option.

Middle is similar to the Center option. Its advantage, however, is that it not only centers the text from left and right, but also up and down. When the text is inserted, it is centered both horizontally and vertically in the text string.

Fig. 12.1. Aligned and fitted text.

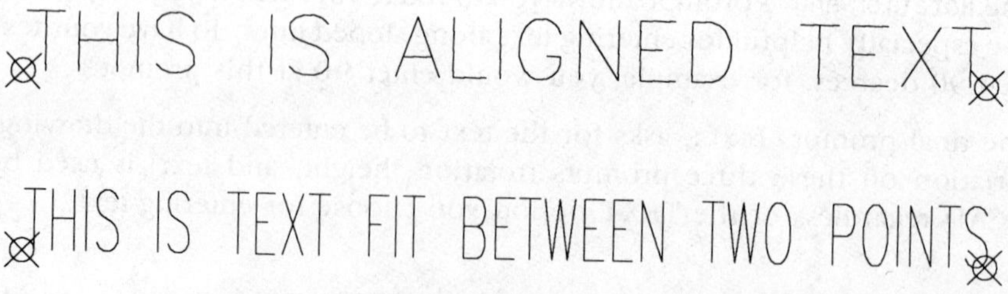

THIS IS ALIGNED TEXT

THIS IS TEXT FIT BETWEEN TWO POINTS

Figure 12.2 shows the effects of the Center and Middle options on text. In this figure, two lines show the point specified as the center point.

Fig. 12.2. Center and middle aligned text.

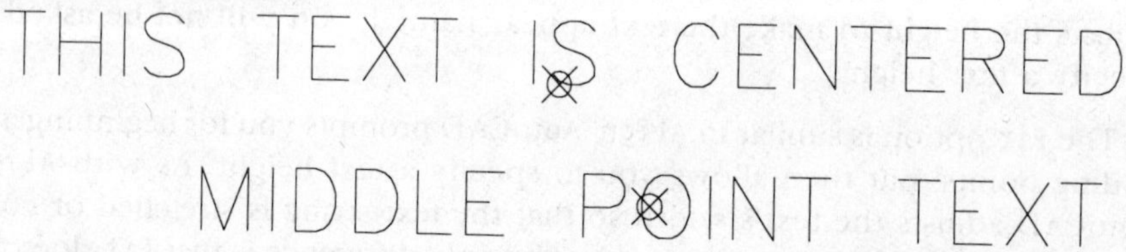

THIS TEXT IS CENTERED

MIDDLE POINT TEXT

Right-justifying Text (TEXT *Right*)

If you used the TEXT option to specify a starting point for your text, you caused the text to be left-justified according to the point you indicated. But what if you want to specify an *ending* point for the text you enter? Like many word processors, AutoCAD lets you right-justify your text; this is done with the Right option.

The example in figure 12.3 shows how right-justified text looks.

Putting TEXT To Work

The TEXT command has no typical defaults (no options enclosed in angle brackets), although once you choose a method of inserting text, you can use default values for rotation angle and text height. If you press Enter (without

Fig. 12.3. Right-justified text.

RIGHT ALIGNED TEXT

explicitly specifying an option), AutoCAD will use the last text entity entered to control entry of the new text. This means that if your last text entity was centered, rotated 50 degrees, and was 1/4 inch in height, AutoCAD creates your next text entity with the same properties (unless you specifically assign new properties to the text).

To insert a paragraph with the TEXT command, type the first line of the paragraph. This will set up the parameters for the text to follow. When you finish typing the first line, press Enter to get back to the Command: prompt. Then press Enter again to execute the TEXT command a second time, and press Enter once more to accept the previous text string's defaults. Notice that when you execute the TEXT command the second time, the most recently entered piece of text is highlighted so that you can easily find its location. The new line of text will be placed immediately below it.

In addition to letters and numbers, you can insert special formatting characters along with your text. To do so, you embed the characters (and the codes that activate them) in the text you type. A list of these codes follows:

Code	Character
%%o	Overscore
%%u	Underscore
%%d	Degrees symbol
%%p	Plus/minus symbol
%%c	Circle diameter
%%%	Percent sign
%%nnn	ASCII character with decimal code "nnn"

To create the lines of text shown in figure 12.4, for example, type the following responses at the Text: prompt:

Prompt:	Response:
Text:	%%oOVERSCORE%%o and %%uUNDERSCORE%%u TEXT
Text:	DEGREE SYMBOLS --> 90%%d
Text:	DIAMETER SYMBOLS --> 4.6"%%c
Text:	TOLERANCES --> %%p.005"

Fig. 12.4. *The results of using special formatting characters.*

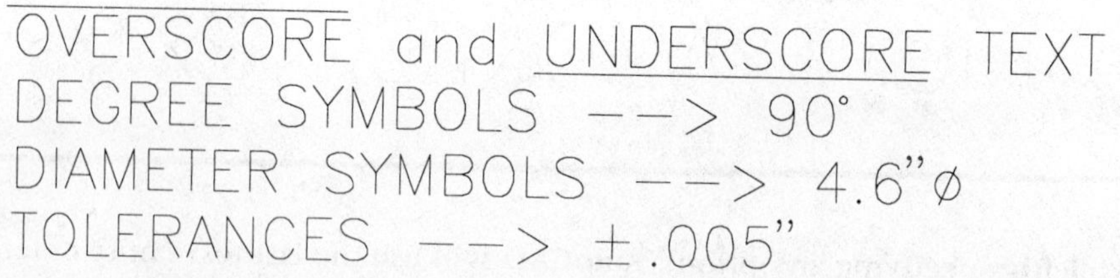

```
OVERSCORE and UNDERSCORE TEXT
DEGREE SYMBOLS --> 90°
DIAMETER SYMBOLS --> 4.6"ø
TOLERANCES --> ±.005"
```

As mentioned in Chapter 8, "Advanced Editing Commands," text entities can be modified through use of the CHANGE command. Properties that can be changed include the insertion point location, style, height, rotation angle, and the text string itself. The only property that cannot be changed is the placement of text (Centered, Fit, etc.) in the drawing. If you want to change the method of placement, you must retype the text from scratch.

The Second Way To Insert Text (DTEXT)

Although TEXT and DTEXT are alike in that they can insert text into a drawing, their main difference lies in the fact that DTEXT (which stands for *Dynamic TEXT*) allows you to enter several lines of text at one time. Not only can you enter several lines, but you also can perform some crude editing of previous lines of text without having to use the CHANGE command.

DTEXT has all of the options available with the TEXT command; functionally, the two commands are the same. As stated previously, however, you can enter more than one line of text at a time by using DTEXT. AutoCAD will even display the text in your drawing as you type it, so that you can be sure it is placed correctly. As AutoCAD displays the text you are typing, a white box is displayed ahead of your letters. This box, which is similar to a cursor, is used to show you where your text is being placed. The example in figure 12.5 shows the location of this box in relation to the text you are typing.

Editing incorrect text is also easier with DTEXT. If you are entering multiple lines of text and notice an error a few lines back, you can use the Backspace key to go backward over previous text to correct the error. This is extremely handy, but unfortunately, as you backspace to reach your error, you erase the text you have just typed. If your error is more than three lines back, it probably will be easier simply to finish typing and then use the CHANGE command to make corrections.

Fig. 12.5. The dynamic text box.

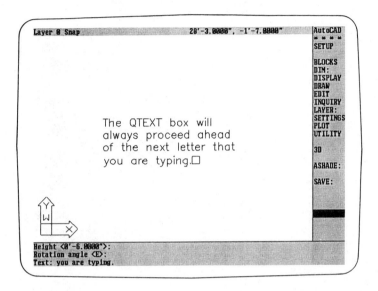

Speeding Drawing Regenerations (QTEXT)

Chapter 8, "Advanced Editing Commands," discussed a method for speeding up drawing regeneration. That method, which uses the LAYER FREEZE command, effectively allows AutoCAD to bypass any entities on frozen layers when recreating the drawing. The QTEXT command does something similar, but only for text entities.

The QTEXT command draws a box where the text string normally is displayed, thus cutting down the time needed for AutoCAD to draw all the lines that make up the text characters. The text is still in the drawing database, but it is not regenerated on the screen—only the box is displayed. This box is the same width and height as the text that normally would occupy that location in the drawing. Figure 12.6 shows the effect of turning QTEXT ON with the text shown in figure 12.5.

QTEXT is similar to the toggle commands described in Chapter 11; its only value is on or off. When you enter **QTEXT** at the Command: prompt, you must specify ON if you want boxes to be drawn, or OFF if you want the text to be displayed normally. *Every* text entity within the drawing will be changed to

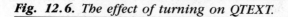

Fig. 12.6. *The effect of turning on QTEXT.*

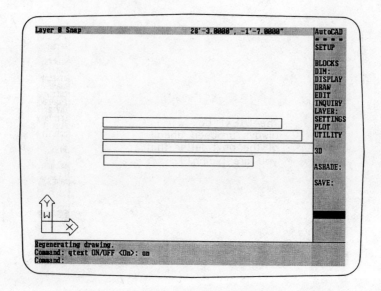

a marking box if QTEXT is turned on. After turning QTEXT off, you may have to use REGEN in order to display the text correctly.

Loading Text Fonts (STYLE)

Although AutoCAD has a few features you could find in a word processing package, it also is somewhat like a desktop publishing package. Within AutoCAD you can manipulate both text and graphics to suit your needs. And, much like a good desktop publishing program, AutoCAD can use different character fonts to show text differently.

To load a different text font, you need to use AutoCAD's STYLE command. This command is different from the Style option found in the TEXT and DTEXT commands. When you ask AutoCAD to load a font into a drawing, you need to know several pieces of information:

❏ The style name: a 31-character name for this font

❏ The name of the *font file* after which you will pattern the font

❏ A fixed or variable text height

❑ Width factor

❑ Slant angle

❑ And, if permitted, whether the text is to be drawn backward, upside down, or vertically

Let's walk through the steps involved in loading a font style that is different from the default font. To do this, use the following command sequence:

Prompt:	Response:	Explanation:
Command:	**STYLE**	Starts STYLE command
Text style name (or ?) <STANDARD>	**OURTEXT**	Name you will call style in drawing
Font File <TXT>:	**ROMANS**	File containing character definitions
Height <0>:	Press Enter.	Letter height (if you need it to stay consistent)
Width factor <1>:	Press Enter.	Value to stretch or compress letters
Obliquing angle <0>:	Press Enter.	Value for a slant
Backwards? <N>	Press Enter.	Don't draw letters backwards.
Upside-down? <N>	Press Enter.	Don't draw letters upside-down.
Vertical? <N>	Press Enter.	Don't draw letters vertically.

The Text style name is a 31-character name with which to call the text file *within* AutoCAD. If, instead of giving a style name, you enter **?**, AutoCAD will list all the font styles currently available in the drawing. Font file is the name of a hard disk file with an .SHX extension. This file contains the actual character definition. The Height option lets you set a permanent height for the style you have selected. Once set, this uniform height will be maintained whenever that style is used; you will not be prompted for a height during future uses of the style in TEXT or DTEXT. It usually is better, however, to leave this setting at

0, so that you can select an appropriate character height whenever you use the font.

The Width factor option allows you to compress or stretch the individual characters' width. A default of 1 means that the characters are not modified at all. You can give the characters a slanted look by setting the value of Obliquing angle between −15 and 15 degrees. All text entered with this style will have that slant. The final three options, Backwards, Upside-down and Vertical, depend entirely on how the character definitions were created in the font file. Many of the AutoCAD-supplied fonts can use these options, but a few, like the map and musical symbols, do not. The only way to find out is to load the font file and see what happens.

As stated earlier, the AutoCAD program comes with more than 15 font files that can be used in a variety of ways. Figure 12.7 shows three of those font styles. Any font style can be loaded as shown in the previous example. The Standard font style is *always* loaded when you create a new drawing. AutoCAD also has font files that contain map and weather symbols. For a complete listing of these font files, see Appendix B of the *AutoCAD Reference Manual*.

Fig. 12.7. Three standard AutoCAD fonts and their font file names.

Just because AutoCAD comes with 15 different text styles, you should not assume that it is limited to just these 15. You can also create your own text fonts or purchase fonts created by others (like symbol libraries). These can be used within your drawings.

If you can use the Advanced User Interface's pull-down menus, there is an easier method for loading fonts. If you select FONTS from the Options pull-down menu, you will be shown slides of the available font styles. You can select a style from this pull-down menu; AutoCAD will automatically load a style name and font file for you. Then, just answer the final STYLE questions, starting with text height. Figure 12.8 shows the dialogue box that appears when you choose this pull-down menu option.

Fig. 12.8. The pull-down fonts menu.

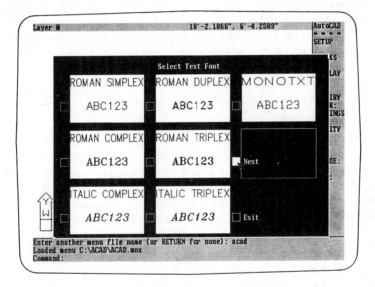

Hatching

Text is effective for indicating items of special interest, but there are times when a simple pattern may more effectively convey what you are drawing. This pattern can be anything—from a brick wall to a piece of metal to sod. With AutoCAD's HATCH command, you can use specially created patterns to indicate different materials or items in your drawing.

Proper Text Height at Any Drawing Scale

Chapter 11, "Customizing Your Drawing Environment," discussed a system variable that controls how linetypes are drawn at differing scales. That variable, LTSCALE, is used to hold a value relating to the scale of the drawing you are creating. The LTSCALE variable can be handy for creating text that has the proper height when your drawing is plotted.

In Chapter 10, "Plotting Your Drawing," and even back in Chapter 2, "AutoCAD—Manual versus Computer Drafting," we discussed how most of a drawing is created at full scale and then, when you plot the drawing, you assign a scale to make the drawing fit your paper. If you use the LTSCALE variable properly within your drawing, your linetypes will have the proper dash and space relationship when the drawing is plotted. Text is a different matter. If you know that you need all your text to be plotted at 1/4 inch, how large does the text need to be in your drawing? This is where LTSCALE, and a little AutoLISP, can come to the rescue.

Assuming that you are plotting your drawing at $1/8'' = 1'-0''$, you calculate the value of the LTSCALE variable to be 96. As you know from our discussion, LTSCALE is a system variable that AutoCAD uses to hold a value that enlarges or reduces the dash-dot spacing of linetypes. AutoLISP, AutoCAD's internal programming language (discussed more fully in Chapter 19) contains a means by which you can retrieve that value and use it in a multiplication equation. The result of this equation can be used to get the proper height needed to draw the text so that it will plot out correctly.

When AutoCAD asks Height <default>:, you should respond with (* *<plot height>* (getvar LTSCALE)), where *<plot height>* is the decimal value of the height at which the text should be plotted. For example, if you need the text plotted at a height of 1/4 inch, you should respond with (* 0.25 (getvar LTSCALE)). This will let AutoCAD find the proper value, if you need a certain text height at plot time.

Using AutoCAD's Hatching Capability (HATCH)

If you can use the Advanced User Interface, a pull-down menu shows each available hatch pattern. To see and select a pattern, pull down the Draw menu and then choose Hatch. When you do, you will see the screen shown in figure 12.9. Use the arrow to select the pattern you want, and then specify the scale, angle, and selections set.

Fig. 12.9. *The pull-down hatch menu.*

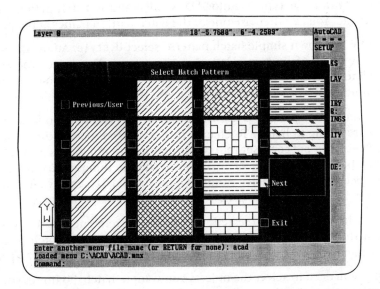

If you cannot use pull-down menus, you can execute the HATCH command by entering the following command sequence:

Prompt:	Response:	Explanation:
Command:	**HATCH**	Starts HATCH command
Pattern (? or name /U,style):	Pattern name	Enter name of hatch pattern
Scale for pattern <current>:	Specify a scaling factor	A scale of 1 is normal size
Angle for pattern <current>:	Specify a hatching factor.	An angle of 0 is normal. Angle is in relation to X axis.
Select objects:	Create a selection set of boundary entities.	

To use a particular pattern, type its name at the first prompt. If you are unsure of the patterns available, you can either look in Appendix A of the *AutoCAD Reference Manual*, or type **?**. AutoCAD will list all the hatch patterns in the ACAD.PAT file. You can then use one of the hatch pattern names at the prompt.

To create your own simple hatch pattern, select U,style. AutoCAD will ask you for the angle of lines in relation to the current X axis, for the spacing between lines, and whether you want the area double-hatched. You can indicate the hatching style (discussed later) that you want, as well.

When your hatch pattern is drawn, it may be too large or too small for the area you are trying to hatch. To change this, you need to set a different value for the Scale for pattern <default>: prompt. Any number is allowable for this value, but negative numbers may cause strange things to happen. If you do not specify a value here, AutoCAD uses the last scale value entered. Remember: because you can UNDO this command, experimentation is easy.

When a hatch pattern is created, it is drawn in reference to the X axis. If you want to hatch parallel to a rotated object, or rotate the hatch pattern as it is drawn, enter a rotation angle at the Angle for pattern <default>: prompt.

Finally, you need to select the objects you want to hatch. To do so, you must be aware of a few rules that apply to hatching. The first is that the entities you pick *must* form a closed boundary. Circles and polygons are great for this, as are closed polylines. If you use normal lines, be sure they all connect end-to-end.

The second thing to remember is that you must select all boundaries that delineate where hatching will begin and end. If you do not want to hatch through internal boundaries of any sort, use the style option. Otherwise, AutoCAD will hatch over them.

One last thing to remember is that a complex hatch style at a small scale will dramatically increase the size of your drawing. Be aware that this may happen; if the drawing file size is too large to work with, try to find a simpler pattern to do the same job.

Hatching Styles

Many of the objects you hatch will be empty entities, with only the hatch pattern within their boundaries. If there are entities you need to hatch around, AutoCAD's style option can help.

There are three styles of hatching:

- ❏ Normal
- ❏ Outermost
- ❏ Ignore

Normal style hatches every other selected hatch boundary, working from the outside in. Outermost style hatches only the outermost selected boundary; the Ignore style ignores and hatches everything inside the outermost hatch boundary.

The Normal and Outermost styles hatch around text, solids, and attributes. If you used Ignore, the hatch pattern would hatch on top of text, solids, and attributes. If you are working with blocks, AutoCAD selects an entire block and hatches according to the individual entities contained in that block. For proper hatching of a block, you may need first to perform the necessary hatching and then create the block (discussed in Chapter 13, "Creating a Symbol Library").

AutoCAD as a Sketch Pad (SKETCH)

The SKETCH command lets you use AutoCAD as a freehand drawing instrument. This can be useful if hatch patterns and other AutoCAD drawing commands are not enough to give your drawing the look you want, or if you want to trace other drawings into the AutoCAD environment. To enter sketch mode, issue the SKETCH command:

```
Command: SKETCH
Record increment <current>:
```

The freehand sketch you create is actually made up of many short line or polyline segments. When AutoCAD asks for a *record increment*, it needs to know how far the crosshairs will travel from the endpoint of the last line or polyline segment before it draws a new segment. The smaller the increment, the better the resolution but the more disk space needed to record these segments. If you are working on a drawing approximately 10 inches square, a record increment of 1/10 inch is sufficient for most applications. For a much larger drawing, you will want to set a larger increment.

Note: Sketching can devour free space on your drawing disk as fast as you can devour a pizza after a good ball game! This occurs because of the many line or polyline segments used to depict your freehand drawing accurately. If you are sketching with a small record increment, be sure to leave SKETCH periodically and use the STATUS command to see how much free space remains.

After you enter the record increment, you will see the following prompt:

```
Sketch . Pen eXit Quit Record Erase Connect
```

To enter selections from this prompt, just type the appropriate uppercase letter (the first letter, except for eXit). You do not have to press Enter.

Sketching in AutoCAD is based on line or polyline segments, determined by the system variable SKPOLY. When SKPOLY is set to 1, AutoCAD treats your drawing as polyline segments; with SKPOLY set to 0, AutoCAD sees your drawing as line segments. If you have a great deal of sketching to do, draw with polyline segments (SKPOLY set to 1)—it is easier on memory and editing.

AutoCAD draws with a "pen." You can control this pen by selecting Pen. Your pointing device's pick button also controls the pen. The pen is down if you are drawing, and up (the default) if you are not. The pen follows the cursor (crosshairs) on-screen as you move your pointing device. To start sketching, move the crosshairs to the location you want to sketch and either "pick" the point or enter **P**. The line (or polyline) segments are recorded as you move.

In sketch mode, the segments you draw are retained in memory until you either end sketch mode (eXit) or record (Record) the segments. Choose eXit if you want to leave sketch mode and return to normal drawing mode; the segments you have drawn will be recorded. If you want to save the segments you have sketched and continue sketching, choose Record. If you do not want to record what you have drawn, you can Quit. You will return to normal drawing mode and the segments you have sketched will not be recorded.

You can erase to some extent in SKETCH (but you cannot erase lines that already have been recorded). Press **E** to enter Erase mode. The cursor will blink as you move across the segments on-screen. To erase in SKETCH, you must backtrack your work from the last segment drawn. To simplify the procedure, make sure that the crosshairs are at the end of your sketch when you enter Erase mode. Press **P** to complete erasing. If you have second thoughts and decide not to erase a line, press **E**.

Connect allows you to connect to previously sketched segments after you have lifted the pen. Making sure that the crosshairs are on the end of the last line you entered, type **C**. AutoCAD will connect to that segment and you can continue sketching.

If you enter a period (.), AutoCAD will connect a line segment from the endpoint of the segment last entered to the cursor's current location. Then the pen will be returned to the up position.

Snap and Ortho modes affect the way SKETCH draws. In Ortho mode you get only horizontal and vertical lines. In Snap mode, all endpoints are locked onto the grid, no matter what your record increment may be. If your sketches are choppy, check the status of these modes.

Dimensioning

To be truly useful, a drawing should show such critical information as lengths, widths, angles, clearances, and tolerances. AutoCAD's *dimensioning* mode provides an excellent means of calculating and annotating this information.

Dimensioning of any drawing is typically the last step in the drawing process. This need not be any different in AutoCAD, but due to AutoCAD's unique drawing environment, dimensioning does not have to be the last step. Because dimensions are like any other entity within a drawing, they can be added, erased, copied, and changed as your drawing develops. The dimensions you use can be made to change as your drawing changes, as well as fit to your particular style of annotating this necessary information.

The next few pages will show you how to use dimensions and customize them to suit your particular needs. The two commands that put you into dimensioning mode are DIM and DIM1, but these are not the only commands involved in AutoCAD's dimensioning process. After you type either of these commands, several dimensioning subcommands do the actual work of dimensioning your drawing. These dimensioning subcommands are

- ❑ HORIZONTAL
- ❑ ALIGNED
- ❑ BASELINE
- ❑ RADIUS
- ❑ ANGULAR
- ❑ NEWTEXT
- ❑ REDRAW
- ❑ STYLE
- ❑ STATUS
- ❑ UNDO
- ❑ VERTICAL
- ❑ ROTATE
- ❑ CONTINUE
- ❑ DIAMETER
- ❑ HOMETEXT
- ❑ UPDATE
- ❑ CENTER
- ❑ LEADER
- ❑ EXIT

These subcommands are discussed on the following few pages. Also, toward the end of the discussion on dimensioning, you will see how AutoCAD's system variables can change the way dimensioning works for you. First of all, you need to know how to get into dimensioning mode.

Entering Dimensioning Mode (DIM and DIM1)

AutoCAD performs dimensioning in a way that separates dimensioning from all other AutoCAD commands. This method, which is called *dimensioning mode*, is a separate set of subcommands and system variables that work *only* when you are dimensioning. AutoCAD's dimensioning is so different from its normal commands that it even has its own command line prompt. The normal drawing and editing commands cannot be used when you are in dimensioning mode, nor can the dimensioning subcommands be used from the `Command:` prompt.

Which command you use to enter dimensioning mode depends on the type of dimensioning you need. When you dimension and edit at the same time, the DIM1 command is handy. DIM1 lets you execute a single dimensioning command, then returns you to the `Command:` prompt. The DIM command places you in dimensioning mode indefinitely. When you enter dimensioning mode, the familiar `Command:` prompt changes to `Dim:`. This lets you know which mode you are in and that only dimensioning commands apply here. When you want to leave dimensioning mode and work with other commands, use Ctrl-C or type **EXIT** at the `Dim:` prompt. Either method will return you to AutoCAD's `Command:` prompt.

Six groups define the AutoCAD dimensioning commands. These groups, and the commands associated with them, are

Type of Dimension	Commands
Linear	HORIZONTAL, VERTICAL, ALIGNED, ROTATED, BASELINE, CONTINUE
Radius	RADIUS
Diameter	DIAMETER
Angular	ANGULAR
Associative	HOMETEXT, NEWTEXT, UPDATE
Utility	CENTER, EXIT, LEADER, REDRAW, STATUS, STYLE, UNDO

Before we look at each of these major dimensioning types and you begin working with the examples in this chapter, you need to do some preparation. First, enter dimensioning mode by typing **DIM** at the `Command:` prompt. The prompt will change to `Dim:` and you will be able to start working with dimensions.

Fundamentals of Dimensioning

What does a dimension look like in AutoCAD? That depends on many factors (which will become apparent as you read on). The simple dimension shown in figure 12.10 is typical. The parts of this dimension have been labeled so that you can understand its composition. These labels will become more important when you work with dimensioning variables.

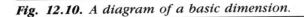

Fig. 12.10. A diagram of a basic dimension.

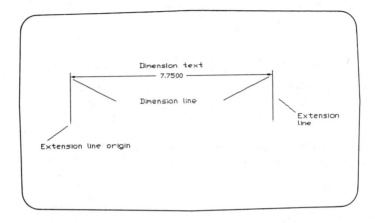

Each type of AutoCAD dimension consists of (at least) dimension text, dimension line, and arrows; extension lines usually are included, depending on which type of dimension is being created.

If extension lines are included in a dimension, there is a somewhat obvious relationship between the dimension line and the extension lines. As you can see from figure 12.11, they are perpendicular to each other. This relationship is important to an understanding of the linear dimension ROTATED command, described in the next section.

There are essentially two types of dimensions in AutoCAD, *normal* and *associative*. In the normal method, the individual entities that make up the dimension are inserted as individual entities—the dimension text is a text entity, the dimension lines are lines, etc.

Associative dimensioning, AutoCAD's default method of inserting a dimension, groups all the entities that make up the dimension and treats them as a single collective entity. Editing this type of entity is easier because the entire dimension acts as a single object. When you use editing commands to modify an associative dimension, AutoCAD modifies the dimension text to reflect the change, and draws the dimension entity to its new location, size, and rotation.

As you insert dimensions, you may decide that you do not like the way a certain dimension was placed, or the way it looks on-screen. There are several things you can do to rectify the situation. First, you can use *U* to undo the last

Fig. 12.11. The relationship between the dimension line and extension lines.

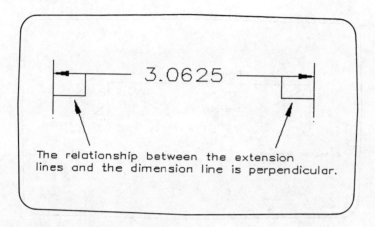

dimension inserted. When you first experiment with dimensioning, this may be the easiest way to eliminate a dimension. You can try reinserting the dimension again until it looks just the way you want.

Another way to modify an associative dimension after insertion is to explode it. The EXPLODE command, which is used to disassemble a collective entity into its base pieces, is described in detail in Chapter 13, "Creating a Symbol Library."

With these fundamentals out of the way, let's look at the various types of dimensioning available in AutoCAD.

Linear Dimensions (HORIZONTAL, VERTICAL, ALIGNED, ROTATED, BASELINE, CONTINUE)

Linear dimensioning, the basic type of dimensioning used by AutoCAD, measures the distance (vertical, horizontal, or inclined) from one point to another. AutoCAD provides several types of linear dimensioning. These types (along with the dimensioning command that affects them) include:

Type	Command
Vertical	VER
Horizontal	HOR
Aligned	ALI
Rotated	ROT
Baseline	BAS
Continued	CON

These six dimensioning commands insert linear dimensions. All of these commands share certain similarities, including some common prompts. For example, after you enter one of the four basic linear dimensioning commands (VERtical, HORizontal, ALIgned, or ROTated), AutoCAD responds:

`First extension line origin or RETURN to select:`

If you specify a point, AutoCAD uses it as the origin point for the first extension line. This can be the endpoint or intersection of a line, the center point of a circle, and even the insertion point of a text entity.

After the first extension line origin has been specified, AutoCAD asks for the `Second extension line origin:`. Again, you should specify the point to be used as the origin of the second extension line.

If you press Enter at the `First extension line...` prompt, AutoCAD responds with the following message:

`Select line, arc, or circle:`

AutoCAD is asking you to select the entity you want to dimension. This feature is handy if all you need to dimension is a wall made up of one line, or another similar object.

If you indicate a line or an arc, AutoCAD uses the endpoints for the first and second extension lines. If you indicate a circle, a diameter is used: 0° for HORIZONTAL, 90° for VERTICAL, a user-defined angle for ROTATED. For ALIGNED, the point used to indicate the circle defines where the dimension is placed.

Whether you select an actual entity or the origin points for the extension lines, AutoCAD will ask you for the `Dimension line location:`. This is the location of the actual line on which the dimension is written. If there is enough room between the extension lines, the dimension text will be centered in or on this line. Otherwise, the text will be placed outside the extension lines. After you specify the dimension-line location, you are prompted for:

`Dimension text <length>:`

AutoCAD is giving you an opportunity to override the calculated dimensioning text. AutoCAD calculates this length based on the distance between the two extension lines. If you have drawn to scale, the default value should be correct; pressing Enter will cause AutoCAD to accept the value. If you want to change the text, you should enter a new text string. When you press Enter, the text will be centered within the dimension line or, if there is not enough room between the extension lines, to the side of the line.

Now that you know some terms, commands, and common prompts for linear dimensioning, let's look at each linear-dimensioning command.

HOR (HORIZONTAL) calculates a horizontal dimension: the X-axis distance between two points. After you enter **HOR** at the Dim: prompt, you define the dimension by responding to the series of common linear-dimensioning prompts. Figure 12.12 shows an example of horizontal dimensioning being used to display the bathroom's width.

***Fig. 12.12.** An example of horizontal dimensioning.*

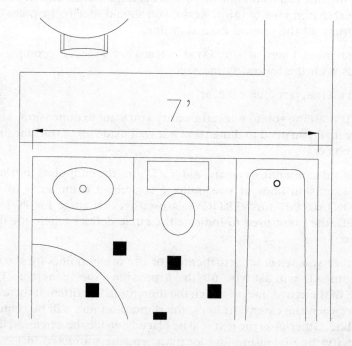

VER (VERTICAL) calculates a vertical dimension—the Y-axis distance between two points. Like the HOR command, VER uses the common linear-dimensioning prompts to define a dimension. In figure 12.13, vertical dimensioning is used to establish the length of the other bathroom wall.

Fig. 12.13. *An example of vertical dimensioning.*

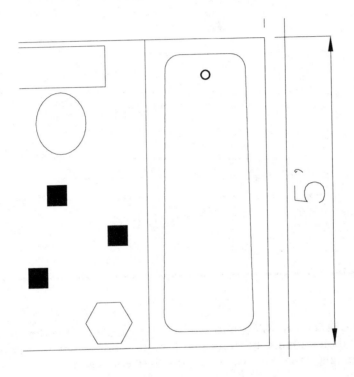

HOR and VER calculate only horizontal and vertical distances. ALI (ALIGNED) places the dimension line parallel to a line drawn through the origin points of the first and second extension lines. The dimension measured is the true distance from the first point to the second. The common linear-dimensioning prompts are used to define a dimension created with ALI. Although nearly all the line work in the sample drawing is strictly horizontal or vertical, the tub's sides do have an angle that can be used to show how the ALIGNED dimensioning works. Figure 12.14 shows how the dimension is kept parallel to the entity that is being measured.

Fig. 12.14. Using ALIGNED to measure the inside of the tub accurately.

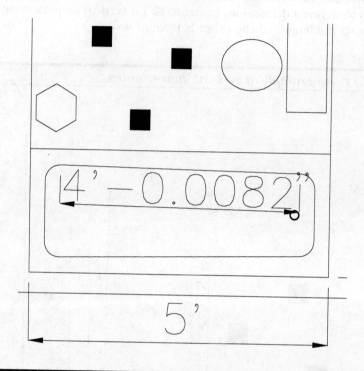

ROT (ROTATED) allows you to set a rotation angle for the dimension line. If you are dimensioning an entity that is neither horizontal nor vertical, and you cannot align the dimension, use the ROT command.

When you enter the ROT command, AutoCAD (before displaying the common linear-dimensioning prompts) will prompt:

```
Dimension line angle <O>:
```

Here you should enter the angle at which you want the dimension line to appear. With ROTATED, the dimension (or length) is measured between the extension line origins at the angle you have defined. For instance, if you have two points, the second directly above the first, and define a rotation angle of $45°$, the dimension text will reflect a length of $1\sqrt{2}$ multiplied by the distance from the first point to the second point.

The BASELINE and CONTINUE linear-dimensioning commands differ only in one detail. The BASELINE command causes the dimension you are defining to share a common first extension line with the previously entered dimension (see fig. 12.15), and will take all its measurements from this first point to any second point you choose. CONTINUE, on the other hand, uses the second extension line of the previously entered dimension as the first extension line of the dimension being defined. This lets you create a string of dimensions, one right after the other (see fig. 12.16).

Fig. 12.15. Dimensioning from a baseline.

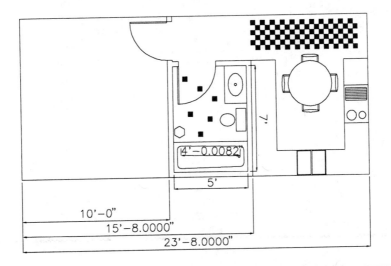

Because BAS and CON take reference points from previously entered dimensions, you must keep two things in mind. First, these commands can be used only *after* another dimension has been entered. Trying to use BAS or CON as your first dimensioning command will generate an error. Second, the first common linear-dimensioning prompt (First extension line...) is not displayed. AutoCAD immediately asks for the second extension-line origin.

Fig. 12.16. Continuous dimensioning.

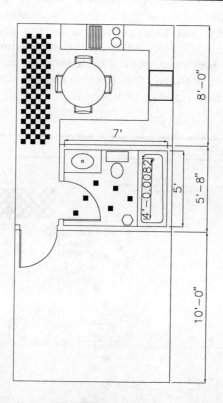

Radius and Diameter Dimensioning (RAD/DIA)

The RAD and DIA dimensioning commands affect radius and diameter dimensioning, respectively, and are used for dimensioning arcs and circles. Both commands share similarities, including common prompts. After you enter either **RAD** or **DIA**, AutoCAD responds:

    Select arc or circle:

Use your pointing device to select the entity you want to work with. (The location of the diameter or radius dimension is determined by the point with which you select the entity.) Then AutoCAD prompts:

    Dimension text <length>:

Here you are given an opportunity to override the calculated dimension text. If you decide to add any notes, remember to enter the necessary dimension text because you are overriding the original dimension. As you can see from figure 12.17, which shows how these dimensioning commands are used to dimension the burners, radii are automatically prefaced by an R, and diameters by a diameter symbol ∅.

Fig. 12.17. Radius and diameter dimensioning.

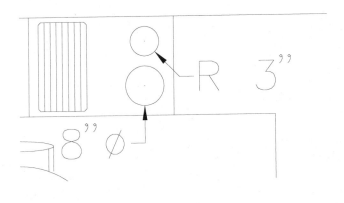

If there is not enough room for the text within the dimension line or entity (a small circle, for instance), you will see this message:

```
Text does not fit.
Enter leader length for text:
```

AutoCAD wants you to specify the length of the leader line, which leads from the entity (at the point of selection) to the dimension text. This is what has happened in figures 12.16 and 12.17.

Angular Dimensioning (ANG)

In *angular* dimensioning, a dimension is applied to the angle between two entities. The dimension line is an arc between the two lines. Although the lines do not have to intersect physically in order for angular dimensioning to be applied, they would have to intersect eventually if they were extended. They cannot be parallel.

In order to apply an angular dimension, AutoCAD provides the ANG dimensioning command. The discussion of the ALIGNED dimensioning command mentioned that nearly all the linework in the sample drawing is strictly horizontal or vertical. In figure 12.18, you can see that two of the lines that define the counter tops are at exactly 90 degrees to each other.

***Fig. 12.18.** Dimensioning an angle.*

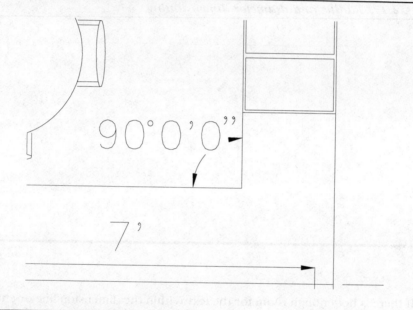

When you enter **ANG** at the Dim: prompt, AutoCAD responds:

Select first line:

This first line must be either a line or a line segment of a polyline. It cannot be an arc, circle, or ellipse. After you select the first line, AutoCAD prompts:

Second line:

Select the second line in the same way you selected the first. This line *must be separate from and cannot be parallel to* the first line. If you select a parallel line, AutoCAD will generate an error message and the ANG command will be canceled.

If there are no problems with the two lines you have selected, AutoCAD asks you to:

`Enter dimension line arc location:`

The dimension-line arc generated by the ANG command will pass through the point you specify, ending with the two lines you selected to define the angle.

If, based on the location you specify, there is not enough room for the dimension-line arc and the arrows, AutoCAD displays the following message:

`Arrows don't fit, will be moved outside.`

and the arrows and arc are placed outside the angle that has been measured.

After you specify a location for the dimension-line arc, you will see the following prompt:

`Dimension text <angle>:`

As it does with other dimensioning commands, this prompt gives you an opportunity to override the calculated dimensioning text. AutoCAD calculates the angle based on the angle between the two lines. If you want to change the dimension text, enter any notes or text and press Enter. AutoCAD will ask you to `Enter text location:`. If you press Enter at this prompt, AutoCAD will place the text in the dimension arc; otherwise the text is entered at the location you indicate, left-justified to the point you select. Again, if the text does not fit, or if AutoCAD had to move the arrows outside the angle being dimensioned, you will see this message:

`Text does not fit. Enter new text location:`

Enter the new location at which you want the dimension text to appear. This step completes the angular dimension. The `Dim:` prompt will reappear on your screen.

Associative Dimension Commands

Although associative dimensions are extremely versatile, changing as a drawing changes, they have their share of difficulties. The main problem is in the placement of text in a dimension. With a normal dimension, if AutoCAD places the text incorrectly, you just move the text string to the position you prefer. But an associative dimension, being a collective entity, is more difficult to change. If text is in the wrong place, you have to use the STRETCH Crossing command (as discussed in Chapter 7, ''Editing Your Drawing'') on the text string. This is a cumbersome task, at best.

The following commands (HOMETEXT, NEWTEXT, and UPDATE) affect only how text, arrows, and extension lines are shown in associative dimensions. With that in mind, you may need to decide whether the usefulness of these commands outweighs the problems of associative dimensions.

Text used in an associative dimension has a default location that can be changed by stretching the dimension. The HOMETEXT command causes the dimension text to return to its "home" location (usually the center of the dimension line). If you stretch or modify the dimension and then want the dimension text to return to its original location, use HOMETEXT. When you enter **HOMETEXT** at the Dim: prompt and select the applicable dimensions, the text string in each of the dimensions you chose will return to its home position.

The NEWTEXT command allows you to change the dimension text within an associative dimension without exiting dimensioning mode. After you type in the new text, you are prompted to select the dimensions to which this text string should be applied. The text in these entities will be changed to match the text you typed.

The UPDATE command causes all associative dimensions to re-create how they are shown, based on the current settings of the dimensioning variables. Dimension variables, which control all aspects of the way dimensions are drawn, are discussed in detail later in this chapter. This variable can be used to change the types of arrows, text style, and other features of a typical dimension all at once, over all of the associative dimensions you choose.

Dimension Utility Commands

The dimension utility commands do not actually dimension entities. They provide handy features not covered under other dimensioning commands.

The REDRAW command should be the most familiar of the utility commands. REDRAW, when used for dimensioning, causes the screen to be cleared and redrawn (just like AutoCAD's regular REDRAW command).

CENTER allows you to place a mark at the center of a circle or arc. When you enter **CENTER** at the Dim: prompt, AutoCAD prompts you to select an entity whose center you want marked. When you select the entity, a center mark (it may be either a + or a -, depending on the rotation of the circle or arc) will be placed at the center.

STYLE lets you change the text font for the dimensions. As long as a font is loaded in the drawing, you can access that font. For more information on fonts and font styles, refer to the discussion of the STYLE command earlier in this chapter.

If you want to put special dimensioning notes (sometimes known as *call outs* or *leader lines*) in a drawing, you can do so with the LEADER command. These notes are handy for referencing portions of the drawing that may need additional explanation. This dimensioning command is used also to show the relationship between a note and a specific object in the drawing.

To create a leader line, enter **LEADER** at the Dim: prompt. AutoCAD responds with:

Leader start point:

This start point is the location at which the arrow will appear. Select a point with your pointing device. At the next prompt, To point:, you specify the next vertex for the leader line.

This process is similar to using the LINE command. You simply continue to specify endpoints until the leader line leads to the desired location. When you have finished, press Enter without specifying a point. AutoCAD then asks you for:

Dimension text <current>:

Here you should enter the text that will appear at the end of the leader line. AutoCAD uses the last dimension you worked with as a default for this text.

The STATUS command will display a list of the current value of the dimensioning variables. The variables control the "look" of a dimension; when used correctly, they can make the process of dimensioning a drawing very easy. The dimensioning variables are discussed in detail in the next section.

As mentioned earlier, the EXIT command removes you from dimensioning mode and takes you back to the familiar Command: prompt. You can exit dimensioning mode also by pressing the Ctrl-C key combination.

UNDO in dimensioning mode, like UNDO at the Command: prompt, allows you to undo all your dimensioning steps. By using UNDO in dimensioning mode, you can step back through your individual dimensioning commands; if you use **UNDO** at the Command: prompt, you undo the effects of the entire dimensioning command.

Controlling Dimensions

AutoCAD uses a series of system variables to control the way dimensions are drawn and what they look like. Each of these system variables can be changed in either of two ways. The normal method of changing the value of dimensioning variables is to use the variables named at the Dim: prompt. The second method is to use the SETVAR command, as described in the "Quick Reference to Autocad's System Variables," available in Part VI of this book.

If you want to change the variable from within dimensioning mode, simply enter the variable name at the Dim: prompt. You will see the current setting and be given an opportunity to make any changes you want.

Many system variables affect dimensioning. They can be separated (according to what each group of variables affects) into the following general categories:

❑ The dimension in general
❑ Dimension text and lines
❑ Arrow heads
❑ Extension lines
❑ Tolerances and limits
❑ Alternate dimensions

Each category of system variable is discussed in some detail in the next several sections.

As mentioned in the discussion on associative dimensions, the UPDATE command can be used to redraw any associative dimensions after changes to the dimensioning variables have been made. When you enter **UPDATE** at the Dim: prompt, you are prompted to Select objects:. The updating will occur after you select the dimensions you want to update.

To list all the dimension variables and their values, use the STATUS command. The list, which also includes a brief description of each variable, is similar to that produced when you enter **SETVAR ?** at the Command: prompt, but is limited to dimensioning variables. Just type **STATUS** at the Dim: prompt and press Enter. Because all the variables cannot fit on the screen at one time, you will need to press Enter to see the rest of the list.

System Variables that Affect the Dimension in General

Three system variables affect the general display of dimensions. There is also one miscellaneous system variable. These four variables are

❑ DIMASO
❑ DIMCEN
❑ DIMLFAC
❑ DIMSCALE

DIMASO controls the generation of associative dimensions. If DIMASO is on, the dimensions are associative; if it is off, the dimensions are normal. (Associative dimensioning is described at the beginning of this chapter.)

DIMCEN controls the size of the + marker used to denote the center of an arc or circle. These marks are placed by the CENTER, RAD, and DIA commands. The value used for this variable is the distance from the center of the mark along one of the line segments that make up the mark. The default is 0.09. If a value of 0 is used, no center marks appear; if the value is negative, only a center line (no cross mark) is used.

Use the DIMLFAC variable if you are drawing in anything other than full scale. The default value for DIMLFAC is 1, indicating a scaling factor of 1, or full scale (one drawing unit equals one object unit). If you are drawing in half scale, you should set this variable to 2. AutoCAD multiplies the calculated dimension values by the value of this variable. Angular dimensions are not affected.

DIMSCALE is an overall scale factor. Use this variable if you are working with a drawing that is quite large or very small. DIMSCALE scales the entire dimension by the same amount. The default value is 1. Entering a value larger than 1 results in a dimension that is multiplied by that factor; the same is true if you enter a value of less than 1. All dimensions are scaled.

System Variables that Affect Dimension Text and Lines

The majority of the system variables that affect dimensioning have to do with the dimension text or the dimension lines. These dimensioning elements are controlled by a series of system variables:

- DIMSOXD
- DIMTIX
- DIMTAD
- DIMTXT
- DIMTVP
- DIMTIH
- DIMTOH

- DIMTOFL
- DIMPOST
- DIMZIN
- DIMRND
- DIMSHO
- DIMDLI

Normally, AutoCAD draws dimension lines between two extension lines. In the space between these lines AutoCAD tries to place the dimension, dimension line, and arrow. If not enough room is available between the extension lines, the text, arrows, and dimension lines will be placed outside the extension lines. DIMSOXD, if set ON, forces AutoCAD to draw only between extension lines. If AutoCAD calculates that not enough room is available between the extension lines, the dimension will not be displayed.

DIMTIX has the same effect on dimension text that DIMSOXD has on dimension lines. If DIMTIX is set ON, dimension text can appear only between extension lines. If AutoCAD calculates that not enough room is available, the dimension text is not displayed. The dimension lines and arrows, however, may appear outside the extension lines while the text is inside.

DIMTAD controls whether the dimension text is placed above the dimension line. If DIMTAD is set OFF (the default), the dimension text is centered in relation to the dimension line, as dictated by the relationship between DIMTVP (the variable controlling vertical placement of the dimension text) and DIMTXT (the variable controlling dimension-text height).

DIMTXT is used to specify the height of the dimension text. The default is 0.18 units. You can change this to a different size as needed. A negative value here would have no practical value.

If DIMTAD is set OFF, DIMTVP controls the placement of dimension text in relation to the dimension line. This is done through the formula *DIMTVP – DIMTXT*. Thus, the default setting of 0 for DIMTVP results in an offset of 0 units above or below the dimension line—the dimension text is centered vertically within the dimension line. As you change DIMTVP, the dimension text's position will change. A positive value for DIMTVP causes the dimension text to move above the dimension line; a negative value causes it to move below.

If DIMTVP has an absolute value of less than 1, the dimension-text line will be split automatically (as needed) to fit within the required dimensioning area.

DIMTIH controls the orientation of text that appears between extension lines. When DIMTIH is set ON (the default), all text between the extension lines is drawn horizontally. If set OFF, the dimension text is aligned parallel to the dimension line.

DIMTOH is similar in function to DIMTIH, but controls all dimension text appearing outside of extension lines. When DIMTOH is set ON (the default), all text outside the extension lines is drawn horizontally. If set OFF, the dimension text is aligned parallel to the dimension line.

Normally, a dimension line is located where the dimension text appears. You can override this location of the dimension line by setting the DIMTOFL system variable. If set ON, DIMTOFL causes the dimension line to appear between the extension lines (if it will fit), even if the text is placed outside the extension lines. The default for DIMTOFL is OFF.

Use DIMPOST to add a default suffix to dimension text. For example, if you wanted to add the characters *approx.* to the end of each dimension, you could do so by setting DIMPOST to approx. The setting of DIMPOST has no effect on angular dimensions. To get rid of the suffix, set DIMPOST to no characters.

DIMZIN affects dimension text only if you are working with architectural units and the calculated dimension has 0 inches. In this case (and with DIMZIN OFF) any dimension with 0 inches is displayed without the inches. For instance, 12 feet 0 inches will be displayed as 12 feet. If DIMZIN is ON, the true 12 feet 0 inches will be displayed.

You can use the DIMRND variable to round all the dimension values calculated by AutoCAD. For instance, if you set the value to 0.5, all the dimensions are rounded to the nearest half unit. The default value for DIMRND is 0, which signifies that no rounding is to occur.

If, when you edit dimensions, the DIMSHO variable is ON and the dimensions are associative, the dimension-text values are updated as the dimension changes. The change in the entity's length is echoed in the dimension text as the rubber band entity is dragged. If DIMSHO is OFF (the default), the dimension text is updated only after the change is complete.

AutoCAD uses the DIMDLI system variable to control the incrementing factor for successive uses of BAS and CON, two linear-dimensioning commands. This variable's value represents units and has a default of 0.38.

System Variables that Affect Arrows

AutoCAD gives you complete control over the size and appearance of the arrows within a dimension. You can even replace the arrows with library blocks, which are discussed in Chapter 13, "Creating a Symbol Library."

The following system variables control the use of arrows within AutoCAD:

❏ DIMASZ   ❏ DIMBLK
❏ DIMTSZ   ❏ DIMSAH
❏ DIMDLE   ❏ DIMBLK1
                ❏ DIMBLK2

The DIMASZ variable is used as a scaling factor for arrow size. The variable's value is multiplied by the size of the arrow or block (whichever is used) to calculate a display size. The default value is a scale factor of 0.18.

You can end dimension lines with any of the following:

❏ Arrows
❏ Tick marks
❏ Dots
❏ Library blocks

DIMTSZ controls whether arrows or tick marks are used. The scaling factor for the tick mark is equivalent to whatever DIMTSZ is set to: if DIMTSZ is set to 0 (the default), arrows are used; if set to a number other than 0, tick marks are used, with a scaling factor equal to the value used in this variable.

If you are using tick marks (DIMTSZ is set to a value other than 0), you can use the DIMDLE variable to extend the dimension line past the extension lines. DIMDLE represents the number of units by which you want to extend the dimension line. The default value is 0.

If you need an indicator other than the arrows or tick marks, you can create a block and indicate its name with DIMBLK. You draw the block for the right side of a horizontal dimension, and it is rotated 180° for the left side. The block must be available at the time it is needed for the dimensioning operation, or AutoCAD will default to either arrows or internally generated tick marks.

If you set DIMBLK to DOT, and no block with that name is available, AutoCAD provides a dot marker for use by the dimensioning commands.

Set DIMBLK to a blank character (nothing) to return to regular arrow use.

If you are using library blocks rather than arrows, you can use different blocks at each end of the dimension line. To do this, set DIMSAH ON and specify (in DIMBLK1 and DIMBLK2, or in DIMBLK) the names of the blocks or block. If DIMSAH is set ON and DIMBLK1 and DIMBLK2 define blocks to be used at the first and second extensions, respectively, the block name stored in DIMBLK is ignored; only DIMBLK1 and DIMBLK2 are used.

System Variables that Affect Extension Lines

The extension lines created by AutoCAD during linear and angular dimensioning can be controlled by the following variables:

- ❏ DIMEXO
- ❏ DIMEXE
- ❏ DIMSE1
- ❏ DIMSE2

When AutoCAD creates an extension line, the distance from the extension line origin to the beginning of the extension line is controlled by the DIMEXO system variable. This variable represents the number of units in the gap between the origin of the extension line and the beginning of the line. The default is 0.0625; if the value is set to 0, the line will touch the origin point.

The distance the extension line extends beyond the dimension line is controlled by DIMEXE. If you set DIMEXE to 0 units, the extension line and the dimension line will form a right angle. The default value for DIMEXE is 0.18. A negative value is not allowed, although setting a negative value through the SETVAR command will not generate an error. If you attempt to change DIMEXE to a negative value from the Dim: prompt, AutoCAD displays an error message and no change is made. If you do the same thing with the SETVAR command, no message is displayed; any negative value is converted to a positive (absolute) value. For instance, if you enter – .1, it will be changed to .1.

You can suppress display of either of the extension lines by changing the settings of DIMSE1 and DIMSE2. If DIMSE1 is set ON, display of the first extension line is suppressed. Setting DIMSE2 ON suppresses display of the second extension line. The default for both variables is OFF, which means that the extension lines are visible.

System Variables that Affect Tolerances and Limits

AutoCAD lets you display regular dimensions as well as dimensions that use tolerances or limits. Four variables affect the display of this information: DIMTOL, DIMLIM, DIMTP, and DIMTM.

If DIMTOL is set ON (normally it is set OFF), tolerances are displayed with each dimension. DIMLIM works the same way for limits; if set ON, limits are displayed. If you are displaying limits (DIMLIM is set ON), the values in DIMTP and DIMTM are used as the limits.

DIMTP and DIMTM are the upper and lower tolerance ranges. DIMTP contains the "plus" portion of the tolerance; DIMTM the "minus" portion. If both DIMTP and DIMTM are set to the same value, the tolerance will appear as a single number preceded by a plus-or-minus sign ($\pm$). DIMTM is assumed to be a negative number; the negative value of whatever you enter is used for the tolerance display. Thus, if you enter a negative value, it is negated and a positive value is displayed.

It is important to remember that any dimension-text suffix specified in DIMPOST is attached to the end of any displayed tolerances or limits.

System Variables that Affect Alternate Dimensions

AutoCAD can be set to use two measurement systems simultaneously during the dimensioning procedure—typically, to provide measurements in SAE and metric units. In order to use the two systems simultaneously, the following system variables must be changed:

- ❏ DIMALTF
- ❏ DIMALT
- ❏ DIMALTD
- ❏ DIMAPOST

Alternate dimensioning has no effect on angular dimensions.

DIMALTF is the conversion factor to be used in calculating the alternate dimension. For instance, if the primary dimensions are provided in inches, and the alternate unit of measure is to be centimeters, DIMALTF should be set to 2.54 (the number of centimeters in an inch). Conversely, if the primary dimension unit is centimeters and the alternate is inches, DIMALTF should be set to

0.3937 (the number of inches in a centimeter). After accounting for the global scaling factor in DIMLFAC, AutoCAD multiplies the calculated dimension by the value in DIMALTF.

DIMALT controls whether the alternate dimensions are displayed. The default is OFF, but if DIMALT is set ON, alternate dimensions are used in addition to the default dimensions.

DIMALTD is used to specify the number of decimal places to be used in the alternate dimension values. The default value is 2.

DIMAPOST is used for adding a default suffix to alternate dimension text. In the previous example (of centimeters used as the alternate dimension unit), setting DIMAPOST to cm would be helpful. To get rid of the suffix, set DIMAPOST to nothing.

Summary

This chapter showed you how several AutoCAD commands can be used to make your drawing come alive. The addition of text and dimensions usually is the final step in the creation of a drawing, and ultimately provides the most information about your design.

In this chapter you have learned how to make the most of your drawings by using the following commands:

❏ TEXT ❏ HATCH
❏ DTEXT ❏ SKETCH
❏ QTEXT ❏ DIM
❏ STYLE ❏ DIM1

These commands let you add the final touches to your drawings.

This chapter also discussed how the dimensioning variables can be used to customize the DIM and DIM1 commands. The dimensions created by using the DIM or DIM1 command then look the way *you* want them to.

In the next chapter you will learn how blocks, which are collective entities much like linear dimensions, can be used to create a "rubber stamp" of a symbol that you may draw quite often. This will allow you to reduce file size while still having many copies of the item in your drawing. You also will discover how certain information can be associated with a block, allowing you to associate test information with block symbols in your drawing.

13

Creating a Symbol Library

In the last several chapters you have seen many of AutoCAD's advanced uses. These have included the use of commands to change entity characteristics, set up layering schemes, and even add dimensions and labels to your drawings. Although a drawing entity called a *block* has been mentioned, this book has neglected to explain what a block really is, and how blocks can help you.

This chapter will show you how to create, manipulate, and attach information to blocks. Basically, a *block* is an entity made up of smaller pieces but drawn and edited as a single entity. To master the use of blocks, you first should learn how to work with the following commands:

❑ BLOCK ❑ UNDO
❑ WBLOCK ❑ REDO
❑ INSERT ❑ ATTDEF
❑ MINSERT ❑ ATTEDIT
❑ EXPLODE ❑ ATTDISP
  ❑ ATTEXT

The Uses of a Symbol Library

An AutoCAD symbol library serves the same purpose as a set of drafting templates: by using it to replicate a standard symbol quickly and as many times as you need it in a drawing, drafting is faster. And, as with many drafting templates today, symbol libraries can be customized to contain only items that are needed for a particular discipline. This gives you the flexibility of being able to choose the symbols that best suit your needs. Appendix B lists additional programs that add functionality to AutoCAD; not surprisingly, most of these packages are symbol libraries.

This chapter does not focus on other people's symbol libraries. It shows you how to create your own. With a customized personal symbol library, you can maintain a standard set of drawing objects that remain the same, no matter who is working on the drawing or which computer system is used to do the drawing.

Creating Library Parts (BLOCK)

In AutoCAD, a block is an entity composed of many individual pieces. The pieces are drawn in the normal way, through AutoCAD's drawing and editing commands, and then are used to represent a meaningful symbol in your drawing. This symbol can be anything, from a simple chair to an engine mounting bracket to a sports car. Remember, however, that the symbol should be something you will use *often* in your drawing.

Why would you want to use blocks? There are several reasons. The first reason has been mentioned already: blocks can provide standard symbols that anyone can use.

The second reason is that blocks can save space in a drawing. When you make a block of an object that you use often, AutoCAD keeps only one copy of the actual block *definition* in the drawing database. The block definition is a description of the pieces that make up the symbol. Any copy of the symbol that you insert into the drawing will refer back to the original definition. Thus, *hundreds* of copies take up very little space in the drawing, because each is patterned after the *one* original definition.

The third reason is ease of change. If midway through your project you decide to change the symbol for a light switch, all you need to do is redefine the block definition (discussed over the next few pages) for a light switch. Every copy of the light switch in your drawing will be updated automatically to show the changes.

In AutoCAD Release 10, blocks are true three-dimensional objects. This means that you can take advantage of AutoCAD's enhanced 3-D capabilities when you insert and manipulate blocks in a three-dimensional drawing. The use of blocks in three-dimensional drawing is discussed in Chapter 15, ''More 3-D Drawing Tools.''

Because blocks usually are made up of individual entities, you can use any of AutoCAD's drawing and editing commands to create the object that will become your block. Once you have drawn an object, you can use the BLOCK command to create the block. However, blocks created with the BLOCK command can be used only in the drawing in which they were created. The WBLOCK command, described in the next section, is used to write these blocks to disk, making them accessible to all drawings.

Figure 13.1 shows the symbol you will create: a chair. Figure 13.2 shows the steps necessary to draw the chair. Take a moment to create this chair within the Drawing Editor, using the commands detailed in figure 13.2. These commands were covered in earlier chapters.

Fig. 13.1. *A basic block.*

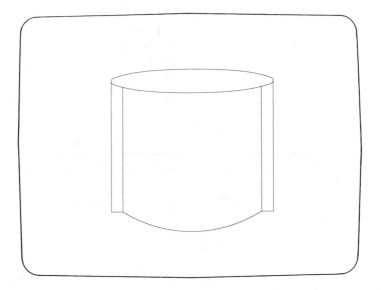

Now that you have drawn the chair, you can create your first block. To create the block, use the following BLOCK command sequence:

Prompt:	Response:	Explanation:
Command:	**BLOCK**	Starts the BLOCK command
Block name (or ?):	**CHAIR**	You name the block "chair."
Insertion base point:	Select the point shown in figure 13.2.	

Prompt:	Response:	Explanation:
Select objects:	**W**	Specifies that you want to use a window to create the selection set.
First corner:	Pick a window box that will enclose the pieces of the chair.	
Other corner:	Digitize window's lower right corner.	
Select objects:	Press Enter.	Indicates that all items are selected.

Fig. 13.2. How to draw the entities that will make up the block.

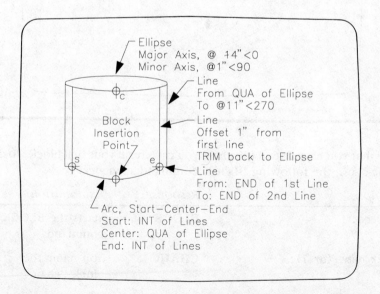

When you press Enter, the BLOCK command is complete. The entities you selected are stored as the block definition in the drawing's database. Later, they will be used to create any copies of the block that you insert into the drawing.

If you want to see a list of all the blocks in the current drawing, enter a question mark (**?**) and press Enter at the first prompt. A complete list of the blocks currently in your drawing will scroll on-screen. To return to the graphics screen, press the F1 function key.

If you enter the name of an existing block at the `Block name` prompt, AutoCAD displays the following question:

```
Block _____ already exists.
Redefine it? <N>:
```

AutoCAD is asking whether you want to *redefine* (replace) the old block with the new one. If you choose to do this, the old block will be replaced by the new one, and every occurrence of that block in the drawing will be changed to match the new block.

AutoCAD also allows you to combine existing blocks to form a new block. This is done by simply including the desired block (or blocks) within the selection set of the new block you are creating. You can form a new block by combining several blocks, provided that the name of the combined block is different from the names of the individual blocks you combine.

The `Insertion base point:` prompt asks you to choose a point of reference that will be used whenever you insert the block into the drawing. AutoCAD uses this point of reference later for inserting the block into the drawing. When you insert the block, the insertion base point is aligned to a point you indicate in the drawing. When you are creating the block, be sure to place this reference point so that it will be convenient for future insertions. The block's center or lower left corner are commonly used points, but you must determine how the blocks will be used, and define the insertion points accordingly.

After you identify the insertion base point, AutoCAD prompts you to select objects. Create a selection set of the entities that you want to include in this block definition, and press Enter at the next `Select objects:` prompt.

The objects you choose to make up the block will disappear from the screen as AutoCAD uses them to create the block definition. Using the OOPS command will cause them to reappear. As you may recall from Chapter 1, "A Quick Start in AutoCAD," OOPS restores the last deleted entities to a drawing. If you were to use U (UNDO) to get the entities back, you would reverse the entire BLOCK command; the block definition would no longer be stored in the drawing database.

Points To Consider When You Create a Block

When you create a block, you need to be aware of the effect that layers and linetypes have within blocks. In the discussion of the CHANGE command in Chapter 8, "Advanced Editing Commands," two keywords for resetting colors and linetypes (BYLAYER and BYBLOCK) were introduced. Because blocks are made up of individual entities, and those entities have layers and linetypes associated with *them*, you should follow a couple of rules when you create blocks.

First, if you want the inserted block to take on the properties of the layer on which it is being inserted (color, linetype, and state), the entities that make up the block must be on Layer 0 when you use the BLOCK command. A block created on Layer 0 can be inserted on any other layer and will adopt the characteristics of that layer. A block created on any other layer(s) will maintain ties to those layers, and will be forced to follow the properties of the layers of which it is made up. If, when inserting a block, the layer(s) that the block is created from do not exist, AutoCAD will create them as it inserts the block.

Second, if you want a block's entities to take on the properties of the layer on which they are inserted, set all entity properties to BYLAYER before you create the block. If the entities within the block have been assigned specific colors or linetypes, these will always be used rather than the default layer properties.

Writing Blocks to a File (WBLOCK)

When you create blocks in AutoCAD, they have effect only within the drawing you are currently using. Thus, the chair block created earlier in this chapter can be used only within the drawing for which the block was created. How do you create blocks that can be used within *other* drawings? By using the WBLOCK command.

The Write BLOCK (WBLOCK) command lets you write blocks to your hard disk so that they can be inserted into other drawings. The WBLOCK command sequence follows:

```
Command: WBLOCK
File name:
Block name:
```

At the File name: prompt, enter the name of the file that will hold the block. This name must comply with DOS file name standards (described in Chapter 4, "Dabble in DOS"). You do not need to add a three-character extension; AutoCAD adds the extension *.DWG* to the file name you specify. As you may suspect, AutoCAD simply creates a new drawing file that will hold the block definition. There is no practical difference between a block file and a drawing file.

The `Block name:` prompt asks you for the name of the block to write to the file. If you have not yet created the block, press Enter. You will see the standard block-creation prompts (refer to the preceding section). If you already have created the block, and both the block and the file have the same name, you can type an equal sign (=) rather than the name.

The WBLOCK command is similar to the PURGE command, in that it also can be used to remove unused layers, blocks, styles, and so forth from a drawing. If you type an asterisk (*) rather than a file name, all the drawing entities used will be written out of the drawing file. You can use this command to purge your drawing of all entities (such as layers, linetypes, styles, blocks, and shapes) that were once defined in the drawing and are saved in the drawing's memory, but which are not actually used. After issuing this command, you should notice that your drawing file is slightly smaller.

Inserting Parts into a Drawing (INSERT)

Now that you have created your first block, the next step is to learn how to use it in a drawing. This is done by using the INSERT command, which copies the block definition from the database and places it at a specified point in the drawing.

When you use the INSERT command, you need to provide the block's name and information about its location, scaling factor, and rotation. Figure 13.3 shows your chair block when it is inserted using the following command sequence:

Prompt:	Response:	Explanation:
Command:	**INSERT**	Inserts the BLOCK
Block name (or ?):	**CHAIR**	The block's name
Insertion Point:	Pick a point in the drawing.	This is the location for the symbol.
X scale factor <1> /Corner /XYZ:	Press Enter.	X scale factor = 1
Y scale factor <default=X>:	Press Enter.	Y scale factor same as X
Rotation angle <0>:	Press Enter.	No rotation

Fig. 13.3. The inserted block.

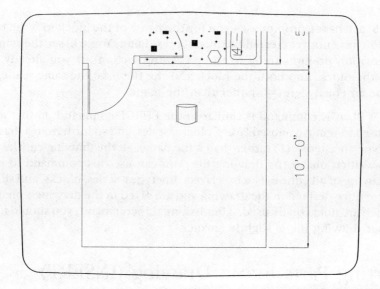

You must type the name of the block you want to insert. (With a block that has been saved to disk with WBLOCK, type the name of the file that contains the block.) As mentioned earlier, a whole drawing can be considered a block; all you need to do is use the drawing's name when you are asked for a Block name.

If you want to modify a standard block after insertion, you can insert the block with its entities separated (exploded). At the Block name (or ?): prompt, type an * followed by the block name. The block will be inserted in its component form, that is, as the individual entities (lines, arcs, and circles) of which it is made. To list the currently available blocks, type a ? at the prompt.

The Insertion point: prompt asks for the location at which the block is to be inserted. This is the point that will be lined up with the block's insertion base point. Remember that each block's insertion base point is defined when the block is created. Notice that a ghosted image of the block appears on-screen; you can use your pointing device to position the block where you want it.

Next, AutoCAD prompts you for scaling information. If you want the block inserted using the same scale at which it was created, press Enter at the following prompt:

```
X scale factor <1>/Corner/XYZ:
```

The default value for the scale factor (1) inserts the block at the scale to which it was originally drawn.

Both two- and three-dimensional blocks can be inserted with different X, Y, and Z scales. Scaling is useful if you want to use a single standard block to meet a variety of situations. If you want to give different scales, you will see the following prompts:

```
X scale factor <1>/Corner:
Y scale factor <default=X>:
Z scale factor <default=X>:
```

Numeric values and points picked in the drawing both can be used to supply scaling information. By typing a scale factor (a number), you give explicit scaling information. Indicating a point can also be considered explicit, but depends on the location of the point you specify.

After you enter the X scale factor (and if you did not use the XYZ option), you are prompted for the Y scale factor:

```
Y scale factor <default=X>:
```

You can enter a Y scale factor that is different from the X scale factor. If you want both factors to be the same, press Enter. Figure 13.4 shows the effect of using different values for the X and Y scale factors. In this case, X was set to 2 and Y was set to 1.

Fig. 13.4. Inserting the block with different X and Y scales.

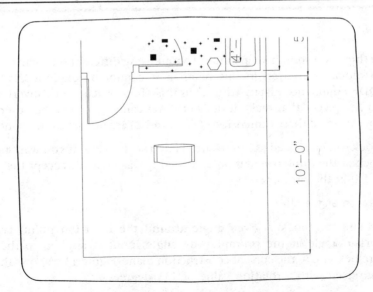

AutoCAD also will accept a negative scale value. A negative X value "mirrors" the block around the Y axis; a negative Y value, the block around the X axis. The block shown in figure 13.5 was inserted with an X factor of 1 and a Y factor of -2. As you can see, it not only stretched the block but also mirrored it.

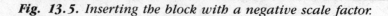

Fig. 13.5. *Inserting the block with a negative scale factor.*

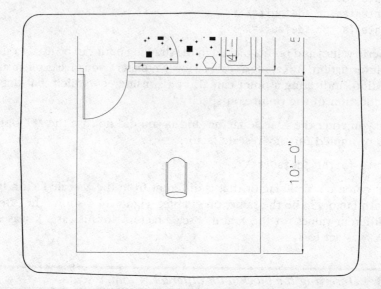

One thing you should keep in mind about using different scale factors is that once a block is inserted in this manner, it cannot be exploded later. The EXPLODE command, discussed later in this chapter, lets you convert a block back to the pieces that make it up. AutoCAD cannot do this, however, if the scale factors in all three dimensions (X, Y, and Z) are not set to the same value.

A block can be rotated as it is inserted into the drawing. If you want to insert the block at the same orientation at which it was created, accept the default angle of 0 at the prompt:

```
Rotation angle <0>:
```

To rotate the block a given angle around the insertion point, type the appropriate angle at the prompt. Any angle input is applied to the block counterclockwise in the current construction plane. Figure 13.6 shows the chair block inserted with a rotation value of 135 degrees.

***Fig. 13.6.** Inserting the chair and giving it a rotation angle.*

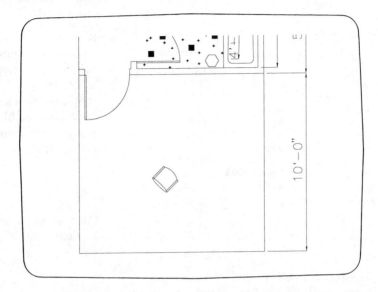

If you update the drawing file from which you inserted a block, as in the case of a block sent to your hard disk by WBLOCK, and you want to change the inserted version of the block to match the drawing file version, you need to follow the next few steps. This will ensure that all the block's definitions match the current "master" definition.

Drawing courtesy of R.L. Tomlinson Drafting & Blueprinting, Inc.
Thunder Bay, Ontario, Canada

Prompt:	Response:	Explanation:
Command:	**INSERT**	Starts INSERT command
Block name (or ?):	**block1= block2**	Replaces "block1" with block name originally inserted in drawing; replaces "block2" with another block name. Both names can be the same.
Block _____ redefined Regenerating drawing. Insertion point:	Press Ctrl-C.	Cancels command. (You do not want to insert anything new.)

All the inserted blocks are updated.

When you want to insert an entire drawing into your other drawings as a block, you can define the insertion base point by using the BASE command. The default base point for a full drawing is at (0,0); that is, as you insert a sheet, the insertion point of that drawing is 0,0 by default. When you issue the BASE command, AutoCAD allows you to give it a new base point.

Inserting More than One Block (MINSERT)

To insert more than one copy of a block at a time, use the MINSERT (Multiple INSERT) command. This will allow you to insert the block in a rectangular array of rows and columns.

The prompts for MINSERT (which combines the INSERT and ARRAY commands) are the same as those for both INSERT and ARRAY. If you need more information on the ARRAY command, refer to Chapter 7, "Editing Your Drawing." The following command sequence shows how the array of chairs shown in figure 13.7 was created:

Prompt:	Response:	Explanation:
Command:	**INSERT**	Inserts the BLOCK
Block name (or ?):	**CHAIR**	The block's name
Insertion point:	Choose a point in the lower left corner of the bedroom.	
X scale factor <1>/Corner/ XYZ:	Press Enter.	X scale factor = 1
Y scale factor <default=X>:	Press Enter.	Y scale factor same as X
Rotation angle <0>:	Press Enter.	No rotation
Number of rows (---) <1>:	5	
Number of columns (|||) <1>:	5	
Unit cell or distance between rows (---)	2'	
Distance between columns (|||):	2'	

As you can see, these are the standard INSERT and ARRAY prompts. The only difference in the way you respond to these prompts with the MINSERT command is that you cannot insert a block in its individual pieces (exploded) by using an asterisk (*) when you enter the block name. If you need to move the individual blocks in the array to different locations, you should not use MINSERT. When AutoCAD performs a MINSERT, the full array becomes a block that cannot be manipulated as individual block entities.

Breaking Apart Blocks and Other Compound Entities (EXPLODE)

Within the AutoCAD drawing environment, several entity types, called *compound entities*, are composed of smaller individual pieces. Sometimes it can be easier to draw and edit this kind of entity, and as we have shown with the BLOCK command, proper use of such entities can even reduce the size of

Fig. 13.7. Using MINSERT to insert multiple copies of the chair.

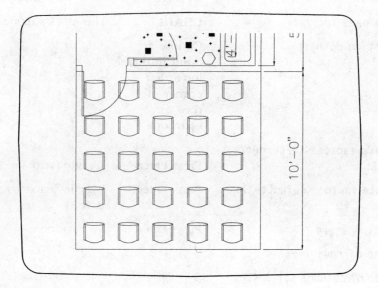

your file. Besides blocks, several other types of compound entities can be created within AutoCAD. They include the following:

❏ Associative dimensions
❏ Hatch patterns
❏ Polylines
❏ Meshes

Each of these compound entities can be treated only as a whole. There may be times, however, when you want to work with the individual entities that make up a compound entity. This can be done only by using AutoCAD's EXPLODE command.

EXPLODE separates compound entities into their original component entity pieces. To use the EXPLODE command, enter **EXPLODE** at the Command: prompt. You then will be prompted as follows:

`Select block reference, polyline, dimension, or mesh:`

You should specify the compound entity that you want to break apart. You can explode only one compound entity at a time. When you have selected it, the block blinks on-screen, indicating that the ungrouping, or explosion, has occurred. The individual pieces of the entity now can be modified as needed.

EXPLODE is particularly useful for working with blocks. Sometimes it is necessary to modify and redefine a block. The easiest way to do this is to insert the block, use EXPLODE, make your modifications, and then redefine the block. When you explode a block, all entities are moved back to the layer on which they were created originally (when the block was defined).

As you may remember from Chapter 12, "Expanding Your Horizons," associative dimensions are also compound entities. When these dimensions are exploded, they revert to the lines, arcs, and text entities that make up the dimension.

You can use EXPLODE to clean up and edit hatch patterns. When a hatch pattern is exploded, all the entities will move to Layer 0, regardless of the layer on which the pattern was created. You then can edit the basic line segments that make up the pattern.

When a polyline is exploded, any information specifying width for the segments is lost. Line segments and arc segments become normal lines and arcs and can be manipulated as such. Remember that ellipses, polygons, and doughnuts are all polylines.

Meshes, which are discussed in Chapter 15, "More 3-D Drawing Tools," also can be exploded. When a mesh is exploded, it becomes a series of individual three-dimensional faces. These entities then can be edited according to the methods of 3-D editing, explained in Chapter 15.

Here are a couple of pointers for using the EXPLODE command. First, exploding compound entities can greatly enlarge your database and take up room on your disk. For instance, exploding a complex mesh that is defined in the database as one entity may add hundreds of bytes of entity information to the database, causing a substantial increase in memory usage.

Second, EXPLODE ungroups compound entities one level at a time. For instance, when you EXPLODE a library block composed of several polylines, the polylines remain intact—they simply are ungrouped from the other entities in the block. You will need to execute the EXPLODE command again to further ungroup the component polylines.

Undoing Commands (UNDO)

A couple of commands (UNDO and U) rightfully belong in the introductory set of AutoCAD commands. They are discussed here because they are useful when you work with library commands.

As you insert blocks within a drawing or use the EXPLODE command to "unblock" a block, sometimes you may go too far. You may remember reading about the U command in Chapter 1, "A Quick Start in AutoCAD." A similar command, UNDO, provides a more versatile means of reversing the steps you have taken in a drawing. With UNDO, you can undo a single command or a group of commands.

You also may recall that the U command (an abbreviated form of the UNDO command) undoes one command at a time and can be used inside other commands. You can use U to step back to the beginning of the current editing session, or to the last time you saved your drawing.

The UNDO command functions differently. If you enter **UNDO** at the Command: prompt, the following prompt is displayed:

Auto/Back/Control/End/Group/Mark/<number>:

The default option, number, allows you to enter the number of commands you want undone at this time. If you are stepping back through your database to a certain point, but are not sure how far back it is, undo a few commands at a time.

The Auto option, which prompts you for an ON or OFF response, controls the handling of menu selections. If Auto is ON, subsequent menu selections are treated as one command. In other words, by properly using UNDO Auto, a set of any number of menu commands can be undone by a single U command.

The Group option is similar to Auto, in that it starts the grouping procedure: you are telling AutoCAD that you want the next series of commands to be considered as a group. These commands usually are entered at the keyboard. To let AutoCAD know that you have finished a group of commands, you enter **UNDO End**. The grouped commands can be undone with a single U command.

You use Mark to indicate a place in a sequence of commands to which you can later UNDO with the Back option. Back undoes all commands back to the point at which you entered the UNDO mark. If there are no marks in the UNDO information, AutoCAD undoes to the beginning of the current editing session. Mark and Back give you a powerful "what if" capability; you can mark your place in a drawing, change the drawing to see whether you want to proceed in a particular way, and later go back to the original place (and condition) that you marked.

The drawback to using U and UNDO is that if you want to undo one particular command, you cannot specify it. Rather, you must backtrack through all the commands you have executed, in order to undo that one command. This is a small price to pay, however, for the ability to correct your mistakes without having to recreate the drawing.

When you UNDO, you should be aware of the way commands—particularly those that create many entities at one time—work in AutoCAD. If you UNDO a command that draws several entities, all drawn entities are undone. The *command* is undone—not the separate entities. Doing a multiple copy is another example. If you UNDO multiple copies, *all* copies (not just the last one) are removed. To get rid of one specific copy, use the ERASE command.

Redoing an UNDO (REDO)

The REDO command, which cancels out the effects of an UNDO and takes you back to where you were before you issued the UNDO, is especially helpful when you step back through many commands at one time. If you go back too far, simply REDO and then step forward one command. Note that you may step forward only once.

In order for REDO to work, you must use it immediately after you use U or UNDO. When you type **REDO** and press Enter, the last U or UNDO is redone. Remember to use REDO immediately following the UNDO command you want redone.

As an example of using UNDO and REDO together, suppose that you use EXPLODE to disassemble several different blocks within a drawing. After doing this to five blocks, you discover that you have exploded one block in error. Simply enter the command **UNDO 5** to undo the last five EXPLODE commands. Now you can use REDO to undo the effects of the UNDO (if necessary). Continue this process until you get to the point where you mistakenly exploded the wrong block, then resume using the EXPLODE command on the blocks you do want to explode.

Adding Information to Blocks

The last few pages have shown you how to create, insert, and manipulate blocks. You have even learned more about AutoCAD's "eraser" commands, UNDO and REDO. Now you will learn how to use commands to store information about a block. These pieces of information, or *attributes*, are stored with a block and are inserted with the block into a drawing. Information may already be stored within attributes, or you can specify the information to be stored at the time the block is inserted. AutoCAD's flexibility lets you insert user-defined questions within attributes. When a block is inserted, AutoCAD asks these questions and adds the user's responses to the block being inserted.

The attribute information can be extracted from the drawing and used to build bills of materials or to quote a job. The extraction procedure, which is discussed later in this chapter, provides a file that can be imported into a word processing program or a database. Attributes can be used to detail the materials, part numbers, and costs of a specific item in the drawing. This information then can be extracted to gather project costs and inventories.

When you work with attributes, you use four basic commands:

- ❑ ATTDEF
- ❑ ATTDISP
- ❑ ATTEDIT
- ❑ DDATTE

You can use the ATTDEF command to define attributes, ATTEDIT and DDATTE to edit them, and the ATTDISP command to control the way they are displayed. These commands are discussed in the next few sections.

Defining Your Information (ATTDEF)

The ATTDEF command may seem confusing at first. In effect, the information you enter is used to set up the attributes. To make attribute extraction easier, the definition created by ATTDEF can be used as a template. (Attribute extraction is discussed later in this chapter.) When you enter **ATTDEF** at the Command: prompt, AutoCAD responds with the following prompt:

```
Attribute modes -- Invisible:N Constant:N Verify:N Preset:N
Enter (ICVP) to change, RETURN when done:
```

AutoCAD is allowing you to specify the attribute modes for the attribute you are about to enter. Let's look at each of these attribute modes.

Invisible mode controls the visibility of attributes when a block is inserted into a drawing. You can see visible attributes after the block is inserted; you cannot see invisible attributes. This is helpful if you have 20 lines of information, but do not want every line shown.

Constant mode lets you specify how accessible you want the attributes to be. Attributes set to Constant always have the same value. If the attributes are not constant, you have the option of being prompted for attribute values when you insert a block and you can edit the attributes after the block has been inserted. AutoCAD allows a mixture of constant and variable attributes in any given block.

Verify mode causes AutoCAD to prompt you for verification that you have entered the attribute value that you want.

With Preset mode, you can have variable attributes without being prompted for a value when the block is inserted. By editing the attributes, you can enter the values after the attributes have been inserted into your drawing. Use Preset mode if you do not anticipate knowing the attribute information for your blocks when you insert them. You can use this mode also to limit the number of attributes to which you respond when inserting the block.

After setting the attribute modes, you will see the following prompt:

`Attribute tag:`

The *attribute tag* is a one-word label for the attribute you are defining. A different attribute tag must be assigned to each attribute associated with a single block. Different blocks may have the same attribute tags for their attributes. These tags are used later in the attribute extraction process.

The next prompts you see depend on which modes you have set for this attribute. If you are working with constant attributes (if `Constant` mode is set to `Y`), AutoCAD simply prompts you for the value to assign to the attribute:

`Attribute value:`

You enter the constant value that you want the attribute to hold.

If, on the other hand, `Constant` mode is set to `N`, AutoCAD will prompt you for two pieces of information. At the first prompt,

`Attribute prompt:`

you specify what you want AutoCAD to use as a prompt when the block is inserted. Enter the wording for this prompt exactly as you want it to appear. If you do not specify a prompt, AutoCAD will use the attribute tag as a default prompt. When the block is inserted, the attribute prompt appears in the command area of your monitor, indicating the information AutoCAD needs for the attribute value.

The second piece of information required if `Constant` mode is set to `N` has to do with the default for the attribute:

`Default attribute value:`

Here you define a default value, typically the most commonly occurring value for the attribute. This value will be used only if, upon inserting the block, another value is not entered.

Suppose, for example, you want to put desks in a school floor plan on which you are working. You begin by creating a block for the desks, then you define the attributes to be used. You might include such attributes as the desks' *type* (whether for students or teachers), the *material* used to make the desks (metal or wood), and desks' *price* ($150 or $300). Any default value for these three attributes would pertain to student desks, because it is more likely that they will be specified due to the greater number of student desks than teachers' desks in the room.

At this point, AutoCAD simply needs to know some specifics about how you want to display the attribute: specifics such as location, height, and rotation angle. This information is gathered through a series of prompts that are the same as several of the prompts for the TEXT command (refer to Chapter 12, "Expanding Your Horizons"):

```
Start point or Align/Center/Fit/Middle/Right/Style:
Height <current>:
Rotation angle <current>:
```

When you reach this part of the ATTDEF command, you must determine where you want the text information to appear. In some cases, the text should be "inside" the entities that make up the block; in other cases, it is best to have the text appear next to the entities that make up the block. When you create the symbol, you must decide which way to place the text.

After you define one attribute, press Enter to execute the ATTDEF command again. If you press Enter when you get to the location prompt, the next attribute will be placed directly below the one most recently entered, much the same as with the TEXT command, and be given the same text properties as the previous attribute.

After you have defined all the attributes for a block, use the BLOCK command to create the new block symbol. When you select the entities to be included in the block, include the attributes you have created. This procedure attaches the attributes to the block.

Let's look at an example of how attributes are used. Earlier, you created a chair to learn how the BLOCK command works. Follow this command sequence to learn how to redefine the block and add the necessary attribute information.

Prompt:	Response:	Explanation:
Command:	**INSERT**	Starts INSERT command
Block name (or ?):	**CHAIR**	The block's name
Insertion Point:	Pick a point near the bedroom door (see fig. 13.8).	
X scale factor <1>/Corner/ XYZ:	Press Enter.	X scale factor = 1
Y scale factor <default=X>:	Press Enter.	Y scale factor same as X

Prompt:	Response:	Explanation:
Rotation angle <0>:	Press Enter.	No rotation
Command:	**EXPLODE**	Executes EXPLODE command
Select block reference, polyline, dimension, or mesh:	Choose the block you just inserted.	

To verify whether the explode was successful, issue a MOVE command and, when prompted to Select objects:, pick one of the lines of the chair. If the entire chair is highlighted, the explode was not successful, and should be tried again.

Fig. 13.8. The chair that will be linked to the attributes.

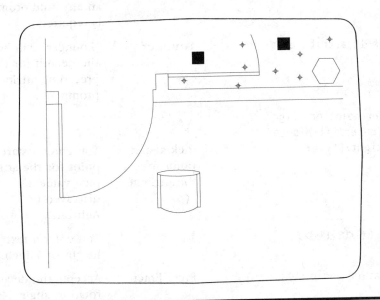

Follow this command sequence to learn how to add the necessary attribute information:

Prompt:	Response:	Explanation:
Command:	**ATTDEF**	Starts the attribute-definition process

Attribute modes --
  Invisible:N Constant:N
  Verify:N Preset:N
  Enter (ICVP) to change,
  RETURN when done:
	Press Enter.	Signifies acceptance of the attribute modes

Attribute tag:	**Type**	The tag for this attribute will be 'Type'.
Attribute prompt:	**Enter chair type**	Because this is not a constant attribute, an attribute prompt is required.
Default attribute value:	**Lounger**	'Lounger' will be the default for the preceding attribute prompt.

Start point or Align/
  Center/Fit/Middle/
  Right/Style:
	Pick a start point for the attribute.	You enter a start point for the attribute value displayed by AutoCAD.

Height <0.2000>:	**1**	You enter a text height of 1 inch.
Rotation angle <0>:	Press Enter.	Accepts the default rotation angle. Now the attribute is completely defined.

Prompt:	Response:	Explanation:
Command:	Press Enter.	Repeats last AutoCAD command (starts the attribute-definition process)

Attribute modes --
  Invisible:N Constant:N
  Verify:N Preset:N
  Enter (ICVP) to change,
  RETURN when done:
	Press Enter.	Signifies acceptance of the attribute modes

Attribute tag:	**Room**	The tag for this attribute will be 'Room'.
Attribute prompt:	**Enter Apt, Room & number**	
Default attribute value:	Press Enter.	No default for the preceding attribute prompt.

Start point or Align/
  Center/Fit/Middle/
  Right/Style:
	Press Enter.	Causes AutoCAD to display the attribute directly below the preceding one. Now the attribute is completely defined.

Command:	**BLOCK**	Starts the BLOCK command
Block name (or ?):	**CHAIR**	Name the block "chair."
Block CHAIR already exists. Redefine it? <N>:	**Y**	You must redefine the block you already created.

Prompt:	Response:	Explanation:
Insertion base point:	Select the point shown in figure 13.2 again.	
Select objects:	**W**	Specifies that you want to use a window to create the selection set
First corner:	Pick a window box that will enclose the pieces of the chair.	
Other corner:	Digitize window's lower right corner.	
Select objects:	Press Enter.	Indicates that all items are selected.

You have created your first block with attribute information! Next, you will learn how to insert blocks with attributes, as well as how to enter and edit attribute information.

Inserting a Block with Attributes

Clearly, blocks are of little value if you cannot later insert them in your drawings. The same is true of attributes. Although the process of inserting blocks into drawings was covered earlier in the chapter, you should take another look at insertion, to see how it is affected by the presence of attributes within the block.

When you insert a block with attributes, AutoCAD has two distinct methods of retrieving variable attribute information. Normally, the attribute prompts are displayed in the screen's command area, and the user can respond to the prompts with the appropriate attribute values.

Prompt:	*Response:*	*Explanation:*
Command:	**INSERT**	Starts INSERT command
Block name (or ?):	**CHAIR**	The block's name
Insertion Point:	Pick a point in the drawing.	This is the location for the symbol.
X scale factor <1>/Corner/ XYZ:	Press Enter.	X scale factor = 1
Y scale factor <default=X>:	Press Enter.	Y scale factor same as X
Rotation angle <0>:	Press Enter.	No rotation
Enter Apt. Room Name & Number:	**Apt #1, bedroom**	First attribute value
Enter chair type <Lounger>:	Press Enter.	Accept default attribute value.

Figure 13.9 shows the inserted block and its displayed attribute values. Notice that the order in which AutoCAD displays the attribute prompts is the reverse of the order in which you created them. As you define and work with attributes, you should keep this ordering system in mind.

Editing Your Attributes (ATTEDIT)

In the discussion of the ATTDEF command earlier in this chapter, you learned that you can insert blocks, including any attributes, and later edit the attribute values. This editing is performed primarily by using the ATTEDIT command, although the CHANGE command also can be used to edit attribute values.

ATTEDIT is quite versatile. With it, you can edit attribute values individually or by tag. If you edit by tag, the attribute tag is used as a reference. Editing all attribute values with the same tag is called *global editing*. You can either edit on-screen attributes or all attributes: visible, invisible, and off-screen.

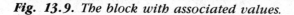

Fig. 13.9. *The block with associated values.*

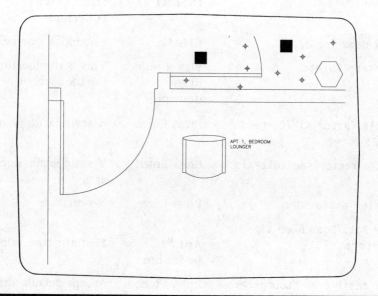

APT 1, BEDROOM
LOUNGER

Editing Attributes by Way of Dialogue Boxes

As you saw in Chapter 9, "Ways To View Your Drawing," AutoCAD provides several dialogue boxes to perform special functions within the Drawing Editor. One of those boxes, which you call with the DDATTE command, allows you to modify attributes as they are inserted into the drawing.

You use the DDATTE command to interact with the attributes of a specific block. Upon issuing this command, you will be prompted to Select Block:. After choosing a block with attributes, you will see a dialogue box that allows you to edit the selected block's attributes.

This command is a nice supplement to the ATTEDIT command. Along with the MULTIPLE command, DDATTE offers the speed and readability not available with ATTEDIT.

The ATTDIA system variable controls the use of a dialogue box for editing attribute variables. If your video display can use the Advanced User Interface (AUI), and ATTDIA is set to 1, AutoCAD prompts for attribute values through the DDATTE dialogue box upon inserting the block. SETVAR can be used to change the value of ATTDIA to turn dialogue-box entry on or off.

When you enter **ATTEDIT** at the `Command:` prompt, AutoCAD responds:

`Edit attributes one at a time? <Y>`

At this prompt, you tell AutoCAD what kind of editing you want to do. Answer **Y** (the default) if you want to edit the attributes individually; answer **N** to enable global editing.

If you choose to edit attributes individually, you are restricted to editing only visible on-screen attributes. You edit each attribute individually and can change the location, angle, height, and other properties, as well as the attribute value. If you want to limit further the set of attributes edited, you can do so by selecting specific tags, values, or block names for the attributes.

Although global editing is not restricted to visible attributes, you can change only an attribute's *value*. The attribute's location, angle, height, and other properties can be modified by the CHANGE command only *before* the attribute becomes part of a block. To specify which attributes you want to edit, you indicate the tag, value, or block name.

Let's look at both the individual and global methods of editing attributes.

Editing Individual Attributes

When you choose to edit individual attributes, AutoCAD asks you to specify the attributes you want to edit. You identify these attributes by providing appropriate block names, tags, and values (if any) at each of the following prompts:

`Block name specification <*>:`
`Attribute tag specification <*>:`
`Attribute value specification <*>:`

Notice that the default response for each prompt is an asterisk (*)—a wild card specifying that you want to edit *all* block names, tags, and values. If you want to limit your editing to selected attributes, you must enter the names of specific blocks, tags, and values.

If you need to enter more than one name, separate the names with commas. You can use the asterisk (*) wild-card character to represent several characters, and the question mark (?) to represent a single character.

At the `Select attributes:` prompt, use your pointing device to digitize each attribute you want to edit. You will not see any on-screen acknowledgment of your selection. After you have selected all the attributes you want to edit, press Enter. AutoCAD will tell you how many attributes have been selected.

Now the editing process begins. AutoCAD highlights the first attribute selected, places an X on the screen at the attribute's text-insertion point, and displays the following prompt:

```
Value/Position/Height/Angle/Style/Layer/Color/Next<N>:
```

Select Value if you want to change the attribute's original value. This assumes, of course, that you have not set the attribute mode as Constant (see the discussion on ATTDEF earlier in this chapter). If you choose to change the value, AutoCAD displays this prompt:

```
Change or Replace? <R>:
```

If you type a **C**, indicating that you are changing the value, you see the prompts:

```
String to change:
New string:
```

Type the string you want to change, press Enter, then type the correction. You need to type only the letters that will be changed. Because the Change option is case-sensitive, be sure to enter the proper mix of upper- and lowercase characters. AutoCAD searches the original attribute value for the first occurrence of the character sequence to be changed, replacing just that portion with the new string. If the string you want to change is not located, AutoCAD issues an error message and returns to the attribute-editing prompt.

If you type **R** (for replace), AutoCAD displays this prompt:

```
New attribute value:
```

Type the new value and press Enter. The entire attribute value is replaced by the new value.

Position prompts you for a new location for the attribute.

With Height, you can change the height of the attribute text. Use Angle to change the rotation angle of the text's base line.

Style refers to the text font or style used. (Styles are discussed with the TEXT command in Chapter 12, "Expanding Your Horizons.")

Layer lets you change the layer on which the attribute resides. (Refer to Chapter 8, "Advanced Editing Commands," for a discussion of layers.)

When you change the Color, the attributes stay that color until you specifically change them later. If you set the color to BYLAYER, the attributes assume the color assigned to the layer on which they reside. (For more information about colors, see Chapters 8 and 11, "Advanced Editing Commands" and "Customizing Your Drawing Environment," respectively.)

When you have finished editing an attribute, select Next. AutoCAD then moves the X to the next attribute to be edited.

Global Attribute Editing

If you want to change only the value of a group of attributes, you should edit the attributes globally. AutoCAD first prompts you for the following information:

```
Global edit of attribute values.
Edit only attributes visible on screen? <Y>:
```

Type **Y** (the default) if you want to edit only the attributes that appear on-screen. If you type **No**, AutoCAD switches the display to text mode and informs you that the drawing will be regenerated after you finish editing.

Then, whether you are editing all attributes or only those that are visible, AutoCAD displays a series of prompts similar to those for editing individual attributes. You are asked for the block names, tags, or values of the attributes to be edited:

```
Block name specification <*>:
Attribute tag specification <*>:
Attribute value specification <*>:
```

Notice that the default response for each prompt is an asterisk (*), a wild card specifying that you want to edit all block names, tags, and values. If you want to limit your editing to selected attributes, enter the names of the blocks, tags, and values AutoCAD will use to select the attributes.

If you need to enter more than one name, separate them with commas. As mentioned earlier, you can use the asterisk (*) wild-card character to represent many characters, and a question mark (?) to represent a single character.

If you are editing visible attributes, you will see a prompt that says Select attributes:. AutoCAD is asking you to select the visible attributes you want to edit. Use the pointing device to digitize each attribute you want to edit. There will be no overt on-screen acknowledgment of your selection. After you have selected all the attributes you want to edit, press Enter. AutoCAD tells you how many attributes have been selected.

If you are editing visible attributes, AutoCAD highlights the first attribute selected, placing an X at the attribute's text-insertion point. This display does not occur if you are editing all attributes.

When AutoCAD asks you for the String to change:, enter the string you want to change, then press Enter. Because you are performing a global edit, the string should be common to all attributes.

Finally, AutoCAD will prompt you to enter the `New string:`, the replacement value for the search string just entered. Because both search and replacement strings are case-sensitive, be sure to enter the proper mix of upper- and lowercase characters.

Now, to find the first occurrence of the character sequence to be changed, AutoCAD searches the original attribute values of each specified attribute. Then the old attribute value is replaced with the new string.

Overriding the Default Display Settings (ATTDISP)

As you may recall from the discussion of the ATTDEF command earlier in this chapter, the visibility of attributes is controlled by an attribute mode. To override the default visibility setting for all attributes, you enter **ATTDISP** at the `Command:` prompt. AutoCAD displays the following prompt:

```
Normal/On/Off <current>:
```

`Normal` defaults to the visibility setting with which the attributes were created. If you created the attributes as invisible, `Normal` sets Invisible; conversely, if you created the attributes as visible, `Normal` sets the attributes Visible.

`On` overrides the display settings and turns on all attributes, making them all visible, whereas `Off` overrides the display settings and turns off all attributes, making them invisible.

Any change to ATTDISP causes a regeneration of the entire AutoCAD drawing. If your drawing is large and contains many entities, you probably will not want to change ATTDISP, unless it is absolutely necessary.

Extracting Attribute Information (ATTEXT)

Attributes allow you to store information with a drawing and then, in a procedure called *attribute extraction*, pull out the information. In this procedure, specified attributes (perhaps all attributes) from a drawing are placed in a disk file according to a layout that you can specify.

The file you extract from the AutoCAD database can be formatted in any of three ways:

❑ CDF, or Comma Delimited Format
❑ SDF, a format compatible with dBASE III PLUS
❑ DXF, a variant of AutoCAD's drawing interchange format

AutoCAD uses the highly structured DXF file format to communicate drawing information to other programs. After reading DXF-formatted files, these other programs (desktop-publishing software, for example) can produce or manipulate AutoCAD drawings.

The CDF and SDF formats are more flexible. CDF is used to output an ASCII file in which each database field is separated by commas. The SDF format is used to communicate directly with a program such as dBASE III Plus. When you choose to extract information in CDF or SDF format, AutoCAD requires you to specify a template file that will be used as a guide for formatting the extracted information. The construction of a template file is beyond the scope of this introductory-level book; if you are interested in learning more about template files, see Chapter 9 of the *AutoCAD Reference Manual*.

To use the ATTEXT command, enter **ATTEXT** at the Command: prompt. AutoCAD responds with the following:

```
CDF, SDF or DXF Attribute extract (or Entities)? <current>:
```

To indicate the type of extract file you want to create, just type the appropriate first letter. Or, you can select entities on-screen to limit what is sent to the extract file. If you select entities (by entering **E**), AutoCAD asks you to create a selection set of the entities, after which you will see the ATTEXT prompt again.

If you choose the CDF or SDF file formats, you will see the following prompt:

```
Template file <current>:
```

As described previously, specify the name of the file to be used as the pattern for creating the extract file. The file must have an extension of *.TXT*.

Attribute extraction is a process that you may use frequently—or not at all. It all depends on whether you need to communicate information about your drawing to other programs. If such a need arises, be sure to leave time for working with AutoCAD and the other software, to ensure that the transfer of information works as expected.

Summary

This chapter has discussed two-dimensional drawing methods, with an overview of how you can produce your own symbol libraries. The usefulness of the BLOCK command, coupled with attributes, is limited only by your imagination. The following commands were discussed in this chapter:

❏ ATTDEF   ❏ INSERT
❏ ATTDISP   ❏ MINSERT
❏ ATTEDIT   ❏ REDO
❏ ATTEXT   ❏ UNDO
❏ BLOCK   ❏ WBLOCK
❏ EXPLODE

You have also discovered that blocks are useful for saving space in a drawing or getting information about symbols that have been inserted. This information can be extracted to a database or word processor for inclusion in project cost estimates or facilities management.

Now it's time to leave two-dimensional space and travel into the reaches of the third dimension. AutoCAD provides you the many tools needed for modeling your designs and discovering how well the object you are creating will really work in a real-life setting. Chapter 14, ''Entering the Third Dimension,'' shows you the basics of how to work in this intriguing environment.

Part IV

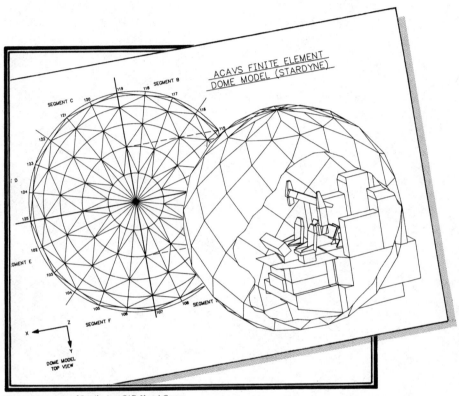

Drawings courtesy of Seattle AutoCAD Users' Group
Seattle, Washington

Working in the Third Dimension

CHAPTER 14

Entering The Third Dimension

This chapter will introduce you to the most exciting part of AutoCAD Release 10: three-dimensional drafting. With the advent of three-dimensional drafting, all CAD users—regardless of the amount of CAD exposure—are seeing a major evolution in the way computerized drawings are prepared.

This chapter will discuss the importance and applications of three-dimensional drafting, and will demonstrate some basic 3-D commands. After completing this chapter, you should understand the usefulness of 3-D, be able to enter elements with X, Y, and Z coordinates, and be able to get around in a three-dimensional environment.

The following 3-D features and commands are discussed in this chapter:

❏ Coordinate systems   ❏ UCSICON
❏ The Right Hand rule   ❏ VPOINT
❏ WCS   ❏ PLAN
❏ UCS   ❏ ELEV
❏ DDUCS   ❏ Point filters

What Is The Third Dimension?

What is three-dimensional drafting, and how will it affect us? The term *three-dimensional drafting* describes the process of entering into a computer any entities that can be recognized as having relative locations in space. Just as our world and the things in it are based in three dimensions, CAD drawings now can be based in three dimensions.

So far, this text has discussed only two-dimensional drafting. You may find that drafting in two dimensions on the computer is similar to drafting "on the boards," or on a two-dimensional sheet of paper. Three-dimensional computer drafting, on the other hand, is like building a model out of toothpicks. Just as a toothpick has beginning and ending points in space, three-dimensional CAD entities also have beginning and ending points. The three dimensions of an entity are its width, length, and height. In computer-aided drafting, these values are called *X, Y,* and *Z coordinates*.

It is important for you to realize that you do not *have* to draw in three dimensions. In fact, most people who draft on the computer will not even consider the Z coordinates of their entities. As a result, their drawings typically look like the older generation sheets of drafted work. They seem flat, unless you look straight down at the drawing.

Three-dimensional CAD work is used mainly for design studies, presentation, or experimentation, but rarely for drafting production documents. Once a project is entered in three dimensions, however, it can be rendered with AutoShade or even animated with AutoFlix. These two programs are discussed in Chapter 18, "Using AutoShade and AutoFlix." Once you understand the power of these programs (and more to come in the future), you will see the importance of three-dimensional work.

Coordinate Systems

One of the most confusing things about working in three dimensions is understanding *how* the computer needs the information entered. Until now, you have been drawing with little regard (and sometimes with no concern at all) for the entities' actual coordinates.

As you discover three-dimensional drafting, you suddenly become much more aware that the computer uses coordinates for all entities in a drawing. As you will see, entering these X, Y, and Z values in three-dimensional space can be a challenge. This is especially true if you are working on odd angles, such as roof planes.

The Right Hand Rule

You will better understand the directions of the positive X, Y, and Z axes, after you learn *the right hand rule*. This rule shows you an easy way to determine the positive direction of an axis. All you need is your right hand (literally!) and the positive direction of any two axes.

To determine the positive direction of the *Z* axis, for example, place your right hand near the screen with the thumb pointing along the *X* axis in the positive direction. Next, place your index finger along the *Y* axis (also pointing in the positive direction). If you curl your other fingers in toward your palm, you will find the direction of the positive *Z* axis. Basically, you make your hand into a play gun (see the *AutoCAD Reference Manual* for an illustration).

You can use this method also to find the positive rotation for a given axis. *Positive rotation* refers to the rotation AutoCAD uses when drawing or editing entities (as with the ROTATE command). Simply point your right thumb along the axis, aiming in the positive direction, and close your fingers into a fist. Your fingers curl in the same direction as the positive rotation along that specific axis.

The World Coordinate System (WCS)

As we discuss drawing in three dimensions and the special approaches to drafting in three dimensions, we should emphasize the fact that you are truly drawing in a unique *world*. In the world of AutoCAD Release 10—a world that has no bounds—you will be locating objects relative to one another.

As you work in this world, you will place items that are relative to each other but in a *specific* location. This location is absolute in AutoCAD's world. A line that runs from the world's coordinates of 4,2,6 to 1701,69,2112 will be located *at that specific location*, no matter which angle you look at it from.

From this thought process comes the term *World Coordinate System* (also called *WCS*). When you work in the world coordinate system, you place each entity in an unmoving, absolute location.

Now you should understand the importance of the X, Y, Z coordinate approach, and the fact that AutoCAD needs this information to put together a three-dimensional picture. Although the WCS holds a drawing's entities, it will soon become apparent that the WCS alone cannot draw three-dimensional entities.

The modern CAD draftsman needs a flexible coordinate system: one with which placing similar entities is faster and easier than working with the WCS. After all, what if you want to copy an item *straight up* to the second floor? You can't use the @*12'<90* for the second point! CAD users need a way to define a temporary coordinate system that has different X, Y, and Z axis locations. This leads us to the User Coordinate System.

The User Coordinate System (UCS)

A *User Coordinate System* (UCS) is a unique X, Y, and Z coordinate reference placed somewhere in the WCS. The CAD user develops the direction and location of the UCS to make entering three-dimensional entities an easier process (an ability you don't need if you're drafting in two dimensions).

An unlimited number of user coordinate systems can be defined in any drawing. If you have multiple UCSs, their specific X, Y, and Z referencing can let you define side, front, and back elevations, or even reflect the plan (straight down). In fact, the UCS command's power comes into play when you are working with inclined planes (such as a roof) of obscure angles in space. The use and definition of UCSs, which may seem difficult to understand now, will become evident in the next section of this chapter.

To repeat—any UCS resides *inside* the world coordinate system. A UCS is temporary; it is defined by the user to help in drafting and editing entities.

Defining a User Coordinate System (UCS)

Using the UCS command, you can create, change, and save user coordinate systems. The syntax of the UCS command is

```
Command: UCS
Origin/ZAxis/3point/Entity/View/X/Y/Z/Prev/Restore/Save/Del/?/<World>:
```

Origin defines a new UCS by moving the origin of the current UCS. Because the orientation of the axes does not change, you can have parallel user coordinate systems without having to redefine the entire coordinate system.

Select ZAxis if you want to define a new UCS with a different positive-Z axis. You define the origin and a point indicating the positive-Z axis. AutoCAD uses a complex method to determine the positive directions in each of the other axes. This is one application in which you can use the right hand rule to determine the new X-Y plane.

Using the ZAxis option may confuse you until you are better acquainted with AutoCAD. Defining a UCS exactly where you want it is easier than trying to figure out where the UCS is.

Select 3point to define a new UCS with three points: the origin, positive-X axis, and positive-Y axis. Be sure that the three points do not form a straight line.

Select Entity to define a new UCS by using an existing entity. The X-Y plane will be parallel to the X-Y plane that was in effect when the entity was drawn; the Z direction will be the same as that of the indicated entity. You must indicate the entity by pointing to it.

In table 14.1, the list of entities includes information about using the Entity option to create a UCS. Information is provided about how the origin and the X axis are determined. (Remember that the Y axis is perpendicular to the X axis and passes through the origin. The Z axis is perpendicular to both the X and Y axes and passes through the origin point.)

Table 14.1. *Using entities to create a UCS.*

Entity	Process
Arc	Center becomes origin, with the X axis through the endpoint of the arc closest to the pick point
Circle	Center becomes origin, with the X axis passing through the point nearest the pick point on the circle
Dimension	Insertion point is origin, with X axis parallel to UCS of the dimension
Line	New origin is endpoint nearest to the pick point. X axis is the other end of line segment indicated.
Point	Origin is the point. X axis derived arbitrarily
2d Polyline	Start point is new origin, with X axis from origin to next vertex
Solid	First point of solid is origin, with the X axis on line between first and second points
Trace	First point is origin, with the X axis along center of trace
3d Face	First point is origin, with the X axis from first two points and Y-positive side from first and fourth points
Shape, Text, Block, Attribute	Origin is insertion point, with the X axis defined by rotation

Select View to define a new UCS whose Z axis is parallel to the direction of the current on-screen view. This is a good way to define a UCS; you can set up your view point and then define the UCS according to the way you want to look at the drawing. Working with the view point, first determine how you want to see the drawing and then define the UCS.

Use the X/Y/Z options to rotate the current UCS around a given axis. When AutoCAD prompts you for the rotation around the indicated axis, you can specify the rotation angle either by typing it or by indicating the angle with the pointing device. The angle is referenced from the current X axis. Use the right hand rule to determine the positive direction for rotation around the given axis.

Previous takes you back to the last UCS in which you worked. This option is useful when you want to work temporarily in one UCS and then return to the current UCS. Simply define the new UCS, do your work, and then select Previous to return to the original UCS.

If you want to use a UCS more than once, you can save it in the drawing and select Restore to return to the stored UCS.

To save the current UCS, choose Save. AutoCAD will prompt you for the name of the UCS. Give the UCS a name, following the standard guidelines for named objects in AutoCAD. A name can be 31 characters long and contain letters, numbers, the dollar sign ($), hyphen (-), and underscore (_).

The Delete option deletes any saved coordinate system. You are prompted:

Name of coordinate system(s) to delete:

You can use wild-card characters to delete more than one system at a time; use a ? to represent one character, an * to represent many characters. Alternatively, you can type a list of the names, placing commas (but no spaces) between the names.

Choose ? to list the saved user coordinate systems (including coordinates for the origin and X, Y, and Z axes relative to the current UCS).

Select World to set the current coordinate system to the World Coordinate System.

For your sample drawing, you need to define one UCS. Use the following command sequence on your current drawing; you will need this specific UCS in upcoming chapters.

Prompt:	Response:	Explanation:
Command:	**UCS**	Begins the UCS command
Origin/ZAxis/3point/ Entity/View/X/Y/Z/Prev/ Restore/Save/Del/?/ <World>:	**ZA**	Choose ZAxis.
Origin point <0,0,0>	Press Enter.	

Prompt:	Response:	Explanation:
Point on positive portion of the Z axis <0,0,1>	**-1,0,0**	Using the Right Hand Rule, you can define the Z axis to be in the negative X axis of the WCS.
Command:	**UCS**	Begins the UCS command
Origin/ZAxis/3point/ Entity/View/X/Y/Z/Prev/ Restore/Save/Del/?/ <World>:	**S**	Saves the UCS
?/Name of UCS:	**L-SIDE**	For the left-side of the drawing

Now that you understand the fundamentals of the UCS command, surely you agree that there should be an easier way to define and restore a given UCS. There is! You can use a display dialogue box.

Modifying User Coordinate Systems with DDUCS

As you learned in Chapter 9, "Ways To View Your Drawing," AutoCAD's display dialogue boxes can simplify your interaction with the computer. Since most of these pop-up boxes were discussed earlier in this text, this chapter focuses on the DDUCS command as it pertains solely to three-dimensional work—namely, the User Coordinate System.

Use the DDUCS command to execute the UCS command through a dialogue box. When you type **DDUCS**, the dialogue box will appear on the screen (see fig. 14.1).

This dialogue box, which lets you do everything the UCS command does, lists the user coordinate systems on file. To make a change, move the arrow to the appropriate box and pick it. You will be prompted for new information. Some boxes are toggles; when picked, they change from ON to OFF or OFF to ON.

If you select the Define New Current UCS located in the lower portion of the box, a *subdialogue* box will appear (see fig. 14.2). Here you will find all the options available for defining a new User Coordinate System.

Fig. 14.1. *The DDUCS: Dialogue box for the User Coordinate System.*

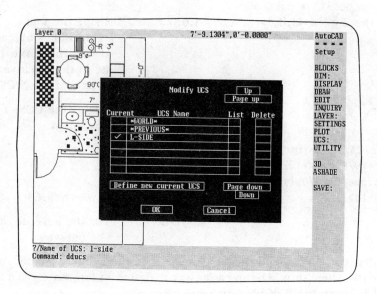

Fig. 14.2. *A subdialogue box: Defining a new current UCS.*

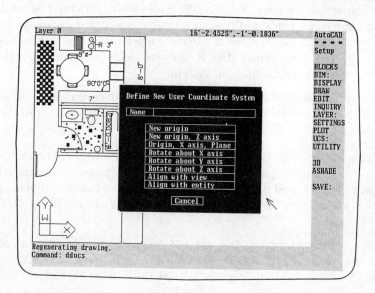

After modifying the current UCS, you will see the change reflected in the UCS icon. The UCS icon normally looks like the one shown at the bottom left of figure 14.3, but may change from time to time to indicate different system conditions. For instance, if you are viewing your drawing from an angle of 0 degrees (AutoCAD's normal viewing angle is 90 degrees), the UCS icon will change to a representation of a broken pencil—a reminder that any coordinates you enter at that angle may have little or no meaning.

Fig. 14.3. *The drafting example with the UCS icon showing the positive X and Y directions.*

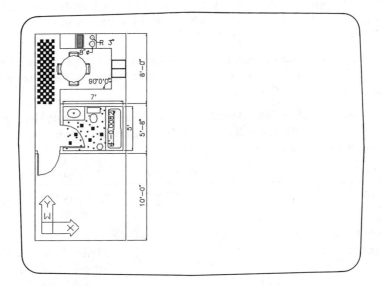

Manipulating the Coordinate System Icon (UCSICON)

To manipulate the coordinate system icon, use the UCSICON command, shown here with its prompts:

Command: UCSICON
All/Noorigin/ORigin/OFF/<ON>:

The All option causes the subsequent UCSICON option to affect the icon displayed in all your viewports. Generally, when you work with viewports, any UCSICON options affect only the icon displayed in the active viewport (viewports are discussed later in this chapter).

If you select Noorigin (the icon's default setting), the icon remains in the drawing's lower left corner (refer to fig. 14.3). Select ORigin when you want to tell AutoCAD to locate the icon at the origin of the UCS.

The default prompt, ON, means that the icon is activated; if you do not need the icon, turn it off by selecting OFF.

Controlling the View Point (VPOINT)

AutoCAD's VPOINT command (the name comes from *View POINT*) lets you look at a drawing in three dimensions. The VPOINT command will display the drawing from any reference point in space. When you start a new drawing, for example, you have a current VPOINT of 0,0,1, which is immediately above the X-Y plane.

Some of this command's features are demonstrated in this chapter. VPOINT is discussed to a greater extent in Chapter 17, "Ways To View Your Three-dimensional Drawing."

If you use the following command sequence on the sample drawing, you will see the image shown in figure 14.4. Notice in this figure the flat image you have been creating.

Prompt:	*Response:*	*Explanation:*
Command:	**VPOINT**	Begins the VPOINT command
Rotate/<Viewpoint> (current):	**-1,-1,1**	This gives you a three-dimensional view from above the lower left corner.

Figure 14.3 represents what is called the *plan view* of your drawing; figure 14.4 represents the screen image after the VPOINT command sequence. This view will become important and will reappear as you proceed to draft and edit in three dimensions.

Fig. 14.4. *A three-dimensional view of the sample drawing.*

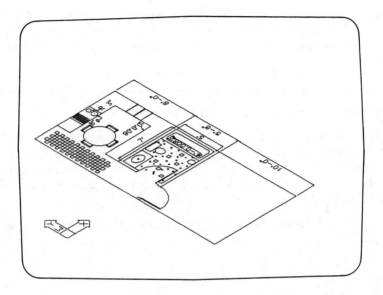

Returning to the World Coordinate System's Plan View (PLAN)

To return to the *plan view*, you can enter **0,0,1** at the VPOINT prompt. An easier way is done with the PLAN command, which is discussed in more detail in Chapter 17, "Ways To View Your Three-dimensional Drawing." If you use the following command sequence, you will return to the display shown in figure 14.3.

Prompt:	Response:	Explanation:
Command:	**PLAN**	Begins the PLAN command
<Current UCS>/Ucs/World:	**W**	You want a plan view of the WCS.

PLAN returns you to the plan view of any saved UCS or the WCS.

Three-Dimensional Drafting

You have just learned about the two coordinate systems you will work with when you draw in three dimensions. Expanding on this concept, the following section describes the different ways of entering entities with three-dimensional properties.

Entering WCS Coordinates while in a UCS

The time may come when you want to enter coordinates or a displacement based on the WCS while you work in a specific UCS. One option is to set the UCS temporarily to *World*, enter the coordinates, and then set the UCS to *Previous*. A better method is to place an * before the X axis' coordinate.

For example, at any To point: prompt, any of the following responses would be based in the WCS:

*5,6,13
@*6<180
@*-6,0,0

The last two designate a six-unit offset parallel to the World's X axis in the negative direction.

Elevation and Thickness (ELEV)

In discussions of three-dimensional properties, you frequently may hear the term *elevation*. This term refers to the entity's distance above (or below) the Z axis. In other words, it is closer to you, or farther away, as if you were looking *through* the screen and not just *at* the screen. So far, you have not had to think about how far above (or below) the Z axis the entities are placed. When you are looking down on a drawing, their position in the Z direction makes little difference; one might consider the entities you have been adding to your sample drawing to be two-dimensional.

You can change these entities from two- to three-dimensional by giving them an elevation. Remember—the Z axis is *always* perpendicular to the current UCS. A positive elevation will move the entities above the current X-Y plane; a negative elevation will move them below.

The second property you can change is the thickness of an individual entity. *Thickness* refers to how far out of its X-Y plane an entity extends. Some people often equate the term *extrusion* with AutoCAD's thickness. An extruded circle provides us with a rod; a circle which has a thickness will provide a similar result. A positive thickness extends an entity *up* by the specified amount; a thickness with a negative value extends *down* by the specified amount.

The following command sequence demonstrates the ELEV command:

Prompt:	*Response:*	*Explanation:*
`Command:`	**ELEV**	Starts the ELEV command
`New current elevation` `<current>:`	**2'6"**	Sets the new elevation to 2'-6" in the Z axis
`New current thickness` `<current>:`	**2"**	Sets the entity's thickness to 2" in the Z axis

After you have entered these values, *all* of the following elements (lines, circles, arcs, etc.) will have a thickness of 2″ and will be placed 2′-6″ in the positive direction in the current UCS.

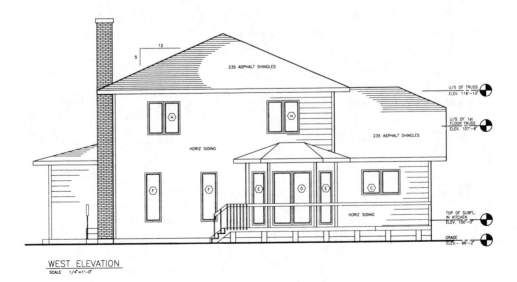

WEST ELEVATION
SCALE   1/4″=1′-0″

Drawing courtesy of R.L. Tomlinson Drafting & Blueprinting, Inc.
Thunder Bay, Ontario, Canada

Although it might seem faster to draft three-dimensional elements correctly the first time, with proper elevations and thicknesses, this is not always the case. As you will see in Chapter 16, "Editing Your Three-dimensional Drawing," it can take less time to modify parts of a drawing *into* three-dimensional space than it takes to draw from scratch in three-dimensional form.

Your use of the ELEV command, therefore, probably will be limited to periods when you work on similar entities, with similar three-dimensional properties. Of course, if you are working solely on two-dimensional drawings, you can have any values for your elevation and thickness, but a professional drawing demands an elevation and a thickness of zero.

Potential Problems With Non-Zero Elevations

If you are like most draftsmen who work in three dimensions, you will continually adjust your elevation, thickness, and UCS while using the OSNAP commands. (You will do so also when you use point filters, which are discussed in the next section.) This is imperative for accurate and speedy drafting, but can lead to confusing results.

Consider this example: You want to draw a line in three-dimensional space, starting at another entity's end point. After choosing the entity's end point, you find that the line does not start where you choose, but rather *in front of* or *behind* that end point. This occurs because your elevation is set to a value other than zero.

When you change your UCS, you should also consider setting the elevation (and possibly the thickness) to zero. This can alleviate potential headaches.

As Autodesk intends to discontinue the use of both the ELEVATION variable and the ELEV command in future releases of AutoCAD, it might well be worth your time to learn alternative ways so that you do not have to rely on these features.

Point Filters

Point filters are another set of important tools you should have when you work in three dimensions. In many ways, the point filters are similar to the OSNAP commands (discussed in Chapter 6, "The Basics of Drawing in AutoCAD"). As you know, the OSNAP commands let you draw more accurately by picking exact locations. AutoCAD's point filters work similarly, yet complement the OSNAP capabilities.

The point filters let you grab a specific coordinate (such as the X coordinate) of any entity. In other words, point filters break a point into its component coordinates—the X, Y, and Z values. Filters are helpful when you need to place points in relation to the current on-screen display. With point filters, for example, you can ask AutoCAD to start a line whose first point begins with the same X coordinate as one entity, whose Y coordinate is the same as the INTersection of two lines, and whose Z coordinate is at 10 feet above the floor.

Before you look at an example, it is important that you realize that point filters can work with or without OSNAP commands, and that they also act transparently.

Now let's look at the sample drawing. In an enlarged view of the toilet (see fig. 14.5), notice that the bowl seems to be off center in relation to the tank. If the image on your screen is not exactly like that in the figure, work through the following command sequence anyway. Move the bowl so that it is exactly centered.

Fig. 14.5. Enlarged view of the toilet, showing the bowl location "off center."

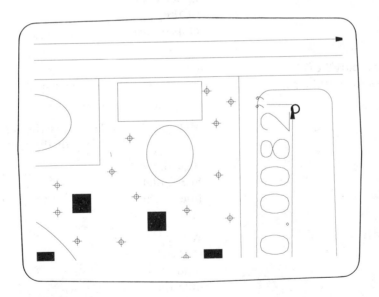

Before you begin, think of how you would move the bowl with the tools you now have. Would you construct temporary construction lines and use OSNAP commands to move it over? Would you find the DISTance (to get the change in the X coordinate, called the *delta X*) and move it a specific value? There are many ways to make this change. Hopefully, you can see why the following procedure might be the easiest.

Prompt:	Response:	Explanation:
Command:	**MOVE**	Begins the MOVE command
Select objects:	Pick the ellipse.	The toilet "bowl"
Select objects:	Press Enter.	Stops the selection
Base point or displacement:	**QUAD**	You want the QUADrant of the arc.
of	Pick the upper edge of the ellipse, near the tank.	
Second point of displacement:	**.X**	"Grabs" the X coordinate
of	**MID**	You want the MID-point of the tank.
of	Pick the horizontal line of the tank.	
(need YZ)	With ORTHO mode ON, drag the crosshairs to the left and pick a point.	

With ORTHO mode on, you can save time on the last part of the command because you do not want to move the ellipse in either the Y or Z direction. By telling AutoCAD to grab the specific coordinates you need, you *filter out* the coordinates you want. The finished drawing should look like the one shown in figure 14.6.

Fig. 14.6. *The bowl's location after the MOVE command and point filters have been used.*

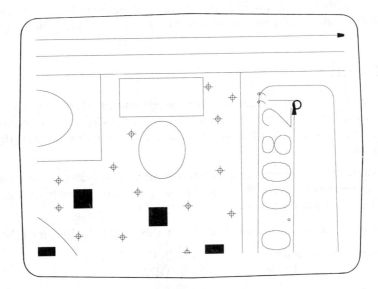

The following filters can be used whenever AutoCAD prompts for location information:

Filter	Meaning
.X	The X value is entered first; you are prompted for the Y and Z values.
.Y	The Y value is entered first; you are prompted for the X and Z values.
.Z	The Z value is entered first; you are prompted for the X and Y values.

Filter	Meaning
.XY	The X and Y values are entered first; you are prompted for the Z value.
.XZ	The X and Z values are entered first; you are prompted for the Y value.
.YZ	The Y and Z values are entered first; you are prompted for the X value.

The point filters are not limited only to three-dimensional work. In fact, you can use them in many ways, such as lining up text or drawing perfect boxes.

Summary

This chapter has started you on your voyage into the third dimension. You have learned the concepts of and considerations for the different coordinate systems, and you have been introduced to some three-dimensional drafting techniques.

It is important to realize the potential of your CAD system's 3-D capabilities. As you experiment, you will quickly come to realize just what an exciting adventure AutoCAD provides.

The commands and concepts developed in this chapter include the following:

❏ Coordinate systems   ❏ UCSICON
❏ The Right Hand rule   ❏ VPOINT
❏ WCS   ❏ PLAN
❏ UCS   ❏ ELEV
❏ DDUCS   ❏ Point filters

The following chapters will build on this foundation. You will be introduced to more powerful 3-D drafting commands in Chapter 15, "More 3-D Drawing Tools." Following that, Chapter 16, "Editing Your Three-dimensional Drawing," covers some important considerations and procedures needed as you modify your 3-D work. Finally, Chapter 17, "Ways To View Your Three-dimensional Drawing," demonstrates the different options you have for seeing your three-dimensional work.

More 3-D Drawing Tools

With the introduction of three-dimensional drafting in AutoCAD Release 10, many new commands were needed. Chapter 14, "Entering the Third Dimension," introduced the concept of three-dimensional drafting and guided you through several examples of 3-D drafting commands.

This chapter will build on that foundation and provide you with more drafting tools. You will learn the importance of the User Coordinate Systems and point filters. You also will learn how to draw involved three-dimensional entities with relative ease.

The following commands are discussed in this chapter:

❑ 3DPOLY   ❑ REVSURF
❑ 3DFACE   ❑ TABSURF
❑ 3DMESH   ❑ RULESURF
                  ❑ EDGESURF

This chapter also features examples that show you how to turn your drafting exercise into a three-dimensional project. Because the scope of creating a three-dimensional project can be extensive, some of these commands can be demonstrated only on a limited portion of the drawing exercise.

After reading this chapter, you should have a good understanding of some of the more involved 3-D commands. With these under your belt, you should be able to draft anything you can imagine.

375

Turning the Sample Drawing into A Three-dimensional Project

Like many three-dimensional projects, you can start by converting parts of a two-dimensional drawing into three-dimensional entities. Such a conversion can be done on the sample drawing you have developed. Before you begin converting some of the objects in the sample drawing (the kitchen table, a three-dimensional light fixture, and the bathroom wastebasket) into three-dimensional objects, you must prepare your current drawing.

Because you will erase some of the entities (and all the text), you should make a *new* drawing and insert your current drawing into it. You can do this at the AutoCAD Main Menu with Option 1 Begin a new drawing. At the prompt, type:

3D-STUFF=*filename*

(Be sure to type the name of the sample drawing in place of *filename*.) AutoCAD will start a new drawing called *3D-STUFF*.

To prepare your drawing for the upcoming three-dimensional work, follow these steps:

1. Erase all text, dimensions, dimension lines, and arrows.
2. Erase all chairs.
3. Erase all door "swings" (the arcs).

The before-and-after drawing files are shown in figures 15.1 and 15.2. You will begin working on this drawing file later in the chapter, as you draft in three dimensions.

Three-dimensional Polylines (3DPOLY)

The PLINE command's advantages and applications were discussed in Chapter 6, "The Basics of Drawing in AutoCAD." Note that the standard polyline will not allow you to enter three-dimensional coordinates. To enter a polyline that has various three-dimensional aspects, you should use the 3DPOLY command.

3DPOLY is less complex than PLINE and, therefore, less powerful. Table 15.1 shows the differences and similarities between the two commands and what they are capable of doing.

Fig. 15.1. *The exercise up to this point.*

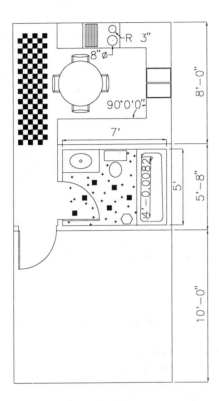

Fig. 15.2. *The exercise after unneeded two-dimensional entities have been erased.*

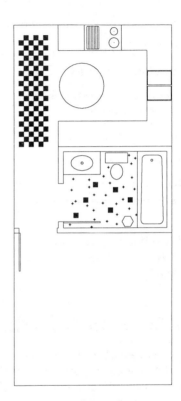

After typing **3DPOLY** at the Command: prompt, you indicate the segment's starting point at the From point: prompt. The following prompt is displayed on-screen:

Close/Undo/<Endpoint of line>:

Choose Close to close the three-dimensional polyline (refer to explanations of the LINE and PLINE commands). To undo the last segment drawn, select Undo. You can use the Undo option also to backtrack to the beginning of the command. At the default prompt (Endpoint of line), you can enter a three-dimensional point (x,y,z); if a two-dimensional point is entered, AutoCAD assumes that the Z coordinate is at the current elevation.

Table 15.1. *Comparison of PLINE and 3DPOLY.*

Drafting Task	PLINE	3DPOLY
Draw elements in two dimensions	YES	YES
Draw elements in three dimensions	NO	YES
Capability to draw arcs	YES	NO
Can close the entity	YES	YES
Draw the new segment with the same Length as the last	YES	NO
Undo the current segment	YES	YES
Modify the Width of the segment	YES	NO
Draw a segment at Halfwidth	YES	NO

Three-dimensional polylines (3DPOLY) can be edited with the PEDIT command. For more information, see Chapter 16, "Editing Your Three-dimensional Drawing."

Three-dimensional Faces (3DFACE)

The next aspect of three-dimensional entities is the 3DFACE command, the three-dimensional equivalent of SOLID. This command is used for drawing flat planes in three-dimensional space. If you need to draw a three-dimensional face that is *not* a flat plane, you should use the EDGESURF command, which is discussed later in this chapter. The area of a three-dimensional face is not filled in, as it is with SOLID. Also, any entities located behind the planes, or that pass through the planes, are removed when the HIDE command (discussed in Chapter 16, "Editing Your Three-dimensional Drawing") is used. You will use 3DFACE also if you are preparing your drawing for a graphics package, such as AutoShade.

You execute the 3DFACE command in much the same way you execute the SOLID command. But with 3DFACE you can enter points either clockwise or counterclockwise *around* the object. Three-dimensional faces can be either three- or four-sided. To enter a three-sided face, press Enter when prompted for the Fourth point:.

After it is drawn, a three-dimensional face looks very much like a polyline, or a line with an elevation. Entering the locations of the corners for a three-dimensional face, however, can be a bit trickier than entering the points of a polyline. With good use of the point filters, you can enter the corners easily in three-dimensional space. Also, the corner (or group of corners) of a three-dimensional face can be stretched (with the STRETCH command) in a given direction. This adds flexibility and ease of modification to your three-dimensional face.

How To Hide The Edges of Your Three-dimensional Face

Sometimes you may want to make one (or all) of the edges of your three-dimensional face invisible. This is especially true if you are placing three-dimensional faces next to each other. To do this, type **I** (for *Invisible*) *before* you pick the starting point of the edge. This edge, and this edge only, will be hidden when you select the next edge's starting point. This invisible procedure must precede any OSNAP modes, filters, or typed coordinates.

If you want to edit a three-dimensional face whose edges are hidden, change the variable SPLFRAME to a nonzero value. (*SPLFRAME*, which stands for *SPLineFRAME*, was discussed in Chapter 8, "Advanced Editing Commands.") After a REGEN, you will be able to see all the edges of the three-dimensional face.

You can practice this command on the top of the kitchen table in the sample drawing. To draw the entire table in three dimensions, you must divide it into three sections. This first section, created with the 3DFACE command, shows the top of the table. In the next step, you use the REVSURF command (which is discussed later in this chapter) to add the table's base. Finally, using the CHANGE command, you add the table top's edge. (The CHANGE command is covered in detail in Chapter 16, "Editing Your Three-dimensional Drawing.")

To draw the first part of the three-dimensional table (the table top), you use the 3DFACE command. Because this command allows only for straight lines—not for curved edges, arcs, or circles—you must divide the table's circular top into triangular shapes (just as you cut a pie or cake into wedges).

There are three basic steps to drawing the three-dimensional faces for the table top:

1. Use DIVIDE to break the circle into equal areas.

2. Draw one three-sided three-dimensional face (using the Invisible option discussed in the preceding sidebar).

3. Use a polar ARRAY to replicate the face.

First, divide the circle into 20 equally spaced parts, ensuring a smooth edge.

Prompt:	Response:	Explanation:
Command:	**DIVIDE**	Begins the DIVIDE command
Select object to divide:	Pick the circie that represents the table.	
<Number of segments>/Block:	**20**	You want 20 wedges.

Next, using the invisible feature of the 3DFACE command, draw a three-sided face that represents a wedge.

Prompt:	Response:	Explanation:
Command:	**3DFACE**	Begins the 3DFACE command
First point:	**I**	This edge to be invisible
no prompt	**CEN**	The center of
of	Pick the circle.	
Second point:	**I**	This edge to be invisible
no prompt	**QUAD**	The quadrant of
of	Pick the right side of the circle.	
Third point:	**I**	This edge to be invisible
no prompt	**NODE**	A node point
of	Pick the first node above the quadrant.	(See fig. 15.3.)
Fourth point:	Press Enter.	Stops the command

To see the wedge shown in figure 15.3, you need to change the variable SPLFRAME to 1, and then regenerate the drawing. SPLFRAME is the variable that lets you see the three-dimensional face's invisible edges. To change SPLFRAME, you need to first type **SETVAR**. This command allows you to change the value of AutoCAD's system variables. (For information about AutoCAD's variables, see the appropriate section of Part VI, ''Reference.'')

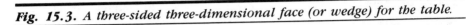

Fig. 15.3. *A three-sided three-dimensional face (or wedge) for the table.*

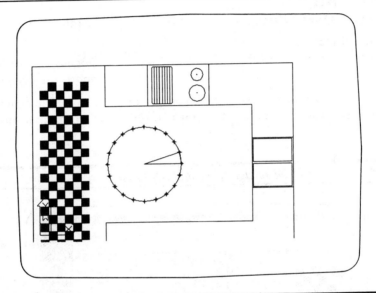

Finally, array the wedge to complete the table top.

Prompt:	Response:	Explanation:
Command:	**ARRAY**	Begins the ARRAY command
Select objects:	**L**	Last object (the three-dimensional face)
Select objects:	Press Enter.	Stops the selection
Rectangular or Polar array (R/P):	**P**	Polar

Prompt:	Response:	Explanation:
Center point of array		
of	CEN	The center of
	Pick the circle.	
Number of items:	20	20 wedges
Angle to fill (+=CCW,-=CW) <360>:	360	A full circle
Rotate objects as they are copied? <Y>:	Y	Rotates the wedge about the center

This command sequence should give you the product shown in figure 15.4. Now you will leave the table; later, you will finish transforming it into three dimensions.

Fig. 15.4. *The arrayed wedge to make a table top.*

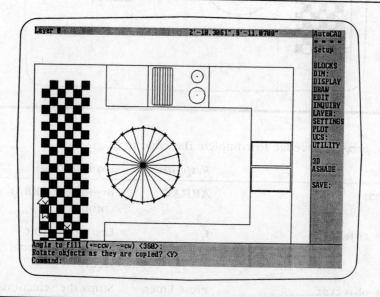

Three-Dimensional Surfaces, or Meshes

The commands in this section use a drawing's entities to create three-dimensional surfaces, or *meshes*. The basic surfacing command (3DMESH) is best suited for LISP programming and for surfaces that do not conform to the other commands (RULESURF, TABSURF, REVSURF, and EDGESURF), all of which use a three-dimensional mesh to create a surface (see fig. 15.5).

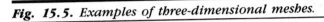

Fig. 15.5. *Examples of three-dimensional meshes.*

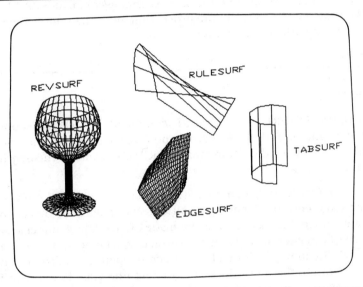

The names of the commands indicate the type of surfaces they create:

Command	Surface
RULESURF	Ruled
TABSURF	Tabulated
REVSURF	Surface of a revolution
EDGESURF	Edge (defined by four entities)

Because these surfaces are created from polygons, they can be edited as polylines. To learn how to edit meshes, see the section on the PEDIT command as it pertains to three-dimensional entities (Chapter 16, "Editing Your Three-dimensional Drawing").

Before you start drawing meshes, you need to know more about their composition. Meshes are a matrix of *M* x *N* vertices, where:

M is the number of vertices in one direction (considered columns)

and

N is the number of vertices in the other direction (considered rows)

The M and N directions are determined differently for each surface and are discussed with each command. Two system variables (SURFTAB1 and SURFTAB2) control the M and N variables. You must define M and N when you use the 3DMESH command; the other surfacing commands (SURFTAB1 and SURFTAB2) define M and N. Before proceeding with the sample drawing, you need to set the variables as follows:

Set variable:	To a value of:
SURFTAB1	6
SURFTAB2	6

With the RULESURF and TABSURF commands, SURFTAB1 controls the density of the mesh. With the REVSURF and EDGESURF commands, SURFTAB1 controls the density of the M direction; SURFTAB2 controls the density of the N direction.

When you use the HIDE command (discussed in Chapter 17, "Ways To View Your Three-dimensional Drawing"), all objects or parts of objects behind a surface are hidden, because surfaces are made of many three-dimensional faces. As a group of three-dimensional faces, surfaces can be open or closed in either the M or N direction (or both). If a surface is open in a particular direction (whether M or N), the mesh does not connect one edge to another, in much the same way that a polyline is not *closed*. A *torus* is closed in both directions, a hemisphere in one; an object that resembles a bundt cake mold is closed in one direction and open in the other.

To construct a surface, all the surface commands except 3DMESH need *boundaries*. These boundaries can include lines, arcs, circles, points, and open or closed polylines. For best results as you practice these commands, use boundaries that are on different user coordinate systems. In this way, you will create true three-dimensional surfaces.

AutoCAD's mesh commands are

- ❏ 3DMESH
- ❏ RULESURF
- ❏ TABSURF
- ❏ REVSURF
- ❏ EDGESURF

General Polygon Meshes (3DMESH)

When you use the 3DMESH command, you create a basic mesh by indicating all vertices (or *corners* of the individual planes) in the mesh. (The vertices are calculated automatically for the other surface commands.) Because of the complexity of entering the information for three-dimensional meshes, they are best suited to LISP programming, or to supplemental programs (see Chapter 19, ''An AutoLisp Primer'') for creating objects that do not conform to the other surface commands. For example, you would use 3DMESH to work with terrain and mapping.

3DMESH creates a general polygon mesh. You specify the mesh's size (in terms of M [columns] and N [rows]), as well as its vertices. AutoCAD assumes that you will input vertices from the top of the first column ''down,'' then move to the second column, progressing ''down'' until all columns have been filled.

For instance, if you want to enter a mesh in which M = 5 and N = 3, the syntax of the 3DMESH command sequence is as follows:

Prompt:	Response:	Explanation:
Command:	**3DMESH**	Starts the command
Mesh M size:	**5**	Mesh will have five columns.
Mesh N size:	**3**	Mesh will have three rows.
Vertex (0,0): Vertex (0,1): Vertex (0,2): Vertex (1,0): Vertex (1,1): Vertex (1,2): Vertex (2,0): Vertex (2,1): Vertex (2,2): Vertex (3,0): Vertex (3,1): Vertex (3,2): Vertex (4,0): Vertex (4,1): Vertex (4,2):	Specify individual coordinates to be used as vertices.	Last vertex. Mesh is finished.

All meshes created with the 3DMESH command are open in both the M and N directions. To close the mesh, use the PEDIT command (see Chapter 16, "Editing Your Three-dimensional Drawing").

Ruled Surfaces (RULESURF)

Use the RULESURF command to create a ruled surface between two entities, such as curves, lines, points, arcs, circles, or polylines. If one of the boundaries you choose is open (a line segment or an arc, for example), the second boundary must also be open. Conversely, if the first boundary is closed (a circle or an ellipse), the second boundary must also be closed. You can use points as a second boundary for either open or closed boundaries (if you want to create a cone, for example).

When you enter **RULESURF**, AutoCAD displays the following prompts:

```
Select first defining curve:
Select second defining curve:
```

You can select any AutoCAD entity for the first defining curve. To start the mesh, RULESURF uses the endpoint closest to the point at which you selected the entity. You select the second defining curve by selecting a point on a second entity. Figure 15.6 shows a RULESURF between two lines.

A closed boundary's surface, such as a circle, starts at 0 degrees. A polygon's surface starts at the first vertex. In figure 15.7, the ruled surfaces' boundaries are closed.

For the sample drawing, you can use the RULESURF command to turn the bathroom wastebasket into a three-dimensional object. First, use the OFFSET command to offset (by one inch) the polygon in the drawing (see figs. 15.8 and 15.9).

Next, move the new element "up" 14 inches, using the following command sequence:

Prompt:	Response:	Explanation:
Command:	**MOVE**	Begins the MOVE command
Select Objects:	Select the larger polygon.	
Select Objects:	Press Enter.	Stops the selection
Base Point or displacement:	*0,0,0	WCS coordinates
Second Point or displacement:	*0,0,14	14 inches up

Fig. 15.6. A RULESURF with open boundaries.

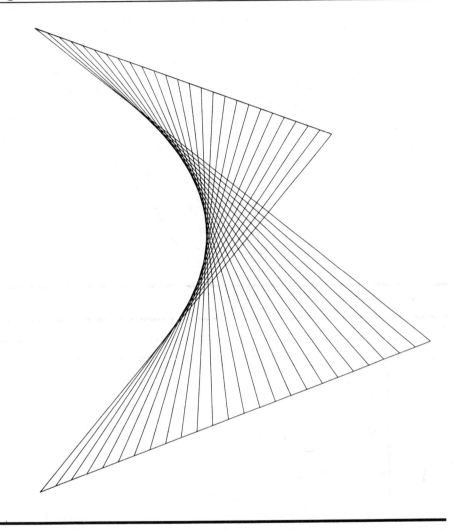

Fig. 15.7. *Ruled surfaces with closed boundaries.*

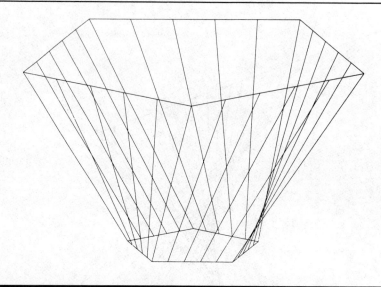

Fig. 15.8. *The original polygon.*

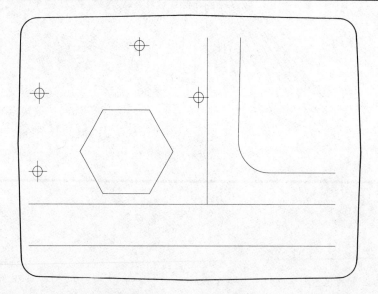

Fig. 15.9. The new polygon, after offsetting the original by 1".

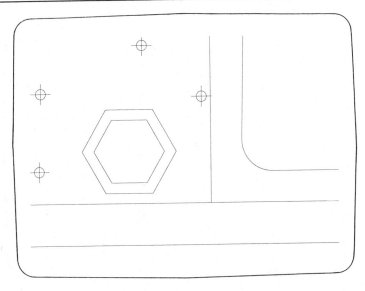

Now create a ruled surface between these two polygons, using the following command sequence:

Prompt:	Response:	Explanation:
Command:	**RULESURF**	Begins the RULESURF command
Select first defining curve:	Select either polygon.	
Select second defining curve:	Select the other polygon.	

The completed figure should look like figure 15.10 in plan view, and like figure 15.11 in hidden isometric view. (For the procedure needed to see the view in figure 15.11, see Chapter 17, ''Ways To View Your Three-dimensional Drawing.'')

Fig. 15.10. *Plan view: Looking down on the three-dimensional waste basket.*

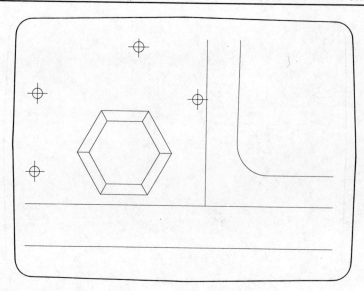

Fig. 15.11. *The three-dimensional wastebasket, seen from the side.*

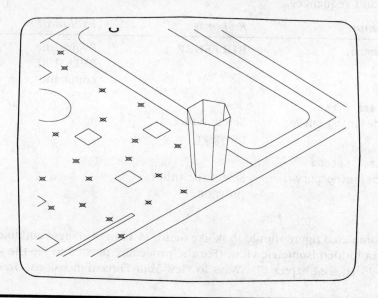

Tabulated Surfaces (TABSURF)

The TABSURF command creates a tabulated surface (see fig. 15.12). This type of surface requires a *path* (a basic entity that will form the surface) and a *direction vector* (or generatrix), which controls the surface's direction and distance. If the path and the direction vector reside on the same UCS, the surface will "smear" across the UCS.

Fig. 15.12. *Examples of tabulated surfaces.*

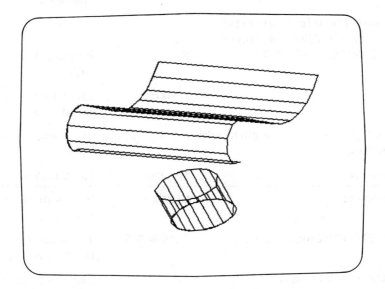

RULESURF creates a mesh to join two entities; TABSURF is used to project a selected entity a specific distance along a chosen angle. TABSURF will extrude *any* shape in *any* direction. This is similar to the ELEV command, in which thickness will extrude an item in the Z direction.

When you enter **TABSURF**, the following prompts are displayed:

```
Select path curve:
Select direction vector:
```

The path curve is the entity used to define the surface. This entity can be a line, an arc, a circle, or a polyline. This shape *cannot* be a point.

The direction vector (a line or an open polyline) indicates the direction and length in which the shape should be extruded. The extrusion's direction depends on the end you select on the line or polyline.

To practice the TABSURF command, place a horizontally tubed light fixture (like a fluorescent tube) over the bathroom sink. First, it is important to restore the *L-SIDE* UCS (as created in the previous chapter) so that you are working with the proper coordinates. To do so, follow this command sequence:

Prompt:	Response:	Explanation:
Command:	**UCS**	Begins the UCS command
Origin/ZAxis/3point/Entity/ View/X/Y/Z/Prev/Restore/ Save/DEL/?/<WORLD>:	**R**	Restores a saved UCS
	L-SIDE	The name of your saved UCS

Next, you will draw a circle with a 1 1/2-inch radius at one end of your future tube:

Prompt:	Response:	Explanation:
Command:	**CIRCLE**	Begins the CIRCLE command
3P/2P/TTR/<Center point>:	***2'6,4'9,5'**	The left edge of the fixture's center
Diameter/<Radius>:	**1.5**	The desired radius

Now that you have the shape you want to tabulate (or extrude), you are ready to use the TABSURF command, as follows:

Prompt:	Response:	Explanation:
Command:	**TABSURF**	Begins the TABSURF command
Select path curve:	**L**	Selects the Last object (the circle) as the shape for extrusion
Select direction vector:	Pick a point on the horizontal line of the sink *on the right half.*	

When completed, your drawing should look like figure 15.13. If your new entity went "the wrong direction" (that is, to the left), you should UNDO and try again. This time, when selecting the *direction vector*, you should be careful to pick on the *right half* of the line. You see, the pick point not only gives AutoCAD the distance by having it compute the line's length; it also determines the direction by calculating the line's closest endpoint.

Fig. 15.13. *Isometric view of the three-dimensional light tube.*

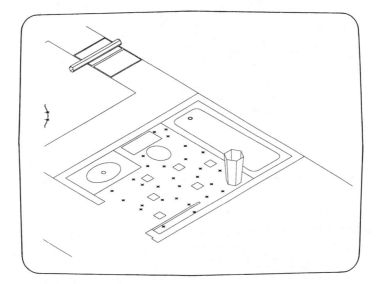

The REVSURF Command

The REVSURF command produces a surface of revolution by rotating an outline, path curve, or *profile* around an axis. A profile is an edge view (cross section) of the surface. This is the defining curve. Two examples of surfaces of revolution are shown in figure 15.14.

Explanations of the REVSURF command's prompts follow:

```
Select path curve:
Select axis of revolution:
Start angle <0>:
Included angle (+=ccw, -=cw) <Full circle>:
```

Fig. 15.14. Examples of surfaces of revolution.

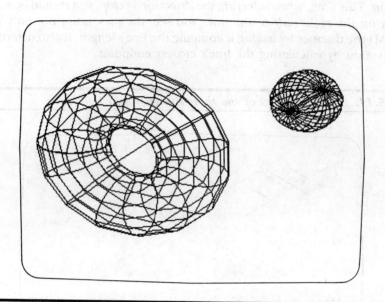

The path curve is the outline of the object you are drawing (a line, arc, circle, or a two- or three-dimensional polyline). The path curve is the *N* direction of the mesh created by REVSURF. If the *path curve* is either a circle or a closed polyline, the revolved surface will be closed in the N direction.

The axis of revolution (the axis around which the path curve revolves) can be a line or an open polyline. It is the *M* direction of the mesh eventually created by REVSURF.

The Start angle: prompt lets you begin the surface at an offset from the defined path curve. You can start the surface offset from the entity creating the surface. Just type an angle at the prompt.

At the Included angle (+=ccw, -=cw) <Full circle>: prompt, you specify how far the entities are rotated around the axis. You can define how far the surface is created and how far the path is rotated.

The direction of revolution is determined by which end of the axis you pick. To determine the direction of revolution, use the "right hand rule"; extend your right thumb along the axis, pointing away from the end closest to the pick point. Then curl your fingers. They will curl in the direction of revolution.

Figure 15.15 shows the axis and path of a surface of revolution before and after the surface is generated.

Fig. 15.15. *The path and axis before and after surface of revolution is generated.*

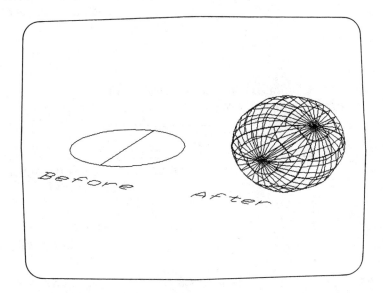

For the sample drawing, you need to create a base for the kitchen table. You can do this with the REVSURF command in the following steps:

1. Draw a construction line straight up in the "middle" of the table's circle. This will be the *axis of rotation* for the REVSURF command.

Prompt:	Response:	Explanation:
Command:	**LINE**	Begins the LINE command
From point:	**CEN**	The Center of
of	Pick the circle.	
To point:	**.XY**	"Grab" the X and Y coordinates of

Prompt:	Response:	Explanation:
of	**CEN**	The Center of
of	Pick the edge of the circle.	
(need Z)	**9'**	The Z coordinate of the line's second point
To point:	Press Enter.	Stops the LINE command

2. Set your view point so that you can see what you are working on. Then draw a polyline in the *L-SIDE* UCS. This represents the cross-section extents of the table's base. This is the *path curve* that will be rotated.

Prompt:	Response:	Explanation:
Command:	**VPOINT**	Begins the VPOINT command
Rotate/<View point> (current):	**-1,-1,1**	Isometric view from lower left corner
Command:	**UCS**	Begins the UCS command
Origin/ZAxis/3point/Entity/ View/X/Y/Z/Prev/Restore/ Save/Del/?/<World>:	**R**	Restores a UCS
?/Name of UCS to restore:	**L-SIDE**	The LEFT view
Command:	**PLINE**	Begins the PLINE command
From point:	**.XY**	Tells AutoCAD to "grab" the X and Y coordinates
of	**CEN**	The center
of	Pick the circle that represents the table top.	

Prompt:	Response:	Explanation:
(need Z)	**35"**	
To point:	**@1"< 0**	The following represents the outline of the table base.
To point:	**@33"< 270**	
To point:	**@2.14"< 315**	
To point:	**@10"< 0**	
To point:	**@1"< 270**	
To point:	Press Enter.	Stops the command

3. Use the REVSURF command to rotate the polyline *around* the construction line.

Prompt:	Response:	Explanation:
Command:	**REVSURF**	Begins the REVSURF command
Select path curve:	Pick the polyline.	
Select the axis of Revolution:	Pick a point on the construction line.	

4. Erase the construction line.

Prompt:	Response:	Explanation:
Command:	**ERASE**	Begins the ERASE command
Select objects:	Select the construction line drawn earlier.	
Select objects:	Press Enter.	

The finished product should look something like the table base shown in figures 15.16 and 15.17. (In Chapter 16, "Editing Your Three-dimensional Drawing," you will use the CHANGE command to finish the table.)

Fig. 15.16. The table base in plan view.

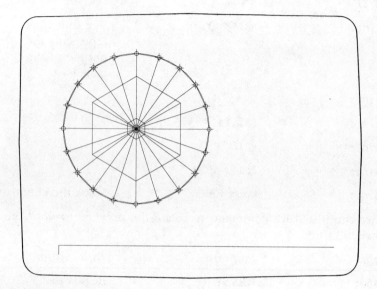

Fig. 15.17. The table base in isometric.

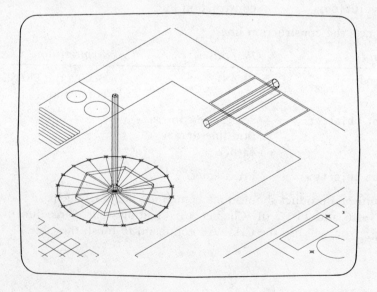

Edge-Defined Surface Patches (EDGESURF)

EDGESURF constructs a polygon mesh that is bounded on four sides by entities. These entities can be lines, arcs, or open polylines. This specific type of mesh is called a ''Coon's surface patch,'' after the professor who defined the algorithm used to create the mesh.

The four defining curves (or edges) must connect end-to-end, forming what Autodesk calls a ''topographically rectangular closed path.'' The path is a general-space curve, which defines the space between the curves. To define this space, the ends of each of the boundaries must touch.

After you enter **EDGESURF** at the Command: prompt, AutoCAD prompts you to select each of the four edges:

```
Select edge 1:
Select edge 2:
Select edge 3:
Select edge 4:
```

The edges may be selected in any order. The M direction is defined by the first entity selected. The N direction is defined by the two edges connected to the first selected edge.

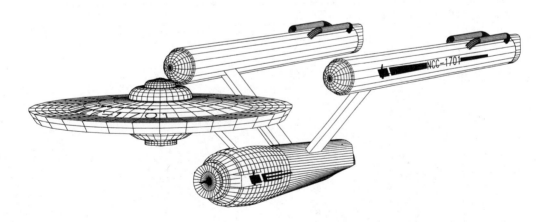

Drawing courtesy of Steven J. Frey
Fort Lauderdale, Florida

Figure 15.18 shows a Coon's patch applied to four curves (edges); figure 15.19, some examples of EDGESURF.

Fig. 15.18. *Four boundary curves (edges), with and without EDGESURF.*

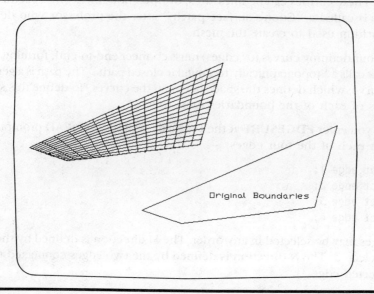

Original Boundaries

Fig. 15.19. *Examples of EDGESURF.*

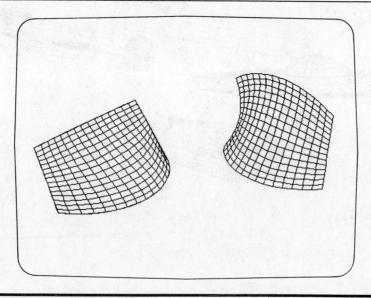

Summary

This chapter has covered the new commands introduced with three-dimensional drafting. And by demonstrating some of the more involved commands of three-dimensional drafting, this chapter has expanded on Chapter 14, "Entering the Third Dimension."

The following commands were discussed in this chapter:

❑ 3DPOLY   ❑ REVSURF
❑ 3DFACE   ❑ TABSURF
❑ 3DMESH   ❑ RULESURF
              ❑ EDGESURF

With their flexibility and power, these commands offer you the ability to construct almost any object. With these commands, and the tools discussed here, you can now draft in three dimensions. The next step is that of editing your three-dimensional drawing.

Chapter 16, "Editing Your Three-dimensional Drawing," covers the commands and steps you need to modify your work in three dimensions. It also demonstrates the differences between editing two-dimensional or three-dimensional entities with the same command.

CHAPTER 16

Editing Your Three-dimensional Drawing

In this chapter you will learn some of the commands that affect three-dimensional entities, and you will develop tools for editing three-dimensional drawings. This chapter will build on the foundation started in Chapter 14, "Entering the Third Dimension," by showing you how to convert a two-dimensional drawing to a drawing with three-dimensional entities.

This chapter complements and further explains some of the commands discussed in Chapter 7, "Editing Your Drawing," and Chapter 8, "Advanced Editing Commands." The commands discussed in this chapter have been grouped in three categories:

1. Editing commands that will not function on two-dimensional entities or on entities not drafted in the current UCS:

   - ❑ CHANGE
   - ❑ BREAK
   - ❑ TRIM
   - ❑ EXTEND
   - ❑ FILLET
   - ❑ CHAMFER
   - ❑ OFFSET

2. Editing commands that affect three-dimensional entities:

   - ❑ CHPROP
   - ❑ PEDIT
   - ❑ EXPLODE

3. Inquiry commands that provide information about three-dimensional entities:

   - ❑ LIST
   - ❑ DISTANCE
   - ❑ AREA

403

After reading this chapter, and after a great deal of practice, you should have a firm grasp of how to edit three-dimensional entities, and a better understanding of how to convert a two-dimensional drawing to a three-dimensional one.

Editing Commands Restricted to Entities in the Current UCS

You learned some of the basic editing commands in Chapter 6, "The Basics of Drawing in AutoCAD," and Chapter 7, "Editing Your Drawing." These rudimentary commands, however, are limited in their capability to modify three-dimensional entities. The following sections discuss a few of these commands and the problems they can cause.

Changing an Entity's Elevation and Thickness (CHANGE)

If you choose `Elevation` when invoking the CHANGE command, the items you are trying to change *must* have the same Z values. If the objects selected have different Z coordinates, AutoCAD will display the following message:

`Cannot change elevation of entities with different Z coordinates.`

Although you can use the CHANGE command to modify the entities' Z coordinate, doing so is not recommended. In fact, Autodesk does not plan to provide this capability in the next version. Rather, you should use the MOVE command to change an object's elevation *above* or *below* the UCS's Z axis.

If you try to use the CHANGE command's `Thickness` option, you soon will learn that it is not possible to modify the thickness of a three-dimensional face, three-dimensional polyline, or polygon mesh.

An example of the CHANGE command is reflected in figures 16.1 and 16.2.

Commands that Need Entities Parallel with the Current UCS

When you execute some of the editing commands discussed in Chapter 6, "The Basics of Drawing in AutoCAD," and in Chapter 7, "Editing Your Drawing," you will find that the entities chosen must be *in* the current UCS. That is, if

Fig. 16.1. The table top before a change in elevation.

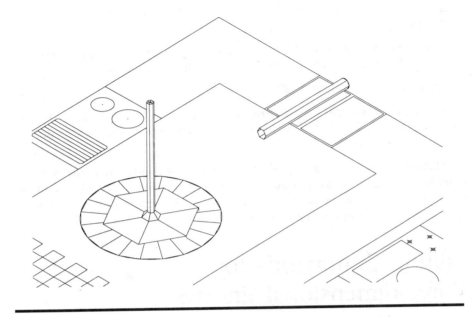

Fig. 16.2. The table top after the elevation has been changed to 30".

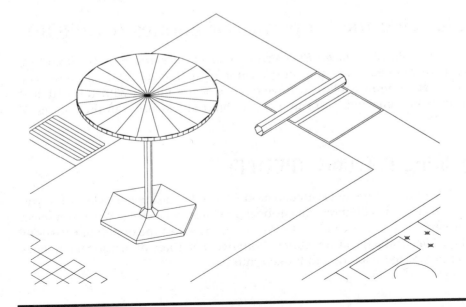

the commands are to have any effect, the entities' *extrusion* direction must be parallel to the current Z axis. These commands are

❏ BREAK ❏ EXTEND ❏ CHAMFER
❏ TRIM ❏ FILLET ❏ OFFSET

When you execute any of these commands, if you select an object that does not lie in the current UCS, you will see the following message:

```
Entity not parallel with UCS
```

For example, you will get this error if the current UCS is parallel with the World Coordinate System and you try to offset the base of the table as drawn in Chapter 15.

When you issue any of these commands, it is safest to alter your current view point so that you are looking "down" at the entity. This way, you will be editing the entity as it lies in the active UCS. (For more information on view points, see Chapter 17, "Ways To View Your Three-dimensional Drawing.")

Editing Commands for Three-dimensional Entities

This section demonstrates commands that have a specific editing effect on three-dimensional entities. These are the commands you execute in order to modify a three-dimensional object directly.

Changing the Properties of Entities (CHPROP)

The CHPROP (*CH*ange *PROP*erty) command lets you modify an entity's properties—specifically, the entity's color, layer, linetype, and thickness. The Thickness option applies to three-dimensional entities. With the CHPROP Thickness command, you can give an object an extrusion in the entities' Z coordinate.

Editing Polylines (PEDIT)

The PEDIT command is used to modify two-dimensional polylines, but you can use it also to edit three-dimensional polylines and meshes. When you select the entity you want to edit, AutoCAD determines the type of polyline (two- or three-dimensional) you are editing. Both two- and three-dimensional polylines can be opened, closed, and broken into parts.

When you use PEDIT to modify three-dimensional polylines, you can do the following:

❏ Open or close polylines
❏ Take out the kinks from a polyline
❏ Separate a polyline into segments
❏ Insert new vertices
❏ Move vertices
❏ Fit a three-dimensional spline curve in the polyline

When you use PEDIT to modify a polygon mesh, you can do the following:

❏ Open or close the mesh in the M or N direction
❏ Move vertices
❏ Fit a smooth surface into the vertices

After having read the following discussions on editing three-dimensional polylines and meshes, you will better understand the PEDIT command and the way it applies to both types of entities.

Editing Three-Dimensional Polylines

Two- and three-dimensional polylines are edited in the same way. You are limited, however, as to how much you can edit a three-dimensional polyline. You cannot edit the width because, by definition, three-dimensional polylines do not have a width. Nor can you add new entities with JOIN. You can, however, open or close the polyline, create a spline, and straighten and edit the vertices.

To use the PEDIT command, enter **PEDIT** at the `Command:` prompt; then select a three-dimensional polyline. The following prompt appears:

`Close/Edit vertex/Spline curve/Decurve/Undo/eXit <X>:`

These options are identical to those for a standard two-dimensional polyline.

Editing Three-dimensional Meshes

If you choose a three-dimensional polygon mesh after you enter **PEDIT**, AutoCAD prompts you with the following:

`Edit vertex/Smooth surface/Desmooth/Mclose/Nclose/Undo/eXit<X>:`

If the three-dimensional mesh were closed in the M direction, you would see the `Mopen` option rather than `Mclose`; if the mesh were closed in the N direction, the `Nopen` option would be seen rather than `Nclose`. These open and close options on the PEDIT option prompt act as toggles; whichever is displayed is based on the current entities' state.

The Smooth surface option allows you to fit a smooth surface into the mesh. The type of surface is determined by the variable SURFTYPE (similar to the SPLINETYPE variable discussed in Chapter 6, "The Basics of Drawing in AutoCAD"). If, for example, this variable is set to "5," the surface's smoothness will take the form of a quadratic B-spline. If the variable has a value of "6," it is similar to the cubic B-spline (refer to Chapter 6). A SURFTYPE variable set to "8," however, creates a *Bezier* surface—the smoothest type of surface, with the fewest "peaks" and "valleys."

After you have used the Smooth option, you can use the Desmooth option to return the three-dimensional mesh to its original condition. The Undo option allows you to undo the PEDIT options. The eXit option will end the command and return you to AutoCAD's Command: prompt.

When you choose Edit vertex, an X appears on a vertex of the given three-dimensional mesh, and you are prompted:

Vertex (*m,n*). Next/Previous/Left/Right/Up/Down/Move/Regen/eXit<X>:

The current vertex's location appears in the Vertex (*m,n*) area. As you use the Next and Previous options, you move through the vertices in order; the *N* direction moves quickest. If you use the Left and Right options, you will see the X move along the *N* direction. The Up and Down options move the marker along the *M* direction of the mesh.

When the X is at the correct location, you can Move the vertex. When AutoCAD displays the following prompt:

Enter new location:

enter the new coordinate in three dimensions.

You also can edit three-dimensional meshes by breaking them into individual lines and then modifying them. To break a three-dimensional mesh into lines, you would use the EXPLODE command.

Breaking Apart Three-dimensional Meshes and Three-dimensional Polylines (EXPLODE)

With the EXPLODE command, you can break a three-dimensional mesh or a three-dimensional polyline into individual entities. If you explode a three-dimensional mesh, the entities will be three-dimensional faces. If you choose a three-dimensional polyline, you will be given lines. When either is exploded, the entities created are placed on the same layer and have the same color and linetype as the original object.

Inquiry Commands Affected by Three-dimensional Entities

The following AutoCAD commands display information about your three-dimensional entities:

❏ LIST
❏ DISTANCE
❏ AREA

The LIST Command

The LIST command gives you a great deal of information about a chosen entity. This command will return the following information about a three-dimensional entity:

❏ Its X, Y, and Z location relative to the current UCS

❏ The X, Y, and Z coordinates

❏ The extrusion direction, in UCS coordinates (if different from the Z axis)

❏ The three-dimensional length for entities such as lines

❏ The angle in the current X-Z plane

❏ The change (called *delta*) in the X, Y, and Z directions

Further, LIST will do the following:

❏ Label three-dimensional polylines as ''space''

❏ Label three-dimensional meshes as ''mesh''

❏ Display the *M* x *N* size of a polygon mesh

❏ Designate whether a mesh is open or closed

The DIST Command

When you use the DIST (DISTance) command, you must consider the *Z coordinate*. If no Z coordinate is given, AutoCAD assumes the current elevation. DIST can create problems if you are grabbing entities with OSNAP commands. If you are using ENDpoint, for example, you can easily get odd values if the entities' elevations are different.

To guard against potential problems, watch not only the *Distance* returned, but also the Delta X, Delta Y, and Delta Z.

The AREA Command

With the AREA command, you can enter either two-dimensional (x,y) or three-dimensional (x,y,z) points, but the points must lie in a plane that is parallel to the X-Y plane of the current UCS.

When you use this command you must give careful consideration also to closed two-dimensional polylines or two-dimensional circles. This is important because the extrusion direction must lie in the Z axis of the current UCS.

Summary

This chapter has continued the discussion of three-dimensional drafting by demonstrating commands for editing three-dimensional entities. Many of these commands were introduced in Chapter 6, "The Basics of Drawing in AutoCAD," and in Chapter 7 "Editing Your Drawing." As you can see, these commands offer three-dimensional editing capabilities as well as two-dimensional capabilities.

Some of these editing commands will not function correctly on some three-dimensional entities, some will affect three-dimensional entities, and several inquiry commands provide information about three-dimensional entities.

The commands discussed in this chapter were

❏ CHANGE	❏ FILLET	❏ PEDIT
❏ BREAK	❏ CHAMFER	❏ LIST
❏ TRIM	❏ OFFSET	❏ DIST
❏ EXTEND	❏ CHPROP	❏ AREA

Your three-dimensional drafting lessons will continue in Chapter 17, "Ways To View Your Three-dimensional Drawing," which will show you how to generate specific views of your three-dimensional model. Chapter 17 will also give you information on image processing and better screen control.

CHAPTER 17

Ways To View Your Three-dimensional Drawing

In Chapter 9, "Ways To View Your Drawing," you learned that being able to see your drawing as you work on it is extremely important. This is especially true in three-dimensional drafting. This chapter covers the commands you use to see a three-dimensional project.

This chapter shows you how to get the on-screen views you need in order to work accurately in three dimensions. You will learn commands that can help you in your two-dimensional work, as well. AutoCAD's commands seldom are limited in their applications. Some of the commands discussed in this chapter are

- ❏ VPORTS
- ❏ REGENALL
- ❏ REDRAWALL
- ❏ PLAN
- ❏ VPOINT
- ❏ DVIEW
- ❏ HIDE

This chapter, which completes this book's section on three-dimensional drafting, builds on previous discussions of 3-D considerations, drafting, and editing and gives you a better understanding of AutoCAD's viewing options. You will learn first about screen-control commands and then about displaying three-dimensional work.

Screen-control Commands

It is important to control the on-screen image when you draft in AutoCAD. Although this may seem basic, it cannot be emphasized enough in three-

411

dimensional drawing. You know that AutoCAD provides new and powerful 3-D drafting and editing commands. But Release 10 also features *screen-control commands*, which are designed to aid with three-dimensional drafting tasks.

These commands let you quickly and easily view a three-dimensional image in whichever way is needed. The following commands can be used for a range of actions—from obtaining multiple images at once, to instant plan views. This section ends by giving you some tips that can help you get the most from AutoCAD's screen-control commands.

Seeing More than One View (VPORTS)

The VIEWPORTS command, introduced in AutoCAD Release 10, is executed by entering **VPORTS** at the Command: prompt. VIEWPORTS allows you to divide your screen into as many as four smaller "screens." You can work in any of the screens; the changes you make in one screen will be reflected in the others.

To understand this command, think of it as giving you the ability to set up windows of any area of your drawing. Each window is isolated from the others, and each one shows you a particular view of your drawing. One "screen" (or window) might contain a plan view, for example, while another could display an isometric view from the left corner. The third screen could show the isometric view of your project from another corner, and the fourth view might be an elevation.

These windows are called *viewports* because they are ports through which you can see your project. If you erase a door from an elevation view of your three-dimensional model, the door also will disappear from the other viewports, such as the plan view.

Within each viewport, you can define the following:

❑ The GRID and SNAP modes and relative spacing
❑ Fast Zoom mode (controlled with the VIEWRES variable)
❑ The Coordinate System Icon (UCSICON)
❑ The three-dimensional view of your project (VPOINT or DVIEW)
❑ The perspective mode (from DVIEW)
❑ The front and back clipping planes (also from DVIEW)

The VPORTS command and its prompts look like this:

```
Command: VIEWPORTS or VPORTS
Save/Restore/Delete/Join/SIngle/?/2/<3>/4:
```

You can work with a viewport configuration and end your work session without saving the configuration, or you can save the configuration so that you can return to it later.

To save a viewport configuration, select Save; then type any name you choose for the configuration. (If you want to see a list of saved configurations, enter ?.) To return to a saved configuration, use Restore, as you would when using the VIEW command.

The VPORTS command's Delete option (like the VIEW command's Delete option) deletes a saved configuration.

Select the Join option to join two adjacent on-screen viewports into one viewport. You must define the viewport that will become the view in the new, combined viewport. The SIngle option returns you to the default configuration.

Select ? for a list of active viewports and currently saved viewport configurations.

The 2, 3, and 4 options allow you to choose the number of viewports you want to use. Select 2 if you want two viewports; the screen can be divided either horizontally or vertically (the default). If you want three viewports, select 3 (the default option). AutoCAD then displays the following prompt:

Horizontal/Vertical/Above/Below/Left/<Right>:

The Horizontal and Vertical options split the screen into thirds in the appropriate direction. The other options allow for one large and two small viewports. You specify the larger viewport's location in relation to the two smaller viewports.

The VPORTS command is useful when you are working with a complex three-dimensional object. This type of work is easier if you can take advantage of multiple views. VPORTS is useful also when you need to show an object from several angles at one time. And VPORTS is helpful when you do two-dimensional drawings. You can use the command to display an entire sheet in one viewport, for example, while showing enlarged drawing details in the other three.

One of the most powerful capabilities of viewports is their *transparency* to most AutoCAD commands. If you have two viewports defined, for example, and you want to place a line within your drawing, you can place one of the line's endpoints in the first viewport and the other endpoint in the second viewport. AutoCAD cleverly will place your line in the intended location. After all, you are working on a single drawing or model.

You also can create viewports while you are using other AutoCAD commands. To carry the preceding example a little farther, suppose that you are entering a line and decide that you need another viewport in order to place the line's other end correctly. Simply enter the VPORTS command, preceded by an apostrophe ('**VPORTS**). AutoCAD lets you create the viewport and, when you finish, returns you to the LINE command so that you can place the second endpoint.

Sometimes, however, you cannot move between viewports. Any of the following commands prohibit you from working in multiple viewports until the command is completed:

❏ SNAP   ❏ GRID   ❏ ZOOM
❏ PAN   ❏ VPOINT   ❏ DVIEW
❏ VIEWPORTS (or VPORTS)

AutoCAD treats each viewport as if it were the only image on the monitor. This means that a REDRAW or a REGEN will affect only the *active* viewport. Likewise, PAN, ZOOM, VSLIDE and other commands that affect the display will act only on the current viewport. But two commands (REGENALL and REDRAWALL) affect *all* the viewports.

Regenerating All the Viewports (REGENALL)

Some AutoCAD commands work only in the current viewport. As mentioned earlier, REDRAW and REGEN work only in the currently active viewport. If you want to regenerate all the defined viewports, use the global REGENALL. This has the same effect as a REGEN for each viewport.

Redrawing All the Viewports (REDRAWALL)

To REDRAW the images seen in all the viewports, use the REDRAWALL (redraw all) command. This command has the same effect as a REDRAW for each viewport.

Returning to the World Coordinate System's Plan View (PLAN)

When you work on a three-dimensional model, you create multiple views, viewports, and different User Coordinate Systems. As you "flip" between UCSs, you need to see the image as if it were in *plan view*.

Suppose, for example, that you want to work on a building's side elevation. It is easiest to modify your UCS so that the X axis is unchanged but the Y axis is along the WCS's Z axis. Therefore, the UCS is "tilted up." Now that you have the right UCS, you probably want to see the side elevation as if you were looking *directly at it*.

In the World Coordinate System, you would be looking at the model from the side. In the current User Coordinate System, however, you look *straight down the Z axis*. This perspective is called the *plan view*.

With AutoCAD's PLAN command, you can tell the display to show the plan view of any of the following:

❏ The current UCS
❏ A predefined UCS
❏ The World Coordinate System

When you enter the PLAN command, AutoCAD prompts you:

```
Command: PLAN
<Current UCS>/Ucs/World:
```

Select Current UCS (the default) to display the current UCS's plan view. The next option in the prompt, Ucs, allows you to see the plan view for a previously saved UCS. This option does not alter the current UCS; it only shows you the image from the plan view of a different UCS. Select World to bring back the World Coordinate System's plan view.

If you want to view the drawing at a perspective different from a plan view, use either the VPOINT (ViewPOINT) command or the DVIEW (Dynamic VIEW) command (discussed later in this chapter).

Generating a Plan View Automatically

By using one of AutoCAD's system variables, you can cause a plan view to be generated whenever you change the current UCS. Use the SETVAR (SET VARiable) command to change the variable UCSFOLLOW to the value 1 (on).

When this variable is set to any nonzero value, a plan view is generated whenever the UCS is altered. This feature can be set separately for each viewport you have on-screen. If you have multiple viewports, you might set up one of them to display the plan view whenever you modify your UCS.

Tips for Better Screen Control of Three-dimensional Work

Now that you have been exposed to many of the commands that influence the display, you should consider how you can use these commands. Think about the viewing commands discussed in Chapter 9, "Ways To View Your Drawing," as well as those discussed earlier in this chapter. You have substantial control over the display when you use all the available options.

The following list includes some of the methods you can use to take full advantage of your display:

❏ Use multiple viewports whenever possible, especially in three-dimensional drawing.

❏ With multiple viewports, use the PAN and ZOOM Previous commands to move the image. This lets you keep a "blow up" at all times in one specific port, and can aid in adding detail.

❏ The saying "less is more" is especially true when you work with three-dimensional drawings. Because processing is faster with fewer faces, lines, and other entities, choose the number of entities carefully. More important, be selective about *what* you display. Having a "tight" zoom on a specific area will reduce the selection time needed.

❏ Because a three-dimensional model typically has more entities than a standard two-dimensional drawing, create and use VIEWS. Named views and named User Coordinates also should be used often. This practice will shorten the time needed to get the correct display.

❏ Slides can be used with good effect in viewports. (Refer to Chapter 9, "Ways To View Your Drawing," for information about slides.) If you have four slides representing four different options on one specific design, why not put them all on the screen simultaneously? With VPORT and VSLIDE, you can.

The items in this list are just examples from our experience. Experiment a little. You certainly will find additional ways to get the views you need.

Displaying Three-dimensional Work

This section of the chapter discusses some of the commands you can use to display your three-dimensional project. Here you will learn how to get an isometric or perspective view from any point in space. This section will show you also how AutoCAD can turn a three-dimensional "wire frame" image into a realistic picture, by removing entities that are behind each other.

Controlling the View Point (VPOINT)

When you draw a CAD image in two dimensions, you view the project from a point directly above it. When you draw in three dimensions, however, you need a different *view point* (the point at which you are "standing," in relation to the object you are drawing). There are several ways to change the view point. To change the current view point to one that is more conducive to drawing in three dimensions, you will use the VPOINT (View POINT) command.

To control the view point (the location from which you see your drawing), use the VPOINT command:

```
Command: VPOINT
Rotate/<View point> (current):
```

This command's default is a three-dimensional location in space. You can enter an X,Y,Z coordinate for an answer. This coordinate refers to the current UCS, not to world coordinates. (If you want to use coordinates based in *world*, type an * before the X coordinate, as in ***39,69,102**.)

`Rotate` allows you to indicate the view point by entering two angles: the first in relation to the current X axis, the second in relation to the current X-Y plane. Both angles start at the current origin, with positive angles going counterclockwise from either the X axis (as with the first angle) or a line along the first angle and the origin (for the second angle).

Note that the second angle is dependent on the first. The angle is referenced from the current X-Y plane along a line that indicates the first angle (see fig. 17.1).

You also can indicate the view point by using AutoCAD's compass and axes tripod (see fig. 17.2), which you can access by pressing Enter at the VPOINT prompt. The *AutoCAD Reference Manual* describes the compass as a two-dimensional representation of a globe: The center is the north pole, or top, the inner circle is the equator, or side, and the outer circle is the south pole, or bottom. Thus, if you choose a point between the two circles, you will be looking "up" at your object from the underside. As you move your pointing device, a cross travels through the compass, and the axes tripod moves accordingly. The tripod shows the directions of the positive X, Y, and Z axes for a given position of the cross in the compass.

Fig. 17.1. *The VPOINT command's* Rotate *options.*

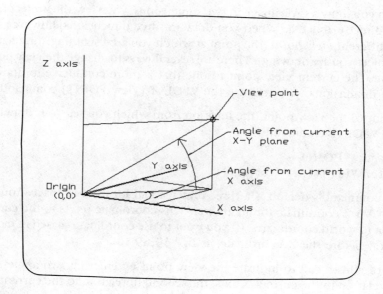

Fig. 17.2. *VPOINT's compass and axis tripod.*

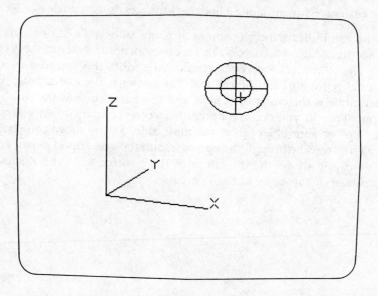

To indicate a new view point, "pick" a point in the compass. AutoCAD will regenerate the drawing based on the viewing location you select.

To change your view point for the sample drawing, follow these steps:

Prompt:	Response:	Explanation:
Command:	**VPOINT**	Starts VPOINT command
Rotate/<View point> <0.0000,0.0000,1.0000>:	**R**	Indicates that you want to rotate the view
Enter angle in X-Y plane from X axis <current>:	**−120**	Indicates new view in relation to X axis
Enter angle from X-Y plane <current>:	**45**	Indicates new view in relation to X-Y construction plane along Z axis

Remember: The current construction plane is the current X-Y plane. Everything you enter is in relation to the current construction plane. The current Z axis is perpendicular to the current X-Y plane.

After you enter the appropriate information, AutoCAD calculates the proper view and regenerates the drawing. Figure 17.3 shows the display before the preceding command sequence; figure 17.4 shows the screen after the view point has been changed.

Although the VPOINT command lets you see the drawing in three dimensions, it is somewhat deceiving because the projected image is in *isometric*. In an isometric view, the image is displayed so that all lines that are parallel in their respective UCSs are seen as parallel. (Autodesk calls an isometric view *parallel projection*.) The image appears to be three-dimensional, but all lines in the image are based on 30°, 60°, or 90° to a horizontal line.

Another disadvantage to the VPOINT command is that you might have to make a trial and error series of pictures before you come up with the view you need. The DVIEW command solves both these problems.

Fig. 17.3. *Plan view of the sample drawing.*

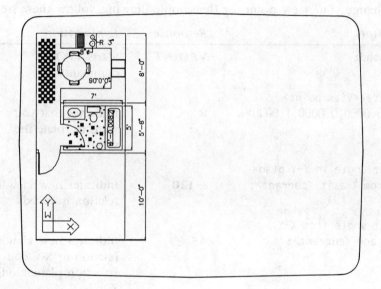

Fig. 17.4. *The sample drawing after the view point has been altered.*

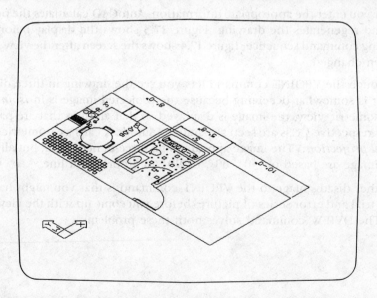

Dynamically Changing Your View Point (DVIEW)

Autodesk's DVIEW command gives you an opportunity never before available in AutoCAD—the ability to see your drawing in perspective. Another important feature of the DVIEW command is that it lets you change the view point *dynamically*; you can watch the view point change on-screen *while* you use the command. This *dynamic* effect means that the entities "move" as the view point changes.

The VPOINT command places limits on the changes you can make. That is, you can change only the location from which you are viewing, and you must remain at a fixed distance. DVIEW, on the other hand, lets you change not only your location but also the objects you are viewing and your distance from them. While you are using DVIEW, you can modify the view as often as you like; you are not limited to a one-shot change.

After typing **DVIEW** at the Command: prompt, you need to indicate the entities you want to see. When you see the Select objects: prompt, you have two choices. The first option is to press Enter without selecting any entities. If you do this, AutoCAD searches for a drawing called DVIEWBLOCK and uses it as a display while in DVIEW mode. If no drawing with this name is located, AutoCAD uses a small house for the DVIEW display. The house has a chimney, window, and open door. By pressing Enter, you tell AutoCAD to use all the drawing entities. AutoCAD then simplifies this display with the house graphic.

Your second choice at the Select objects: prompt is to create a selection set of entities from your drawing. You should select the entities you want to work with and a few additional entities, as well. This will give you a bearing on how you are looking at the entities. Choose carefully, because AutoCAD displays only those entities selected during DVIEW operations. If you select too many entities, you will slow down the DVIEW command; if you select too few entities, you will have difficulties understanding the changes in view point. The number of entities you should select for the command depends on the number of variables, not the least of which are the size of your drawing, the complexity of the entities, and the type of computer you are using. We recommend that you follow the principle of "less is more" when working with three-dimensional images. Remember—you can always cancel the command and try again.

Whether you choose to create your own selection set or to use AutoCAD's default display, you will be able to manipulate your view of the display. You can do this by adjusting the target (the object at which you are looking) and the camera (the direction from which you are looking). You do this from the DVIEW prompt:

```
CAmera/TArget/Distance/POints/PAn/Zoom/TWist/CLip/Hide/Off/Undo/<eXit>:
```

To facilitate changing the view point to the location you want, this prompt is repeated whenever you make a selection (until you eXit DVIEW).

DVIEW is an involved command. Because several of the prompt selections make similar changes to the drawing, similar selections are grouped together in the following sections; whenever possible, they are explained together.

DVIEW's *CAmera*, *TArget*, and *POints* Options

These three options deal with the same pieces of information: the target and the camera. In AutoCAD, the term *target* is used to define the object at which you are looking. *Camera* refers to the point from which you are looking (your *station point*). The target and camera determine how you look at a drawing; they calculate your line of sight, called the *viewing direction*.

The CAmera option allows you to change you station point's location while maintaining a fixed target. In other words, select CAmera when you want to view the same point in space from a different position.

The TArget option lets you change the object you are viewing, without changing your camera location. With TArget, you can "look around" a room, for example.

To change both camera and target locations simultaneously, select the POints option. By using this option, you can totally change the way you are looking at a drawing.

DVIEW's *Distance*, *Zoom*, *PAn*, and *TWist* Options

These four options are similar in that they do not change the target and camera locations as described in the preceding section. Rather, they change their positions by altering the image itself. Although the four options are similar, each changes the view in a different way.

Distance allows you to move the camera along the line of sight (the line between the camera and the target). This command can be used to change the camera location while retaining the current line of sight. Because the change is relative to the target, you must define a new camera-to-target distance.

The Distance feature also turns on perspective. To remind you that perspective is on, the UCS icon changes to a special perspective icon that resembles an elongated cube. The perspective view mode is disabled by the Off option, discussed later in this chapter.

The Zoom option's function depends on whether perspective is on or off. If you are viewing in perspective, you can use Zoom to adjust the length of the camera lens. The default (50mm) simulates the view through a 35mm camera with a 50mm lens. Using a lens with a lower number (25mm, for example) is similar to using a wide-angle lens. A higher lens length is analogous to using a telephoto lens, because it increases your viewing area.

If you are not working in perspective, the effects of the Zoom option are similar to those of ZOOM Center. AutoCAD magnifies the drawing while retaining the current center point of the screen. In other words, whatever is in the center of the screen stays there; you zoom in on that part of the screen.

The PAN command and DVIEW's PAn option react in the same way. With the PAn option, however, you are working in a dynamic mode—you see the changes occur as you enter information. The PAn option shifts the drawing without changing the zoom factor. This is useful if you are working with entities that are only partially on-screen. You can use PAn to move them completely on-screen, as long as they are in the selection set.

TWist allows you to tilt the view around the line of sight. Only the view is tilted; the camera and target remain the same. The line of sight is the axis of tilt (or twist). The angle you indicate (if positive) is taken counterclockwise (ccw) around this line.

DVIEW's *Hide, Off,* and *Undo* Options

These three options provide different capabilities to the DVIEW command.

The Hide option removes hidden lines in the current view. After hidden lines have been removed, a regeneration will restore all hidden lines. This option is similar to the HIDE command (discussed later in this chapter) issued at the Command: prompt.

If you choose the Off option, you tell AutoCAD to turn off perspective mode (which was turned on automatically when you selected Distance). If perspective mode is not on (that is, if you are working with parallel projection), this command will have no effect.

The Undo option, which allows you to undo the last DVIEW selection and any changes you may have made, is wonderful when you experiment with DVIEW.

DVIEW's *CLip* Option

CLip lets you add *clipping planes* to a drawing. Of all the DVIEW command's options, this one is the most involved. When you select this option, you are given the following options:

```
Back/Front/<Off>
```

The Back and Front options refer to *clipping planes*. A clipping plane blocks whatever is behind (back clipping plane) or in front of it (front clipping plane). Clipping planes are perpendicular to the line of sight and can be applied anywhere between the camera and target. This is a nice feature when you want to show one part of a drawing and the rest of the drawing is in the way.

When you are working in perspective, the front clipping plane is turned on automatically and is located at the camera. Anything behind the camera is not seen when you are in perspective. (Ordinarily, these entities are not seen, because they are behind the camera. The clipping plane eliminates any possible strange projections of these entities during perspective.)

By selecting the Off option, you totally disable the front and back clipping. Choosing this option returns the DVIEW command to the default setting for CLip.

Working with DVIEW's Options

Now that you have been introduced to the DVIEW options, let's look at a few examples of how they are used. The examples are based on the drawing shown in figure 17.5.

The examples are grouped similarly to the options. The first set of examples deals with moving the camera and target; the second set, with the Distance, Zoom, PAn, and TWist options. Finally, the CLip and Hide options are discussed. If you are working along with the examples, use the Undo option to return to the drawing shown in figure 17.5.

First, let's look at how the CAmera option is used. The screen shown in figure 17.6 allows you to change the view in a "vertical" direction; the second screen (see fig. 17.7) allows you to make changes in the "horizontal" direction. You make the changes by using *slider bars* (bars marked with angle measurements and located at the side and top of the screen). Alternatively, you can type a new angle for the camera.

Fig. 17.5. *The original drawing.*

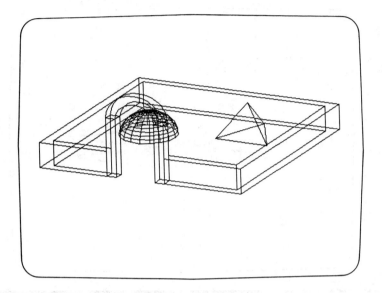

Fig. 17.6. *Modifying the vertical location of the camera.*

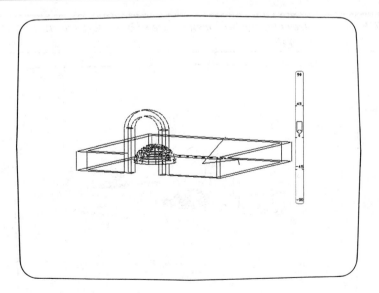

Fig. 17.7. Modifying the horizontal location of the camera.

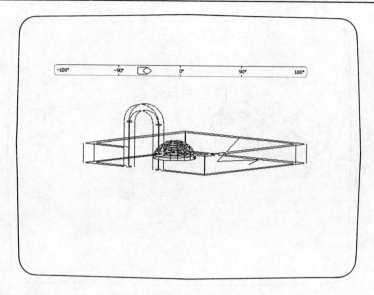

In figure 17.8, the camera location reflects a change of 15 degrees in both the vertical and horizontal directions. Compare this view with the view shown in figure 17.5.

Fig. 17.8. A 15-degree change has been made to both vertical and horizontal camera angle.

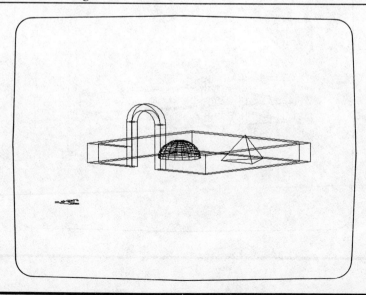

Changing the target can create confusion at first, especially if the new location is nowhere near the entities. The new target location is rotated around the current camera location, just as the new camera location was rotated around the current target location. The effect is the same as that of turning your head to see a different part of a room. Starting with the drawing in figure 17.5, we will maintain the target's vertical location (see fig. 17.9) while changing the horizontal location (see fig. 17.10).

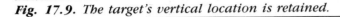

Fig. 17.9. *The target's vertical location is retained.*

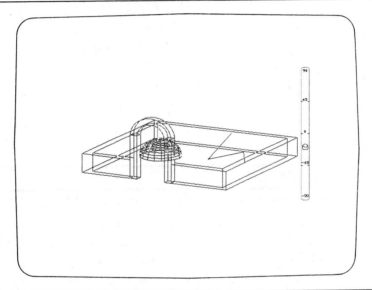

Figure 17.11 shows the changes made to the original drawing by modifying the horizontal target location by 15 degrees. Compare figure 17.11 with figure 17.5.

As you may recall, the POints option allows you to change both camera and target at the same time. The new target point is specified first, with the default target indicated in your current view port. You can use the "rubber band" connected to the current target location to help place the new target, or you can enter an X,Y,Z coordinate.

Next you are prompted for the new camera location. As you can see from figure 17.12, the "rubber band" is connected to the new target location for easier placement of the camera. (Basically, you are defining the line of sight.)

Fig. 17.10. Changing the horizontal location of the target.

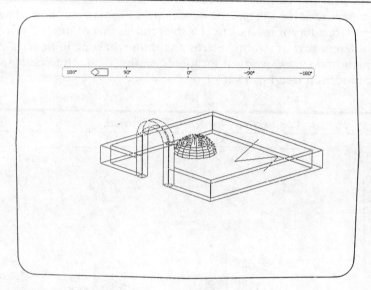

Fig. 17.11. A 15-degree change has been made in the horizontal location of the target.

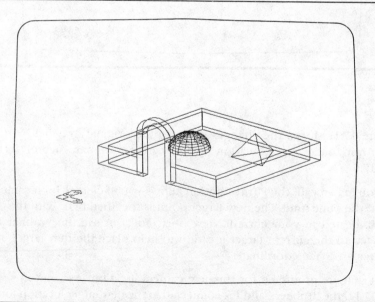

Fig. 17.12. *Changing the camera location with* POints.

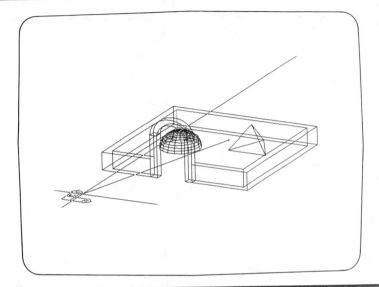

Distance, as you will recall, changes the camera location along the line of sight. We will change the camera distance to 5 feet from the target (see fig. 17.13).

Fig. 17.13. *Distance changed to five feet from target.*

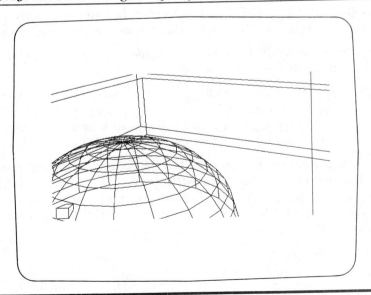

It is 15′ from the target in figure 17.14.

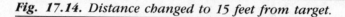

Fig. 17.14. *Distance changed to 15 feet from target.*

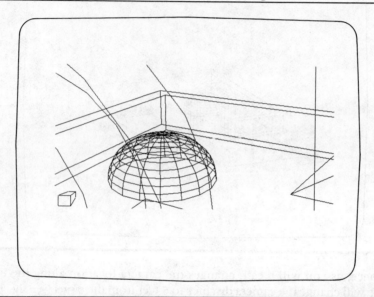

PAn, like the PAN command, allows you to shift on-screen images without changing the zoom factor. This feature is handy when you have made changes and the image is off-screen. You can use this option to move it back on-screen.

TWist allows you to tilt the view by rotating it around the line of sight. Figure 17.15 shows the original drawing, twisted 25 degrees.

CLip and Hide allow you to modify your view to describe more accurately what you are seeing. You can apply two clipping planes: front and back. The front plane blocks anything in front of it (between it and the camera, as in fig. 17.16); the back plane blocks whatever is behind it (see fig. 17.17).

Select Hide if you want to remove hidden lines from the currently selected entities. This option is similar to the HIDE command, which is discussed in the next section. With DVIEW's Hide option, however, you can see the image with the hidden faces while still in the dynamic view. This allows you to adjust your view in order to get the right image.

Fig. 17.15. *The effect of twisting the drawing by 25 degrees.*

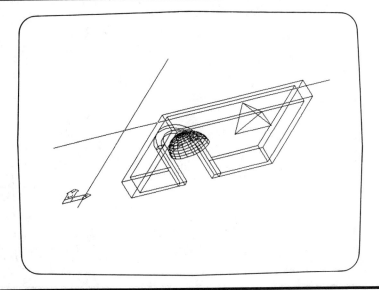

Fig. 17.16. *Front clipping plane in the original drawing.*

Fig. 17.17. Back clipping plane in the original drawing.

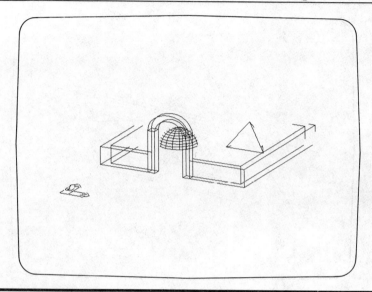

Removing Hidden Lines (HIDE)

Working in three dimensions can be confusing, especially if your drawing has many lines. You can clear up some of the confusion by using the HIDE command to remove hidden lines and faces from your drawing. You simply type **HIDE** and press Enter. AutoCAD does all the work.

The terms *hidden lines* and *hidden faces* describe entities that lie behind other entities. Whether an entity lies behind another depends solely on your current view point. Entities on layers that are turned off are still calculated by AutoCAD during the HIDE command. Although these entities will not be plotted or drawn on-screen, they may obscure other entities and cause confusion. To overcome this problem, *freeze* these layers.

The HIDE command will not process any entity that is made up only of text. Blocks that contain attributes, and Attribute Definition entities alone, are drawn without regard to their ''visibility.'' For information about these items, see Chapter 8, ''Advanced Editing Commands.''

Figure 17.18 shows a drawing before hidden line removal; figure 17.19 shows the same drawing after the hidden lines have been removed.

Fig. 17.18. *A set of three-dimensional shapes before HIDE.*

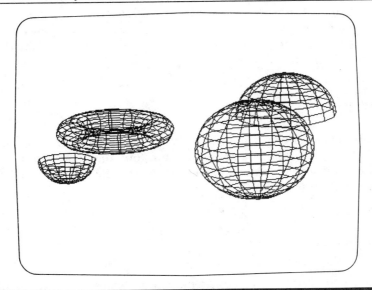

Fig. 17.19. *The shapes after HIDE.*

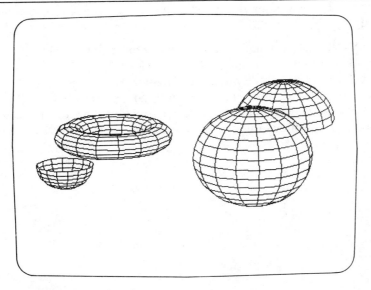

Generally, you should restrict your use of the HIDE command, because the process can be time consuming. But some applications may help in three-dimensional drafting as planes and surfaces are located in relation to each other; should their locations be incorrect, this command will quickly show it. Without question, this command (along with the MSLIDE and VSLIDE commands) can be a powerful presentation tool.

Summary

This chapter has shown you different ways to look at a three-dimensional drawing. It has covered commands for controlling the on-screen image and commands for displaying three-dimensional work. The following commands were discussed in this chapter:

❑ VPORTS   ❑ VPOINT
❑ REGENALL   ❑ DVIEW
❑ REDRAWALL   ❑ HIDE
❑ PLAN

This concludes Part IV, "Working in the Third Dimension." You should now have a firm grasp of three-dimensional drafting, editing, and viewing. As you can see, it truly is an exciting extension of the way CAD drawings were once put together. The future looks bright as the features of three-dimensional work, such as ways to view your three-dimensional drawing, are developed and improved.

In Part V, "Branching Out," you will learn about two programs, distributed by Autodesk, that transform your three-dimensional image into a presentation tool. These programs are discussed in Chapter 18, "Using AutoShade and AutoFlix." Then, in Chapter 19, "An AutoLISP Primer," you will explore AutoCAD's programming language. Here you will find the tools that take users far beyond just "pushing buttons" in AutoCAD to get the most from the CAD station.

Part V

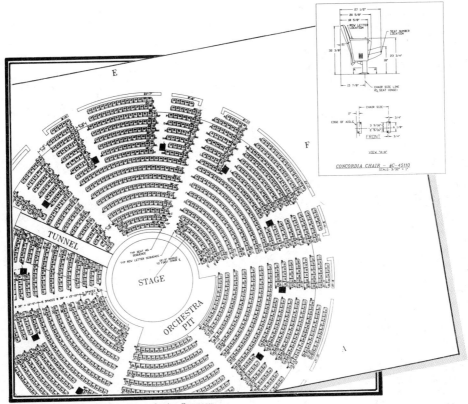

Drawing courtesy of Tom Melvin, Hussey Seating Company
North Berwick, Maine

Branching Out

18

Using AutoShade
and AutoFlix

This chapter will introduce you to two three-dimensional rendering tools: AutoShade and AutoFlix. These Autodesk programs let you create presentations of the three-dimensional drawings you prepare in AutoCAD. AutoShade can be purchased from Autodesk; AutoFlix is shareware that comes free with AutoShade or can be purchased as an inexpensive stand-alone program from Autodesk.

Not every design or drawing needs to be viewed three-dimensionally. Traditionally, the need for three-dimensional representations has been based on the requirements of communicating—and to a lesser degree, designing and drawing—an idea. With the advent of PC-based CAD, however, three-dimensional designing is going to become a reality and, eventually, the standard. Draftsmen and designers will originate their ideas in three dimensions, reversing the traditional order of design sketches, drawings, prototype construction, design revision, and drawing completion.

Autodesk recently added the Renderman Interface to its product line. This standard was originated by the developers of the Renderman software, Pixar. The interface allows renderings created in AutoShade to be exported to other software packages that use the Renderman Interface as their standard. As a result, you can create practically photoreal images of your AutoShade renderings. This is a substantial development; many others certainly will follow. If you already are a 3-D user, you should try to keep up with these developments; if you do not use 3-D, you should begin experimenting with it. AutoShade and AutoFlix are an excellent and economical introduction to three-dimensional presentation and analysis of your AutoCAD drawings.

An Introduction to AutoShade

AutoShade is designed to work with IBM (or IBM-compatible) PCs; this program and AutoCAD run in basically the same environment. AutoShade is available also in a 386-specific version, which creates images much faster than its 286 predecessor. AutoShade cannot, however, input from and output to as many different peripherals as AutoCAD can. AutoShade also introduces some new hardware terms that you may not know.

To better understand this discussion, you should be familiar with four of these terms:

❑ AutoShade's *pointing device* must be a Microsoft-compatible mouse, an Autodesk Device Interface pointer, a joystick or Koala pad, or the keyboard. (If your digitizing tablet will emulate a Microsoft mouse, you may be able to use the mouse option for the AutoShade pointing device.)

❑ The *interactive display device* is simply the monitor and graphics card you use to view and adjust your renderings. AutoShade supports many AutoCAD-compatible displays for this purpose.

❑ The *rendering display device* is used to show the renderings you create with AutoShade. With separate interactive and rendering displays, you can create images that can be viewed on a system other than the one you are using. Renderings can be stored in a file and viewed later from within AutoShade. If you do not save the renderings you create in AutoShade, they are viewed only through your interactive display (and cease to exist after you exit AutoShade). Soon you will see why this feature is important.

❑ The *hard copy device* is used for creating paper or film copies of a rendering. AutoShade creates a file that can be used by a variety of devices to create "prints" of your renderings.

Be sure to read about your devices in the *AutoShade Installation and Performance Guide*. With the variety of options available for many devices, you can adjust the quality of the program's output. Your goals may change once you better understand AutoShade's capabilities. The following sections will introduce you to some of these capabilities.

What AutoShade Does

To display your three-dimensional drawing, AutoShade approximates a photography studio, with one notable exception—AutoShade does not cast shadows. Through the use of lights, a target point, and a camera, AutoShade creates a shaded view of a three-dimensional AutoCAD drawing. The image will have light and dark areas based on the amount of light striking its surfaces. This light may be from general sources (*Ambient* light), or from specific lights placed in the drawing (*Directed* or *Point* light sources). Depending on the capabilities of your display device, AutoShade can display up to 256 colors, or create 256 colors from 16 colors by *dithering* (mixing pixels of color to create the illusion of 256 colors).

Instead of creating its own entities, Cameras, Scenes, or Light sources, AutoShade does most of its work by processing the AutoCAD drawing. In fact, everything in an AutoShade image must be placed there by using AutoCAD. Once the image's elements are in place, AutoShade's only creative role is the management and manipulation of the shading objects. This is an important fact to remember when you are working with AutoShade. AutoShade's only permanent contribution is the rendering or the hard-copy files you initiate within AutoShade. When you exit AutoShade, all other aspects of the AutoCAD drawing return to their original state.

AutoShade converts the three-dimensional faces, extrusions, meshes, lines, and polylines created in AutoCAD into triangulated surfaces. Then AutoShade determines which objects are visible, which are not, and how much light is on them. After making these calculations, AutoShade projects a perspective image of the objects. This is all done by *algorithms*. Algorithms are mathematical formulas that calculate a three-dimensional drawing's composition in a variety of ways and combine the results into one image. Because the image is a mathematical one, its quality relies on the quality of the algorithms. Just as you design or draw objects with AutoCAD, the designers of these algorithms had to take into account the speed and capabilities of the AT and the peripherals you use. The final result is a compromise of these considerations; clearly, it will not compare to images created by bigger, faster computers. Nevertheless, AutoShade can produce a respectable image when its capabilities are fully implemented.

A Little Help from Release 10

A Release 9 user must place a Camera and a Target in the drawing, create a file (called a *filmroll* file), and then view it within AutoShade in order to be sure that the image created is what he or she wants.

Release 10's display capability is quite similar to that of AutoShade, with the exception of shading. This AutoCAD enhancement makes the use of AutoShade much more predictable and reduces the amount of experimentation you had to go through with a Release 9 drawing to achieve the view you wanted. Release 10 places a Target, a Camera, and applies a perspective view to your three-dimensional drawing within AutoCAD. Before you create the file AutoShade will use to project renderings of your drawing, you can preview much of what you will do in AutoShade.

If you have practiced viewing your drawings in three dimensions with AutoCAD's DVIEW command, you are well on your way to using AutoShade. If not, you should spend some time working with DVIEW. This chapter includes a brief discussion of the use of DVIEW, but is not a tutorial on the three-dimensional use of AutoCAD.

Let's get started. You are going to create an AutoCAD drawing that can be used by AutoShade.

Setting Up the Scene

For the purposes of this exercise, pick one of your favorite (but simple) three-dimensional drawings created with AutoCAD. If you do not have one, take the time to create one before you continue with this chapter. The example used in this book is displayed in side, plan, front, and three-dimensional views in figure 18.1.

Fig. 18.1. *Side, plan, front, and three-dimensional views of the sample drawing.*

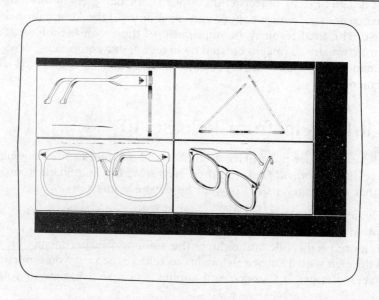

Both AutoShade and AutoCAD Release 10 use Cameras and Targets to set up the view that will be projected. AutoShade also uses Lights and Scenes, which are discussed later in this chapter. Before worrying about Lights, however, you must make sure that the objects you are going to view are reasonably accurate and look real.

Like a real camera, AutoCAD's Camera lens size, distance to target, and distance to object combine to determine how much of an object can be seen in a picture, and how distorted that object will appear.

If you have Release 10, you should try placing the Camera and Target in the DVIEW option until you get the view you want of the object(s) in your drawing. Write down the Camera and Target locations, for later use.

If you don't have Release 10, the following guidelines will help you focus on a setup that will start you out closer to the final results you want. (Release 10 users also can benefit from following these guidelines.)

❑ A 50mm lens (the standard lens for most 35mm cameras) creates the generally accepted "real life" view of objects in the camera's frame. This fact of photographic technology is true in AutoCAD, as well. If you can imagine taking a picture of the viewed object in real-world conditions, you should do your best to place objects in the drawing and create views that are in scale with a real condition. You can't take a picture of the entire front of a house, for example, while you are standing on the front steps of that house. You could come close with an 8mm fish-eye lens, but the distortion would be grotesque.

❑ The relationship between the Camera point and the Target point will determine how much perspective is applied to the objects in the drawing and how much distortion occurs.

❑ AutoCAD drawings are in real-world units. For example, an eye-level view of a building will be at about 5 feet above ground level. Furthermore, the Target and Camera points will be at considerable distances from the building. On the other hand, if you are shooting a picture of a bolt in a photo studio, you may take the picture from as little as 12 inches away from the object, and the Target point will be on the bolt's surface.

❑ Don't be too concerned about the initial view of the object filling up the screen. Just as you can magnify a photograph, you can use AutoCAD to zoom in on the object after you have created the view you want. Maintaining proper Camera/Target relationships reduces distortion, especially in large objects.

❏ Don't be afraid to experiment. Once you have some practical experience with AutoShade, you will find that the more you press the envelope of AutoShade's capabilities, the faster you will be able to achieve the results you want.

❏ Remember to make notes. Neither AutoCAD nor AutoShade keeps track of your experimental views, lighting, camera settings, etc. If you don't keep track of what you are doing, you may not be able to retrieve a previous setup that you liked.

❏ Although AutoCAD has an almost infinite capacity for detail, the camera, the human eye, and your patience do not. In your drawing, put only the detail you need for the view you want to create. For closer views, create other drawings that contain less of the overall object but greater detail.

Figure 18.2 shows a final view of the sample drawing.

Fig. 18.2. *Final DVIEW display of the sample drawing for rendering use.*

Remember that this view was selected by simply manipulating AutoCAD's DVIEW command; you don't need AutoShade to do this—you can do it with Release 10 of AutoCAD. If you don't have Release 10, you should review the Camera placement, lens size, and Target location for your drawing by using AutoShade's wire-frame imaging function, which is discussed in more detail later in this chapter. Figure 18.3 shows the placement of the Camera and the Target for this view. These locations also will be used for the AutoShade Camera and Target block placement. AutoShade uses an icon to show the Camera placement, but it does not show the Target's placement. The Target icon in figure 18.3 is for the purpose of clarification in this discussion only.

Fig. 18.3. *The sample drawing with Target and Camera icons inserted.*

Once you set the Camera and Target locations, use the DVIEW command's Distance option to view your drawing with perspective mode on. Using the DVIEW Zoom option gives you an idea of different lens sizes that will enhance or detract from the view with which you are working. Some experimentation with lens sizes and Camera placement will provide you with the best combination for your needs. Figures 18.4 and 18.5 show two different lens settings for the view shown in figure 18.3.

Fig. 18.4. Sample drawing with lens set at 70mm in DVIEW ZOOM.

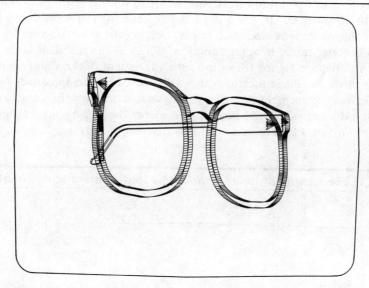

Fig. 18.5. Sample drawing with lens set at 120mm in DVIEW ZOOM.

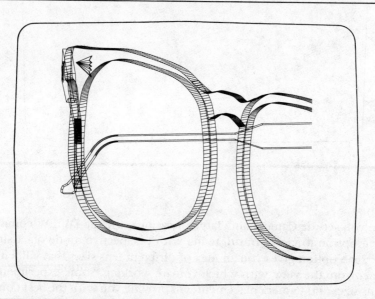

Remember, AutoCAD's default view resembles a picture of the object taken by a 35mm camera using a 50mm lens. If you use a wide angle or telephoto shot of your drawing, be sure to write down the lens setting you selected with the DVIEW Zoom option. Again, if you are using Release 9, you can accomplish the same thing in AutoShade. You will learn how to do this later in this chapter.

The main difference in the way AutoShade and AutoCAD Release 10 display a drawing is that, unless you tell it to do otherwise, AutoShade always tries to fill the screen with the image. It will take some time for you to get a feel for AutoCAD's Camera placement and how it relates to AutoShade. Don't worry, though, because you can change the Camera's distance from the Target in AutoShade. You will learn how to do that a little later in this chapter.

Using the Lights and Camera

The next step in preparing a file for use by AutoShade is to insert the block that will be used to retrieve the Camera's location, and its target. If you are using Release 10, select the ASHADE command from the OPTIONS pull-down menu or, if you prefer using your digitizing tablet, select Camera from the AutoShade section of the tablet menu. (If you are using Release 9, load the ASHADE.LSP function and type **CAMERA** at the Command: prompt.) Using the coordinates from the Camera position you established with Release 10 DVIEW, locate the Target point and insert the Camera icon at the proper X, Y, and Z coordinates. (If you use Release 9, you will have to make an educated guess at a Camera location, based on the guidelines presented earlier in this chapter.)

You may find it helpful to use AutoCAD's .XY filters to locate the Camera, and then type the Z coordinate you want. Release 9 will always place the .XY coordinates in the World Coordinate System. If you are using Release 10, make sure that the UCS (User Coordinate System) is set to the WCS (World Coordinate System) before you use filters to insert the Camera icon. Then, when you are prompted for the Camera icon's insertion point, type **.XY**, press Enter, and pick a point on the screen. AutoCAD prompts you for the Z coordinate to complete the insertion. In some instances, you can use existing objects in a drawing for the Camera's X, Y, or Z coordinates. Another way to position the Camera is to use the required point filters and select existing objects by using an OSNAP option. Take the time to experiment with a number of different Camera locations and view the results.

Once a Camera block is in place, you need to insert lighting. AutoShade uses two types of lights. The first thing to understand about AutoShade and these light sources is that the light will illuminate *all* surfaces facing its location and direction of illumination in the drawing, regardless of any intervening objects.

It takes considerable practice to be able to predict what these lights will do to the shaded image you intend to create. Unlike the Camera location and DVIEW, you cannot get a preliminary view of a light's effect on your image. The best technique for handling lighting, therefore, is to create more than one image; use lights in different locations, including some lights in one image and excluding them from another. You can do this by using what AutoShade calls a *Scene*. Scenes let you group different combinations of lights and cameras in a drawing so that you can limit the number of times you have to go back and forth between AutoCAD and AutoShade. You will learn how to set up a Scene later in this chapter. For now, it is important for you to realize that you can work within your AutoCAD drawing just like a director or professional photographer, setting up different layouts to get the best results. As you use AutoShade, you will learn how to brighten some lights and dim others. The creative use of lighting adds to the flexibility available when you use AutoShade and lets you be more creative in the ways you use your AutoCAD drawings.

The first type of light, a *Point* light, illuminates the shaded image in all directions from the light's location. This type of light is used for the general illumination of the drawing. Although AutoShade does not cast shadows, parts of your drawing that do not face a light source may sometimes be prohibitively dark. You may find also that adjusting the other lights and lighting factors in the drawing causes you to lose contrast. In such cases, a Point light is used to provide backlighting in addition to general illumination. Point lights are placed in the drawing in the same way that the Camera block is inserted, by using X, Y, and Z coordinates and any point filters that you may be able to use.

The second type of light, a *Direct* light, illuminates all objects that face it directly. A Direct light acts like the sun or a spotlight. You place Direct lights in the drawing with X, Y, and Z coordinates as well as a Target, in exactly the same way you insert the Camera block. The difference between a Direct light and a Camera is that the light ''sees'' all the objects in front of it in the drawing; also, unlike the Camera, the light is not affected by anything like lens focal length.

Try inserting both kinds of lights in your drawing, using the AutoLISP command LIGHT. When you type **LIGHT** at the Command: prompt, and press Enter, you are prompted to select a Direct light or a Point light. You can use point filters for inserting lights just as you use them to insert the Camera block. Figure 18.6 shows the location of the lights that have been added to the sample drawing. The Direct lights radiate light in one direction; the Point lights, in all directions.

Fig. 18.6. The sample drawing with Light icons in place.

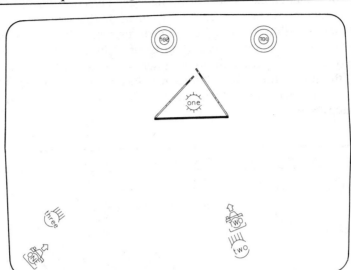

Setting Scenes and Making a Filmroll File

Now that you have the Camera and the Lights in your drawing, you must add a block that collects the Camera and Lights into a Scene. The Scene is simply a block (called *Clapper*) that uses attributes to record which Camera and Lights are to be included in the shaded image prepared by AutoShade. The X, Y, Z, and Target coordinates, where applicable, are part of the attributes of the Camera and Light blocks you place in your drawing. AutoShade reads the attributes of the Clapper block so that the proper coordinates and Targets are included in the Scene. It is important for you to understand that the information is passed to AutoShade from the block attributes. Moving a Camera icon will not have any effect on the shaded image, for example, because the attributes of the block will not be changed. It is better, therefore, to erase the Camera or Light you want to move and then insert another one at the new coordinates.

More than one Scene can be recorded in each drawing, with different Camera and Light blocks associated with each Scene (Clapper block). If you intend to process more than one image, or if you aren't sure which approach to the image is best, you can create a variety of Scenes containing different options for creating a range of images. Then you can choose from among those images.

To create a Scene, use the SCENE command and follow the prompts. You will be asked to pick the Camera and Lights that you want to include in the

Scene. When you are prompted for an insertion point for the Clapper block, pick any convenient location for the Scene icon. The coordinates of the block insertion point have no bearing on the final image in this instance. If you decide to experiment with different Lights, you can use the SCENE command again and select the same Camera icon and different Light icons for the next Scene. If you have included more than one Camera to create different views of the drawing, the procedure remains the same; just remember which Lights and Camera went in each Scene. The Scenes in place in figure 18.7 will be used for the sample drawing.

Fig. 18.7. The sample drawing with Scene icons in place.

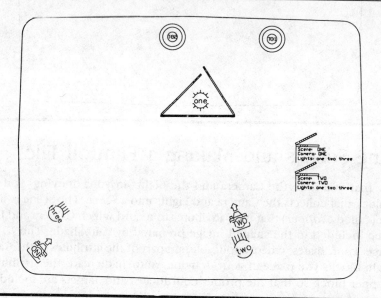

Before you leave AutoCAD and enter AutoShade, your final task is to execute the FILMROLL command, which causes the AutoLISP routine to create a file with a .FLM file extension. You can give this file any name, provided that it follows your operating system's file conventions.

The Ins and Outs of AutoShade

If you have already installed AutoShade, all you need to do is copy the Filmroll file you just created in AutoCAD to the subdirectory in which you have placed AutoShade. Make sure that you are in the AutoShade subdirectory. Then type

SHADE at the operating system command prompt, and press Enter. If you have not installed AutoShade, you will have to answer some configuration questions after you start AutoShade. Refer to the *AutoShade Installation and Performance Guide* for further instructions.

Once in AutoShade, you will see a blank screen with a menu line across the top and a message area across the bottom. A cursor arrow should be somewhere on the screen. If you do not see it, move your mouse or cursor keys until you do. You will view the image in the blank area of the screen. Before you start rendering, however, you must learn about AutoShade's menu options and how to use the pull-down menus and pop-up dialogue boxes that help you visualize your design.

If you have a mouse, you can move the pointer and click your choices from the AutoShade menu. If you do not have a mouse, you must use the keyboard's cursor, Insert (Ins), Page Down (PgDn), Page Up (PgUp), and Enter keys. In either case, you can also use the function keys to operate the pull-down menus. Each cursor key moves the on-screen arrow in the appropriate direction (up, down, right, and left); use the PgUp and PgDn keys to increase or decrease the distance the arrow moves when the cursor key is pressed. You use the Ins key to select highlighted items in the pull-down and pop-up menus; the Enter key confirms your selections. If you need more information about the operation of your mouse or the keyboard, refer to the *AutoShade User's Guide*. From now on, all you will be asked to do is make the appropriate selection from the menu.

Loading a File and a Scene

The first thing you have to do is load the Filmroll file you just created in AutoCAD. From the File menu, either select OPEN or press F10 to display the Filmroll files available in the AutoShade subdirectory. To select the Filmroll you just created, place the arrow on the corresponding menu cell next to the Filmroll file and press Ins or click your mouse. Then select OK from the menu icon. AutoShade will load the Filmroll file you selected.

The Scenes in your Filmroll file appear automatically in a dialogue box. Select the Scene you want to use. If no dialogue box appears, you must return to AutoCAD and make sure that you have placed the Scene icons properly in your drawing and that they are displayed. If the Scenes were missing, you must create new ones. Then you must make another Filmroll file. You may discover that the names of the Scenes you have created in the Filmroll file have become *just words*, and that you cannot remember the differences between the Scenes by just looking at their Scene names. The best solution to this problem is to order the Scenes by number in the direction of movement about the object, or in the order of the lighting changes you have made. As you create each Scene, jot down notes about it on a pad. If you forget what a Scene contains, you can create a plan view (in AutoShade) that will give you a quick look at the Scene's contents.

To create a plan view, select Display from the menu and select Plan View from the pull-down menu, or press F5. It is better to use a plan view than a wire frame, because the Lights and Camera locations are indicated in the plan view. Their use is not as obvious in a wire frame.

If you know what is in the Scene and you want to take a quick look at the effect of the view point location and Camera lens setting, select the Display menu and then Wire Frame, or press F2.

Basic Commands

In addition to the OPEN, Plan View, and Wire Frame commands, you must learn several other basic commands before you start shading your drawing.

When you want AutoShade to create a shaded image of your drawing, select either the Fast Shade or Full Shade command from the Display menu. Just as its name implies, Fast Shade is a quick shading of your drawing that skips over the detailed intersections and overlapping faces. Fast Shade creates a shaded image much faster than Full Shade does. Use Fast Shade to check all the Camera and Light settings, and to make sure that you have established the right colors for your image. Full Shade is used when you have the desired final image.

Later in this chapter, you will learn more about the remaining Display menu commands, shown in figure 18.8.

When you are ready to start shading your drawing, use the Select Scene and Lights options from the Settings menu. Figure 18.9 shows the Settings menu, which includes many advanced fine-tuning options. These options are discussed later in this chapter.

If you do not like the Scene you viewed with the Wire Frame command, you can select another Scene by picking Select Scene or by pressing F6. You can review the newly selected Scene with Plan View and Wire Frame in the manner you learned earlier.

Remember, if you need to review the Camera and Light locations, you should use Plan View to look at the current Scene (refer to fig. 18.7).

The Lights command lists the lights you have placed in the scene, the type of light used (Point or Directed), and each light's intensity level. The intensity level works like a dimmer switch. You can adjust the amount of light from each

Fig. 18.8. *AutoShade's Display menu.*

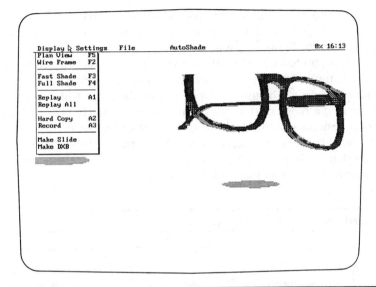

Fig. 18.9. *AutoShade's Settings Menu.*

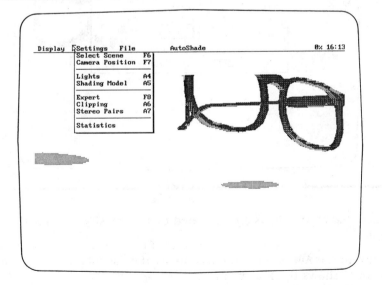

source, thereby controlling the amount of illumination on each face of your drawing.

Any light source's range of intensity levels is relative to all other lights in the drawing. This is an important fact that is easy to overlook. AutoShade's camera adjusts for lights and will not allow you to over- or underexpose the image, unless you force AutoShade to override the camera's automatic adjustments. This means that you can set each light to a range of 0 (Off) to 1, in increments of one-tenth, and the scene will be the same as if you set each light to a value in the range of 0 to 10, in increments of 1. The value of one light's brightness remains *relative* to all the other lights. You can also assign a negative value to the light intensity, causing light to be subtracted from the lighted surface. Any light that has been assigned a negative value will not show up in the Plan View option. The Lights dialogue box is shown in figure 18.10.

Fig. 18.10. AutoShade's Lights dialogue box.

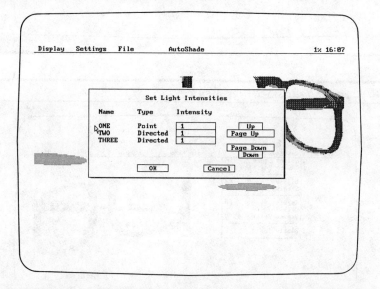

Notice that all the lights are defaulted to an intensity of 1 for the sample drawing.

Finally, to exit AutoShade, you need to use the File menu's Quit command. Figure 18.11 shows the File menu.

Fig. 18.11. AutoShade's File menu.

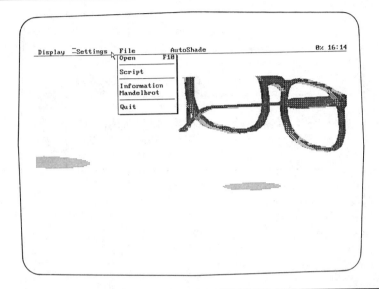

These basic commands will let you experiment with shading one of your AutoCAD drawings. When you feel comfortable with these commands, you can go on to AutoShade's more detailed fine-tuning commands.

A Review of the Settings

When you have loaded the Scene you want to shade, it is best to review the Scene's default settings so that you have an overview of the Scene. As you learn more about the use and effects of AutoShade's settings, this review will become even more important. If you forget to make minor adjustments to a complex drawing, you can tie up your computer waiting for a Fast Shade to be created, only to learn that you must go back and make those adjustments. Thus, it is a good idea to develop the habit of reviewing settings before you proceed with Fast Shade or Full Shade.

The Settings menu is deceptively simple in appearance. Each listed command can have a dynamic and specialized effect on the image. Let's review the default settings for the sample drawing illustrated in figure 18.1.

Figure 18.12 shows the Camera Position dialogue box for the sample drawing.

Fig. 18.12. *AutoShade's Camera dialogue box.*

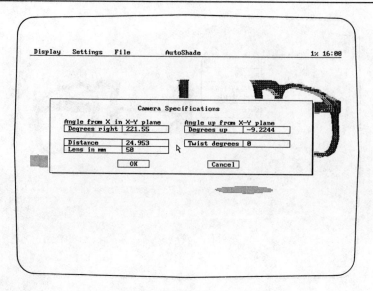

Notice that Degrees right, Degrees up, and Twist degrees indicate the Camera's position. Degrees right is the actual Camera location from zero degrees. Degrees up indicates whether the Camera is pointing up, level, or down. Twist degrees indicates whether the Camera is turned to one side or the other. These settings are the results of your placement of the Camera block in your AutoCAD drawing. You can change them if you want, but the results may be hard to predict without experimentation.

Most important, the Lens length and the Camera Distance are indicated in this dialogue box. If you need to correct the view you obtained when looking at your Wire Frame image, you can move the Camera in and out along the line of view, and you can change to a telephoto or wide-angle lens. You will make these adjustments to the sample drawing a little later in the chapter. These adjustments will be similar to those made with the DVIEW command in figures 18.4 and 18.5.

Figure 18.13 shows the Shading Model dialogue box. This is one of AutoShade's most complex setting groups. It will take quite some time and a considerable amount of experimentation for you to master all these settings. Fortunately, you do not have to adjust all the settings to achieve acceptable results in shading your drawing.

Fig. 18.13. *AutoShade's Shading dialogue box.*

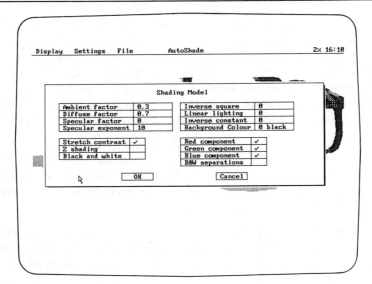

Initially, the portions of the Shading Model dialogue box you should be concerned with are the Ambient factor, Diffuse factor, Specular factor, Specular exponent, Stretch contrast, and Z shading settings.

The Ambient factor setting can have a value from 0 to 1. Ambient lighting is the general lighting of the Scene; it is developed from general sources rather than from any one light you may place in the drawing. Increasing the value of the Ambient light will uniformly brighten all objects in the drawing. The default setting for the sample drawing is 0.3.

The Diffuse factor setting controls the reflectivity of the surfaces in the drawing. Diffuse light is generally dispersed throughout the image, not reflected from a shiny surface. (The Specular factor setting controls a surface's shininess.) If you want surfaces with a great deal of life (surfaces that reflect most of the light that strikes them), set the Diffuse factor to a higher number. The default setting for the sample drawing is 0.7.

The Specular factor setting controls the "hardness," or light-reflecting characteristics of a surface. A matte surface has a Specular factor of 0 (the default setting). By increasing the setting, you increase the amount of glare on the surface.

The Specular exponent setting controls how mirrorlike the surface is. Most images fall within the range of 3 (similar to stainless steel) to 20 (mirrored).

AutoShade uses the Specular exponent to adjust the width of the light beam reflected from a surface. The higher the number, the narrower the beam.

Stretch contrast does just what the name implies. This effect makes sure that your image has the maximum available differentiation in light values, based on the number of lights in the drawing. The results of using this factor vary. If you have only one light in a drawing, for a mood setting, Stretch contrast may make part of the image too dark. On the other hand, if you have many light sources in the drawing to make everything visible, Stretch contrast improves the quality of the image. The default value of Stretch contrast is ON.

Z shading is used to adjust the image's illumination levels, based on the distance of each surface from the Camera. If you are creating an image of a large object, such as a building, Z shading makes the image more lifelike by decreasing the light as the distance from the Camera increases. The default value of Z shading is OFF.

Using Fast Shade, you should experiment with these basic settings in your image until you understand their capabilities. When you have mastered these six basic settings, you can move on to the more advanced uses in the Settings menu.

Figure 18.14 represents the default Expert dialogue box for the sample drawing. This dialogue box lets you make detailed, advanced adjustments to your rendering. For the time being, however, you should concern yourself only with moving the Camera, setting the screen space that AutoShade will fill with the image, turning perspective on and off, and turning intersection calculation on and off.

As you can see from figure 18.14, the Target location in the sample drawing has an X, Y, and Z value; note specifically that the Target is located with a Z value of 0. This means that the Camera's target point is not elevated or lowered with respect to the objects in the drawing, assuming that they are resting on a Z elevation of 0. Further, the Camera location has negative X, Y, and Z values. This simply means that the Camera is outside the drawing's 0,0 origin point and is below the drawing's Z plane. From these settings, it can be derived that the image is being viewed from below the horizontal 0 plane. You will learn how to adjust these settings in the next part of this chapter.

The default setting for Perspective mode is ON. Perspective mode is like using the Distance option of DVIEW in AutoCAD Release 10. If you are viewing a small object, you may get a more accurate view of the object by turning Perspective mode OFF and forcing AutoShade to use parallel projection of the image.

Fig. 18.14. The AutoShade Expert dialogue box.

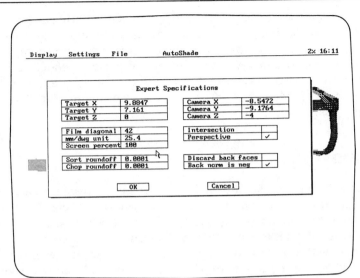

As was explained earlier, AutoCAD Release 10 (unlike AutoShade) does not automatically fill the screen with the image when you view an object with DVIEW. By adjusting the Screen percent setting, which has a default of 100 percent, you can obtain a view of the object with some empty space around it. In addition, if you want AutoShade to treat the image in exactly the same way AutoCAD's DVIEW command does, set the Screen percent to 0. This forces AutoShade to view the object as though the program were a 35mm camera at the distance you specify.

Intersection tells AutoShade whether you want the intersections of two planes calculated. If you created your drawing without representing the actual intersection of three-dimensional faces with an edge, you must turn Intersection ON, so that AutoShade will calculate the intersection of the faces. The default is OFF.

The final menu option, Clipping, is beyond the scope of this chapter and represents advanced adjustments to the AutoShade image. You will find a detailed discussion of clipping in the *AutoShade User's Guide*.

Taking a First Look

Now that you have reviewed your image's default settings, you can better understand your starting point. This review should help you understand why you are, or are not, seeing what you expected to see when you completed your first Fast Shade of the image. Now it is time to create a rendering, using the settings that you have worked with up to this point. Renderings are created using the `Full Shade` option from the Display menu. But first, a quick look using `Fast Shade` is appropriate.

Shading

Using the F3 function key, or the `Fast Shade` option from the Display menu, create a shaded image of your drawing. While the image is being created, review in your mind the default settings you have just checked, and try to create a mental picture of what is happening. As you gain experience with AutoShade, your mental picture and the final results should become more and more alike. Figure 18.15 shows the results of a Fast Shade for the sample drawing.

Fig. 18.15. A Fast Shade of the sample drawing's Scene 1.

One element missing from this figure (because of the limitations of this book) is color. AutoShade creates colors based on the type of display you use. If you have an EGA display, or want to use VGA in the highest resolution mode, you will see as many as 256 dithered colors. The best way to estimate which color you want to assign to each element of your AutoCAD drawing is to use the color chart in the *AutoShade Users Guide*. All colors must be assigned while you are creating the image in AutoCAD and before you create the Filmroll file.

Critiquing the Results

Once you have the first Fast Shade image on-screen, decide what you do and do not like about the image, and jot down your best estimate of the changes you will have to make. If you have a complex image and a complex set of lights, it may be best to use AutoCAD to plot the drawing with the AutoShade Camera and Light blocks visible. You can make notes on the plotted drawing. This will become even more important if you intend to use AutoFlix, which is discussed later in this chapter.

In the sample drawing, the lighting values and the Camera/Target position could use some fine tuning. The lens size may have to be adjusted to get the proper view of the entire image, and the screen percentage definitely needs to be changed. These changes can be made without leaving AutoShade, but if the Camera/Target position is to be changed permanently, the changes must be made in the original drawing and a new Filmroll file must be created.

Experimenting with the Settings

The sample drawing should have slightly reflective surfaces, and the lights in the drawing need to be amplified from one side so that they increase the contrast in the image. To do this, you should experiment with the Intensity, Ambient, Diffuse, Specular, and Specular Exponent settings. There is no best way to experiment, and no best place to start. Because these settings have an interrelated effect on the image, getting one part right may render another part unacceptable. The most important thing to do is to make a chart of the settings you are adjusting; record the changes you make, and include notes on the positive and negative effects your experiments have on the image. In this way, you can ensure that the image will improve.

The first adjustment that should be made to this rendering is to get the entire object into the view of the screen (Camera). To do so, you use two settings in the Expert dialogue box (F8). First, to create some open space around the image, you set the screen percent to 0. Next, you should move the Target location to a Z value of 3.000, so that the camera looks at a more upward angle. When the Target location is moved, AutoShade automatically changes the Camera position values by adjusting the degrees up and the distance, in this case. Note that this adjustment could have been accomplished in AutoCAD by inserting a new Camera block and creating a new Filmroll file, or the lens could have been made a wide angle lens within AutoShade, to increase the Camera's field of view. Because a wide angle lens would have resulted in greater distortion of the image, the Target and screen percent were adjusted instead. Figure 18.16 shows the results of these adjustments.

Fig. 18.16. *The Screen percent is set to 0 and the Target location has a Z value of 3.000 in this view.*

Next, the image must be made crisper, to give the surfaces of the glasses a harder, more reflective quality. To achieve crisper lighting, the intensity of the lights should be adjusted by using the Lighting dialogue box, setting Point light ONE (an overhead general illumination light) to an intensity of .1. Next, Directed light THREE should be set to an intensity of .2, with Directed light TWO left with the default value of 1. This creates a definitive lighting atmosphere, rather than the more general effect of the default settings. Figure 18.17 shows the effect of these adjustments to the intensity settings.

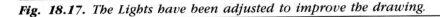

***Fig. 18.17.** The Lights have been adjusted to improve the drawing.*

Now, the surfaces need to be more reflective. Using the Shading Model dialogue box (Alt F5), the Diffuse light should be increased to 0.7, the `Specular factor` set to 0.7, and the `Specular Exponent` set to 18. The result is an image with more sparkle (see fig. 18.18). The Specular settings and the diffuse setting will vary, depending on the value of the hue that is used (the color's lightness or darkness). Each rendering you create will require lighting experimentation to achieve the best image.

Changing the View Entirely

When, after your experimentation, you arrive at the image's characteristics, the final viewing location should be analyzed. Further, if you plan to use AutoFlix to create a movie, you should experiment with the Camera/Target locations, distance, lens settings, and even the Camera's tilt angle. For example, figure 18.19 shows a change in the target location and a change to a 150mm lens so that a detail of the glasses can be seen.

Perhaps you would prefer the effect of putting the Camera above the object and the Target below the object. This can be done by swapping the `Camera` and `Target Z` settings used for figure 18.16 (see fig. 18.20).

Fig. 18.18. *The Specular and Specular Exponent settings have been adjusted to add "hardness" to the surfaces.*

Fig. 18.19. *The Target has been moved and the lens set to 150 mm to provide this detail shot.*

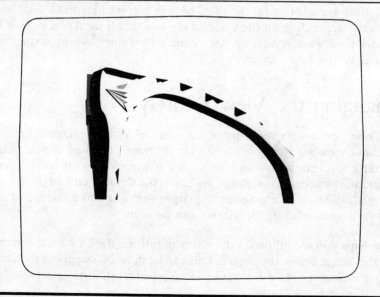

Fig. 18.20. The Camera and Target have swapped Z axes from their original settings.

Fig. 18.20. The Camera and Target have swapped Z axes from their original settings.

Just in case you want to view the object from a different vantage point, you should create other Scenes from which to view the object. If you have changed settings, AutoShade resets some of them to default when a new Scene is loaded. You should review the settings again, to retrieve the image you developed with the first Fast Shade. Figure 18.21 shows an example of the second Scene created for the sample drawing.

When To Start Over

If you have made extensive adjustments to the Camera and Target settings in your rendering from within AutoShade, or if you have made dynamic changes to Light settings (such as turning off a light and creating a large disparity in intensity among the others), you should go back to AutoCAD, make adjustments to the drawing, and create a new Filmroll file. AutoShade will need less time to calculate the rendering image, and you will be able to use more of AutoShade's default settings.

If you must make major adjustments to your settings, remember that you will have to retrieve these settings from notes whenever you want to create a new image. No matter how many permanent images you make, it always seems

Fig. 18.21. *A Fast Shade of Scene 2 with the same adjustments made to Scene 1.*

that just one more is needed. If you intend to create an AutoFlix movie of your image, you will have to retain the settings you develop through experimentation. When you create a movie, changing the AutoCAD drawing to accurately reflect your final image and keeping good notes are both musts.

Getting the Final Picture

Now that you have used `Fast Shade` to develop the image for your drawing, it is time to create a Full Shade. A Full Shade will reveal any minor inconsistencies in your drawing, and will present all the faces properly displayed with their assigned colors. More adjustments may be needed when you finally get to see the Full-Shaded image. Only practice will lessen the effect of these late discoveries; the attention to detail in your drawings will be paramount to your success.

Full Shading

If your image is complex, make yourself some coffee or tea, get a good book or rent a movie for the VCR, and press F4. If you are fortunate enough to have a 386-based machine and are using AutoShade 386, developing the Full Shade

Fig. 18.22. The final Full Shade for the rendering of the design.

may not be quite as slow as this book implies, but the process is still very complex. You should be aware of this complexity so that you do all your homework before you start a Full Shade. Be forewarned—the process requires extensive calculations that can take hours (even days) to complete on a 286 AT. Full Shades can take as much as ten times longer to complete than Fast Shades, depending on the complexity of the intersections and placement of three-dimensional entities in the drawing. You may even want to schedule unattended shading for the computer while you sleep.

Figure 18.22 shows the final Full-Shaded image of the sample drawing. Notice that some of the faces completely conceal those that lie behind them. This happens because the Full Shade command is more accurate than the Fast Shade command.

Saving the Results

To save the results of your Full-Shaded rendering, make sure that AutoShade is configured for a rendering device and a hard copy device. The rendering device may be the same as the display device, or you may want to display the renderings on a different computer with a higher-resolution monitor. Instructions for configuring AutoShade are included in the *AutoShade Installation and Performance Guide*.

If you use the Record option to save the Full Shade, the image will be created for the monitor you are currently using as well as for a file for later display of the rendering (using the Replay option). This fact is important when you create hard copies. By using the same monitor for Interactive and Display work, you create the files for retaining the image while the Full Shade is being completed. Otherwise, the file to which the image is recorded is created independently of the screen image. If you have to look at a screen image of a Full Shade before you want to record the image, AutoShade must take time to create the images *twice* if the display and rendering devices are different.

If you want to make a hard copy for a display device with higher resolution or more colors than the device you are using as the Interactive display, or if you want to send the output to a PostScript device, the Full Shade and the hard copy must be created separately. This means that calculations of the image must be performed twice: once for you to look at and once for you to keep. To create a hard copy (the way the images were created for this book), make sure that Record is OFF and select Hard Copy from the Display menu, or press Alt-F2.

Moving on to AutoFlix

If you create AutoShade renderings, you may want to use them for a presentation that is more dynamic than simply using Replay from AutoShade's Display menu. AutoFlix (which is shipped with AutoShade) automates, for the most part, the process of creating a movie from your AutoShade images. Just remember— AutoFlix is meant to be used with an EGA monitor connected to an IBM or compatible XT, AT, or PS/2.

How AutoFlix Works

AutoFlix can create three types of movies from your three-dimensional AutoCAD drawings, or it can automate AutoCAD or AutoShade Slide (.SLD) files. It can also incorporate wire-frame graphics, text, renderings, music, and other programs into an interactive presentation (one from which the user can make choices and that he or she can view at his or her own pace).

The three types of movies are *Walkthrough*, *Kinetic Animation*, and *Interactive*. In a walkthrough movie, the camera is the only object that moves. A kinetically animated movie can include movement of objects in the drawing, as well as the movement of the camera. Kinetic movies are much more complex than walkthroughs; to achieve predictable results, you must have considerable experience with AutoCAD, AutoShade, and AutoFlix. Interactive movies include *Vector Slides* that use *Button* definitions which are placed next to text, vector images, or renderings. Selecting a `Button` allows the viewer to interact with the movie, asking questions or choosing which direction in the presentation he or she wants to proceed. These three movie types can also be combined into one complete movie for final viewing.

All the movies include a *Motion Path*, a two-dimensional polyline (three-dimensional polylines cannot be used in Release 10) that describes the motion of the object or the camera in the movie. AutoFlix divides the motion path polyline equally into the same number of spaces as there are frames in the movie. AutoFlix projects movies at about 5 frames per second, so a 50-frame movie will be 10 seconds long.

AutoFlix writes a script (.SCR) file, which AutoShade uses to create the images used in the movie, and an AutoFlix command file (.MVI) that is used to compile the AutoShade renderings into a final movie (.MOV) file. The script file is based on the number of frames from which you chose to make the movie, and includes other instructions to AutoShade. Normally, you would enter these instructions manually from the AutoShade menus. Remember that if you have a rendering (.RND) file containing, say, 60,000 bytes, a one-minute movie will require AutoShade to write 11,800,000 bytes (11M) of rendering files to your disk before they are compiled into the EGA movie file, which is much smaller. A great deal of disk space and time are required to prepare an AutoFlix movie. In addition, because the .MVI, .SCR, .MOV, and .FLM files are added to this total, the required disk space can easily be 22M for an animated version of this movie. AutoFlix automates most of this work—you can let your computer create the movies unattended.

AutoFlix is extremely flexible. Its uses are limited only by your imagination and the time available to you. The program has many optional effects that can be combined in different ways to create deceptively simple, yet professional, presentations.

If you have not reviewed the demo movies provided with AutoFlix, you should do so before continuing with this chapter. You can do this by setting the current directory to the one that contains AutoFlix and typing **AFEGA DEMO**. As you watch the movie, try out the control keys to learn how the movie projector works. The keys and their functions are listed in table 18.1.

Table 18.1. *AutoFlix control keys and their functions.*

Key	Use To
Space bar	Toggle start and stop
H	Halt projection
R	Resume projection
–	Slow projection
+	Speed up projection
Q	Quit and return to DOS
Esc	Quit and return to DOS
Home	Return to first frame. (Stops running projector)
End	Go to last frame. (Stops running projector)
→	Next frame (Stops projector)
←	Previous frame (Stops projector)
↑	Next cue mark (Stops projector)
↓	Previous cue mark (Stops projector)

In the demo movie, you will see many of AutoFlix's capabilities as well as examples of both a Walkthrough and a Kinetic movement.

When To Make a Movie

Whenever you want to replay a set of rendering files in AutoShade, you can use AutoFlix. AutoFlix creates a file that takes up less space than the rendering files, and replays them with much greater flexibility than AutoShade can. AutoFlix's only drawback is that it works only in EGA mode.

If you want to create a presentation to explain a design you have created in AutoCAD, AutoFlix can accomplish the task in an automated fashion, leaving you with time to go to the game or take a nap. If a picture is worth a thousand words, a movie is worth ten thousand. The capability to move a three-dimensional object does a great deal for the viewer and helps him or her understand the design.

Finally, if you want to keep up with the latest developments in PC-based animation, AutoFlix is a good training tool. Autodesk recently announced a brand new product for the VGA. Called Animator, it promises to be even more amazing than AutoFlix. (The primary difference, of course, is that you get AutoFlix free with AutoShade; besides VGA specialization, Animator is not free.)

What To Do in Preparation

As you have already read, you must take certain preparatory steps before creating a movie. These can be summarized and expanded on as follows:

❏ Create a drawing that has only the detail required for your purposes. You can add details to partial drawings that can be used in a different movie and spliced in. (This is discussed in the section on Optional Effects.)

❏ Make sure that you prepare your drawings accurately, verifying intersections and a complete use of three-dimensional faces as you go.

❏ While in AutoShade, preview your drawing and the settings you want to use, selecting Scenes along the motion path you will use. (Be sure to erase the Scenes from the drawing before you start using AutoFlix.)

❏ Don't make your movie too long. As you learn more about AutoFlix, you will be able to create movies in segments, piecing them together as they are perfected.

❏ Make a plot of your drawing, and design the movie from this plot. Note the camera's general position and elevation. Note also the direction in which the camera should face from each view point along the motion path.

❏ If you want objects to move in the movie (Kinetic motion), you must place these objects together on their own layer, separate from anything else in the drawing.

❏ Real directors use storyboards of the production they plan to create. A storyboard can help you, too. Draw a set of sketches that show what will happen at major points in the movie, especially if you intend to make an interactive movie, or splice together several types of movies and special effects.

❏ Determine what should happen along the way. You can even turn lights on and off in the movie, once you become advanced enough. If you want to incorporate a musical score, you have to choreograph the movie with the score in terms of beats per minute. This movie business can get serious!

❏ If you are doing a walkthrough movie, choose your light settings with the stretch contrast turned OFF. Similarly, be sure that your camera locations will work with a reasonable lens setting (AutoFlix defaults to a setting of 50mm) and that the screen percent is set to 0 or −1.

❏ Most important, make sure that you have enough disk space available for the rendering files as well as the AutoFlix files.

The best approach is to start with a simple drawing that contains the elements of what you want to do. AutoFlix has an option for using Fast Shades. If you use a simple, representative drawing, along with Fast Shades, you can create a movie that includes all the planned events without sacrificing a great deal of time and disk space.

Finally, make sure that you have the correct AutoLISP files in place on your disk for the version of AutoCAD you are using (see Appendix A of the *AutoFlix Guide*). Also, if you are using Release 9 of AutoCAD, make sure that you have the lines:

```
SET LISPHEAP=40000
SET LISPSTACK=5000
SET ACADFREERAM=24
```

in your AUTOEXEC.BAT or ACAD.BAT file.

Making the Movie

The first step in making a movie is to enter the Drawing Editor and open a drawing file you have used to create a suitable rendering in AutoShade. All the Lights, Cameras, and Scenes that you placed in the drawing should be displayed. If they are not, thaw the layer ASHADE to display them. Then, using AutoCAD's ERASE command, erase all the Scenes, Cameras, and any Lights you don't want to use in the movie.

Use AutoCAD's PLINE command to draw a polyline that represents the motion path of the Camera you want AutoFlix to incorporate. In Release 10, this *must* be a two-dimensional polyline and should be drawn at the base elevation from which you want the Camera to be placed on the path. In Release 9, the current elevation sets the Camera's base elevation. It is all right if the polyline has a number of steps, or vertices. When you have finished drawing the polyline, use PEDIT and FIT CURVE or SPLINE to create a curve from the polyline. Figure 18.23 shows the Camera motion path that was used for the sample drawing.

Next, if you intend to animate objects in the drawing, you must draw a polyline that represents the motion you want the objects to make. Note that AutoFlix will create a separate AutoCAD Filmroll file for each frame of the rendering when animation is present. If you are not using animation, AutoFlix simply creates a Scene for each Camera position along the Camera motion path. In the sample drawing, the glasses will fold up as the Camera moves around the frame design. Figure 18.24 shows the motion path for the stems of the glasses.

Finally, if you want the *look-at* point to move, you must draw a polyline for the look-at path. Like the camera motion path, the look-at path is divided equally, with each division representing a frame. If the look-at path is shorter

Fig. 18.23. *The sample drawing with the AutoFlix camera motion path added.*

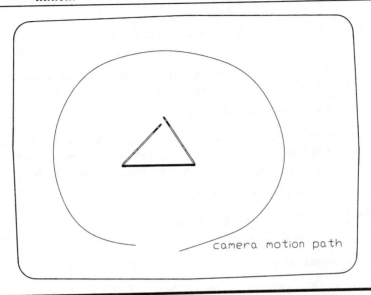

camera motion path

Fig. 18.24. *The sample drawing with the AutoFlix object motion path added.*

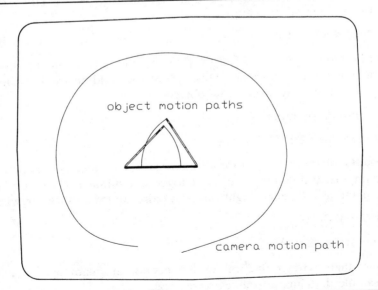

object motion paths

camera motion path

than the motion path, the camera spends a much longer period of time looking at the same general vicinity of the drawing. Conversely, if the look-at path is the same length as the camera path, the objects will move by the viewer at the same pace the camera moves through the image (like riding on a train and looking out the window.) Because the sample drawing uses a fixed look-at point, no polyline is drawn.

At the AutoCAD Command: prompt, type **(load "afkinet")** and then type **ANIMLENS**. When AutoFlix replies:

```
Animation lens focal length in mm <50>:
```

enter the setting that will work in all locations. (You should have determined this setting beforehand, while you tried out various Scenes in preparation for making the movie.) A setting of 35mm was used for the sample drawing.

Next, type **ANIMATE**. AutoFlix replies:

```
Choose the camera path polyline:
```

Do so. Then AutoFlix prompts you to:

```
Choose the look-at point (or Path or Same):
```

You can answer this prompt in one of the following three ways:

1. Type **P** and select a polyline that represents the look-at path.

2. Use AutoCAD XY filters and enter a Z coordinate value. (This was done for the sample drawing.)

3. Type **S** and select the camera path.

The third option (typing **S**) causes the Camera to look at the next point along the camera path for each frame. (This is similar to holding a video camera to your head and walking around the objects.)

AutoFlix then prompts:

```
Base name for path (1-3 characters):
```

You should reply with an appropriate name for the current camera path. This name is important if you want to splice together a number of movies. Do not use the name of a Camera, Light, or Scene already used in the drawing.

Next, AutoFlix asks:

```
Number of Frames:
```

Remember that there are five frames per second, and many bytes per frame. In the sample drawing, 20 frames were used.

Now AutoFlix prompts you for:

```
Initial Camera Elevation of <0">:
Final Camera Elevation of <0">:
```

The base Camera elevation is 0″. If you set the current elevation in Release 9 to 60″ or draw the polyline in Release 10 at an elevation of 60″, the Camera will remain at 60″ if you reply 0″. If you want the Camera to move up and down as it goes along the camera motion path, enter the appropriate starting and ending elevations. If you want the Camera to move up and down several times during the movie, you will have to splice movies together to achieve that effect. In the sample drawing, the Camera started out below the glasses (as in fig. 18.15) and finished above the glasses (as in fig. 18.21).

Next, AutoFlix asks for the layers of the objects that are to move kinetically:

```
Layer to move:
Chose motion path for <layer name>:
Rotations <0>:
Z translation <0>:
```

This sequence is repeated until you enter a null response to the Layer to move: prompt. As you may recall, each group of moving objects must be on a unique layer. You will select the polyline you used to establish the motion path; then you can have the object rotate around its center. To do so, enter the number of rotations you want to achieve during the movie. You can also enter partial rotations. To make the object move up or down, use a *Z translation value*. This value can be any amount, entered in drawing units, and can be positive or negative. Again, if you want the object to move both up and down during a movie, you must splice together more than one movie.

Finally, AutoFlix asks you to identify the Lights to be used in the movie:

```
Select a light:
```

AutoFlix needs at least one Light to create the movie. When you enter a null value for the Light selection, AutoFlix begins creating the Filmroll file(s) required for your movie.

If you are not using animation of objects in your movie, the procedure is similar to the one just described except that you enter **(load ''afwalk'')** and **WALKTHROUGH**. Then, since everything will be placed in one Filmroll file, you must enter the AutoShade FILMROLL command.

The next step is to exit AutoCAD and enter AutoShade. Load the Filmroll file (or one of the Filmroll files for animation movies) and set up the lights with Stretch contrast turned off. Set the screen percent to −1. Finally, from AutoShade's File menu section, pick the Script option. The script file will have the name XXX.SCR, where *XXX* is the name of the camera path you have given AutoFlix.

Next, you must compile the movie by using the AutoFlix program. To do this, enter the following at the DOS command prompt from the AutoFlix subdirectory:

AFEGA −MXXX <XXX.MVI

where *XXX* is the camera path name.

Finally, to view the movie, enter:

AFEGA XXX

AutoFlix will display your movie on-screen!

Optional Effects

You can achieve many subtle variations by creating Buttons on AutoCAD slides or by editing the .MVI files created by AutoFlix. These are advanced techniques that require extensive study of the AutoFlix manual. (The relatively thin AutoFlix manual contains an incredible amount of information.) Here, to inspire your creativity, is a sampling of what you can do:

❏ Create interactive tutorials that let the user exit the movie at any point and enter AutoCAD to edit a drawing that represents the area from which the user left the movie.

❏ Splice previously created movies into the final movie.

❏ Change the lighting during a movie by editing the AutoShade script file created by AutoFlix. In fact, you can change many things throughout the movie by editing the script files as indicated in the *AutoShade User Guide*.

❏ Create pauses, cue marks, speed variations, and delays in the movie by editing the .MVI file.

❏ Write a musical score by using a set of commands in the .MVI file. (You'd better check with the piano teacher you had way back when!)

❏ Create fades and dissolves in the movie by using different image controls in the .MVI file.

❏ Overlay more than one image to create a notated rendering, and have the notes fade away, leaving a new image.

These are only some of the possibilities AutoFlix offers. AutoFlix applications are quite extensive and can become a full-time activity for you.

Summary

This chapter introduced you to the basic concepts of using AutoShade and AutoFlix. These two programs represent a wealth of capabilities and deserve extensive study. It is not possible to discuss all the possibilities in this chapter, but you have been introduced to AutoShade and AutoFlix.

You have seen what AutoShade can do and you have learned a little about the following:

- ❏ Setting up Scenes
- ❏ Using the Lights and a Camera
- ❏ How Release 10 can help
- ❏ Making a Filmroll file
- ❏ Loading a file and a Scene
- ❏ Basic commands
- ❏ The settings
- ❏ Shading
- ❏ How to critique the results
- ❏ Experimenting with the settings
- ❏ Changing the view completely
- ❏ When to start over
- ❏ Refining the image
- ❏ Full shading
- ❏ Saving the results

You know something about how AutoFlix works, including the following:

- ❏ When to make a movie
- ❏ What to do in preparation
- ❏ Making the movie
- ❏ Optional effects

It is a good idea to start learning now about three-dimensional design, which will be the reality of the future. Soon you will be able to simulate and try out your design, conducting wear tests, stress tests, thermal expansion analysis, tolerance design, and other experiments that currently are attempted only on mainframe computers.

CHAPTER 19

An AutoLISP Primer

This chapter will introduce you to the AutoLISP programming language and to the basic concepts involved in using it. Even if you don't want to be a programmer, you can benefit greatly from understanding just the basics of AutoLISP. A few keystrokes in AutoLISP can save you hours and hours of work. A few lines of AutoLISP can make a tedious task fun.

You will be presented with introductory information about the following:

❏ Explanations of what AutoLISP is and when, where, and how to use it
❏ How to create AutoLISP routines
❏ Basic AutoLISP syntax, definitions, and formats
❏ How to use AutoLISP at the keyboard
❏ How to use AutoLISP in menu macros
❏ Some useful AutoLISP routines to help you in your work

What Are LISP and AutoLISP?

AutoLISP is a programming language that is included with AutoCAD. It can be used to write custom programs, or routines, to manipulate both AutoCAD and the database AutoCAD creates. AutoLISP is important to AutoCAD designers and drafters because it can have a tremendous effect on their productivity and enjoyment as they use AutoCAD.

Learning to use AutoLISP is not particularly difficult, but requires study, practice, and an understanding of many programming concepts for the effective and detailed development of capabilities. Fortunately, AutoLISP can enhance AutoCAD by returning benefits commensurate with the user's skill level. Even better, many free or economical AutoLISP routines are available—you need no programming skill to put them to work.

477

The History of AutoLISP

AutoLISP is based on XLISP, written by David Betz. LISP is an acronym for *LISt Processing*; the general programming language has many dialects. AutoLISP, which is patterned after Common LISP (one of those dialects), does not include all the capabilities of Common LISP. Nor does AutoLISP use all the LISP program-language features in the same way as Common LISP.

What Are Programs and Routines?

You may be intimidated by the idea that AutoLISP involves *programming*, but you shouldn't be. A program is simply a set of instructions, processed one at a time. The difficult part of programming is learning the language. Think of it this way—you had to learn that the word *blue* meant a color, and what that color looked like; later, you also found out that *blue*, when used in a particular way, could mean a state of mind. In the same way, learning AutoLISP means learning a language with a simple set of words that can do many things, depending on how and when they are used.

To *program* a computer, you create a logic framework on an essentially blank blackboard that is made up of the computer's random access memory (RAM). This framework consists of a set of rules, instructions, and definitions that govern the manipulation of data (input) and the output of data as results. Fortunately, the rules, instructions, and definitions are already available in the form of AutoLISP. All you have to do is write a *routine*—a particular order of those rules, instructions, and definitions defined by AutoLISP. So, you see, you have nothing to fear; you won't be programming after all! Why should you learn to write a routine? Because AutoLISP can save you time and effort, and because AutoLISP can lend support to and extend the capabilities for drawing with AutoCAD.

What AutoLISP Does for AutoCAD

AutoLISP is a powerful tool for adding to your AutoCAD production capabilities. AutoLISP can implement changes, create new images, and record information about your AutoCAD drawing. Here is a list of just some of the things you can do with AutoLISP:

❑ Create macros: A *macro* is a list of commands that are fed automatically to their parent program (in this case, AutoCAD) for processing as if only one command was entered. AutoLISP can combine many AutoCAD commands into a single command macro.

❏ Change existing drawing entities: AutoLISP can access the drawing database directly and change the characteristics of the drawing entities (lines, arcs, circles, polylines, 3-D faces, etc.) stored there.

❏ Create new drawings: using a procedure known as a *parametric routine*, AutoLISP can create new drawings based on user input of variable quantities. In this way, for example, AutoCAD can use the same routine to automatically draw screws with a different number of threads per inch and in different sizes.

❏ Create and import databases: AutoLISP can write to separate files information about what you are drawing, so that you can use this data as a supplement to your drawing. The program can also import notes, model numbers, and a variety of other data stored in files outside your AutoCAD drawing.

❏ Sort and manage a database: AutoLISP can sort the AutoCAD drawing database in different ways. For example, it can gather all entities displayed as the color red, or all objects on a certain layer, or all blocks whose name starts with the letter *A*.

The use of AutoLISP is as varied as the use of AutoCAD. You can develop AutoLISP routines to accomplish almost anything you can imagine. However, AutoLISP is not always the fastest or most appropriate method for the task.

Where and When To Use AutoLISP

How you use AutoCAD and what you use it for will be the determining factors in deciding what benefits you get from AutoLISP. Applying the following general considerations to your own situation may help you decide what you want to do with AutoLISP:

❏ Repetitive tasks
❏ Unpleasant tasks
❏ Error-prone activities or calculations
❏ Work requiring consistent applications of standard practices
❏ Time-saving command enhancements
❏ Customization of AutoCAD for your specific uses

You can use AutoLISP in many different circumstances. This chapter will show you how to use AutoLISP in each of the following areas:

❏ At the AutoCAD Command: prompt
❏ In a stored routine file (.LSP)
❏ In an AutoCAD script file
❏ In a menu macro
❏ In the ACAD.LSP file

Word Processors and Editing

You can create AutoLISP routines by typing them in at the AutoCAD Command: prompt. This is fine for "on the fly" work, but unless you intend to leave your computer on indefinitely, you need a way to store the routines for repeated use. To create a permanent AutoLISP routine you must use a word processor or DOS's EDLIN. Some DOS shell programs also have extremely basic text editors that will suffice for small routines. Major AutoLISP editing is best handled by a text editor with search-and-replace functions, block-editing functions, and the capability of writing blocks of text to a different file. Added features that are helpful are the capability to edit two files at once and to merge files.

Most word processors use special characters to format text so that your documents look nice when they're printed, have bold or underlined text, and have the text justified on both the left and right margins. AutoLISP cannot use these special characters; the program will generate error messages when it finds these characters in a file. It is easy to forget this fact and ruin a routine that you have spent hours editing. AutoLISP routines must be written using a word processor in nondocument or programming mode. Make sure that your word processor has this capability.

You can use almost any of the popular word processors to edit AutoLISP files, whether they are high-end commercial products or low budget public domain software products. The extent to which you will be writing AutoLISP routines may warrant the purchase of a text editor with the specific features listed earlier in this section. It will pay for itself many times over in terms of ease of use and efficiency in routine writing. You should also consider a text editor that is efficient in its use of memory. As your AutoLISP routine writing becomes more advanced, you will need to incorporate the editor into your ACAD.PGP file (you will find out how to do this later in this chapter). Low memory use is desirable in this instance.

AutoLISP Basics

The essence of AutoLISP is list processing. AutoLISP's flexibility and its ability to "think" come from the way it manipulates *lists* of data. You will learn more about lists in a moment.

AutoLISP is actually a command interpreter that is included within AutoCAD. AutoLISP contains a number of predefined functions, known as *subroutines*, that you can use to manipulate and evaluate your data. These subroutines are interpreted by AutoLISP and sent to the computer's Central Processing Unit (CPU) for evaluation. If it weren't for AutoLISP, the only way you could get any response to your requests would be to send everything to the CPU in a series of 0s and 1s known as machine language. You are going to learn to "speak" AutoLISP because it is much simpler to understand and record than machine language.

Since AutoLISP is a language, you must make certain that your instructions are phrased in the exact way AutoLISP communicates. Unfortunately, computers and the program languages used with them are not yet capable of dependable independent thought processes. You can venture a guess that "ornges" may actually mean "oranges," but AutoLISP cannot guess about anything. The fact that the phrasing in a program must be exact is the reason that "debugging" a program or routine has become a principal task for the author of the program. No matter how precise you are, you will spend time debugging your routines. Consequently, it is a good idea to develop habits that will ensure care and deliberation in the development of your routines. Otherwise you will spend many frustrating hours trying to find errors in your work.

Definitions

You will find that understanding AutoLISP is easier if you are familiar with several basic definitions. A partial list of definitions is included here; you will add to these definitions as you gain experience with AutoLISP.

Data, at least in AutoLISP, can be formatted in different ways as *data types*. Some of the data types used by AutoLISP follow:

❏ **Real:** A number that has decimal precision. For example, *7.017* is a *real* number; *7* is not.

❏ **Integer:** A number that does not have decimal precision, but can represent the count of objects or dates and time, and so on. For example, *7* is an *integer*; *7.017* is not.

❏ **String:** A collection of numeric or alphabetic characters that are not evaluated by AutoLISP but are retained by AutoLISP with a unique identity. *Strings* are enclosed in quotation marks so that you, as well as AutoLISP, can recognize them as strings. For example, *"7.017"* is a string and *7.017* is not. *"Seven"* is a string and *Seven* is not.

❏ **Symbols:** A collection of alphabetic characters that AutoLISP uses to store variables. A value that is stored is said to be bound to a *symbol*. *Seven* is a symbol; *"Seven"* is not.

❑ **Lists:** AutoLISP evaluates "phrases" of *symbols*, *reals*, *integers*, and *strings* as a set of actions. The organization of these phrases or *lists* and their relationship to each other determine the order of the actions AutoLISP takes to execute a routine. The boundary of the list is denoted (delimited) by left and right parentheses.

AutoLISP recognizes other types of data, but they are for advanced use and you won't need them right away. You can find more information about them by looking at the *type* function in your *AutoLISP Programmer's Reference*.

You should be familiar with some definitions of general terms. Keep in mind that the use of these terms varies slightly from one programmer to another since there is no formal single source standard for AutoLISP. A little later in this chapter, you will find examples that further explain these definitions. These general definitions follow:

❑ **Program, routine, and subroutine**: A *program* (such as AutoCAD) is a collection of *routines*. Programs, which generally provide the user with a range of actions and options, are what the user generally interacts with.

A *routine* generally is a set of activities collected into something called a *function*, and is part of a program. The terms *program* and *routine* are sometimes used interchangeably.

A *subroutine* is a collection of activities, bound together within a *routine*, that provides a result for use by the routine.

❑ **Function:** In AutoLISP, a subroutine is called a *function*. A *function* is a defined set of commands that AutoLISP will carry out when the function is called by your routine. AutoLISP has a set of built-in functions (listed in the *AutoLISP Programmer's Reference*). *Functions* are also routines you can define.

❑ **Nesting**: Lists can be *nested* to improve the execution speed of AutoLISP. AutoLISP evaluates lists from the innermost list outward. In the following example, each number represents a list. The numbers show the order in which AutoLISP would evaluate a set of *nested lists*:

```
( 4 ( 3 ( 2 ) ( 1 )))
```

Nesting also helps reduce the number of variables you must bind to symbols. If, instead of maintaining the value of a variable in memory, you want to use the result of AutoLISP's evaluation of a set of variables, you can nest them within other lists and avoid using time and memory to assign a symbol to any of those variables. The use of nesting, lists, and parentheses is discussed in more detail a little later in this chapter.

❏ **Atoms:** An *atom* is the smallest element AutoLISP recognizes as a unit. An atom can be a single number, a symbol, a variable, or a specific set of characters.

❏ **Bound:** If a value is assigned to a symbol, that value is said to be *bound* to that symbol.

❏ **Expression:** A list that has been put together into an executable collection of instructions for AutoLISP's action is called an *expression*. The term can be used also to describe nested lists. You may find that an entire routine written in AutoLISP will be used as an *expression* to another function.

❏ **Argument:** An *argument* is a conditional parameter that governs how an expression is to be evaluated.

❏ **Loop:** A set of expressions that are repeated an explicit number of times is called a *loop*. The number of repetitions in a loop can be determined in a variety of ways by using different conditions to establish how many repetitions will be completed. An *iterative loop* is repeated a predetermined number of times; a *recursive loop* is repeated a conditional number of times, based on other calculations and variables.

❏ **Null and nil:** The term *null* generally is used to denote explicitly that nothing exists in a phrase, or that a symbol is bound to nothing. This is required because in programming, as well as in mathematics, the value of *0* is not interchangeable with *nothing* or *empty*. *Nil* is the value returned by AutoLISP when a symbol is bound to nothing. *Null* is a resident function of AutoLISP; it tests to see whether a symbol is bound to *nil*.

Special Characters

In AutoLISP, certain characters can be used only for a specific purpose. For example, the following characters are the math functions:

```
= + - < > * / /= ~ >= <=
```

They work exactly as they did in your math courses. For a detailed explanation of these characters, see your *AutoLISP Programmer's Reference*.

Other special characters include the following:

```
( ) . " ' ;
```

As you may recall, parentheses separate (*delimit*) lists for AutoLISP. If you don't include a balanced number of right and left parentheses when you create a routine, AutoLISP will let you know that there is a problem by displaying one of two error messages when you try to execute the routine.

If you see a number followed by a > (1>, for example), AutoLISP is telling you that you have one less right parenthesis than you do left. The message extra right paren tells you that you have too many right parentheses.

You will see the first error message also if you omit a closing quotation mark (") in a string statement. Doing so will cause AutoLISP to ignore all the parentheses following the omitted quotation mark.

Although you will not be able to access AutoCAD if your routine is missing one or more right parentheses, don't be alarmed. To solve the problem, type the number of right parentheses that AutoLISP shows are missing and then press Enter or, if adding the proper number of right parentheses doesn't fix the problem, type "). Then, before trying the routine again, go back and find out what you did wrong.

Periods, which are used as decimal points, are used also to create *dotted pairs*. Dotted pairs are used in the AutoCAD drawing database as association lists, allowing you to retrieve certain information about an entity in the drawing. This is an advanced usage that you will have to work up to.

An apostrophe (') is used in the same way that the resident AutoLISP function quote is used. The quote forces AutoLISP to view the characters that follow it exactly as they appear, instead of evaluating what may have been assigned to the variable.

Quotation marks (") are used to tell AutoLISP that a string is included between each pair of quotation marks.

Semicolons (;) are special characters that let you add comments to your routine. These comments, which won't disrupt AutoLISP while it processes the instructions, can help you keep track of your intentions, the status of long lists, and whether those lists have the proper number of closing (right) parentheses.

Parentheses, apostrophes, quotation marks, a space, and an end-of-line character will all terminate a symbol name or numeric constant in AutoLISP.

Within strings, backslashes (\) are used to tell AutoLISP that a special control character follows. Two of those control characters are a second backslash (\\) and a character that causes AutoLISP to print a new line to the screen (\n). You will see how each of these is used in the examples later in this chapter.

General Syntax

In simple terms, AutoLISP's syntax amounts to the proper placement of parentheses and the proper use of the symbols, functions, and special characters of AutoLISP. That sounds simple, but the power of AutoLISP can create situations where things get a little complex. It is important that you strive to do two things as you learn AutoLISP. First, learn new "words" (functions) every chance you get, and second, make sure that you understand the "grammatical rules" for the use of those words. It is best to take each part of AutoLISP one step at a time and build your ability along with your understanding of the ways AutoLISP can be used. After all, when you learned the word "blue," you could describe a number of objects without being concerned whether it had other meanings!

Before you learn more about AutoLISP syntax, you should note two things about AutoLISP. First, it *generally* doesn't matter whether you enter AutoLISP phrases, symbols, etc. as upper- or lowercase text. AutoLISP is case sensitive in the use of the open function, when you are trying to tell AutoLISP to read ("r"), write to ("w"), or append ("a") a file.

Another important aspect of AutoLISP is that it does not understand the DOS path you have set up on your computer. For this discussion, it is assumed that your AutoLISP routines are stored in the same directory in which you are loading AutoCAD, or that they are in the directory you have assigned to the SET ACAD = environment variable in your AUTOEXEC.BAT or ACAD.BAT file. For more information, refer to your *AutoLISP Programmer's Reference*.

When you create AutoLISP routines, you start with the AutoLISP function defun. This function *de*fines a *func*tion by establishing the symbol that will be used to call the routine. The routine starts out with something like (defun tick (). This phrase sets up a routine called *tick*. When you define a new function, be sure not to use the name of any of AutoLISP's built-in functions.

Following the defun statement and the name of the routine, AutoLISP is told of any arguments that should accompany the function and the name of any variables that will be used in the execution of the routine. These variables, known as *local* variables, have no meaning outside the routine in which they are named. The value of a local variable is set to nil when the routine has completed its work. The arguments and variables might look like this:

```
(defun tick (x / etl tlw ntl ss1 ctr sl)
  (....
```

Let's say that you often have a drawing which was prepared with arrows for the AutoCAD dimensioning blocks and that you want to replace all of those blocks with a tick (a slash). Furthermore, you want to replace the arrows only on a particular layer, the name of which changes from time to time. You want any other arrows in the drawing to remain in place. You could execute this routine by typing **(load "tick")** at the AutoCAD Command: prompt, pressing Enter, and then typing **(tick dimension)** and pressing Enter again to let the routine know that it is supposed to look for the arrows on a layer named *dimension*. The x in the routine's definition is replaced by the string dimension, in this case; dimension is used as an argument to the AutoLISP function defun. Following the / are several symbols that will be used as local variables in the tick routine.

Listing 19.1 is an example of a typical LISP routine.

Listing 19.1. *The* frlayer *routine.*

```
(defun frlayer (/ ss1 e# ent names lyr)
 (prompt "/nSelect objects on layers to be frozen: ")
 (setq ss1 (ssget)
   setq e# (sslength ss1))
 (if (> e# 0)
   (progn
    (setq ent (ssname ss1 (setq e# (1- e#))))
    (setq ent (entget ent))
    (setq names (cdr (assoc 8 ent)))
    (setq e# (1- e#))
   )
 )
 (while (> e# -1)
    (setq ent (ssname ss1 e#))
    (setq ent (entget ent))
    (setq lyr (cdr (assoc 8 ent)))
    (setq names (strcat names "," lyr))
    (setq e# (1- e#))
 )
 (command "layer" "f" names "")
 (princ)
)
```

This is a routine for freezing layers by selecting objects in a drawing. It has been formatted in *pretty printing*, which means that spaces and returns have been added to help clarify the activities that occur during execution of the routine. The frlayer routine could be written so that all of its instructions are on one line. Any extra spaces that don't separate symbols, functions, and numeric entries can be removed. Removing this *white space* from a routine makes the routine load a little faster, but after the routine is loaded into memory, the format used does not affect the run time.

Take some time and look at how the parentheses have been balanced in listing 19.1. Each parenthesis on a balanced line remains on the same line with its mate. Parentheses that close functions which were requested a few lines earlier in the routine are on lines by themselves and aligned with the opening parenthesis. You will see many examples of this type of formatting when you study AutoLISP. As you become more advanced, you won't need pretty printing for your routines, although using this format for setting up routines you write for others is a good idea.

Parentheses and Lists

As you have read, the use of *lists* is central to AutoLISP routines. AutoLISP expects to find lists properly formatted and divided by parentheses. The following is an example of a set of lists nested into one list:

```
(long (sorta long (medium (shorter (really short))))) still longer)
```

The most basic of these nested lists contains two atoms: really and short. The next list in order of evaluation is the shorter list, which is made up of the two atoms: shorter, and the really short list. Note that after AutoLISP is outside the first set of parentheses, the really short list is an atom. The next list also contains two atoms: medium, and the shorter list. Stepping out farther, the list becomes three atoms: sorta, long, and the medium list. The last list contains four items: long, the sorta long list, still, and longer. When you begin to analyze and write AutoLISP routines, you will realize that all you are doing is manipulating lists. In fact, the frlayer routine (see listing 19.1) is a single list.

Lists also can be grouped together without being nested. For example, consider the following:

```
((list one) (list two) (list three))
```

This list consists of three atoms, each of which is a list made up of two atoms. You will also see many examples of these.

Finally, a special kind of list, known as a *dotted pair*, is used to associate *group codes* with the data that defines a drawing entity within the AutoCAD drawing database. Dotted pairs look like the following line:

```
(0 . "LINE")
```

which is part of the entity list that describes a LINE. The group code 0 is associated with the name of the entity (LINE, in this case). Note that the entity name is a string.

A Keyboard Tutorial

One of the best ways to learn how AutoLISP works is to enter directly (at the AutoCAD Command: prompt) examples of what you are trying to learn. As your programming skills improve, you will find that the length of the list you are working with will become too long for this technique. But for now, you should try to enter your experiments at the Command: prompt. Try this example by typing the following line at the Command: prompt:

(setq ball (* 2.0 4.0))

Then press Enter.

If you typed everything correctly, AutoLISP should return 8.0. If you type **!ball** and press Enter, AutoCAD should return 8.0. You just used the AutoLISP functions setq and * to bind the symbol ball to the value of 2 times 4, or 8. AutoCAD recognizes an ! accompanied by a symbol and returns the value AutoLISP has bound to that symbol. If you needed to enter the value *8.0* for an offset amount, for example, you could type **!ball** instead. You can test many of your ideas about the syntax of an AutoLISP function by entering them at the AutoCAD Command: prompt.

AutoLISP at the Command Prompt

After you master a little bit of AutoLISP, you can use it just like any other AutoCAD command at the AutoCAD Command: prompt. This can be a real bonus to your productivity.

Let's say, for example, that you want to convert quite a few lines to polylines, set them a specific width, and join them with other lines so that they will become one line of uniform width. You could issue a PEDIT command, select the line, tell AutoCAD that you want to turn the line into a polyline, change the width, and then join the line with other lines. You would have to do this for several lines, repeating the command every time. Alternatively, you could type the following line at the AutoCAD Command: prompt:

(defun C:PE ()

Press Enter. AutoLISP returns:

1>

Then type:

(command "pedit" pause "y" "w" "0.20" "j" pause ""))

and press Enter. AutoLISP returns:

```
C:PE
```

This quick routine will automate all of your entries so that all you have to do is type **PE** at the AutoCAD Command: prompt and press Enter. You can keep pressing Enter to repeat the command. There are several things about this entry that you should notice. First, by using the prefix *C:* before *PE*, you tell AutoCAD to recognize *PE* or *pe* as a command *for the duration of the current editing session only*. If you decide that you want to use this command more often, you can create the file with your word processor and store it on your hard disk. More about that in a moment.

Next, notice that the empty parentheses *()* had to be placed after the routine name, even though no arguments or local variables were defined.

Notice also that you can type a line and press Enter before the available space on the command line is filled. This allows you to check your typing and use backspace, delete, and so forth before going on to the next line. AutoLISP lets you know how many outstanding right parentheses you have in your "balance." (In this case, it was 1.)

Finally, the routine gets to the real action. Using the AutoLISP function, command, which calls AutoCAD commands from within AutoLISP, the PEDIT command is issued. Notice that pedit is enclosed in quotation marks. This indicates that you are providing a reply to the AutoLISP request for a command name, just as though you had typed it at the Command: prompt. The next statement, pause, is an AutoLISP function that causes AutoLISP to wait for you to answer a question posed by the PEDIT command, namely, Select object: .

The rest of the line in this quick routine answers the normal sequence for the PEDIT command, including a pause for the selection of the objects to JOIN with the PEDIT command. Notice again that all of the responses you normally would type in are enclosed in quotation marks as strings.

You can type AutoLISP routines of any length in this manner, provided that you don't make any errors. This is the manual version of the AutoLISP load command. Instead of AutoLISP reading a file, you are loading the routine at the Command: prompt. Good AutoLISP programmers ordinarily can enter six or more lines of AutoLISP code as they use AutoCAD. You can use this technique to do many unique tasks with AutoLISP, without ever saving the routine to disk.

AutoLISP can be used in AutoCAD script (.SCR) files in the same way it is used at the keyboard. The script file "types" the AutoLISP routine for you (just as it does other AutoCAD commands). You can experiment with this feature in the same way you have been experimenting with AutoLISP at the keyboard, but you must use a word processor to create a script file. Just pretend that you are actually in AutoCAD when you are typing the script file. The only thing missing will be the AutoCAD prompts; you might want to have your *AutoCAD Reference Manual* handy to make sure that you are replying properly to AutoCAD command requests. Review your *AutoCAD Reference Manual* for more information about writing script files.

AutoLISP in Menu Macros

The next step in your development as an AutoLISP user is to start using simple AutoLISP routines in your own custom menus. This use of AutoLISP is similar to typing the routine at the Command: prompt, except that the routine is stored permanently in your menu. (If you need to learn more about menu customization, refer to the appropriate appendix in your *AutoCAD Reference Manual*, or read *AutoCAD Advanced Techniques*, published by Que Corporation.)

The key to writing AutoCAD menu macros is to keep in mind that, with a few exceptions, you compose a menu macro in exactly the same sequence you type the commands and AutoLISP phrases at the AutoCAD Command: prompt. Menu macros have some special characters for pauses, extensions of command lines, returns, and the screen, pull-down, and icon menu-selection procedure. Refer to the *AutoCAD Reference Manual* for an explanation of the menu syntax.

Let's assume that several parts in your drawings have a leader pointing at the part, with a letter or number identifying the part. Because you frequently have to insert a number of these parts to create the drawing, you normally create a block and name the block with the part number or letter. It would make sense, then, for you to have a menu macro that automatically accomplishes this sequence for you. A screen macro for this purpose might look something like the following:

```
[ MARKBLK]^C^C(progn (prompt "\nSelect the mark that you wish+
to name the block with: ")(setq bnm (cdr (assoc 1 (entget (car+
(entsel))))))) (prompt "\nSelect Block Entities: ")+
(setq s1 (ssget))(if (= (type bnm) 'STR)+
(progn (menucmd "S=OSNAP")(command "block" bnm pause s1 ""))+
(prompt "\nMark not found..."))(setq bnm nil s1 nil)(princ)) $S=
```

Here is a line-by-line explanation of the MARKBLK (markblock) menu macro. In the first line:

```
[ MARKBLK]^C^C(progn (prompt "\nSelect the mark that you wish+
```

the screen displays MARKBLK so that the user can select this macro within the screen-menu portion of the AutoCAD screen. The macro then issues two ^Cs (cancels) to cancel any other command that is in effect (except for a transparent command in progress during a dimensioning command, which would require three ^Cs). Next, the AutoLISP function progn starts the AutoLISP macro. This function simply tells AutoLISP "more commands follow, so make sure that you look at all of them before returning control to AutoCAD." Next, the prompt function issues a message that asks the user to select the mark after which he or she wants to name the block. The plus sign (+) tells AutoCAD that the next line should be included in the macro.

In the next line:

```
to name the block with: ")(setq bnm (cdr (assoc 1 (entget (car+
```

The setq function tells AutoLISP to bind the results of the next list to the symbol bnm. The cdr function returns all but the first atom of a list. In this case, it will return the second part of a dotted pair associated with the group code 1, which you find by using the function assoc on the next list. The next list is found by using the function entget on the entity whose name is retrieved by using car, an AutoLISP function that returns the first atom of a list.

Finally, we get to the innermost list of the original setq list:

```
(entsel))))))(prompt "\nSelect Block Entities: ")+
```

This list is created by the AutoLISP function entsel, which prompts the user to Select an object: and then returns the name of the entity selected along with the coordinates of the point used to select the entity. Since you don't need those coordinates, the function car was used so that AutoLISP would retrieve only the name of the entity from the list returned by entsel. To understand this a little better, make sure that you have a text mark already in the drawing; then enter the following at the AutoCAD Command: prompt:

(entget (car (entsel)))

Press Enter, and select a mark in the drawing. You will see the complete data list of the text entity you picked. Look for the list that includes something like (1 . "FF"), which is the label that will be selected for the block name. This is the string associated with the text entity you picked; the string is stored in the data list associated with the group code 1. For more information about group codes, refer to the appendixes of your *AutoCAD Reference Manual*.

In the next line:

```
(setq s1 (ssget))(if (= (type bnm) 'STR)+
```

the function setq binds the name of a selection set to the variable s1, using the function ssget. The ssget function is the same as the AutoCAD command SELECT. The name of the selection set will be something like (<Selection Set 1>). AutoLISP will wait patiently while you pick any number of objects, using the Window, Individual, Previous, Last, Crossing, Add, or Delete options just as you would in AutoCAD.

The if function tests to see whether something is true or false. If the test returns true (T), if then executes the next list within the if function; if the test returns false (nil), the second list within the if function is executed. Note that these must be complete lists, properly organized between a pair of parentheses. The test phrase, in this instance, is (= (type bnm) 'STR). This phrase uses the type function to see whether the symbol bnm is bound to a value that is a string ('STR). The single quotation mark (') makes AutoLISP read the phrase STR literally, without trying to evaluate it. This happens to be the same phrase AutoLISP would return if the function type were used to evaluate the symbol bnm when it is bound to a string. This if test is executed to ensure that the user selected a text string instead of a different type of entity when he or she was prompted to select the mark for the block name.

As you have seen, the if function can use only two lists as its choice for execution. If a true test is found, the if function can use just one list for execution, as the lack of a second list will cause AutoLISP to continue as if nothing happened upon finding a false test result.

To get around this condition, you need the next line:

```
(progn (menucmd "S=OSNAP")(command "block" bnm pause s1 ""))+
```

in which progn is used again to make the statements included with it a single list.

First, menucmd calls a screen menu that contains OSNAP settings. (You may or may not have the same screen submenu included in your menu. If you don't have it, you may have to create one.) Next, the command function is used to start the AutoCAD BLOCK command. The block name is provided by the string bound to the symbol bnm, and a pause is executed to allow the user to select an insertion point. Then AutoLISP passes all the entities in selection set s1 to AutoCAD, creating the block with the name of the mark associated with it. Finally, the command "block" section is completed with a pair of quotation marks, which is the same as pressing the space bar during an AutoCAD command procedure. This completes the true choice for the if condition.

If the entity selected for the block name was a different data type than a string, the false (nil) side of the if condition uses the prompt function to present a message telling the user that the mark was not found:

```
(prompt "\nMark not found..."))(setq bnm nil s1 nil)(princ)) $S=
```

This completes the if list. Then both of the symbols used in this routine (bnm and s1) are set to nil using setq. This is necessary because the symbols will retain their values after the AutoLISP commands are completed and might provide false information the next time the routine is used. (This would happen only under unique circumstances, but it's better to be safe than sorry.) Finally, princ is used to exit the AutoLISP routine without displaying the nil that AutoLISP returns upon setting the symbols to nil. This is only required for a better "look" to the routines. The $S= returns the screen menu that was displayed prior to the selection of the OSNAP menu, so that this routine can be used again immediately.

This fairly short routine gives you a macro that improves execution speed for the user. If you find that your routine is getting larger than this, consider making it a permanent file on disk and simply loading the routine from the menu. The size of your menu file comes into play also when you are considering whether you should use AutoLISP to create a menu macro or a routine on disk. The amount of time it takes your computer to page through your menu will increase as you add more and more macros. Only experimentation will tell you when to start placing macros on disk instead of using the menu.

An AutoLISP Routine

You can create an AutoLISP routine and store it in an ACAD.LSP file or in a file unique to the routine that is stored on disk. The difference in this case is that you should use the space in the ACAD.LSP file judiciously. If your routine is used constantly, relatively short, and/or if it applies to several other uses, you should consider storing it in your ACAD.LSP file. Doing so will make the function defined by the defun statement instantly available to every drawing session you begin. Too many routines in the ACAD.LSP file will cause the execution speed of those routines to deteriorate, since the routines are all stored simultaneously in memory. Listing 19.2 is an example of an AutoLISP routine. The MARKBLK menu macro discussed in the preceding section has been turned into a routine (with a few added features) that is stored on disk.

This routine, which you could name BMK.LSP, can be stored on disk. If you use the routine's name for the file name, you can execute the routine by typing (load "bmk"), pressing Enter, typing **BMK**, and pressing Enter again.

Once the routine is loaded, all you have to do to start it is type **BMK** and press Enter. Because the disk file version of the routine starts with C:BMK, the routine is executable at the command line.

Notice that, following the defun statement, an argument has been added, along with local variables. The argument (x, in this case) allows the addition of an optional block name to the execution of the routine. To use this routine with a predetermined block name, type **BMK B104**, for example, and a block can be created using the name B104. Essentially, this routine automates AutoCAD's BLOCK command, with some custom features.

Listing 19.2. *The* `C:BMK` *routine.*

```
(defun C:BMK (x / bnm s1 echo)
(setq echo (getvar "cmdecho"))
(setvar "cmdecho" 0)
(if (= x nil)
 (progn
  (prompt "\nSelect the mark that
     you wish to name the block with: ")
  (setq bnm (cdr (assoc 1 (entget (car (entsel))))))
 )
 (setq bnm x)
)
(prompt "\nSelect Block Entities: ")
(setq s1 (ssget))
(if (= (type bnm) 'STR)
 (progn
  (menucmd "S=OSNAP")
  (command "block" bnm pause s1 "")
 )
 (prompt "\nMark not found...")
)
(setvar "cmdecho" echo)
(princ)
)
```

By including the local variables bnm and s1 in the list following the defun statement, you tell AutoLISP to set these variables automatically to nil upon exiting the routine. Next, two new functions (getvar and setvar) have been added. These two phrases store the current value of the AutoCAD variable CMDECHO to the symbol echo and then set the variable CMDECHO to OFF (0). This makes the routine run faster and hides unnecessary command echoing from the user.

The use of the routine is now governed by an if statement that tests to see whether a value was assigned to the x argument with the phrase (= x nil). This test allows the user to include a block name with the execution of the routine, or continues with the mark option as the original routine did. The if statement says to AutoLISP, "if x is bound to nil, then get a string from the user; but if x has a value, set the value of the symbol bnm to the value bound to x". The routine proceeds as before, except that you can remove the setq functions which reset the symbols to nil and the AutoCAD CMDECHO variable is reset to the stored value of echo.

You can enhance this routine even further by adding other options, such as letting the user decide whether to create a block in the drawing or write it to file and letting the user type a string instead of using a mark in the drawing for naming the block. The true power of AutoLISP is revealed in the wide range of possibilities available.

Useful Examples

The *AutoLISP Programmer's Reference* lists the basics of every function but offers little explanation of what each function does. You have to learn AutoLISP on your own or from AutoCAD training centers that provide courses in AutoLISP. Even if you take a course, you will learn AutoLISP by experimenting at the keyboard and studying other examples. *CADENCE* and *CADalyst* magazines both publish AutoLISP articles and examples every month. If you want to become a more proficient writer of AutoLISP routines, *AutoCAD Advanced Techniques*, published by Que Corporation, contains detailed discussions of AutoLISP functions and their practical use. Let's take a look at some examples that you may find helpful in your everyday use of AutoCAD.

A Routine for Checking Dimensions

If you don't use Associative Dimensions, it is possible that the dimensions for the components of your drawing won't get updated if changes are made to your drawings. The routine described in the following sections lets the user pick dimension extension lines or drawing entities and then select the dimension text that goes along with them. Then the routine prompts the user to see whether he or she wants to update the dimension text string.

This routine will work only in cases in which dimension extension lines or the drawing entities are used to check the dimension and whether the drawing entities or dimension extension lines are parallel to each other. With some additional expansion, checking dimensions from nodes, arcs, circles, and so on can be added to this routine.

To create this routine, with your word processor in programming mode, start a file named DIMCHK.LSP. Type in the following, exactly as you see it:

```
(defun C:DIMCHK (/ echo ose dmpt1 dmd dmt dmtxt yn)
   (setq echo (getvar "cmdecho"))
   (setvar "cmdecho" 0)
   (setq ose (getvar "osmode"))
   (prompt "\nSelect one extension line or drawing line: ")
   (setvar "osmode" 512)
```

DIMCHK routine continues

DIMCHK routine *continued*

```
(setq dmpt1 (cdr (entsel)))
(setvar "osmode" 128)
(prompt "\nSelect the other extension line or drawing line: ")
(setq dmd (distance dmpt1))
(setvar "osmode" 0)
(prompt "\nSelect the dimension text string to verify: ")
(setq dmt (car (entsel))
   dmtxt (cdr (assoc 1 (entget dmt))))
(if ( = "TEXT" (assoc 0 dmt))
   (if ( = (rtos dmd (getvar "lunits")) dmtxt)
     (prompt "\nDimension checks out O.K.")
     (progn
      (prompt "\nThe dimension currently reads ")
      (princ dmtxt)
      (prompt " and the actual dimension is ")
      (princ dmd)
      (prompt ".")
      (initget 1 "Y y N n")
      (setq yn (strcase
          (getkword "\nDo you wish to change it? <Y> or N: ")))
      (if (or (equal yn "Y") ( = yn nil))
        (command "CHANGE" dmt "" "" "" "" ""
           (rtos dmd (getvar "LUNITS")))
      )
    )
  )
  (prompt "\nDimension text not found...")
 )
 (setvar "cmdecho" echo)
 (setvar "osmode" ose)
 (princ)
)
```

To execute this routine from the AutoCAD Command: prompt, type **(load
"DIMCHK")** and press Enter. Then type **(DIMCHK)** and press Enter.

Here is an explanation of the way this routine works. In the first three lines:

```
(defun C:DIMCHK (/ echo dmpt1 dmpt2 dmt vdmt yn)
  (setq echo (getvar "cmdecho"))
  (setvar "cmdecho" 0)
```

the defun function, local variables, and getvar and setvar work as described
earlier in this chapter.

The next sequence of phrases:

```
(setq ose (getvar "osmode"))
(prompt "\nSelect one extension line or drawing line: ")
(setvar "osmode" 512)
(setq dmpt1 (cdr (entsel)))
(setvar "osmode" 128)
(prompt "\nSelect the other extension line or drawing line: ")
(setq dmd (distance dmpt1))
(setvar "osmode" 0)
(prompt "\nSelect the dimension text string to verify: ")
(setq dmt (car (entsel))
    dmtxt (cdr (assoc 1 (entget dmt)))))
```

is used to set up the principal elements used for the dimension check, namely the lines dimensioned or the dimension extension lines that reference those lines, and the text which is in the drawing as the current dimension. These three `prompt` functions, each with slight variations in use, let the user know what AutoLISP is looking for.

The first `setq` stores the current value of the AutoCAD variable osmode bound to the symbol ose. The user is prompted to select the first line, after which `setvar` is used to set OSNAP mode to nearest. A point is retrieved using `cdr` and `entsel` and binding the value to the variable dmpt1. This sequence was required to make sure that the point is on the desired line and that no rounding of the point by system settings will create a point which is no longer on the line.

Next, the OSNAP is set to perpendicular using `setvar` again, and the user is prompted to select the second line. The `distance` function returns the distance from the first point perpendicular to the second line which is bound to the variable dmd.

Finally, OSNAP mode is turned off and the user is prompted to select the dimension text. Using `entsel`, the variable dmt is bound to the entity selected. Remember, because `entsel` returns both the entity name and the point by which the user selected it, `car` is used to return only the entity name. In addition, the string value of dmt is bound to the symbol dmtxt so that AutoLISP will know what the dimension string actually says, as well as which entity in the database is being reviewed.

This `if` test:

```
(if (= "TEXT" (assoc 0 dmt))
```

checks to make sure that the entity type which is bound to the symbol dmt is indeed a text entity. The entity type is always a string associated with the group code 0 in the entity data list.

The next if statement:

```
(if (= (rtos dmd (getvar "lunits")) dmtxt)
  (prompt "\nDimension checks out O.K.")
  (progn
   (prompt "\nThe dimension currently reads ")
   (princ dmtxt)
   (prompt " and the actual dimension is ")
   (princ dmd)
   (prompt ".")
```

tests to see whether the distance found by the distance function (and bound to the symbol dmd) is equal to the dimension string you are checking, bound to the symbol dmtxt. Distance returns a real number that cannot be compared to a string unless it is converted to one. Rtos converts the real number to a string and, by checking the setting for the AutoCAD variable ''LUNITS'' with getvar, the real number is converted to a string that is in the same format as the drawing units setting.

If both dmd and dmtxt have equal string values, the if statement returns the message Dimension checks out O.K. If the values aren't equal, progn allows a series of prompts and princs to be executed as one list that tells you not only what the current dimension text says but also the value of the actual distance between the two lines. Princ is used to display on the screen the value that is bound to a symbol. Prompt will only display strings on the screen. Princ and prompt are intermixed to create a complete message on the screen.

Now to explain the next four lines in the routine:

```
(initget 1 "Y y N n")
  (setq yn (strcase
    (getkword "\nDo you wish to change it? <Y> or N: ")))
  (if (or (equal yn "Y") (= yn nil))
```

Initget is an AutoLISP function that predetermines the format many of the AutoLISP get functions can receive. The use of initget with the mode flag 1 in this instance will allow a null reply or one of the string characters (Y y N n). Next, the symbol yn is bound to the uppercase value, using strcase, of a keyword, using getkword, that will be supplied by the user. Since the function initget was used, the symbol yn will be bound to nil, Y, or N. In this case, because you only want to know whether the dimension needs to be changed, the routine uses another if statement to test whether the symbol yn is bound to "Y" or to nil, either of which would indicate a ''yes'' response.

If a yes response is found, the AutoCAD CHANGE command is executed, selecting the dimension text entity that was bound to the symbol dmt:

```
(command "CHANGE" dmt "" "" "" "" ""
    (rtos dmd (getvar "LUNITS")))
  )
 )
)
```

Remember that empty pairs of quotation marks have the same effect as pressing the space bar. The number of quotation marks in this code is the same as the number of times you would have to press Enter to change the string value of a text entity. When the AutoCAD CHANGE command prompts for the new text string, the same rtos conversion of dmd that was explained earlier is executed, supplying a new value for the text string. The remaining parentheses close an if, progn, and another if list, respectively.

Finally, the false option of the first if test is a prompt that tells the user he or she didn't select a text entity for the dimension text:

```
    (prompt "\nDimension text not found...")
  )
 (princ)
)
```

Princ provides a quiet exit to the routine.

A Multiple Trim Routine

This routine allows you to make a group selection of objects to be trimmed, instead of selecting them one at a time. It first prompts the user for a trimming edge and then continues, trimming each "trimmable" selected object. To create this routine, start a file (MTM.LSP) in programming mode and type the following exactly as you see it:

```
(defun c:mtm (/ echo te s1 tpt ctr)
  (setq echo (getvar "cmdecho"))
  (setvar "cmdecho" 0)
  (prompt "Select edge(s) for trimming with: ")
  (setq te (ssget))
  (prompt "\nSelect object(s) for trimming: ")
  (setq s1 (ssget))
  (setq tpt (getpoint "\nIndicate the side to be removed: "))
  (setq ctr 0)
  (command "TRIM" te "")
```

MTM routine continues

MTM routine continued

```
(repeat (sslength s1)
 (command (list (ssname s1 ctr) tpt))
 (setq ctr (1 + ctr))
)
(command "")
(setvar "cmdecho" echo)
(princ)
)
```

To execute this routine from the AutoCAD Command: prompt, type **(load "mtm")**, press Enter, type **(mtm)** and press Enter again. The following sections describe in detail how this routine works.

These statements:

```
(defun c:mtm (/ echo te s1 tpt ctr)
 (setq echo (getvar "cmdecho"))
 (setvar "cmdecho" 0)
 (prompt "Select edge(s) for trimming with: ")
 (setq te (ssget))
 (prompt "\nSelect object(s) for trimming: ")
 (setq s1 (ssget))
 (setq tpt (getpoint "\nIndicate the side to be removed: ")
 (setq ctr 0)
```

are similar to those discussed earlier; the getpoint function has been added in this routine. The getpoint function allows you to prompt the user with a message that defines exactly what he or she is looking for (in this case, a point that indicates which side of the objects is to be trimmed). So, we have values bound to five symbols: echo, which we have used before; te, the trim edge; s1, the selection set of objects to be trimmed; tpt, the point indicating the trimmed side; and ctr, which will be used as a counter in a loop. As you will see, the symbol ctr is important to the functioning of this routine.

The next sequence:

```
(command "TRIM" te "")
(repeat (sslength s1)
 (command (list (ssname s1 ctr) tpt))
 (setq ctr (1+ ctr))
)
```

is unique to AutoCAD commands that suspend operation for multiple selection of entities which are then acted on, either one at a time or as a group. Since the TRIM command remains active, AutoLISP phrases can be used to satisfy input to the command in a group fashion instead of one at a time as required by the normal AutoCAD TRIM command response. Some AutoCAD commands, such as LINE, can also accept AutoLISP code for input in a similar fashion, but many of the commands will accept only single points or entities from AutoLISP. You must experiment with each AutoCAD command, investigating all the possibilities for your particular application.

Here, the `command` function is being used to begin the TRIM command, providing the symbol `te` to select the trimming edge, and then executing a `repeat` loop while TRIM is active. `Sslength` retrieves the length of the selection set that is bound to `s1`, which is all of the entities that are to be trimmed. To ensure that all entities in the selection set are trimmed, the length of the selection set must be used for the number of times the loop will repeat.

Within the `repeat` loop, the `command` function is used in a unique fashion. First, the `list` function creates a list of the entity name found by the `ssname` function and the point which is bound to the symbol `pt`. (The list will look something like *((<6000014>) (568.000000 720.187500))*.) Ssname looks at a selection set, which is bound to `s1` in this case, and returns the name of the entity that is located in the set in accordance with a number provided as an argument to the function. The entities in a selection set are numbered from 0 to the total number of entities in the set, less one. (One is subtracted from the total because AutoLISP starts counting at 0. Thus, if there are 5 entities in a set, they are numbered 0 through 4.) In this case, the symbol `ctr` is being used to provide the number of the entity which, if you recall, starts out at 0. Next, the value of `ctr` is incremented by the `1+` function, which adds 1 to the counter each time AutoLISP reads the `setq`. Since the repeat loop executes this `setq` once for each member of the selection set, the value of `ctr` matches the number of each entity in the selection set.

The `command` function works in this case as if the user were typing the entity name and a general point for use by the TRIM command. The results are similar to the use of the AutoCAD BREAK command, but this aspect of the TRIM command is available only through AutoLISP.

Once the `repeat` loop has counted through the set, AutoLISP returns to the TRIM command, which is waiting for another object to trim. In the next few lines:

```
(command "")
(setvar "cmdecho" echo)
(princ)
)
```

`command` issues a space bar ("") to the TRIM command, thereby ending the command. Finally the AutoCAD variable CMDECHO is returned to its pre-routine value, and `princ` exits the routine quietly.

Summary

This chapter introduced you to the concepts behind AutoLISP and provided an elementary review of the way AutoLISP works. You were also shown the important uses of AutoLISP in menu macros, at the Command: prompt, in script files, in the ACAD.LSP file, and as stored routines on the disk.

Remember that learning AutoLISP is the same as learning a new language. Start out by learning to use new functions in AutoLISP, then putting them together in groups, and finally writing complete AutoLISP routines. You will find that having at least a basic understanding of AutoLISP is well worth your while. If you can imagine what is possible with AutoLISP, you can communicate it to a friend or consultant who will write the routines for you. If you find that you enjoy writing AutoLISP routines, you can create whatever you want with just a little practice and study.

This chapter gave you a brief look at some of AutoLISP's functions. Entire books have been written on AutoLISP, so you can imagine the complexity and flexibility of AutoLISP. If you want to learn more about AutoLISP, the ACAD.LSP file, and how to write menus and script files, you will find more detailed discussions of these and other topics in *AutoCAD Advanced Techniques*, which is available at your bookstore or from Que Corporation.

Part VI

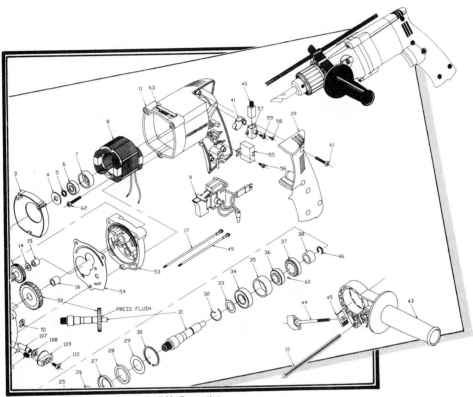

Drawing courtesy of Dwayne Gould, Porter-Cable Corporation
Jackson, Tennessee

Reference

Troubleshooting Guide

One nice thing about computers is that for every effect, there is a predictable cause, even though the cause may seem obscure at times. This section describes several general pitfalls, their causes, and possible solutions.

AutoCAD is a large program with an impressive range of features and potential applications. But AutoCAD's dynamic nature can create problems for its users. If troubles arise, however, do not let yourself become too distraught. Remember that problems are not unusual when you use complex computer systems. Rather, try to approach your problem from an analytical standpoint, and take the following steps:

1. Identify the nature of the problem.

2. Identify the steps you took that made the problem occur, and determine whether these steps will re-create the problem every time they are followed.

3. Determine the scope of any damage (to your drawing or other files).

4. Find a solution.

This process should not be foreign to you. Indeed, it is a variation of the same process used to solve most business problems.

Typically, the errors you encounter will fall into one (or more) of the following general classifications:

❏ **Configuration errors.** These errors are symptomatic of an improperly installed system or a system that has been upgraded without changing AutoCAD's configuration parameters. Otherwise, AutoCAD may be looking for a file that is not where it is supposed to be.

505

❑ **Hardware errors.** These errors can be caused by hardware that is not suited to your task, improperly installed, or just plain faulty.

❑ **Input errors.** These errors are caused by something you input into the computer. The solution generally involves changing your input to something that AutoCAD can use.

❑ **Software bugs.** These can be errors with AutoCAD itself, with a software add-on package used with AutoCAD, or with an AutoLISP program written to work with AutoCAD. Solution options for errors in this category may be limited.

❑ **System errors.** These errors are caused by the operating system you are using. Your options here may be limited and generally are outside the scope of this section. System errors may require that your computer or its operating system be replaced.

Although determining which type of error has occurred can be difficult, figuring out the problem is frequently easy. You should be able to fit an error condition pretty quickly into one of the preceding categories. Just consider the nature of the problem. Ask yourself questions like: "Am I able to enter AutoCAD, and does the Main Menu appear correctly? Am I able to enter the Drawing Editor? With a previous drawing? With a new drawing? Am I able to enter commands from the keyboard, but not from the menu?" This kind of questioning will lead you to the appropriate area of your computer's hardware or software, where you can investigate further.

The preceding paragraph gave you an example of a logical train of thought. Clearly, you cannot enter the Drawing Editor if you cannot even enter AutoCAD. If you hop around from one possibility to another, you probably will waste valuable time looking in the wrong place for your answer. Your best bet for finding the problem is to keep a cool head and try to re-create the problem. Start at the point at which the problem may have occurred, or do something that may cause the problem to occur. Then move ahead in a linear fashion. Only then, with these facts in mind, can you arrive at a solution.

You should get into the habit of backing up your work often. This means saving your drawing not only to the hard drive, but also to a floppy disk. For safety's sake, do not leave the floppy disk in the drive with the latch closed. If your computer system malfunctions, the data on the floppy disk can become scrambled, negating all your efforts to prevent a disaster. Leave the disk drive latch open, except while saving your work. That should be protection against all possible data-destroying problems.

Configuration Errors

Configuration Problem #1: My display screen does not make any sense when I enter the Drawing Editor. It is full of squiggly lines, and I cannot read any letters on the screen.

POSSIBLE CAUSE: AutoCAD is configured for the wrong display device.

SOLUTION: Return to the Main Menu, and choose to configure the system. Specify the display device option that represents your hardware.

Configuration Problem #2: When I reconfigured AutoCAD, I could not find my device listed in the configuration choices.

POSSIBLE CAUSE: The appropriate driver is either missing from the directory in which you are keeping drivers or has been discontinued, or you have an ADI-type device.

SOLUTION: Ask your dealer to verify the name of the driver you need; then check for the file on your original AutoCAD disks. If you do not find it, look in a directory (called *OBSOLETE*) on your original AutoCAD disks.

Configuration Problem #3: When I run AutoCAD, I see a message that indicates I am out of RAM.

POSSIBLE CAUSE: The ACADFREERAM variable in your AUTOEXEC.BAT file is not set or is set improperly.

SOLUTION: In your AUTOEXEC.BAT file, change the line that controls the ACADFREERAM variable. This line looks like the following:

```
SET ACADFREERAM=28
```

Experiment with the value to the right of the equal sign, alternately increasing or decreasing it until the error message disappears. Remember, this value is a multiplier; it tells AutoCAD to set aside the number times 1,000. In this case, AutoCAD will set aside 28,000 bytes of RAM.

Configuration Problem #4: I have extra memory installed in my computer system; but when I run AutoCAD, I get a message indicating that extra memory is disabled.

POSSIBLE CAUSE: A variety of factors can cause this message to appear.

SOLUTION: Review the settings for ACADXMEM, ACADLIMEM, and LISPXMEM in your AUTOEXEC.BAT file. The use of extra memory is covered in Chapter 4 of the AutoCAD *Installation and Performance Guide*.

Configuration Problem #5: AutoCAD cannot find the overlay (.OVL), shape (.SHX), or menu (.MNX) files.

POSSIBLE CAUSE: Either the files have been erased from the \ACAD directory, or the environment variable SET ACAD = is missing from the AUTOEXEC.BAT or ACAD.BAT file.

SOLUTION: If you are using a third-party menu system or loading AutoCAD onto a RAM disk, you may have to provide an environment setting for the directory that contains these files. Review the literature from the menu system you are using, or ask your dealer about the RAM disk installation.

Configuration Problem #6: My digitizer menu does not work in the proper squares.

POSSIBLE CAUSE: The menu overlay on your digitizer has moved.

SOLUTION: Using the TABLET command, reconfigure your digitizer.

Configuration Problem #7: My cursor freezes on-screen, or my keyboard seems sluggish.

POSSIBLE CAUSE: An interrupt conflict or more than one device assigned to the same communications port

SOLUTION: Check the AutoCAD configuration and any driver addresses you may have provided, to see whether the digitizer is installed properly.

Configuration Problem #8: The text I had in a file will not display on-screen.

POSSIBLE CAUSE: AutoCAD uses a shape file (.SHX) to create the text style in your drawing. This file is missing.

SOLUTION: Make a new copy of the required .SHX file in your ACAD directory.

Configuration Problem #9: I receive a message stating that my AutoCAD prototype drawing is not on file.

POSSIBLE CAUSE: You attempted to begin a new drawing from the AutoCAD Main Menu when ACAD.DWG was not stored in the proper directory.

SOLUTION: In the configuration section, specify the ACAD.DWG file's location, or copy ACAD.DWG to the current subdirectory.

Configuration Problem #10: I receive a message indicating that setup is not loaded.

POSSIBLE CAUSE: AutoCAD cannot locate the file SETUP.LSP while loading AutoLISP.

SOLUTION: Make sure that SETUP.LSP is available in the current subdirectory or that your DOS PATH is set to include the subdirectory in which SETUP.LSP is located.

Hardware Errors

Two types of hardware generally cause problems in the use of AutoCAD: plotters (or printer plotters) and display devices. These devices use drivers, written by Autodesk or the manufacturers of the devices, that determine AutoCAD's output format. If there are bugs in the drivers themselves, strange things can happen to your display or plots.

Display Device Errors

Display devices have graphics cards that may not be totally compatible with the system in which they are installed. Normal software use will not point out these discrepancies, but AutoCAD will. AutoCAD is a demanding program, especially where visual graphics are concerned. Your display device may need a new driver in order to work with a new version of AutoCAD. When a display adapter conflicts with AutoCAD, the problem may manifest itself as a locked-up display, an inactive Advanced User Interface, a malfunctioning digitizer or mouse (due to interrupt problems), colors that do not display properly, or a "cursorless" or blank screen.

Some graphics cards have a feature called *display-list processing*. A display list, which is a virtual screen of the AutoCAD drawing, controls what is seen on the display independent of AutoCAD. Display-list processing uses either extra memory, your hard disk, or memory on the graphics card to store the virtual screen image. AutoCAD never knows (except in general terms) what is going on concerning the display, and speed is dramatically improved. These cards require drivers that use a great deal of RAM; they can have a variety of bugs in their software. Problems with display-list processing cards should be taken up with the manufacturer.

Display Device Problem #1: My display screen does not make any sense when I start my computer. It is blank or full of gibberish.

POSSIBLE CAUSE: Generally, this is due to improperly installed or faulty hardware.

SOLUTION: Refer to your computer system manuals for a possible solution. If this does not help, consult the dealer who provided you with the system.

Display Device Problem #2: My system has two monitors, but the drawing does not come up on either monitor or comes up on only the smaller of the two.

POSSIBLE CAUSE: Improper configuration of the software or hardware.

SOLUTION: If you can, have the dealer perform the installation correctly. If this is not possible, check the *Installation and Performance Guide* for instructions on configuring AutoCAD for a dual-screen setup. If your graphics card uses the ADI interface, the card's manufacturer should have instructions on how to set it up correctly for dual-screen operation. If necessary, ask someone who is using the same setup.

Plotter or Printer Plotter Errors

Plotters use a method called "handshaking" to make sure that the computer is ready to send information and that the plotter is ready to receive it. The plotter driver must recognize how the system is set up, which communications port the plotter is connected to, and other factors such as parity, baud rate, and stop bits. For proper handshaking to occur, the correct lines within the plotter cable must be connected to the computer's communications port, and the wires must be shielded from outside electrical interference. Problems with drivers and cabling can show up as loss of plot origin, lack of activity, erratic pen behavior, and failure to respond to pen-change commands from AutoCAD. If you have such problems, check your cable design. It should be the same as the one shown in the AutoCAD *Installation and Performance Guide*.

Plotter Problem #1: The plotter seems to be skipping over certain lines and text on my plots.

POSSIBLE CAUSE: AutoCAD's pen-width setting does not match the actual width of your plotter's pens.

SOLUTION: Try to plot again, but change the pen width to one that is equal to (or smaller than) your actual pen width.

Plotter Problem #2: While attempting to plot, I receive a message indicating that there is no response from the controller and that my plot is canceled.

POSSIBLE CAUSES: The plotter is not connected or has not had time to warm up completely.

SOLUTION: Check the plotter connections to make sure that they are firm and secure. Some plotters also require a warm-up period before plotting can begin. Check your plotter manual to see whether this is necessary. If all else fails, check the actual cable connected to the plotter; it may be wired incorrectly.

Plotter Problem #3: My plots are fine if they are smaller than a certain size; a larger plot will start drawing unwanted lines in unwanted places while skipping other lines that should be there.

PROBABLE CAUSE: The plotter driver has become scrambled.

SOLUTION: Recopy the plotter driver from the proper AutoCAD distribution disk to your hard disk and reconfigure AutoCAD to use the new copy of the driver.

Printer Plotter Problem #1: When I attempt to use a printer plotter, I receive a message stating that the printer is not ready.

POSSIBLE CAUSES: The printer is not connected properly, is not turned on, is out of paper, or is off line.

SOLUTION: Check the printer to make sure that it is correctly set up and connected to the computer. Try the plot again.

Other Hardware Errors

Hardware Problem #1: When running AutoCAD, I see a message similar to Error: FMTOUT.

POSSIBLE CAUSE: Your math coprocessor is not installed correctly or is faulty.

SOLUTION: Check your math coprocessor. It may not be seated properly. If this does not seem to be the case, replace it and try again. If the error goes away, the first math coprocessor is bad and should be retired.

Input Errors

Input Problem #1: When I insert a block into my drawing, nothing appears.

POSSIBLE CAUSE: The block contains entities that are on a layer which currently is turned off or frozen.

SOLUTION: Check to see which layers are off or frozen. Entities will not appear if they are in a block on a layer that is off or frozen.

If no layers are off or frozen, you may have made a common mistake when creating the block. When you were prompted for an insertion point, you may have failed to specify the entities to be defined as a block. This results in a block of "nothing." In this case, you will need to define the block again.

Input Problem #2: When I insert a block, I get an old version rather than the latest version that's stored on disk.

POSSIBLE CAUSE: Your drawing has not been updated to include the current disk version of your block.

SOLUTION: To force the Drawing Editor to redefine the block by reading the new one from the disk, use the command

INSERT *BLOCKNAME = BLOCKNAME*

where *BLOCKNAME* is the name of the block definition you want to update.

Input Problem #3: When AutoCAD tries to load the menu file I have been using, the program reports Incompatible Menu File.

POSSIBLE CAUSE: The proper .MNX file was erased, and you copied an out-of-date .MNX file to the hard disk.

SOLUTION: Erase the .MNX file, and have AutoCAD recompile the .MNU file when you load a new drawing.

Input Problem #4: When I pick a menu choice, some of the prompts are out of sequence, or the commands do not work.

POSSIBLE CAUSE: You are using a menu from a previous version of AutoCAD.

SOLUTION: AutoCAD redesigned the prompting sequence order for most commands in Version 2.1. In the unlikely event that you are using a menu from that version, you must reprogram your menu to match the current prompting sequence. A menu from Version 2.5 will work correctly with Release 9 or Release 10, but some commands have been eliminated since then. Look for the REPeat and ENDREPeat commands, in particular, and make the appropriate changes.

Input Problem #5: When I Zoom All, my drawing appears (very small) in one corner of the screen, but I cannot find anything else on the screen.

POSSIBLE CAUSE: When you did a Copy or Move, you picked a Base Displacement Point and then pressed Enter, rather than Ctrl-C, to cancel the command. This sent the objects off into space a distance equal to the value of the point you picked for the Base point. Later, you froze or turned off a layer with that object on it.

SOLUTION: Thaw and turn on all layers, and execute a REGEN command. Then erase the offending entity (which may be impossible to see if you are zoomed *way* out) and execute another ZOOM All.

Input Problem #6: When I am working in the Drawing Editor, I receive a message indicating that I am outside limits.

POSSIBLE CAUSE: The last entity you created extended outside your defined drawing limits.

SOLUTION: Turn the limits off, using the LIMITS command.

Input Problem #7: I cannot find the proper divisions using the DIVIDE command.

POSSIBLE CAUSE: Your POINT type setting is not visible at the drawing scale you are using.

SOLUTION: Using PDMODE and PDSIZE, reset the POINT type.

Input Problem #8: The circles on my screen seem to be many-sided polygons. Sometimes, my picks do not find them.

POSSIBLE CAUSE: The VIEWRES setting is too low.

SOLUTION: Change VIEWRES to 500. You might experiment with this value. A higher number will slow down redraw and regeneration times.

Input Problem #9: My polylines are hollow.

POSSIBLE CAUSE: FILLMODE is set to OFF.

SOLUTION: Turn on FILLMODE.

Input Problem #10: My drawing contains unnamed user blocks, and I cannot purge them from the drawing.

POSSIBLE CAUSE: Not only Hatch patterns but also Dimension blocks that are created when DimAso is turned on are unnamed user blocks that cannot be purged.

SOLUTION: There is no solution to this problem unless you erase or explode the Hatch pattern or Dimension block.

Input Problem #11: I cannot purge a block from a drawing even though I am not using the block.

POSSIBLE CAUSE: The block is nested within another block you are using.

SOLUTION: By extension, you are using the block in question. If you believe that this block does not enhance the value of the drawing, explode the block that contains the block you don't want, erase the unwanted block, and redefine the first block.

Input Problem #12: AutoCAD does not change some items I select with the STRETCH command.

POSSIBLE CAUSE: The items to be stretched must be within the LAST window with which you select them. If they are part of a block, they will not move unless the block's insertion point is within the stretch window.

SOLUTION: Make sure that you use the proper stretch window, or use more than one STRETCH command.

Input Problem #13: When I change an object to a different layer, its linetype and/or color don't change.

POSSIBLE CAUSE: The objects are not colored or linetyped "BYLAYER."

SOLUTION: Use the CHGPROP command to make the object's property definition "bylayer."

Input Problem #14: I cannot get any objects on my screen with the DVIEW command.

POSSIBLE CAUSE: The target and camera positions are not located properly to display drawing objects.

SOLUTION: Use the DVIEW command's POints option.

Input Problem #15: When I use a particular AutoLISP routine, AutoCAD locks up and displays a 1>.

POSSIBLE CAUSE: The LISP routine is missing either a right parenthesis or a quotation mark (").

SOLUTION: Enter a quotation mark and then a right parenthesis from the keyboard. Then press Enter.

Input Problem #16: Some of the AutoLISP routines I use abort, saying that they cannot find a specific layer.

POSSIBLE CAUSE: You have renamed or purged from your drawing a layer that the LISP routine expects to find.

SOLUTION: Review the LISP routine's requirements, or insert a new copy of your prototype drawing by using **INSERT xxx=xxx**, where *xxx* is the name of your prototype drawing.

Input Problem #17: When loading the AutoLISP file ACAD.LSP, AutoCAD reports an unrecognized character and displays the message Unable to enter AutoLISP.

POSSIBLE CAUSE: The file has been edited by a word processor in document mode rather than nondocument or programming mode. *High ASCII* characters have been left in the file; although you cannot see these characters, AutoLISP can.

SOLUTION: Recopy the original ACAD.LSP file to the proper directory on your hard disk.

Input Problem #18: When I use the IGESIN command, I get a drawing that does not resemble the original in any way.

POSSIBLE CAUSE: The IGES file was written by another CAD system that does not know how to implement the IGES standard correctly.

SOLUTION: Although there is an IGES standard, not many CAD systems implement it correctly. You will have to perform some manual clean-up after you import a drawing from such a system. Look for blocks that are not defined correctly, layers that are not named correctly, incorrect linetypes, circles and arcs that actually are many short line segments, text that is the wrong style or size, etc.

Input Problem #19: When I build a block with attributes for later extraction, the ATTEXT commands put the information into a file in an incorrect order.

POSSIBLE CAUSE: The ATTEXT command is using a template file that is not designed correctly.

SOLUTION: Check the template file you have designed for this particular use. You may have specified extraction of an attribute that does not exist in a given block, thereby causing a skipped field.

System Errors

Many users expect Autodesk to solve problems with their operating system. This is appropriate to an extent, because Autodesk knows what AutoCAD needs from the operating system. Autodesk cannot always accommodate operating system problems, however; these problems must be solved through a joint effort between the operating system's creators, your dealer, and Autodesk. These problems generally are similar to those that arise from system configuration conflicts, except that their cause may require the manufacturer of your computer to do some redesigning and rewriting of the operating system. As you can imagine, the manufacturer may not choose to follow through on this solution. Your only recourse may be to swap your system for a different computer.

System Problem #1: My computer locks up when I try to use AutoCAD.

POSSIBLE CAUSE: This is a tough one because there are literally hundreds of possible causes.

SOLUTION: Because there are so many possible reasons for this error, the best solution is to contact someone who is extremely knowledgeable about AutoCAD and your type of computer system. That person will need to perform some tests on your computer, but probably will come up with a solution fairly quickly. Perhaps your AutoCAD dealer can help you or give you the name of someone who can.

System Problem #2: When I start my computer (or AutoCAD), I see a message that says I am out of environment space.

POSSIBLE CAUSE: The normal memory area used by your operating system for environmental variables is too small.

SOLUTION: Increase the environment space by using the appropriate command in your CONFIG.SYS file.

With DOS V3.2 or later, use:

SHELL=c:\command.com /p /e:512

With DOS V3.0 or V3.1, use:

SHELL=c:\command.com /p /e:32

Both of these statements expand the area for storing environment variables to 512 bytes. For more information, refer to your *Installation and Performance Guide* and your DOS manual.

Software Bugs

If you suspect that you have encountered a software bug, double-check your reasoning. It is easy to fall into the trap of blaming errors on the software, when in fact the error falls into a different category, such as an input error. If, after careful analysis, you determine that you have a real software bug, you should do the following:

1. Make a detailed, written list of your system hardware, software, any TSR programs you may have installed, memory configuration, etc. Include anything that affects your computer environment.

2. Write down every step you took that led up to the error. These should be steps that other users can take to make the error occur on their system.

3. Contact the software authors (either Autodesk or a third-party software vendor) to let them know of the bug. They will want all the information you have detailed in Steps 1 and 2.

4. Sit back and wait. Fixing software errors takes time. You should, however, expect the software authors to give you an estimate of when they will have a fix; then you should expect them to perform accordingly.

Error Messages

AutoCAD issues a variety of error messages from a continually evolving list of messages. Some of those messages and their possible causes are listed in this section. Many of the messages can be triggered by a number of situations, including file corruption.

INTERNAL ERROR: FREE

`Internal error: FREE` indicates that AutoCAD is trying to free a temporary work buffer but cannot do so. This message can be caused by a software bug or by faulty memory (parity error).

SMIO 1 or *GETSM*

This message can indicate an Input/Output (I/O) error when reading one of the drawing's layer, linetype, text style, view, or other tables. It could indicate corruption of the drawing file or of a temporary file maintained in I/O page space or on the hard disk by AutoCAD.

FMTOUT 2

This error is typical of hardware in which the coprocessor switches are not set correctly. Check the switches on the motherboard, and make sure that the coprocessor is seated correctly.

FMTOUT 1

FMTOUT 1, a new error message in Release 10, is issued by some initialization code that is trying to compute various constants based on the computer's mathematical precision. The message usually indicates a problem with the math coprocessor.

HMATH

This message indicates that the database contains an inappropriate number, which AutoCAD does not know how to use. Negative radii, coordinates such as 1e+98, can cause this to occur. You may be able to find the problem by editing a DXF file and looking for the offending digits.

MWRITE

An MWRITE failed m,n error indicates that AutoCAD was trying to write the header portion of the drawing file to disk (as for SAVE, END, or WBLOCK), but that the operation failed for some reason. The numbers indicate the expected file position following the write (the drawing file header's length) and the actual file position.

SCANDR

This error message indicates a corrupted file that was improperly written to disk. As was mentioned earlier, you may be able to save the drawing with a third-party software package.

DISK FULL

The DISK FULL error message indicates that your hard disk is full or that AutoCAD cannot handle the number of available files in the File Allocation Table (an AutoCAD Release 10 bug for large hard disks of 100M or more). Although you may have thought that you had plenty of space when you started the drawing, you must realize that AutoCAD also opens many temporary files. If you do not get any error message, but the Drawing Editor is locked up, the disk was filled when a temporary file was opened.

EREAD

EREAD errors occur when AutoCAD tries to read the drawing file and encounters some type of file or data error when reading entities from the file. In other words, the file was stored with unreadable data or data that AutoCAD does not know how to interpret. The data may be garbled because of extended memory handling problems, hard disk error, power surge, damaged floppy disk, or some other factor (an act of God, for example).

TCODE

This indicates a bad header record written in the drawing file. You may be able to insert the drawing into another drawing and create a DXF file that can be edited with a text editor to correct the problem.

LTINIT

The linetype table section of the drawing database has improper definitions.

RFSubs

This message indicates faulty handling of on-screen image refreshing. It indicates a hardware problem in the storage of the temporary file containing the virtual screen image. Faulty memory boards or bad hard disk controllers can cause this message to appear.

EREGEN

This message shows that errors were encountered while obtaining an entity definition for display purposes from the temporary drawing files. EREGEN is similar to RFSubs.

SHELL: "Insufficient memory to continue"

This message appears if AutoCAD detects a conflicting interrupt in RAM while paging to disk during execution of the SHELL command. This can indicate a problem with a terminate-and-stay-resident program.

SHELL: "Error swapping temp file"

This message indicates that a hardware error was encountered while you paged out to extended or expanded memory—or to the hard disk during execution of the SHELL command.

Summary

Many errors can occur while you use AutoCAD. This chapter has introduced you to some of them and to their possible causes and solutions.

Remember that when a problem occurs you should use the information in this chapter as a basis for making your own determination of the problem. Stop what you are doing and think back through the steps you have taken recently. In this way, you can determine not only the precise cause of the problem but also a solution.

As your AutoCAD skills grow, your problems will become more complex. The more experienced you are, the harder you will push AutoCAD; problems increase when the limits of a system are pushed.

Where To Get Help

In this section, you will learn how to get additional help when you are working with AutoCAD. The AutoCAD HELP facility (discussed in Chapter 1, "A Quick Start in AutoCAD") can get you through minor problems when you are using the program. As any computer user knows, however, more problems can arise than are covered by any one manual. With that in mind, this guide should help you find additional support when the *AutoCAD Reference Manual* cannot answer your questions.

You have already taken the first step in your search for better AutoCAD support. You are using this book to gain a degree of proficiency that you cannot get with just the "Getting Started" training manual. Many fine training and tutorial manuals are available for AutoCAD. We also recommend *Advanced AutoCAD Techniques*, published by Que Corporation.

If a tutorial manual cannot answer your questions, you can try to solve your problem by trying one or more of the following options:

❏ Contact your local AutoCAD dealer or training center.

❏ Join the local AutoCAD Users' Group.

❏ Join the Autodesk forum on CompuServe, or contact one of the many AutoCAD bulletin boards.

If you turn for help to any of these three resources, you will be able to contact experienced AutoCAD users. Their knowledge can be invaluable in either helping you solve your problem or directing you to someone who can answer your questions.

AutoCAD Dealers and Training Centers

Like many CAD programs on the market today, AutoCAD is only as good as the people who support it. Autodesk has a worldwide network of salespeople and training centers that can help you get the most from the program.

When you have trouble solving a problem or answering a question about AutoCAD, talk first to the dealer who sold you the program. Autodesk has always striven to maintain a well-informed sales staff that is not only knowledgeable about the program itself but also is willing to steer you toward third-party packages that can make your AutoCAD work easier.

If you need training, Autodesk maintains authorized training centers across the United States. These centers provide classes that show you how to work from the beginner's level (simple drawing and editing commands) to more advanced levels (manipulating attributes, modeling in three dimensions, and even creating hatch patterns and linetypes). Training centers are useful if you want to learn to work with AutoCAD in a short time.

AutoCAD Users' Groups

AutoCAD Users' Groups are probably the most enjoyable way to get answers to your AutoCAD problems. Members typically share the same interests and are willing to meet other people and discuss problems, find solutions, and even trade tips.

Most users' group meetings are informal; they frequently are held at local universities or companies. A group's membership can range from 10 to more than 100 people. At a meeting, you can find expert users, as well as those who casually dabble in AutoCAD. All of them are there, however, to share their common experiences.

The following list of North American AutoCAD Users' Groups is current. This list includes the names of local AutoCAD Users' Groups and the names and telephone numbers of people to contact if you are interested in joining. This list includes only groups, names, and numbers that could be verified.

Alabama

Bobby Benson
Birmingham AutoCAD Users' Group
P.O. Box 43462
Birmingham, AL 35243
(205) 995-0190

Arizona

Brian Goelz
AutoCAD Users' Group
CAD Institute
4100 East Broadway Road, Suite 150
Phoenix, AZ 85040
(602) 437-0405

California

Lee Walker
Orange County AutoCAD Users' Group
15342 Gemini Lane
Eltoro, CA 92630
(714) 455-1179

Genevieve Katz
East Bay AutoCAD Users' Group
1970 Broadway, Suite 320
Oakland, CA 94612
(415) 832-2153

Volker Ackermann
Marin County AutoCAD Users' Group
8 West Street
San Rafael, CA 94901
(415) 331-9466

Chuck Handel
AutoCAD Users' Group of Santa Cruz
105 Cooper Street, Suite 206
Santa Cruz, CA 95060
(408) 425-3630

John Weitzel
Sonoma County AutoCAD Users' Group
5003 Rick Drive
Santa Rosa, CA 95403
(415) 777-9144

Christopher DeLucchi
San Diego AutoCAD Users' Group
122 Nardo Avenue
Solana Beach, CA 92075
(619) 755-0854

Colorado

Bernd Hoffmann
N. Colorado AutoCAD Users' Group
636 Powder Horn
Ft. Collins, CO 80526
(303) 229-0314 (h)

Connecticut

Jorge Guillen
Greater Hartford AutoCAD Users' Group
SL/AM Architects
100 Allyn Street, 4th Floor
Hartford, CT 06103
(203) 525-8651

Dan Cummings
Micro Tech Training Center
(203) 234-9490

Delaware

Mel Sloan
Brandwine Area AutoCAD Users' Group
W.L. Gore and Associates Inc.
750 Otts Chapel Road
Newark, DE 19714
(302) 368 2575

Florida

Craig Lojewski
Broward County AutoCAD Users' Group
RH Miller and Associates
4800 SW 64th Avenue, Suite 103
Davie, FL 33314
(305) 791-2900

Tom Kaley
Tampa Bay AutoCAD Users' Group
P.O. Box 12248, Mail Station 15
St. Petersburg, FL 33733
(813) 381-2000

Georgia

James Orrison
Southern Electric Users' Group
Southern Company Services
64A Perimeter Center East BIN 203
Atlanta, GA 30346
(404) 668-2756

William Bland
Macon AutoCAD Users' Group
Architects
348 Cotton Avenue
Macon, GA 31201
(912) 745-4945

Ronald Kolman
Savannah AutoCAD Users' Group
Ronald Kolman Architects
P.O. Box 23192
Savannah, GA 31403
(912) 233-9003

Idaho

Mark Forbord
SE Idaho Area Users' Group
Walker Engineering
1035 Yellowstone Avenue
Pocatello, ID 83201
(208) 233-9800

Illinois

Dean Williamson
A.E. Staley
Central Illinois AutoCAD Users' Group
2200 East Eldorado Street
Decatur, IL 62521
(217) 421-2100

Greg Gooch
John Deere Co.
1600 First Avenue East
Milan, IL 61264
(309) 756-1445

Indiana

Mark Kitt
Dedicated Registered ACAD Professionals
701 E. South Street
Albion, IN 46701
(219) 693-2167

Rick Oprisu
Indy AutoCAD Users' Group
CAD/CAM Plus, Inc.
122 West Carmel Drive
Carmel, IN 46032
(317) 575-9606

Kansas

Brad Swanson
KC-CAD 417 Rawhide, Suite H
Olathe, KS 66061
(913) 764-2203

Kentucky

Dennis Marshall
Bluegrass AutoCAD Users' Group
Lexington Community College
Cooper Drive, Room 103
Lexington, KY 40506
(606) 257-3650

Greg Heitzman
Kentuckiana AutoCAD Users' Group
Louisville Water Company
435 South Third Street
Louisville, KY
(502) 569-3600, Ext. 248

Louisiana

Renso Spanoff
Baton Rouge AutoCAD Users' Group
MicroCAD
7290 Exchange Place
Baton Rouge, LA 70806
(504) 387-0303

Maine

Dan Moreno
AutoCAD Users' Group
2 Great Falls Plaza
Auburn, ME 04210
(207) 784-2941

Dick Staples
AutoCAD Users' Group of Maine
East Maine Vo Tech
354 Hogan Road
Bangor, ME 04401
(207) 941-4619

Martha Kleinschmidt
South Maine AutoCAD Users' Groups
Wright-Pierce Engineers
99 Main Street
Popsham, ME 04086
(207) 725-8721

Maryland

David Drazin
CAD/CAM Special Interest Group
Capital PC Users' Group, Inc.
15 Orchard Way, North
Rockville, MD 20854
(301) 279-7593

Mark Glick
Gibraltar Construction
Baltimore Area AutoCAD Users' Group
836 Ritchie Highway
Severna Park, MD 21146
(301) 647-8686

Massachusetts

Al Folan
Greater Boston AutoCAD Users' Group
Stone & Webster Engineering
245 Summer Street (4th Floor)
Boston, MA 02107
(617) 589-1535

Michigan

Frank Conner
West Michigan AutoCAD Users' Group
Grand Rapids Junior College
1234 Ball Avenue N.E.
Grand Rapids, MI 49505
(616) 456-4274

Dave Johnson
Iron Mountain AutoCAD Users' Group
M.J. Electric
200 West Frank Pipp Drive
Iron Mountain, MI 49801
(906) 774-8000

Kenneth Hornfeld
Main.Mnu
DiClemente Siegel Engineering, Inc.
22255 Greenfield, Suite 500
Southfield, MI 48075
(313) 275-5226

Minnesota

Wayne Hobbs
Lakes Area AutoCAD Users' Group
HCR121 G
Merrifield, MN 56465
(218) 829-9891

Hani Ayad
AutoCAD.EXE Users' Group
Ellerbee Becket Architects
One Appletree Square
Minneapolis, MN 55425
(612) 853-2104

Missouri

Randy Turner
Pfizer, Inc.
1107 South 291 Highway
Lee Summit, MO 64081
(816) 524-5580

Keith Wallace or Chris Talbert
Prestress Casting Company
P.O. Box 3499
Springfield, MO 65808
(417) 869-7350

Nebraska

Leendert Kersten
AutoCAD Users' of Nebraska
3721 Chapin Circle
Lincoln, NE 68506
(402) 472-2384

New Jersey

Richard Finch
South New Jersey AutoCAD Users' Group
49 Park Street
Bordentown, NJ 08505
(609) 298-7449

Robert Weissner
Computer Users' Group
Architects League of Northern NJ
120 North Route 17
Paramus, NJ 07652
(201) 599-0030

Mark Meara
Princeton Area AutoCAD Users' Group
CUH2A
600 Alexander Road
Princeton, NJ 08543
(609) 452-1212

New York

Rochelle Borgen
Albany AutoCAD Users' Group
40 Colvin Avenue
Albany, NY 12206
(518) 438-6844

Michael Geyer
New York AutoCAD Users' Group
20 West 20th Street
New York, NY 10011
(212) 691-4722

Bob Schellinger
Rochester Area AutoCAD Users' Group
Olin Corporation
P.O. Box 205
Rochester, NY 14601
(716) 436-3030

North Carolina

Steve Frick
Piedmont AutoCAD Users' Group
Draper Corporation
P.O. Box 16341
Greensboro, NC 27416
(919) 852-4200, Ext. 356

David Jerolle
Triangle AutoCAD Group
7416 Chapel Hill Road
Raleigh, NC 27602
(919) 851-3455

North Dakota

David Bauman
Mid-Con AutoCAD Users' Group
616 Main Avenue
Box 44
Fargo, ND 58103
(701) 232-3271

Ohio

Janak Dave
Cincinnati AutoCAD Users' Group
OMI College of Applied Science
2220 Victory Parkway
Cincinnati, OH 45206
(513) 556-6573

Wes Eichelman
Dayton Area AutoCAD Users' Group-DaCad-
6001 B. North Dixie Drive
Dayton, OH 45414
(513) 228-4007

Thomas Altman
Cleveland Computer Aided Design Society
1501 Spring Garden Avenue
Lakewood, OH 44107
(216) 521 2574

Ted Gentsch
Akron Area AutoCAD Users' Group
Linden Industries
4020 Bellaire Lane
Peninsula, OH 44264
(216) 928-4064

Ron Harp
NW Ohio AutoCAD Users' Group
P.O. Box 23332
Toledo, OH 43623
(419) 242-7405

Oklahoma

Dr. Ginger Benedict
AutoCAD Users' Group
East Central University
Ada, OK 74820
(405) 332-8000

Chuck Earnhart
AutoCAD ACE Users' Group
AAE, Incorporated
P.O. Box 32797
Oklahoma City, OK 73123
(405) 949-1442

Pennsylvania

Jeff Chambers
Presque Isle AutoCAD Users' Group
Van-Air Systems
2950 Mechanic Street
Lake City, PA 16423
(814) 774-2631

Kenn Anderson
KEYstone ACADemy AutoCAD Users' Group
Keystone Junior College
Box 149
LaPlume, PA 18440
(717) 945-3232

Howard Fulmer
Phila AutoCAD Users' Group
HMF Consulting
161 Jefferson Court
Norristown, PA 19401
(215) 275-9866

Al Scheib
Southeast Pennsylvania AutoCAD Users' Group
(717) 872-8167

South Carolina

John Watts
Piedmont AutoCAD Users' Group
Spartanburg Technical College
P.O. Drawer 4386
Spartanburg, SC 29305
(803) 591-3674

South Dakota

Jeff Manley
Black Hills Power and Light
P.O. Box 1400
Rapid City, SD 57709
(605) 342-3200

Gene Murphy
Sioux Falls Area AutoCAD Users' Group
Architecture Automated
600 West Avenue North
Sioux Falls, SD 57104
(605) 336-3722

Tennessee

Barbara Gatlin
Dyersburg Area AutoCAD Users' Group
Dyersburg State Community College
P.O. Box 648
Dyersburg, TN 38025
(901) 285-6910, Ext. 209

Don Boston
Jackson Area AutoCAD Users' Group
Porter Cable Corporation
Youngs Crossing at Highway 45
Jackson, TN 38305
(901) 668-8600

Joe Cook
Nashville Area AutoCAD Users' Group
120 White Bridge Road
P.O. Box 90285
Nashville, TN 37209
(615) 353-3462

Mike Nichols
NW Tennessee AutoCAD Users' Group
166 Brook Street
Paris, TN 38242
(901) 642-4251

Texas

Clyde Brothers
Brazos Valley AutoCAD Users' Group
Route 3 Box 297
College Station, TX 77840
(409) 776-8820

Dan Luce
PRO-CAD Users' Group
Houston Community College
12601 High Star
Houston, TX 77072
(713) 463-0196 (h)
(713) 933-8050 (w)

Mike Salars
Pasadena-Clear Water AutoCAD Users' Group
Dixie Chemical
10701 Bay Area Boulevard
Pasadena, TX 77507
(713) 474-3271

Virginia

Tom Tulloch
Northern Virginia AutoCAD Users' Group
Helbing Lipp, Ltd.
7929 Westpark Drive
McLean, VA 22102
(703) 556-0700

Dale Campbell
Norfolk Area AutoCAD Users' Group
Joe D. Glenn & Associates
P.O. Box 12154
5 Kroger Executive Center
Norfolk, VA 23502
(804) 461-9130

Michael Farmer
Central Virginia AutoCAD Users' Group
12343 Sir James Court
Richmond, VA 23233
(804) 360-4764 (h)
(804) 756-7743 (w)

Washington

Dick Vogel
Bellingham Users' Group (BUG)
Western Washington University, Technology
Bellingham, WA 98225
(206) 676-3380

Dan Flanagan
Seattle Area AutoCAD Users' Group
4301 230th Place S.W.
Mountlake Terrace, WA 98043
(206) 771-5334

Jeff Waymack
Architects/Engineers/Planners Users' Group
2102 North 52nd St.
Seattle, WA 98103
(206) 634-0849

West Virginia

Max Dent
Greater Tri-State AutoCAD Users' Group
P.O. Box 53
Scott Depot, WV 25560
(304) 757-9217

Wisconsin

Ron Zenke
Fox Valley Area AutoCAD Users' Group
Fox Valley Tech Institute
1825 North Bluemound Drive
Appleton, WI 54913
(414) 735-2519

David Regge
Apache Stainless Equipment
3103 Baskerville Avenue
Middleton, WI 53562
(414) 887-3721

Gene Roseburg
NorthStar AutoCAD Users' Group
WITI
600 North 21st Street
Superior, WI 54880
(715) 394-6677

CompuServe's Autodesk Forum and AutoCAD Bulletin Boards

If you have a modem (a device that lets your computer communicate with other computers over a telephone line), you can contact other AutoCAD users across the country and find answers to your questions.

The forums on CompuServe are the largest clearinghouses of information on computing and society today. These forums are meeting halls; you can walk into any meeting hall and speak to other people who are there to discuss their use of programs or computing services.

CompuServe's Autodesk Forum is composed of message forums and data libraries. The message forums currently are divided into 12 sections, each of which deals with a different aspect of AutoCAD or the Autodesk product line. There are sections on AutoCAD, AutoLISP, AutoShade, AutoFlix, general Autodesk news, utilities, and third-party products, to name just a few.

When you need to find an answer through one of the forum sections, leave a message in that particular area. Your message should include your question, state whether you are addressing the question to a particular person, and include a heading that may interest others reading the section messages and cause them to reply to you. The Autodesk Forum can bring you information from many people, including those who directly support the products at Autodesk, as well as "power users," who may choose to answer your question. One of the nicest things about the CompuServe forums is that you normally can expect a reply to your message in 24 to 48 hours.

The forum data libraries are arranged much like the message sections. Typically, a data library is associated with each message section. The data libraries contain hundreds of utilities, AutoLISP routines, hatch patterns, and other information that can be helpful to any AutoCAD user. Any of the programs in the data libraries can be downloaded to your computer and used as you need them.

Although AutoCAD bulletin boards may not have the storage capacity or the traffic of CompuServe, they are similar to the Autodesk Forum. These computers are located around the country and are maintained by individuals whose interest is to see AutoCAD proliferate through the free exchange of information.

The list in Table R.1 was taken from a CompuServe file that usually is updated quarterly. The list includes the names and telephone numbers of many bulletin boards. Most bulletin boards are set up to communicate at a minimum of 1,200 baud, no parity, 8 data bits, and 1 stop bit (sometimes known as 1200,N,8,1). The use of these parameters will guarantee you the best transmission of data between your systems.

Table R.1. *AutoCAD Bulletin Boards.*

Name	Telephone Number
The University BBS	1-201-544-8193
Alacrity BBS	1-206-643-5477
Synthesis BBS	1-206-671-6576
AEPUG BBS	1-206-682-4465
CAD Plot Shop	1-206-839-4970
The Maine PC Connection	1-207-854-3928

New York AutoCAD BBS	1-212-980-0770
Computer Corner	1-215-641-9273
BOLDER Designs	1-215-988-9761
Akron A.U.G	1-216-673-1088
PainFrame	1-301-488-7461
Arcadia Systems	1-305-445-3123
XEROX Service Centre	1-306-934-2919
Greater Chicago A.U.G.	1-312-395-0920
Backstreet BBS	1-315-593-1589
Central NY AutoCAD BBS	1-315-593-3561
Applied Software Tech	1-404-633-2197
The Drafting Board	1-407-862-2124
Comp-U-Ease	1-408-286-8332
Exec-PC	1-414-964-5160
Off Broadway Business	1-415-547-5264
ThelemaNET	1-415-548-0163
DATADRAFT AutoCAD	1-503-232-5641
Koh-i-noor BBS	1-503-747-2593
IBM Tech Fido	1-508-433-8452
Salem Adventure BBS	1-508-745-4892
CADENCE	1-512-258-9532
T.A.C.O. BBS	1-512-349-4086
ZAP TPBoard	1-514-324-9031
PC COMM DZ	1-514-989-9450
FOGLINE Something	1-515-964-7937
Leased Squares	1-603-332-9969
DataNET	1-604-276-8088
TRIUMF BBS	1-604-590-6405
Central Kentucky C.S.	1-606-293-0154
Nick's Nest	1-612-490-1187
LandLine	1-616-942-4044
Digital Control Systems	1-617-344-8140
IntelliCADD	1-619-460-1568
LightSpeed BBS	1-619-697-9840
Techmail	1-703-430-2535
The Other Woman	1-707-938-3508
Kingdom Productions	1-713-630-0553
Mark's BBS	1-816-941-7549
NightLine-1	1-916-362-0715
Galaxy Computer	1-918-835-8933
TAG Board	1-919-544-7533

Summary

There are many ways to get help when you use AutoCAD. This chapter has discussed three of those methods:

❑ Contact your local AutoCAD dealer/training center.

❑ Join your local AutoCAD User Group.

❑ Join the Autodesk Forum on CompuServe, or contact one of the many AutoCAD bulletin boards.

Add to this the many fine tutorial manuals (one of which you now have in your hands), and you begin to see why AutoCAD has become so popular. Not only is it a good drafting package, but the support from other users and the third-party vendors virtually guarantees that no matter what your question may be, finding an answer will be fairly easy.

Quick Reference to AutoCAD's System Variables

This section contains a complete list of all AutoCAD system variables. AutoCAD maintains these variables in order to facilitate execution of the program. Typically, variables are set in one of three ways:

- ❏ Through use of the SETVAR command
- ❏ Through use of an AutoCAD or subsystem command
- ❏ Through use of AutoLISP

Conversely, you can read the current values of the system variables by using the same methods.

Not all variables can be accessed in each of these methods. Some variables can be set only with AutoCAD commands, but not directly with SETVAR. This accessibility varies depending upon the variable.

Why would you want to change system variables? There is no good, identifiable reason if you are a novice with AutoCAD. As you become more adept at using AutoCAD and you begin to "branch out," stretching the limits of built-in AutoCAD functions, you will find a greater need to work with system variables.

The table that makes up the bulk of this section lists every AutoCAD variable. Please note that the information in the table is correct as of Release 10. If you are using an earlier version of AutoCAD, some variables may not be available, or they may not store information as indicated here. (For example, the variable may be 2D under an earlier AutoCAD version, but 3D under Release 10.)

This variable table lists the following information about each variable:

- ❏ The variable's name
- ❏ The variable's type
- ❏ Where the variable is saved
- ❏ The default value for the variable
- ❏ A short description of what the variable is for

The variable's name is the name you use when accessing the variable through the SETVAR command or through AutoLISP.

The variable's type has one of the following designations:

- ❏ I   Integer
- ❏ R   Real
- ❏ S   Text String
- ❏ 2 D Two-Dimensional Point
- ❏ 3 D Three-Dimensional Point
- ❏ T   Toggles On or Off

Many of these variables are saved across editing sessions. Some are saved in the drawing and a few are saved in the ACAD.CFG configuration file; these variables are marked with a *D* or *C*, respectively, in the list. Other variables may not be saved or may be hard coded into AutoCAD. No saving is indicated for these variables.

The default value field is the most fluid field in this table. It is difficult to say what the default value of a system variable may be, because the "out-of-the-box, plain vanilla" value of a variable can be modified by configuration options or default drawing values. These may have been set up by someone else (by the person who installed AutoCAD, for example). Take this column with a grain of salt; the values listed here refer to the default values as set with an out-of-the box copy of AutoCAD Release 10.

Many of the system variables are alluded to elsewhere in this book, either in the tutorial portion (earlier chapters) or in the Command Reference section. The descriptions in this section are quite terse. Only a quick statement about the purpose of the variable is given here, although additional helpful information may be provided. For instance, if the variable is read-only, this information is noted. Variables that are not read-only can be changed with AutoCAD's SETVAR command.

Variable	Type	Saved in	Default	Meaning
ACADPREFIX	S		(Nothing)	If you specified a directory other than the AutoCAD directory for your drawing, that information is stored here. (Read-only)
ACADVER	S		Your version	The current release of AutoCAD. (If you are using Release 10, the default should be *10*.) (Read-only)
AFLAGS	I		0	Contains information that determines whether attributes are 1 = invisible, 2 = constant, 3 = verify, 4 = preset. This information is set when ATTDEF command is first executed.
ANGBASE	R	D	0	Defaults to 3 o'clock. Contains the direction for angle 0. This is used to calculate all angles in AutoCAD.
ANGDIR	I	D	1	Defines whether angles entered in AutoCAD will default to clockwise (0) or counterclockwise (1).
APERTURE	I	C	10	Defines OSNAP target (aperture) height. Set with APERTURE command.
AREA	R		0	Holds value of the true area from the most recent of any of these commands: AREA, LIST, or DBLIST. (Read-only)
ATTDIA	I	D	0	Controls whether INSERT command displays a dialogue box for any attributes defined with a given block. A value of 1 displays dialogue box; 0 does not.
ATTMODE	I	D	1	Holds value of ATTDISP command. 0 = off, 1 = normal, 2 = on.

Variable	Type	Saved in	Default	Meaning
ATTREQ	I	D	1	Controls whether all attributes are set to their defaults (a value of 0) or whether you are prompted for attributes (a value of 1).
AUNITS	I	D	0	Holds angular units for UNITS command: 0 = decimal degrees, 1 = degrees/minutes/seconds, 2 = grads, 3 = radians, 4 = surveyors units.
AUPREC	I	D	0	The precision of the angular units
AXISMODE	I	D	0	Controls axis display (AXIS command). 0 = off, 1 = on.
AXISUNIT	2D	D	0,0	Holds spacing of tick marks for AXIS command. Changes to this variable are not reflected in the displayed axis until a redraw operation is performed. AutoCAD does not perform an automatic redraw when this variable is changed, because you may be changing several variables in quick succession.
BACKZ	R	D	0	The offset for back clipping plane, set with DVIEW command. The units are drawing units. The distance from target to clipping plane can be found by using the following formula: camera-to-target distance – BACKZ. (Read-only)
BLIPMODE	T	D	1 (ON)	Holds value that controls whether blips appear on-screen. Set with BLIPMODE command.
CDATE	R		Varies	Holds current date and time for drawing. (Read-only)
CECOLOR	S	D	BYLAYER	Holds color with which you currently are drawing. (Read-only)

Variable				Description
CELTYPE	S	D	BYLAYER	Holds linetype with which you currently are drawing. (Read-only)
CHAMFERA	R	D	0	Holds first chamfer distance.
CHAMFERB	R	D	0	Holds second chamfer distance.
CLAYER	S	D	0	Holds name of current layer. (Read-only)
CMDECHO	I		1	Controls whether commands are echoed to (appear on) the screen as you use them. Used for programming purposes.
COORDS	I	D	0	Controls coordinate display at top of screen. If 0, updated only when you pick a point; if 1, updated as crosshairs travel around screen; if 2, functions as though set to 1, except relative polar coordinates are displayed after first point requested by an AutoCAD command has been picked.
CVPORT	I	D	4	Holds identification for current viewport.
DATE	R		Varies	Holds current Julian calendar date and time for drawing. (Read-only)
DIMALT	T	D	Off (0)	Controls generation of alternate dimensions.
DIMALTD	I	D	2	Controls decimal places for alternate dimension value.
DIMALTF	R	D	25.4	AutoCAD multiplies this value (the alternate units scale factor) with value determined by current dimension. If DIMALT is on, alternate value will appear along with normal value.
DIMAPOST	S	D	(Nothing)	Holds the suffix for alternate dimensions. (Read-only at the Command: prompt; can be set only at the Dim: prompt)

Variable	Type	Saved in	Default	Meaning
DIMASO	T	D	On (1)	Controls generation of associative dimensions. If on, dimensions are associative; if off, dimensions are normal.
DIMASZ	R	D	0.18	Controls arrow size. AutoCAD uses this size, the size of the text, and a default minimum length for the dimension line to determine whether dimension text will be inside or outside the dimension.
DIMBLK	S	D	(Nothing)	If you need an indicator instead of the arrows or tick marks, you can create a block and indicate its name here. (Read-only at the Command: prompt; can be set only at the Dim: prompt)
DIMBLK1	S	D	(Nothing)	If you want one arrow on the dimension line to be different from the other arrow, DIMBLK1 is placed on the end of the dimension line that extends to the first extension line. (Read-only at the Command: prompt; can be set only at the Dim: prompt)
DIMBLK2	S	D	(Nothing)	If you want one arrow on the dimension line to be different from the other arrow, DIMBLK2 is placed on the end of the dimension line that extends to the second extension line. (Read-only at the Command: prompt; can be set only at the Dim: prompt)
DIMCEN	R	D	0.09	Changes size of center mark AutoCAD inserts with CENTER command. The size is the distance from center mark along one of the line segments.

Variable			Default	Description
DIMDLE	R	D	0	If you are using tick marks, this variable can be used to extend the dimension line past the extension lines.
DIMDLI	R	D	0.38	Controls increment size AutoCAD uses to offset dimensions when using BAS and CON.
DIMEXE	R	D	0.18	Controls extension above dimension line of extension lines. If you do not want an extension, set this variable to 0.
DIMEXO	R	D	0.0625	Controls extension line offset from origin. If you do not want an offset, set this variable to 0.
DIMLFAC	R	D	1	Sets scale factor for the drawing. The default (1) is to full-scale (one drawing inch equals one object inch). If you are drawing in half-scale, set this variable to 2; AutoCAD will multiply the measured values by this variable. Angular dimensions are not affected. This variable lets you have several different scale details within the same drawing, and dimension them correctly. When drawing to half-scale, draw the object at full size and let the plotting routine set the correct scale. DIMSCALE takes care of dimension scaling. When plotting at half-scale, DIMSCALE should be set at 2. You should change DIMLFAC only if you need to show a small detail at a different scale on the same sheet (for instance, a blow-up done at 1:4 on a sheet that is 1:96).
DIMLIM	T	D	Off (0)	Generates limits, using the values in DIMTM and DIMTP.

Variable	Type	Saved in	Default	Meaning
DIMSOXD	T	D	Off (0)	Suppresses outside-extension dimension lines.
DIMPOST	T	D	(Nothing)	Holds default suffix for dimension text. You can enter a suffix to be attached to dimensions as they are inserted. (Read-only at the Command: prompt; can be set only at the Dim: prompt)
DIMRND	R	D	0	Rounds all dimension values you insert. If you set value to 0.5, all dimensions will be rounded to nearest half unit.
DIMSAH	T	D	Off (0)	Tells AutoCAD to use block names in DIMBLK1 and DIMBLK2 as arrow heads for the dimension.
DIMSCALE	R	D	1	Scales entire dimension by same amount. This variable is useful when you are working with a large drawing or an extremely small drawing.
DIMSE1	T	D	Off (0)	Suppresses first extension line.
DIMSE2	T	D	Off (0)	Suppresses second extension line.
DIMSHO	T	D	Off (0)	When this variable is on, dimension values are updated as dimension changes. If off, dimension text will be updated after the change.
DIMTAD	T	D	Off (0)	Places dimension text above dimension line.
DIMTIH	T	D	On (1)	Draws all text horizontally inside the dimensions (parallel to bottom edge of paper). When this variable is turned off, text is inserted aligned to dimension line and is readable from bottom or right side of the drawing.

Variable			Default	Description
DIMTIX	T	D	Off (0)	Draws dimension text between extension lines, even if dimension line and arrows do not fit.
DIMTM	R	D	0	Sets negative tolerances for dimensions.
DIMTOFL	T	D	Off (0)	Draws dimension line between extension lines, even if dimension text is forced outside.
DIMTOH	T	D	On (1)	Draws all text horizontally outside the dimensions. When this variable is set to off, dimension text is drawn in alignment with dimension line and is readable from bottom or right side of page.
DIMTOL	T	D	Off	Generates tolerances, using tolerance settings defined in DIMTP and DIMTM.
DIMTP	R	D	0	Sets positive tolerances for dimensions.
DIMTSZ	R	D	0	Sets a size for tick marks. If you want arrow heads, type 0 for tick mark size.
DIMTVP	R	D	0	Allows you to place dimension text above or below dimension line. AutoCAD uses the calculation DIMTVP × DIMTXT to place the text. To use this variable, DIMTAD must be off. If value of DIMTVP is positive, text is placed above dimension line; if negative, text is placed below dimension line.
DIMTXT	R	D	0.18	Controls text size for dimensions. Type the text size you want, and press Enter.

Variable	Type	Saved in	Default	Meaning
DIMZIN	I	D	0	Controls AutoCAD's zero-inch editing feature of dimensioning when you are working with architectural units. If 0, zero feet and zero inches not placed in dimension. If 1, both zero feet and zero inches placed in dimension. If 2, only zero feet placed in dimension; if 3, zero inches are placed in dimension.
DISTANCE	R		0	Last value computed by DIST command. (Read-only)
DRAGMODE	I	D	2	Controls the dragging of entities.
DRAGP1	I	C	10	Controls speed at which entities being dragged are redrawn.
DRAGP2	I	C	25	Controls speed at which entities being dragged are redrawn.
DWGNAME	S	D	Varies	Name of current drawing. (Read-only)
DWGPREFIX	S	D	Varies	Holds path for current drawing. (Read-only)
ELEVATION	R	D	0	Holds value for current elevation.
EXPERT	I	D	0	Controls issuance of Are you sure? prompts. 0, the default, issues all prompts normally; 1 suppresses About to regen, proceed? and Really want to turn the current layer off?; 2 suppresses preceding prompts and BLOCK's Block already defined. Redefine it? and SAVE/WBLOCK's A drawing with this name already exists. Overwrite it?; 3 suppresses preceding prompts and those issued by

LINETYPE if you try to load a linetype that is already loaded or create a new linetype in a file that already defines it; 4 suppresses preceding prompts and those issued by UCS Save and VPORTS Save, if the name you supply already exists. When a prompt is suppressed by EXPERT, the operation in question is performed as though you had responded **Y** to the prompt.

Variable	Type		Value	Description
EXTMAX	3D	D	X = $-1.0E+20$ Y = $-1.0E+20$ Z = $-1.0E+20$	Upper right coordinate of area in which you have drawn. (Read-only)
EXTMIN	2D	D	X = $1.0E+20$ Y = $1.0E+20$ Z = $1.0E+20$	Lower left coordinate of area in which you have drawn. (Read-only)
FILLETRAD	R	D	0	Holds radius used by FILLET command.
FILLMODE	I	D	1	Holds value that controls whether polylines and solids are filled with color.
FLATLAND	I	D	0	Allows you to draw in two-dimensions. Default of 0 allows Release 10 capabilities.
FRONTZ	R	D	0	Location of front clipping plane, defined with DVIEW command. (Read-only)
GRIDMODE	I	D	0	Controls whether grid is on or off. Default is off.
GRIDUNIT	2D	D	0,0	Grid spacing for current grid. Changes to this variable are not reflected in the displayed axis until a redraw operation is performed. AutoCAD does not perform an automatic redraw when this variable is changed, because you may be changing several variables in quick succession.

Variable	Type	Saved in	Default	Meaning
HANDLES	I	D	0	Turns handles on or off. (Read-only)
HIGHLIGHT	I		1	Controls whether entities selected for a particular operation are highlighted.
INSBASE	3D	D	X = 0 Y = 0 Z = 0	Insertion base point for entire drawing. Default = 0,0,0 in World Coordinate System.
LASTANGLE	R		0	End angle of last arc entered, relative to X-Y plane of current UCS. (Read-only)
LASTPOINT	3D		X = 0 Y = 0 Z = 0	Last point entered, in UCS coordinates
LASTPT3D	3D		X = 0 Y = 0 Z = 0	Same as LASTPOINT
LENSLENGTH	R	D	50	Length of lens, in millimeters. Used in perspective viewing. Set during DVIEW command. (Read-only)
LIMCHECK	I	D	0	Controls limits-check alarm.
LIMMAX	2D	D	12,9	Upper right drawing limits, in World coordinates
LIMMIN	2D	D	0,0	Lower left drawing limits, in World coordinates
LTSCALE	R	D	1	Global linetype scale factor
LUNITS	I	D	2	Holds value set for units with UNITS command.
LUPREC	I	D	4	Holds decimal places for linear units.

Variable	Type		Default	Description
MENUECHO	I		0	Menu echo/prompt control. Sum of the following: 0, the default, displays all menu items and system prompts; 1 suppresses echo of menu items; 2 suppresses printing of system prompts; 4 disables ^P toggle of menu-item echoing.
MENUNAME	S	D	ACAD	Holds name of menu file currently in use. Set with MENU command. (Read-only)
MIRRTEXT	I	D	1	Controls whether text is mirrored when MIRROR command is used. If 0, text will retain its "direction" and be mirrored but readable.
ORTHOMODE	I	D	0	Toggle for Ortho mode
OSMODE	I	D	0	Holds values for OSNAP modes currently in use.
PDMODE	I	D	0	Holds value of point-entity display.
PDSIZE	R	D	0	Holds value that defines point-entity size.
PERIMETER	R		0	Perimeter computed by one of the following: AREA, LIST, OR DBLIST. (Read-only)
PICKBOX	I	C	3	Object selection target height, in pixels
POPUPS	I		1	Defines whether dialogue boxes, menu bar, pull-down menus, and icon menus are supported. (Read-only)
QTEXTMODE	I	D	0	Holds value for QTEXT command.
REGENMODE	I	D	1	Holds value for REGENAUTO.
SCREENSIZE	2D		Varies	Current viewport size, in pixels. (Read-only)
SKETCHINC	R	D	0.1	Sketch record increment

Variable	Type	Saved in	Default	Meaning
SKPOLY	I	D	0	Determines whether lines or polylines are created during Sketch mode.
SNAPANG	R	D	0	Snap/grid rotation angle for current viewport. Changes to this variable are not reflected in the displayed axis until a redraw operation is performed. AutoCAD does not perform an automatic redraw when this variable is changed, because you may be changing several variables in quick succession.
SNAPBASE	2D	D	0,0	Snap/grid origin point for current viewport. Changes to this variable are not reflected in the displayed axis until a redraw operation is performed. AutoCAD does not perform an automatic redraw when this variable is changed, because you may be changing several variables in quick succession.
SNAPISOPAIR	I	D	0	Isoplane currently in use
SNAPMODE	I	D	0	Snap mode toggle
SNAPSTYL	I	D	0	Holds value for SNAP style: standard = 0, isometric = 1.
SNAPUNIT	2D	D	1,1	Snap spacing. Changes to this variable are not reflected in the displayed axis until a redraw operation is performed. AutoCAD does not perform an automatic redraw when this variable is changed, because you may be changing several variables in quick succession.
SPLFRAME	I	D	0	Controls display of spline frame.
SPLINESEGS	I	D	8	Number of line segments to be generated for each spline patch

Variable	Type		Default	Description
SPLINETYPE	I	D	6	Type of spline curve to be generated by PEDIT Spline: 5 = quadratic B-spline, 6 = cubic B-spline
SURFTAB1	I	D	6	Number of tabulations to be generated for RULESURF and TABSURF; also, mesh density in M direction for REVSURF and EDGESURF
SURFTAB2	I	D	6	Mesh density in N direction for REVSURF and EDGESURF
SURFTYPE	I	D	6	Type of surface fitting to be performed by PEDIT Smooth: 5 = quadratic B-spline surface, 6 = cubic B-spline surface, 8 = Bezier surface
SURFU	I	D	6	Holds value for M-direction density of meshes defined by 3DMESH command.
SURFV	I	D	6	Holds value for N-direction density of meshes defined by 3DMESH command.
TARGET	3D	D	X = 0, Y = 0, Z = 0	Holds location of target. Set with DVIEW command. (Read-only)
TDCREATE	R	D	Varies	Time and date of drawing creation. (Read-only)
TDINDWG	R	D	Varies	Total editing time. (Read-only)
TDUPDATE	R	D	Varies	Time and date of last update/save. (Read-only)
TDUSRTIMER	R	D	Varies	User elapsed time. (Read-only)
TEMPPREFIX	S		(Nothing)	Directory name configured for placement of temporary files. (Read-only)
TEXTEVAL	I		0	Used for programs in AutoLISP.
TEXTSIZE	R	D	0.2	Default height for new text entities drawn with current text style

Variable	Type		Default	Description
TEXTSTYLE	S	D	Standard	Current text style. (Read-only)
THICKNESS	R	D	0	Current three-dimensional thickness
TRACEWID	R	D	0.05	Default trace width
UCSFOLLOW	I	D	0	If set to 1, allows automatic viewing of plan view for new UCS.
UCSICON	I	D	1	Controls location of UCS icon.
UCSNAME	S	D	(Nothing)	Holds name of current UCS. (Read-only)
UCSORG	3D	D	X = 0 Y = 0 Z = 0	Holds origin (0,0,0) of current UCS, in World Coordinates. (Read-only)
UCSXDIR	3D	D	X = 0 Y = 0 Z = 0	X-direction of current UCS. (Read-only)
UCSYDIR	3D	D	X = 0 Y = 0 Z = 0	Y-direction of current UCS. (Read-only)
USERI1-5	I	D	0	Five variables for storage and retrieval of integer values. (Intended for use by third-party developers)
USERR1-5	R	D	0	Five variables for storage and retrieval of real numbers. (Intended for use by third-party developers)
VIEWCTR	3D	D	X = 7.219 Y = 4.5 Z = 0	Center of view in current viewport, in UCS coordinates. (Read-only)

Variable			Default	Description
VIEWDIR	3D	D	X = 0 Y = 0 Z = 1	Viewing direction of current viewport, in World coordinates. (Read-only)
VIEWMODE	I	D	0	Viewing mode bit-code for current viewport. Sum of the following: 1 = perspective view active; 2 = front clipping on; 4 = back clipping on; 8 = UCS follow mode on; 16 = front clip not at eye. If on, FRONTZ (the front clip distance) determines front clipping plane. If off, FRONTZ is ignored and front clipping plane is set to pass through camera point (vectors behind camera are not displayed). This flag is ignored if front clipping bit (2) is off. (Read-only)
VIEWSIZE	R	D	9	Height of view in current viewport, in drawing units. (Read-only)
VIEWTWIST	R	D	0	Defined in DVIEW command. (Read-only)
VPOINTX	R	D	0	X component of current viewport's viewing direction, in World coordinates. Describes "camera" point as a three-dimensional offset from target point. (Read-only)
VPOINTY	R	D	0	Y component of current viewport's viewing direction, in World coordinates. Describes "camera" point as a three-dimensional offset from target point. (Read-only)
VPOINTZ	R	D	1	Z component of current viewport's viewing direction, in World coordinates. Describes "camera" point as a three-dimensional offset from target point. (Read-only)

VSMAX	3D	X = 14.4381	Upper right corner of the Y = 9 current viewport's "virtual Z = 0 screen," in UCS coordinates. (Read-only)
VSMIN	3D	X = 0 Y = 0 Z = 0	Lower left corner of current viewport's "virtual screen," in UCS coordinates. (Read-only)
WORLDUCS	I	1	If 1, current UCS is the same as World Coordinate System; if 0, it is not. (Read-only)
WORLDVIEW	I	D	0	DVIEW and VPOINT command input is relative to current UCS. If this variable is set to 1, current UCS is changed to WCS for duration of a DVIEW or VPOINT command. (Read-only)

AutoCAD
Command Reference

This command reference serves as a guide for both new and experienced AutoCAD users. For the sake of defining commands for new users, this reference includes some programming commands.

Some AutoCAD commands may be used within other commands. These commands are commonly referred to as *transparent* or *internal* commands. The internal format is expressed by preceding the regular command with an apostrophe. The apostrophe is not necessary when the command is being used at the `Command:` prompt. AutoCAD recognizes the following commands with or without the preceding apostrophe:

```
DDEMODES
DDLMODES
DDRMODES
GRAPHSCR
HELP or ?
PAN
REDRAW
REDRAWALL
RESUME
SETVAR
TEXTSCR
VIEW
ZOOM
```

557

Most AutoCAD commands in this reference section are presented with the associated icons (the same image used on the AutoCAD digitizer template). The icons and the template coordinates are used so that you can locate the commands quickly.

ALIGNED

Places the dimension line parallel to a selected entity or to a line drawn through the first and second insertion points.

Syntax

```
Dim: ALIgned
First extension line origin or Enter to select:
Select line, arc, or circle:
Dimension line location:
Dimension text <measured length>:
```

Template Coordinates

Y 6

Description

This dimensioning subcommand is available only after you enter the DIM or DIM1 command. This subcommand lets you align a dimension with an entity or along a line you select.

You can pick points to locate dimension lines, or you can select an entity, just as with other linear dimension commands (HORIZONTAL, VERTICAL, ROTATED, BASELINE, and CONTINUE). To select an entity, you must point to it.

To use this command, specify the location for the extension lines by picking the extension lines on the screen or by entering numeric coordinates.

If you press Enter at the first ALIgned prompt, you will have an opportunity to select an entity to dimension.

<measured length> is the length of the entity or the length between the extension lines you specified. It is the default dimension text.

Hint

Only the first three letters of the command are required for AutoCAD to initiate this command.

Error Messages

Ambiguous response, please clarify... You did not enter enough letters to let AutoCAD know you want to use this command. Enter at least **ALI** to remove the ambiguity. Pressing Ctrl-C at this point aborts the command and exits the dimensioning subsystem.

Invalid You provided an invalid response.

Entity selected is not a line, arc, or circle. You chose to dimension an entity but did not select one that can be dimensioned with this command. Choose again, ensuring that the selected entity is a line, an arc, or a circle.

ANGULAR   *Measures the angle between two lines.*

Syntax

Dim: **ANGular**
Select first line:
Second line:
Enter dimension line arc location:
Dimension text <measured angle>:
Enter text location:

Template
Coordinates

Y 4

Description   This dimensioning subcommand is available only after you enter the DIM or DIM1 command.

The dimension line is an arc showing the angle between two lines. <measured angle> is the angle between the two lines you specified. It is the default dimension text.

If you press Enter at the Enter text location: prompt, AutoCAD places the text within the dimensional arc. Otherwise, the text will be entered at the location you indicate. If the text does not fit, AutoCAD prompts you to enter a new text location.

If the dimensional arc line cannot be drawn between the two lines, an extension line is drawn from the center point of the dimensional arc to an intersection with the arc itself. This extension line is, as the name suggests, simply an extension of one of the lines you chose with the ANGULAR command.

Hints   Only the first three letters of the command are required for AutoCAD to initiate this command.

ANGULAR works with nonparallel lines only. Trying to dimension parallel lines with this command results in an error message.

Error
Messages

Lines are parallel.*Invalid* You selected two lines that are parallel. Parallel lines cannot be given an angular dimension. Try the command again, choosing two lines that are not parallel.

Entity selected is not a line. You chose an entity that is not a line. Choose again, ensuring that the selected entity is a line.

APERTURE   *Controls the size of the aperture box in OSNAP modes.*

Syntax

Command: **APERTURE**
Object snap target height (1-50 pixels) <current>:

Template
Coordinates

Y 10

Description

The APERTURE command lets you change the size of the aperture to fit the way you want to work. An aperture is used within the OSNAP commands to select entities. A small aperture locates points quickly but requires precision when you line up the crosshairs to select an entity; a large aperture is slower and less precise in dense drawings but makes it easier to line up the crosshairs.

The aperture is always square, so you need to specify only the height; the width will equal the height. The aperture height is specified in pixels, each pixel being a resolution dot on your video monitor. The default aperture height is 10 pixels (for out-of-the-box AutoCAD) or the last setting you used for the aperture.

The aperture value is saved in the APERTURE system variable in the ACAD.CFG configuration file. When the aperture size is set, it does not change for different drawings.

Hints

You may want to experiment with the size of the aperture. If the aperture is too small, it will be difficult for you to determine whether entities pass through it. If it is too large, too many entities will pass through, and you may select the wrong one.

You can change aperture size by using the SETVAR command to change the APERTURE system variable.

Error
Messages

Value must be between 1 and 50. You specified a number outside the valid aperture size range. Choose a number between 1 and 50.

Requires an integer value. You did not use a whole number (for instance, you entered a number such as 2.2), or you gave a non-numeric response. Try again with a whole number between 1 and 50.

ARC   *Draws an arc segment.*

Syntax
```
Command: ARC
Center/<Start point>:
Center/End/<Second point>:
End point:
```

Template
Coordinates   L 10

Description   This command allows you to enter an arc segment. At each prompt, you can easily enter a point to define an arc, or you can begin by selecting the center point first. If you choose to specify the center point first, you will see the following prompts in turn:

```
Center:
Start point:
Angle/Length of chord/<End point>:
```

You will see a similar series of prompts (less the Start point: prompt) if you start your arc by first indicating a start point and then specifying the center point.

If you choose to enter the end point for the arc, you will see the following prompts in turn:

```
End point:
Angle/Direction/Radius/<Center point>:
```

Possible
Responses

Response	Meaning
A	Indicate the included angle for the arc. Available only if you specified the center for the arc.
C	Specify the center point for the arc.
D	Specify the arc by the tangent direction from the start point. Available only if you specified the end point for the arc.
E	Specify the end point for the arc.
L	Specify the arc by entering the length of the chord for the arc. Available only if you specified the center for the arc.
R	Enter a radius for the arc.
Return	Sets start point (as reply to Start point: prompt) and direction as end of last line or arc.

Hints The easiest way to create an arc is with the default three-point ARC. The first and last points define the arc's chord, and the second and third points define its curvature. After you enter the second point, AutoCAD automatically drags the arc to help you see where it will fall—unless you have previously turned off DRAGMODE.

AutoCAD does not recognize a straight line as an arc of infinite radius. If you attempt to enter points which lie in a straight line, AutoCAD responds with an error message.

Error Messages `2D point or option keyword required.` You gave a non-numeric response to a prompt that requires a point be picked on-screen or entered numerically.

`Point or option keyword required.` You gave a non-numeric response to a prompt that requires a point be picked on-screen or entered numerically.

`*Invalid*` You entered points that lie in a line. Try again, but provide a different set of points for the arc.

AREA *Calculates the area of an object.*

Syntax
Command: **AREA**
`<First point>/Entity/Add/Subtract:`

Template Coordinates U 2

| AREA |

Description This command computes the area and perimeter, circumference, or length of an entity or a series of points you specify. The area becomes the system variable AREA, and the perimeter becomes the system variable PERIMETER. The add/subtract options let you add or subtract areas from a running total of measured areas.

`First point` is the default. You can enter points clockwise or counterclockwise. You do not have to reenter the first point; AutoCAD automatically closes the area.

Use the `Entity` option to compute the area of a circle or polyline.

If you select a point or an entity, the area and perimeter values are reset to zero before computation. If you select `Add` or `Subtract`, AutoCAD modifies the previous values by the new area and perimeter values.

The Add option sets add mode and switches between adding areas and subtracting areas. If you want to add and subtract areas, enter add mode first. The prompt changes to this:

```
<First point>/Entity/Subtract:
```

The Subtract option sets subtract mode and results in the following prompt:

```
<First point>/Entity/Add:
```

This command returns one of the following responses, depending on what you select for the computation. In each response, x.xxxx represents the computed values:

```
Area = x.xxxx, Perimeter = x.xxxx
Area = x.xxxx, Circumference = x.xxxx
Area = x.xxxx, Length = x.xxxx
```

Possible
Responses

Response	Meaning
A	Add mode
S	Subtract mode
E	Compute area of circle or polyline

Hints

If you choose to compute the area of an open polyline, AutoCAD returns an area as if the polyline were closed and a length equal to the actual polyline length.

Enter points in an organized fashion (clockwise or counterclockwise), or the results may be meaningless. If you want the area of a square and you enter the points (2,2), (4,2), (2,4), and (4,4), you get an area of 0 and a perimeter of 9.6569. If entered in a clockwise rotation of (2,2), (2,4), (4,4), and (4,2), you get an area of 4 and a perimeter of 8, the proper results.

Error
Messages

Entity selected is not a circle or 2D/3D polyline. You chose to compute the area of an entity but did not select a circle or a polyline. Try again, but select a proper entity.

Point or option keyword required. You have entered a point coordinate that is invalid or a keyword that AutoCAD cannot understand. Try again.

ARRAY
(Rectangular)

Makes multiple copies of entities, placing them within a user-defined circular or rectangular pattern.

Syntax

Command: **ARRAY**
Select objects:
Rectangular or Polar array (R/P):**R**
Number of rows (---) <1>:
Number of columns (|||) <1>:
Unit cell or distance between rows (---):
Distance between columns (|||):

Template Coordinates

W 21

Description

Rectangular arrays are based on horizontal rows and vertical columns. The *unit cell* refers to the vertical and horizontal distances between entities. If you indicate opposite corners of the array at the Unit cell: prompt, AutoCAD skips the prompt for column distances.

You can specify only up to 32,767 rows or columns.

Possible Responses

Response	Meaning
P	Polar (circular) array
R	Rectangular array

Hints

Using ARRAY to create even a single row or column of entities is quicker than using COPY MULTIPLE.

To create a rotated array, use the Rotate option of the SNAP command, and rotate your snap grid.

If you mistakenly create an array that is too large, use **U** to Undo the entire array.

Error Messages

If you set up a large array, AutoCAD may ask whether you really want to make so many copies of the selection set. You can use Ctrl-C to stop.

Array expansion terminated. You canceled the ARRAY command by pressing Ctrl-C while AutoCAD was filling out the array. The portion of the array already expanded remains in your drawing.

Invalid option keyword. You have not selected either **R** or **P** as prompted.

Requires an integer value. When prompted for the number of rows or columns, you entered a value which is not a whole number, is out of bounds, or is non-numeric. Enter a whole number less than 32,767.

Value must be positive and nonzero. When prompted for the number of rows or columns, you entered a negative or zero value. Enter a whole number between 1 and 32,767.

Requires number or two 2D corner points. When specifying the unit cell or distance between two rows, you entered a non-numeric response. Try again, providing a numeric distance or selecting two on-screen points that define the size of the unit cell.

Requires numeric distance or two points. When specifying the distance between columns, you entered a non-numeric response. Try again, providing either numeric distance or picking two on-screen points that define the distance between two columns.

ARRAY
(Polar)

Makes multiple copies of entities, placing them within a user-defined polar pattern.

Syntax

```
Command: ARRAY
Select objects:
Rectangular or Polar (R/P):P
Center point of array:
Number of items:
Angle to fill (+=CCW, -=CW) <360>:
Angle between items:
Rotate objects as they are copied? <Y>:
```

Template
Coordinates

W 21

Description

Center point of array: is the point around which all entities are copied. First point is the default.

Number of items: is the number of copies you want.

Angle to fill: is the number of degrees you want these copies to fill. This can be a number or a second point defining the angle. This number will be assumed to be counterclockwise, unless it is entered as a negative number.

Angle between items: is the angle that separates the entities in the array.

The last prompt asks whether the objects are to be rotated. AutoCAD will rotate the objects in accordance with the polar array.

You must provide information for at least two of these three prompts: `Number of items:`, `Angle to fill:`, and `Angle between items:`. If you do not want to give information at a prompt, press Enter; the next prompt will appear.

Possible Responses

Response	Meaning
P	Polar (circular) array
R	Rectangular array

Hint

When you use the ARRAY command on `Dimension` entities in a rotated polar array, the dimension will adapt to the new dimension angle or length. It will be regenerated with the current settings of dimensioning variables, text style, and UNITS.

Error Messages

`Invalid option keyword.` You have not selected either **R** or **P** as prompted.

`Requires numeric angle or second point.` You responded with a non-numeric response when prompted for an angle to fill. Try again, providing either a numeric value or a second point that defines the angle.

`Invalid 2D point.` When prompted for the center point, you entered a single numeric value (two are needed for a coordinate) or a non-numeric value. Try again, providing a valid coordinate either through numeric input or by picking an on-screen point.

`Requires an integer value.` When prompted for the number of items, you entered a noninteger value or an integer greater than 32,767. Try again using a whole number between 1 and 32,767.

`Value must be positive and nonzero.` When prompted for the number of items, you entered a number which is less than 1. Try again using a whole number between 1 and 32,767.

`Yes or No, please.` You responded incorrectly when asked whether the objects should be rotated as they are copied.

ATTDEF

Creates an attribute definition that controls aspects of textual information that you assign to a block.

Syntax

```
Command: ATTDEF
Attribute modes - Invisible:N Constant:N Verify:N Preset:N
Enter (ICVP) to change, Return when done:
Atribute tag:
Attribute prompt:
Default Attribute value:
```

```
Start point or Align/Center/Fit/Middle/Right/Style:
Height <current>:
Rotation angle:
```

If you are working with `Constant` attributes, the following prompt will appear (instead of `Default attribute value:`):

```
Attribute value:
```

Template Coordinates Q 3 - R 3

Description Attributes are entities that contain text used for labeling purposes. They are used with blocks.

`Attribute modes` are settings that control various aspects of the attributes. There are four modes: `Invisible`, `Constant`, `Verify`, and `Preset`. These modes are set for each attribute you assign to a block and may be different for each attribute in the block.

`Invisible` mode controls the visibility of the attributes when the block is inserted in the drawing.

`Constant` mode gives attributes a fixed (unchangeable) value.

`Verify` mode prompts you for the value you entered for the attribute so that you can verify the value.

`Preset` mode allows you to have variable attributes without being prompted for the value upon insertion of the block.

`Attribute tag:` is the label for the attribute you are defining. All attributes associated with a single block must have different tags. However, different blocks may have the same tags for their attributes.

`Attribute prompt:` depends on the setting for `Constant` mode. If the attribute is constant, there is no need for a prompt; the attributes do not change when the block is inserted. If the attributes are variable, the prompt is used when the blocks are inserted. You create this prompt, which appears at the command area to indicate what information the attribute needs. Spaces are accepted as spaces. Be sure to state clearly the information in the prompt so that other operators will understand and be able to use your library parts.

`Attribute value:` is the actual piece of information in the attribute. If your attributes are set constant, this information remains the same whenever you insert this particular block.

The remaining prompts are the same as the TEXT command prompts.

Possible Responses	Response	Meaning
	I	Control visibility
	C	Control accessibility
	V	Control verification
	P	Control preset mode
	A	Align attribute text between two points
	C	Center attribute text horizontally
	F	Fit attribute text between two points
	M	Center attribute text horizontally and vertically
	R	Right-justify attribute text
	S	Select attribute text style

Hints
Attribute commands are not grouped on a single screen menu. They usually appear as one of the first few items on a menu.

Attribute tags cannot contain blanks.

Error Messages
Tag cannot be null. When prompted for an attribute tag, you pressed Enter with no input. You must enter an attribute tag.

Point or option keyword required. When prompted to specify the start point for the attribute, you entered a letter that did not correspond to the option keywords displayed. Try again.

Value must be positive and nonzero. When prompted to enter the text height, you specified a height that is out of range. Enter a height greater than zero.

Requires numeric distance or second point. When prompted to enter the text height, you entered a non-numeric value. Enter a numeric distance representing the height, or select two on-screen points defining the text height.

Requires numeric angle or second point. When asked to enter a rotation angle, you entered a non-numeric character. Try again.

ATTDISP

Overrides the default display visibility setting for all attributes.

Syntax
Command: **ATTDISP**
Normal/On/Off <current setting>:

Template Coordinates
None. See the DISPLAY menu.

Description	ATTDISP controls an attribute's display visibility. `<current>` is the ATTDISP current setting—`Normal`, `On`, or `Off`.

Normal defaults to the display settings at which the attributes were created.

On overrides the display settings and turns on all attributes, making them visible.

Off overrides the display settings and turns off all attributes, making them invisible.

Possible Responses	*Response*	*Meaning*
	ON	Make all attributes visible.
	OFf	Make all attributes invisible.
	N	Normal visibility (user-defined)

Hints

When editing attributes, you may want to display them even though some are set to be invisible.

When indicating `On` or `Off`, type as much of the word as possible; the letter *O* is insufficient and will cause an error message. However, you can abbreviate `Off` as `Of`.

Error Messages

`Ambiguous response, please clarify...` When prompted to enter a new setting, you entered the letter *O*. This can mean either `On` or `Off`; you need to spell out as much of the word as necessary to remove any ambiguity.

`Invalid option keyword.` When asked to clarify your option setting, you entered a letter that does not correspond to a valid option keyword. Try again.

ATTEDIT
(One-by-one)

Allows you to edit attributes one at a time once the attribute text has been inserted into a drawing.

Syntax

Command: **ATTEDIT**
Edit attributes one at a time? <Y>: **Y**
Block name specification <*>:
Attribute tag specification <*>:
Attribute value specification <*>:
Select Attributes:

Template Coordinates

Y 18

Description   At the `Edit attributes one at a time? <Y>:` prompt, you tell AutoCAD whether you will edit one-by-one or globally. If you answer `Yes` (for one-by-one editing), you are restricted to visible attributes. If you answer `No` (for global editing), you have more options, which are covered in the next section.

Prompts at each attribute allow you to change the location, angle, height, and other properties as well as the value. You can further limit the attributes edited by selecting certain block names, tags, or values for the attributes.

To edit attributes one-by-one, you need to specify block names, attribute tags, and attribute values. Use a comma to separate two or more names. You may use wild-card characters in the names—the asterisk (*) for many characters and the question mark (?) for a single character. Only the attributes you specify will be edited.

After you select the attributes to be edited, AutoCAD lets you edit them in reverse order; the last attribute selected is the first attribute you edit. This attribute is marked X, and the following prompt appears:

```
Value/Position/Height/Angle/Style/Layer
/Color/Next<N>:
```

`Value` allows you to change the value set when you originally inserted the block, provided that the value is not constant. AutoCAD prompts:

```
Change or Replace? <R>:
```

If you select `Change`, the following prompt appears:

```
String to change:
New string:
```

Type the string you want to change, press Enter, and then type only the letters that need to be changed.

If you select `Replace`, AutoCAD prompts:

```
New attribute value:
```

Type the new value, and press Enter.

`Position` allows you to specify a new location for the attribute.

`Height` allows you to change the height of the attribute text.

`Angle` allows you to change the angle of the text's baseline.

`Style` refers to the text font or style used.

`Layer` allows you to change the layer on which the attribute resides.

`Color` allows you to change the color for the attributes.

When you finish with one attribute, AutoCAD moves the X to the next attribute to be edited. The same series of prompts is displayed for each attribute.

Hint The ATTEDIT command terminates when you enter **Next** after editing the last attribute you selected. You can also stop the ATTEDIT command from executing by entering Ctrl-C.

Error
Messages `Yes or No, please.` You entered an invalid character when prompted for a Yes or No response. Try again, using either **Y** or **N**.

`0 attributes selected.*Invalid*` When prompted to select attributes, you did not specify any. After this error, AutoCAD returns to the `Command:` prompt. Try again.

`*Invalid selection*`
`Expects a point or Window/Last/Crossing/BOX` When prompted to select attributes, you entered an invalid character. Try again.

ATTEDIT
(Global)

Allows you to edit attributes once the attribute text has been inserted into a drawing.

Syntax
```
Command: ATTEDIT
Edit attributes one at a time? <Y>: N
Global edit or attribute values.
Edit only attributes visible on screen? <Y>
Block name specification <*>:
Attribute tag specification <*>:
Attribute value specification <*>:
Select Attributes:
```

Template
Coordinates Y 18

Description At the `Edit attributes one at a time? <Y>:` prompt, you indicate whether you will edit one-by-one or globally. If you answer `Yes` (for one-by-one editing), refer to the previous command section. If you answer `No` (for global editing), you can edit all attributes, visible or invisible. Specify the attributes you want to edit by indicating tag, value, or block name. When you edit globally, you can change only the value of the attribute. To change more than the value, you must edit attributes one-by-one.

After you select an editing mode, indicate whether you wish to edit visible attributes only. If you answer Yes, AutoCAD prompts you for any block names, tags, or values for restricting the editing of the attributes. Use a comma to separate names. You can use wild-card characters (the asterisk [*] for multiple characters and the question mark [?] for a single character) in the names. Only the attributes you specify will be edited.

If you answer No, AutoCAD indicates that the drawing will be regenerated after the editing process and prompts you to select any block names, tags, or values for restriction of the editing process.

As you edit each attribute you selected, AutoCAD indicates with an X the attribute currently being edited. You are prompted:

```
String to change:
New string:
```

These prompts continue until all indicated attributes been edited.

If you edit all the attributes, AutoCAD switches to text mode. You are prompted:

```
String to change:
New string:
```

AutoCAD searches the attributes you select. The first time it encounters a string to change, AutoCAD replaces that string and prompts you for a new string to change. If you press Enter at the String to change: prompt, AutoCAD places the new string at the beginning of all the attributes. When you finish editing, press Enter at both prompts.

Hint

You can stop the ATTEDIT command from executing by pressing Ctrl-C.

Error Messages

Yes or No, please. You entered an invalid character when prompted for a Yes or No response. Try again, using either **Y** or **N**.

0 attributes selected.*Invalid* When prompted to select attributes, you did not specify any. After displaying this error message, AutoCAD returns to the Command: prompt. Try again.

Invalid selection
Expects a point or Window/Last/Crossing/BOX When prompted to select attributes, you entered an invalid character. Try again.

ATTEXT

Allows you to extract attribute information from a drawing for use outside the drawing.

Syntax

Command: **ATTEXT**
CDF, SDF, or DXF Attribute extract (or Entities)? <C>
Template file <default>:
Extract file name <drawing name>:

Template Coordinates

None. See UTILITY Menu.

Description

This command lets you extract attribute information for use outside the drawing in one of three formats. Indicate the form you want the extracted file to take: CDF (Comma Delimited Format), SDF (similar to dBASE III's SDF format), or DXF (AutoCAD's Drawing Interchange file format).

Specify a template file that indicates how the data in the extract file is to be structured. Information contained in the template file might include which attributes to extract, what information about the blocks containing those attributes should be incorporated, and how the extracted information should appear in the file. The default extension for the template file is .TXT. (See *AutoCAD Reference Manual* for information about creating a template file.)

Enter the extract file name for the extracted information. If you accept the default by pressing Enter, the extract file is given the same name as your drawing.

Possible Responses

Response	Meaning
CDF	Comma-delimited format
SDF	SDF format
DXF	DXF format
E	Select particular entities

Hints

If you type **E** to select particular entities, ATTEXT prompts you to select the objects whose attributes will be extracted. After you respond to this prompt, the CDF, SDF, or DXF prompt will redisplay without the Entities option.

To send the attribute extract directly to the screen, enter **CON:**.

To send the extract file to a printer, make sure your printer is connected and ready to print, then enter **PRN:**.

Error
Messages

Invalid option keyword. You entered a character that does not correspond to any currently offered option. Check the available options, and try again.

Invalid file name You entered a file name that is not allowed. Check your spelling, and try again.

Can't open file You entered a template file name that AutoCAD cannot find on the disk. Check your spelling, and try again.

** Invalid field specification: Your template file has an error in it. Check the contents of this file, and try again.

AXIS

Sets up an axis of tick marks on the bottom and right side of the drawing area.

Syntax

Command: **AXIS**
Tick spacing (x) or ON/OFF/Snap/Aspect <current>:

Template
Coordinates

X 8

Description

Tick spacing is the default. Type a value at the prompt to set the spacing for both X- and Y-axis ruler lines.

On turns on the axis after the spacing is set; Off turns off the axis.

Snap sets the axis to the current snap value.

Aspect allows different X and Y values for spacing.

Possible
Responses

Response	Meaning
ON	Turn on axis.
OFf	Turn off axis.
S	Set axis to current snap value.
A	Establish different tick aspects for X and Y axes.
number	Set tick spacing to this number.
numberX	Set tick spacing to multiple of snap spacing.

Hints

Tick marks make it easier to line up the crosshairs at grid points.

If you use the Snap option or specify a tick spacing of zero, the axis will adjust automatically if the Snap resolution is changed.

The Aspect option, which sets different spacings for horizontal and vertical axis ticks, is not available when the Snap style is isometric.

To display the axes, you must have a single viewport configuration active.

The axis can also be controlled by using the SETVAR command or AutoLISP.

Error
Messages

Requires a distance, numberX, or option keyword. You entered an improper response to the AXIS prompt. Check your spelling, and try again.

Ambiguous response, please clarify... When prompted to enter a new setting, you entered the letter *O*. Since this can mean either On or Off, you need to spell out as much of the word as necessary to remove ambiguity.

Requires a distance (or numberX). When prompted for horizontal or vertical spacing, you entered a non-numeric response. Try again.

BASE

Creates the insertion point when you want to insert one drawing into another or use the BLOCK command to create a Block from objects in the current drawing.

Syntax

Command: **BASE**
Base point <current>:

Template
Coordinates

X 3

Description

BASE is closely related to library blocks. You use the BASE command to set an insertion (base) point for the current drawing. This three-dimensional coordinate is stored with the drawing and is used if you insert the current drawing into another drawing.

The base point defaults to three-dimensional coordinates 0,0,0 in the World Coordinate System. If you change the current elevation, the default Z coordinate will match this elevation. <current> indicates, in three-dimensional coordinates, the default (current) base point setting.

Hint

Use this command to change the insertion point of a library block once it has been defined. Load the block as a drawing, and then do the change.

Error
Message

Invalid point. You specified an invalid base point or entered a non-numeric character when prompted for a base point. Check your entry, and try again.

BASELINE

Allows you to utilize the last dimension you input as a base point for the next dimension entered.

Syntax

```
Dim: BASELINE
Second extension line origin:
Dimension text <value>:
```

Template Coordinates

X 3

Description

This dimensioning subcommand is available only after you enter DIM or DIM1.

AutoCAD uses the first extension line origin of the last dimension you input as the base point, so it prompts you for the second extension line origin without prompting you for the first origin.

<value> is the measured value of the newly computed dimension. It is the default dimension text offered by AutoCAD.

Hints

BASELINE repeats the last entered linear dimensioning subcommand (HORIZONTAL, VERTICAL, ROTATED, or ALIGNED) so that all dimensions originate at the same place.

BASELINE cannot be used after any other dimensioning commands, such as ANGULAR.

Error Messages

`No dimension to continue.` You used BASELINE as the first command on entering the dimensioning subsystem or after a dimensioning command that cannot be continued with BASELINE. Since BASELINE is intended to continue a previous dimensioning command, use it only after you used another valid dimensioning command.

`*Invalid*` When prompted to enter the second extension line origin, you entered a non-numeric character or an invalid coordinate. Check your entry, and try again, or select an on-screen point.

BLIPMODE

Toggles blip markers on and off.

Syntax

```
Command: BLIPMODE
ON/OFF <current>:
```

Template Coordinates	None.
Description	Blips are the small **+** marker symbols that AutoCAD inserts to record the location whenever you select a point or entity. They appear on the screen as visual aids; they do not appear on drawings. <current> is the current BLIPMODE setting.

Possible Responses

Response	Meaning
ON	Turn on marker blips.
OFf	Turn off marker blips.

Hints	Since BLIPMODE is a system variable, you can also turn it on and off with SETVAR. Blips serve only as markers; they do not affect the operation of AutoCAD. Your screen will look less cluttered if you work with Blips off. Since blips are not entities, they cannot be erased using ERASE.
Error Messages	Invalid option keyword. You have not selected either On or Off as prompted. Try again. Ambiguous response, please clarify... When prompted to enter a new setting, you entered the letter *O*. Since this can mean either On or Off, you need to spell out as much of the word as necessary to remove ambiguity.

BLOCK   *Creates an object from existing entities.*

Syntax	Command: **BLOCK** Block name (or ?): Insertion base point: Select objects:
Template Coordinates	Q 1 BLOCK
Description	Blocks are library parts created from objects existing in AutoCAD. AutoCAD Release 10 shows three-dimensional blocks; earlier releases have two-dimensional blocks only.

The BLOCK command lets you create new blocks from parts of existing drawings.

To list all the blocks you created in a drawing, enter a question mark (?) at the first prompt. AutoCAD will switch to the text screen, and you will see a complete list of the blocks currently in the drawing. After this list is finished, the Command: prompt is returned to the screen.

The Block name can be 31 characters long and contain letters, numbers, the dollar sign ($), the hyphen (-), and the underscore (_). AutoCAD automatically converts letters to uppercase.

If the block exists, AutoCAD prompts:

```
Block _____ already exists.
Redefine it? <N>
```

When you redefine a block, be sure not to redefine it to itself; that is, do not take an inserted block and redefine the block to its current name. To redefine a block, either redraw the entire block, or use EXPLODE.

Insertion base point: is the reference point AutoCAD uses when inserting the library part back into the drawing. After you identify the insertion base point, AutoCAD prompts you to select the objects that comprise the block.

Possible Response

Response	Meaning
?	List names of defined blocks.

Hints

Use WBLOCK to write the block to disk if you want to use it in a different drawing.

You can use entire files as blocks in other drawings.

To make multiple copies of a block, use INSERT to copy a block back into the drawing from which it was created.

Although block names may be 31 characters long, you may want to limit them to fewer than 8 characters if there is a chance you may want to WBLOCK them later.

Use the RENAME command to rename blocks.

When naming blocks, keep in mind the potential for using wild cards. You may want to use common prefixes to group related blocks into categories.

Error Messages

Invalid point. When asked to select the insertion base point, you specified an invalid location. Check your entry, and try again.

```
*Invalid selection*
Expects a point or Window/Last/Crossing/BOX/Add/Remove/Multiple/
Previous/Undo/AUto/SIngle
```
When prompted to select objects, you entered an option keyword AutoCAD does not understand. Try again.

BREAK

Removes parts of an entity or separates an entity into segments.

Syntax

```
Command: BREAK
Select object:
Enter second point (or F for first point):
Enter first point:
Enter second point:
```

Template Coordinates

X 13 (BREAK F)
X 14 (BREAK @)

Description

On the tablet menu, there are two BREAK commands: BREAK F and BREAK @. BREAK F removes parts of an entity, and BREAK @ separates the entity without removing a part.

If you use BREAK F or enter BREAK at the Command: prompt, AutoCAD assumes that the point at which you select an object is the first break point unless you choose the F option. If you do this, you will be instructed to choose the first point and then the second, and the break will occur between the two points selected.

BREAK affects different entities differently:

❑ Lines: The segment between the two points is removed.

❑ Arcs: The segment between the two points is removed.

❑ Circles: The segment counterclockwise from the first point to the second is removed.

❑ Polylines: The segment between the two points is removed. If the polyline has a nonzero width, the ends are cut square. If you fit a curve to the polyline and then break the fitted polyline, the fitting information becomes permanent, and you cannot later decurve the polyline.

Other types of entities cannot be broken.

If you are using BREAK @, AutoCAD will prompt you for a first point. That first point is where the entity will be divided.

Possible Response	Response	Meaning
	F	Respecify first point.

Hints

The easiest way to select objects for breaking is by picking, although you can select objects with any object selection method.

When you enter a second point to remove one end of an object, the second point can be beyond the end of that object.

Break cannot be used to break blocks, solids, three-dimensional lines, or three-dimensional faces.

When breaking circles, select the first and second points in counterclockwise order.

Error Messages

Invalid selection

Expects a point or Window/Last/Crossing/BOX When prompted to select an object, you entered an option keyword AutoCAD does not understand. Try again.

2D point or option keyword required. You did not specify a break point correctly. Try again.

Need a line, 2D polyline, trace, circle, or arc. When prompted to select an object you selected an entity that cannot be broken. Try again.

CENTER *Marks center of a circle or arc.*

Syntax

Dim: **CENTER**
Select arc or circle:

Template Coordinates

Y 1

Description

CENTER, a dimensioning subcommand, is available only after entering DIM or DIM1.

This subcommand places a cross (+) at the center of the arc or circle you select.

The size of the center mark is determined by the dimension variable DIMCEN. The smaller the value, the smaller the center mark.

If you assign a negative value to DIMCEN, the center mark will be the same size as the absolute value of DIMCEN, but AutoCAD will add extension lines that extend from close to the end of the center mark to just past the circumference of the circle.

Hint

When you are erasing center marks (using ERASE), remember that either two or six objects make up a center mark: the horizontal portion and the vertical portion and the extensions (if DIMCEN is negative). Make sure you select all these lines for complete erasure.

Error Messages

`Ambiguous response, please clarify...` You have not entered enough letters to let AutoCAD know you want to use this command. Enter at least **CEN** to remove the ambiguity. Pressing Ctrl-C at this point aborts the command and exits the dimensioning subsystem.

`Invalid point.` When prompted to select an arc or circle, you entered an invalid point. Try again.

`Object selected is not a circle or arc.` When prompted to select an arc or circle, you chose a different type of entity. Make sure the object you select is really an arc or circle.

CHAMFER

Trims or extends two lines until specified distances are met and then connects the lines with a line segment, squaring or beveling the corner where the lines intersect.

Syntax

`Command: `**`CHAMFER`**
`Polyline/Distances/<Select first line>:`
`Select second line:`

Template Coordinates

X 21

Description

Chamfering trims or extends two lines so that they intersect. Then it trims them a distance you specify with an option of this command and connects them with a new connecting line.

CHAMFER distances default to 0. To set these distances to the correct value, type **D** at the chamfer prompt. You will see the following prompts, in turn:

`Enter first chamfer distance <current>:`
`Enter second chamfer distance <current>:`

The first distance is applied to the first line you select; the second, to the second line selected. After specifying the distances, repeat the CHAMFER command, and select the lines.

If you type **P** at the chamfer prompt, AutoCAD will prompt for the polyline you want to chamfer. Select the entity, and AutoCAD will chamfer every vertex possible. After completion of the CHAMFER command, you are informed of how many lines (in the polyline) AutoCAD could chamfer, along with how many were too short.

AutoCAD will not chamfer parallel or divergent lines.

Possible Responses	*Response*	*Meaning*
	D	Set distances
	P	Chamfer polyline

Hints

Generally, a chamfer will be at a 45-degree angle to the base angle (equal distances).

You can use this command to adjust two lines so they end at the same point by specifying both chamfer distances as zero. In this case the two lines are extended without a chamfer being drawn.

The FILLET command works similarly to the CHAMFER command, except that it produces rounded, instead of squared, intersections.

Error Messages

Lines diverge
Invalid You chose to chamfer two lines AutoCAD cannot use. Select two lines that are not divergent.

Lines are parallel
Invalid You chose to chamfer two lines AutoCAD cannot use. Select two lines that are not parallel.

If you are viewing from a direction oblique to the X-Y plane of the current User Coordinate System, you will receive a message warning that the results may be unpredictable. At this point you may want to alter your viewing direction.

Chamfer requires 2 lines. *Invalid* You did not specify two lines to be chamfered. Try again (from the beginning).

CHANGE   *Modifies entities.*

Syntax

Command: **CHANGE**
Select objects:
Properties/<Change point>:

Template
Coordinates

Y 16 - 17

```
CHANGE
```

Description

There are two ways to change entities: by indicating a change point or by changing the properties. A change point will modify the physical entity. Properties that can be changed include color, elevation, layer, linetype, and thickness.

The effect of using a change point differs slightly among entities:

❑ Line: The end of the line closest to the change point will move to the change point. Several lines may be included in the selection set.

❑ Circle: The radius is changed so that the circumference passes through the change point.

❑ Text: The location of the text is changed by moving the insertion point to the change point. If you press Enter at the Properties/<Change point>: prompt, AutoCAD will prompt for a new text style, text height, rotation angle, and text string. You can change nearly all aspects of text. An exception is when text is defined with a fixed height, then you cannot change the height of that particular font.

❑ Block: You can provide a new insertion point by indicating a change point.

If you select properties, AutoCAD displays the following prompt:

Change what property (Color/Elev/LAyer/LType/Thickness)? :

Color changes the color of an entity. If you have overridden the layer color and want the entity to default to the layer color, type **BYLAYER**. This tells AutoCAD to set colors by layer. You will be prompted with the following:

New color <current>:

If the current color is BYBLOCK, the entities are set to the color of the block in which they reside. You can also use this setting to override the layer color setting. Type the color, by number or by name, that you want the entity to have:

1 Red
2 Yellow
3 Green
4 Cyan
5 Blue
6 Magenta
7 White

Elev stands for elevation and will change the location of the entities with respect to the Z axis.

LAyer changes the layer on which an entity resides. If the destination layer is off, the entity will disappear from the screen when you are finished with CHANGE. If the entity's color and linetype are set BYLAYER, the entity will acquire the settings for the new layer.

LType changes the linetype of the entities. The comments listed under the LINETYPE command apply here. If you change the linetype of an entity, you are overriding the layer setting unless you are changing the linetype to BYLAYER.

Thickness modifies the thickness of the entities.

Possible Responses	*Response*	*Meaning*
	P	Change properties.
	C	Change color.
	E	Change elevation.
	LA	Change layer.
	LT	Change linetype.
	T	Change thickness.

Hint   Several properties can be changed at once by replying null to the Change what property? prompt. This allows multiple changes you request to take place.

CHANGE can be used to alter volumes and shapes in the Z axis.

Error Messages   *Invalid selection*
Expects a point or Window/Last/Crossing/BOX/Add/Remove/Multiple/Previous/Undo/AUto/SIngle When prompted to select objects, you entered an option keyword AutoCAD does not understand. Try again.

n selected, *n* found, (*n* not parallel with UCS). When prompted to select objects, you selected at least some entities that that do not have an extrusion direction parallel to the Z axis of the current UCS. Either reselect the objects, or use the CHPROP command, which does not have this limitation.

`Point or option keyword required.` You selected an option keyword AutoCAD does not understand. Review the possible responses, and try again.

`Invalid option keyword.` When you chose to change properties, you entered an invalid keyword to the `Change what property?` prompt. Review the possible responses, and try again.

CHPROP — *Modifies properties of entities.*

Syntax	Command: **CHPROP** Select objects: Change what property (Color/LAyer/LType/Thickness)?:
Template *Coordinates*	None
Description	CHPROP is a subset of the CHANGE command, changing only a few of the properties of entities. See the description for the CHANGE command.

Possible
Responses

Response	Meaning
C	Change color.
LA	Change layer.
LT	Change linetype.
T	Change thickness.

Hints

CHPROP modifies entity properties without limiting changes to entities with extrusion directions parallel to the Z axis of the current UCS.

Elevations may not be changed using CHPROP.

Error
Messages

`*Invalid selection*`
`Expects a point or Window/Last/Crossing/BOX/Add/Remove/Multiple/`
`Previous/Undo/AUto/SIngle` When prompted to select objects, you entered an option keyword AutoCAD does not understand. Try again.

`Invalid option keyword.` You entered an invalid keyword. Review the possible responses, and try again.

CIRCLE   *Draws a circle.*

Syntax
```
Command: CIRCLE
3P/2P/TTR/<Center point>:
```

**Template
Coordinates**
M 10

Description

3P prompts you for three points. The circle is drawn with its circumference lying on the three points. You will see a ghosted, rubber-band circle after entry of the second point.

2P prompts you for two points. The two points define the circle's location and its diameter, which equals the distance between the two points. You will see a ghosted, rubber-band circle after entry of the first point.

TTR is the Tangent/Tangent/Radius selection. The entities to which you want the circle to be tangent must be on-screen.

Perhaps the easiest way to create a circle is to specify a center point for the circle and then respond to the following prompt:

```
Diameter/<Radius>:
```

Tell whether the second point you specify indicates the diameter or the radius. In either case, you will notice a ghosted, rubber-band circle on the screen to assist you in placement of the circle.

**Possible
Responses**

Response	Meaning
2P	Specify two endpoints of diameter.
3P	Specify three points on circumference.
D	Enter diameter instead of radius.
TTR	Specify two tangent points and radius.

Hint

You can indicate the radius by designating a point on the circle circumference.

**Error
Messages**

Point or option keyword required. You entered an option keyword AutoCAD does not understand. Try again.

Requires a TAN object-snap and selection of Circle, Arc, or Line. After selecting the TTR method of specifying a circle, you entered an invalid tangent specification. Try again.

Circle does not exist. After selecting the TTR method of specifying a circle, you provided tangent points and a radius that do not allow a circle to be created. Try again, either changing the tangent points or the radius.

*Requires numeric radius, point on circumference, or "D". After selecting a center point for your circle, you entered a non-numeric value, with which AutoCAD cannot work. Check your entry, and try again.

Value must be positive and nonzero. You specified an illegal diameter or radius. Try again, using a number greater than zero.

COLOR   *Establishes the color for an entity.*

Syntax

Command: **COLOR**
New entity color <current>:

Template Coordinates

None

Description

You can respond to the prompt by typing the name (for standard colors) or the number of the color you want to draw with, by pressing Enter to accept the current setting, or by typing **BYLAYER** or **BYBLOCK**.

You can specify colors from 1 to 255 by number but only seven by name.

Number	Color
1	Red
2	Yellow
3	Green
4	Cyan
5	Blue
6	Magenta
7	White

For information about specifying colors 8 through 255, refer to the CHROMA.DWG file on the Sample Drawings disk supplied with AutoCAD.

BYLAYER causes the color of entities to default to the layer color setting. This means the entities will be the color assigned to the layer on which they reside.

BYBLOCK causes the color of the entities to default to the color set for the block definition. The color of the block is determined when you create the block.

	Response	Meaning
Possible ***Responses***	*number*	Entity color number
	name	Entity color name
	BYBLOCK	Floating entity color
	BYLAYER	Match layer's color

Hint

In addition to setting the color used for an entity on drawings, COLOR also affects the color for the entity's display on your graphics monitor. Of course, on monochrome monitors all colors display the same, and on color monitors the display is constrained by the number of colors the monitor allows.

Error Message

A color number or standard color name is required. You entered a color not recognized by AutoCAD. Check your spelling, and try again.

CONTINUE

Allows you to use the last dimension inserted as a reference for the next dimension. The second extension line of the first dimension is used as the first extension line for the new dimension.

Syntax

```
Dim: CONTINUE
Second extension line origin:
Dimension text <value>:
```

Template Coordinates

X 4

Description

This dimensioning subcommand is available only after you enter DIM or DIM1.

CONTINUE is similar to BASELINE, except that CONTINUE uses the second extension line origin of the last dimension as the first extension line origin of the current dimension. This keeps the dimension lines the same distance from the extension lines when possible.

This subcommand repeats linear dimensioning subcommands such as HORIZONTAL, VERTICAL, ROTATED, or ALIGNED. It cannot be used to continue other dimensioning subcommands.

Use CONTINUE to dimension several linear points on the same line.

<value> is the measured value of the newly-computed dimension. It is the default dimension text offered by AutoCAD.

Hints   The distance between the dimension lines is determined by the DIMDLI variable.

If you dimension an entity, exit the dimensioning subsystem, return to the dimensioning subsystem, and then use CONTINUE, AutoCAD will not function as you would expect. Instead CONTINUE uses the first extension line of the last dimensioning command as the first extension line of the continuation; in this way, it is the same as BASELINE. The difference is that the dimension text is not offset from the previous dimension text; the dimension text overwrites the previous dimension text.

Error   Ambiguous response, please clarify... You did not enter enough letters
Messages   to let AutoCAD know you want to use this command. Enter at least **CON** to remove the ambiguity. Pressing Ctrl-C at this point aborts the command and exits the dimensioning subsystem.

No dimension to continue. You used CONTINUE as the first command upon entering the dimensioning subsystem or after a dimensioning command that cannot be continued. Since CONTINUE is intended to continue a previous dimensioning command, use it only after you used another valid dimensioning command.

Invalid When prompted to enter the second extension line origin, you entered a non-numeric character or an invalid coordinate. Check your entry, and try again, or select an on-screen point.

COPY *Copies selected objects.*

Syntax
```
Command: COPY
Select objects:
<Base point or displacement>/Multiple:
```

Template   X 15
Coordinates

Description   COPY is similar to MOVE but leaves the original entity in place. Each copy can be changed without affecting the original copy or other copies.

Base point provides AutoCAD a reference from which to act on your selection set. displacement allows you to enter a displacement for X, Y, and Z coordinates. If you indicate a Base point or displacement, you will be prompted:

    Second point of displacement:

With Base point, indicate a second point; with displacement, press Enter.

Multiple lets you make multiple copies at one time. If you indicate Multiple, you will be prompted:

Base point:

AutoCAD still needs a reference. With Multiple, you may want the base point to be on the object you are copying. This will make the copying easier to calculate. You are then prompted:

Second point of displacement:
Second point of displacement:
Second point of displacement:

AutoCAD lets you place copies as many times as necessary. When you finish copying the object, press Enter.

Possible Response

Response	Meaning
M	Make multiple copies.

Hints

COPY has an option not available with MOVE. This Multiple option lets you make multiple copies of an entity without respecifying the entity.

Use COPY when you want to place copies of entities in an irregular pattern; use ARRAY when you want to make multiple copies in a rectangular or circular pattern.

Error Messages

Invalid selection
Expects a point or Window/Last/Crossing/BOX/Add/Remove/Multiple/Previous/Undo/AUto/SIngle When prompted to select objects, you entered an option keyword AutoCAD does not understand. Try again.

Point or option keyword required. When prompted for a base point or displacement, you entered an option keyword AutoCAD does not understand. Check your entry, and try again.

DBLIST   *Lists information about all the entities in your drawing.*

Syntax   Command: **DBLIST**

Template Coordinates   U 1

Description   DBLIST stands for DataBase LIST. When this command is executed, AutoCAD switches to the text screen and lists the database information on the screen. You can pause the listing with Ctrl-S; press any key to resume. Use Ctrl-C to cancel the listing and Ctrl-Q to echo the listing to your printer.

Hint   For drawings with many entities, DBLIST takes a long time to execute because it scrolls through the entire database. Use Ctrl-C if you decide to cancel.

Error
Messages   None

DDATTE   *Allows attribute editing by means of a dialogue box.*

Syntax   Command: **DDATTE**
Select block:

Template
Coordinates   None

Description   Use of the dialogue box lets you alter the defaults in any order you choose.

Hints   Limit attribute prompts to fewer than 24 characters with the DDATTE dialogue box; additional characters will be truncated.

You can edit only text string values, one block at a time.

DDATTE works only with the Advanced User Interface.

Error
Messages   *Invalid selection*
Expects a point or Window/Last/Crossing/BOX When prompted to select a block, you entered a character or value at the keyboard. Pick a block on-screen.

Entity is not a block. You selected an entity DDATTE cannot use. Check your selection, and try again.

Block has no attributes. You selected a block that has no attributes to edit.

DDEMODES   *Allows changing of entity properties by means of a dialogue box.*

Syntax   Command: **DDEMODES**

Template   None
Coordinates

Description   You can use DDEMODES as an internal command within another AutoCAD command by preceding it with an apostrophe: 'DDEMODES.

DDMODES lets you establish five entity properties: layer, color, linetype, elevation, and thickness. The values you set with DDEMODES may not take effect until you type the next AutoCAD command.

Hints   DDEMODES works only with the Advanced User Interface.

DDEMODES can also be accessed through the Entity Creation option of the Settings pull-down menu.

Error   None
Messages

DDLMODES   *Changes layer properties by means of dialogue box.*

Syntax   Command: **DDLMODES**

Template   None
Coordinates

Description   You can use DDLMODES as an internal command within another AutoCAD command by preceding it with an apostrophe: 'DDLMODES.

DDLMODES displays a dialogue box with all the LAYER command capabilities and also lets you rename any of the layers used in the drawing.

Field lengths in the dialogue box limit how many characters of the layer and linetype names are displayed.

Hints   As with other dialogue box commands, DDLMODES relies on features of the Advanced User Interface and only works on systems supporting AUI.

DDLMODES can also be accessed through the Modify Layer option of the Settings pull-down menu.

Error Messages	None

DDRMODES   *Sets drawing aids by means of a dialogue box.*

Syntax

Command: **DDRMODES**

Template Coordinates

None

Description

You can use DDRMODES as an internal command within another AutoCAD command by preceding it with an apostrophe: 'DDRMODES.

DDRMODES lets you set the following drawing aids from within a dialogue box: Snap, Grid, Axis, Ortho, Blipmode, Isoplane.

Hints

As with DDEMODES and DDLMODES, this command relies on features of the Advanced User Interface and only works on monitors supporting AUI.

If you want to use this dialogue box to establish different spacings for X and Y, set the X value first, then the Y value; otherwise the Y spacing is set equal to X.

Changing Snap, Grid, or Axis spacing with this box does not turn the corresponding mode on or off. To change modes, use the toggle buttons.

DDRMODES can also be accessed through the Drawing Aids option of the Settings pull-down menu.

Error Messages

None

DDUCS   *Controls User Coordinate System by means of a dialogue box.*

Syntax

Command: **DDUCS**

Template Coordinates

None

Description

The DDUCS command provides the same functions as the UCS command. It can also be used to name or rename existing coordinate systems. Naming or renaming is accomplished by entering the new name in the UCS Name field.

Although it was developed primarily for three-dimensional use, USC can be used to create coordinate systems for two-dimensional drawings as well.

Hints   This command relies on features of the Advanced User Interface and only works on monitors supporting AUI.

DDUCS can also be accessed through the UCS Dialogue option of the Settings pull-down menu.

Error   None
Messages

DELAY   *Delays execution of the next command; used in scripts.*

Syntax   Command: **DELAY**
Delay time in milliseconds:

Template   None
Coordinates

Description   DELAY allows you (in a script file) to cause AutoCAD to delay execution of the script a specific period of time. It is particularly useful when you are designing a slide presentation and want the display to pause between commands.

Delay time is input in milliseconds. If you want a delay of about a second, type **1000** at the Delay time in milliseconds: prompt.

Hints   The maximum delay time allowed is 32,767 milliseconds, approximately 33 seconds.

Negative or zero values result in no delay at all.

Error   Requires an integer value. You entered a value that is not a whole number
Message   or is above 32,767. Enter another delay value that is an integer between 1 and 32,767.

DIAMETER   *Provides diameter dimensions.*

Syntax   Dim: **DIAMETER**
Select arc or circle:
Dimension text <measured diameter>:

Template Coordinates	Y 3

Description   DIAMETER, a dimensioning subcommand, is available only after you enter DIM or DIM1.

The point at which you select the arc or circle determines where the dimension appears, since AutoCAD uses this point as the diameter endpoint. AutoCAD locates the second endpoint automatically and draws a line between the two points.

If there is not enough room to insert the dimension text, AutoCAD notifies you and asks you to enter the leader length for the text.

Hint   If the diameter of the arc or circle is less than four arrow lengths, the diameter line will not be drawn; however, an arrow will be appended to the text leader.

Error Messages   `Object selected is not a circle or arc.` When prompted to select an object, you selected one that is not a circle or arc. Try again.

`Block references not permitted.` When prompted to select entities, you chose a block. Select again.

DIM, DIM1   *Sets dimensioning mode for one dimension (DIM1) or multiple dimensioning commands (DIM).*

Syntax
```
Command: DIM
Dim:
```
or
```
Command: DIM1
Command:
```

Template Coordinates	X 1 (DIM1)

Description   DIM1 allows you to enter only one dimension and then returns you to the `Command:` prompt. DIM places you in dimensioning mode so that you can execute several dimensioning commands. Once you enter the DIM command, the typical `Command:` prompt is replaced with the `Dim:` prompt, indicating you are in dimensioning mode.

To return to the `Command:` prompt after using the DIM command, type **EXIT** at the `Dim:` prompt, or press Ctrl-C.

Following are the DIM subcommands:

ALIGNED	NEWTEXT
ANGULAR	RADIUS
BASELINE	REDRAW
CENTER	ROTATED
CONTINUE	STATUS
DIAMETER	STYLE
EXIT	UNDO
HOMETEXT	UPDATE
HORIZONTAL	VERTICAL
LEADER	

For detailed information about each of these dimensioning commands, see the appropriate command description in this Command Reference.

Hints

The DIM subcommands, which allow you to create dimensions in numerous ways, can be executed by entering the first three letters of the subcommand.

The DIM subcommands constitute a command language within the AutoCAD command language. Once you enter the DIM command, you cannot use other AutoCAD commands (except transparent commands) until you exit dimensioning mode.

Error Messages

None

DIST

Calculates the distance from one point to another.

Syntax

```
Command: DIST
First point:
Second point:
```

Template Coordinates

U 3   [DISTANCE]

Description

DIST returns the angle in the X-Y plane; the angle from the X-Y plane for a line drawn between the two points; and the change in X, Y, and Z values for both points. These values are expressed in current drawing UNITS.

DIST calculates the three-dimensional distance between two points. With three-dimensional points, the current elevation is used if you omit the Z coordinates.

DIST returns the following values: distance, angle on X-Y plane, angle from the X-Y plane, and delta values for X, Y, and Z.

Hints

Once you have used DIST, you can use SETVAR to see the current DISTANCE system variable setting.

Use DIST to calculate line lengths.

Error Message

Requires numeric distance or two points. When prompted to insert a point, you entered a non-numeric character. Check your entry, and try again.

DIVIDE

Divides an entity into equal parts.

Syntax

```
Command: DIVIDE
Select object to divide:
<Number of segments>/Block:
```

Template Coordinates

W 22

Description

If you type the number of segments, point entities will be used to mark the divisions. If you select Block, you will be prompted for the name of the block to use in place of the points.

If you type **B** in response to the <Number of segments>/Block: prompt, the following prompts appear:

```
Block name to insert:
Align block with object? <Y>
Number of segments:
```

If you answer **No** to the second prompt, the Block is inserted with a rotation angle of zero.

Possible Response

Response	Meaning
B	Use specified block as a division marker.

Hint

You can use library blocks with DIVIDE to evenly space entities along a line, arc, or circle.

Error Messages

Cannot divide that entity. When prompted to select an entity, you chose one that cannot be divided. You may select only a line, arc, circle, or polyline. Try again.

Cannot find block _____. You entered the name of a block AutoCAD cannot locate. Check your spelling, and include a library name if necessary.

Invalid block name. You did not provide a block name in a valid format. Check your spelling, and try again.

Yes or No, please. You entered an invalid character when prompted for a Yes or No response. Try again, using either **Y** or **N**.

Requires an integer value. When prompted for the number of segments, you entered a decimal number, a number greater than 32,767, or a non-numeric character. Check your entry, and try again.

Value must be between 2 and 32767. You cannot specify a number of segments outside this range. Try again.

DONUT or DOUGHNUT *Inserts a solid filled or unfilled ring in your drawing.*

Syntax

Command: **DONUT** or **DOUGHNUT**
Inside diameter <current>:
Outside diameter <current>:
Center of doughnut:
Center of doughnut:

Template Coordinates

Q 10

Description

Inside diameter is the inside diameter of the doughnut (that is, doughnut hole). For solid, filled circles, set the inside diameter to zero.

Outside diameter is the outside diameter for the doughnut.

<current> is the current inside or outside diameter values (the values that were set last).

Center of doughnut allows you to enter as many doughnuts as you need with a single command. If you undo this command, all doughnuts drawn with this command are undone.

To exit the DOUGHNUT command, press Enter at the Center of doughnut: prompt.

Hints	If you enter an outside diameter smaller than the inside diameter, AutoCAD accepts your input but assigns the values to the logical diameters. This means the smaller value is assigned to the inside diameter, which means the outside diameter is always the largest.
	You can edit doughnuts with PEDIT and other editing commands that work on polylines.
Error Messages	`Value must be positive.` You specified a negative diameter. Try again.
	`Requires numeric distance or two points.` You provided non-numeric input when prompted to enter a diameter. Check your entry, and try again.
	`Invalid 2D point.` As a location for the center of a doughnut, you entered an invalid location. Check your entry, and try again.

DRAGMODE *Modifies dragging.*

Syntax	Command: **DRAGMODE** ON/OFF/Auto <current>:
Template Coordinates	Y 9
Description	The `On` option permits dragging when appropriate. The `Off` option disables all dragging. With the `Auto` option, all commands that support dragging will drag.
	When working with complex objects, it may be less time-consuming to turn DRAGMODE off until you finish.

Possible Responses	*Response*	*Meaning*
	ON	Turn on dragmode.
	OFf	Turn off dragmode.
	A	Use auto mode.

Hints	DRAGMODE can also be controlled as a system variable. Use SETVAR to change the DRAGMODE variable.
	When an entity is dragged, only part of it is redrawn immediately. When you are satisfied with the new location, press the pick button to redraw the whole entity.

Error
Messages

Ambiguous response, please clarify... When prompted to enter a new setting, you entered the letter O. Since this can mean either On or Off, you need to spell out as much of the word as necessary to remove ambiguity.

Invalid option keyword. You entered a letter that does not correspond to a valid option keyword. Try again.

DTEXT   *Draws text dynamically.*

Syntax

Command: **DTEXT**
Start point or Align/Center/Fit/Middle/Right/Style:
Height <current>:
Text:

Template
Coordinates

None

Description

The difference between the DTEXT and TEXT commands is that DTEXT echoes the text on-screen as you type and allows you to create multiple lines of text (by pressing Enter at the end of the current line). DTEXT also lets you edit using Backspace. AutoCAD gives you the same prompts for DTEXT as for TEXT, and all selections have the same meaning.

When using the Align, Center, Fit, Middle, or Right options, you must finish typing your text and press Enter before AutoCAD will adjust the text. (See the TEXT command.)

Possible
Responses

Response	Meaning
A	Align text between two points.
C	Center text horizontally.
F	Fit text between two points.
M	Center text horizontally and vertically.
R	Right-justify text.
S	Select text style.

Hints

With DTEXT the final Text: prompt is issued repeatedly until you exit the command by pressing Enter.

Use DTEXT to enter left-justified text. If you use it with another text alignment, the text appears left-justified first and is then redrawn correctly (that is, realigned) when you exit the command.

Error
Messages

Point or option keyword required. When prompted to specify the start point for the text, you entered a letter that did not correspond to the option keywords displayed. Try again.

Value must be positive and nonzero. When prompted to enter the text height, you specified a height that is out of range. Enter a height that is greater than zero.

Requires numeric distance or second point. When prompted to enter the text height, you entered a non-numeric value. Enter a numeric distance representing the height, or select two on-screen points defining the text height.

Requires numeric angle or second point. When asked to enter a rotation angle, you entered a non-numeric character. Try again.

DVIEW   *Defines parallel or perspective screens dynamically.*

Syntax

Command: **DVIEW**
Select objects:
CAmera/TArget/Distance/POints/PAn/Zoom/TWist/CLip/Hide/Undo/<eXit>:

Template
Coordinates

L 4 - M 6

Description

DVIEW allows you to change dynamically how you view your drawing. When executed, you are asked first to create a selection set of the objects that are dynamically displayed during execution of this command. After that, you see the DVIEW prompt, at which point you can select how you want to modify your view.

DVIEW works on the principle of a target (what you are looking at, typically your selection set) and a camera (your eye).

To use the options at the DVIEW prompt, you need enter only the letters that are capitalized.

CAmera (template coordinate L-5) allows you to change the angle, from the X-Y plane and within the X-Y plane, at which you view the selected objects. You can do this by using the on-screen slider bars or by typing in the new angle. The camera is rotated around the target.

TArget is the opposite of CAmera. It allows you to change your target. The target is rotated around the camera when you enter numeric coordinates or use the slider bars.

Distance changes the distance between the camera and the target. This option turns on perspective view.

POints allows you to change the location of both camera and target using X, Y, Z coordinates. The target point is specified first; the default target is located in the center of the viewport on the current UCS X-Y plane.

PAn (template coordinate M-6) is like standard PAN, only dynamic. You effectively change the location within your field of vision of what you are viewing. Do this by specifying a displacement base point and then moving the crosshairs until the view is satisfactory.

Zoom (template coordinate M-5) allows you to adjust the camera's lens length if perspective is on. If perspective is off, you have a standard zoom center. The default camera length is approximately 50mm long—or what you would see through a normal lens on a 35mm camera. This option is similar to the regular ZOOM command yet is limited to entering only a zoom factor. You can do this numerically or with the slide bar at the top of the screen.

TWist allows you to tilt or twist the view around the line of sight. (This command uses a camera-target setup to define the line of sight.)

CLip allows you to define clipping planes. This is how you define cutaways in your drawing. AutoCAD blanks whatever is in front of the front clipping plane or whatever is behind the back clipping plane. You receive the following prompt:

    Back/Front/<Off>:

Back blocks objects behind the back clipping plane. The following prompt appears:

    ON/OFF/distance from target <current>:

Front blocks objects between you (the camera) and the front clipping plane. The following prompt appears:

    ON/OFF/Eye/distance from target<current>:

If you select Eye, AutoCAD positions the clipping plane at the camera.

Off turns off perspective view; use Distance to turn on perspective.

Hide removes hidden lines from the currently selected entities. This is similar to the regular HIDE command but affects only the entities in the selection set. Typically, this is used after setting the clipping planes.

Undo will undo the last DVIEW option executed. If you use more than one option, you can step back through the whole command.

eXit ends the DVIEW command and regenerates the drawing with the modified view.

Possible *Responses*	*Response*	*Meaning*
	CA	Select camera angle.
	CL	Set clipping planes.
	D	Set distance, turn on perspective.
	H	Remove hidden lines.
	OFF	Turn off perspective.
	PA	Pan drawing.
	PO	Specify camera and target points.
	TA	Rotate target point.
	TW	Twist view.
	U	Undo.
	X	Exit.
	Z	Zoom.

Hints

With DVIEW, there is a viewing direction or line of sight between the camera and the target. To change the viewing direction, move the camera, the target, or both.

Slider-bar icons appear in several places on the screen to help set an aspect of the view as it moves, regenerating the view as the slider moves.

To see an approximation of your drawing with clipping planes in place, use the Hide option.

F1, usually used to switch between text and graphics displays, will not work while you are using DVIEW.

Error *Messages*

Ambiguous response, please clarify... When prompted to enter an option keyword, you did not enter enough letters to let AutoCAD know what you wanted. You need to spell out as much of the word as necessary to remove ambiguity.

Invalid option keyword. You entered a letter that does not correspond to a valid option keyword. Try again.

Requires numeric angle or point. You entered a non-numeric character when prompted for an angle. Check your entry, and try again.

Angle must be in range ____ to ____. You entered an angle outside the valid range for the prompt. Check your entry, and try again.

Value must be positive and nonzero. You entered a negative, zero, or non-numeric response to a prompt that requires positive, nonzero responses. Try again.

Invalid point. You entered a point AutoCAD does not understand. Try again.

Requires numeric angle or point pick. When working with TWist, you entered a non-numeric character. Check your entry, and try again.

Requires numeric distance, point, or option keyword. When entering a clipping plane, you entered an illegal character. Check your entry, and try again.

DXBIN

Loads compacted binary files such as those produced by the AutoShade program.

Syntax

Command: **DXBIN**
DXB file:

Template Coordinates

None

Description

DXB is the extension used to indicate files saved in a specific binary format. It is typically used for exchanging files between different CAD systems.

After executing DXBIN, enter the name of the binary file you want to load. For a more detailed description of this file, see *AutoCAD Reference Manual*.

Hints

Do not type the DXB extension as part of the file name you specify. AutoCAD assumes this extension and inserts it automatically.

If you block a DXB image before you import it, the image will be easier to position and scale.

Error Message

Can't open file. The file name you specified cannot be located by AutoCAD. Check your spelling, and try again.

DXFIN

Loads drawing-interchange or normal binary files into AutoCAD.

Syntax

Command: **DXFIN**
File name:

Template Coordinates

None

Description   DXF files are ordinarily created by applications other than AutoCAD. You can use DXFOUT to get AutoCAD to create a DXF file.

To convert a drawing interchange file into an AutoCAD drawing, enter the Drawing Editor by selecting `Create new drawing` in the Main Menu. Then type **DXFIN** and the name of the file to be loaded.

Hint   Use an empty or new drawing to load an entire DXF file to ensure that any layering, blocks, linetypes, text styles, named views, and coordinate systems are generated correctly. If you are working in a drawing that is set up with layers, linetypes, and so on, only entity information should be loaded.

Error   `Can't open file.` AutoCAD cannot locate the file you specified. Check your
Messages   spelling, and try again.

`*Invalid*` An error was discovered while loading a drawing. The drawing is discarded; no loading takes place. Typically, this happens if blocks are referenced in an entities-only or binary DXF file when corresponding blocks are not available in the current drawing.

`Not a new drawing -- only ENTITIES section will be input.` You specified a file that was saved with DXFOUT for entities only. This message is informational only.

DXFOUT

Writes the current drawing file to a drawing interchange file or a binary file.

Syntax
```
Command: DXFOUT
File name <default>:
Enter decimal places of accuracy (0 to 16)/Entities/Binary <6>:
```

Template   None
Coordinates

Description   Enter the name of the file to contain the drawing information. The `Enter decimal places of accuracy` prompt defines the accuracy of the stored information. The greater the number of decimal places you specify, however, the more memory needed for the file. You can indicate specific `Entities` to be written, or you can specify a `Binary` file to export a full ASCII text description of the drawing.

If you choose to save entities, DXFOUT will prompt you to select entities you want in the DXF file. Then you will again be prompted for numeric accuracy.

Possible Responses	*Response*	*Meaning*
	E	Select specific entities.
	B	Specify binary file.

Hints

If you specify a file name, omit the .DXF extension; AutoCAD inserts it automatically. CAUTION: If a file with the same name already exists, it will be overwritten.

If you do not specify a file name, it will default to the name for the current drawing.

Error Message

Requires an integer value or an option keyword. You entered an invalid value or option when asked to enter the number of decimal places. Check your entry, and try again.

EDGESURF

Constructs a Coons surface patch—a polygon mesh bounded on four sides by entities you select.

Syntax

Command: **EDGESURF**
Select edge 1:
Select edge 2:
Select edge 3:
Select edge 4:

Template Coordinates

O 4

Description

EDGESURF creates a mesh pattern using four individual edges you specify. Edges can be two-dimensional or three-dimensional lines, arcs, or open polylines and must connect end to end. Closed polylines cannot be used.

After picking the final edge, AutoCAD uses the system variables SURFTAB1 and SURFTAB2 to determine how many divisions are in the M and N directions, respectively. The M direction is determined by the first edge you indicate; the N direction is determined by the two entities connected to the first edge.

Hints

Select edges by pointing to them. You can select the edges in any order, but the first one you select determines the M direction of the mesh.

A polyline is a single edge, regardless of the number of its vertices.

Error
Messages

Entity not usable to define surface patch. When prompted to select an edge, you chose an entity that cannot be used as such. Try again.

Invalid point. When prompted to select an edge, you entered an invalid point or a non-numeric character. Check your entry, and try again.

Edge n does not touch another edge. AutoCAD is not able to create the desired mesh because the edges you specified do not intersect (or would not intersect if extended). Use different edges.

ELEV

Controls where the current X-Y construction plane is located on the Z axis.

Syntax

Command: **ELEV**
New current elevation <current>:
New current thickness <current>:

Template
Coordinates

J 3

Description

This command affects the elevation and thickness system variables and may adversely affect the entry of Z coordinates.

Release 11 of AutoCAD is expected to eliminate the ELEV command and its corresponding elevation system variable. SETVAR is a good alternative for setting elevation and thickness.

Hint

The X-Y plane can be moved up and down the Z axis (elevation), and subsequently drawn entities can extrude above or below the construction plane (thickness).

Error
Message

Requires numeric distance or two points. When asked to enter a new elevation or thickness, you entered a non-numeric character. Check your entry, and try again.

ELLIPSE

Draws ellipses.

Syntax

Command: **ELLIPSE**
<Axis endpoint 1>/Center:
Axis endpoint 2:
<Other axis distance>/Rotation:

or

```
Command: ELLIPSE
<Axis endpoint 1>/Center: C
Center of ellipse:
Axis endpoint:
<Other axis distance>/Rotation:
```

Template   N 10
Coordinates

Description   There are two ways to create ellipses with AutoCAD:

❏ Specify two axis endpoints. To draw the ellipses, AutoCAD uses the major and minor axes. AutoCAD uses the axes distances to set up the ellipse. The default prompts ask you to indicate one axis and then the endpoint for the other axis. After you indicate the first axis, AutoCAD prompts you for the endpoint of the second axis. AutoCAD is looking for a distance to apply to the second axis. If the distance is shorter than half of the first axis, the first axis is the major axis. If the distance is longer, the first axis is the minor axis.

❏ Enter the center of the ellipse. AutoCAD prompts you for a point to define one of the axes and then prompts you for the endpoint of the second axis.

Regardless of the method you use to establish an ellipse, the last prompt line has another selection—Rotation. Using the first axis as the major axis, AutoCAD rotates the ellipse around that axis.

Possible | Response | Meaning |
Responses | --- | --- |
| | C | Specify center. |
| | R | Rotate ellipse around first axis. |

Hint   The ELLIPSE command actually draws an ellipse by drawing a polyline of short arc segments.

Error   2D point or option keyword required. When prompted to enter the first
Messages   axis endpoint, you entered an invalid point or a non-numeric character. Check your entry, and try again.

Invalid 2D point. When asked to enter the second axis endpoint, the center of the ellipse, or an axis endpoint after specifying the center of the ellipse, you entered an invalid point or a non-numeric character. Check your entry, and try again.

Requires numeric distance, second point, or option keyword. When prompted for the other axis distance, you entered a non-numeric character that could not be recognized as a valid option keyword. Check your entry, and try again.

Value must be positive and nonzero. When asked to enter the other axis distance, you entered a negative number or a zero. Enter a value greater than zero.

Requires numeric angle or second point. When asked to enter a rotation value, you entered something AutoCAD cannot use, such as a non-numeric character. Check your entry, and try again.

Invalid You entered values from which AutoCAD cannot make an ellipse. This typically happens when you specify two axis endpoints at the same location. Change your parameters, and try again.

END — *Saves your drawing and returns you to the Main Menu.*

Syntax Command: **End**

Template U 24   [END]
Coordinates

Description In contrast with SAVE, which saves your file and leaves you in the Drawing Editor, END saves your file, exits the Drawing Editor, and returns you to the Main Menu. (See also the QUIT command.)

A temporary name for the drawing file is used while the drawing is being edited. When you type **END**, AutoCAD renames the file as you specify. If you specify a name AutoCAD cannot use for some reason, END will try another name, such as *dwg.$$$* or *8ef.$ac*. Your drawing will be saved, and messages will inform you of the file name.

Hint Your drawing files will generally be smaller if you use SAVE and QUIT to exit the Drawing Editor.

Error None
Messages

ERASE

Removes entities from your drawing.

Syntax
Command: **ERASE**
Select objects:

Template Coordinates
W 16 – 17 | ERASE |

Description
After you create a selection set of objects, AutoCAD erases these objects from the drawing.

Hints
Use any selection method to select objects.

To erase the last object drawn, type **L** (for ERASE Last) in response to the Select objects: prompt. You can continue using **L** to erase previously drawn objects.

Use OOPS to restore anything you wish you had not erased.

Error Message
Invalid selection
Expects a point or Window/Last/Crossing/BOX/Add/Remove/Multiple/ Previous/Undo/AUto/SIngle When prompted to select objects, you entered an option keyword AutoCAD does not understand. Try again.

EXIT

Returns you to the Command: *prompt.*

Syntax
Dim: **EXIT**

Template Coordinates
W 5 - W 6 | EXIT |

Description
This dimensioning subcommand is available only after you enter **DIM** or **DIM1**.

Use EXIT when you finish working in the dimensioning subsystem and want to return to the Command: prompt.

Hint
You can also press Ctrl-C to return to the Command: prompt.

Error Messages
None

EXPLODE   *Separates a block into its original entities.*

Syntax
```
Command: EXPLODE
Select block reference, polyline, dimension or mesh:
```

Template
Coordinates

W 20

Description   Select the block you want to break apart. The block will blink on the screen. Special color or layer assignments no longer exist. All entities are moved to layer 0 and become white.

When you need to modify a block, you must explode the block, modify it, and then redefine the block. Each exploded part must be edited separately.

If you explode a polyline that has previously been fit to a curve, the original uncurved polyline is lost and the exploded version matches the curve-fitted polyline.

Hint   You cannot explode a block inserted with MINSERT, a mirrored block, or a block with different X and Y scales.

Error
Messages
```
*Invalid selection*
Expects a point or Last
```
When prompted to select an entity, you entered a response AutoCAD cannot understand, such as an invalid point or a non-numeric character. Check your entry, and try again.

`X, Y, and Z scale factors must be equal.` You tried to explode a block that had its scale factors changed when inserted. These blocks cannot be exploded. Select another entity to explode.

EXTEND   *Extends entities to a boundary.*

Syntax
```
Command: EXTEND
Select boundary edge(s)...
Select objects:
```

Template
Coordinates

X 16

Description   The entity or entities to be extended must be visible on the screen, and there must be a boundary. The first two prompts request the boundaries to which you will extend. When all boundaries have been selected, press Enter. Respond to the second prompt, and you will be prompted to select the object to extend. Point to the part of the entity you want to extend.

Entities can be selected as boundaries and as entities to be extended.

Hint   Use this command to extend entities to already-established boundaries such as walls, ceilings, or floors.

Error Messages   `*Invalid selection*`
`Expects a point or Window/Last/Crossing/BOX/Add/Remove/Multiple/ Previous/Undo/AUto/SIngle` When prompted to select objects, you entered an option keyword AutoCAD does not understand. Try again.

`Cannot extend a closed polyline.` You selected an invalid entity as the object to extend. Select again.

`Entity does not intersect an edge.` The entity you selected to extend, if extended, will not intersect any of the boundary edges you previously specified. Select a different entity to extend.

`Cannot EXTEND this entity.` You are trying to extend an entity that cannot be extended, such as a block or text. Select again.

`Entity not parallel with UCS.` You are trying to extend entities whose extrusion direction is not parallel to the current UCS. Select again.

`No edge in that direction.` You selected an entity that cannot extend toward the desired boundary. Select again.

`No edges selected.` After selecting an edge to use as a boundary, and upon attempting to go to the next prompt, AutoCAD discovered that none of the entities you selected can really be used as a boundary. Try the command again, selecting a valid boundary edge.

FILES

Allows you to accomplish some limited system operations while still in AutoCAD.

Syntax   `Command: FILES`

Template Coordinates   V 24 - V 25

FILES

Description   Displays the AutoCAD File Utility Menu, which provides options that let you list, delete, rename, and copy files.

Hint   This menu is the same regardless of whether you invoke it with the FILES command or from the Main Menu.

Error Messages   None

FILL   *Controls the solid fill of polylines and solids.*

Syntax
```
Command: FILL
ON/OFF <current>:
```

Template Coordinates   None

Description   If FILL is On, the objects are filled with color; if FILL is Off, the outlines of the entities appear on the screen.

Possible Responses

Response	Meaning
ON	Fills solids and wide polylines.
OFf	Outlines solids and wide polylines.

Hint   The FILLMODE system variable must be set to On for fills to be drawn during plotting. To save plotting time, you might want to turn FILL MODE off when generating test plots.

Error Messages   Invalid option keyword. When asked to clarify your option setting, you entered a letter that does not correspond to a valid option keyword. Try again.

Ambiguous response, please clarify... When prompted to enter a new setting, you entered the letter O. Since this can mean either On or Off, you need to spell out as much of the word as necessary to remove ambiguity.

FILLET   *Trims or extends two entities and places a fillet between them.*

Syntax
```
Command: FILLET
Polyline/Radius/<Select two objects>:
```

Template
Coordinates

X 19 - X 20

Description

FILLET causes two intersecting entities, two entities that would intersect if extended, or each vertex of a polyline to be trimmed or extended, as required, so that an arc of a defined radius connects the entities.

When you select Polyline, AutoCAD prompts for the two-dimensional polyline to fillet. All segments that are long enough will be filleted. When AutoCAD is completed filleting a polyline, you are notified of how many segments were filleted.

The default radius for the fillet arc is zero; filleting entities with this radius causes the entities to be trimmed or extended to a sharp corner, the same as using CHAMFER with chamfer distances of zero.

To change the fillet radius, type **R** at the prompt. AutoCAD prompts for the new radius:

    Enter fillet radius <current>:

After you enter the radius, AutoCAD returns the Command: prompt to the screen. The radius you entered remains until you change it.

Possible
Responses

Response	Meaning
P	Fillet polyline.
R	Set fillet radius.

Hints

FILLET works better in plan view than in oblique views.

If the fillet is not drawn, your objects may be spaced too far apart to be joined.

Using FILLET with a radius of zero results in a square corner. A shortcut for this is to use the FILLET 0 icon on the AutoCAD template.

Error
Messages

Requires numeric distance or two points. When specifying the fillet radius, you entered an invalid response. Enter a distance or select two points on-screen that define the distance for the radius.

Value must be positive. You attempted to enter a negative fillet radius. Try again, ensuring that your response is zero or greater.

Fillet requires 2 lines, arcs, or circles.*Invalid* You did not select two objects to be filleted. Try again.

Invalid selection
Expects a point or Window/Last/Crossing/BOX/Polyline/Radius You entered an invalid character as an option keyword. Check your entry, and try again.

Entity selected is not a 2D polyline You selected to fillet a polyline but then selected an entity that is not a two-dimensional polyline. Select again.

If you type the FILLET command with a viewing direction that is oblique to the X-Y plane for the current UCS, a message displays to warn that the results may be unpredictable.

FILMROLL — *Generates a file used for rendering if you are using AutoShade.*

Syntax

Command: **FILMROLL**
Enter the filmroll file name <default>:
Creating the filmroll file
Processing face: *xx*
Filmroll file created

Template Coordinates

None

Description

FILMROLL converts the current drawing into a file that can be used with AutoShade. The current drawing file name is the default provided; AutoCAD automatically appends an extension of .FLM to the file name.

Hints

You must convert an AutoCAD drawing into a shade file before using it in AutoShade.

When entering a file name, do not type the .FLM file extension. AutoCAD appends it automatically.

Error Message

Invalid file name You provided a file name that AutoCAD cannot use. Check your entry, and try again.

GRAPHSCR — *Switches a single-screen system from text display to graphics display.*

Syntax

Command: **GRAPHSCR**

Template Coordinates

N 8

Description   You can use GRAPHSCR as an internal command within another AutoCAD command by preceding it with an apostrophe: **'GRAPHSCR**.

GRAPHSCR causes display of the graphics screen of the Drawing Editor on single-screen systems. On dual-screen systems, GRPHSCR is ignored.

See also TEXTSCR.

Hint   You can also toggle between graphics and text screens using F1.

Error Messages   None

GRID

Sets up a rectangular array of reference points within the drawing limits.

Syntax
```
Command: GRID
Grid spacing (x) or ON/OFF/Snap/Aspect <current>:
```

Template Coordinates   P 8, W 10 | GRID |

Description   A grid within AutoCAD is used to set up reference points on-screen to aid in drawing. The reference points are not entities.

If you enter a numeric value, this becomes the X and Y spacing value for the grid. Using any option except Off results in the grid becoming visible—being turned on. When you enter a value and press Enter, the grid automatically turns on at your setting.

When the grid is set up, you can toggle it on and off. The On option toggles the grid on; the Off option toggles the grid off.

By default, the grid setting equals the snap setting. If you want your grid to default to the snap setting, use the Snap option. (See the SNAP command.)

Aspect is used to set different X and Y values for the grid. You are prompted separately for the X value and then for the Y value. Remember to respond to both prompts.

Because the points on a grid are not drawing entities, you cannot reference them physically.

Possible Responses	*Response*	*Meaning*
	ON	Turn on grid.
	OFf	Turn off grid.
	S	Default grid to snap setting.
	A	Change X-Y values.
	number	Set X-Y values.
	numberX	Set spacing to multiple of snap spacing.

Hints   Since the grid displays only within the drawing limits, you can use this option to show your drawing limits.

Many users find it handy to set their grid values to 2X—twice their snap value.

Error Messages   Requires a distance, numberX, or option keyword. You entered a response AutoCAD does not understand. Try again.

Ambiguous response, please clarify... When prompted to enter a new setting, you entered the letter *O*. Since this can mean either On or Off, you need to spell out as much of the word as necessary to remove ambiguity.

Requires a distance (or numberX). When setting the grid aspect, you entered a non-numeric character. Check your entry, and try again.

Value must be positive. When entering a value, you entered a negative number. Grid values must be positive; try again.

Grid too dense to display You set the grid spacing too close to view at the current zoom factor. Zoom in, or try again.

HANDLES   *Controls the system variable for unique identifiers for entities.*

Syntax   Command: **HANDLES**
Handles are disabled.
ON/DESTROY:

Template Coordinates   None

Description   AutoCAD uses a handle to identify each entity in a drawing. On is the default. All entities have a handle defined.

DESTROY destroys all entity handles in the drawing. Because this option is potentially dangerous, AutoCAD switches to the text screen and displays the following special message:

```
* * * * *  W A R N I N G  * * * * *
Completing this command will destroy ALL
database handle information in the drawing.
Once destroyed, links into the drawing from
external database files cannot be made.

If you really want to destroy the database
handle information, please confirm this by
entering 'I AGREE' to proceed or 'NO'
to abort the command.

Proceed with handle destruction <NO>:
```

In order to destroy the handles, you must enter the phrase shown (a different phrase may appear each time you use this command). All database handles are then removed, and you are informed of this fact.

If you enter **NO** (or any other characters), the destruction process is aborted.

Possible Responses	Response	Meaning
	ON	Assign handles to all entities.
	DESTROY	Discard all entity handles.

Hint   Exercise caution when destroying handles.

Error Message   Invalid option keyword. When asked to clarify your option setting, you entered a letter that does not correspond to a valid option keyword. Try again.

HATCH   *Performs hatching.*

Syntax
```
Command: HATCH
Pattern (? or name/U,style) <default>:
Scale for pattern <default>:
Angle for pattern <default>:
Select objects:
```

Template Coordinates   None

Description   Type a question mark (?) to display a list of hatch patterns available with AutoCAD.

name,style. When you want to change the hatching style, type the name of the pattern followed by a comma and the first letter of the style type: N for normal, O for outermost, or I for ignore. The default style is normal.

U,style allows you to describe your own pattern. You are prompted for the angle for the lines, the spacing between lines, and whether you want the area double-hatched:

```
Angle for crosshatch lines <default>:
Spacing between lines <default>:
Double hatch area? <default>:
```

Scale. If you are working with a large or small drawing, you will want to change the scale of the hatch pattern. You may have to experiment to determine which scale is best.

Angle. All hatch patterns are created with reference to the X axis. If you want to hatch a rotated object and you want the pattern to align with the object, enter the rotation angle here.

Possible Responses

Response	Meaning
name	Use hatch pattern name from library file.
U	Use simple, user-defined hatch pattern.
?	List names of available hatch patterns.

name and U can be followed by a comma and a hatch style from the following list:

I	Ignore style.
N	Use normal style.
O	Hatch outermost portion only.
?	List available style types.

Hints

Hatch patterns are really specialized blocks that you can scale and rotate as you would other blocks. They require special attention when you are setting up boundaries since HATCH has trouble recognizing the interior boundaries of entities. Consider using BREAK to create boundaries for hatching.

Use Ctrl-C to stop a pattern fill in process. Use UNDO to undo hatching.

Error Messages

```
Unknown pattern name.
```
Invalid You entered a pattern name that AutoCAD cannot locate. Check your entry, and try again. You can use the ? option to see what hatch patterns are available.

```
Improper line style. Must be:
    N = Normal (invert in odd areas)
    O = Fill outermost areas
    I = Fill through internal structure
```
Invalid You specified an invalid fill style. You can specify only one of those shown. Try again.

Value must be positive and nonzero. You entered a negative scale for the hatch pattern. Enter a positive number.

Requires numeric value. You entered a non-numeric response when prompted for the pattern scale. Check your entry, and try again.

Requires numeric angle or two points. You entered a non-numeric response when prompted for the pattern rotation angle. Check your response, and try again.

Invalid You did not select any objects to be hatched. Try the command again, selecting the objects to be considered in the hatching.

HELP, ?   *Provides on-line documentation.*

Syntax

Command: **HELP** or ?
Command name (Enter for list):

Template Coordinates

T 5 - U 6

HELP

Description   If you enter a command, you will receive the documentation for it. If you press Enter, you will receive a listing of all the commands currently available in AutoCAD, as well as some general information. To use HELP within a command, the apostrophe ('HELP or '?) is required.

When you first enter the Drawing Editor, the HELP command is activated whenever you press Enter without typing anything else.

Hint   When HELP has displayed all the information it has on your topic, it returns you to the Command: prompt.

Error Message   No help found for _____. You entered a command for which AutoCAD can locate no help. Check your entry for spelling, and try again.

HIDE   *Removes lines that are hidden by three-dimensional surfaces or extruded shapes.*

Syntax

Command: **HIDE**
Regenerating drawing.
Removing hidden lines: *nnn*

Template *Coordinates*	J 1	HIDE

Description   Many times you can benefit from seeing what your drawing looks like when lines that would normally not be visible are removed. HIDE removes lines from view on the screen without removing them from the drawing database.

Hint   With complex drawings, removing hidden lines can take an hour or more.

Error   None
Messages

HOMETEXT   *Returns dimension text to its home (default) position.*

Syntax
```
Dim: HOMETEXT
Select objects:
```

Template   None
Coordinates

Description   This dimensioning subcommand is available only after you enter DIM or DIM1.

Dimension text has a default location. This is its home position. HOMETEXT returns dimensioning text to its default location if it has been positioned somewhere else.

Hint   HOMETEXT is useful if you used STRETCH on a dimension entity and want to cancel its effect.

Error   None
Messages

HORIZONTAL   *Gives the horizontal (X) distance from one point to the next.*

Syntax
```
Dim: HORIZONTAL
First extension line origin or RETURN to select:
Second extension line origin:
Dimension line location:
Dimension text <value>:
```

Template
Coordinates   X 6

Description   This dimensioning subcommand is available only after you enter DIM or DIM1.

You can specify the origins for the extension lines manually, or press Enter to dimension an entity automatically. The only entities you can dimension with this subcommand are lines, arc, and circles.

Hints   The last two prompts allow you to use the derived dimension text or enter your own.

HORIZONTAL has the same result as the ROTATED subcommand with an angle of zero.

Error
Messages   *Invalid* You entered a response that AutoCAD cannot understand. Try again.

Entity selected is not a line, arc, or circle. You chose to dimension an entity but did not select a valid entity. Select either an arc, line, or circle.

ID   *Returns the coordinates of a point.*

Syntax   Command: **ID**
Point:

Template
Coordinates   T 2

Description   This command allows you to determine the exact coordinates of a point. There need not be an entity at the point you select. You can use OSNAP modes to snap onto parts of entities to define specific points.

When prompted for a point, selected any point desired. You are then shown the three-dimensional coordinates for the point.

Hint   To make it easier to pick a point accurately, you might want to use an AXIS ruler or set up a grid with the GRID command.

Error
Message   Invalid point. You entered an invalid point specification. Try again.

IGESIN

Converts and loads files in Initial Graphics Exchange Standard (IGES).

Syntax

Command: **IGESIN**
File name <current>:

Description

This command allows you to load a drawing that was saved in IGES format. Many CAD systems support this file type to promote cross-sharing of drawing files.

The default file name displayed is the same as the current drawing name. Enter the name of the IGES file to import. If you do not specify a file extension, AutoCAD automatically uses the extension .IGS.

You can use the IGESIN command only within a new drawing.

Hints

Drawings imported with IGESIN typically require editing.

IGESIN can be a time-consuming command. The file loading and translation will take a great deal more time than loading a native AutoCAD drawing.

Error
Messages

IGES input may be done only in a new drawing.
Invalid This error message is self-explanatory. Return to the Main Menu (use QUIT or END), and start a new drawing. Then try IGESIN again.

Invalid file name You have entered a file name that is not valid. File names must conform to DOS standards. Check your entry, and try again.

When a serious error occurs while importing a drawing, input is stopped and an error message reports where the error was found. AutoCAD saves the resulting partial drawing.

IGESOUT

Converts the current drawing to Initial Graphics Exchange Standard (IGES) format.

Syntax

Command: **IGESOUT**
File name <current>:

Description

This command is used to save the current drawing in a file format (IGES) that can be used by other CAD packages. For complete compatibility, you must check the specifications for the other software.

The default file name shown (<current>) is the same as the current drawing name. You can replace this with any file name you desire. There is no need to use an extension; AutoCAD automatically appends a .IGS extension.

Hint   Drawings exported with IGESOUT lose attribute definitions and solid fills. There are also problems with three-dimensional representation.

Error   Invalid file name You entered a file name that is not valid. File names must
Message   conform to DOS standards. Check your entry, and try again.

INSERT   *Inserts previously defined block.*

Syntax
```
Command: INSERT
Block name (or ?) <current>:
Insertion point:
X scale factor <1> /Corner/XYZ:
Y scale factor (default=X):
Rotation angle <0>:
```

Template   Q 2
Coordinates

Description   At the Block name (or ?): prompt, type the name of the block you want to insert. Use the question mark to see a list of the currently-defined blocks. This list will not include blocks saved as separate drawing files on disk or within libraries. The default block name is shown only if you have previously inserted blocks within the current editing session.

Insertion point: prompts you for the location of the block. This is the point that will be aligned with the insertion base point you defined when you created the block. Notice that when this prompt is visible, a ghosted version of the block can be dragged to various locations on-screen.

At the X scale factor <1>/Corner/XYZ: prompt, you can enter a number or a point, or you can press Enter if you want the block inserted at the scale drawn. If you enter a point, you can show AutoCAD the X and Y scales at the same time. The default value for the scale factor is one; this value causes the block to be inserted at the scale used when it was drawn. (The XYZ option is available only with the ADE-3 package.)

At the Y scale factor (default=X): prompt, you can enter a Y scale factor different from the X factor. If you want the X scale factor to be the same as the Y scale factor, press Enter. This prompt is not displayed if, at the X scale factor prompt, you entered a point on-screen.

Negative scale values are acceptable. A negative X value mirrors the block around the Y axis; a negative Y value mirrors the block around the X axis.

With the Rotation angle <0>: prompt, the block is rotated around the insertion point at the given angle. If you accept the default angle of zero, the block is inserted at the orientation created. Angle input is applied counterclockwise.

After each of these prompts has been answered, AutoCAD gives you a chance to respond to any attribute prompts attached to the block.

Possible Responses

Response	Meaning
name	Load block file name.
name=f	Create block name from file f.
*name	Retain individual part entities.
?	List names of defined blocks.
C	Specify corner of scale.
XYZ	Readies INSERT for X, Y, and Z scales.

Hint

You can remove blocks you inserted by using UNDO or ERASE Last command.

Error Messages

Can't open file You provided a block name AutoCAD cannot locate. Check your entry, and try again.

Point or option keyword required. When asked to pick an insertion point, you failed to do so. Pick a valid point, or use an option keyword to help you pick a point.

Value must be nonzero. When asked to specify a scale factor, you entered a zero value. Try again, ensuring that the value is nonzero.

Requires numeric scale factor, 2D corner point, or option keyword. When asked to specify an X scale factor, you entered a response AutoCAD does not understand. Check your entry, and try again.

Requires numeric angle. When prompted for the Y scale factor, you input a non-numeric character. Check your input, and try again.

Requires numeric angle or second point. When prompted for a rotation angle, you entered an invalid angle or point. Check your entry, and try again.

ISOPLANE
Changes the orientation of the crosshairs when you are working in isometrics.

Syntax

Command: **ISOPLANE**
Left/Top/Right/<Toggle>:

Template Coordinates	None

Description

The ISOPLANE command is a toggle; to change among the three different settings, press Enter at the prompt. AutoCAD informs you of the current isometric plane.

The current isometric plane is stored as the system variable SNAPISOPAIR.

Possible Responses

Response	Meaning: Plane (grid axes)
L	Left plane (90 and 150 degrees)
R	Right plane (30 and 150 degrees)
T	Top plane (90 and 30 degrees)
Enter	Toggle to next plane

Hint

Isometric planes have grid axes in pairs of 90 and 150 degrees, 30 and 150 degrees, or 90 and 30 degrees. These planes can be changed using the ISOPLANE command, the Isoplane toggle key, the SETVAR command, or AutoLISP.

Error Message

Invalid option keyword. You made an invalid response. Check your entry, and try again.

LAYER
Creates and modifies layers.

Syntax

```
Command: LAYER
?/Make/Set/New/ON/OFF/Color/Ltype/Freeze/Thaw:
```

Template Coordinates

Q 5 - R 6

LAYER

Description

Layers help you control the complexity of your drawing; you can turn layers off when a drawing becomes too complex. Layered drawings are like acetate sheets stacked or superimposed to compose a single image.

The LAYER command lets you create new layers, change layers, and make layers visible or invisible.

Each layer has a name, color, and linetype. Each entity is associated with the layer on which it was drawn.

? gives you a listing of layers and their status.

The New option creates new layers. AutoCAD prompts you for the layer names. To enter more than one layer name at a time, type the name followed by a comma and the next name; no spaces are allowed. Do not end your list with a comma.

Set identifies the layer on which you want to draw.

Make is a combination of Set and New. When you use Make, you are prompted for the layer you want to be the current layer. AutoCAD searches for the layer name. If the layer name is not found, AutoCAD creates a new layer with that name and sets that layer. Check your spelling with this option carefully; AutoCAD can be unforgiving and will create a new layer if you inadvertently misspell the name of an already existing layer.

On turns on layers. When you create a new layer, it defaults to On. Off turns off layers. When layers are off, you cannot see the entities, if any, that exist on those layers.

The Color option allows you to set the layer color. AutoCAD is capable of producing 255 colors. You will be limited, however, if your graphics card and monitor are not capable of producing that many colors. The following colors are standard and can be referred to by number or by name:

1	Red
2	Yellow
3	Green
4	Cyan
5	Blue
6	Magenta
7	White

The default color for new layers is white. Setting the color also defines the color of the entities that reside on a given layer.

Ltype sets the linetype for the layer. The default is the solid linetype. You can enter a question mark as a linetype and you will see a list of the currently available linetypes.

Freeze. Freezing layers is a timesaving option. When you freeze a layer, AutoCAD ignores the entities on that layer, which reduces the time required for a regeneration.

Thaw allows you to access frozen layers. AutoCAD automatically turns on thawed layers.

Possible Responses	*Response*	*Meaning*
	?	List defined layers.
	C	Set current layer to a specific color.
	F	Freeze layers.
	L	Set current layers to a specific linetype.
	M	Make a layer (create, if necessary, and set to that layer).
	N	Create new layers.
	OFf	Turn off layers.
	ON	Turn on layers.
	S	Set current layer.
	T	Thaw layers.

Hint   When you are naming layers, consider using wild cards. You can perform certain operations on more than one layer at a time by using wild cards when you are prompted for a layer name or by listing more than one layer. Separate layer names with commas and no spaces. (You cannot use wild cards with the Make, Set, or New options.)

Error Messages   is an invalid layer name. You ended your list of layers (when using New) with a comma. All other layers were created, but AutoCAD was expecting one more name (because of the comma). Thus, you get this message; it is more an informational message than a critical error.

Cannot find layer _____. You entered a layer name that is nonexistent in the current drawing. Use the question mark (?) to list the defined layers. Check your entry, and try again.

Invalid layer name. When using the Make option, you entered more than one layer name. Check your entry, and try again.

Layer _____ not found. You specified a nonexistent layer name in response to a prompt. Try again.

A color number or standard color name is required. When prompted for a layer color, you entered a color name AutoCAD does not recognize. Check your entry, and try again.

Invalid color number. When prompted for a layer color, you specified a color number AutoCAD cannot recognize. Try again.

Linetype _____ not found. Use LINETYPE command to load it. You specified a linetype not currently loaded. Exit the LAYER command and use LINETYPE to load the linetype, or check the spelling of your entry, and try again.

Ambiguous response, please clarify... When attempting to enter a new setting, you entered the letter O. Since this can mean either On or Off, you need to spell out as much of the word as necessary to remove any ambiguity.

Really want layer _____ (the CURRENT) layer) off? <N> You indicated that you want to turn off the current layer. AutoCAD wants to confirm this. Answer appropriately.

Yes or No, please. You entered an invalid character when prompted for a Yes or No response. Try again, using **Y** or **N**.

LEADER   *Allows you to place notes in a drawing.*

Syntax

Dim: **LEADER**
Leader start:
To point:
To point:
Dimension text <last dimension entered>:

Template Coordinates

X 2

Description   This dimensioning subcommand is available only after you enter DIM or DIM1.

LEADER lets you add a note connected by an arrow to the entity the note describes. You specify the location of the leader by picking points that define the line segments making up the leader line. When you finish entering end points, press Enter. AutoCAD prompts you for the text you want inserted. The default text is the last dimension text entered.

Hints   Respond to the To point: prompts as you would for a normal LINE command. You can undo LEADER segments if you want.

You can enter only one line of text using the LEADER option.

Error Message   *Invalid* You have not specified a valid point for the leader. Try again.

LIMITS   *Controls drawing size.*

Syntax

Command: **LIMITS**
ON/OFF/<Lower left corner> <current>:
Upper right corner <current>:

Template Coordinates	None

Description The limit of your drawing is basically the drawing area you have defined with a previous use of LIMITS or in your ACAD.DWG default drawing file. The drawing area is always rectangular, and the limits are defined by two points that define the rectangle.

ON engages the limits check; a beep warns you that you are outside the limits of your drawing area. OFF turns off the limits-check warning.

<Lower left corner> is the lower left corner of your drawing area. The default (0,0) is the standard setting for LIMITS. Press Enter to accept 0,0 as the lower left corner, or enter a point by either digitizing or typing the X and Y values.

Upper right corner: is where you set the upper right corner of your drawing. Remember that the X (horizontal) value comes first, followed by the Y (vertical) value.

To see the new drawing size, use ZOOM All.

Possible Responses

Response	Meaning
ON	Turn on limits checking.
OFf	Turn off limits checking.

Hints If you use LIMITS to match your drawing size to your plotter paper, be sure to leave as much room at the borders as the plotter needs to hold the drawing paper.

LIMITS affects the following system variables: LIMCHECK, LIMMIN, and LIMMAX.

Error Messages 2D point or option keyword required. You entered a character to the LIMITS prompt that AutoCAD cannot recognize. Check your entry, and try again.

Ambiguous response, please clarify... You entered the letter O at the LIMITS prompt. Since this can mean On or Off, you need to spell out as much of the word as necessary to remove ambiguity.

Invalid 2D point. When prompted for the upper right corner, you entered an invalid point. Try again.

LINE

Draws a straight line.

Syntax

```
Command: LINE
From point:
To point:
To point:
```

Template Coordinates

J 10

Description

This command lets you draw the most basic of entities in AutoCAD: a line.

From point: prompts you for the beginning of the first line segment. You can enter this point by using any of the methods available for entering points. Press Enter to inform AutoCAD that you wish to continue from where you last stopped drawing entities.

To point: You are being prompted for the end of the current line segment. The point you enter at this prompt is used as the beginning for the next line segment. If you press Enter without entering a point, you end the LINE command.

Type **U** at the To point: prompt to undo the last line segment you drew. If you remain in the LINE command while you undo the segment, AutoCAD allows you to pick up the line segments at the previous point entered.

Type **C** at the To point: prompt to close the sequence of lines (draw a line from the end of the last-defined line segment to the point used at the beginning of the LINE command). You must have two or more line segments to close the LINE command.

Possible Responses

Response	Meaning
Enter	Start at end of previous line or arc (as reply to From point:).
C	Close polygon (as reply to To point:).
U	Undo segment (as reply to To point:).

Hint

You can continue undoing while you are in the LINE command if you have not exited by pressing Enter, space bar, or Ctrl-C.

Error Messages

Invalid point. You have not specified a valid point when prompted for the starting point of the line.

No line or arc to continue. When prompted for a starting point for your line, you pressed Enter. AutoCAD assumes that you want to continue with a line from where you last drew an entity. This message indicates that there was no valid last entity from which to continue. Enter a starting point for your line.

Point or option keyword required. When prompted for a To point, you entered a character AutoCAD does not understand. Enter a point, or use the option keywords U or C.

LINETYPE   _Creates, loads, and sets linetypes._

Syntax

Command: **LINETYPE**
?/Create/Load/Set:

Template Coordinates

None

Description

LINETYPE lets you set the current linetype, define linetypes, get linetypes from libraries, and list linetypes available.

? lists the linetypes available in a linetype file on disk. You will be prompted:

File to list <default>:

Standard linetypes are stored in the default file, ACAD.LIN. If you supply a different file name, there is no need to use the .LIN extension; AutoCAD appends this automatically.

Create enables you to create primitive linetypes.

If a linetype is in a file other than ACAD.LIN, you must use the Load option to load it. You will be prompted:

Name of linetype to load:
File to search <default>:

The Set option sets the linetype with which you will be working. All the entities you draw from this point will be drawn in the linetype you set. If you draw a block with some entities set to layer default linetypes (some with linetype overrides, and some set to linetype by block), there will be confusion when the block is inserted. Some entities retain the linetype you want; other entities change to the layer default. You are prompted:

New entity linetype <current>:

Be careful about changing the entities in your drawing. Use overrides with caution.

Possible Responses	Response	Meaning
	?	List available linetypes.
	C	Create linetype.
	L	Load linetype.
	S	Set current entity linetype.

Hints   LINETYPE affects only lines, arcs, circles, and polylines.

The following suboptions are available for the `Set` option:

name	Entity linetype name to set
BYBLOCK	Entity linetype for the block
BYLAYER	Layer's linetype for entities
?	Lists loaded linetypes

Error Messages   `Invalid option keyword.` You did not use a valid option for the LINETYPE command. Try again.

`Invalid file name` You entered an invalid file name when trying to use the ? or Load option. Check your entry, and try again.

`Can't open file` You entered a file name AutoCAD cannot locate. Check your spelling and make sure you use the full path of the linetype file; try again.

`Linetype _____ not found. Use the LOAD option to load it.` When setting the linetype, you specified a linetype not currently loaded. Use the `Load` option to load the linetype, or check the spelling of your entry, and try again.

LIST   *Lists information for entities in your drawing.*

Syntax
```
Command: LIST
Select objects:
```

Template Coordinates   T 5 - U 5

LIST

Description   This command lists information for all the entities in a drawing. Included are entity type, layer, and location relative to the User Coordinate System. Other information is included selectively, based on the entity type.

Hints   To pause the information displayed on your screen, use Ctrl-S or Pause. Press any other key to start the display again.

To echo information to your printer, use Ctrl-Q before the command is executed.

Error
Message

```
*Invalid selection*
Expects  a  point  or  Window/Last/Crossing/BOX/Add/Remove/Multiple/
Previous/Undo/AUto/SIngle
```
When prompted to select objects, you entered an option keyword that AutoCAD does not understand. Try again.

LOAD

Loads compiled shape and font files.

Syntax

```
Command: LOAD
Name of shape file to load (or ?):
```

Template
Coordinates

None

Description

This command loads shape files or font files for use within AutoCAD. Only shape files that have been successfully compiled at the Main Menu can be loaded.

Possible
Response

Response	Meaning
?	List loaded shape files.

Hint

When typing the name of a file to be loaded, do not type the .SHX extension; AutoCAD appends this automatically.

Error
Messages

`Invalid file name` You entered an invalid file name. Check your entry, and try again.

`Can't open file` You entered a file name AutoCAD cannot locate. Check your spelling, and make sure you use the full path of the linetype file; try again.

LTSCALE

Changes the scale of linetypes in your drawing.

Syntax

```
Command: LTSCALE
New scale factor <default>:
```

Template
Coordinates

None

Description

Enter a value greater than zero for the scale; the default for new drawings is one. The higher the value of LTSCALE, the larger the dashes and spaces between dots and dashes in your line.

If all the lines you draw look similar regardless of the linetype, try increasing the LTSCALE value.

You must execute the REGEN command after you set LTSCALE, for the new scale to take effect.

Hints

You may have to set the scale a few times to get the correct spacing on your linetypes.

You can also use the SETVAR command to change LTSCALE as a system variable.

Error Messages

Requires numeric value. You entered non-numeric characters when prompted for the scale factor. Check your entry, and try again.

Value must be positive and nonzero. When prompted to enter a scale factor, you specified one that is out of range. Enter a value greater than zero.

MEASURE

Measures a distance, placing points or markers at intervals.

Syntax

```
Command: MEASURE
Select object to measure:
<Segment length>/Block:
```

Template Coordinates

X 22

Description

Select the object with which you will work. Type the length or **B** for Block. The lengths will be measured from the end of the entity nearest the point at which you selected that entity. If you use the Block option instead of specifying a segment length, the following additional prompts will display after the <Segment length>/Block: prompt:

```
Block name to insert:
Align block with object? <Y>:
Segment length:
```

MEASURE can use only a block that has been created and is already in the drawing.

Possible Response

Response	Meaning
B	Use specified block as marker.

Hints	MEASURE can be used to mark intervals at which you will later insert blocks.
	Circles are always measured counterclockwise.
Error Messages	Value must be positive and nonzero. You entered a negative, zero, or non-numeric response to a prompt that requires positive, nonzero responses. Try again.
	Requires numeric distance, two points, or option keyword. When entering a segment length or the Block option, you entered an illegal character. Check your entry, and try again.
	Object isn't that long. You entered a number greater than the length of the object you are measuring. Enter a number equal to or smaller than the object's length in current units.
	Cannot measure that entity. You selected an entity that AutoCAD cannot measure, such as a single point.

MENU

Allows you to work with menus other than the standard AutoCAD menu.

Syntax	Command: **MENU** Menu file name or . for none <current>:
Template Coordinates	None
Description	This command lets you use a menu system such as one you have developed or one developed by a third party. When prompted, enter the name of the new menu. AutoCAD supports screen, button, tablet, and pull-down menus.
Hints	When you are specifying a menu name, omit the .MNU extension; AutoCAD inserts this automatically.
	You can also load a menu by selecting Menu from the Utility screen menu.
Error Messages	Can't open file You entered a menu name not in your menu files, or you did not yet create a menu file.

MINSERT

Makes multiple inserts of a block.

Syntax

```
Command: MINSERT
Block name (or ?):
Insertion point:
X scale factor <1>/Corner/XYZ:
Y scale factor <default = X>:
Rotation angle <0>:
```

Template Coordinates

R 2

Description

MINSERT is like INSERT; with MINSERT, however, you can insert an array of multiple block copies. You could think of MINSERT as a command combining both INSERT and ARRAY. However, MINSERT can create rectangular arrays only, not polar arrays.

The prompts shown are the standard INSERT prompts; see INSERT in this command reference for an explanation of the options. The only difference with MINSERT is that you cannot enter a block name with an asterisk (*) to insert the block exploded.

Following are the prompts for the array part of the MINSERT command:

```
Number of rows (---) <1>:
Number of columns (|||) <1>:
```

These are the same prompts that follow ARRAY. Type the number of rows and the number of columns; responses must be positive, whole numbers. If the number of rows is greater than one, you will be prompted for the distance between the rows or for a unit cell:

```
Unit cell or distance between rows (---)
```

A unit cell includes the block and the distance between the rows. AutoCAD needs to know the distance from one entity in the first block to the same entity in the second block.

Possible Responses

Response	Meaning
name	Load block file name, and form a rectangular array.
name = f	Create block name from file f, and form a rectangular array.
?	List names of defined blocks.
C	Specify corner of scale.
XYZ	Ready MINSERT for X, Y, and Z values.

Hint   When you specify a rotation angle in response to the Rotation angle <0>: prompt, the array (if any) is rotated as well as the blocks it contains.

Error Messages   *Invalid* You entered an invalid block name. Check your spelling, and try again.

Point or option keyword required. You entered an invalid insertion point. Select an insertion point, or enter coordinates separated by commas.

Requires numeric scale factor, 2D corner point, or option keyword. Reenter the X scale factor, a two-dimensional corner point, or an option keyword indicated in the prompt.

Required numeric angle or second point. You made a non-numeric entry when prompted for a rotation angle. Try again, providing a numeric value or a second point that defines the angle.

Requires an integer value. When prompted for the number of rows or columns, you entered a value that is not a whole number, is out of bounds, or is non-numeric. Enter a whole number less than 32,767.

Value must be positive and nonzero. When prompted for the number of rows or columns, you entered a number less than one. Try again, using a whole number less than 32,767.

MIRROR   *Reflects entities on an axis, making mirror images (either deleting or retaining the original entities).*

Syntax   Command: **MIRROR**
Select objects:
First point of mirror line:
Second point:
Delete old objects? <N>:

Template Coordinates   X 12

Description   MIRROR allows you to create duplicates of an entity by use of a *mirror line*. The new entity is created as a reflection of the original as if a mirror had been placed at the mirror line you specify.

At the prompts, select the objects with which you want to work. Because the mirror line is a line of symmetry in the final object, its placement is important. At the next two prompts, specify the first and second points that will define this line.

You can retain the original entities or delete them with the `Delete old objects? <N>:` prompt. If you answer **Y**, only the mirror image will remain.

Hint

You are not limited to using mirror lines on the horizontal or vertical axis. By experimenting with mirror lines at various angles, you can create interesting effects and perhaps save a great deal of drawing time.

Error Messages

`Invalid 2D point.` When prompted for the first or second point of the mirror line, you entered a single numeric value (two are needed for a coordinate) or a non-numeric value. Try again, providing a valid coordinate either through numeric input or by picking an on-screen point.

`Yes or No, please.` You entered an invalid character when prompted for a Yes or No response. Try again, using either **Y** or **N**.

`Expects a point or Window/Last/Crossing/BOX/Add/Remove/Multiple/ Previous/Undo/AUto/SIngle` When prompted to select objects, you entered an option keyword AutoCAD does not understand. Try again.

MOVE   *Moves entities in the drawing.*

Syntax

```
Command: MOVE
Select objects:
Base point or displacement:
Second point of displacement:
```

Template Coordinates

W 15

Description

AutoCAD does not limit you to keeping entities where you first create them. This command allows you to change the location of an entity within a drawing.

`Base point` gives AutoCAD a reference for moving the entities. This is equivalent to the insertion base point for blocks.

`displacement.` AutoCAD will accept displacements for the entities. You must enter at least an X and Y value; AutoCAD will accept X, Y, and Z values. The displacement should correspond to the X, Y, and Z displacements for the entities.

Second point. No matter how you respond to the previous prompt, you will be prompted for a second point. If you entered a displacement, press Enter at this prompt. If you indicated a Base point, show AutoCAD where you want the entities by dragging them, or indicate the coordinates for the second point.

Hints

You can move entities by dragging them.

If you are moving a group of entities that comprise a larger object (for example, a series of entities that may collectively define a floor plan), make sure you select all the objects to be moved so that they retain their relationship to each other. This is perhaps best done by selecting the objects with a window or by crossing.

Error Message

Invalid point. When prompted for the base point or second point of displacement, your response was invalid. Select a point on-screen, or enter two or three coordinates. For the second point, you can show AutoCAD the coordinates by dragging the entity.

MSLIDE   *Makes a slide of a drawing or part of a drawing.*

Syntax

Command: MSLIDE
Slide file <default>:

Template Coordinates

None

Description

Before you execute the MSLIDE command, bring the drawing into the Drawing Editor, and zoom in on the area you want to be the slide.

You must provide the name of the slide file. The name must be a DOS file name—up to eight characters, with the standard DOS limitations. AutoCAD creates the slide from what is currently displayed on-screen.

Hints

If you want to edit the drawing, do so before using MSLIDE because slide files cannot be edited.

The SLIDELIB program, an AutoCAD utility, can be used to combine slide files into slide libraries.

Error *Messages*	Invalid file name *Invalid* The file name you entered does not conform to AutoCAD file naming conventions, or else it exceeds the number of characters allowed by your operating system. Check your spelling and the number of characters you entered, and try again.

MULTIPLE   *Repeats another command until canceled.*

Syntax	Command: **MULTIPLE**
Template Coordinates	U 16
Description	This command is used in concert with another command and keeps repeating the other command until Ctrl-C is executed. For example, if you are inserting several blocks and will be using INSERT often, type **MULTIPLE INSERT** at the Command: prompt; AutoCAD will keep repeating INSERT until you cancel.
Hints	You can type any AutoCAD command following the MULTIPLE command. MULTIPLE only repeats the command, not any associated parameters. For each repetition of the command, you must respond to the prompts. MULTIPLE saves one keystroke each time you repeat a command because you do not have to press Enter.
Error Messages	Error messages vary, depending on the command you are repeating. For help interpreting these messages, refer to the Error Messages section in this Command Reference for the command you are repeating. Unknown command. Type ? for list of commands. The command you entered is invalid. Check your spelling and retype it, or enter **?** to see a list of valid commands.

NEWTEXT   *Allows you to change the text in an existing dimension.*

Syntax	Dim: **NEWTEXT** Enter new dimension text: Select objects:
Template Coordinates	None

Description   This dimensioning subcommand is available only after you enter DIM or DIM1.

This subcommand allows you to change the text within a dimensioning string. It substitutes new dimension text for dimension entities you select.

Hints   If you use angle brackets (<>) as a prefix or suffix when you enter the new text, the dimension measurement will be drawn in the dimension string in place of the brackets.

Press Enter to restore NEWTEXT to the dimension measurement.

Generally, your text style should be horizontal when you are executing any of the DIM commands because AutoCAD writes dimension text horizontally unless you change dimension variables.

Error Messages   Unknown command. Type ? for list of commands. The command you entered is invalid. You may have entered NEWTEXT without first entering DIM or DIM1. Enter one of these commands first, then enter **NEWTEXT** at the Dim: prompt. Otherwise, check your spelling, and retype the command, or enter ? to see a list of valid commands.

Unknown command: ">____<". Type EXIT to return to COMMAND prompt. You typed the angle brackets in reverse order when entering dimension text.

If the alarm sounds, you entered too much text.

OFFSET   *Creates a parallel entity next to the original.*

Syntax
```
Command: OFFSET
Offset distance or Through <last>:
```

Template Coordinates   W 14

Description   If you type an Offset distance, all offsets will be that distance. The following set of prompts appears:

```
    Select object to offset:
    Side to offset:
```

You select the entity to offset and then specify a point on the side of that entity on which you want to place the offset.

If you selected Through, you will be prompted for the point through which the new entity will pass. The following prompts appear for each entity:

```
Select object to offset:
Through point:
```

AutoCAD looks for the entity to offset and the point through which the new entity will pass.

One problem arises in OFFSET when you try to offset complex curves such as ellipses and other polylines and arc generations. If you offset to the interior of the curve, AutoCAD, reaching a point at which it is not sure how to draw the next curve, improvises.

Possible Responses

Response	Meaning
number	Specify offset distance.
T	Specify point through which offset curve will pass.

Hint   You can specify only one entity each time you use the command.

Error Messages   `Entity not parallel with UCS.` The extrusion direction of the entity you select is not parallel to the Z axis of the current User Coordinate System. Select another object to offset, making sure its extrusion direction is parallel to the Z axis of the current UCS.

`Invalid through point.` You tried to offset a line that would draw a new line over the original. Select another through point.

`No parallel at that offset.` You tried to offset a circle or arc and specified an offset that would result in a negative radius. Specify an offset with a positive radius.

`Cannot offset that entity.` You tried to offset an entity other than a line, arc, circle, or two-dimensional polyline. Select a line, arc, circle, or two-dimensional polyline.

`Invalid 2D point.` You entered a non-numeric character, one coordinate, or more than two coordinates in response to the `Through Point:` prompt. Select a point on-screen, or enter two coordinates.

OOPS   *Brings back the last group of entities erased.*

Syntax   Command: **OOPS**

Template Coordinates   W 18 | OOPS |

Description   OOPS is one of several ways within AutoCAD to undo commands. OOPS is used to undo the effects of ERASE; it must be used immediately after you use ERASE.

Hints	You can restore only entities erased with the last ERASE command. If you need to restore something prior to the last ERASE command, use the UNDO command.
	OOPS also reverses the effects of BLOCK and WBLOCK commands.
Error Message	OOPS *Invalid* You entered the OOPS command before erasing anything during the current work session.

ORTHO   *Restricts user to horizontal or vertical movement of the cursor.*

Syntax	Command: **ORTHO** ON/OFF:
Template Coordinates	J 8 - K 8 [ORTHO]
Description	When it is on, ORTHO confines lines drawn with rubber-banding to the current snap grid's horizontal and vertical directions, so you can draw only right angles.
	Pressing Enter at the prompt toggles ORTHO on or off, changing the ORTHOMODE system variable.

Possible Responses	Response	Meaning
	ON	Turn on horizontal/vertical constraint.
	OFF	Turn off horizontal/vertical constraint.

Hints	ORTHO is useful when your drawing consists mainly of horizontal and vertical lines.
	You can use SETVAR or AutoLISP to change the ORTHOMODE system variable, and you can toggle ORTHO mode with F8—even in the middle of another command.

Error
Messages

Ambiguous response, please clarify... When prompted to enter the ORTHO setting, you entered the letter O. Since this could mean either On or Off, you need to spell out as much of the word as necessary to remove ambiguity.

Invalid option keyword. You entered a letter that does not correspond to a valid option keyword. Try again.

OSNAP   *Sets global Object SNAP modes.*

Syntax

Command: **OSNAP**
Object snap modes:

Template
Coordinates

X 10

Description

OSNAP modes can be used globally, as with the OSNAP command, or individually. If the mode is set globally, the mode will be invoked whenever AutoCAD looks for point information. To use the modes selectively, type the appropriate mode at the prompt for point information, and press Enter. You will be prompted for the entity with which you want to work.

NEArest (Template coordinates: T 18) locates a point visually nearest the crosshairs on the entity and snaps to that point.

ENDpoint (Template coordinates: T 14) is the closest endpoint of a line or arc or the closest defining point of a solid or three-dimensional face. You can snap to the extruded points of these entities.

MIDpoint (Template coordinates: T 17) snaps to the midpoint of lines, arcs, polyline segments, and the extruded sides of entities. It can be applied to solids and three-dimensional faces by snapping to the midpoint between the two nearest corners.

CENter (Template coordinates: T 13) snaps to the center of arcs and circles. When using this OSNAP mode, you must indicate the entity by digitizing the circumference. AutoCAD locates the center; you indicate the entity with which you want to work.

NODe (Template coordinates: T 19) locks onto a point entity.

QUAdrant (Template coordinates: T 21) locks onto the closest point on a circle or arc at 0, 90, 180, or 270 degrees. You can use this mode only with entities in the current UCS or entities whose extrusion direction is parallel to the Z axis of the current UCS.

INTersection (Template coordinates: T 16) locks onto an intersection only if it is a true intersection in three-dimensional space. For extruded entities, you can lock onto the intersection of the entity and the extrusion lines. If two entities intersect on a UCS and extrude in the same direction, AutoCAD can locate the intersection of the extruded edges. If there is a difference in the amount of extrusion, the shorter extrusion defines the intersection. Make sure both entities are in the aperture when you indicate the intersection.

INSert (Template coordinates: T 15) locks onto the insertion points of blocks, text, and shapes.

PERpendicular (Template coordinates: T 20) locks onto an existing entity in such a way that the new entity is perpendicular to the last point entered on the existing entity. Any extrusion must be parallel to the current UCS Z axis. This mode is used in reference to the last point entered.

TANgent (Template coordinates: T 22) locks to a point on an entity tangent to the last point entered. Any extrusion must be parallel to the current UCS Z axis.

NONe (Template coordinates: T 12) cancels any globally set OSNAP modes. Type **NONE** at the Object snap modes: prompt and press Enter.

Possible Responses

Response	Meaning
CEN	Center of arc or circle
END	Closest endpoint of arc or line
INS	Insertion point of text, block, or shape
INT	Intersection of arc, circle, or line
MID	Midpoint of arc or line
NEA	Point nearest crosshairs on entity
NOD	Node (point)
NON	None; cancel OSNAP mode
PER	Perpendicular to arc, circle, or line
QUA	Quadrant mode of arc or circle
QUI	Quick mode
TAN	Tangent to arc or circle

Hints

Object snap takes place when you answer a To point: prompt by picking a point close to an entity. With object snap, you can snap to a particular part of the entity or to a point having a specific spatial relationship to the entity.

When OSNAP is enabled, a target box will appear where the crosshairs intersect.

You can execute any OSNAP option by typing the first three letters of the option.

It may be easier to use OSNAP through the Tools pull-down menu. Each OSNAP option is listed, and you can select the one desired with your pointing device.

Error
Message

Invalid object snap modes. When prompted for object snap modes you typed an invalid response. Type one of the following: CEN, END, INS, INT, MID, NEA, NOD, NON, PER, QUA, QUI, TAN.

PAN

Allows you to move around in the drawing without changing the zoom factor.

Syntax

Command: **PAN**
Displacement:
Second point:

Template
Coordinates

Q 9

Description

PAN needs two points to make different parts of your drawing appear in the viewport. The first is a reference point; the second point indicates the direction and distance you want to pan.

At the Displacement: prompt, type a displacement in X,Y,Z fashion, or indicate a point. If you type a displacement, press Enter. If you indicate a point, type another point at the Second point: prompt to show the direction and displacement.

You can use PAN as an internal command within another AutoCAD command by preceding it with an apostrophe: 'PAN.

Hint

You can mimic the effects of PAN by using dynamic zoom with a constant-sized window. Rather than indicating the window each time you want to zoom, you can name and save a window as a named view with the VIEW command.

Error
Messages

** Requires a regen, cannot be transparent. You tried to use 'PAN within another AutoCAD command. Since the displacement and second points you entered require a regeneration, the PAN command was ignored.

Requires two points, or a displacement followed by RETURN. Your response to the Displacement: or Second Point: prompt was inappropriate. Either select a point on-screen, or enter two or three coordinates or a displacement.

PEDIT

(2-D or 3-D, polyline or nonpolyline entities)
Allows you to edit polyline entities and to connect nonpolyline entities into a polyline.

Syntax

Command: **PEDIT**
Select polyline:

If the entity you select is not a polyline, you see the next prompt:

Entity selected is not a polyline.
Do you want to turn it into one? <Y>:

A **Y** response turns the entity into a polyline. If the object you select is a polyline, you see the following prompt:

Close/Join/Width/Edit vertex/Fit curve/Spline curve/
Decurve/Undo/eXit <X>:

Template
Coordinates

W 19

Description

If the entity you select is not a polyline, you can turn it into one with a **Y** response to the Do you want to turn it into one? <Y>: prompt.

If the polyline is not closed, you can close it with the Close option. If the polyline is closed, the Close option becomes the Open option, and you have the option of opening the polyline. These two options toggle to offer you the choice of opening or closing.

Join attaches separate line and arc segments to one another, forming a polyline.

Width sets a uniform width for the entire polyline.

When you select the Fit curve option, AutoCAD fits a curve to the polyline. The curves are drawn to tangent points and pass through the vertices.

A Spline curve is different from a Fit curve. A spline is a best-fit curve to the polyline. This selection uses the vertices of the polyline as a frame to draw the spline. The more vertices there are, the more the curve will be pulled in that direction.

Decurve removes the fit curve or the spline from the polyline.

Undo will undo the last PEDIT operation you performed. You can use it to step to the beginning of the PEDIT editing session.

To keep changes you have made, you must use the eXit option to exit the PEDIT command.

Edit vertex allows you to edit individual segments by using the vertices. When you enter this selection, an X appears at the start of the polyline. The X indicates which segment you will be working with. When you select Edit vertex, AutoCAD displays the following prompt:

Next/Previous/Break/Insert/Move/Regen/Straighten/
Tangent/Width/eXit <N>:

Next moves the indicator to the next vertex.

Previous moves the indicator to the previous vertex.

Break removes a segment of the polyline or breaks the polyline into separate entities. You will see a new prompt:

Next/Previous/Go/eXit <N>:

Next and Previous move the indicator. The command will be executed for the segments you cross while at this prompt. Go executes the selection, and eXit leaves the selection without executing.

Insert inserts a new vertex between the current vertex and the next vertex. Move the cursor to the vertex directly before the new vertex, then select Insert.

Move moves the current vertex to the specified new location.

Regen acts like the normal REGEN. After you change a segment's width, use Regen to see your changes.

Straighten removes all vertices between two indicated vertices. You are prompted:

Next/Previous/Go/eXit <N>:

Tangent provides the polyline tangent information used in Fit curve. You can define the angle to which you want the fitted curves to be tangent. Move to the vertex, and enter the tangent angle; an indicator will appear on your screen.

Width allows you to change the width of individual segments. You must do a REGEN to see the change in the width. You will be prompted for both a new beginning width and a new ending width.

eXit returns you to the basic PEDIT prompt.

After you change the polyline, you can use other editing commands. You can COPY, MOVE, ERASE, ARRAY, MIRROR, ROTATE, and SCALE the polyline. If these commands are executed, the Spline retains its frame. If you BREAK, TRIM, or EXPLODE the polyline, the frame will be deleted. OFFSET creates a polyline fit to the Spline.

Possible Responses

Response	Meaning
C	Close open polyline.
D	Decurve polyline.
E	Edit vertex.
F	Fit curve to polyline (not in 3-D).
J	Join to polyline (not in 3-D).
O	Open polyline.
S	Use vertices as frame for spline curve.
U	Undo.
W	Set uniform width for polyline (not in 3-D).
X	Exit.

Options for vertex editing:

B	Set first vertex for break.
G	Go.
I	Insert new vertex after current vertex.
M	Move current vertex.
N	Make next vertex current.
P	Make previous vertex current.
R	Regenerate.
S	Set first vertex for straighten.
T	Set tangent direction (not in 3-D).
W	Set new width for following segment (not in 3-D).
X	Exit vertex editing; cancel break or straighten.

Hint

PEDIT toggles between Open and Close. When the polyline is open the prompt displays Close, and when it is closed the prompt displays Open.

Error Messages

Expects a point or Window/Last/Crossing/BOX When prompted to select a polyline, you entered an invalid character. Select a point on-screen, enter coordinates, or use the Window, Crossing, or Box methods of entity selection. You can also use the Last option to select the same entity you last selected.

Yes or No, please. When prompted to answer whether you want to turn an entity into a polyline, you typed a character other than *Y* or *N*. Type **Y** or **N**.

You cannot join a 3D Polygon Mesh.
0 segments added to polyline You tried to join a three-dimensional mesh with another entity. Join only line and arc segments.

Can't join to a closed polyline You tried to join an entity with a closed polyline. Join only line and arc segments.

Requires numeric distance or two points. Your response to one of the width prompts was invalid. Try again, providing either a numeric distance or picking two on-screen points that define the width.

Value must be positive. You entered a negative value in response to one of the width prompts. A segment cannot have a negative width. Enter a positive value.

Invalid option keyword. When asked to select an option, you did not give a response that corresponds with a valid option keyword. Select a response from the options shown in the prompt. Pressing Enter when a response is required displays this message.

Invalid 2D point. You entered a non-numeric character, one coordinate, or more than two coordinates in response to one of the location prompts. Select a point on-screen, or enter two coordinates.

Requires numeric angle or second point. You responded with a non-numeric response when prompted for the direction of tangent. Try again, providing a numeric value or a second point to define the tangent direction.

Command has been completely undone. You selected the Undo option when there was nothing to undo.

PEDIT

(Mesh or surfaces)
Allows you to edit three-dimensional polygon meshes.

Syntax   Command: **PEDIT**

Template   W 19
Coordinates

Description   You can use PEDIT to edit three-dimensional polygon meshes as well as two-dimensional and three-dimensional polygons. The command options function in the following ways with a three-dimensional polygon mesh:

`Decurve` restores the original mesh.

`Edit` vertex edits the mesh vertices individually.

`M` opens or closes the mesh in the M direction.

`N` opens or closes the mesh in the N direction.

`S` fits a smooth surface, using the SURFTYPE system variable.

Vertex Editing

`D` moves down in the M direction to the previous vertex.

`L` moves left in the N direction to the previous vertex.

`M` moves the indicated vertex.

`R` moves right in the N direction to the next vertex.

`RE` redisplays the mesh.

`U` moves up in the M direction to the next vertex.

Possible Responses

Response	Meaning
D	Desmooth—restore original.
E	Edit vertex.
M	Open or close mesh in M direction.
N	Open or close mesh in N direction.
S	Fit a smooth surface.
U	Undo.
X	Exit.

Options for vertex editing:

D	Move down to previous vertex in M direction.
L	Move left to previous vertex in N direction.
M	Reposition vertex.
N	Move to next vertex.
P	Move to previous vertex.
R	Move right to next vertex in N direction.
RE	Redisplay polygon.
U	Move up to next vertex in M direction.
X	Exit vertex editing.

Hint

Editing vertices when the M and N factors are small can be difficult. You may wish to adjust the ZOOM factor while editing.

Error Messages   Expects a point or Window/Last/Crossing/BOX When prompted to select a polyline, you entered an invalid character. Select a point on-screen, enter coordinates, or use the Window, Crossing, or Box methods of entity selection. You can also use the Last option to select the same entity you last selected.

Requires numeric distance or two points. Your response to one of the width prompts was invalid. Try again, providing either a numeric distance or picking two on-screen points that define the width.

Value must be positive. You entered a negative value in response to one of the width prompts. A segment cannot have a negative width. Enter a positive value.

Invalid option keyword. When asked to select an option, you did not give a response that corresponds with a valid option keyword. Select a response from the options shown in the prompt. Pressing Enter when a response is required displays this message.

Invalid 2D point. You entered a non-numeric character, one coordinate, or more than two coordinates in response to one of the location prompts. Select a point on-screen, or enter two coordinates.

Requires numeric angle or second point. You responded with a non-numeric response when prompted for the direction of tangent. Try again, providing a numeric value or a second point to define the tangent direction.

Command has been completely undone. You selected the Undo option when there was nothing to undo.

PLAN

Provides a plan view of the drawing relative to the current UCS, a specified UCS, or the World Coordinate System.

Syntax   Command: **PLAN**
<Current UCS>/Ucs/World:

Template Coordinates   J 4 - K 6

Description   The <Current UCS> option provides the plan view with respect to the current User Coordinate System (UCS).

With the UCS option, AutoCAD prompts you for the name of the previously saved UCS for which you want a plan view. You can enter a question mark (?) for a list of currently defined UCSs.

World regenerates the drawing to a plan view of the World Coordinates.

Possible	*Response*	*Meaning*
Responses	C	Display plan view of current UCS.
	U	Display plan view of specified UCS.
	W	Display plan view of World Coordinate System.

Hints   PLAN automatically resets the viewport to 0,0,1.

PLAN turns off perspective and clipping but does not change the current UCS. Consequently, when you enter or display coordinates after the PLAN command, they relate to the current UCS rather than to the PLAN viewport.

If you want the plan view displayed regardless of the viewport you select, set the UCSFOLLOW system variable to one.

Error   Invalid option keyword. When asked to select an option, you gave a
Messages   response that does not correspond to a valid option keyword. Press Enter to accept the default, or type **C**, **U**, or **W**.

Regenerating drawing. AutoCAD is regenerating your drawing to produce the plan view you requested.

PLINE   *Draws straight or curved polylines.*

Syntax
```
Command: PLINE
From point:
Current line-width is ___
Arc/Close/Halfwidth/Length/Undo/Width/<Endpoint of line>:
```

Template   K 10
Coordinates

Description   The PLINE command needs a starting point for the segments. Indicate a starting point at the From point: prompt.

The default drawing segment is a line. You can indicate the <Endpoint of line>:, or select one of the other options.

The Arc option provides a different prompt:

```
Angle/CEnter/CLose/Direction/Halfwidth/Line/Radius
/Second pt/Undo/Width/<Endpoint of arc>:
```

You can draw arc segments in any of several ways: Angle, CEnter, Direction, Radius, and Second pt options all work as they would for the ARC command.

Close closes the current polyline.

Halfwidth allows you to specify half the width of a wide polyline. You are prompted:

> Starting half-width <current>:
> Ending half-width <current>:

Length lets you enter the length of the segment. AutoCAD draws the segment at the same angle as the last segment.

Undo is used to undo the last part of the PLINE command. Undo in PLINE reacts the same as Undo in the LINE command.

Width lets you assign widths to polyline segments.

Endpoint is the default. AutoCAD looks for the end of the line segment.

	Response	Meaning
Possible Responses	H	Set new half-width.
	U	Undo last PLINE command.
	W	Set new line width.
	Enter	Exit.

Options for line mode:

A	Change to arc mode.
C	Close with straight segment.
L	Enter previous segment length.

Options for arc mode:

A	Angle
CE	Center point
CL	Close with arc segment
D	Starting direction
L	Length of chord; switch to line mode R Radius
S	Second point of three-point arc

Hints   You can draw lines and arcs with PLINE much the same as with the LINE and ARC commands, with three important differences:

❑ All the prompts display each time you enter a new polyline vertex.

❑ Additional prompts, like Halfwidth and Width, control segment width.

❑ You can go back and forth between drawing straight and curved segments.

Error
Messages

2D point or option keyword required. Type one of the choices indicated in the prompt, or select a two-dimensional point as the endpoint of a line or arc.

Cannot close until two or more segments drawn. You tried to close an entity with fewer than two segments. Draw another segment, and try again.

Invalid point. You responded inappropriately to the From Point: prompt. Select a point on-screen, or enter two or three coordinates.

Requires numeric distance or second point. When prompted to enter the halfwidth, length, or width, your response was invalid. Enter either a numeric distance representing the halfwidth, length, or width; select on-screen points; or enter coordinates.

All segments already undone. You requested Undo when there were no segments to undo.

PLOT

Plots a drawing on a pen plotter.

Syntax

Command: **PLOT**
What to plot -- Display, Extents, Limits, View, or Window <D>:

Template
Coordinates

W 24

Description

Display plots the current display—that part of the drawing displayed on-screen when the command is executed.

Extents plots the extents of the drawing. Before you plot extents, it is a good idea to ZOOM extents. If any entities lie beyond the drawing limits, they are included in the extents.

Limits selects the limits you set up for your drawing. If you are using a title block, use this selection.

View plots a defined view. Use this for preliminary drawings in large projects.

Window plots an area that you window. You are prompted for two corners of the window.

After you specify what you want plotted, you are prompted with the parameter values (similar to the following) established when you last configured AutoCAD:

```
Plot will NOT be written to a selected file.
Sizes are in Inches
Plot origin is at (0.00,0.00)
Plotting area is xx wide by yy high (MAX size)
Plot is NOT rotated 90 degrees
Pen width is 0.010
Area fill will be adjusted for pen width
Hidden lines will NOT be removed
Plot will be scaled to fit available area
Do you want to change anything? <N>
```

Values in these prompts vary depending on how your AutoCAD is configured. To accept the values, press Enter at the prompt. To alter them, type **Y**, and press Enter. AutoCAD will prompt for changes to the parameter values.

The `Do you want to change anything? <N>` prompt is where you set the speed of your plotting, pen numbers for layers, and linetypes. Pen numbers determine the colors of the entities. If you want to change any of the pen settings, type **Y** at the prompt. You are prompted for the pen number, linetype, and pen speed for entity color 1. You can respond to these prompts in five ways:

❏ Change the value.

❏ Press Enter to retain the current value.

❏ Type **Cn** where *n* is the pen number to which you want to change.

❏ Type **S** to show the updated table.

❏ Type **X** to resume the PLOT prompts.

Entity Color	Pen No.	Line-type	Pen Speed
1 (red)	1	0	38
2 (yellow)	2	0	38
3 (green)	3	0	38
4 (cyan)	4	0	38
5 (blue)	5	0	38
6 (magenta)	6	0	38
7 (white)	7	0	38
8	8	0	38
9	1	0	38
10	1	0	38
11	1	0	38
12	1	0	38
13	1	0	38
14	1	0	38
15	1	0	38
16	1	0	38

After you enter any changes for the pens, AutoCAD prompts you for basic plotting specifications.

At the Write the plot to a file? <current> prompt, you can send plots to a file instead of to the plotter. This can save time while you are working; plotting can be done later. You can work in inches or millimeters. The Size units (Inches or Millimeters) <current>: prompt lets you change the size units.

Regarding the Plot origin in units <default X,Y>: prompt, with pen plotters the origin is usually the lower left corner of the paper. This is the *home* position for the pen. For printer plotters, home is the upper left corner. The plot origin corresponds to the lower left corner of the drawing. AutoCAD allows you to move the plot origin. If you are working with D-size paper, you can plot four A-size drawings on the same paper by moving the plot origin.

With the Enter the Size or Width,Height (in units) <default>: prompt, AutoCAD lets you determine the plotting area with which you want to work. The maximum size for plotting depends on the physical size of your plotter. Plotting size is measured from the plot origin; you can create a margin around the drawing by setting a new plot origin.

The Rotate 2D plots 90 degrees clockwise? <N> prompt allows you to rotate the plot 90 degrees. This means the point that would have been in the lower left corner will be in the upper left corner, and all other corners will be rotated accordingly.

If you are using wide polylines and solids, you may want to adjust the pen width with the Pen width <default>: prompt. This affects the amount of work necessary to fill in these areas.

The Adjust area fill boundaries for pen width? <N> prompt adjusts the plotting of wide polylines and solids by half a pen width. This adjustment provides a more accurate plot. If you are plotting printed circuit artwork, for example, you will want to change the setting by typing **Y**. If you do not need the additional accuracy, respond **N**.

When you are plotting three-dimensional objects, you can remove the hidden lines by entering **Y** at the Remove hidden lines? <N> prompt. (You cannot do this for two-dimensional plots.)

With the Specify scale by entering: prompt, you can set the scale for the plot. This scale is independent of the drawing scale. You can scale either the drawing or the plot. You are prompted:

```
Specify scale by entering:
Plotted Inches=Drawing Units or Fit or ? <F>:
```

If you are working with millimeters, the prompt says Plotted Millimeters instead of Plotted Inches.

Hints

You can plot from the Main Menu instead of using the PLOT command from within a drawing, but you must specify the name of the drawing to plot.

Ctrl-C aborts the plot at any time, plotting only the contents remaining in the data buffer.

Plan ahead for your title block and border margins when establishing your plotting size, and be sure to leave room for the plotter to grasp the edges of your paper.

Error Messages

Invalid You responded inappropriately when prompted for what to plot. Type **D**, **E**, **L**, **V**, or **W**, or press Enter to accept the default.

View___ not found
Invalid You requested a plot of a nonexistent view. Retype the view name, or create a view before trying to plot.

Invalid window specification. You responded inappropriately to one of the corner prompts for a Window plot. Select a point on-screen, or enter two or three coordinates.

POINT

Inserts point entities into your drawing.

Syntax

Command: **POINT**
Point:

Template Coordinates

P 10

Description

Any method of indicating point locations is acceptable: OSNAP modes, absolute coordinates, or relative coordinates. The point will be drawn using the current color on the current layer. How the point appears is determined by system variables you can change with the SETVAR command.

Hints

To change the size of points, change the value of the PDSIZE system variable.

To specify how points should be displayed, change the PDMODE system variable.

Error Message

Invalid point. You responded inappropriately to the Point: prompt. Select a point on-screen, enter two or three coordinates, or use OSNAP modes.

POLYGON   *Draws polygons.*

Syntax

```
Command: POLYGON
Number of sides:
Edge/<Center of polygon>:
```

Template Coordinates

O 10

Description

After specifying the number of sides, type **E** if you want to specify the edge, or else select the center point for the polygon. If you select a center point you are prompted:

```
Inscribed in circle/Circumscribed about circle (I/C):
Radius of circle:
```

```
Enter I or C and then the radius of the circle.
```

With the Edge option, you are indicating one side of the polygon, not the center point and radius. AutoCAD prompts you:

```
First endpoint of edge:
Second endpoint of edge:
```

AutoCAD is looking for two points to define one side of the polygon.

Possible Responses

Response	Meaning
E	Specify edge of polygon.
C	Circumscribe (if specifying center point).
I	Inscribe (if specifying center point).

Hints

Use POLYGON to help you draw regular polygons.

For both the Circumscribe and Inscribe methods of drawing polygons, you can drag the circle radius. For the Edge method, you can drag the second endpoint.

Error Messages

Requires an integer value. When prompted for the number of sides for a polygon, you entered a value that is not a whole number, is out of bounds, or is non-numeric. Enter a whole number between 3 and 1024.

Value must be positive and nonzero. When prompted for the number of sides for a polygon, you entered zero or a negative number. Type a positive integer between 3 and 1024.

Value must be between 3 and 1024. When prompted for the number of sides for a polygon, you entered a value outside this range. Type a positive integer between 3 and 1024.

2D point or option keyword required. In response to the Edge/<Center of polygon>: prompt, you typed something other than the choices allowed. Type **E**, or specify a two-dimensional point for the center of the polygon.

Invalid 2D point. When prompted for one of the endpoints of the edge, you gave an inappropriate response. Select a point on-screen, or enter two coordinates.

Invalid option keyword. When asked to select an option, your response did not correspond with a valid option keyword. Select a response from the options shown in the prompt. Pressing Enter when a response is required will also display this message.

PRPLOT — *Sends a plot to a printer that accepts graphics information.*

Syntax	Command: **PRPLOT** What to plot -- Display, Extents, Limits, View or Window <D>:
Template Coordinates	W 25
Description	See the options for the PLOT command.
Hint	Use your printer instead of your plotter for quick, economical, preliminary plots.
Error Messages	*Invalid* You responded inappropriately when prompted for what to plot. Type **D**, **E**, **L**, **V**, or **W**; or press Enter to accept the default. View___ not found *Invalid* You requested a plot of a nonexistent view. Retype the view name, or create a view before trying to plot. Invalid window specification. You responded inappropriately to one of the corner prompts for a Window plot. Select a point on-screen, or enter two or three coordinates.

PURGE

Cleans up the drawing database by removing unused entities.

Syntax

Command: **PURGE**
Purge unused Blocks/LAyers/LTypes/SHapes/STyles/All:

Template Coordinates

None

Description

Unused Blocks, LAyers, LTypes, SHapes, and STyles can be purged. All searches the database for all unused, named objects and presents them for purging.

You must use this command before making any changes to the database (including adding entities to or removing them from the database).

Certain parameters—layer 0, the continuous linetype, and the standard text style—are basic to the drawing and cannot be purged.

Possible Responses

Response	Meaning
A	Purge all unused, named objects.
B	Purge unused blocks.
LA	Purge unused layers.
LT	Purge unused linetypes.
SH	Purge unused shapes.
ST	Purge unused text styles.

Hints

All entities you create while working on a drawing use space in your drawing database and clutter your storage list of names even if you never use them in your drawing. Use PURGE to weed out unnecessary entities.

It is a good idea to use PURGE before making backup diskettes.

Error Messages

The PURGE command cannot be used now.
Invalid You issued the PURGE command when there were no unused blocks, layers, linetypes, shapes, or styles in your drawing. PURGE is unnecessary when there are no unused entities.

Invalid option keyword. When asked to select an option, you gave a response that did not correspond with a valid option keyword. Select a response from the options shown in the prompt. Pressing Enter when there is no default and a response is required displays this message.

QTEXT	*Replaces each text string with a box the same size as the text.*

Syntax

Command: **QTEXT**
ON/OFF <current>:

Template
Coordinates

Y 8   QTEXT

Description   QTEXT saves time when you are working with large drawings that contain a great deal of text. When QTEXT replaces the text with a box, the text is still in the database but does not regenerate on-screen.

Possible
Responses

Response	Meaning
ON	Turn on quick-text mode.
OFF	Turn off quick-text mode.

Hints   QTEXT does not take effect until the next regeneration of the screen.

You can also control quick-text mode by using the SETVAR command or AutoLISP to change the QTEXTMODE system variable.

Error
Messages

Ambiguous response, please clarify... When prompted to enter the QTEXT setting, you typed the letter O. Since this could mean either On or Off, you need to spell out as much of the word as necessary to remove ambiguity, or press Enter to accept the default.

Invalid option keyword. When prompted to enter the QTEXT setting, your response was invalid. Try again.

QUIT	*Ends the editing session and returns to the Main Menu without saving changes to the drawing.*

Syntax

Command: **QUIT**
Really want to discard all changes to drawing?

Template
Coordinates

U 25   QUIT

Description   This is one of two commands you can use to end a session in the Drawing Editor. (The other command is END.)

Use QUIT if you do not want to save changes to your drawing or if you have already used the SAVE command to do so.

If you respond **Y** when prompted whether you want to discard drawing changes, AutoCAD returns to the Main Menu with no changes saved to your drawing.

If you type **N** or an invalid response to this prompt, the QUIT command is cancelled and the AutoCAD Command: prompt redisplays.

Possible Responses

Response	Meaning
Y	Discards all changes made during current work session.
N	Cancels QUIT command.

Hint

Any .BAK file associated with the drawing is preserved unchanged along with the drawing.

Error Messages

None

RADIUS
Provides radius dimensions for circles and arcs.

Syntax

```
Dim: RADIUS
Select arc or circle:
Dimension text <measured radius>:
Text does not fit. Enter leader length for text:
```

Template Coordinates

Y 2

Description

This dimensioning subcommand is available only after you enter DIM or DIM1.

This option draws a radius dimension from the center of an arc or circle to the point you select on the perimeter. If you need to modify the dimension, you can STRETCH, CHANGE, or EXPLODE it.

If the text you enter does not fit within the arc or circle you selected, you will be prompted for the length of a leader line from the entity to the text. You can use a positive number or a negative number for leader length. If the length is positive, the leader is drawn to the right of the point where you selected the entity; if negative, to the left.

Hint	You can enter your own text or accept the default. Default text begins with an *R*, indicating a radius dimension.
Error Messages	Invalid point. When prompted to select an arc or circle, you responded inappropriately. Select an arc or circle.
	Object selected is not a circle or arc *Invalid* You selected an entity other than an arc or circle. Select an arc or circle.
	Invalid You entered an invalid response for the leader length for text. Try again.

REDEFINE

Allows you to reset to its original definition a standard AutoCAD command that has been defined with a LISP routine.

Syntax	Command: **REDEFINE** Command name:
Template Coordinates	None
Description	Enter the name of the command that has been defined to a LISP routine or has previously been the subject of the UNDEFINE command. The command will be reset to its original definition.
Hint	If you used UNDEFINE to make an AutoCAD command invisible, you can make it visible again with REDEFINE.
Error Message	Unknown command name. You tried to redefine an unknown command. Check your spelling, and try again.

REDO

Reverses an UNDO command.

Syntax	Command: **REDO**
Template Coordinates	U 15

Description   This command must be used immediately after the **U** or **UNDO** command; otherwise, it will not work.

This command is especially helpful when you step back through your work five commands at a time. When you overshoot the commands you want to undo, use the REDO command; then step back one command at a time.

Hints   When you undo more than you planned, you can continue to use REDO repetitively until you enter another command. At this point the commands previously undone are lost.

When you want to show someone else the sequence of steps you went through, you can use UNDO to undo a certain number of steps and then REDO them one at a time.

Error Message   Previous command did not undo things You entered the REDO command without first entering the UNDO command. Undo a command, and then try again.

REDRAW   *Redraws entities on the screen.*

Syntax   Command: **REDRAW**

or

Dim: **REDRAW**

Template Coordinates   J 11 - R 11, W 4

Description   REDRAW causes the display within the current viewport to be regenerated, resulting in a cleaner display. It is a good idea to use this command periodically; it takes less time than a REGEN command.

You can use REDRAW as an internal command within another AutoCAD command by preceding it with an apostrophe: **'REDRAW**.

This command can be used from the normal AutoCAD prompt or within the dimensioning subsystem. It functions the same way in both contexts.

Hint   REDRAW reduces screen clutter by erasing any point selection blips.

Error Messages   None

REDRAWALL *Redraws all the viewports at one time.*

Syntax   Command: **REDRAWALL**

Template   None
Coordinates

Description   REDRAWALL is similar to REDRAW, except it affects all viewports.

                      You can use REDRAWALL as an internal command within another AutoCAD
                      command by preceding it with an apostrophe: **'REDRAWALL**.

Hint   In contrast to the REDRAW command, REDRAWALL does not work as a DIM
                      subcommand. However, you can use REDRAWALL as a transparent command
                      at the Dim: prompt ty typing **'REDRAWALL**.

Error   None
Messages

REGEN *Regenerates the drawing and redraws the current viewport.*

Syntax   Command: **REGEN**

Template   None
Coordinates

Description   REGEN causes AutoCAD to search through the drawing database and
                      recalculate the positions of all entities in the drawing. REGEN can take a
                      long time to execute. The larger your drawing, the more time REGEN takes.

Hints   To abort REGEN, press Ctrl-C.

                      When you change system variables, you may want to use REGEN to ensure
                      that the entire drawing is current.

                      REGEN affects only the current viewport.

Error   None
Messages

REGENALL *Regenerates all viewports.*

Syntax	Command: **REGENALL**
Template Coordinates	None
Description	REGENALL is similar to the REGEN command, except it affects all viewports.
Hint	To abort REGENALL, press Ctrl-C.
Error Messages	None

REGENAUTO *Limits automatic regeneration by issuing a prompt.*

Syntax

```
Command: REGENAUTO
ON/OFF <current>:
```

Template Coordinates None

Description On enables automatic regeneration. AutoCAD proceeds without prompting for REGEN. Off disables automatic regeneration. When a command would ordinarily regenerate the drawing, AutoCAD asks whether regeneration should occur by issuing the following prompt:

```
About to regen-proceed? <Y>
```

REGENAUTO resets the REGENMODE system variable.

Possible Responses

Response	Meaning
ON	Enables automatic regeneration
OFF	Disables automatic regeneration

Hint The REGEN command always overrides REGENAUTO, forcing a regeneration even when REGENAUTO is turned off.

Error ***Messages***	Ambiguous response, please clarify... When prompted to enter the REGENAUTO setting, you typed the letter *O*. Since this could mean either On or Off, spell out as much of the word as necessary to remove ambiguity, or press Enter to accept the default.

Invalid option keyword. When prompted to enter the REGENAUTO setting, you gave an invalid response. Try again.

Yes or No, please. When prompted to answer whether you want the regeneration to proceed, you typed something other than *Y* or *N*. Type **Y** or **N**.

RENAME   *Renames entities.*

Syntax	Command: **RENAME** Block/LAyer/LType/Style/Ucs/VIew/VPort: Old (object) name: New (object) name:
Template ***Coordinates***	None
Description	This command lets you rename several elements of an AutoCAD drawing. You can rename blocks, layers, linetypes, text styles, coordinate systems, views, and viewports.

When prompted, enter the type of entity you want to rename. Then enter the current name at the Old (object) name: prompt and the new name at the New (object) name: prompt.

Possible ***Responses***

Response	Meaning
B	Rename block.
LA	Rename layer.
LT	Rename linetype.
S	Rename text style.
U	Rename UCS.
VI	Rename view.
VP	Rename viewport.

Hints	You can use up to 31 characters in a name, including letters, digits, the dollar sign ($), the hyphen (-), and the underscore (__).

If you type a name in lowercase characters AutoCAD will automatically convert it to uppercase.

Three things cannot be renamed: CONTINUOUS linetype, layer 0, and shape entities.

Error Messages

```
Old (object) name ___ not found.
```

Invalid The object name you entered is invalid. Valid names may contain up to 31 characters including letters, digits, the dollar sign ($), the hyphen (-), and the underscore (__). To see a list of names for blocks, layers, or linetypes, issue the BLOCK, LAYER, or LINETYPE command and then enter a question mark (?).

RESUME   *Continues an interrupted script file.*

Syntax

```
Command: RESUME
```

Template Coordinates

None

Description

You can use RESUME as an internal command within another AutoCAD command by preceding it with an apostrophe: 'RESUME.

Hints

To interrupt a script of AutoCAD commands, press Ctrl-C or Backspace. To resume running the script, use RESUME (or 'RESUME if you interrupted the script in the middle of a command).

RESUME also works to resume running a script file that was stopped when an error was encountered.

Error Messages

None

REVSURF   *Generates a surface of revolution by rotating an outline around an axis.*

Syntax

```
Command: REVSURF
Select path curve:
Select axis of revolution:
Start angle <0>:
Included angle (+=ccw, -=cw) <Full circle>:
```

Template Coordinates	N 5	

Description   REVSURF stands for revolution surface. This command creates a surface by revolving a path curve around an axis, allowing you to select the path curve and the axis of revolution. The path curve can be a line, arc, circle, two-dimensional polyline, or three-dimensional polyline. After specifying the path and axis, you indicate the angle to which you want the surface rotated. If the angle is positive, the surface will be created counterclockwise. If the angle is negative, the surface will be generated clockwise.

Surfaces are drawn as polygon meshes, which always have N and M directions. The N direction of the mesh is determined by the path curve, and the M direction by the axis of revolution.

`Select path curve:` prompts for the outline of the object you are drawing, which can be a line, arc, circle, two-dimensional polyline, or three-dimensional polyline. This is the N direction of the resulting mesh.

`Select axis of revolution:` prompts for the axis around which the path curve is revolved. This axis, which can be a line or an open polyline, is the M direction of the resulting mesh.

`Start angle <0>:` allows you to begin the surface at an offset from the defined path curve.

`Included angle (+=ccw, -=cw) <full circle>:` specifies how far the entities are rotated around the axis.

Hint   The size of the mesh representing a surface is determined by the system variables SURFTAB1 and SURFTAB2. Large numbers for these variables result in small mesh cells and more processing time.

Error Messages   `Entity not usable as a rotation axis.` The entity you selected for the rotation axis is invalid. Select a line or an open polyline.

`Entity not usable to define surface of revolution.` Your response to the `Select path curve:` prompt was invalid. Select a line, arc, circle, two-dimensional polyline, or three-dimensional polyline to determine the N direction of the mesh.

`Invalid point.` Select a point, or enter two or three coordinates.

`Requires numeric angle or two points.` Your response to one of the angle prompts was invalid. Enter a numeric angle, two points, or press Enter to accept the default.

ROTATE   *Rotates the entities in your drawing.*

Syntax

```
Command: ROTATE
Select objects:
Base point:
<Rotation angle>/Reference:
```

Template Coordinates   W 13

Description   Select objects: prompts for the point around which the entities will rotate.

Base point: prompts for the base point.

<Rotation angle> prompts for the rotation angle.

Reference: allows you to reference an entity in the drawing as the current angle and then tell AutoCAD the new rotation. To do this, indicate the ends of the source entity, using OSNAP modes if necessary. Then type the angle to which you want the entities rotated.

Possible Response

Response	Meaning
R	Rotate to referenced angle.

Hints   ROTATE lets you turn an entity at a precise angle rather than guessing how much to rotate it.

Negative angles are rotated counterclockwise; positive angles, clockwise.

Error Messages   Invalid point. Your response to the Base point: prompt was invalid. Select a point on-screen, or enter two or three coordinates.

Requires numeric angle second point or option keyword. Your response to the <Rotation angle>/Reference: prompt was invalid. Specify the angle, or type **R**.

Requires numeric angle or two points. When prompted for the reference angle, you gave an invalid response. Enter a numeric angle or two points that define the angle, or press Enter to accept the default.

ROTATED   *Sets a rotation angle for the dimension line.*

Syntax
```
Dim: ROTATED
Dimension line angle <0>:
First extension line origin or RETURN to select:
Second extension line origin:
Dimension line location:
Dimension text <1.19>:
```

Template Coordinates   Y 5

Description   This dimensioning subcommand is available only after you enter DIM or DIM1. It draws a dimension line rotated to an angle you specify. You can indicate the angle for the dimension line by specifying it explicitly or by dragging the entity.

If the part you are dimensioning is not horizontal or vertical, and you cannot align the dimension, use the ROTATED linear dimension.

Hints   This is the only linear dimensioning subcommand that prompts you for an angle.

Using the ROTATED subcommand with an angle of zero is equivalent to the HORIZONTAL subcommand; both draw a horizontal dimensioning line.

Error Messages   `Unknown command. Type ? for list of commands.` You entered the ROTATED command without first entering DIM or DIM1. Enter a DIM command and then the ROTATED command.

`Invalid point.` Your response to one of the extension line origin prompts or the dimension line prompt was invalid. Select a point on-screen, or enter coordinates.

`*Invalid*` When prompted for a dimension line angle, you responded inappropriately. Try again, providing either a numeric value or a second point that defines the angle.

`*Invalid*` When prompted for the first extension line origin, you entered an invalid response. Select a point on-screen, or enter two or three coordinates.

`*Invalid*`
`dimension line location:` When prompted for the dimension line location, you entered an invalid response. Select a point on-screen, or enter two coordinates.

RSCRIPT · *Reruns a script file.*

Syntax	Command: **RSCRIPT**
Template Coordinates	None
Description	This command is typically used within script files to rerun the script.
Hint	If the last command in a script is RSCRIPT, it will loop the script to start over.
Error Message	*Invalid* You entered the RSCRIPT command when there were no script files to rerun.

RULESURF · *Creates a ruled surface between two curves, lines, arcs, circles, or polylines, or between any one of these and a single point.*

Syntax	Command: **RULESURF** Select first defining curve: Select second defining curve:
Template Coordinates	N 4
Description	If one of the boundaries is closed, the other must be closed also. AutoCAD starts the surface from the endpoint of the entity nearest the point used to select the entity. With circles, the start is zero degrees; with polygons, the start is the first vertex. The word *curve* in the two defining curve prompts may be misleading because you can also select defining lines or polylines and a defining point in addition to arcs and circles. RULESURF is similar to REVSURF, but since it does not produce a surface of revolution, you need to set only one system variable, SURFTAB1.
Hint	You may inadvertently create twisted meshes with closed entities if you do not pick the nearest endpoints on the entities you want to connect with meshing, or if your zero points are not aligned when you try to connect two circles.

Error
Messages
Invalid point. In response to one of the curve prompts you selected an invalid point. Select another point, or select a line, arc, circle, or polyline.

Two points don't define a surface. You selected points for both defining curves. Select no more than one point and another entity—a line, arc, circle, or polyline.

That's the same entity you picked last time. You selected the same invalid entity twice. Select a line, arc, circle, polyline, or point.

SAVE

Saves the changes you made to the drawing without returning to the Main Menu.

Syntax
Command: **SAVE**
File name <current>:

Template
Coordinates
T 24 - T 25

```
SAVE
```

Description
To increase execution speed, AutoCAD does as much work in the computer's Random Access Memory (RAM) as possible. If your power fails, or the computer is turned off, changes saved only in RAM are lost. SAVE is used to commit to disk all changes to a drawing made since the last time you saved.

SAVE works like END except that it leaves the Drawing Editor on the screen, so you can continue editing.

Hint
It is a good idea to save your work every 10 to 20 minutes, depending on how much time you can afford to spend reconstructing a drawing if you lose it for some reason.

Error
Messages
A drawing with this name already exists.
Do you want to replace it? <N> When saving a file, you specified a different output file name and a drawing with a preexisting file name. Consider your naming choice again, and enter **Y** only if you want the current drawing to replace the one whose name you specified; otherwise, type **N**, and save the file under another name.

Invalid file name
Invalid The file name you entered does not conform to AutoCAD file naming conventions, or else it exceeds the number of characters allowed by your operating system. Check your spelling and the number of characters you entered, and try again.

SCALE   *Scales what you have drawn.*

Syntax

```
Command: SCALE
Select objects:
Base point:
<Scale factor>/Reference:
```

Template Coordinates   W 12

Description   If you want the finished drawing to be at a particular scale, you can draw at full scale and then use the SCALE command to scale your drawing up or down. You need a base point, and you can indicate the scale factor, or reference part of the object.

At the `Select objects:` prompt, select the entities you want scaled.

`Base point:` is the point from which AutoCAD will scale the entities. If the base point is inside or on the object, the entity changes size at its present location. If the base point is outside the object, the object moves from its original location in accordance to the scale factor.

`<Scale factor>` is looking for a relative scale factor. All selected entities are multiplied by this factor. A factor of less than one shrinks the entities, whereas a factor greater than one increases the size of the entities.

`Reference:` allows you to reference the length of an entity to indicate the new length. All other entities indicated will change size according to the scale generated by the reference. When you select this option, you will see the following prompts:

```
Reference Length <1>:
New Length:
```

Possible Response

Response	Meaning
R	Scale to referenced length.

Hint   SCALE lets you change the size of individual entities already in your drawing. It also lets you change the size of the entire drawing.

Error Messages   `Requires numeric distance, second point, or option keyword.` When prompted to enter the scale factor or select the reference option, you entered a non-numeric value other than the R option keyword (for Reference). Enter a scale factor, or type **R** to select the reference option.

Invalid point. Your response to the Base point: prompt is invalid. Select a point on-screen, or enter two or three coordinates.

Value must be positive and nonzero. When prompted for the reference length or new length, you entered zero or a negative number. Enter a positive number.

Requires numeric distance or second point. When prompted for the reference length or new length, you entered something other than a numeric distance or second point. Enter a number, or select two points to indicate the length.

SCRIPT
Runs script files inside the Drawing Editor.

Syntax
Command: **SCRIPT**
Script file <default>:

Hints
Script files can be created containing commands, input, and responses. These scripts can be run subsequently using the SCRIPT command.

Script files, recognizable by their .SCR extensions, are often useful for demonstrations and presentations. Use of DELAY is often needed so that viewers have time to observe the sequence of commands, input, and responses.

Error
Messages
Can't open file
Invalid You entered a script file name for which no script file exists. Check your file name, and try again. If you have not yet created a script file, do so before using this command.

Invalid file name
Invalid The file name you entered does not conform to AutoCAD file-naming conventions or exceeds the number of characters allowed by your operating system. Check your spelling and the number of characters you entered, and try again.

SELECT
Creates a selection set for use in subsequent commands.

Syntax
Command: **SELECT**
Select objects:
Select objects:

Template Coordinates	None
Description	SELECT presents an alternate way of creating a selection set that can be used by AutoCAD commands. This command is not used too often because all commands that need selection sets allow you to build those sets when you use the command.
	If you use SELECT to build a selection set, you can subsequently use this predefined selection set with another command by entering **P** when prompted to select objects.
Hint	It is generally safer to build your selection set as you are executing an AutoCAD command. This is because SELECT allows you to add any entity to the selection set; even those that are not legal for the command with which you subsequently use the selection set.
Error Messages	None

SETVAR *Accesses system variables.*

Syntax	Command: SETVAR Variable name or ? <current>:
Template Coordinates	None
Description	SETVAR lets you read the values of system variables and change most of them. In response to the Variable name or ? <current>: prompt, enter the name of the variable you want to view or change. Then enter the new value (if any).
	You can use SETVAR as an internal command within another AutoCAD command by preceding it with an apostrophe: 'SETVAR.
Hints	In response to the Variable name or ? <current>: prompt, you can type ? to list variable names available.
	Many AutoCAD commands set system variables automatically.
Error Messages	(read only) You tried to use SETVAR on a read-only system variable. This message indicates that the value of this variable cannot be changed with the SETVAR command.

Unknown variable name: Type SETVAR? for a list of variables. You entered an invalid variable name. Check your spelling, and retype your entry, or type ? to see the list of variables.

SH   *Allows a partial shell to the operating system.*

Syntax	Command: **SH** DOS Command: Command:
Template *Coordinates*	None
Description	The SH command allows you to execute a single command at the system level and then returns you to AutoCAD, displaying the AutoCAD Command: prompt.
Hints	SH works only with DOS internal commands, not external commands. When you are running the SHELL command, your system may run out of memory. The SH command is a useful alternative for running internal commands in such instances because it requires less memory.
Error *Messages*	Bad command or file name You entered an invalid command at the DOS Command: prompt. Enter a valid command.

SHAPE   *Inserts shapes into a drawing.*

Syntax	Command: **SHAPE** Starting point: Height <1.0>: Rotation angle <0.0>:
Template *Coordinates*	None
Description	You must LOAD shape files before you can use the shapes. Type **LOAD**, press Enter, and type the name of the file you want to load. You can use the question mark (?) to list available shape file names.

The Starting point: prompt is looking for a location at which to insert the shape. This point corresponds to the first vector in the shape definition.

Height <1.0>: is used to scale the shape.

Rotation angle <0.0>:. The shape can be rotated at a given angle.

Possible Response

Response	Meaning
?	List shape names.

Hints

SHAPE works only with previously-defined shapes you LOAD into the drawing.

Shapes are symbols much like blocks but more difficult to create.

Error Messages

Shape (*name*) not found. You tried to load a shape name that is not found. The Shape name (or ?): prompt redisplays so that you can enter a valid shape name.

No default established yet. You pressed Enter at the Shape name (or ?): prompt without first entering a shape name. The shape name you enter here will become the default until you enter another shape name.

Not a valid shape/font file. You tried to load a file that is not a valid shape file. Edit the shape file so that it is valid, and try loading again, or load another valid shape file.

SHELL *Provides full access to operating system commands.*

Syntax

Command: **SHELL**
DOS command:

Template Coordinates

None

Description

At the DOS Command: prompt, you can execute one command, after which AutoCAD will automatically return, or you can press Enter to get to the system level. At the system level, you can execute as many commands as you want. You can even run programs. Return to AutoCAD by typing **EXIT** at the DOS prompt.

Hints

Do not try to execute AutoCAD while using this command. You can permanently corrupt your AutoCAD files by doing this. You are already in AutoCAD; you have temporarily shelled out to DOS.

The prompts may differ slightly with operating systems other than DOS.

SHELL can execute utility programs while you are in the Drawing Editor, providing access to all normal DOS commands.

This command is not for novices. SHELL requires caution so that you do not affect files and devices AutoCAD is using. Use this command only when you know the potential effect the DOS commands inside the shell may have on AutoCAD while SHELL is running.

Be sure not to delete any of AutoCAD's temporary files, recognizable by their .$ac or .$a file type extensions.

Error
Message
Bad command or file name You entered an invalid command at the DOS Command: prompt. Enter a valid command.

SKETCH   *Allows freehand drawing.*

Syntax
Command: **SKETCH**
Record increment <current>:
Sketch. Pen eXit Quit Record Erase Connect

Template
Coordinates
None

Description
SKETCH lets you draw as you would on a piece of paper. Use only the CONTINUOUS linetype for sketching.

In Sketch mode AutoCAD ignores all input except Sketch mode options and toggle commands, like SNAP and ORTHO.

To select an option while you are in Sketch mode, all you need to do is type the capitalized letter. You do not need to press Enter.

Record increment <current>:. AutoCAD sketches with line or polyline segments. Record increment is the length of these segments. Both Snap mode and Ortho mode affect the way segments are drawn.

The Pen option is a toggle that alternately raises or lowers the pen. If the pen is up, you can move the cursor on the screen without drawing. When the pen is down, AutoCAD accepts cursor movement as the drawing.

eXit records the segments permanently and ends Sketch mode.

Quit ends Sketch mode without saving any of the work.

Record saves the segments without exiting.

Erase erases segments as you backtrack through the drawing.

Connect connects new segments to existing segments. Make sure that the pen is up, position the cursor next to an existing segment, and then type **C**.

Sketch is not an option. It is merely a label indicating that you are working in Sketch mode.

	Response	Meaning
Possible		
Responses	C	Connect new segments to existing segments.
	E	Erase.
	P	Raise or lower pen.
	Q	Exit Sketch mode without saving.
	R	Save without exiting.
	X	Save and exit.
		Draw line to current point.

Hint   Freehand drawing generates a large number of lines, so it should be used only when AutoCAD's normal data entry is ineffective—for instance with signatures, maps, and other highly irregular shapes.

Error   Requires numeric distance or two points. When specifying the record
Messages increment, you gave an invalid response. Try again, entering a numeric distance for the increment or a point. If you select a point, you will be prompted for a second point.

Nothing recorded. You did not sketch anything before recording, or you entered an invalid response to the Sketch. Pen eXit Quit Record Erase Connect prompt.

n lines recorded. <Pen current> The number of lines you sketched is indicated here. Your response to the Record increment <current>: prompt determines the line length.

SNAP   *Provides an invisible grid that determines the smallest increment AutoCAD recognizes when you move the pointer.*

Syntax   Command: **SNAP**
Snap spacing or ON/OFF/Aspect/Rotate/Style <current>:

Template   Q 8 - R 8, W 9
Coordinates

Description   You can toggle Snap mode on and off inside commands as you are working. You can toggle Snap mode on and start to draw, then toggle Snap mode off while still in the command. Snap mode is used also when you need a rigid area in which to draw.

Snap mode and Grid mode can be compared to using graph paper in your drawings. You can choose to stay on the graph lines or draw between the lines. This is true of both Snap mode and Grid mode.

SNAP determines the shortest distance AutoCAD will recognize when you move your pointer. Pick points will be limited to multiples of the snap value. When you want to pick a point between snap points, use Ctrl-B or F9 to toggle out of Snap mode.

Snap mode has no effect in perspective views.

Snap spacing is the default. Just like the GRID command, Snap spacing will set both the X and Y values. Type the values you want, and press Enter. Values may be as large or as small as needed in the drawing.

SNAP is a toggle. You can turn it on and off from the command (with the On and Off options) or by pressing one of the function keys (F9 on IBM and compatible machines).

Aspect sets the X and Y spacings to different values. AutoCAD prompts you first for the X value and then for the Y value. This option is not available if Style is set to isometric.

Rotate. If you need to draw at an angle other than horizontal, you can rotate the grid and snap to accommodate. Rotate affects both the visible grid and the invisible Snap mode. You are prompted for a base point, around which the grid will be rotated. If you want to align the point with an entity, indicate the entity for the rotation angle. Otherwise, it is a good idea to leave the base point at 0,0.

Style allows you to choose between standard drawing mode (the default) or isometric mode. An isometric grid contains angles that are multiples of 60 degrees, in contrast with the normal 90-degree grid for standard drawing mode.

Possible | Response | Meaning |
Responses | --- | --- |
number	Set alignment.
ON	Turn on snap mode.
OFF	Turn off snap mode.
A	Change X-Y spacing.
R	Rotate snap grid.
S	Select standard or isometric style.

Hints	If you magnify your drawing, the snap setting remains the same. You may need to change the setting when you are doing detail work.

Changes in the snap setting do not affect entities already in the drawing, only the entities or processes that will happen after the changes are made.

Grids with small snap values take longer to redraw. As an alternative, reduce the axis spacing, and increase the snap value.

Error Messages

Ambiguous response, please clarify... When prompted to enter the snap spacing or other options, you typed the letter O. Since this could mean either On or Off, you need to spell out as much of the word as necessary to remove ambiguity, or select one of the other options indicated in the prompt.

Requires numeric distance, two points, or option keyword. When prompted for snap spacing, you entered an illegal character. Check your entry, and try again.

Invalid option keyword. When prompted to enter snap spacing or another option, your response was invalid. Try again, either indicating spacing or selecting a keyword from the prompt.

Invalid 2D point. When prompted for a base point, you entered something invalid. Select a point on-screen, or enter two coordinates.

Requires numeric angle or second point. You responded with a non-numeric response when prompted for a rotation angle. Try again, providing either a numeric value or a second point that defines the angle.

SOLID

Draws solid rectilinear and triangular areas.

Syntax

Command: **SOLID**
First point:
Second point:
Third point:
Fourth point:
Third point:
Fourth point:

Template Coordinates

None

Description

To draw solids, you indicate the corners of the area. It is important to indicate the corners correctly to achieve the shape you want. You may indicate three or four corners.

To obtain a rectilinear solid, the points must be selected so that the first and third points lie on the same edge. If you indicate the points in a clockwise or counterclockwise direction, you will get a bow tie.

If you are drawing only a four-point solid, press Enter when prompted the second time for the Third point:. If you are drawing a three-point solid, press Enter at the Fourth point: prompt. You will still be prompted for the continuation of the command. If you use the continuation, the solids will be connected.

Hints   To terminate the command, enter two null responses in a row.

If you want the figures filled, use Fill mode. Even if you aren't in Fill mode when you draw a figure, you can fill it by subsequently turning on Fill mode and then using the REGEN command. Fill mode increases regeneration time.

Error   Invalid point. Your response to one of the point prompts was invalid. Select
Message   a point on-screen, or enter two or three coordinates for each point.

STATUS   *Displays drawing information.*

Syntax   Command: **STATUS**

Template   T 3
Coordinates | STATUS |

Description   STATUS tells you what your toggles read, what your drawing extents and limits are, the number of entities, insertion base point, snap resolution, grid spacing, how much disk space is available, and how much I/O page space is available. It also shows current layer, color, linetype, elevation, and the on or off status for axis, fill, grid, ortho, qtext, snap, and tablet.

Hints   There is a subset of the STATUS command—actually a Dimension subcommand—that shows the current values of all dimensioning variables. The template coordinates for this subcommand are W 1.

Values displayed by the STATUS command are expressed in units established with the most recent UNITS command.

Error   None
Messages

STATUS **(Dimensioning Subcommand)**
Lists dimension variables and their values.

Syntax Dim: **STATUS**

Template Coordinates W 1

Description This dimensioning subcommand is available only after you enter DIM or DIM1.

Values displayed for dimensioning variables are expressed in units established with the most recent UNITS command.

There are more variables than will fit on the screen at one time. Press Enter to see the rest of the list.

Hint The DIM: STATUS subcommand is different from the STATUS command you enter the Command: prompt. DIM: STATUS shows only the current status of all dimensioning variables.

Error Messages None

STRETCH *Changes entities while retaining connections with other entities or points.*

Syntax Command: **STRETCH**
Select objects to stretch by window...
Select objects:
Base point:
New point:

Template Coordinates X 17

Description The first selection must be made by a window or crossing. If you select with a window, you will select all objects contained entirely in the selection box. With crossing, you will select all objects inside or crossing the selection box. (Crossing is only available with the Advanced User Interface.) Subsequent selections may be made by pointing. Another window or crossing selection will negate the first window or crossing selection.

With STRETCH you can stretch entities to make them smaller or larger, or you can realign those entities any way you want.

`Base point:` is a reference point for the stretch.

`New point:` is the point to which you want the base point moved.

Hint

You can't stretch text, although you can move it with the STRETCH command.

**Error
Messages**

`You must select a window to stretch.` You tried to stretch an entity without using a window or crossing when making your selection.

`Invalid window specification.` When using a window to select objects, your selection was invalid. Try again.

`Invalid point.` Your response to one of the point prompts was invalid. Select a point on-screen, or enter two or three coordinates for each point.

`0 found.` No objects were found within the window or crossing you specified. Try again.

`Expects a point or Window/Last/Crossing/BOX/Add/Remove/Multiple/ Previous/Undo/AUto/SIngle` When prompted to select objects, you entered an option keyword AutoCAD does not understand. Try again.

STYLE

Loads text fonts into your drawing.

Syntax

```
Command: STYLE
Text style name (or ?) <current>:
Font file <default>:
Height <default>:
Width factor <default>:
Obliquing angle <default>:
Backwards? <Y/N>:
Upside-down? <Y/N>:
Vertical? <Y/N>:
(name) is now the current text style.
```

**Template
Coordinates**

None

Description

STYLE can be used to modify fonts by changing the height, width, and obliquing angle. You can also specify that the text be drawn backward, upside down, or vertically.

Style names may contain up to 31 characters.

The Vertical? prompt appears only if the font you selected allows dual orientation.

When responding to the Font file: prompt, omit the .SHX extension, as AutoCAD inserts this automatically.

Possible Response

Response	Meaning
?	List text styles.

Hints

The style you establish with the STYLE command becomes the current style for TEXT and DTEXT commands.

When you change the font with the STYLE command, AutoCAD regenerates your screen, replacing all occurrences of the former style with the new style. Only the font changes.

Error Messages

Invalid text style name. The name you entered does not conform to naming conventions. Check your typing, and try again.

Requires numeric distance or two points. When specifying the height or obliquing angle, you entered an invalid response. Try again, providing a numeric distance or picking two on-screen points that define the height or angle.

Requires numeric value. When prompted for the width factor, you entered one or more non-numeric characters. Try again with a numeric response.

Yes or No, please. When prompted to answer whether you want the text produced backward, upside down, or vertically, you typed something other than Y or N. Type **Y** or **N**.

Invalid file name. The font file name you entered was invalid. Check your spelling, and try again.

Can't open file The file you specified cannot be used by AutoCAD as a font file. Check the file, or specify another font file.

No such text style. Use main STYLE command to create it. You tried to create a new text style at the DIM subcommand level. Instead, use the STYLE command at the Command: prompt to create a new style.

STYLE

(Dimensioning Subcommand)
Changes the text font for the dimensions.

Syntax

```
DIM: STYLE
New text style <current>:
```

Description

This dimensioning subcommand is available only after you enter DIM or DIM1.

Dimension text uses the current text style unless you change it using the `DIM: STYLE` subcommand.

Hint

After you use `DIM: STYLE` to change dimensioning text style, it will remain the same until you change it again.

Error Messages

`Invalid text style name.` The name you entered does not conform to naming conventions. Check your typing, and try again.

`Existing style.` You entered the name of an existing style.

`New style.` The style name you entered does not refer to a style you established previously.

TABLET

Allows you to turn the tablet on and off, calibrate the tablet for digitizing drawings, or configure the tablet for a menu.

Syntax

```
Command: TABLET
Option (ON/OFF/CAL/CFG):
```

Template Coordinates

None

Description

ON returns the tablet to menu use after it has been turned off. OFF turns off the tablet menu and allows you to use the entire tablet area for digitizing. Use the OFF option before calibrating.

CAL allows you to calibrate the tablet to a given paper drawing for the purpose of digitizing the paper drawing into AutoCAD. You are prompted for the following:

```
Digitize first known point:
Enter coordinates for first point:
```

```
Digitize second known point:
Enter coordinates for second point:
```

Secure the paper drawing to the digitizing tablet so that no movement will occur. On the drawing, select two points you know, and decide what coordinates those two points should have in AutoCAD. These are your first and second points and define the scale of the drawing.

CFG lets you configure the tablet for different menu areas when you switch between menus. If the menus are defined with the same areas and the same number of squares in each area, you do not need to reconfigure the tablet. CFG also lets you respecify the screen pointing area. Be sure the menu areas and pointing area do not overlap. You are prompted for the following:

```
Enter number of tablet menus desired
    (0-4) <default>:
```

If you enter the number of tablet menus you currently have, you will be prompted: Do you want to realign tablet menu areas! ‹N›

```
Digitize upper left corner of menu area n:
Digitize lower left corner of menu area n:
Digitize lower right corner of menu area n:
Enter the number of columns for menu area n:
Enter the number of rows for menu area n:
Do you want to respecify the screen pointing area? <N>:
Digitize lower left corner of screen pointing area:
Digitize upper right corner of screen pointing area:
```

n represents the number of the particular tablet area you are defining. If you make a mistake defining one of the corners, you must execute the command again. The screen pointing area specified includes the area used for the screen menu, which can be reached through the tablet or other pointing device.

Possible
Responses

Response	Meaning
ON	Turn on tablet mode.
OFF	Turn off tablet mode.
CAL	Calibrate tablet.
CFG	Configure tablet for tablet menus.

Hints

If you customize your tablet menu, it is a good idea to work on a copy of TABLET.DWG, give it a new name (such as CUSTOM.DWG), and save the original.

The template coordinates given for each item in this command reference pertain to the command definitions in the AutoCAD TABLET.DWG menu.

When respecifying the screen pointing area, make sure it doesn't overlap tablet menu areas.

See Chapter 5 for more information on configuring a tablet menu.

Error Messages

Ambiguous response, please clarify... When prompted to enter a tablet option, you typed **O** or **C**. Since *O* could mean either ON or OFF, and *C* could mean either CAL or CFG, you need to spell out enough of the command to remove ambiguity.

Invalid option keyword. When prompted for a tablet option, you entered a response that does not correspond to a valid option keyword. Try again, selecting an option indicated in the prompt.

Invalid 2D point. When prompted for a corner, you entered something invalid. Select a point on-screen when digitizing.

Alarm sounds. If you try to type coordinates when prompted to digitize a point, the alarm sounds. Digitize by selecting a location on your tablet.

Value must be between 0 and 4. When specifying the number of tablet menus, you entered a number outside the range of 0–4. Enter a positive integer within this range.

Requires an integer value. Your response was not an integer, or it was outside the range of integers allowed. Enter a positive integer within the range indicated in the prompt.

Points must form a 90 degree angle, try area again... The points you selected do not form a 90-degree angle. Try again.

Value must be positive and nonzero. The value you entered is negative, zero, or non-numeric. Enter a positive number.

Too many rows for the selected area. You specified too many rows to fit in the area you selected. Try again with fewer rows.

TABSURF

Creates a tabulated surface with a path curve and a direction vector.

Syntax

Command: **TABSURF**
Select path curve:
Select direction vector:

Template Coordinates

O 5

Description   TABSURF stands for *tab*ulated *surf*ace. This command extrudes a curve through space along a direction vector, allowing you to select the path curve and the direction vector. The path curve can be a line, arc, circle, two-dimensional polyline, or three-dimensional polyline. After you select the curve and direction vector, a tabulated surface is drawn from the point you pick on the curve to the point you pick for the direction vector.

Surface lines are drawn parallel to the direction vector. The tabulated surfaces are created as polygon meshes, with mesh density controlled by the SURFTAB1 system variable.

`Select Path curve:` is used to define the surface. Lines, arcs, circles, and polylines may be used.

`Select direction vector:` is a line or an open polyline that indicates the direction and length of the surface.

Hint   Large values for SURFTAB1 will result in dense meshes and more processing time.

Error Messages   `Invalid point.` Your response to the `Select path curve:` prompt was invalid. Select a point on-screen, or enter two or three coordinates for each point.

`Entity not usable to define tabulated surface.` The entity you selected for the path curve cannot be used for that purpose. Select a line, arc, circle, or polyline.

`Entity not usable as direction vector.` The entity you selected for the direction vector cannot be used for that purpose. Select a line or open polyline.

TEXT   *Places text in your drawing.*

Syntax
```
Command: TEXT
Start point or Align/Center/Fit/Middle/Right/Style:
```

Template Coordinates   W 8 | TEXT |

Description   The TEXT command is used to place text within your drawing. Text can be placed with this or with the DTEXT command; they are similar in function and purpose. Text is treated like another entity; it can later be selected and functioned upon by other AutoCAD commands.

Start point is the default for the TEXT command. AutoCAD is looking for the starting point for the text you will insert. The text you enter will be left-justified.

Align prompts for a starting point and an ending point for your text. The overall size of the text you enter will be adjusted so that it prints between the two points. Although you are prompted for the second text line, this is actually the last line of text.

Center centers the text. AutoCAD prompts you for the center point for the text.

Fit is similar to the Align option. AutoCAD prompts you for a starting point, an ending point, and for a height for the text. AutoCAD adjusts the width of the text to fit between the two points.

Middle is similar to Center. The difference is that Middle centers text both horizontally and vertically around the point, whereas Center centers text only horizontally. AutoCAD prompts for a middle point.

Right right-justifies your text. AutoCAD prompts you for an endpoint for the text.

Style allows you to switch between the loaded text fonts. To load or modify a text font, see the STYLE command.

If you press Enter at the TEXT prompt, AutoCAD will prompt for text and place any text you enter below the last piece of text entered. The new text will retain all the parameters of the last text including font, height, rotation, and color.

After you respond to the preceding prompt, you will either be prompted for the endpoints of the base line, or you will see the following prompts:

```
Height <current>:
Rotation <current>:
Text:
```

Spaces are allowed for the text you input. When you finish typing text, press Enter.

To insert a paragraph with this command, execute the command and set up the parameters for the text. Then execute the TEXT command a second time; the parameters default to the last text inserted.

The default text font (called STANDARD) is used unless other fonts have been loaded with the STYLE command. There are special characters you can insert with your text. These characters are embedded in the text and need codes to activate them. The following table shows the codes and the special characters they activate:

Code	Character
%%o	Overscore
%%u	Underscore
%%d	Degrees symbol
%%p	Plus/minus symbol
%%c	Circle diameter
%%%	Percent sign
%%*nnn*	ASCII character with decimal code *nnn*

When you have inserted your text in the drawing, you can use the CHANGE command to change everything about the text.

Possible Responses

Response	Meaning
A	Align text between two points.
C	Center text horizontally.
F	Fit text between two points.
M	Center text horizontally and vertically.
R	Right-justify text.
S	Select text style.

Hint

If you press Enter at the Start point prompt, the next text will start one line below the last text you entered in the drawing and will share the same height, style, justification, and color.

Error Messages

Invalid point. Your response to one of the point prompts was invalid. Select a point on-screen, or enter two or three coordinates for each point.

Requires numeric distance or second point. When prompted for a distance, you entered something other than a numeric distance or second point. Enter a number, or select two points.

Value must be positive and nonzero. The value you entered is negative, zero, or non-numeric. Enter a positive number.

TEXTSCR
Flips from graphics to the text screen on a single-screen system.

Syntax

Command: **TEXTSCR**

Template Coordinates

None

Description   This command is used for single-display systems to switch from the graphics screen to the text screen. See also GRAPHSCR.

TEXTSCR and GRAPHSCR flip back and forth between text and graphics mode. Although you could toggle back and forth on a single-screen system by pressing F1, you cannot use F1 in a command script or menu item.

This command has no effect on a dual-screen system.

You can use TEXTSCR as an internal command within another AutoCAD command by preceding it with an apostrophe: 'TEXTSCR.

Hint   Using F1 is quicker and easier than typing in the command.

Error Messages   None

TIME   *Keeps track of time spent in a drawing.*

Syntax   Command: **TIME**

Template Coordinates   T 1

Description   TIME is a management tool to help you track the times, dates, and durations of edit sessions for drawings. It has potential use for client billing purposes, as well.

You can turn the timer on and off, and reset it.

When you enter the TIME command, AutoCAD responds with the following display:

Current time: *time and date*
Drawing created: *time and date of creation*
Drawing last updated: *last time in editor*
Time in drawing editor: *total time in editor*
Elapsed timer: *current session time*
Timer on.

Drawing created: is the date and time the current drawing was created.

Drawing last updated: is the last time you updated the current file.

Time in drawing editor: is the total amount of time you spent in the Drawing Editor with this drawing.

Elapsed timer: is the time you spent in the Drawing Editor during the current session.

Display/ON/OFF/Reset:Display redisplays the time. ON turns on the timer; OFF turns off the timer. Reset causes the time to be reset to zero.

Possible Responses

Response	Meaning
D	Display time
ON	Turn on timer
OFf	Turn off timer
R	Reset timer

Hint

Times are expressed to the nearest millisecond in 24-hour military format; for example, 13:01:00 means 1:01 in the afternoon.

Error Message

Invalid option keyword. When prompted to select an option, you entered a response that does not correspond to a valid option keyword. Try again, selecting an option indicated in the prompt.

TRACE   *Draws a line of a specific width.*

Syntax

Command: **TRACE**
Trace width:
From point:
To point:
To point:

Template Coordinates

None

Description

A *trace* is a solid line with a constant width you can determine. Traces are drawn like lines—by selecting the points where the lines begin and end. Traces can be as wide as you want. They are solid unless Fill mode is off; then only the outlines are drawn.

Traces have a number of disadvantages in comparison with lines: you can't curve, close, continue, or undo a trace or trace segment. These limitations hamper the command's usefulness to the extent that it may be eliminated from future versions of AutoCAD.

Hints   The current default trace width is determined by the TRACEWID system variable.

All traces drawn by one TRACE command have the same width, and all traces are squared off at both ends.

As an alternative to using traces, you can get thick lines by using thick technical pens for plotting, or you can create thick lines with the PLINE command.

Error
Messages   Requires numeric distance or two points. When prompted for the trace width, you responded with something other than a number or two points. Try again, providing a numeric distance or picking two on-screen points that define the trace width.

Value must be positive. A trace cannot have a negative width. Enter a positive value.

Invalid point. Your response to one of the point prompts was invalid. Select a point on-screen, or enter coordinates for each point.

Invalid 2D point. Your response to the To Point: prompt was invalid. Select a point on-screen, or enter two coordinates for the point.

TRIM

Trims entities back to a boundary.

Syntax
```
Command: TRIM
Select cutting edge(s)...
Select objects:
```

Template
Coordinates   X 18

Description   TRIM is used to trim entities to a boundary you define. It works with lines, arcs, circles, and polylines. You can also use any of these entity types for your cutting edge boundaries.

The *cutting edges* are the boundaries to which you are trimming. When all the boundaries have been selected, you are prompted:

```
Select object to trim:
```

Hint   You can trim inside or outside the cutting edges, depending on where you select the entity to be trimmed. Select inside the cutting edges to retain what's inside the edges and delete what falls outside. Select the object to trim outside the cutting edges to retain what's outside the edges and delete what falls inside.

Error Messages	3D Polygon Mesh entities may not be used as edges. When prompted to select the cutting edge, you selected a three-dimensional polygon mesh. Select a line, arc, circle, or two-dimensional polyline.

Error Messages (continued):

3D Polygon Mesh entities may not be used as edges. When prompted to select the cutting edge, you selected a three-dimensional polygon mesh. Select a line, arc, circle, or two-dimensional polyline.

Cannot trim this entity. The entity you selected cannot be trimmed. Select only lines, arcs, circles, and two-dimensional polylines.

Select objects: n selected, 0 found, (n) not parallel with UCS) For your cutting edge you selected an entity whose extrusion direction is not parallel to the Z axis of the current User Coordinate System.

Entity not parallel with UCS. You tried to trim an entity whose extrusion direction is not parallel to the Z axis of the current User Coordinate System.

Entity does not intersect an edge. The entity you want to trim does not intersect any of the cutting edges.

U — *Reverses the effect of the most recent command.*

Syntax	Command: **U**
Template Coordinates	None
Description	This command is one method AutoCAD provides for correcting mistakes. U will undo the most recent command; it has the same effect as UNDO 1. It can be used repeatedly to single-step back through previous commands.
Hint	Use UNDO if you want to reverse the effects of more than one command at a time.
Error Messages	Nothing to undo U was the first command entered since you accessed this drawing. Type another command before using the U command. Everything has been undone. You have undone all commands entered during this work session.

UCS — *Defines or modifies User Coordinate Systems.*

Syntax	Command: **UCS** Origin/ZAxis/3point/Entity/View/X/Y/Z/Prev/ Restore/Save/Del/?/<World>:

***Template
Coordinates***

J 4 - K 6

```
UCS
```

Description

Origin defines a new UCS by moving the origin of the current UCS. The orientation of the axis remains the same.

ZAxis defines a new UCS using an origin and a point indicating the positive Z axis. You are prompted:

```
Origin point <0,0,0>:
Point on positive portion of Z-axis <default>:
```

3point defines a new UCS with three points: origin, positive X axis, and positive Y axis. OSNAP modes can be used to indicate a UCS that corresponds to entities in the drawing. You are prompted:

```
Origin point <0,0,0>:
Point on positive portion of the X-axis <current>:
Point on positive-Y portion of the UCS X-Y plane <current>:
```

The three points must not form a straight line.

Entity defines a new UCS using an existing entity. The X-Y plane is parallel to the X-Y plane that was in effect when the entity was drawn and has the same Z direction as that of the indicated entity. The entity must be selected by pointing. The following list describes the process of creating the UCS from each type of entity:

- ❑ Arc. The center becomes the origin; the X axis passes through the point on the arc closest to the pick point.

- ❑ Circle. Same as arc.

- ❑ Dimension. The insertion point is the origin; the X axis is parallel to the UCS of the dimension.

- ❑ Line. The endpoint nearest the pick point is the new origin; the Y axis is the other end of the line segment indicated.

- ❑ Point. The origin is the point; the X axis is derived arbitrarily.

- ❑ Polyline and Mesh. The start point is the new origin; the X axis lies between the origin and the next vertex.

- ❑ Solid. The first point of solid is the origin; the X axis is on the line between the first and second points.

- ❑ Trace. The first point is the origin; the X axis lies along the center of the trace.

❏ 3D Face. The first point is the origin; the X axis is from the first two points; and the positive Y side is from the first and fourth points.

❏ Shape, text, block. The origin is the insertion point; the X axis is defined by the rotation.

View defines a new UCS whose Z axis is parallel to the direction of view—that is, perpendicular to the current view.

X/Y/Z rotates the current UCS around the specified axis. (Enter only one.) You are prompted for the rotation around the axis you indicate.

Previous takes you back to the UCS in which you last worked.

Restore restores a saved UCS.

Save saves the current UCS. You are prompted for a name; the standard conventions apply.

Delete removes the specified UCS from the list. You are prompted for the name of the UCS to delete.

? lists the UCSs that are saved.

World sets the current coordinate system to the World Coordinate System.

Possible Responses

Response	Meaning
D	Delete specified UCS.
E	Use existing entity to define UCS.
O	Define new UCS by moving origin of current UCS.
P	Make previous UCS current.
R	Restore a saved UCS.
S	Save current UCS.
V	Define new UCS with Z axis parallel to view direction.
W	Set current UCS to World Coordinate System.
X	Rotate current UCS around X axis.
Y	Rotate current UCS around Y axis.
Z	Rotate current UCS around Z axis.
ZA	Define new UCS with specified origin and positive Z axis.
3	Define new UCS with specified origin, positive X axis, and positive Y axis.
?	List saved UCSs.

Hints

When you begin a new drawing, its World Coordinate System and User Coordinate System are the same, with X, Y, and Z coordinates of zero.

You can change the UCS from the SETTINGS screen menu.

Although UCS was developed for three-dimensional drawing, it can also be used to change the orientation of two-dimensional drawings.

**Error
Messages**

`Invalid option keyword.` When prompted to select an option, you entered a response which does not correspond to a valid option keyword. You may have typed **X/Y/Z** instead of just entering one axis at a time, as AutoCAD requires with the UCS command. Try again, selecting an option indicated in the prompt.

`Invalid point.` Your response to one of the point prompts was invalid. Select a point on-screen, or enter coordinates for each point.

`Coincident with first point` When specifying the point on the positive-Y portion of the plane, you selected the same point as for the X axis. Select a different point.

`Points are colinear` You entered points that form a straight line. Select or enter points that do not form a straight line.

`No object found` You tried to select an entity by some method other than pointing.

`Requires numeric angle or two points.` When prompted for the rotation, your response was invalid. Enter a numeric angle or two points that define the angle.

`Invalid UCS name.` You entered a UCS name that does not conform with AutoCAD file-naming conventions. Try again, using a valid file name.

`____ not found.` You entered a name for which no UCS exists. Enter the name of an existing UCS.

UCSICON   *Controls the User Coordinate System icon.*

Syntax

`Command:` **UCSICON**
`ON/OFF/All/Noorigin/ORigin <current>:`

**Template
Coordinates**

None

Description

The UCS icon is typically located in the bottom left corner of the viewing screen. It is used by AutoCAD Release 10 to indicate the axis directions for the current user coordinate system.

`ON` turns the icon on; `OFF` turns the icon off.

`All` activates the icon change in all viewports, not just the current port.

Noorigin (the default) displays the icon at all times in the screen's lower left corner.

ORigin displays the icon at the origin of the current UCS.

	Response	Meaning
Possible Responses	A	Change icon in all viewports.
	N	Display icon in lower left corner of screen.
	O	Display icon at origin of current UCS.
	OFf	Turn off icon.
	ON	Turn on icon.

Hints

This icon shows the current UCS origin and orientation for the current viewport.

If the icon has a plus sign (+) it means that the icon is located at the origin of the current UCS. The letter *W* indicates that the current coordinate system is the World Coordinate System (WCS). A box at the base of the icon indicates you are looking at the UCS from above; absence of a box indicates you are looking from below.

Error Messages

Ambiguous response, please clarify... When prompted to turn the UCS icon on or off, you typed the letter *O*. Since this could mean either ON or OFF, you need to spell out as much of the word as necessary to remove ambiguity, or select one of the other options indicated in the prompt.

Invalid option keyword. When prompted to select an option, you entered a response that does not correspond to a valid option keyword. Try again, selecting an option indicated in the prompt.

UNDEFINE

Allows advanced programmers to define standard AutoCAD commands with a new definition.

Syntax

```
Command: UNDEFINE
Command name:
```

Template Coordinates

None

Description This command is used to make an AutoCAD command invisible. This invisibility is commonly desirable if you used LISP to define a function with the same name as a current AutoCAD command.

If you use this command, and you did not define a LISP routine by the same name as the command being undefined, the AutoCAD command corresponding to the name entered is disabled.

Hints UNDEFINE works only on commands available from the Command: prompt. It does not work with subcommands, including those in the dimensioning subsystem.

See REDEFINE in this command reference for help in restoring AutoCAD's built-in command definitions.

You can execute an AutoCAD command that has been undefined if you precede the command name with a period. For example, if you inadvertently undefine the REDEFINE command, you can still use REDEFINE by entering the command as **.REDEFINE**.

The effects of UNDEFINE apply only to the current editing session. All AutoCAD commands return to normal operation the next time you enter the Drawing Editor.

Error Message Unknown command name. You tried to undefine an unknown command. Check your spelling, and try again.

UNDO   *Reverses the effect of previous commands and provides control over the undo feature.*

Syntax
Command: **UNDO**
Auto/Back/Control/End/Group/Mark/<number>:

Template Coordinates W 3

Description UNDO is another command you can use to correct mistakes. It is similar in function to the U command but gives you greater control over how many steps you undo at a time.

UNDO differs from ERASE in that it undoes zooms and screen settings, whereas ERASE only erases entities.

<number>: is the default. You can enter the number of commands you want undone at this time.

Auto is the part of UNDO that controls how menu selections and other multiple commands are handled. If Auto is on, the menu selections are treated as one command.

Group starts the grouping process. When you tell AutoCAD to open a group, the next commands you execute become part of that group. When you have entered all the commands you want in that group, you must End the group.

End ends the grouping process. If you start the grouping process, you must end that process. When commands have been grouped together, they are undone with one UNDO command.

Mark allows you to mark a place in your UNDO information to return to through the UNDO command. You can mark more than one place at a time. When you go back to that mark, the mark is removed. If you want to keep a mark there, you mark the place again. By marking the information, you can experiment in your drawing without worrying about getting back to a particular spot.

Back takes you back to the mark you placed in the UNDO information. If there are no marks in the UNDO information, AutoCAD will undo to the beginning of the editing session.

Control allows you to limit the UNDO and U commands. AutoCAD prompts you

> All/None/One:

All is the default, allowing you all of the different UNDO functions. None disables the command, and One allows one undo at a time. Both None and One free any disk space used for storing previous UNDOs.

Possible Responses	Response	Meaning
	number	Undo specified number of commands.
	A	Control treatment of menu selections.
	B	Undo to previous mark.
	C	Toggle undo feature off and on.
	E	End UNDO group.
	G	Group commands.
	M	Mark a place in UNDO information.

Hint   If you want to step back through your drawing to a particular point but are not sure how many commands back you need to go, undo a specific number of commands, and then use REDO to undo the effects of the UNDO.

Error
Messages

Requires an integer value or an option keyword. You entered an invalid value or option. Select an option keyword displayed in the prompt, or enter the number of commands to undo. Check your entry, and try again.

Value must be between 1 and 32767. You entered a number outside the valid range. Enter a positive integer between 1 and 32767.

Nothing to undo UNDO was the first command entered since you accessed this drawing. Type another command before using the UNDO command.

Everything has been undone. You have undone all commands entered during this work session.

Yes or No, please. When prompted to answer Yes or No, you typed something else. Type **Y** or **N**.

Ambiguous response, please clarify... When prompted to turn Auto on or off, you typed the letter *O*. Since this could mean On or Off, you need to spell out as much of the word as necessary to remove ambiguity.

Invalid option keyword. When prompted to select an option, you entered a response that does not correspond to a valid option keyword. Try again, selecting an option indicated in the prompt.

UNDO

(Dimensioning Subcommand)
Undoes the last dimension inserted in the drawing.

Syntax

Dim: **UNDO**

Template
Coordinates

W 3 | UNDO |

Description

This dimensioning subcommand is available only after you enter DIM or DIM1.

Hints

You can undo the effects of a single dimensioning command, or cancel the entire current dimensioning session.

To undo the effect of the last dimensioning command, type **UNDO** at the Dim: prompt.

To cancel the entire dimensioning session, exit dimensioning mode (by typing **EXIT** or pressing Ctrl-C), and type **UNDO** at the AutoCAD Command: prompt.

Error
Messages

Command has been completely undone. Any effects of the command you undid have been reversed.

UNITS

Sets the display format and precision of your drawing units.

Syntax Command: **UNITS**

Template Coordinates None

Description This command allows you to specify your preferences in measurement systems. When you enter the UNITS command, AutoCAD provides a whole dialogue of prompts to allow you flexibility in entering and viewing information. You have the opportunity to change the following:

❑ How linear measurement units are displayed

❑ The number of decimal digits or fractional divisor displayed

❑ How angular measurements are displayed

❑ The number of decimal digits in angular displays

❑ The angular direction of measurement

You are prompted for each of these areas in turn. The effects of the UNITS command is global; all measurement displays throughout AutoCAD are affected.

When you enter the UNITS command, you are greeted by the following series of prompts:

```
Systems of units:        (Examples)

    1.   Scientific      1.55E+01
    2.   Decimal         15.50
    3.   Engineering     1'-3.50"
    4.   Architectural   1'-3 1/2"
    5.   Fractional      15 1/2

Enter choice, 1 to 5 <2>:
```

The main type of unit is determined here. The examples were added to this prompt in AutoCAD Release 2.6 for clarification. The Fractional selection displays units in whole and fraction parts. If this system of units is selected, AutoCAD makes no assumption as to whether the units being used are inches or millimeters.

With the exception of Engineering and Architectural units, these display units can be used with any measurement system. For example, Decimal mode is perfect for metric units as well as decimal English units.

The next prompt depends on the system of units you selected. The following prompt appears if you choose selection 1, 2, or 3:

Number of digits to right of decimal point (0 to 8) <default>:

The following prompt appears for selection 4 or 5:

Denominator of smallest fraction to display
       (1, 2, 4, 8, 16, 32, or 64) <default>:

Next, you are prompted for angle format:

Systems of angle measure:
  1.   Decimal degrees   42.5
  2.   Degrees/minutes/seconds   42d30'0.00"
  3.   Grads   47.2222g
  4.   Radians   0.7418r
  5.   Surveyor's units   N 47d30'0" E

Enter choice, 1 to 5 <default>:

When you work with Surveyor's units, the display will be

N or S   angle   E or W

The angle is input the same as Degrees/minutes/seconds. If the angle you are working with lies on a compass point, simply identify the compass point. For example, zero degrees would be equivalent to E in Surveyor's units.

The precision of the angle measurement is selected next. The prompt is

Number of fractional places for display of angles (0 to 8)<>:

Next, you are prompted for the direction of angle zero. The default in AutoCAD is for angle zero to be at three o'clock, and for the angles to be figured counterclockwise. The next prompt in the UNITS command follows:

Direction for angle 0:
  East   3 o'clock   = 0
  North 12 o'clock   = 90
  West   9 o'clock   = 180
  South   6 o'clock   = 270
Enter direction for angle 0 <default>:

If you want to specify an angle other than those listed here, and you have a single-screen system, use F1 to flip to the graphics screen. Then indicate the angle with two points. If you indicate an angle in this manner, remember what you have done; you may become confused with a nonstandard angle as your zero angle.

The last prompt in the UNITS command controls the direction of angles. By default, AutoCAD works counterclockwise. You can work clockwise or counterclockwise. The prompt follows:

```
Do you want angles measured clockwise? <N>:
```

Hints

You can create a drawing with one UNITS setting and then alter the UNITS later. For instance, you could draw a machine part in decimal notation and later convert to feet and inches.

Any precision you set with the UNITS command affects only the display of values. AutoCAD internally always keeps track of values to a precision of 16 decimal places.

Error Messages

`Value must be between 1 and 5.` When prompted to select the system of units or of angle measure, you entered something other than an integer between one and five. Type a positive integer within this range.

`Value must be between 0 and 8.` When prompted to select the number of fractional places for display of angles, you entered something other than an integer between zero and eight. Type a positive integer within this range.

`Requires an integer value.` Your response was not an integer or was outside the range of integers allowed. Enter a positive integer within the range indicated in the prompt.

`Invalid choice.` Your response was invalid. Choose from the options in the prompt.

`Yes or No, please.` When prompted to answer Yes or No, you typed something else. Type **Y** or **N**.

UPDATE

Updates dimensions to current settings for dimension variables, text style, and UNITS.

Syntax

```
Dim: UPDATE
Select objects:
```

Template Coordinates

None

Description   This dimensioning subcommand is available only after you enter DIM or DIM1.

UPDATE causes AutoCAD to recalculate dimensioning information. This is done for the selection set you specify.

Hint   Only dimensioned entities are updated with this subcommand.

Error Messages   Unknown command. Type ? for list of commands. You entered the UPDATE command without first entering the DIM or DIM1 command. Enter a DIM command and then the UPDATE command.

Expects a point or Window/Last/Crossing/BOX/Add/Remove/Multiple/ Previous/Undo/AUto/SIngle When prompted to select objects, you entered an option keyword AutoCAD does not understand. Try again.

VERTICAL   *Gives the vertical (Y) distance from one point to the next.*

Syntax   DIM: **VERtical**
First extension line origin or RETURN to select:
Second extension line origin:
Dimension line location:
Dimension text <value>:

Description   This dimensioning subcommand is available only after you enter DIM or DIM1.

VERTICAL is used to generate dimensioning vertical to the selected entities. It is similar to the HORIZONTAL dimensioning command.

Hints   You can press Enter in response to the First extension line origin or RETURN to select: prompt to select an object. The vertical dimension of the selected entity will be used to derive the dimension. Alternatively, in response to the first prompt, you can pick a point to be used as the dimension origin.

Only the first three letters of the command (VER) are needed to use this command.

Error Messages   Unknown command. Type ? for list of commands. You entered the VERTICAL command without first entering the DIM or DIM1 command. Enter a DIM command and then the VERTICAL command.

Invalid option keyword. When prompted to select an option, you entered a response that does not correspond to a valid option keyword. Try again, selecting an option indicated in the prompt.

Invalid When prompted for the first extension line origin, you entered an invalid response. Select a point on-screen, or enter two or three coordinates.

Invalid
Select line, arc, or circle: When prompted for the first extension line origin, you entered an invalid response. Select a line, arc, or circle.

Invalid
dimension line location: When prompted for the dimension line location, you entered an invalid response. Select a point on-screen, or enter two coordinates.

VIEW

Creates views of zoomed work areas.

Syntax

Command: **VIEW**
?/Delete/Restore/Save/Window:
View name:

Template Coordinates

None

Description

A VIEW is simply that—a defined, named view of a drawing. Using VIEW to store drawing views can reduce the number of times you need to pan or zoom, saving the time it would take to regenerate your drawing with each pan or zoom.

? lists all the views that currently exist in the drawing.

Delete removes from the list the reference for the specified view.

Restore causes the view to be restored to the screen after it has been defined. Restore is used to flip between the views.

Save saves whatever is currently on-screen as a view. You are prompted for a view name, which can be 31 characters long and may contain letters, numbers, dollar signs ($), hyphens (-), and underscores (__). You reference the view by its view name.

Window allows you to make several views without zooming in on a view. First you enter the name under which you want the view saved. Then you put a window around the area you want included in the view.

You can use VIEW as an internal command within another AutoCAD command by preceding it with an apostrophe: `'VIEW`.

Possible Responses	*Response*	*Meaning*
	D	Delete specified view.
	R	Restore specified view.
	S	Save current screen display as view.
	W	Make area in window a view.
	?	List views.

Hints
As an alternative to entering the command, you can select VIEW from the DISPLAY screen menu.

You can store a window as a named view, and you can change the name of a view with the RENAME command.

Error Messages
`Cannot find view...` You tried to delete or restore a nonexistent view.

`Invalid view name.` You tried to save a view under a name that does not conform to AutoCAD file naming conventions. Rename the view.

VIEWPORTS or VPORTS *Controls the number of viewports on the screen at a given time.*

Syntax
Command: **VPORTS**
`Save/Restore/Delete/Join/SIngle/?/2/<3>/4:`

Template Coordinates
O 1 - 3

Description
The rectangular portion of the graphics screen that displays your drawing is called the *viewport*. You can divide the screen into more than one viewport to display portions of your drawing. You can also set the Snap mode, grid spacing, and three-dimensional view point independently for each viewport. VPORT lets you change the number of viewports on the screen. It also lets you save and restore viewports.

Save saves the current viewport configuration for future use. You are not limited to the number of viewports that can be saved. You are prompted for viewport names; standard naming requirements apply.

Restore restores a saved viewport.

Delete deletes a saved viewport configuration.

Join merges two adjacent viewports into one larger viewport. The resulting viewport is inherited from the dominant viewport. You are prompted:

```
Select dominant viewport <current>:
Select viewport to join:
```

SIngle returns you to single viewport (normal) viewing.

? lists the viewports currently saved.

2,3,4 allows you to define two, three, or four viewports in a configuration of your choice. Two viewports are defined with either a vertical or horizontal configuration. Three viewports are defined with one large port next to two small ports. Four viewports divides the screen into four equal areas.

Possible Responses	*Response*	*Meaning*
	D	Delete saved viewport configuration.
	J	Join two viewports.
	R	Restore saved viewport.
	S	Save current viewport.
	S1	Display single viewport filling the entire graphics area.
	2	Divide current viewport into two viewports.
	3	Divide current viewport into three viewports.
	4	Divide current viewport into four viewports.
	?	List saved viewports.

Hints

If you use the pull-down menus for VPORT, choosing the configuration is easier.

View names can be up to 31 characters, including letters, numbers, dollar signs, hyphens, and underscores. AutoCAD automatically converts view names to uppercase characters.

Once you have named views in a drawing, you can specify a view when the Drawing Editor loads the drawing, and you can plot portions of the drawing using view names.

Error Messages

Requires an integer value or an option keyword. You entered an invalid value or option. Select an option keyword displayed in the prompt, or enter the number of viewports you want to define.

Cannot find viewport configuration____. You entered a valid name, but no viewport configuration exists under that name. Check your typing, and try again.

Invalid viewport configuration name. You entered an invalid name. Check your typing, and try again.

`Only one viewport is active.` You tried to join two viewports when only one was active. To define additional viewports, use the 2,3,4 option with this command. Then you can join the viewports.

`Invalid viewport I.D.` Your response to one of the select viewport prompts was invalid. Specify a valid name.

`The selected viewports must be distinct.` You selected the same viewport twice when trying to join viewports. Select two different viewports.

VIEWRES

Controls AutoCAD's fast regeneration and the resolution of circles and arcs as they are drawn and represented.

Syntax

```
Command: VIEWRES
Do you want fast zooms? <Y>:
Enter circle zoom percent <1-20000> <100>:
```

Template Coordinates

None

Description

VIEWRES stands for *view resolution*. VIEWRES controls regeneration and the smoothness of curves. The more segments or vectors you specify with `circle zoom percent`, the smoother curves appear. The effect of the number of segments drawn becomes increasingly apparent as the size of the curved entity increases.

If you respond with **Y** to the first prompt, AutoCAD allows fast regenerations. The `circle zoom percent` is the value that determines the resolution of circles and arcs on your graphics monitor. The default setting is 100. This default value causes AutoCAD to use its internal algorithm to compute the optimum number of vectors for each circle or arc so that it appears smooth at the current zoom magnification.

For fast drawing, you can set `circle zoom percent` to a number less than 100. There is no point in setting it higher than 100 because AutoCAD never uses more than the number of vectors it determines to be optimal for the entity, given the zoom magnification.

`circle zoom percent` is ignored during plotting and printer plotting; arcs and circles are always plotted with the optimal number of vectors.

Hint   There is a trade-off relationship between resolution and regeneration time. The larger your zoom percentage, the more line segments in a circle, and, therefore, the better the resolution. However, regeneration time increases with the number of segments in a circle.

Error Messages   `Yes or No, please.` When prompted to answer Yes or No, you typed something else. Type **Y** or **N**.

`Value must be between 1 and 20000.` When prompted to enter the center zoom percent, you entered something other than an integer between 1 and 20000. Type a positive integer within this range.

`Requires an integer value.` When prompted to enter the center zoom percent, you responded with something other than an integer. Enter a positive integer between 1 and 20000.

VPOINT   *Allows you to see your drawing in three dimensions.*

Syntax
```
Command: VPOINT
Rotate/<View point> <current>:
```

Template Coordinates   None

Description   The default view point is plan view with coordinates of 0,0,1, which means that your view is over the X-Y plane origin. When you want to return to the plan view of your drawing, type those coordinates at the prompt. You can also use the pull-down menus to determine your view point.

Possible Responses

Response	Meaning
R	Select view point by way of rotation angles.
Enter	Select view point by way of compass and axes.
x,y,z	Specify view point.

Hints   You can establish a view point for each viewport. Points and angles entered with this command relate to the current UCS.

If you are unfamiliar with this command, you may find it helpful to establish the X-Y angle first and then adjust the view point.

The drawing is regenerated each time you use the VPOINT command.

Error	*Invalid* It appears that V (for View point) is an option keyword in the
Messages	Rotate/<View point> <current>: prompt, but to select this option, you need to press Enter.

Requires numeric angle or second point. You responded with a non-numeric response when prompted for a rotation angle. Try again, providing a numeric value or a second point that defines the angle.

VSLIDE — *Allows you to view previously created slides.*

Syntax

Command: **VSLIDE**
Slide file <default>:

Template Coordinates

None

Description

VSLIDE allows you to view slides you created previously with the MSLIDE command. When prompted for a slide file, you should enter the name of the singular slide file or (if the slide you want to view is part of a library) the name of the library file followed by the slide name in parentheses.

Possible Responses

Response	*Meaning*
file	View slide.
*file	Load slide for next VSLIDE.

Hints

To clear a slide from your screen, use REDRAW.

Since slides appear in the current viewport over your drawing, it is difficult to edit a drawing while a slide is displayed. Using additional viewports lets you see both the slide and the drawing.

Error Message

Can't open file
Invalid You entered an unknown VSLIDE file name. Try again, and be sure not to use the .SLD file extension.

WBLOCK — *Creates blocks that can be used in all drawings.*

Syntax

Command: **WBLOCK**
File name:
Block name:

| Template
Coordinates | R 1 | |

Description When you create blocks using the BLOCK command, AutoCAD saves the defined block with the current drawing. This means it can be used within the current drawing only. To make the block more widely available, you can write the block to a disk file by using the WBLOCK command.

File name. AutoCAD requests the name of the file it is creating to hold the block. The file name must comply with DOS conventions.

Block name. AutoCAD requests the name of the block to write to the file. If the block does not exist yet, press Enter. You will see the standard BLOCK creation prompts for insertion base point and object selection. If the block and the file have the same name, you can type the shorthand character, the equal sign (=); if the entire drawing is being written out, use the asterisk (*); otherwise, type the name of the block to be written to file.

Possible Responses

Response	Meaning
name	Write file name for block.
=	Block name is same as file name.
*	Write entire drawing.
Enter	Write specified block.

Hints After you create a WBLOCK, you can INSERT it in drawings. To orient the block appropriately when you insert it, set the UCS for the host drawing before entering the INSERT command.

After saving a block with WBLOCK, you can subsequently edit the block by loading the file as you would any other drawing.

Error Messages A drawing with this name already exists.

Do you want to replace it? <N> You tried to create a block with the same name as one that already exists. Answer *Yes* only if you want to replace the old block with the new one; otherwise, answer *No*, and rename the new block.

Yes or No, please. When prompted to answer Yes or No, you typed something else. Type **Y** or **N**.

Block ___ not found. No block was found under the name you specified. Try again.

Invalid point. Your response to the insertion base point prompt was invalid. Select a point on-screen, or enter two or three coordinates.

ZOOM — *Allows you to magnify or condense parts of the drawing.*

Syntax

Command: **ZOOM**
All/Center/Dynamic/Extents/Left/Previous/Window/ <Scale(X)>:

Template Coordinates

J 9 - P 9

Description

ZOOM, one of the most frequently used commands in AutoCAD, lets you magnify portions of your drawing for easier editing.

All (Template coordinate M 9) returns you to your drawing limits or the extents, whichever is larger.

Center allows you to identify a new center point for the screen and then enter the height. This height is the factor that determines the zoom scale.

Dynamic (Template coordinate L 9) causes a new screen to appear on the monitor.

Extents (Template coordinate N 9). The extents of the drawing are the precise area in which you have drawn. The X and Y values make up the drawing extents. Extents pulls all entities in the drawing onto the screen. This is a good way to see whether any rogue entities are floating around in the drawing.

Left allows you to set a new lower left corner and height.

Previous (Template coordinate N 9) returns you to the previous screen. You can restore up to 10 previous views.

Window (Template coordinates J 9 and K 9) allows you to place a window around the area in which you want to work.

Scale (Template coordinate P 9) allows you to zoom by a scale factor.

You can use ZOOM as an internal command within another AutoCAD command by preceding it with an apostrophe: 'ZOOM. ZOOM can be used as an internal command only if no regeneration is necessary to display the newly specified ZOOM area.

Possible Responses

Response	Meaning
number	Zoom by a factor from original scale.
numberX	Zoom by a factor from current scale.
A	All

C	Specify new center point.
D	Dynamic
E	Extents
L	Set new lower left corner.
P	Return to previous screen.
W	Place window around working area.

Hints

The All and Extents options always regenerate your drawing. Use ZOOM Previous whenever appropriate since it does not necessarily regenerate your drawing (although it may).

Use ZOOM Extents before exiting from a drawing session to see whether you "colored outside the lines" of your drawing limits.

ZOOM Previous does not restore any entities you erased. Use UNDO for this purpose.

Error Messages

Requires a distance, numberX, or option keyword. You responded with something other than the options displayed in the prompt. Try again, selecting from the options indicated or specifying the scale.

Redisplay required by change in drawing extents. AutoCAD has redisplayed your drawing according to changes you made in the drawing extents.

Invalid point. Your response to the center point prompt or a corner point prompt was invalid. Select a point on-screen, or enter two or three coordinates.

Invalid window specification. Your response to the corner point prompts for a window was invalid. Either select points on-screen, or enter two or three coordinates for each corner.

3DFACE

Draws three-dimensional flat planes.

Syntax

Command: **3DFACE**
First point:
Second point:
Third point:
Fourth point:
Third point:
Fourth point:

Template Coordinates

N 6

Description The 3DFACE drawings are similar to the SOLID drawings created in the X-Y plane. The prompts are similar to those for the SOLID command. The difference is in the point input sequence: the points used to define the 3DFACE must be indicated clockwise or counterclockwise—not randomly, as with the SOLID command.

To make an edge of the 3DFACE invisible, type **I** before specifying the first point of that edge in the following format:

```
First point: I (point coordinates)
```

You can also type **I** before selecting the point on-screen.

Possible   *Response*   *Meaning*
Response   I   Make following edge invisible.

Hints Specify points in clockwise or counterclockwise order but not randomly. This is in contrast with the SOLID command, where entering points clockwise or counterclockwise draws a bow tie.

Unlike Solid faces, 3D faces are not filled.

To use AutoShade on entities you create with 3DFACE, use the FILMROLL command.

Error Point or option keyword required. Your response to one of the point
Message prompts was invalid. Select a point on-screen, or enter two or three coordinates for each point.

3DMESH

Creates a general polygon mesh by specifying the size of the mesh (in terms of M and N) and the vertices for the mesh.

Syntax
```
Command: 3DMESH
Mesh M size:
Mesh N size:
Vertex (0, 0):
Vertex (x, y):
Vertex (x, y):
Vertex (x, y):
```

Template   None
Coordinates

Description	The 3DMESH command, used for specifying arbitrary meshes, is best used in LISP. For easier use of meshes, see RULESURF, TABSURF, REVSURF, and EDGESURF in this command reference.

M size and N size define how many vertices the mesh will have (M × N vertices).

Vertex. Default vertices correspond to the current UCS and to the M and N sizes. Vertices may be two- or three-dimensional points.

Hint 3DMESH creates a mesh using the system variables SURFTAB1 and SURFTAB2 rather than relying on entities in the drawing to establish characteristics of the mesh surface. Since dense meshes increase your drawing time, low values for these two variables save drawing time.

Error Messages Requires an integer value. When prompted to enter the Mesh M or N size, you responded with something other than an integer. Enter a positive integer between 2 and 256.

Value must be between 2 and 256. You entered a value out of range. Enter a positive integer between 2 and 256.

Value must be positive and nonzero. The value you entered is negative, zero, or non-numeric. Enter a positive number.

3DPOLY *Draws three-dimensional polylines.*

Syntax
```
Command: 3DPOLY
From point:
Close/Undo/<Endpoint of line>:
```

Template Coordinates O 6

Description A three-dimensional polyline is a polyline with independent X, Y, and Z axis coordinates. Three-dimensional polylines are oriented in space rather than confined to a single X-Y plane like two-dimensional polylines. They have no thickness and can contain only straight line segments. Although you can use PEDIT to spline curve fit a three-dimensional polyline, the curve will actually consist of straight segments. Three-dimensional polylines are useful when you want to cross a three-dimensional space in multiple planes.

From point: is the start of the polyline.

Close closes a polyline with two or more segments.

Undo undoes the last endpoint.

<Endpoint of line>: option prompts for the next endpoint for the polyline.

Points may be two- or three-dimensional. Use the PEDIT command to edit three-dimensional polylines.

Possible *Responses*	*Response*	*Meaning*
	C	Close polyline.
	U	Undo last endpoint.
	Enter	Exit.

Hint 3DPOLY is the three-dimensional counterpart of the two-dimensional command PLINE.

Error *Messages* Point or option keyword required. Your response to one of the point prompts was invalid. Select a point on-screen, or enter two or three coordinates for each point.

Invalid point. Your response to the center point or a corner point prompt was invalid. Select a point on-screen, or enter two or three coordinates.

AutoCAD's Menus

This appendix discusses the major programs Autodesk has included in the Release 10 pull-down menus, as well as two from the screen menu. The programs from the pull-down menu are for three-dimensional construction, three-dimensional view point, viewports, and setting up UCSs. Also discussed are the screen-menu's Setup program and the screen menu's three-dimensional construction complement to the pull-down three-dimensional construction program. This appendix is intended as a quick reference for the programs, not an in-depth discussion of programming.

Pull-Down Menu Programs

A large program for three-dimensional construction is located under the pull-down menu's DRAW option. This program allows you to create several objects in three dimensions by entering information about a specific object. Figure A.1 shows the dialogue box for this command. Following is an explanation for each of the objects, including the prompts you will see and directions for answering them.

The following explanations for the dialogue box start from the top, reading from left to right.

Box: Designers will find this option helpful for work involving simple figures. When planning a project, architects will want to use it for working with masses.

Select Box if you want to draw a rectilinear shape or a cube. You are prompted for a corner for the box, and for a length and width, after which you are prompted for a height. You also have the option of rotating the box around the current Z axis.

Fig. A.1. *Dialogue box for three-dimensional construction (under pull-down menu's* DRAW *option).*

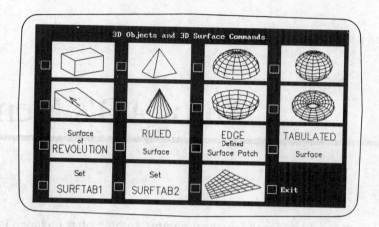

Pyramid: This option allows you to draw a pyramid, either a tetrahedron (three-sided pyramid) or a four-sided pyramid. The top can end either in an apex or a flat plane.

The first four prompts ask for the bottom corners of the pyramid. (The fourth prompt allows you to select a fourth corner or a tetrahedron.) You are next prompted for the top—a flat plane or an apex. If you select a flat plane, you are prompted for the three or four corners that define the top plane.

Dome: This option draws a dome. The edges of the dome default to the current UCS. You are prompted for the center of the dome, a diameter or radius, and the number of segments (both longitudinally and latitudinally). The two prompts with which you select segments define the density of the mesh that makes up the dome.

Sphere: Both the dome and the dish are based on the sphere. Because the center of the sphere defaults to the current UCS, half of the sphere is above the current UCS and half below. To change this, enter a point with a Z value when AutoCAD prompts you for the center point. If the Z value is equal to or greater that the radius of the sphere, the sphere will lie above the UCS. If the Z value is less than the radius, the sphere will either intersect the current UCS or lie below the current UCS. In addition to the center and the radius or diameter, you are prompted also for the number of longitudinal and latitudinal segments, which define the density of the mesh used to define the sphere.

Wedge: This option allows you to draw a wedge-shaped object. You are prompted for the wedge's lower left corner, a length and width, and the height of the end. As with the box, you can rotate this object around the current Z axis.

Cone: This option (like Pyramid) allows you to draw a cone with either a point or flat plane for its apex. You are prompted for the center of the base, a diameter or radius for the base, a diameter or radius for the top (use 0 for a point), and a height for the cone. You are prompted also for the number of segments to define the cone.

Dish: The dish, like the dome, is based on the sphere. The default location for the rim of the dish is the current UCS. To change this, enter a center point for the dish with a Z-axis coordinate. In addition to the center of the dish, you are prompted for a diameter or radius, and for the number of both longitudinal and latitudinal segments to define the density of the mesh.

Torus: A torus is shaped like a doughnut. You are prompted for the center of the torus, the diameter or radius of the torus (the outside diameter or radius), the diameter or radius of the tube (the inside diameter or radius), and for the segments around the circumference of the tube and the torus circumference. These segments define the density of the mesh that defines the torus.

The next four options on the dialogue box (Surface of REVOLUTION, RULED Surface, EDGE Defined Surface Patch, and TABULATED Surface) execute the commands that create those types of surfaces. The standard command prompts are the same as those discussed in Chapter 15.

The Set SURFTAB1 and Set SURFTAB2 options allow you to change the values of these two system variables, just as though you were using the SETVAR command.

The box displaying the mesh allows you to define four corners, an M density, and an N density, and then calculates the three-dimensional mesh which fits that area. This is handy for those who do not want to use the 3DMESH command to calculate a mesh for an area. You can always modify the mesh with the PEDIT command. The last option returns you to a normal screen without having executed any commands.

The next major program in the pull-down menu is under the heading DISPLAY. The Vpoint 3D option allows you to select a three-dimensional view point from some preset selections shown in the dialogue box (see fig. A.2). After you select one of these view points, you are prompted for the angle from the current UCS. This angle defines how far up from the current UCS you will view the objects.

Fig. A.2. *Dialogue box for pull-down menu's* DISPLAY, Vpoint 3D *option.*

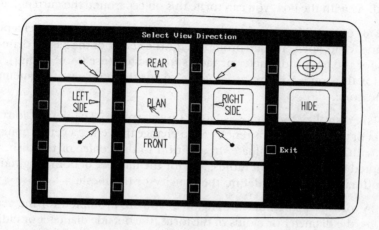

When you select one of these view points, AutoCAD automatically sets up the direction from the object in the current X-Y plane. You set up the vertical direction by entering an angle at the prompt that follows your selection.

Another program under DISPLAY is that for setting up viewports. If you select Set Viewports, a dialogue box (see fig. A.3) allows you to select preset layouts for viewports. By selecting a layout from the dialogue box, you cause that particular layout to become the current layout for viewports. Remember: to switch between viewports, simply digitize the viewport in which you want to work.

The final major pull-down menu program discussed here is under SETTINGS. If you select UCS Options, a dialogue box displaying preset UCS options appears on-screen (see fig. A.4). This option is handy because the preset selections are standard views for basic drafting (including top, back, left, front, right, and bottom). Also included are the options of the World Coordinate System (WCS) or the current view on-screen.

Screen-Menu Programs

The two programs discussed here are the main programs located in the screen menu. The first, Setup, is a program that allows you to set up a drawing by answering three questions. The second program, 3D, is the complement of the pull-down menu's 3D construction program.

Fig. A.3. *The* Set Viewports *dialogue box.*

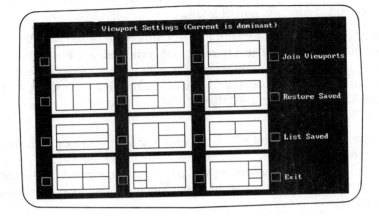

Fig. A.4. *Pull-down menu's dialogue box for UCS options (under* Settings*).*

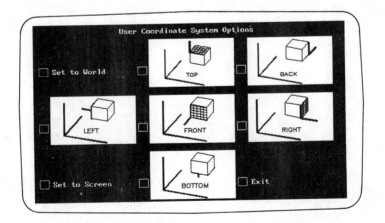

Setup prompts for units, the scale for your drawing (this can be very helpful if you are not drawing full scale), and for the size of your drawing. With this program you can use one command for setting up part of the drawing, instead of having to execute several commands.

The Root menu's 3D command is the complement of the pull-down menu's 3D construction option. The difference is that the dialogue box does not appear on-screen. The screen menu displays the selections (box, pyramid, dome, sphere, wedge, cone, dish, and torus) and you also can select REVSURF, RULESURF, EDGESURF, TABSURF, and 3DMESH. You can also set the system variables (SURFTAB1 and SURFTAB2).

The programs described in this appendix are the main ones in AutoCAD's pull-down and screen menus. There is some programming in all AutoCAD menus. This programming—from the repetition of commands in the pull-down menu to the simplicity of using the tablet menu—is intended to enhance your productivity.

B

Useful Additional Programs

O ne of the reasons for AutoCAD's tremendous success among all the CAD packages on the market is its support from third-party developers. While the basic AutoCAD package provides drafting utilities, the packages discussed here cover certain areas of drafting in more depth.

The current copy of the *AutoCAD Applications Guide* lists over 200 third-party packages. This appendix lists several packages, available both commercially and as shareware, that enhance AutoCAD's effectiveness.

AutoCAD AEC Architectural

The AEC Architectural package, developed by Autodesk, provides a custom template and symbol library for architectural and construction firms. The package provides library symbols in both two- and three-dimensional versions and allows you to switch back and forth so that your design may be viewed as either a plan or a model. The template contains many helpful routines for placement of structural grids, room creation, wall intersection cleanup, and storefront creation.

AutoCAD AEC Mechanical

The AEC Mechanical package, also developed by Autodesk, is appropriate for mechanical engineers and similar in capabilities to the AEC Architectural template. The largest difference is that the symbol libraries are geared more towards piping, duct work, HVAC, and fire protection. The template comes complete with an interface to a popular duct-analysis software package, which may be used to accurately design duct networks.

AutoSolid

AutoSolid, another Autodesk product, is a *solids modeling* package. Solids modeling is important in the design and analysis of objects, their properties, and how those objects fit together. The AutoSolid package can perform analysis operations (such as volume, surface area, mass, and finite-element mesh analysis) that help determine how a product can best be manufactured. The beauty of using a computer for these prototyping operations is that if a design doesn't work, scrapping the time to build a computer "model" costs less than if you had built the model in the more traditional clay or plastic.

AutoSketch

AutoSketch is sometimes thought of as AutoCAD's younger sibling. Developed by Autodesk, this package contains much of the functionality of AutoCAD without a lot of the drafting extras supplied in the full AutoCAD package. Drawings created in AutoSketch can be exported to AutoCAD by means of the DXF format. AutoSketch is most useful for developing preliminary drawings that will later be enhanced with the more robust AutoCAD package.

DCA Engineering Software

The DCA Civil Engineering package by DCA Engineering, Inc. is a group of programs that run from within AutoCAD and customize AutoCAD for civil engineers. The different modules allow for profile and cross-section generation, three-dimensional mesh creation from points, lot sizing, complete drawing annotation, and other specific civil engineering requirements.

LandCADD Professional Land Planner

The LandCADD Professional Land Planner package by LandCADD, Inc. allows you to perform site design and land planning from within AutoCAD. The template contains a complete symbol library of plants and trees as well as routines to simulate growth of the flora over extended periods. These simulation capabilities, coupled with routines for landscaping design, irrigation design, and many standard construction details, make the package extremely helpful to the landscape architect.

CAD Letterease

As you know from Chapter 12, "Expanding Your Horizons," AutoCAD can use multiple text styles within a drawing. The CAD Letterease template, developed by CAD Lettering Systems, Inc., is a series of custom-designed fonts that mimic many of the typefaces available in press-on lettering. This add-in program allows you to place lettering along arcs and polylines and to control the spacing between individual letters. Each Letterease lettering style comes in 5 different forms which can be reproduced accurately (from 1/16 inch up to 5 feet high) with no distortion.

Quicksurf

If you need to create 3-D meshes from a series of random points within a drawing, Quicksurf is the fastest method available. The Quicksurf program by Schreiber Instruments is available as a demo version from many bulletin boards. The program will read random points or contour lines and create the matching 3-D mesh surface model. Its speed comes from the use of an external module to perform all calculations instead of relying on AutoLISP routines as many other surface-modeling packages do.

AutoManager

AutoManager, by CYCO Automation, is a drawing management program for AutoCAD. It allows you to open DWG files, turn layers on and off, and even view blocks within a drawing—all without ever entering the AutoCAD program. AutoManager contains super-fast routines for erasing, copying, and renaming multiple files across different directories. This makes it easier to keep your CAD workstations cleaned up.

AutoDC

The AutoDC program by the Memphis Software Company decrypts encrypted AutoLISP files. Encryption, like copy protection, is becoming a thing of the past. Software vendors find that providing users with maximum flexibility is often more productive. This program is still helpful for customizing routines in commercially available packages that still use encryption.

Checklsp

The LISP programming language has long been called one of the most difficult languages to use, mainly because it relies heavily on properly balanced parentheses that maintain data integrity within the interpreter. Any AutoLISP programmer knows that the minute AutoCAD finds a mismatched parenthesis or quotation mark, it will cancel loading an AutoLISP routine.

The Checklsp program, created by Computer Projects Unlimited, provides syntax-checking of LISP source files and notifies the user of any errors as it finds them. The program, which is small enough to be run from within most programming editors, can even be added to the ACAD.PGP file for syntax checking from within AutoCAD.

Herman Miller AutoCAD Template

The Herman Miller Systems Furniture Division created the Herman Miller Template more than four years ago. This template, one of the first of its kind, heralded a new type of product specification. Instead of creating symbol libraries to match the different types of furniture from a manufacturer, the manufacturer created the library and distributed it free of charge so that more people would specify the product line.

Andersen Windows CADD-I

One of the newer generation of computerized product lines available from a manufacturer, the CADD-I template contains window details, elevations, and sections that help shorten your design time. This package contains the same information found in the Andersen specifications booklets as well as routines for insertion of custom windows and doors, and storefront design.

TED

TED (for Text EDitor) is a shareware product that can be found on CompuServe. TED was designed from the ground up to be as similar as possible to a normal full-screen text editor that you would use when you are not in AutoCAD. It has color capabilities, can do search-and-replace, will break apart lines of text or put two lines together, can cut and paste from the middle of one line to the middle of another, and uses intuitive cursor-control keys. In addition, TED can import text from outside AutoCAD. And, by using the SHELL command, you can do all of this without leaving AutoCAD. TED is not a TSR; it requires no additional memory.

Summary

The many products available to enhance AutoCAD are too numerous to mention here. The products listed in this section should give you an idea of the diverse number of products and programs available to make AutoCAD more productive for you.

A Portfolio of Drawings

The drawings in this appendix were submitted by individuals, firms, and AutoCAD users' groups across North America. We thank those who have shared their creative talents so that you, the reader, might have an idea of the types of drawings possible with AutoCAD.

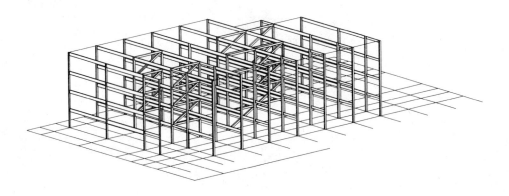

Drawing courtesy of Seattle AutoCAD Users' Group
Seattle, Washington

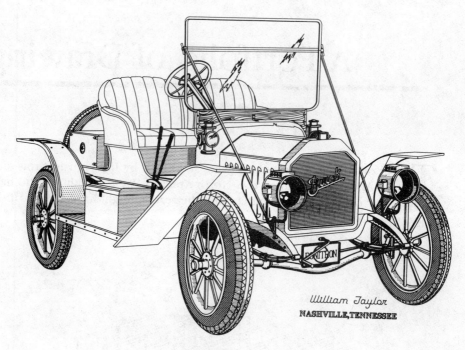

William Taylor
NASHVILLE, TENNESSEE

1910 BUICK

Drawing courtesy of William Taylor, Bonitron, Inc.
Nashville, Tennessee

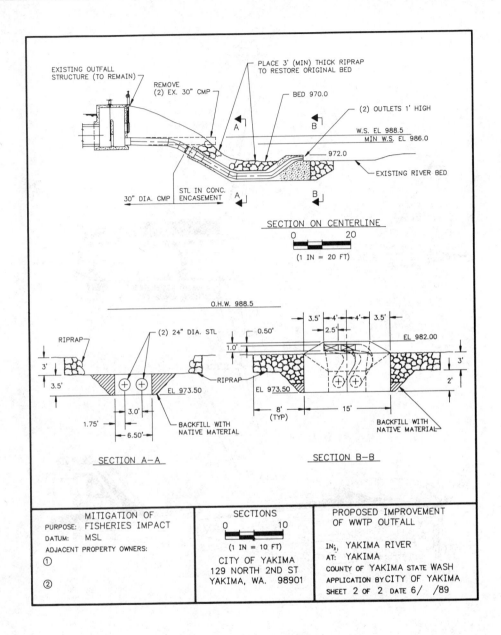

EXISTING OUTFALL
STRUCTURE (TO REMAIN)

REMOVE
(2) EX. 30" CMP

PLACE 3' (MIN) THICK RIPRAP
TO RESTORE ORIGINAL BED

BED 970.0

(2) OUTLETS 1' HIGH

W.S. EL 988.5
MIN W.S. EL 986.0

972.0

EXISTING RIVER BED

30" DIA. CMP

STL IN CONC.
ENCASEMENT

SECTION ON CENTERLINE

0   20

(1 IN = 20 FT)

O.H.W. 988.5

RIPRAP

(2) 24" DIA. STL

0.50'

1.0'

3.5' | 4' | 4' | 3.5'
2.5'

EL 982.00

3'

3.5'

RIPRAP

EL 973.50

EL 973.50

3.0'

1.75'

6.50'

BACKFILL WITH
NATIVE MATERIAL

8'
(TYP)

15'

3'

2'

BACKFILL WITH
NATIVE MATERIAL

SECTION A–A

SECTION B–B

MITIGATION OF	SECTIONS	PROPOSED IMPROVEMENT OF WWTP OUTFALL
PURPOSE: FISHERIES IMPACT DATUM: MSL ADJACENT PROPERTY OWNERS: ① ②	0 10 (1 IN = 10 FT) CITY OF YAKIMA 129 NORTH 2ND ST YAKIMA, WA. 98901	IN: YAKIMA RIVER AT: YAKIMA COUNTY OF YAKIMA STATE WASH APPLICATION BY CITY OF YAKIMA SHEET 2 OF 2 DATE 6/ /89

Drawing courtesy of Seattle AutoCAD Users' Group
Seattle, Washington

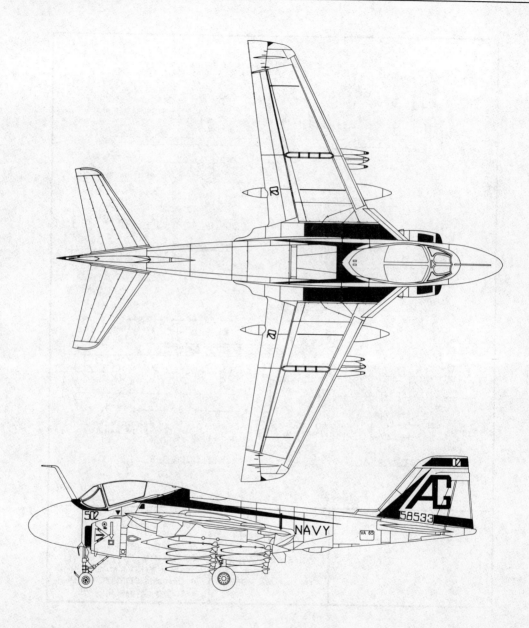

Drawing courtesy of Kenn R. Anderson, Jr. (ACSI)
La Plume, Pennsylvania

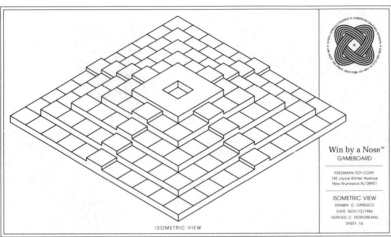

Win by a Nose™
GAMEBOARD

PRESSMAN TOY CORP.
745 Joyce Kilmer Avenue
New Brunswick,NJ 08901

ISOMETRIC VIEW
DRAWN: O. OPRESCO
DATE: NOV/12/1986
VERIFIED: C. ROSIOREANU
SHEET: 1b

ISOMETRIC VIEW

"Win by a Nose" is a registered trademark of Pressman Toy Corporation

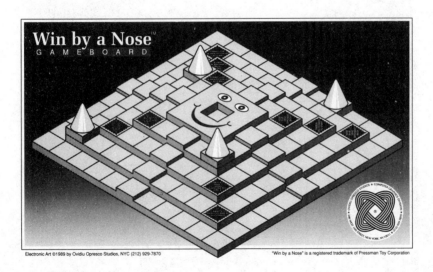

Electronic Art ©1989 by Ovidiu Opresco Studios, NYC (212) 929-7870   "Win by a Nose" is a registered trademark of Pressman Toy Corporation

Drawing courtesy of Ovidiu Opresco Studios
New York, New York

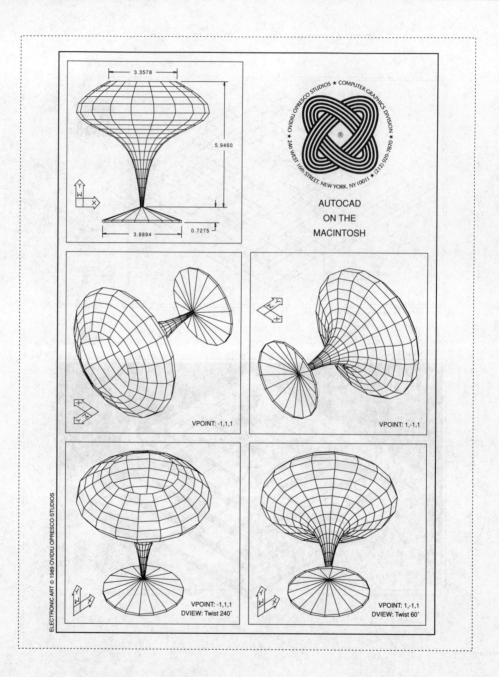

AUTOCAD
ON THE
MACINTOSH

VPOINT: -1,1,1

VPOINT: 1,-1,1

VPOINT: -1,1,1
DVIEW: Twist 240°

VPOINT: 1,-1,1
DVIEW: Twist 60°

ELECTRONIC ART © 1989 OVIDIU OPRESCO STUDIOS

Drawing courtesy of Ovidiu Opresco Studios
New York, New York

Drawing courtesy of Ovidiu Opresco Studios
New York, New York

ARCH OF SEPTIMIUS SEVERUS ROME

Drawing courtesy of Kenneth A. Rogers & Associates
Santa Cruz, California

HAMPSTEAD DOORWAY

Drawing courtesy of Kenneth A. Rogers & Associates
Santa Cruz, California

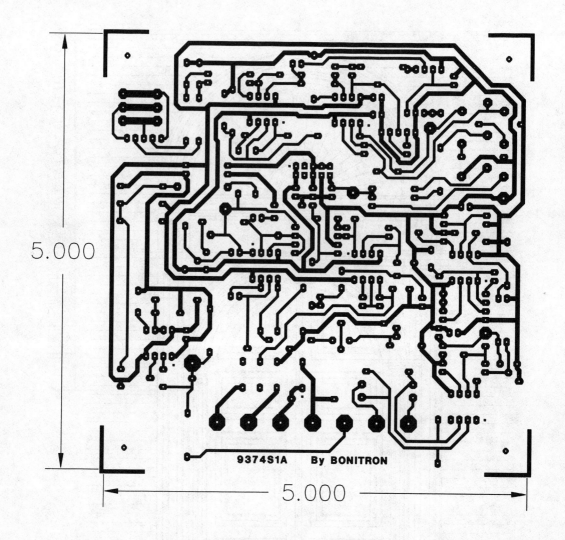

5.000

5.000

9374S1A   By BONITRON

Drawing courtesy of Marty Hart, Bonitron, Inc.
Nashville, Tennessee

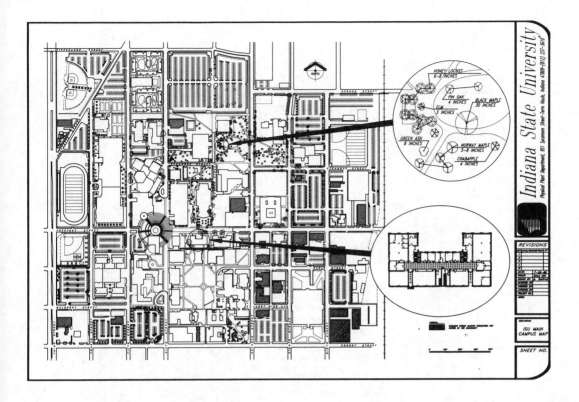

Drawing courtesy of Paul F. Beima (Indiana State University)
Terre Haute, Indiana

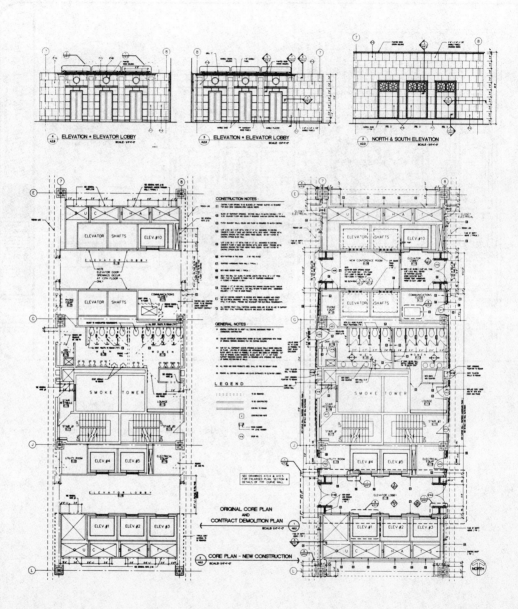

Drawing courtesy of Jorge L. Guillen, Stecker LaBau Arneill McManus
Hartford, Connecticut

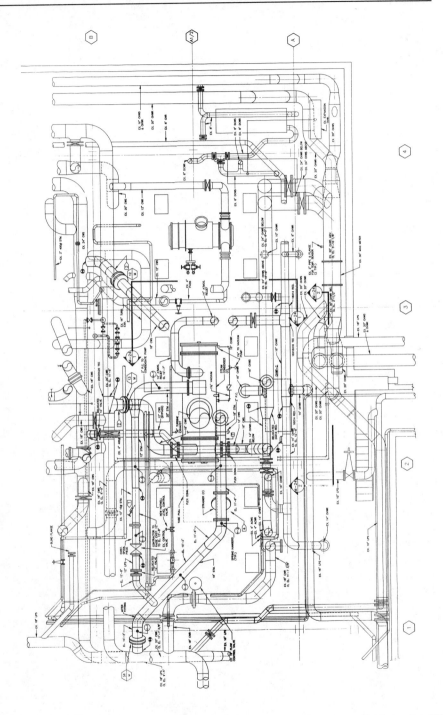

Drawing courtesy of Ellerbe Becket
Minneapolis, Minnesota

Glossary

Absolute coordinate. The absolute location of a point in the current X-Y plane, with reference to a fixed origin point. Can be either Cartesian or polar. These coordinates are treated as X,Y displacements from 0,0.

Aperture. A target box that encloses the intersection of the crosshairs, used to select entities on-screen.

Array. Multiple copies of entities in rows and columns arranged in rectangular or polar patterns.

Associative dimension. A dimension stored as an entity rather than as individual lines, areas, solids, and dimension text. The associated values are updated automatically to reflect modifications to a dimensioned entity.

Attribute. A special AutoCAD entity in which you can store any type of information associated with a block.

Attribute mode. Four attribute mode toggles are available to control the handling of attributes: Invisible, Constant, Verify, and Preset.

Attribute tag. A one-word label for the attribute being defined.

Axis of revolution. The axis around which a path curve revolves.

Base point. A reference point, located anywhere in a drawing, that AutoCAD needs in order to copy or move entities from this point to a second point.

Blip. A symbol—usually a small cross (+)—which AutoCAD places on-screen to indicate points that have been digitized. Although they appear on the screen whenever you select a point, blips are not part of your drawing.

Block. A special set of grouped entities treated by AutoCAD as a single object. A block can contain part of a drawing or an entire file. Blocks can be used to insert components of one drawing into another drawing or to make copies of a component in the same drawing.

Boundary. The outline of an area to be hatched, including any internal outlines of areas that should not be hatched. Boundaries must be closed figures.

CAD. An acronym for *Computer-Aided Design*.

Camera. The name of the location from which you are looking at an object.

Cartesian coordinate system. A coordinate system that uses two or three axes to locate any given point in three dimensions. The origin of this system is 0,0 or 0,0,0 (X=0, Y=0, and Z=0).

Cell. See *Unit cell*.

Chamfer. A beveled edge between two intersecting lines which ''squares'' their intersection.

Chord. A straight line segment that connects the endpoints of an arc.

Clipping plane. A plane, perpendicular to the line of sight, which can be applied anywhere between the camera and target point so that it blocks whatever is behind or in front of it. Two clipping planes can be used to show only objects between them. Clipping planes are used to show views that would otherwise be hidden by objects in the foreground.

Compression factor. With text, a factor of the default setting that determines whether the text will be normal or compressed. (See *Expansion factor.*)

Construction plane. The X-Y plane at the current elevation.

Continuation. The process of drawing a line or arc that starts at the end of the most recently drawn line or arc and continues from that point.

Coons surface patch. The surface created by using the EDGESURF command. An interpolated bicubic surface between four adjoining curves; the curves may be in any alignment in the drawing.

Coordinate system icon. An on-screen symbol that indicates the orientation of the X and Y axes as you change coordinate systems.

Corrupt. To mix up or partially erase information in a file so that your computer no longer understands it.

Crosshairs. A cursor (two perpendicular crossed lines inside the aperture or target box) used to select coordinate locations on-screen.

Delta. The change in the X, Y, and Z values from one point to another (delta x, delta y, and delta z); the change in distance in the X, Y, and Z directions.

Dialogue box. A temporary overlay that provides prompts with which you can respond to a command.

Digitizing. The process of using a pointing device in order to randomly but accurately indicate points in a drawing and to select coordinates on an AutoCAD template.

Digitizing tablet. A flat, electronic surface used in conjunction with a mouse or puck to enter commands and select points on-screen.

Dimensions. Measurements (usually in the form of extension lines) of the angles and distances between points in a drawing.

Dimension line. A line showing the distance or angle the dimension measures.

Dimension variables. System variables that affect the way dimensioned entities act and appear.

Dimensioning commands. Commands used to add dimensioning to a drawing.

Direction vector. A line or an open polyline with an exact direction and length but without an exact location.

Displacement. The distances along the X, Y, and Z axes when an entity is moved from one location to another. These distances are expressed as delta x, delta y, and delta z.

Dragging. The process in which AutoCAD draws a ''shadow'' (or tentative image) of an entity as that entity is drawn or edited so that you can see the effect of the change before it takes place.

Drawing commands. Commands used to create an entity.

Editing commands. Commands used to modify or change previously created entities.

Elevation. The location of entities on the Z axis.

Entity. A graphic element such as a line, circle, arc, text, attribute, or dimension.

Expansion or compression factor. With text, a factor of the default setting that determines whether the text will be normal, expanded, or compressed.

Extents. The area in which you have drawn. The drawing limits determine the potential size of a drawing; drawing extents indicate its actual size.

Extrusion. An entity's thickness or extension from its X-Y plane along the Z axis of the UCS. Always parallel to the Z axis of the UCS in which the entity was created.

Fillet. The representation of a filled-in or rounded intersection of two entities. (See *Chamfer*.)

Flip screen key. On a keyboard, the F1 function key, which "flips" between AutoCAD's text screen and graphics screen.

Global editing. The process of editing all attributes at one time.

Grid. A rectangular array of reference points that lie within a drawing's limits.

Hatching. The process of filling an area with a design for purposes of identification.

Insertion base point. A reference point used as the 0,0 origin point when an entity is inserted into a drawing. Inserting, scaling, and rotating are relative to the insertion point.

Isometric. A two-dimensional representation of a three-dimensional object.

Layer. In a drawing, an overlay on which specific data can be stored.

Leader. A dimension line that connects text with the entity being dimensioned or labeled.

Library part. (Also called *block*.) A special entity used often in your drawings and created from other entities or blocks. Several add-on software packages provide symbol libraries for use with AutoCAD. You may want to catalog blocks in a library for easier access and reuse.

Limits. The boundaries that determine the potential size of a drawing. (See *Extents*.)

Menu. A series of program choices presented in such a fashion that selecting any function is done by selecting a number or letter corresponding to the function desired.

Mesh. A pattern of intersecting lines used to indicate a three-dimensional surface.

Mirroring. Process of producing a mirror image of an entity.

Mouse. A hand-operated pointing device used to position the cursor on the computer screen.

Multiple insert. An insertion of more than one copy of a block at a time.

Nest. To place one block inside another in a drawing. (A basic part defined as a block can be used in the subsequent creation of new blocks.)

Object Pointing. Using your pointing device to move the pickbox until it is over a portion of the entity you want to select.

Obliquing angle. An angle, taken from the vertical, that determines the slant of letters for a text font.

Orientation. The location or position of an entity. The UCS icon shows the orientation for the current viewport.

Ortho. (Short for *Orthogonal.*) In AutoCAD, a mode that permits only horizontal or vertical pointer movement and input.

Path curve. The arc, circle, line, or polyline revolved around an axis to define a surface; the outline of the object you are drawing.

Picking. The process of using a pointing device to select commands from the tablet or screen and to indicate entities or locations on-screen.

Pickbox. A small box that appears on-screen at the intersection of crosshairs when AutoCAD prompts you to select objects.

Plan view. The view of the current construction plane from the positive Z axis. The plan view is determined by the coordinate system.

Pointing device. A hand-held device (a puck, mouse, or stylus) used for digitizing.

Point filter. A means of selecting a point by entering one coordinate preceded by a period (*.x*, for example) and then responding to prompts for the other coordinate points. Used to align new parts of a drawing with existing entities in the current construction plane.

Polar. Resembling a pole or axis; relating to polar coordinates.

Polar coordinate. A coordinate system defined in reference to a specific origin and based on distances and angles rather than on X, Y, and Z coordinates. The angles are relative to 0 degrees, with positive angles measured counterclockwise.

Polyline. A special entity composed of connected lines and arcs. Polylines can have width and can be tapered. They can be open or closed figures.

Primitive. A simple entity (such as a line, circle, or arc) on which other, more complex entities are based.

Profile. Synonymous with *Path curve*.

Properties. Characteristic qualities of an entity (endpoints, color, linetype, etc.).

Prototype drawing. A drawing in which the default information used by AutoCAD is stored. Used for creating a new drawing.

Puck. A pointing device, resembling a mouse, with one or more buttons. Used in conjunction with a digitizing tablet to move crosshairs on-screen and execute commands.

Record increment. The distance your pointing device must travel in order for a line or polyline segment to be drawn in Sketch mode. The smaller the increment, the shorter the line segments and the smoother the appearance of curved lines on the screen.

Rectangular. One of two types of AutoCAD arrays: rectangular and polar. Rectangular arrays are composed of repetitive objects arranged in rows and columns.

Relative coordinates. Points located in relation to another, specified point (usually the last point entered). The last coordinate point entered is treated like 0,0.

Right hand rule. A method of determining the direction of the positive Z axis, in which you extend your right thumb along the positive X axis and point your index finger in the positive Y direction so that when you curl your fingers, they point along the positive Z axis. Especially useful when you want to visualize UCS orientation.

Rotation factor. The number of degrees an entity is rotated.

Rubber band effect. The way a line appears to stretch and contract when the cursor, attached to a fixed display point, is moved.

Selection set. A collection of one or more objects to be processed.

Shading. Alteration of a drawing to suggest three-dimensionality or shadows.

Slide. A snapshot of the screen that can be used in presentations.

Slider bar. Adjustment controls presented on-screen when using DVIEW. These slider bars allow you to adjust your view of a selection set when using specific DVIEW options.

Snap. To lock on to an entity or grid at a snap point. The SNAP command establishes the smallest increment AutoCAD recognizes when you move the pointer.

Stylus. A hand-held pointing device resembling a fancy pen with a spring-loaded or electronic tip. Used like a puck to enter commands or points from a digitizing tablet.

System variable. A variable that contains information (grid, snap, and axis information, for example) about a drawing's environment settings and their values.

Tabulated surface. A surface defined by a path curve and a direction vector. These surfaces are represented as polygon meshes.

Tangent. A line through a point on the circumference of a circle (or other curved line) perpendicular to the radius at that point.

Target point. Name of the location of the object (point) at which you are looking.

Template coordinates. X and Y coordinates for a menu item on a template for an AutoCAD digitizing tablet.

Thickness. The distance an entity extends from its X-Y plane.

Three-dimensional face. A flat plane in three-dimensional space.

Three-point definition. A method of defining a UCS with an origin, a positive X axis, and a positive Y axis.

Torus. A geometric surface shaped like a doughnut and generated by rotating a circle around an axis in its plane that doesn't intersect the circle.

Transparent command. An AutoCAD command which can be used within another AutoCAD command. Transparent commands are invoked by preceding the command name with an apostrophe ('). The transparent commands are DDEMODES, DDLMODES, DDRMODES, GRPAHSCR, HELP, ?, PAN, REDRAW, REDRAWALL, RESUME, SETVAR, TEXTSCR, VIEW, and ZOOM.

UCS. An acronym for *User Coordinate System*.

UCS icon. See *Coordinate system icon*.

Unit. Usually, the distance from one known point to another, such as one inch or one centimeter. Also refers to the system of measurement with which you are working (metric, for example).

Unit cell. In an array, the sum of the distance between the row and the column distances and the area occupied by the entity or block.

User Coordinate System (UCS). A user-defined coordinate system (or plane), defined within the World Coordinate System used by AutoCAD.

View. A graphical representation of a 2-D drawing or 3-D model from a specific location (view point) in space.

View point. The direction and elevation from which you view a drawing; your location in relation to the object you are drawing.

Viewport. A portion of the screen's graphics area; different views of a drawing may be displayed simultaneously in separate viewports.

WCS. An acronym for *World Coordinate System*.

Wild-card character. A symbol (* or ?) used in file names and extensions to represent any other string of characters (*) or any other single character (?).

Window. A framelike area in which you can enclose a small part of your drawing for modification or zooming.

World Coordinate System (WCS). In AutoCAD, a fixed Cartesian coordinate system consisting of absolute coordinates: a horizontal X displacement, a vertical Y displacement, and a positive Z displacement for 3-D. The WCS is the default User Coordinate System, but you can create other UCSs at any angle or location in 3-D space relative to the WCS.

X-Y plane. (See *Construction plane*.)

Command Index

AutoCAD commands

Index

B

More Computer Knowledge from Que

Lotus Software Titles

1-2-3 QueCards	21.95
1-2-3 for Business, 2nd Edition	22.95
1-2-3 QuickStart	21.95
1-2-3 Quick Reference	7.95
1-2-3 Release 2.2 Quick Reference	7.95
1-2-3 Release 2.2 QuickStart	19.95
1-2-3 Release 3 Business Applications	39.95
1-2-3 Release 3 Quick Reference	7.95
1-2-3 Release 3 QuickStart	19.95
1-2-3 Release 3 Workbook and Disk	29.95
1-2-3 Tips, Tricks, and Traps, 2nd Edition	21.95
Upgrading to 1-2-3 Release 3	14.95
Using 1-2-3, Special Edition	24.95
Using 1-2-3 Release 2.2, Special Edition	24.95
Using 1-2-3 Release 3	24.95
Using 1-2-3 Workbook and Disk, 2nd Edition	29.95
Using Lotus Magellan	21.95
Using Symphony, 2nd Edition	26.95

Database Titles

dBASE III Plus Applications Library	21.95
dBASE III Plus Handbook, 2nd Edition	22.95
dBASE III Plus Tips, Tricks, and Traps	21.95
dBASE III Plus Workbook and Disk	29.95
dBASE IV Applications Library, 2nd Edition	39.95
dBASE IV Handbook, 3rd Edition	23.95
dBASE IV Programming Techniques	24.95
dBASE IV QueCards	21.95
dBASE IV Quick Reference	7.95
dBASE IV QuickStart	19.95
dBASE IV Tips, Tricks, and Traps, 2nd Edition	21.95
dBASE IV Workbook and Disk	29.95
dBXL and Quicksilver Programming: Beyond dBASE	24.95
R:BASE User's Guide, 3rd Edition	22.95
Using Clipper	24.95
Using DataEase	22.95
Using Reflex	19.95
Using Paradox 3	22.95

Applications Software Titles

AutoCAD Advanced Techniques	34.95
AutoCAD Quick Reference	7.95
CAD and Desktop Publishing Guide	24.95
Introduction to Business Software	14.95
PC Tools Quick Reference	7.95
Smart Tips, Tricks, and Traps	24.95
Using AutoCAD	29.95
Using Computers in Business	24.95
Using DacEasy	21.95
Using Dollars and Sense: IBM Version, 2nd Edition	19.95

Using Enable/OA	23.95
Using Excel: IBM Version	24.95
Using Generic CADD	24.95
Using Managing Your Money, 2nd Edition	19.95
Using Q&A, 2nd Edition	21.95
Using Quattro	21.95
Using Quicken	19.95
Using Smart	22.95
Using SuperCalc5, 2nd Edition	22.95

Word Processing and Desktop Publishing Titles

DisplayWrite QuickStart	19.95
Microsoft Word 5 Quick Reference	7.95
Microsoft Word 5 Tips, Tricks, and Traps: IBM Version	19.95
Using DisplayWrite 4, 2nd Edition	19.95
Using Harvard Graphics	24.95
Using Microsoft Word 5: IBM Version	21.95
Using MultiMate Advantage, 2nd Edition	19.95
Using PageMaker: IBM Version, 2nd Edition	24.95
Using PFS: First Choice	22.95
Using PFS: First Publisher	22.95
Using Professional Write	19.95
Using Sprint	21.95
Using Ventura Publisher, 2nd Edition	24.95
Using WordPerfect, 3rd Edition	21.95
Using WordPerfect 5	24.95
Using WordStar, 2nd Edition	21.95
Ventura Publisher Techniques and Applications	22.95
Ventura Publisher Tips, Tricks, and Traps	24.95
WordPerfect Macro Library	21.95
WordPerfect Power Techniques	21.95
WordPerfect QueCards	21.95
WordPerfect Quick Reference	7.95
WordPerfect QuickStart	21.95
WordPerfect Tips, Tricks, and Traps, 2nd Edition	21.95
WordPerfect 5 Workbook and Disk	29.95

Macintosh and Apple II Titles

The Big Mac Book	27.95
Excel QuickStart	19.95
Excel Tips, Tricks, and Traps	22.95
HyperCard QuickStart	21.95
Using AppleWorks, 2nd Edition	21.95
Using dBASE Mac	19.95
Using Dollars and Sense	19.95
Using Excel: Macintosh Verson	22.95
Using FullWrite Professional	21.95
Using HyperCard: From Home to HyperTalk	24.95

Using Microsoft Word 4: Macintosh Version	
Using Microsoft Works: Macintosh Version, 2nd Edition	
Using PageMaker: Macintosh Version	
Using WordPerfect: Macintosh Version	

Hardware and Systems Title

DOS QueCards	
DOS Tips, Tricks, and Traps	
DOS Workbook and Disk	
Hard Disk Quick Reference	
IBM PS/2 Handbook	
Managing Your Hard Disk, 2nd Edition	
MS-DOS Quick Reference	
MS-DOS QuickStart	
MS-DOS User's Guide, Special Edition	
Networking Personal Computers, 3rd Edition	
Understanding UNIX: A Conceptual Guide, 2nd Edition	
Upgrading and Repairing PCs	
Using Microsoft Windows	
Using Novell NetWare	
Using OS/2	
Using PC DOS, 3rd Edition	

Programming and Technical Titles

Assembly Language Quick Reference	
C Programmer's Toolkit	
C Programming Guide, 3rd Edition	
C Quick Reference	
DOS and BIOS Functions Quick Reference	
DOS Programmer's Reference, 2nd Edition	
Power Graphics Programming	
QuickBASIC Advanced Techniques	
QuickBASIC Programmer's Toolkit	
QuickBASIC Quick Reference	
SQL Programmer's Guide	
Turbo C Programming	
Turbo Pascal Advanced Techniques	
Turbo Pascal Programmer's Toolkit	
Turbo Pascal Quick Reference	
Using Assembly Language	
Using QuickBASIC 4	
Using Turbo Pascal	

For more information, cal

1-800-428-5331

All prices subject to change without notice
Prices and charges are for domestic order
only. Non-U.S. prices might be higher.

Free Catalog!

Mail us this registration form today, and we'll send you a free catalog featuring Que's complete line of best-selling books.

Name of Book _____

Name _____

Title _____

Phone (____) _____

Company _____

Address _____

City _____

State _____ ZIP _____

Please check the appropriate answers:

1. Where did you buy your Que book?
   - ☐ Bookstore (name: _____)
   - ☐ Computer store (name: _____)
   - ☐ Catalog (name: _____)
   - ☐ Direct from Que
   - ☐ Other: _____

2. How many computer books do you buy a year?
   - ☐ 1 or less
   - ☐ 2-5
   - ☐ 6-10
   - ☐ More than 10

3. How many Que books do you own?
   - ☐ 1
   - ☐ 2-5
   - ☐ 6-10
   - ☐ More than 10

4. How long have you been using this software?
   - ☐ Less than 6 months
   - ☐ 6 months to 1 year
   - ☐ 1-3 years
   - ☐ More than 3 years

5. What influenced your purchase of this Que book?
   - ☐ Personal recommendation
   - ☐ Advertisement
   - ☐ In-store display
   - ☐ Price
   - ☐ Que catalog
   - ☐ Que mailing
   - ☐ Que's reputation
   - ☐ Other: _____

6. How would you rate the overall content of the book?
   - ☐ Very good
   - ☐ Good
   - ☐ Satisfactory
   - ☐ Poor

7. What do you like *best* about this Que book?
   _____
   _____

8. What do you like *least* about this Que book?
   _____
   _____

9. Did you buy this book with your personal funds?
   - ☐ Yes   ☐ No

10. Please feel free to list any other comments you may have about this Que book.
   _____
   _____
   _____

Que

Order Your Que Books Today!

Name _____

Title _____

Company _____

City _____

State _____ ZIP _____

Phone No. (____) _____

Method of Payment:

Check ☐   (Please enclose in envelope.)

Charge My: VISA ☐   MasterCard ☐

American Express ☐

Charge # _____

Expiration Date _____

Order No.	Title	Qty.	Price	Total

You can **FAX** your order to **1-317-573-2583**. Or call **1-800-428-5331, ext. ORDR** to order direct.
Please add $2.50 per title for shipping and handling.

Subtotal _____

Shipping & Handling _____

Total _____

Que

BUSINESS REPLY MAIL
First Class Permit No. 9918   Indianapolis, IN

Postage will be paid by addressee

11711 N. College
Carmel, IN 46032

BUSINESS REPLY MAIL
First Class Permit No. 9918   Indianapolis, IN

Postage will be paid by addressee

11711 N. College
Carmel, IN 46032